VHS NASTY: THE VIDEO NASTIES
Budget B&W Limited Edition

The Essential Guide to Video Nasties, Banned films and Censorship.

by
Tony Newton and David Bond
With special guest contributors.

TONY NEWTON & DAVID BOND

**A HellBound Books LLC
Publication**
Second Edition Copyright © 2020 by HellBound Books Publishing LLC
All Rights Reserved

Cover and art design
By Stephen Gilliam

All illustrations are reproduced here in the spirit of publicity and for review purposes of the films themselves.
Images and artwork reproduced in this book are in the spirit of publicity and are used as historical illustrations alongside the text in the book.
All images used under the fair use disclaimer all images are used as research, criticism and comment alongside the text within this book.
Fair Use Disclaimer
Copyright Disclaimer under section 107 of the Copyright Act of 1976, Allowance is made for "fair use" for purposes such as criticism, comment, news reporting, teaching, scholarship, education, and research.
All rights reserved copyright respective owners.
Picture Credits:
Wizard Video,VIPCO,Troma Entertainment, Entertainment International, Atlantis Video Productions, Gorgon Video, Video Programme Distributors, Canon, Go Video, Media Entertainment,EMI, Replay, Intervision, Cinehollywood, Manson International, America International Pictures, Arcade Video, Videospace, New Line Cinema, 21st Century Film Corp, CBS, New Line, VTC, MPM, Fox Video, Twentieth Century Fox Film Corp, Anchor Bay Entertainment, Orion, Erocine, J.E Films, Intervision, Sony, Vipco,CIC, Full Moon Features, Warner Brothers, Original art, Ash Loydon, Paul Draper, Shane Ryan, Tony Newton.
Edited by Tony Newton

Video Nasty black and white image by Shane Ryan.

All other original artwork featured by Ash Loydon, Paul Draper and Tony Newton.

Most of the original VHS distributing companies are now no longer active companies.
Any Omissions will be corrected in future editions.

No part of this book may be reproduced, stored in a retrieval system, or transmitted by any means, electronic, mechanical, photocopying, recording or otherwise without written permission from the author
This book is a work of fiction. Names, characters, places and incidents are entirely fictitious or are used fictitiously and any resemblance to actual persons, living or dead, events or locales is purely coincidental.

Printed in the United States of America

www.hellboundbookspublishing.com

TONY NEWTON & DAVID BOND

Contents

Foreword by Lloyd Kaufman and Taylor Sprow	Page 7
Foreword by David Del Valle	Page 12
Introduction by Tony Newton	Page 14
Introduction by David Bond	Page 15
Chapter 1 Seize the Video Nasties	Page 17
Chapter 2 Moral Panic in the UK	Page 24
Chapter 3 Public Concern Video Nasties in the Media	Page 25
Chapter 4 Video Nasties Confiscated	Page 28
Chapter 5 Nasty Nasty	Page 34
Chapter 6 Cheap Thrills and Visceral Spills	Page 42
Chapter 7 Ban This Vile Filth	Page 52
Chapter 8 The Final Cut, Censorship No More	Page 62
Chapter 9 VHS Memories	Page 85
Chapter 10 Prosecuted Video Nasties	Page 101
Chapter 11 Non-Prosecuted Films	Page 221
Chapter 12 Video Nasties: The DPP section 3 list	Page 295
Chapter 13 VHS Lives	Page 475
Your Video Nasty Checklist	Page 485
Top Ten Video Nasty Lists	Page 487
Top Ten Classic Nasties (Pre 1999)	Page 490

VHS NASTY

Foreword #1

The late, trailblazing filmmaker Samuel Fuller once shared with me a piece of wisdom. It was that life's problems boil down to two things: women and money. Regarding censorship and the evils that come with it, my fifty years of moviemaking suggests to me MONEY is the root. Here, money serves as a catalyst, a tool, or more accurately, a *weapon*. When thinking about the state of the industry, I'm reminded of a Golden Rule. Not that ol' "Do unto others…" one—that would be too noble to describe the crooked, perverse industry in which we, the little guys, are trying to create our art. I'm talking about the one that goes something like: "He who has the gold rules."

In this business, it is not you or I who have this "gold." Rather, it is a concentrated cartel of devil-worshipping, international media elites who sit above the rest of us, not just possessing the wealth of the industry but also using it as a means of control. This grasp the small group of elites has on various aspects of the entertainment market often works to squeeze the life out of the films produced within it. With that wringing out of our art, filmmakers are also often then robbed of their integrity and individuality…and we independent artists of our livelihood.

Nowadays, it would seem reasonable to expect the various forms of entertainment we experience and interact with daily to be rather unrestrained in what they show and how they show it. The media elites are comprised of labor leaders (sexist, racist, closed shops), corporate leaders (you know who they are), and bureaucratic leaders (elected officials who are bought by the other two segments). The seemingly uninhibited tone throughout the media is accented by the likes of reality television stars naked on magazine covers, pseudo-politicians screaming tyrannical intentions, and graphic violence being shown to us through outlets like the TV news or whatever serial-killer-detective-police-procedural dud is airing at the time. Add in the availability and accessibility of the World Wide Web, and it would be easy to assume we have moved into a less restricted era of media consumption.

Little do people know that they are often, if not always, being spoon-fed a diet of media cartel-approved, big union friendly, artistically, politically, and socially stripped bits of media. Blindly consumed and rarely questioned, the breadth and popularity of pieces of mainstream entertainment reinforce the power the corporate cartel has over the industry. These Rupert Murdoch-types save face and win by often disguising their attempts to censor and tailor the markets to their advantage. These corporate conglomerates try to say censorship is necessary to protect the public from damaging and inappropriate content. Instead, it is my opinion the power of the elite exercised through censorship is done so to protect the status quo. The half-hearted attempts at shielding the public's eyes are truly part of the elite's method to keep themselves in power and continue feeding at the oligopoly trough.

It's a fixed system.

While the cartel schemes to remain at the top of the market food chain, they are working simultaneously to keep the independent artists starving at the bottom. I have spent my entire career at Troma Entertainment, and even after more than 40 years of being in business, we are still in the midst of a corporate-driven shitstorm with no umbrella or clear sky in sight. No other truly independent studio in the United States has survived as long as Troma. I want to stress that this is not because those other independent studios were making bad movies. It is because they could not make a living due to the power of the media cartel. Censorship is a tool of the labor, bureaucratic, and corporate elite to keep the independent artist out of competition.

When Michael Herz and I started Troma in 1974, there were antitrust rules in place, having been established during a restructuring of the film industry in the 1940s. These worked to prevent the sort of vertically integrated cartelism and oligopolies that burden the industry today. In that regard, these rules allowed for easier access to the market. However, the industry also created the Motion Picture Association of

America, or the MPAA, which did much to destroy independent movie studios through the use of the rating system. When we started Troma in the 1970s, without an R-rating or milder, your movie could not be shown in theaters. Therefore, at the hands of the MPAA, many independent films were disembowelled and released as only the remnants of the filmmaker's original vision deemed acceptable.

There was a clear MPAA double standard. Mainstream movies would be permitted much more latitude regarding sex and violence compared to independent ones. In blockbusters like *Die Hard*, there was considerably more blood and guts than there was in *Troma's War*, both released in 1988. *Troma's War*, however, did not have a big Hollywood studio star like Bruce Willis to stand behind and was subjected to such eviscerating edits that it was chopped to bits. In order to get an R-rating, we had to cut out almost all of the fun stuff; bullet hits, corpses, bodies aflame, even cartoon-like punches! We brilliantly (and luckily) had used our own money to finance *Troma's War*, whereas these other independent studios usually borrowed from a bank [1]. Then, when the MPAA ratings board gutted their movies, they would fail at the box office. Indie studios and producers would be unable to pay back their debts and quickly went bankrupt.

When tied to a major studio, producers are given the opportunity to screen their unfinished films for the MPAA. The MPAA then gives them advice about where changes are needed. If you are an independent filmmaker, however, the ratings board requires you to present a completed film, does nothing to help you figure out the problems, and makes you edit in the dark. This is done so you will over compensate and cut out the maximum amount of your movie in order to get the process over with as quickly and cheaply as possible.

Before going on to make the animated series *South Park*, creators Trey Parker and Matt Stone worked with Troma on their film *Cannibal! The Musical*, which we began distributing in 1994. A year later, upon their second encounter with the ratings board with their film *Orgazmo*, Parker had said because of their status as independent filmmakers without the support of a studio, they were given an NC-17 rating without any advice on what was needed to receive an R. The popularity of the *South Park* series resulted in the creation of a Paramount feature-length film titled *South Park: Bigger, Longer, and Uncut* in 1999. As their first movie with a major studio, they saw first hand the difference in the treatment of independent versus mainstream filmmakers.

In an interview I conducted with Parker and Stone on the set of their film *Team America: World Police*, Parker had this to say: "The problem was, what we learned later because we were still independent filmmakers then [at the release of *Orgazmo*], was that the ratings board just works for the studios. So, it was basically because we didn't have a studio behind us. We had nobody to fight for us." Elaborating on the pair's experience on either side of the corporate divide, he added that with the NC-17 rating originally given to *South Park: Bigger, Longer, and Uncut*, "the studio was saying, 'We need it to be rated R' and they [are part owners of ratings board] like [The MPAA's Ratings Board says], 'Ok, well let's work together', it's sick."

Ever the rule followers at Troma, we found a way around the cartel's method of controlling competition, for a while at least. To temporarily appease them, we would make the cuts deemed necessary in the print to achieve an R-rating. Then, after receiving the R, we would replace some of the deleted into the 35mm print and show the movie with what we felt was a fair R-rating based on what the MPAA was allowing at the time. Unfortunately we got caught doing this with a little family-friendly movie called *Bloodsucking Freaks*. Originally 95 minutes long, the MPAA R-rated approved version was cut down to 54 minutes. Having faith in the original, we ended up showing the 95-minute version with the R-rating tag on it at a movie theater in the Bronx. All was well until a very attentive mother complained after taking her five-year-old child to see *Bloodsucking Freaks*[2]. Of course, the MPAA was going to sue us. Not, though, based on censorship but for copyright infringement based on the fact that they own the R-rating. Seriously…they own the letter 'R'.

As the laws on copyright infringement are incredibly strict, especially back in the 1970s and 1980s, you can pay a lot for violating them. To make amends, we were forced to spend several thousand dollars and to

---

[1] Here the other independent studios abided by one of the most familiar laws in the business: "OPM", or "Other People's Money".

[2] We would like to retroactively present this mother with the dual honor of Parent of the Year and TromaVillage Idiot of the year.

take out advertisements in various publications such as Variety and the Hollywood Reporter apologizing for being so naughty.

The wrath of unfair, double standard censorship does not just stop at the content within the films. It extends to advertising too; with the release of my brother Charles Kaufman's satire of wilderness movies, *When Nature Calls,* in 1985 came controversy over the film's poster. A satirical rendering of the *Gone With the Wind* poster depicted a bear in the position of Clark Gable embracing a beautiful woman with a medley of crazy cartoon figures scattered beneath. Satire is clearly protected under United States law, yet MGM sent over lawyers as a threat to sue us. Their reasoning? Our poster was misleading, and people would go to see *When Nature Calls* thinking they were going to be seeing *Gone With the Wind.* Never mind the large black bear in place of a classic Hollywood star, and the tag line "When Nature Calls…You've Gotta Go!". MGM mentioned that audiences would be too incompetent to differentiate between the *When Nature Calls… You've Gotta Go* and *Gone With The Wind.* MGM's lawyers basically outright admitted to Troma's lawyers we were in the right, but that at the end of the road, our victory in court would wind up costing us half a million bucks. Not exactly in the place to spend that type of petty cash, we agreed to pull the advertisements and redo the campaign. In the end, we were still hit economically because of having to make new advertisements and having to pay our lawyers. [3]

Another instance with a major studio occurred a few years later with the release of Troma's *Toxic Crusaders* animated series. The series was about to begin airing on the Fox Network while already airing on The WB when the *Tiny Toon Adventures* series started toying with a character named the Toxic Revenger, blatantly similar to our beloved Toxie. Fox complained, thinking we went behind their backs and licensed our cartoons with Warner Bros. Unlike the situation with the *When Nature Calls* poster, this incident actually caused real confusion. In an attempt to stop *Tiny Toons* from using the Toxic Revenger, our lawyers approached Warner Bros. who agreed to stop including the character in their cartoons. However, they refused to give Troma any money and, furthermore, would not agree to stop airing the Toxic Revenger cartoons already in existence. Once again, we were told the same thing as were in the situation with MGM; we were in the right, but to prove it in court, we were going to have to spend hundreds of thousands of dollars.

It would be nice to say these were the only situations where we have been artistically and economically censored but that would be a flat out lie. The vassals of the Hollywood elite reach much further than the rating board and the studios. When Troma released *Surf Nazi's Must Die* in 1987, we attempted to place a full-page advertisement in Variety. Variety, though, being the house organ for the major studios and living off the advertising of these conglomerates, refused to take our advertisement. Again, we were in the right in this situation and yet, again, we were forced to secede to the powers at be.

Our 1979 film, *Squeeze Play,* was also a victim of an utterly ridiculous means of censorship. The poster for the film featured three bikini-clad young women and one lucky young man in various baseball positions. A movie theater in Buffalo was playing it, but without our consent or even our knowledge, they defaced *Squeeze Play*'s poster by painting Bermuda shorts over the women's bikini bottoms. Can you imagine that happening to a major studio film's advertisement? It would never happen without permission, but because Troma does not have the backing of one of the greedy gatekeepers of the industry, we were and are fair game for injustice.

During the Reagan administration, the weight that antitrust laws held shifted significantly. Once again, through the weakening of decrees established in the 1940s, major studios were allowed to become vertically integrated conglomerates. The studios became corporate powerhouses, controlling various means of the market and making it so that there is no way for an independent film to get to the public without being bought over as part of the system.

As recently as 2013 with our film *Return to Nuke 'Em High, Volume 1*, we found ourselves enmeshed in the corporate world. We made the film in association with STARZ, a vassal of Liberty Media, a giant devil-worshipping dynamo. Because we partnered with them, though, *Return to Nuke 'Em High, Volume 1* has been

---

[3] A few years after our scuffle with MGM, the Chevy Chase flop *Fletch Lives* (a sequel to *Fletch*) was released with a poster imitating *Gone With the Wind*'s with Chase in place of Gable. Though it was incredibly more akin to the original than Troma's was, and actually could have confused the picture because it had the backing of cartel member Universal Pictures, MGM did not object.

screened and seen everywhere, and we made a modest profit. Wonderfully, I did not find myself censored as an artist by the corporation, that is, as long as I kept to an extremely low budget.

By contrast, with another somewhat recent Troma film, *Poultrygeist: Night of the Chicken Dead* in 2006, we did not see a fraction of the success that we did with *Return to Nuke 'Em High, Volume 1*. Though *Poultrygeist* was arguably a better movie, or at least less objectionable from a point of censorship, we distributed it ourselves and, inevitably, lost pretty much all our money. Having no major studio support, we were unable to get the movie into any chain stores or even to air on any sort of television channel, not even shitty Cinemax[4].

You might be wondering since Troma has experienced so much difficulty and bias in the industry as an independent studio, how have we survived for over 40 years? Without a doubt, our longevity is a reflection of the dedication of our global fan base. We are so fortunate that there are fans in every corner of the world helping us to spread our art through less restricted channels. For example, a group of Troma super fans invited me to Moscow to direct and star in a music video for the Russian group Korable. The band put up posters around the neighborhood telling of Troma's involvement and inviting people to come be in the music video, like we do with most of our events. The place ended up being full. A number of people who came to participate brought with them videotapes of our movies with shitty, xeroxed covers for me to autograph. It is important to note that we had no distribution in Russia meaning that the fans' awareness were due to the wonderful world of piracy. It might seem odd to praise the act of bootlegging but that's how so many of our international fans got around their country's censorship statues and, therefore, how Troma's popularity spread. It was thanks to these acts of piracy that, around the same time, some Russian distributors began paying us because our movies had become so popular.

We owe a great deal when it comes to our popularity and longevity as an independent studio to the power of the Internet. Despite publications from Fangoria to the New York Times raving about our movies to the screening of them at the Metropolitan Museum of Art, we are still about ready to move the company into a giant refrigerator cart under the overpass of Route 95. The only reason we have been able to survive in this harsh, megacorp-ruled industry is, again, because of our legion of fans that often gain access to our art online.

In an age of tremendous technological innovation, the Internet continues to offer invaluable opportunities for independent artists and for the public in general. With websites such as Kickstarter and Indiegogo, people have the opportunity to independently execute their ideas without necessarily being tied to some corporate weight, dragging them to their inevitable creative demise. Through a wildly successful Kickstarter campaign, Troma was able to raise over $60,000 to help finish our new movie *Return to Nuke 'Em High, Volume 2*. It was our fans and the power of the Internet, not the studios and major corporations, who made that possible.

Beyond the opportunities and innovations offered to artists, the Internet allows for so much vital progression. In the fields of technology, science, and medicine, for example, ideas and information can be explored and shared with the click of a mouse. These things are able to happen because we have access to a free, open Internet. Yet, as I sit here praising all the good the Internet does and can bring, millions and millions of dollars are being spent in Washington to eliminate its democratic nature. The death of net neutrality would make the Internet into just another method of control for the rich and powerful, marginalizing the potential for smaller sites and publications to compete side by side with larger, more corporately tied ones. No longer will the input of the pimply-faced, teenage Troma fangirl blogging from her bedroom be equal to the stream of garbage spewing from the mouths of Donald Trump and Co. Instead, the little guys will be, once again, squashed by the oppressive big business methods that fuel our society.

Unsurprisingly, the MPAA and the elites of the film industry are all for the elimination of the open Internet. Without net neutrality, the public would have less of a chance to even know about Troma movies, let alone watch them. As the seemingly last frontier for any possible acquisition of truth, the Internet is a threat to the cartel, not just in the film industry but overall. For us at Troma, it is the last tool we have to get our art to

---

[4] "Cinemax": An American premium cable and satellite television network and also the lowest form of American cable-movie entertainment.

the public. If net neutrality is taken away, the elites will finally have their superhighway, accessible only to the rich and powerful, while the rest of us will be on the dirt roads in a decrepit rickshaw.

These giant conglomerates do not just sit pretty at the top of the market, making it more difficult to succeed as an "indie". They instead serve as the sole handful of gatekeepers to the industry, persecuting not just through artistic censorship but also by its economic counterpart. Any wholesome purpose that is supposedly reached through the act of censorship is a farce. These wicked gatekeepers, equipped with the necessary wealth and supremacy, are in reality using the convenience of media censorship to feed the corporate machine that does nothing but keep them in power and those of us working as independent artists in artistic and economic captivity.

-Lloyd Kaufman President & Co-Founder, Troma Entertainment, American film Director, Producer, and Documentarian with Taylor Sprow.

VIDEO NASTY

Foreword #2

My very first viewing experience with a horror film that I know must qualify as a "Video Nasty" has to be Michael Powell's PEEPING TOM—an acknowledged masterpiece that almost destroyed Powell's career, so great was the backlash against the violence towards women and children as viewed by the public at that time...

Anglo Amalgamated had released three films in row—the most infamous being PEEPING TOM, then CIRCUS OF HORRORS, and finally, the campy and violent HORRORS OF THE BLACK MUSEUM. These films became known as a "Sadian trilogy" since they all dealt with themes of torture and disfigurement in very graphic terms for the early sixties. However, when we discuss the term "Video Nasties," a decidedly colloquial term used in the UK, we are really discussing the period of the early 1980's of certain VHS releases. BLOOD FEAST and/or any low budget horror film after PSYCHO were enough to create a negative emotional response from customers outside of the loyal and rabid fan base of horror fans that want to see and collect such films, regardless of how far out the filmmaker might take them in terms of sexuality and violence.

My first up close and personal experience with a Video Nasty came in the guise of a British director named Mike Armstrong who wrote several screenplays before getting a deal with Tigon pictures of England—just before they made their most famous video nasty of all: WITCHFINDER GENERAL. It is now regarded as somewhat of a masterpiece from another Mike from the same period, Michael Reeves, a 24-year-old boy genius who had the misfortune to die before his career could take off. Mike Armstrong, on the other hand, lived to see his video nasty become a cult film for many of the same reasons as WITCHFINDER, since they both shared the same themes (at least on the surface). MARK OF THE DEVIL was nasty and violent in a way that was new and daring for the times, and even went so far as to offer vomit bags to patrons who simply could not take seeing a woman tortured and her tongue ripped out. The film also did well enough to begat a sequel, and MARK OF THE DEVIL part Two came out the following summer. The first film starred Herbert Lom as the witch hunter and, as his assistant, Udo Keir. Udo would one day soon star in the 3-D FLESH FOR FRANKENSTEIN.

The only reason these films caused such drama during the 1980's was the moral panic outraged parents were coping with as more and more teenagers began to own videos and realized what was out there to watch, which had been unavailable to them until the advent of VHS. Of course, today, the Internet and the vast amount of films available has all but made the 1980's seem like a part of the dark ages; present day films such as THE HUMAN CENTIPEDE and NEKROMANTIK push the boundaries far more than anything that frightened the horses in the 80's!

It has taken me a decade or two to appreciate these orphans of the cinema, and I had to go through the maze of European trash cinema of equally mad auteurs like Jess Franco and Coffin Joe to savor such titles as ZOMBIE, SLAVE OF THE CANNIBAL GOD, I SPIT ON YOUR GRAVE, and LAST HOUSE ON THE LEFT.

I recently wrote a foreword to a book on the films of Dario Argento entitled: THE ARGENTO SYNDROME. What I realized at that moment about Horror films in general, and the Italian giallo films of the 60's in particular, was how almost all of those films operate on a dream logic that allows atmosphere to transcend self-contained scripts and lacklustre performances. Argento's DEEP RED is a great film and a video nasty if ever there was one.

I am utterly delighted to have survived the dark ages of home video and the moral panic of parents and teachers that spilled paranoia into the public forums until, at last, the Internet and social media opened the floodgates—just as HP Lovecraft might have done in his fiction to allow the Old Ones into our universe. As the wise and all-knowing Oz of my generation, the ever-groovy Dr. Timothy Leary once observed: "Don't take other people's word for an experience—judge for yourself." I tried that on the good Dr. one afternoon, showing him BLOOD FEAST. The one line he thought was out of sight was when the mad caterer asks a customer (while wearing huge eyebrows like beetles): "Have you ever had an EGYPTIAN feast?"

Well, have you?

-David Del Valle
Producer of Sinister Image, Author of Six Reels Under.

Introduction

VHS Nasty is hard to sum up in a few words. Writing and putting the book together has been a very fun and reminiscent journey through video nasties and VHS.

This book isn't just a guide with appraisals of video nasties, but a doorway into the world of the video nasty and the draconian days; a snapshot of an era told by filmmakers and horror fans. A doorway that can't be boarded up or even bricked, video nasties are a part of celluloid horror history.

VHS Nasty is an insight into the greatest era in horror and home video, told through the eyes of filmmakers, producers, authors, and horror fans.

Whether you are discovering these titles for the first time or reminiscing about the good old days, this book features insights on *all* of the video nasties, appraisals and essays on video nasties and banned cinema, censorship and the memories that stand out, the culture, and the driving forces behind them.

This is not a detail-by-detail account on the subject, but a look into the era and films in a similar vein to the classic un-edited horror VHS zines that were published by VHS and horror fans across the globe in the 1980's. Think of this as the biggest VHS horror zine on the subject of video nasties ever produced!

Throughout the book, DPP and the BBFC are mentioned (DPP stands for Director of Public Prosecutions.) It was the Director of Public Prosecutions that released the lists of films that were believed to violate the Obscene Publications Act of 1959. BBFC stands for The British Board of Film Classification, which was previously named The British Board of Film Censors.

I would like to personally thank every contributor to this book, and I know readers and horror fans will enjoy reading the essays and contributions as much as I have enjoyed collecting them to add to my schlock ramblings.

Now is the time for the resurrection of the Video Nasty. VHS is more popular than ever, and the ultimate collection a VHS afficianado can own is a full set of the video nasties—something I am still searching for. Collecting the Video Nasties is like hunting down the back of the sofa for the last few remaining pieces of your jigsaw puzzle; only, VHS collectors have to hunt in the wild at car boot fares, garage sales, collectors' fares, and dreaded online auctions.

Sit back as we enter the world of the video nasty with films deemed to deprave and corrupt, and gain an insight into censorship and why the video nasties and these cult-banned horror films are so important today.

Dedicated to:

George A. Romero (1940-2017)
Tobe Hooper (1943-2017)
Herschell Gordon Lewis (1926-2016)
Wes Craven (1939-2015)
Graham Fletcher-Cook (1963-2019)
Ulli Lommel (1944-2017)
John Alan Schwartz (1952-2019)
Andrzej Żuławski (1940-2016)
Umberto Lenzi (1931-2017)
And horror fans across the globe.
#HorrorFamily   #VHSLives

-Tony Newton

Writer, Director, Producer: VHS Lives: A Schlockumentary, VHS Lives 2: Undead Format, VHS Lives 3:VHS Nasty Documentary, 60 Seconds to Die, Virus of the Dead, Welcome to Hell, Troma's Grindsploitation film series, Trashsploitation, 2 Die for, Toxic Schlock and Creepy pasta.

Author of the books Horror Movie Poetry, Terror Rhymes, Splatter Video, The Zombie Rule Book: A Zombie Apocalypse Survival Guide and #I'm Zombie: A zombie mosaic novel.

Introduction
The Nietzschian gaze

The history of horror storytelling began with the first Neolithic man huddling around the fire, telling of all the monsters and evil forces that exist outside the protective ring of light and warmth as the darkness beyond concealed the sum of their fears.

We progressed as a species, and the world got bigger. The monsters now existed on maps of the unknown world, bestowed with legends like "Here be Dragons," but we ultimately explored those lands as well, and the darkness disappeared. We began to explore monsters in verse, prose, and the oils of the painters. By the end of the 19th century, the written word and the hands of artisans created a home in our minds for that last vestige of darkness.

At the beginning of the 20th century, a new art form emerged to bring the monsters to life: it started with celluloid reflections in a darkened room – and would ultimately give birth to the most popular art form that frightens us today. As independent cinema rose out of the studio system in Hollywood, Paris, Berlin, and London, filmmakers begin to push boundaries, until monsters of every kind and new visual stories of darkness took a wide variety of forms.

In the 1970s, with the advent of VHS and Betamax video machines, for the first time, motion pictures were not purely consumed in a dark room among a group of strangers but on a comfortable couch in our own homes. The medium quickly insinuated itself into modern society – not only entertaining us but serving as a teacher, babysitter, and sexual aid.

Because there were no controls regulating the content and dissemination of this new media, it was only a matter of time before the censors stepped into the fray. The 1980s gave birth to the UK's Video Recording Act – thanks to self-proclaimed moral crusader Mary Whitehouse and her supporters. Passed in 1984, the act stated that all commercial video recordings offered for sale or for hire/rental must carry a classification agreed upon by an authority designated by the Home Office. This would give widespread power of censorship to a small department, which was originally created in 1912. In 1985, the British Board of Film Classification (BBFC) would be given that authority. According to Wikipedia: "works are classified by the BBFC under an age rated system; it is an offence under the act to supply video works to individuals who are (or appear to be) under the age of classification designated."

Works that are refused classification cannot, under this act, be legally sold or supplied to anyone of any age unless the content is deemed educational, or to do with sport, religion, or music, and does not depict violence, sex, or incite a criminal offence. The BBFC may also require cuts made – either to receive a certain age rating or to be even allowed classification at all.

The reaction to this new wave of controversial films stirred a moral panic in the UK, which was spurred further by the tabloids. During this time, however, I was halfway around the world in Canada, where no one had even heard of these draconian laws.

I first discovered VHS in a small oil town in the frozen north of Canada. In the beginning, it was just one location – an appliance store that sold VCRs and rented videotapes. Its horror section was probably 90 titles at most. But within a year, at least 15 new video rental shops had opened in that small town, and this new world opened up to me. My journey through the "fascination of the flesh" may have begun as an easy way to see naked women… but soon grew into the love for this genre.

My favorite among these long-gone video stores was "Jumbo Video," which contained 15 rows of horror videotapes. It was from these viewings, supplemented by the help of magazines like *Fangoria* and Chas Balun's *Deep Red* (I still drink coffee every morning from my *Deep Red* mug Chas gave me at the beginning of my career). My love affair truly began in those days, and like any first love, it has stayed with me my whole life… scars and all.

Over the years, I have owned all of these films in a range of different formats and region codes. After innumerable viewings, they have changed my perception. They started as mere gore-fests, but now are something else: in many cases, they posed deep political and philosophical diatribes. These films became an examination of our own humanity - through the eyes of the voyeur.

I have been very lucky. I get to make films, talk about them, and teach about them all over the world. Horror is a mirror to show us the truth about ourselves. Nietzsche noted when man looks into the abyss, it is himself that looks back, and these films can provide that view. Horror is not merely about grisly shock value and lurid exploitation – it's about the simple truth. Tennessee Williams said it best when asked why he so often wrote about humanity's darker impulses:

"A life is long and a book is short, and to truly understand he human experience we must see it all at it darkest."

So sit back, dear reader - this will be one dark ride!

Dedicated to my mentor, the late Phil Nutman.

-David Bond

David Bond is an award-winning scriptwriter, author, essayist, film producer and festival curator, David Bond recently produced the feature EXTREMITY for Dark Elegy Films, co-writing the screenplay with Rebecca Swan (MASTERS OF HORROR) for acclaimed director Anthony DiBlasi (DREAD, LAST SHIFT).

Bond also co-produced the legendary extreme-cinema anthology THE PROFANE EXHIBIT, and oversaw the reboot of Ulli Lommel's 1980 cult horror hit THE BOOGEYMAN. He currently has multiple film and television projects in development through his own production company.

Chapter 1: Seize the Video Nasties!

"There must be no place in Britain for the video nasty"
-Margaret Thatcher

The Rise of VHS!

Flashback to 1976.

The technological breakthrough of VHS (Video Home System) marked the start of a new era. The format was pioneered by the Victor Company of Japan (JVC), who introduced the first VHS recorders to the consumer market in 1976. One of the most exciting inventions in decades, VHS brought movies home, giving consumers unprecedented control over their media consumption.

VHS held its own as the dominant home entertainment video format and for almost 30 years, winning what became known as the first "Format War" against Betamax and Laserdisc. Sony initially monopolized the market with the release of the Betamax machine in 1975, thus JVC came up with their own system, VHS, which proved the winner of the "War" despite the superior image quality of the Betamax. JVC however, cleverly designed VHS technology to license to companies on a global scale, which resulted in competitive pricing for consumers. Also cited as a significant detail to the victory of VHS was the fact Betamax failed to equal the recording time of VHS. VHS was capable of holding an entire movie, and as a result was embraced by the video rental industry. This would prove to be the nail in the coffin for Betamax as their shelf space in stores dwindled. So began the demise of Betamax. In the 1980s, VHS became affordable and available to the masses with the introduction of video stores. Movie rental giants and independently owned video stores popped up on most street corners, offering the consumer a tantalizing glimpse into the taboo world of towering video nasty mania.

The release of VHS marked a pivotal time in history. VHS was catapulted into the homes of a generation - for whom it would change their lives forever. The home video market would change Britain in more ways than one with not only the introduction of VCRs becoming the medium of choice for home viewing, but unleashed low budget horror films filled with nudity and violence to the masses - they are now known as the video nasties. The introduction of the internet brought about a media consumption frenzy, and nowadays we're never more than a click away from watching a movie - but where's the fun in that?

For the video nasty fan, the magnetic tape of VHS is embedded in the core of their very being.

Video Nasty

A video Nasty is a colloquial term used in the United Kingdom and Europe to describe a number of films distributed on VHS video in the early 1980s, which were heavily criticized by the press, parliament, and various religious organizations for their content: strong use of violence, sex, nudity and gore. At the time of the introduction of home VCR video players and recorders in the United Kingdom during the late 1970s, no legislation was in place to regulate home video content. This meant any films on the market and available from video rental stores had no certification like we know today. The Obscene Publications act was in place and had been since 1959 (The Obscene Publications act 1959), although it did not govern home video. During the rise of the porn film industry in the late 1970s, in 1977 the act was amended to cover erotic/porn films - but still not horror films. At this time, the British Board of Film Censorship, which was established in 1912 and only governed theatrical cinematic releases, was not in force to censor home video; this was due to a loophole within film classification laws at the time. Because of this, in the early 1980s, the market was flooded with low-budget horror films featuring gore, violence, and graphic nudity. It didn't help that major film distributors were reluctant to join the VHS revolution due to fears that less bums would be on seats in the cinema and fears their content would be pirated on video.

Due to the video nasty debate in both the media and parliament, a number of films were prosecuted in the early 1980s by the Director of Public Prosecutions; following this, the government passed the Video Recordings Act 1984, which meant in Britain all video releases had to appear before the BBFC for certification at a cost to the film's distributor. The reason the Video Recordings Act 1984 was in place was to protect children within the home, so we saw a much stricter code and more censorship with home video than theatrical releases.

With campaign leader Mary Whitehouse, and with the help the likes of MP Graham Bright - and even the support of Prime Minister Margaret Thatcher - they won the Video Nasty War. The Director of Public Prosecutions released an official list of 72 films - a list that would end up being amended as more films were added and dropped as the decision to whether a title was successfully prosecuted or dropped from it with unsuccessful prosecution. The courts prosecuted certain video releases, known as the video nasties, for obscenity believed to violate the Obscene Publications Act 1959. The Video Recordings Act 1984 was then put into place - an act that governed film censorship in Britain and relieved the courts of their duty with the matter. With the implement of the Video Recordings Act 1984, the courts destroyed the video nasty lists. The courts have no records of the VN DPP section 2 and 3 video nasty lists on file within their archives to this day.

The 1980s was the video nasty era; the release of VCR players gave viewers the opportunity to enjoy the cinematic experience in their own homes. Sure, it was a far cry from the HD/3D, curved, 4K TVs and wall-to-wall surround sound systems we have today, but that wooden-cased Pye TV which took forever to warm up brought endless hours of entertainment when accompanied by the latest technology the VCR. Britain owned more VCR players and recorders than any other country at the time, though many families invested in Betamax rather than VHS (which is kind of like investing in gold instead of bit-coins today).

There were big bucks to be made in the home video arena; it took off way faster than anyone could have anticipated. When VHS and Betamax home video tapes were first released there were no laws in place to regulate any kind of classification. Alongside the big budget classics came a flood of small, indie, low budget titles containing explicit gore, sex, and violence. These horror films found their way onto video shop shelves across the UK. Not all video nasties were small budget, gore-fuelled offerings featuring explicit violence and/or cannibalism, but when a horror film was released on VHS in the 1970s or 80s, it was more often than not tarred with the same brush. Video shop walls were lined with these classic VHS covers depicting rotting flesh, traumatised women, impaled bodies, and otherwise disturbing images to catch the attention of their customers.

In the UK, fans of violence, gore, and horror were used to tamer horror films, such as the universal monsters and prime time TV mysteries or Amicus and Hammer horror films. But, if they were lucky enough to own a VCR player in the early 80s, they could view uncut, extreme horror and violence in all its uncensored glory. From press to parliament, the video nasty was thrust into the public eye and every gore hound would be on their own personal quest to view and own all those titles on VHS. Video nasties (love them or hate them) are a part of British history and a global phenomenon that hit the country like a tsunami.

Video nasties are as iconic to Britain as fish and chips - only this dish is served on a skewer and comes complete with the head, eyes, and a very bitter aftertaste!

The video nasty era of the 1980s left a legacy of films in somewhat of a time capsule, so much so that the viewer of these films, irrelevant of age, will still experience the chills down the spine, the anticipation of what gruesome images will feature on screen next, along with good old' fashioned shocks and gore - thank you, Mary Whitehouse, for giving the *Video Nasties* the exposure horror films truly deserve!

It doesn't matter how old you are; if you were around at the time of the release of the video nasties, or watched them in the 90s, or are even watching them for the first time now, you still feel that little bit sick to the stomach on the first watch because some of the films are actually quite nasty indeed! *Every* horror film fan has a connection with video nasties! You may feel nauseous at the sight of blood, intestines being torn out or consumed by cannibals, and if you're a hardcore gore hound you might feel queasy at the bad acting or crazy dialogue in some of the movies - and at some points may feel sick to your stomach from laughing so hard!

The 1980s saw the arrival of the shady and, quite frankly, dubious video store owner. With an almost covert look, those men were generally heavily bearded, sported thick, black rimmed NHS style glasses, constantly chain-smoked roll ups, had a penchant for horror films, and were rumoured to partake in under the counter pornographic film dealings! But, that wasn't the scariest thing in your local video shop - no! Far worse was what adorned the shelves of the store itself! If you could find the tapes through the mist of cigarette smoke, you were in for one hell of a shock! Those films featured extreme violence, graphic nudity, blood and gore scenes, psycho killers, maniacs, Nazis, zombies, witches, animal cruelty, and sadomasochism!

Home video took off in Britain, and that meant the small indie distributors and filmmakers had as much as a chance of getting their film viewed as the old guard, big players in the industry. It was a game changer, and meant money could be lost that would normally end up in their fat pockets, and it quickly became a big threat to the big players like Warner Brothers - they even held back titles while we saw an onslaught of independent VHS releases being distributed in the UK. Most were foreign cinema, mainly low budget horror and pornography, although horror was definitely the dominant force; a lot of those titles ended up on the video nasty list. The advent of home video put indie filmmakers' movies side by side on the video shelves with the big boys. So, you would have a multi-million pound movie next to a ultra low budget film costing anywhere from £25,000 upwards competing for attention - much like the times we are living in nowadays with streaming services like Amazon Prime, where indie offerings sit alongside blockbusters. Video nasties were just that. They were *made* to be viewed on VHS, which adds to the pure grindhouse feel of the viewing experience! Pristine Blu-Rays for low-budget schlocky horror is just that little bit to clean for me.

The so-called video nasties caused an outright media frenzy during the early 1980s. Was the influx of cheap foreign horror and soft-core porn films to blame? Or was it simply the nanny state attempting to control our every move, as predicted by George Orwell? Whatever the reason, video nasties made a huge impact! Videos with images of blood, guns, knives, gore, nudity, whips, demons and zombies, or busty females all fought for attention upon the shelf of the video store. If you were lucky enough to be a member of a local video store, all this - and more - could be yours; you could be thrust into the middle of a jungle in "Cannibal Holocaust," be a survivor trying to escape from zombies in "Zombie Flesh Eaters," or be thrust into the world of sleaze and sadomasochism in a Nazisploitation nasty.

So, just what is it we all love so much about horror films? Specifically the video nasty? Well, for me, horror films offer a completely unique cinematic experience to standard comedy, romance, or drama films. It's like comparing watching "Doctor Who" as a kid from behind the sofa to watching "Candid Camera." There's just no comparison! There aren't many films that can crawl deep under your skin, reach right into the hidden depths of your soul, and provoke and intensify your fears whilst making your heart pound and your palms sweat all at the same time!

But horror films, particularly video nasties, can than do just that.

Video nasties are more than just films. They are a global phenomenon. Growing up in Britain where you virtually had to be told when you could wipe your own arsehole, they became part of a ritual of growing up. If you grew up in the 1980s, or even the early 1990s, you couldn't escape the media frenzy surrounding them. There were also rumours from the schoolyard and down the local pub, where somebody would more often than not be talking about a video nasty. In the 80s and 90s, home viewing choice was VHS, and sometimes the selection on the shelves after certification in 1984 would not quite hit the spot. So, tracking down one of the banned titles was a must. Video nasties where like a drug - once you saw one, you were as hooked as many of the victims of the films! It may sound masochistic, wanting to feel and experience fear through the medium of home cinema, but many of us enjoy the thrill and adrenaline rush those films provide, along with the sudden bump back to the safety of your environment once it's over. It's through such films we can embrace our fears safe in the knowledge we're one step removed from the situation on screen. When watching a horror film, we are not seeking just entertainment but a thrill ride, a roller coaster journey of excitement scares and shocks that no other genre of film can provide. What would be your knee jerk reaction if someone were to say, "Don't look over there?" You immediately want to look over there. It's like being told that a horror film is too sick for you to watch.

If a film has been banned, you will instinctively want to watch it; you want to see what all the fuss is about. In a lot of cases, there was actually no good reason for banning the title, and it's then you realise you've spent months (even years) tracking down a low budget film from the 1970's you would be hard pushed to pay a £1 for (let alone the £50 you paid at a specialist market or collectors fair) all those years ago. It was worthwhile to find that hidden gem which popped up on the banned video list, and you would definitely have your money's worth making duplicate copies for friends and family! As a child in the 1980s, video nasties were harder to find than that final Garbage Pail Kid collectors card to complete your collection.

One thing we all have in common is death, although no one likes to talk about it. We are all going to die, and there's no exception to that rule; most of us are afraid of dying. Horror films, in a way, desensitize us to death, violence, and disease, which is a very powerful tool. Horror films evoke various emotions in the viewer - fear and anxiety to name just two. We love horror films because we know they aren't real, but they play on our deepest darkest fears and insecurities. As a youngster, the scariest film ever was "Jaws." It's not strictly a horror film (some say), but just the thought of sharks eating me alive makes my skin crawl even now! I grew up in a seaside town, so many weekends and summer holidays were spent at the beach, even putting my feet in to paddle, and all I could see was Jaws lunging out of the water at me! It didn't help that the local pier was home to Orca the killer whale - there was a huge sign at the front of the pier with the titular whale with his mouth wide open. I remember when I was about 10-years-old going onto the pier with some friends: we climbed up on the railings so we could get a glimpse of that killer whale - I think it scarred me for life.

Fear will be different for every individual, and will depend on a number of things (including upbringing, experiences, and personal circumstances). Fear creeps up on you when you least expect it, fear builds and plays on your own personal anxieties, fear can happen at any moment and anytime! While lying in bed at night, the darkness and silence brings fear disguised as shadows, which quickly turn into monsters and demons. The sound of the water heater, clocks, and creaking bring fears of intruders... or something far worse. Your imagination begins to run wild as you become overwhelmed and frozen with fear. Horror films play on such fears as they draw you into the characters, world, and you, too, begin to feel claustrophobic, alone and scared with no signs of hope. Thanks to the cinematography and heart-pounding score, you feel your pulse race as you experience *real* fear - your subconscious mind can't tell the difference between what you are experiencing for real or what you are watching in the movie. Fear is something you can relate to - we have all felt pain, cut ourselves, and broken bones; just by watching someone in pain or experiencing fear, we easily relate to what we see up on the screen.

Horror films provide escapism from our everyday lives; you need only turn to the news channel to see just how cruel real life is. Many horror films carry a hidden message about current news and affairs - they play on our fears of war, greed, lust, sin, corruption, murder, death, torture, rape, consumerism, and conformity.

You may say life is short, and if that is the case, why spend hour after hour watching horror movies?

Because we enjoy them!

Horror films aren't just murder, violence, and gore for gore's sake, as is the popular belief. In actual fact, many of the films are actually incredibly artistic, well-crafted pieces of art, which use talented writers, groundbreaking special effects, camera angles, lighting, and music along with hard-working actors and crew to ensure the quality of your viewing experience. All the while, they tread new ground and break barriers along the way.

Okay not *all* of them, but there are many titles that do just that. Many of the films on this list are the staple for filmmakers to learn from and be inspired by to create their own masterpieces. "The Evil Dead" was the first film that really sparked my passion for horror - I was blown away by it! The film is a feast for the eyes and candy for the soul! Most kids watch horror films to rebel against their parents' requests for them not to! Just like having a crafty smoke behind the bike sheds at school! At a young age, the threat of being caught watching the film is more heart-poundingly scary than the film itself. Studies show viewing horror films as a child can cause nightmares -both as a child and an adult, I say bring on the nightmares! Perhaps those nightmares will provide inspiration for a much-needed generation of upcoming writers and film directors. I'm certain monster films such as "Frankenstein" and "The Wolfman" would have been just as spine chilling to children and teenagers of their time as "Cannibal Holocaust" and "The Evil Dead" were in the 1980s.

Some people watch horror films to satisfy a morbid curiosity (even those who don't necessarily appreciate them). Those same people stop to inspect the remains of a horrific car crash or a dead animal tossed at the side of the road. Watching horror films can actually be a kind of therapy to some people; it can help them come to grips with fears and anxieties and be a way of dealing with grief. But, at the opposite end of the spectrum, viewers can also become desensitized to the horrific violence and exploitation featured throughout the genre. This increasing desensitization can lead the viewer on an unrealizable search to evoke those same reactions and emotions as when they watched a horror film for the very first time. That feeling of euphoria, that thrill can never be replicated. The thrill ride that is horror at times provides suspense, and at others leaves you literally watching the film from the edge of your seat. I (and most horror fans) enjoy putting themselves in the shoes of the victim, screaming at the screen whilst devising a plan to escape the situation.

Commercially successful indie horror films of recent years are increasingly predictable, but there are a few breaking new ground and making the headlines: "Get Out," "It Follows," The Babadook," "Hereditary," "Mandy," and "Baise-Moi," to name but a handful. Over the last decade there has been some really crazy, bizarre horror films - it seems like they have to break the rules and then take a shit on them as well. One thing is for sure, by doing this, not only will the film get exposure (although not always for the right reasons), but the viewer will be left thinking (and in most cases left in a state of shock).

I look out for unique films that offer unforeseen twists. I enjoy the use of unique camera angles and effects to create ambience, suspense, and fear, as well as the various ways in which each director endeavors to build suspense. Writers and directors of the horror genre have the opportunity to unleash their full potential of creativity and imagination to impress, shock, and terrify the viewer, whilst providing unforeseen twists and turns. Ninety nine percent of horror films are made with the sole intention of scaring the audience!

The reason for our global love of horror films is really of no consequence. They bring audiences pleasure, pain, fear, suspense, terror, and inspire the viewer to unleash their own creativity in the genre. Horror is like Marmite: you either love it or you hate it. Horror has dedicated fans unlike fans of any other film genre - they're great, passionate people. When you are a horror fan, you're a horror fan for life!

We seem to take advancements in technology for granted nowadays, as though it's always been there! In fact, it's hard to remember a time when horror movies weren't available at the click of a button or video on demand, a time when downloading the latest gore fest on your smartphone whilst commuting on the train, from the comfort of your armchair, or even on the toilet at home wasn't an option. In the 80s, audiences had to wait patiently for films to be released in cinemas, a further two years for the movie to be released on home video, and even longer for it to be broadcast on terrestrial TV. It sounds old fashioned to say, "They don't make them like they did in the good old days," but video nasties were fresh, they were new, they were breaking the rules, and making new ones along the way.

I crave for a era in film like it again!

A lot of today's horror films like Hostel, Paranormal Activity, and even The Saw films, started out as great ideas. They were very entertaining horror films, but copycat filmmakers re-hashed the same ideas and have since milked them to death - though they still pull in large numbers at theatres and in DVD sales. The strange thing is there's far less to the story, plot, and characters in those films than there was in the classic video nasty films of the early 80s! Most of the video nasties laid the foundation for the filmmakers who were certainly inspired by them. In the latest wave of torture porn flicks, gore is featured just for gore's sake ninety percent of the time. Not that I mind at all as I'm a lover of gore, but I love seeing new stories and not the same old same old. I think in order for horror to evolve, we need new ideas; I think we are finally going to realize in cinema that the scariest thing isn't the monster in the closet or the ghoul under your bed, -but we ourselves are really the true monsters to be scared of.

Just turn on the news!

Video nasties in Britain always had a bitter aftertaste; there was always that feeling of rebelling against the system by even owning certain VHS tapes and that any minute you might be raided! Okay, we are long past that era, but I know friends who were raided 19/20 years ago! It seems so bizarre now.

I think every generation holds a special place in their heart for the times they grew up in. The 1980s for me screams video nasties, VHS, and horror films! Who would have thought at the time video nasties would have had the impact they did, and have continued to have, on fans and filmmakers? Those films have become immortalized, and it's great to see new generations discovering the titles (even if it is on Blu-ray!). I see so many posts on social media of video nasty collectors - people trying to get full sets on DVD and Blu-ray, and still VHS collectors across the globe trying to complete their VHS nasty collection, which is almost impossible unless you are mega-rich because the VHS copies are worth so much and they are rare.

Video nasties have become part of my life. They which have managed to creep right under my skin and into the darkest depths of my soul…

-Tony Newton

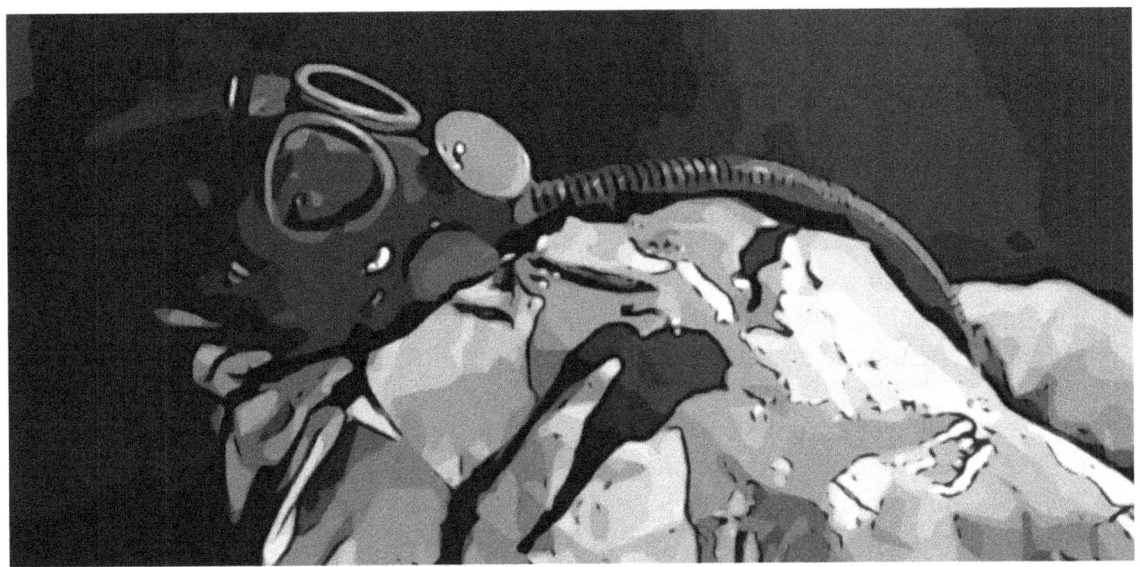

VIDEO NASTY

*I am the one that Mary Whitehouse hated,
I am the reason teenage boys masturbated.
I am the cannibal hunting for flesh,
I am the Driller Killer wearing a mesh,
I am the guts and I'm the glory,
I am the soft-core porno story.*

I am a video nasty.

*I am the reason Margaret Thatcher got you castrated,
I am the one your mother hated,
I am the Chainsaw massacre,
I am the Giallo Italian Whore,*

I am the snuff movie in the video store.

I am a video nasty.

*A Video Nasty,
A Video Nasty,
A Video Nasty.*

-Tony Newton

Chapter 2: Moral Panic in the UK!

"Mutilations of bodies. Cannibalism. Gang rape. That is what a video nasty is."
-Graham Bright MP

Moral panic is a highly intense feeling expressed by a mass movement over something deemed to threaten the social order. Moral panics are controversies that usually include social tension over a taboo subject; the term itself has been widely adopted over the last few decades by the media itself—it generally refers to bringing mass media attention to any subject matter, thus magnifying and bringing mass anxiety and concern around the subject being talked about. The term "moral panic" was originally coined by Stanley Cohen in his writings "Folk Devils and Moral Panicism" in 1972.

There has never been a bigger media publicized, so-called moral panic than the early 1980's video nasties campaign. The only other similar occurrence was around a decade earlier in 1973, when media attention surrounded Stanley Kubrick's film "A Clockwork Orange," with an MP even stating that the film would magnify teenage violence (in reference to the section of the film in which a tramp is beaten to death on the streets—there were reports of teenagers beating tramps in the street!). This followed the media frenzy over "The Exorcist," but even that could not even compare to the mass hysteria we saw in the early 1980's!

In 1982, Vipco placed an advertisement for "The Driller Killer" in a VHS magazine. It served to raise the awareness of such films to the attention of the masses.

What happened next was moral panic!

The whole genre of rental videos was criticized by MP's, Religious Groups, and The Press—along with numerous other groups and influential individuals; it was at that point the term "video nasty" was born.

A rating system had previously been in place at cinemas, but home videos were at that time unclassified. Consequently, the films were falling into the hands of unsuspecting children all around the UK. In some cases, the video covers themselves were enough to cause nightmares! The films quickly began to receive increased attention, including from the likes of Mary Whitehouse, who led a moral campaign to prosecute such VHS releases for their obscene content. Mary Whitehouse's campaigning received mass media attention from leading daily Newspapers and TV and subsequent involvement of MPs caused some horror films to be banned in the UK by the DPP (The Director of Public Prosecutions). In July 1983, those films were listed and their prosecution was pursued. The list of "video nasties" altered somewhat as changes and cuts were made to the films, and subsequently not all films on the "VN1 Video Nasty" list were prosecuted; films not prosecuted by 2009 were abandoned. Since 2001, a number of films from the banned list have been released uncut.

The main list of section 2 "Video Nasties" (the *infamous* list) features 72 films—39 of which were prosecuted and 33 of which either had unsuccessful prosecutions made against them or were not prosecuted at all.

-Tony Newton

Chapter 3: Public Concern—Video Nasties in the Media

"There was no need for them. They were unnecessary… and they were evil."
Graham Bright MP

The hype, panic, and sheer hysteria evoked by the media surrounding video nasties altered the face of the UK video market forever. But was the hype justified? Furthermore, are films containing explicit content *really* capable of influencing people to commit serious crimes—or even murder?

"Video nasties" was the term used to describe a specific group of videos deemed too explicitly violent for release in the UK; they thrived on shocking the audience with gore, sadism, and depravity

During the video nasty era, the films became an all too easy target to blame for violent crime that was occurring on the streets of the UK—with the media even going so far as to pin the blame for murders, such as that of little James Bulger, on the lack of censorship and exposure of unsuitable material to influential young minds. It was widely reported in the media that the 10-year-old murderers of 3-year-old James in 1993 re-enacted scenes from the film "Childs play 3" during the abduction, torture, and horrific murder of their victim. Were video nasties really to blame, or did they become a convenient scapegoat for the rise in violent crime in the UK?

NASTY

Following the introduction of video in the late 1970s, it rapidly became a popular medium that allowed people to watch their favorite films and TV shows in the comfort of their own home. However, it was closely followed by the criticism of graphic violence, gratuitous sex scenes, and satanic plot lines. At that point in time, the content of these video nasties had no specific legislation governing content, and the media, politicians, etc. began a strident campaign for firm legislative measures to be put into place. Although the measures served a purpose, they also served to fuel the public fascination with horror and violent movies. In 1981 the first complaints were made to the Advertising Standards Authority regarding concerns about the advertising of so-called video nasties. On the 12th May 1982 The Daily Mail featured an article outlining the dangers of domestic video with a piece entitled: "The Secret Video Show." The article highlighted the growing fears of the public concerning the availability of such terrible films to children in the home. The video nasty era emerged following an advertising campaign by distributors Vipco featuring several full-page adverts in a number of magazines portraying the explicit poster art of "The Driller Killer." The images showed a man with a drill being driven into his brain and led to numerous complaints to the Advertising Standards Agency—and war was declared on video nasties. Popular cult classics such as "I Spit on Your Grave," "The Driller Killer," and "The Last House on the Left" still somehow managed to find their way onto the shelves of UK video shops, although many of them had actually been banned from being released at the cinema. The moral panic surrounding video nasties that began with a few select films soon grew into a censorship frenzy, which had a huge impact on a generation of film viewers. As the medium of home video grew evermore popular—with video players featured in most homes throughout Britain—media attention grew and newspaper articles fuelled the fire with headlines such as in The Sunday times (1983): "The Seduction of the Innocent!"

Obscenity and Video

In August 1983, The Daily Mail's article "Taken Over by Something From the TV Set" featured claims one young boy had actually been *possessed* by a video nasty!

In November 1983, The Daily Star claimed video nasties had replaced party games and conjurers at children's parties.

In March 1984, The Daily Express claimed one in two children had seen a video nasty.

In May 1982, The Sunday Times used the term "video nasties" for the first time in an article entitled: "How Horror is Invading the Home." The article emphasized the explicit themes and content the videos provided, which could be viewed by minors throughout the UK within their own homes.

With video becoming increasingly popular, this and similar articles began to add fuel to the fire for the debatable campaigns for censorship and certification to be applied to videos, and with various politicians and social activist Mary Whitehouse (founder of the National Viewers and Listeners Association) they were a contributing factor into the frenzy of fear and trepidation surrounding video nasties.

The Express joined the campaign, and on May 28th it carried the headline: "This Poison Being Peddled as Home Entertainment." The head of the "Clean up TV" campaign, Mary Whitehouse, was granted an abundance of press exposure, despite the fact she openly admitted to not having viewed the videos she referred to as "Appalling and Utter filth." Mary Whitehouse played an important role in driving the moral hysteria surrounding video nasties forward, though there's no doubt the public hysteria was fuelled by the misrepresentation and exaggerations of the national press.

These campaigns, coupled with the media coverage and public concern, pushed politicians into creating and supporting the Video Recordings Bill. Labor MP Gareth Wardell described the video recorder as "a potential weapon that may be used to attack the motions of our children and young persons."

Mary Whitehouse wrote to each MP appealing for support and received 150 responses to back the legislation. For years, controversy surrounded the subject of violence in the media having a detrimental effect on society. The Video Recordings Act gave the BBFC (British Board of Film Classification) statutory power over the censorship of videos, requiring each and every feature film due to be released on video to be classified—with nonfiction and documentary films being the exception to the rule. Naturally, it brought about an underground market for the films, which were either sold from the back of a van or under the counter at video stores.

The DPP list of video nasties was made public in June 1983; 72 films appeared on the list at one time, and 39 of them were successfully prosecuted under the Obscene Publications Act. 33 of the films were removed from the list, after initially being part of it.

MP Graham Bright explained video nasties had a negative impact on children as well as pet dogs! For me, MP Graham Bright's comment neatly sums up the whole banning of video nasties! With people like that running the country—it really does say it all!

1984 and the classification rating system was not the end for video nasties—in some ways, it was just the beginning. With all the titles being prosecuted under the obscene publications acts, the hunt, the myths, the legends of the video nasty and the quest for horror fans to watch and own the banned titles had begun!

-Tony Newton

Chapter 4: Video Nasties confiscated!

It's actually amazing to think of small video distributors distributing exploitation and foreign horror films in the early 1980's against major blockbuster releases on home video and actually making a dent in sales—as well as changing the face of home cinema along the way!

Fast forward to today, and we see a very similar pattern. We are seeing something new, just as the home viewing medium was at the time VHS hit, with changes in digital and streaming technology. It's not only the big players—the branded big boys—who can grab all the attention. It's never been so easy to self-promote—with social media, anyone can get a book or film or album out there, be it through YouTube, print on demand, video on demand, watch per pay, Netflix, Hulu, Vimeo, Amazon Prime, VHX, etc.—all of those sites are game-changers. Just like with the video nasty era, we are entering into the unknown, and it's a huge worry for the big guys when the public can choose between an indie film and a generic blockbuster. The big companies are lowering their budgets for making films, and indie filmmakers are becoming the staple for horror once again—it is a very exciting time for indie horror, and you literally can't keep up with all the new releases! The change from filming on reel, shot to video, and now to digital has had a monumental impact and means low budget films can be made by anyone.

The banning of video nasties paved the way for the horror movies we have today, which have influenced directors, actors, and writers alike from all over the globe. The special effects used in some of the video nasties were highly original and groundbreaking; they not only paved the way but also broke pre-existing boundaries.

With the release of home video with no laws in place for their classification (apart from the obscene publications act from 1959, which was later amended in 1977 and only covered erotic and pornographic films), times were a'changing—but was Britain *really* ready for the video nasty?

The DPP were of the opinion the banned films were capable of corrupting the viewer, and were deeply concerned for the minds of young children who were allowed to view them.

In 1984, the BBFC recordings act enforced certification on all video media:

U- Universal (Suitable for all ages).
PG- Parental guidance for general viewing though some scenes may be unsuitable for young children.
15- Suitable for an audience aged 15 or above.
18- Suitable for an audience aged 18 or above.
Restricted 18 – (Blue stickers) Only available to those aged eighteen and over at licensed sex shops and cinemas.

All VHS video titles had to be classified and the correlating sticker placed on tapes on the shelves. These were later released with a sticker of the certification imprinted on both the cassette and the cover. From 1984, in the UK, video stores had to apply for a special license in order for the public to be able to rent 18-rated films. Video shops across Britain were forced to change: a driver's license was required as proof of age for customers to rent an 18-certified film. It was only in 1984 that the Video Recordings Act introduced power to certify and rate every new video release in the UK. In late 2009, it was disclosed that the 1984 video act for sale or rental classification never actually had any legal effect; this was discovered to be a so-called "technical error," with the terms not being communicated to the European commissions. Changes were brought in and the relevant steps were taken rectify this in the Video Recordings Act 2000: every title in the video shop had to be classified by the BBFC, whose staff increased as well as (one assumes) their turnover. At this point in time, a fee of approximately £10 per minute was charged to certify films.

James Furman came in as head of the British Board of Censorship in 1974, replacing Stephen Murphy as secretary of the board who allowed "The Exorcist" to be shown in cinemas with an X certification. It was "The Exorcist" that sealed Stephen Murphy's fate as secretary of the board of censors! A number of the films from the video nasty list were banned either due to explicit cover images or their themes. It was almost impossible to get a horror film through the strict guidelines of the BBFC at the time; it felt almost as though film was being made an example of, as if the BBFC were saying "don't even try to make a film with extreme violence or rape or similar themes, or at least try to have it released in the UK, because we are just not standing for it."

Often, I'll sit watching some of those films and wonder if anyone actually watched the film in full at the BBFC before deciding to ban it? In most cases, it feels like they merely tossed a coin. The DPP list allowed police officers across the UK to seize any titles on the banned film list; not all video rental stores removed banned titles, as they knew there was money to be made thanks to the media attention surrounding them. Many video store owners would rent the titles from behind the counter (a brown paper bag job!), much like renting an X-rated pornography title, as was the standard at the time.

The BBFC had to make the decision to cut the film, classify it, or ban the film completely. It's obvious they weren't going to get *every* decision right, but it's crazy to think the decisions the BBFC were making would have such a huge impact on our lives (video nasties and banned films have certainly been such a big part of my life!).

With all the rumors surrounding which parts of the films were actually real, it felt weird watching them—as if you needed to be cleansed afterwards and say a few Hail Mary's. I remember after watching "Snuff" on a very bad, 3rd rate reproduction cassette, my friend pulled the cassette out of the slow-moving VHS player and started to rip the tape itself 'til there was just masses and masses of it on the floor. He then put it in the garden bin, added some paper, and burnt the lot! Although the film itself was actually a complete let-down, the premise of actually murdering a cast member the way they did in "Snuff" was a very clever marketing tool; although it wasn't real, the debate lasted a while.

Most people today use the term "video nasty" on a broader scale; it can mean any horror film featuring exploitation of some form, gore, blood, and extreme violence. Films will continue to be censored and banned, though it's much harder to shock and scare the viewer nowadays. I really do think Britain is going to enter a new era of censorship: in some ways reverting back to how we used to be—or maybe even worse!

Recently, new rules have come into play in porn films. They prevent the portrayal of a huge number of sex acts, including those that may be dangerous or appear violent towards women. It's strange to think of all the films on the DPP list that now have a part in history and new a generation of horror films fans will enjoy for centuries to come. Without the BBFC, most of those films would have been simply low budget 80's horror movies, but they are now immortal, surrounded by myth and secrecy and will always have a place in the hearts of horror film fans across the globe. If you were lucky enough to be the owner of a VCR player back then, it was the key to the gateway to the world of the video nasty. Okay, you could opt for a kids' cartoon, but why would you? In the early 1980's, you could so very easily get your hands on uncensored unregulated horror films, exploitation films, giallo classics, and a whole host of videos that were doing the rounds.

The introduction of home VCR players brought with it thousands of video rental stores all across the UK. Most towns had more than 3 video rental shops, along with newsagents and even corner shops that stocked VHS rentals; many of those stockists had no idea exactly what the tapes themselves contained. Most video stores welcomed the BBFC act as it gave stockists peace of mind that they wouldn't be prosecuted, it didn't matter if the cover had a drill penetrating someone's head as long as the film had the correct classification sticker on it.

Pre-cert films are pre-certified films released by the distributor before the 1984 Video Recordings Act came into place. Pre-cert VHS films are highly collectable, many have uncut footage or an alternative cut to the cinema and DVD release, and are a great way to view some of the more obscene titles that were floating about. This helped my collection of VHS videos as, around 1999-2000, DVD quickly replaced VHS as the medium of choice for home entertainment, and VHS vanished as quickly as it had appeared. In the late 1960's and 1970's, the British censors had their work cut out preventing viewers from watching sexual violence, graphic nudity, violence, and gore. Prior to this, the censors concentrated mainly on religion, politics, and nudity, and this era brought along with it a new beast: sexual violence, which would be the theme around many of the films that even to this day are considered masterpieces (like "Clockwork Orange," "Straw Dogs," "I Spit on Your Grave," and "The Last House on the Left").

Personally, I would always chose to watch a video nasty on video; VHS tape not only adds to the nostalgia but the experience is so much better all round. Having a full set of the English releases of the "video nasties" pre-cert originals is the holy grail of the collecting world. Some of these tapes can fetch as much as £1500 each, though many of the tapes in circulation are actually copies. The price of such tapes are going up in value, as more and more people are collecting them, and with a limited amount in circulation, completing the whole set is nigh-on impossible! A few years ago, you could go to a car boot or trade fair and purchase tapes from as low as £1; now you just don't see them—except on eBay and fetching high prices!

Home video was reinventing home entertainment, and it was as powerful as the beginning of cinema. It's rumored the distributor of "Cannibal Holocaust," Go Video, sent an anonymous complaint to Mary Whitehouse in a bid to boost the popularity of their own film!

Home video as a medium was a concern for the UK, though many countries—including those in the EU—managed to cope with the introduction of VHS on a huge scale without the need for censorship, which caused questioning of over-censorship in the UK. The UK has always had strict laws regarding censorship, but it seems ironical in the UK that only a relative few years after the video nasty era there came the Internet, which remains largely uncensored.

Though there have been recent changes in torrent and peer-to-peer sharing sites for music and video downloads, which are being blocked in the UK by broadband providers, there are now talks in progress about putting certification on music videos and talk of opting-in for pornography. In my opinion, over the next few years in the UK, we are going to see big changes with censorship online, where up until now there has been little or none.

How would Mary Whitehouse enforce a ban of video nasties in this day and age? Every child and adult would rush to the Internet and find a way to access a film through downloads, online streaming, through a proxy server, peer-to-peer, or even via the Dark Web. Censoring video nasties just wouldn't work today!

With gruesome, yet enticing, video nasty cover art, it was almost a test of stamina to see who could watch the whole film without either leaving or even being sick. It became my obsession to complete my VHS collection of video nasties (of course, bootleg and copies counted). The only other obsession I had was with Garbage Pail Kids, which were equally disgusting in their own way; it wasn't until I was older I could appreciate just how clever some of those were (ironically it was 1988 film of the Garbage Pail Kids that basically killed the franchise)!

I became obsessed with the art of horror films, and this led to my bedroom walls and ceiling being covered in video nasty and classic horror film posters—my favorites being the art of Graham Humphries, who provided the art for "Evil Dead" 1 and 2 and "The Return of the Living Dead," along with "A Nightmare on Elm Street." These works of art capture not only the essence and feel of the movie but of the particular time period. For me, a video cover or poster art can take you directly back to a moment in time and evoke the feelings—just like a certain smell or a song can take you right back to your childhood.

VHS collecting is growing evermore popular in the UK and the US. There are a number of companies releasing titles strictly on VHS as a limited edition alongside either DVD or Blu-ray—like the remake of "Maniac," with great cover art, large, big box, clam shell case, and even a limited edition purple VHS.

One of the films I have just produced is "Grindsploitation," which is homage to exploitation 70's and 80's cinema, and is packed with faux film trailers (released by Troma entertainment). It also had a limited release on VHS video by Sub Rosa, and was actually one of—if not *the*—last VHS tapes released while VCR players were still in production.

In 1981, UK home video distribution rights could be bought for as little as £1000, meaning video rental shop shelves would be full of exploitation horror and soft core pornography VHS tapes. The films were making large amounts of money, with horror even overtaking porn films in the home rental market.

Panic

In 1982, MP Gareth Wardell—with full support—introduced the ten-minute rule bill. The bill made it an illegal offence to rent and sell adult movies to children. He also went as far as to say home video recorders were potential weapons that may be used to attack the emotions of our children and young persons.

The BBFC continued into the late 1980s and beyond into the 1990s. Nunchucks were a no-go, along with large knives and exploitive sex. Sex scenes were always looked at carefully and scandalous scenes of orgies were cut. The head of the BBFC said he could see actual penetration—whether it was a trick of the light or (as the director claimed) a candle mattered not; the scene would be instantly cut. Exploitation, sex, and nudity are considered acceptable in certain environments: For example, men in white coats telling people in an educational way how to have sex. The sex in films such as "The Karma Sutra" 1 and 2 is graphic but accepted within its context. It seems as though the BBFC have been making their own rules as they go; I wonder how many minutes of the video nasties were actually watched by them to justify their arbitrary actions?

In 1970's Britain, it seemed, as a nation, we were becoming more liberal. But, the 1980's and the BBFC soon put a stop to all that. Censorship in Britain, in my opinion, is far too harsh. To me, it seems like it was all for nothing, a waste of time and money, as in today's Internet age, literally anything goes. Censorship through the decades has been harsh, such as the banning of Tod Browning's cult classic "Freaks." That film was outright refused a certificate and would not be shown in the UK in 1932. In fact, the film would not be shown in the UK until *1963*, when it was given an X certificate, and even then the public questioned the BBFC for allowing the film to be shown. In 1970, the age limit for certificates at the cinema changed from 16 – 18. This meant films were passed with an X-certificate that previously would have been refused a certificate at all. Also, films were given an X-certificate and passed with minor cuts; those films also would have not made the cut when the X-certificate was intended for 16-year-olds.

As crazy as it sounds, during 1980 and 1984, film distributors would cut films themselves—worried the movies they were distributing would get caught up in the net along with other video nasties, which would mean dire consequences. Those titles included "Halloween 3: Season of the Witch," "Videodrome," "Children of the Corn," and even "The Dead Zone," to name just a few. There were many more casualties on the cutting list—distributors literally slashed segments out of them, which they deemed to be too nasty.

As the home video market exploded, so did moral panic across the country. There were many titles that got tarred with the same brush as the video nasties—even the likes of "The Best Little Whorehouse in Texas," "Lassie Come Home," and "The Big Red One" got pulled off the shelves with the mix-up as people thought the titles were porn-related films! (Well, The "Big Red One" you can understand!). The video dealers themselves were charged under the section 2 of the Obscene Publications Act for carrying certain titles in stock.

A large number of other titles not related to video nasties were refused certification on VHS by the beloved BBFC during the mid 80's and early 90's. They included the titles: "Back in Action," "Caligula," "Curfew," "The Evil Protector," "Hidden Rage," "House of Hookers," "Target Massacre," "Class of 1984," "The Trip," and "Savage Streets." That's just a very small sample and, strangely enough, it wasn't just horror films. "Kickboxer 4," "Angel of Vengeance," and "Bare Behind Bars" were also refused. Although, on the outside, Britain may have seemed more relaxed with the introduction of a rating system, they certainly were very far from it—it was a war only the BBFC were winning!

Some of my favourite childhood memories were walking around the video rental store; the dark dingy space with covers that would shock you. I think I actually had nightmares over "Driller Killer," even before I saw the actual film—just because I had seen the cover art on a poster in the video store. Even cover art for "Ghoulies" and "Critters" were enough to give me nightmares, but only for a few nights. Freddy Krueger, however, had staying power to give me nightmares for years on end! Trading VHS tapes between friends at trade stalls, collectors fairs, and car boot sales was a great way of getting your hands on titles that were hard to get hold of. Sometimes you would get lucky and find a copy of "Driller Killer," "I Spit on Your Grave," or something like "Anthropophagus" just looking up at you from the bargain bin in its original ex-rental big box. You wouldn't question how it got there; you'd just quickly pay for it and get out of the shop with a big smile on your face. A lot of my friends would always make about 10 copies from the master tape, sell the original from around £50, and easily get £5-£10 for the copies at collectors fairs and through targeted wanted-VHS ads in magazines. A lot of VHS peddlers not only sold bootleg horror and video nasty VHS tapes but pornographic VHS collections—but what young, self-respecting lad would choose "Deep Throat" over "Cannibal Holocaust?"

So many people were raided, and most suppliers had a list with all their contacts, including addresses, so it was not only the dealer who got fucked. This went on until the late 1990's, and in some cases beyond that as the majority of the video nasties were banned between 15 - 20 years. It wasn't just the so-called video nasties that were traded under the radar. It was also titles like "The guinea Pig films," "A Clockwork Orange," "Nekromantik 1 and 2," "The Texas Chainsaw Massacre 1 and 2," and even films like "Death Wish" and "Dawn of the Dead" and shot-on-video indie horror films. At most trade fairs, it paid if you knew the person running the stall, or at least had a mutual friend in common, as most of the good stuff was hidden behind the stalls in boxes and was not blatantly on display. Some stallholders would just have the VHS sleeve in an empty box on display so if they had anyone official investigate they could say it was only the sleeve for sale. Classified ads in popular horror magazines and fanzines were a good source, too; trading VHS through ads in the back of magazines such as "Darkside," "Fear," and many others was a great way to acquire more titles. Even if most of them were dreadful copies, at least you would get to see the film. Fanzines were a huge part of the underground horror scene—like-minded individuals, who all had one thing in common; a quest to own, or at least *view*, all the video nasties and other banned films. I was always a huge addict of fanzines; there was nothing more exciting than getting a fresh copy hot from the homegrown press. With access to the Internet today, we have lost the need for fanzines and have hundreds upon hundreds of websites, which are their equivalent, but I much preferred having a late night read of that loosely bound black-and-white paper filled of trash cinema, extreme horror, awesome art, and classified ads. Even to this day, I try to collect classic fanzines—including the likes of "Gorehound," "European Trash Cinema," "the Missing Link," "Burning Desirez," "Post Mortimer," "Critical Wave," and "Street Meat".

It's a shame the 1980's video nasty era brought along peddlers of untold shit on VHS, including what were rumored to be *real* snuff tapes and every other horrible thing imaginable. Initially, Video nasties and the other banned films were the only problem in the early 80s, but as the years passed by VHS was the medium for sharing some really nasty shit—including some very sick pornography. Dealers and anyone with a tape-to-tape set up had potential to capitalize on the video nasty ban and make money from VHS. People were making a lot of money, not me in the school yard selling VHS nasties for £1 upwards, or swapping a copy of "Driller killer," "I spit on Your Grave" or some Eurotrash with no English subtitles taped direct from the German channels from Sky TV for a bag of Munch Bunch crisps or a few cigarettes. Even to this day, I'm amazed when I look at my DVD/Blu-Ray cabinet that I am legally able to own all those titles, and how today's generation can click "buy it now" at £15 or nip to one of the last remaining music and video stores to acquire the previously banned video nasties. As I walk past titles like "Cannibal Holocaust" and "Nekromantik," it is the most bizarre feeling; the inner kid in me wants to buy every copy just in case we see the so-called video nasty era again—though I suppose it would be called "Blu-ray nasty," which hasn't quite got that ring to it, has it?

Thinking back, "Beast in Heat" took 8 years of hunting for me to finally get to watch it, and a further 8 years to own a copy—and that was just a bootleg copy. Perverts and fuck-wits ruined it for serious horror fans. I would say it was 50/50: 50% was banned horror dealing and 50% was smut and shit peddlers. So, you had the police looking for so-called "real" snuff films, extreme fucked-up pornography, and a number of illegal VHS tapes. If they did enquire or close your mini VHS nasty trading system, they would be relieved all you had on you was "Cannibal Holocaust" and not something far more sinister. The police hunted down dealers and investigated anything suspicious, and so many people were raided and had their VHS tapes confiscated. Thus, a lot of horror collectors would try to get friends from other countries to send over VHS cassettes, and a lot of those were seized, confiscated, and destroyed by Customs. It's a shame video nasty collecting was tainted with a seedy, blood-soaked brush. But, as with anything else, people will try to cash in on any market. Not all underground video dealers were pumping hard-core porn, so-called snuff tapes, and far worse, though—most were hard-core horror fans.

To be honest, I think during the 1980s and 90s and from experience with myself and friends owning video nasties, it did seem as if you got a smacked wrist by the police and your films taken away if you were trading e banned horror tapes (Video Nasties), The police would check over other VHS titles in your collection and maybe confiscate any duplicating equipment.

From what I can make out after speaking with the police at the time, they literally didn't know what the fuck was real snuff or not on the tapes because, as the years progressed, so did the makeup FX. The police were not only on the hunt for video nasties and horror films being sent through customs but child pornography, illicit porn films, and real snuff being traded on VHS. I think the sick bastards of this world made the whole thing ten times worse than it actually would have been; the police had very little control. I mean, I managed to watch and have copies of *all* the video nasties without spending a single night in a cell! There were a lot of raids in the UK between the early 80s and late 90s; I recall a big newspaper article in 1993 about a mass raid in the war on trading video nasties, and the headlines made it sound far worse than it actually was! "Videos Seized Depicting Torture, Bestiality, Animal Killings, Necrophilia, and Disembowelment!" A video may be depicting it, but apart from the animal killings in films like "Cannibal Holocaust" and "Cannibal Ferox," It was all faux, all special make up FX!

Looking back, I'm actually glad to have lived through those decades, and have an appreciation for the video nasties and VHS. I can't see a time in the future when I will be walking away from a film fair or a friend's house with a VHS tape stuffed down my pants anytime soon; the buzz of owning the original video nasties was an adrenaline-filled high, much like the ones I would get from watching the films themselves. As most of the titles were recently granted certification in the UK, these once illegal videocassettes, original big box releases, and copies that filled my bedroom now fill my lounge. Sadly, part of my collection has succumbed to mold, and only the VHS sleeve remains—the rest are in large boxes of mold-ridden tapes that now fill my loft, which I don't have the heart to part with.

The war I face now is keeping the mold and not the fuzz away from my prized big box original VHS nasty collection!

-Tony Newton

Chapter 5: Nasty, Nasty

"The more you try to ban it, the more it grows!"
-James Ferman

When a Video Nasty is Not Really Nasty!

It's a strange phrase, 'video nasty.' Coined by the adorably judgmental Mary Whitehouse and popularized by the reactionary media of the early 1980s, it manages to suggest titillation and outrage in equal measure. 'Nasty' is one of those quaint British words—of Middle English origin apparently (as in: "Did you see those *Hobbit* films? What a nasty piece of cynical money-spinning.")—conjuring up images of school bullies or smelly stink bombs. As to the word 'video,' that has now passed into the mists of time—something to do with unwieldy blocks of black plastic I think. Or am I thinking of cell phones?

And while we're on the subject, why wasn't it 'nasty videos'? Or better still, the more satisfyingly alliterative 'vile videos' or 'violent videos'? However, 'video nasty' it is. Admittedly it does have a certain ring to it; it might not be on a par with Film Noir or Grand Guignol, but in a cheap Essex car boot sale sort of way, it works.

The truth is that these so-called nasties were a ragbag of exploitative horror/sex films, some good, one or two brilliant, but mostly bad. Ineptly acted and staged, with gratuitous gore effects, the best reasons for watching any of these were usually the enthusiasm of the filmmakers. Faced with the challenge of producing an 80-minute flick on a pocket-money budget, things like tripods, retakes or well-honed dialogue all came under the heading 'Unaffordable Under Any Circumstances'.

But then again, I haven't seen many, and there plenty I don't want to see. Anything portraying cruelty to animals just seems wicked and morally reprehensible. It may be controversial to say it, but I strongly believe those sorts of films should be banned. I will take any amount of tasteless blood-drenched perversity—and I often do—but the moment an animal is harmed (or killed) for entertainment then that's just plain wrong. In any walk of life. Of course the same goes for humans, but 'snuff' movies have now been established as an urban myth, and actors who get injured for our enjoyment have all done it through choice and get paid for it anyway. So that rules out me ever watching films like *Cannibal Holocaust* (1980) or *Deep River Savages* (AKA *Man From Deep River*, 1972). But it's not just this sort of vile garbage that mistreats animals—*Walkabout* (1971) and the otherwise wonderful *Journey To the Centre of the Earth* (1959) also have their problematic moments.

Some of the more controversial titles turn out to be surprisingly well-made and engaging pieces. *I Spit on Your Grave* (1978) is an extremely accomplished film by director Meir Zarchi, who features a very strong woman protagonist. Its theme of (multiple) rape, and subsequent bloody revenge is the stuff of Jacobean drama. It's no worse than *Straw Dogs* (1971) in its casual brutality, and the rape scene is nowhere near as graphic as the one in the still-disturbing Jodie Foster movie *The Accused* (1988). Its 1980 re-release title was of course a calculated effort to court controversy—the original *Day of the Women* was far more representative of the material. *The Driller Killer* (1979) is another good film, containing a strong plot and decent characterization. You don't see as much drill-based mayhem as you think you're going to, even in the uncut version. It has a story, which is more than the first four *Friday the 13th*s could boast, much as I love them.

The most bizarre entry on the 'official' list of video nasties is of course Sam Raimi's *The Evil Dead* (1978). There's not a lot to say about this hugely enjoyable slice of hokum except that it's about as harmless as a goldfish and as scary as a jack-in-the-box. It's all about tension and atmosphere and semi-believable characters panicking in a remote TARDIS-like log cabin. Editing and cinematography is key to its success—it just moves at *such* a pace and it looks beautiful. The 'tree rape' scene is a minor lapse of taste, but its roots (sorry) are to be found in Celtic myths and ancient folklore, so I think we can forgive it. And, of course, it introduces Bruce Campbell, who comes into his own in the gorgeously self-indulgent sequel, which gives us exactly the same again - only better.

What else have we got? *The Living Dead at Manchester Morgue* (1974) perhaps, which I was introduced to only recently. A genuinely unsettling film, unerringly directed by Jorge Grau, it made this particular viewer deeply depressed. It's all so damned nihilistic. Shot in muted colour, with the Yorkshire countryside looking as bleak as *Straw Dogs*' Cornwall, it makes 1970s England look like the Dark Ages. Outrageous dubbing aside, this is hard to fault. Strange that its original title (it's had many) was *Let Sleeping Corpses Lie*. James Herriot it isn't.

Not a video nasty as such is *Xtro* (1983), as bad a British horror film as it's possible to imagine. A woman giving birth to an adult man is one of its *good* moments. The reason copies were seized by police in raids up North can only have been for its crimes against filmmaking in general. I wish I could expunge all memories of watching it, alongside such execrable British 'horror films' as *Paper Mask* (1980) and *Paperhouse* (1988). It's almost as boring as *Local Hero* (1983), but not quite.

More mainstream efforts, which are sometimes lumped in with the nasties, include *The Exorcist* (1973) and *The Texas Chain Saw Massacre* (1974). I have it on good authority that anyone who worked on the former film, and anyone who has ever seen it, will die. Shocking true fact. As to the latter, it really is very funny indeed.

My experience of video nasties is, as you can probably tell, hardly exhaustive. I have only seen a few. But the ones I have seen I have generally admired, if not actively enjoyed. As a sub-genre, they form an unusual footnote in the history of film. Perhaps they say more about the newspapers and the 'moral majority' than they do about the filmmakers. There really isn't anything equivalent in these days of fibre optic broadband and Netflix. Charlie Brooker's *Black Mirror* series has pushed the boundaries far more than any 1980s gore-fest. 'Torture porn' has been and gone.

In terms of bad taste, what next? *Operation Yewtree: The Musical?* It would make a nice change from *Frozen*.

-Mark Campbell   Author, Writer.

The Video Recordings Bill: An Exercise in Nasty language and Nastier Politics

"It is common ground that videos depicting violence and sadism are evil, because those who perform in them, or produce, or publish, or distribute, or sell them become, by that participation, less than human. I can think of no other form of words in which to express the repugnance we all have for these productions and reiteration would certainly not strengthen the feeling of horror."
Lord McGregor of Durris

"Personally, I do not have the slightest hesitation in joining in a war of extermination against those who trade in true video nasties. I do not have the slightest hesitation in doing that. I do not find myself troubled by liberal concepts in this regard. To me liberal concepts mean guarding values. I do not put any value upon the trade in video nasties."
Lord Mishcon: Video Recordings Bill, 02 April 1984

Politics, whatever your leanings, is in practice an exercise in the strategic deployment of words. This is to such a high degree that it's painfully obvious when a politician is out of his or her depth as was so often embarrassingly the case for the US when George W Bush was president.

Like him or loathe him his ability to mangle his home language was legend across the world. Language is the key to selling the ideas and ideals and he was frankly terrible at this fundamental political skill, at least for all but the most entrenched republicans to be frank. Other politicians could sell you the worst deals and make you feel like you won the lottery, suffice to say language is the primary tool of the politician and the Nasties scare was a prime example of the deployment of rhetoric. We have already seen some quotes from various members of parliament of the time and the transcript of video recordings bill readings from around late 1983 to mid 1984 are frankly a gold mine of the worst in political show boating and wagon jumping.

The issue of video violence and censorship in general was, and still is on occasions a familiar story that is nearly always attached to the back of concerns for or about youths or children and indeed the lower classes. Censorship has also more often than not tended to follow the popular medium and of course now it's the internet that's the boogyman, one which is sliding quickly into (and in fact beyond) the kind of censorship that befell the humble video cassette with many of the same hysterical worries of piracy and child protection etc. all the same arguments that were deployed against video and this is why it's so important to remember what happened then. The worries, threats, language and excuses almost exactly the same every time and even as I write there are new acts being passed though the US and the UK that threaten to add deep layers of censorship and corporate control over the internet the likes of which are reflective of the Chinese censorship that the western world condemned.

The language of the pro censorship players in the Nasties Scare is, particularly with the distance of time, utterly ridiculous and unnervingly familiar when given a little scrutiny. We have the tabloid press who presented the public with the heightened hysteria and catchphrases that many are familiar with, then of course there are pressure groups such as the festival of light who introduced a forced morality that Margaret Thatcher latched on to and of course this leads us to the politicians. For all the loftiness of their position it stands as a surprisingly shocking peek into the world of the politician when you take time to look at the words delivered in parliament, words that even then were well trodden roads having been uttered and indeed shouted across political battlefields throughout the history of published media. These words can be heard in debates about theatre, literature, television, comic books and cinema amongst other things from the early 19th century and before and the arguments are almost verbatim the same every time this happens. Mostly the concerns are for and about kids and the lower classes, the risk to the feeble of mind or morality, crime will be increased and our kids corrupted, your homes will not be safe and the streets will run red with the blood of the innocent and if we don't act now we would and should live in fear of the deviants, the perverts and the criminals.

First off let's take a look at how the Tabloids presented the case for the 'moral majority.'

When it comes to players in the Nasties scare it should come as no surprise that the lowest of the low tended to come from the Daily Mail. For those who are not familiar with the Daily Mails brand of journalism the fairest description would have to be a tabloid with pretensions to, or aspirations toward broadsheet quality. Unfortunately, it's all too often the case that the Daily mail tends to have to cater for the lowest common denominator and becomes like the Sun newspaper in disguise. During the nasties scare (amongst many other occasions) it became painfully obvious just what level of journalism they were practising.

Tabloid Terror

Amongst the media of the world the newspapers of the United Kingdom, as has been noted by many a commentator of foreign lands, is an almost uniquely vicious animal. In the early 80's this was particularly true of the tabloids that had a reputation for being particularly vicious and sensationalist in their approach to their journalistic output. The main players in these respects were of course The Sun, The Express, The Mirror and the infamous Daily Mail

The commentary coming from the Tabloids made even the outrageous statements emanating from the house of lords sound sane by comparison, at least for the most part, and of course given the level of trust many have in the printed word it was something that seemed to give the arguments, or rather assertions, credibility.

The Daily Mails campaign was, as I've said, the most infamous.

The Daily Mail ran with the campaign title of "Ban The Video Nasties" and took the campaign so apparently personally that claims of "The Rape of our Children's Minds" were even made.

What was happening here was beyond the norm, even for the Mail. The kind of language usually deployed by the tabloids was always vicious but equating a horror film to a rapist, a paedophile rapist at that, even to this day seems quite extraordinary. Considering the events that were unfolding in the country, with social self destruction going on around us, there suddenly seemed to be a disproportionate focus on home entertainment.

While it would be disingenuous to deny that these films could often be disturbing, even quite vile to the uninitiated, it is obvious with even minimal research to see that these claims have been made in the past about whatever media happened to be popular at the time.

Politically speaking the Mail was at the time aligned towards the Conservative Party and of course given that the political and social situation seemed to be going down the toilet with often frightening consequences then it seemed only proper to be looking for the cause. The Mail jumped on this sideshow of a campaign promise entirely willingly and with a fervour that matched that of a rabid dogs interest in a postman's leg.

Once again the familiar concerns of censorship campaigns were to be deployed and it's apparent when looking at historical censorship campaigns that more often there's a latent fear of class in the background of this censorious behaviour. Some of the most obvious examples of this can be seen in the censorship of such films as Battleship Potemkin which was rejected due to the BBFC's hang ups about political films particularly those with socialist concerns (concerns that were exacerbated by the political climate of the country at the time).

The other and most divisive propaganda tool of the censoriously inclined is the image of the child. In most cases it's quite clear that adults don't like to be told what they can and can't watch. This usually leads to the political party or activist group being told to mind their own business and it's a rather risky position to take in terms of PR and popularity. However... take the same goal, say the banning of sexually explicit or violent movies, and throw children into the mix and suddenly you've hit a raw nerve with the general populace. This is understandable and one should certainly not sneer at the human nature of wanting to protect children but it is also an easily exploitable facet of our nature, which can be used to manipulate opinion without much effort.

The main concern of the Tabloids however seemed far from being that interested in investigating any actual harm more than they seemed to be manipulating public opinion by emotional blackmail. This was and is not only dishonest but also utterly complacent as it neither tackles the true causes of the perceived problem nor offers any effective solutions. So the main thrust of the campaign turned from film piracy (an early concern amongst the media) towards projecting a concern for children and vulnerable adults. The language began to evolve to liken the use of VHS cassettes, specifically those featuring sex and violence, to being exactly akin to drug abuse, and this is not hyperbole. The early 80's was a particularly paranoid time when it came to drug abuse, conservative sensibilities were running high in the face of high crime and civil unrest so all the 'ills' of society were blamed on these few social issues. Likening violent videos to drugs lent them an extra air of being the causal element in the problems of the time without even considering that if you were to link them at all they could just as justifiably be described as a symptom. Linking video viewing habits to violence was rather tenuous at best anyway but the tabloids made confident though ultimately spurious claims, as did the authorities that they were quoting. Rapists were now being partly excused by the evil influence of horror films and the viewing of video horror was according to some the same as shooting up with heroin, it was apparently as addictive and corrupting.

The Express joined in on several occasions with the spurious claims of a causal link between the crime of rape and the viewing of video horror, for instance on the 28th of June 1983 they reported on a large article on page 3 "Sick videos lead youth to commit double rape."

This headline was based on hearing evidence of the young man Martin Austin, then aged 18, Who had spent some time watching violent videos after which he went out and raped a couple of women on separate nights in their houses. Austin had watched this "Unremitting diet of violence."

Of course this was also front page news for the Daily Mail who proclaimed that "Boy, 18, attacked women after seeing films" seemingly implying a causal link between the two perhaps suggesting that he was 'normal' beforehand, though a brief look into his history reveals a deeply troubled past that cannot be blamed on videos. The young man had a history but it was, according to the press, the activity of watching the films that lead to the crime. He'd watched the films and THEN gone out and committed the rape. With this kind of thinking they seem remiss in not mentioning that he'd probably eaten a meal, drank a drink and spent every night of his life previous to this indulging in hours of sleep at a time.

A pattern of relating crimes committed to the activity of watching videos crops up on many occasions and the act of watching video violence and sex was claimed to be an act of grooming and even training for a life of depravity. The Daily Express reported on the 24th of August 1983 in a piece entitled "Vile harvest of the porn peddlers" that "In the last few decades we have developed a vast multi-million-pound industry which uses powerful techniques to educate people in the excitements of violating others". Holbrook, in a report that makes claims of "government reports" and "overwhelming evidence" and even asserts that when a group of soldiers raped a girl that they were making some kind of symbolic statement by putting "a pornographic magazine between her legs and [photographing] her."

It seems remarkable given the brutality of such an offence to imply that the soldiers were in some way making an overt, if ironic political statement about pornography and the link between the offence and the presence of pornography is given no more support than the opinion of the writer.

Fans of logical fallacies will be quick to note the 'appeal to authority' fallacy with multiple references to reports and studies that are not named or given citation in any form other than the Williams report which refers to an out of context quote.

"There are no characters or genuine human presence…the whole effect is dehumanising- destructive of any sense of personal individuality or life"

Williams report as referenced by David Holbrook [Dexp 24/08/1983]

In another case the actions of 22-year-old Kenneth Smart was introduced when an increasingly familiar defence was used once more in court. "Video nasties 'led to killing'" proclaimed the headline of a small report when the defence for Mr Smart, accused of murdering his friend, stated that they had been at a club where they had viewed "the sort of nasties about which we have heard so much" [Dexp 06/071983 pg. 7].

As is so often—if not nearly always—the case, however the offender in question usually has and, in this case, certainly had a long track record of behaviour, which makes it less surprising that they have done what they have done.

It seemed that when the purpose suited them the tabloids and other interested parties were only too willing to take the word of a murderer as being gospel. Far from being skeptical at such an offhand excuse for his crimes the reportage was such as to validate this claim, after all it made their lives easier if they could concisely report that the cause was known, that it was simple and obvious and of course ask 'why was no one doing anything about it?'

Then when the youths of this country were not actually committing bloody murder they of course were being seduced, degraded and defiled by the vile and seditious nasties...

BAN VIDEO SADISM NOW

"Four children in ten watch video nasties" cried the Express in November of 1983 following up that sensational and alarming statistic with the claim that "Six year-olds are hooked on violence sex and horror films" [My emphasis]

And on the 26th April 1984 they also ran a story about the plight of a young boy apparently so traumatised by the video nasties that he required tranquillisers in order to continue watching them. The headline ran "Boy takes drugs to see videos." While one could argue semantics regarding the use of the word drugs it at least superficially seems to be used in a fashion that would provoke thoughts of class A narcotics. Despite his apparently being traumatised by the videos he is also reported to have enjoyed them even though he had the apparent need to be sedated to watch them.

While it's not unusual for the tabloids to rely on sensational language to hook in the reader, it has always been a feature of newspaper reporting, all the news papers seemed to be singing from the same song sheet and the Soprano among them was eventually to be The Daily Mail. The earliest reports and some of the most vicious in the early days however were not just from the Daily Mail; in particular they were from the Daily Express, another right leaning tabloid. However it's very important to point out that tabloid involvement with the issue was not a single allegiance issue. The press in general were laying into the video industry. The Mirror, another early player in the campaign, were also particularly dogged in its attacks and the broadsheets where one would expect a higher degree of journalistic responsibility were often either repeating the same arguments or being very quiet in their responses which would mostly be buried deep in the news paper. This is not to say the broadsheets were even nearly as bad in their general coverage of the story as the tabloids but certainly they were not challenging or questioning the push nearly as much as they should have been. Unfortunately the majority of the serious discussion was left to the periodicals to explore and of course the audiences for such reading was relatively limited.

Martin Barker, one of the leading voices in the anti censorship campaign writes in New Society [Nov 1983 pg 231-233] an article which he later says he was 'Stitched up' on over a dramatic illustration that the magazine used.

A familiar weapon in censorship debates was levelled against Barker and anyone who spoke out against the government and tabloid stance on the issue. Anti intellectualism and claims of academic elitism came and those who stood against the idea of the VRA were branded as either misguided 'dupes' or implied to be collaborators in some sort of conspiracy to corrupt the nation. The implication of this approach is that anyone who considers censorship as anything other than a positive thing should be ignored at best or preferably vilified. They were to be labelled as being complicit, as being responsible for actual crimes as Meir Zarchi, director of I spit on your Grave found when he was put in front of Martin Austin's mother as she blamed him for her sons behaviour.

It's this war of character that seemed particularly odious and one that the Tabloids were typically at the front of and of course there were very few forums for the anti censorship side or indeed the directors of these films to respond to these allegations. To be fair we have to acknowledge that the filmmakers were making these films for a wide range of reasons from the purely financial to the real desire to make a serious film but the suggestion that there was some kind of plot to deliberately corrupt their audiences is libellous and fantastical, the worst kind of conspiracy theory tripe. The media though chose to focus on what they saw as the most egregious examples, the ones with shocking sounding titles or premises. They simply didn't care what was actually in them any more than the politicians did, an example of this being Evil Dead and of course the infamously mistaken titles of The Big Red One, and The Best Little Whore House in Texas. When it came to one of the most emotively preached about title on the nasties list, Faces of Death the houses of commons were alight with indignation and disgust about one scene in particular which was entirely fake, a not uncommon practice in Mondo style film making. The leaders of our country had been treated to a 'gag reel' of the highlights of the video nasties including a rape scene from I Spit on your Grave and the most spoken about Faces of Death's monkey brains eating scene. It's understandable that these scenes would shock the uninitiated members of parliament (despite their many protestations they personally would not be affected by such material). The scene in question, set in an obviously fake restaurant in which the exotic dish of monkey brains would be served, is quite difficult to sit through even if you know its fake but the viewers at this out of context clip show didn't know and didn't care to know what was actually going on. The whole issue of the Peter Kruger's montage of the worst of the nasties is illustrative of the whole approach to the nasties, take the worst they have to offer to heart and don't consider the rest. This is exactly why there were going to be problems if these films were to be processed via the OPA which had a specific clause to ensure consideration of the film as a whole and not just these moments that some found so offensive.

The clause in question in the Obscene Publications Act states that the work as a whole must be taken into consideration. The fact that this legislation was being pushed through so fast, that the public, politicians and activists felt the OPA was inadequate, was precisely because they were taking these shocking moments out of context. The OPA's built in protection of freedom of speech was an obstacle for the censorious precisely because it pushed the juries towards being more critical of rather than reactionary to the content and to be successful in their campaign they would have to circumvent it.

"The objective is to establish an obligatory system of classification for video works and to outlaw the small minority that go beyond the pale. The main beneficiaries, obviously, are the children who will be protected from seeing material that might injure their young minds."

"(The) VCR, as I shall call it for short, is to be found in something like one in four homes in the country, mostly in urban rather than rural areas"

-Lord Nugent of Guildford

What is a less remembered aspect of the whole Nasties scare is that it wasn't exclusively to do with horror films. A few of the Tories, including some of the most prominent figures, were also pushing to ban soft core sex videos and the shift from the position of banning adult entertainment, something that was clearly and obviously aimed at consenting adults to swinging the focus to horror films was something that was traceable in the very language that was used. Bernard Braine, Margaret Thatcher, Leon Britain and by association, Mary Whitehouse were quickly defeated in the motion to ban R18 material from the video format, clearly the idea that the government were to meddle in the availability of soft core pornography was something that plenty of MP's were opposed to. [Christopher Meyhew House of Commons Hansard 20 Oct 1982]

Does my hon. friend agree that the Lord Chief Justice, when presenting the Darwin lecture, gave it as his opinion that there was a direct link, albeit imitative, between the sex and brutality depicted in pornography and films and the rise in the number of sex crimes and crimes of violence? If the Lord Chief Justice is right, is there not a moral imperative on the Government to take further action?

Mr. McNair-Wilson
House of Commons Debate 01 December 1983 vol 49 cc976-7
Mr. Gareth Wardell asked the Secretary of State for the Home Department what information he has as to the number of cases brought under section 2 of the Obscene Publications Act 1959 regarding video cassettes which were (a) heard before magistrates and (b) tried at Crown court; and if he will name the film titles in respect of each successful prosecution. Mr. Mellor: The information collected centrally on prosecutions under this Act does not distinguish separately offences involving video cassettes and does not record the titles of video cassettes in respect of which successful prosecutions have been brought. Records available to us for

1982, which may be incomplete, of proceedings under section 2 of the Obscene Publications Act 1959 show that 282 defendants were proceeded against summarily in magistrates' courts, of whom 121 were found guilty, and that of the 257 defendants who appears for trial at the Crown court, 113 were found guilty.

House of Commons Debate 10 November 1933 vol 48 c200W 200W

So soft core pornography, and R18 material were off the table and now the attention of the politicians was turned towards a more vague target, vague in the sense that the genre and material was intended for a less marginalised and certainly younger audience than pornography. However the language that was used against violent horror videos certainly made no distinction between the sight of two people having sex, consensual, real, fake or otherwise, and the fantasy worlds that the Nasties provided. Indeed the violent acts that took place in the video movies were even spoken about in terms that suggested that they were a document of reality.

This projection of fantasy into reality is rather troublesome coming from a section of society that is supposed to be dealing with the real world. The video industry was one of the most successful business enterprises in a time that found the country mired in all manner of social and financial difficulties. It seemed at odds with the Conservative parties ideals to be adding in a layer of legislation that would stifle one of the few successful industries of the time that was creating jobs. When you look to just before the main campaign began it is obvious that the government had no interest in statutory censorship and indeed were aware of the implications that such actions would take.

When the anti video campaign began it's a matter of fact, given this quote that the politicians were aware of the difficulties that legislation would present not least morally but also practically. These concerns were astonishingly set aside and while most politicians across the party lines were towing the line there were some still expressing concerns.

Lord Houghton of Sowerby in particular took a remarkably brave, and all too unusual, stand against the bill, constantly urging caution and highlighting the less than palatable possibilities and implications of the bill. His comparatively reasoned approach to the discussion was immediately ridiculed by the following speakers, who offered little more than patronising responses. This was now to be expected during the debate where anyone who argued against the supposed consensus was either naïve, corrupt or in league with criminals and child abusers, and this is not an exaggeration. Martin Barker found himself under constant attacks during television debates and any attempt to introduce nuance to the discussion was responded to with what was referred to as "Common Sense", the by word for gut feeling.

It's this 'common sense' this gut feeling that informed almost the entirety of the debate. Facts be damned, facts be made up for that matter, and those who decided to speak from a skeptical point of view where dismissed as being either ignorant of real life or of being complicit in the evil deeds of the video industry.

-Glenn Criddle Writer/Critic.

Chapter 6: Cheap Thrills and Visceral Spills

Being a horror movie fan, for me, is all about looking for the next thrill. I want to be scared. I want to be disturbed.

As a teenager I became sick of watching PG-rated horror movies that claimed to be the "Scariest Movie Ever!" I wanted something with real bite! I wanted something that would reach out of the TV and slap me in the face!

That's when I found video nasties.

These movies were something I could sink my teeth into! Something that really got in under my skin, making me shiver with repulsion and glee combined. Those grainy, amoral, gore-soaked reels of celluloid were truly disturbing in their day, and they still have the ability to freak out jaded horror fans nearly four decades later!

Take this quick anecdote for example:

When I was nineteen, my best friend Cameron and I decided to watch *Zombie Flesh-Eaters* and get deliriously high. I was really enjoying it, up until the scene where a naked Italian girl gets her eye impaled by a ten-inch splinter of wood jutting out of a doorframe!

That scene really fucked me up. I mean *really*. The blood, the pus, the screaming… when the scene was over I found myself staring breathlessly at the screen, my face flushed, tears threatening to spill from my eyes.

What the hell had I just witnessed?

I turned to look at Cameron. He glanced at me from the corners of bloodshot eyes and said, "You felt it too?"

After that night, I didn't watch another horror movie for about six months, and I never smoked weed again.

That's the power that *Zombie Flesh-Eaters* had over me. It made me feel powerless and small, like a frightened child.

That's the magic of video nasties! They're the ultimate horror movie thrill. The ultimate test for any newbie horror fan trying to prove his worth.

If you can sit through forty minutes of rape in *I Spit on Your Grave*, scenes of real-life animal slaughter in *Cannibal Holocaust* or the aforementioned "eyeball" scene in *Zombie Flesh-Eaters*, then you can pretty much handle anything that life throws at you.

If you can survive all 39 prosecuted Video Nasties (as well as the 33 that weren't prosecuted), then you truly are made of stern stuff.

Seriously, you deserve a fucking medal or something.

-Joe Ramshaw   Writer, author.

When I was growing up in the South Wales valleys with two older brothers in the house, there were some absolute truths that I learnt to live by very quickly.

If they were having a bad day, I was having a bad day.

If they got beat up, I got beat up.

If they wanted to watch Swap Shop instead of Tiswas, I am watching Swap Shop.

But having brothers aged eight and ten years older than me had its good points too. Especially the VHS tapes they brought home twice, sometimes three times, per week. Because wound away in those surprisingly heavy black plastic cassettes were the stories, stars and slayings that would thirty years later inspire me to write my own horror stories and hopefully scare a new generation into loving the horror genre.

I was just becoming a teenager when the video nasty boom hit its peak. I can say with some confidence that I think my first erection was triggered by five seconds of nipple and three butt thrusts. I can certainly say with extreme confidence that a video nasty put me in hospital.

My eldest brother 'acquired' a pirate copy of Friday 13th Part 3 along with a few sets of horrendous cardboard 3D glasses with flimsy red and blue vinyl lenses. It was 1982 and the grainy copy of a copy of a copy was hard to watch but squint through our spasticated glasses we did as Jason really came into his own, stepping out from the shadow of his sweet, caring and misunderstood mom Pamela (also my mum's name, much to me and my brothers' amusement) to become the world's most recognised slasher.

The movie ended and bedtime approached. I was shitting it. I knew my brothers would try to scare me but they didn't need to. There were shadows in my room. If I fell asleep, like a resident of Elm Street, I was a dead man. My stomach began to churn. My pulse went through the roof. Sweat poured down my face. The pain in my belly got worse. And worse. And worse. Twenty minutes later and I was in hospital with a doctor's finger going where not even Jason would dare to venture. They said it was appendicitis, but I knew it was something far more (video) nasty.

-Craig Jones   Writer, Author: OUTBREAK: The Zombie Apocalypse, the vampire hitwoman series, GEM, Secret of Skerries: Son of Blood.

When I was a kid, my parents weren't too clever when hiding presents. At a very early age I discovered their hiding spot in the back of my dad's closet, and I would frequent this stash often around birthdays and holidays. I must have been about 14 years old when I found *Cut! Horror Writers on Horror Films* among my Hanukah gifts. I thumbed through the book, eager for a sneak peek at what authors like Anne Rice, Clive Barker, and Ramsey Campbell had to say about horror films.

But all this flew out the window when I came across a chapter by Stanley Wiater called "Disturbo 13: The Most Disturbing Horror Films Ever Made." Every chance I got, I would sneak into my dad's closet to drool over these forbidden flicks, most of which I had never heard of. Then the book was wrapped, and I waited anxiously until it was finally gifted to me, and I made it my goal to view each and every one of these films.

Some were easy to find. *I Spit on Your Grave* and *Henry: Portrait of a Serial Killer* were available at my local video store. *Bloodsucking Freaks* and *Combat Shock* were available on VHS by the then-unknown Something Weird video. *Last House on the Left* was practically mainstream by then. A few of the selections took a while to track down, and I never did find *Man Behind the Sun* (but I also haven't looked in a while). But one piqued my interest, above all others: *Cannibal Holocaust*.

I'm not sure what it was about Wiater's description that drew me in. It certainly wasn't the "explicit scenes of live animal slaughter." There are mentions of "unending scenes of cruelty," and the fact that, unlike other cannibal films at the time, the "civilized" white man was at least as savage as the natives. Add to that the description of a girl being "punished by her tribe by being impaled on a massive pole - which is driven up through her vagina right out through her mouth," and I was in.

At that time, *Cannibal Holocaust* was banned in a dozen or more countries. I assumed it was banned in the United States, but I now suspect that it may have simply been unreleased. In the mid-1990s, distributors weren't eager to release a film so violent, its director was indicted for murder. It took me about a year - maybe two - to find a bootleg of *Cannibal Holocaust*. It was a copy of a copy of a copy on an unmarked VHS tape that I got at a local horror convention. It was a few more days before I could watch it - I had to wait until my parents were out of the house - but I was astonished by what I saw.

Being a bootleg, the tracking warbled and the image was fuzzy. I couldn't clearly see a lot of things, namely the animal mutilation (thankfully) and the climactic orgy of dismemberment, but I could see the impaled woman very clearly, an image that stuck with me for years. (I included it in an art portfolio the next year. Unsurprisingly, my teacher nearly failed me.)

I was so proud of my illicit video that I took pleasure in talking it up to all my friends. Only one took me up on the offer to watch it, and it was with glee that I showed it off to him. He was horrified.

Cannibal films are one of my favorite horror subgenres. I have always loved extreme films - the weirder and more perverse the better. Despite recent popularity in projects like *The Walking Dead* and *Hannibal*, cannibalism still remains a very taboo subject. Over 30 years after its release, *Cannibal Holocaust* maintains its shock value and its cultural significance. It is considered the first "found footage" film, paving the way (for better or for worse) for films like *The Blair Witch Project* and *Paranormal Activity*. But nothing has ever matched the brutality of *Cannibal Holocaust*.

-Alyse Wax   Editor, Freelance writer including ShockTillYouDrop.com, Bloody-Disgusting.com, SuperHeroHype.com, DailyDead.com, and Fangoria Magazine. Author: Curious Goods: The Complete Friday the 13th: The Series.

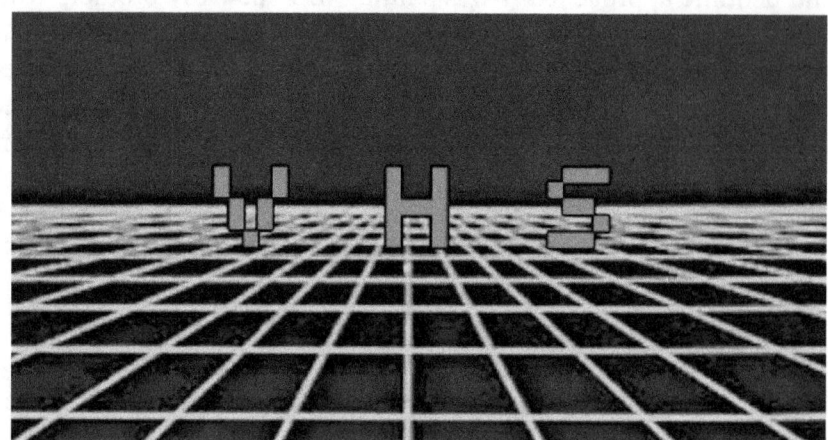

Nostalgia ain't what it used to be! However, the mere mention of VHS brings back blurred and fuzzy feelings of warmth and happiness.

The first video recorder in our household was from Radio Rentals and it was precisely that, a rental. Not many people could afford to own one in those days so you paid on the never-never. In addition to the usual tracking, rec, play, rew, and ff buttons it also had an audio dub option, which meant we could add a soundtrack to our old super 8 silent films once they had been converted to video.

I might be mistaken, but as I recall there was a £40 joining fee to get you membership of the first video shops. You then became part of a faux library set up, you were in effect swapping your tape with the other members of the 'club' for a couple of quid fee each time. Pretty sure this is how it worked until 'Free Membership' became the next big draw to get you to defect to a rival shop. The actual videotapes were securely stashed behind the counter with just the bright boxes on display although even those were soon replaced with black and white photocopies. You took the box of your choice up to the desk and were given the valuable corresponding tape from the vault in a cover emblazoned with the shop's name. If you failed to take it back on time you were soon racking up fines that increased on a daily basis. When a week or more had passed that was it, you could never afford to go back to the shop again and pay the hefty fine. So you spent the rest of your life avoiding the local video shop owner, which involved taking long diversions to avoid walking past the shop and ducking behind cars if you had the misfortune to run into him/her in the street. So then one of your friends would become a member of the video shop and start the entire process all over again. There was this one kid that used to go to our school though, he had two video machines and could make copies of films. Thus, seventh generation copies of A Clockwork Orange and The Long Good Friday were circulated alongside the usual blockbusters of the day. Then the banning started. Much like horror comics in the 1950's or computer games now, the youth were being corrupted and the blame had to lie somewhere. So the films that disappeared off the shelves such as Cannibal Holocaust, I Spit On Your Grave, Driller Killer and Zombie Flesh Eaters became much copied and sought after items. The grainy, lo resolution of videotape only enhanced the shock value of the films of this era. Back then the demagnetised heads on a VHS player gave the images a dream like quality so lacking in today high definition. Add to that the intrigue of a 3rd generation copy and you held in your hands something exciting, daring and illegal. The ability to rewind and replay the highlights empowered the viewer further and went onto inspire a generation of filmmakers.

In this day and age, with media available at everyone's fingertips it is hard to imagine what life was like back then. Prior to the arrival of video shops, there was no other way to watch 18 rated material, except for sneaking into a cinema, which was probably the stuff of urban legend anyway. Either that or get the tallest, oldest looking kid in your year at school to buy the tickets to a AA film whilst you nonchalantly hovered around the concession stand trying to look mature whilst perusing the Paynes Poppets and Kiora. This was the successful method that enabled me to see Rollerball aged 12. Also, if you missed the first run of a movie, unless it cropped up on a cinema double bill some years later, you were looking at a minimum 5 year wait to see it on TV, if at all, because, let's face it, most 'video nasties' would never turn up on late night TV anyway. Even with the advent of Channel 4.

Which brings us to Flesh For Frankenstein.

"To know death Otto, you have to fuck life… in the gall bladder."

Andy Warhol's name is the first thing that appears in this film, although I would hazard a guess that he had absolutely nothing to do with it in any way, shape or form. It still is somewhat baffling that by the early 1970's Warhol had scaled this kind of dizzying commercial heights. Wasn't he the guy who made a film of the Empire State building that ran for 24 hours straight and made movies of his lowlife, drug addled friends in a rundown loft in New York? I say 'made movies' but the reality is more likely that he stood around whilst Paul Morrissey did all the actual work. He was the person amongst Warhol's coterie who knew how to load a 16mm film mag and went on to create a genre and eventually direct movies in his own right.

So, what is the nastiest thing about Flesh For Frankenstein? The wooden acting perhaps? Or the exposition laden dialogue?

Well for the price of admission you get a generic mad scientist, Udo Kier's unforgettable Baron Frankenstein played like a young Dieter Laser from The Human Centipede. The Baron works in his castle laboratory trying to create a master race of 'ZOMBIES' by sewing together parts of mannequins and stuffing them with offal. Ably assisted by his gurning, bug eyed assistant, Otto, a stand out performance from what appears to be a young Harry Enfield, they have created a female 'ZOMBIE' and just need a head to complete the male equivalent. Soon they are joined by a wandering New York hustler, Joe Dallesandro, looking just like Tom Hardy straight off the set of The Revenant and wearing much the same costume - although he's had a shave for the sake of characterisation. He soon gains employment servicing the baron's wife, who is also his sister - don't ask. Around this point the Baron decides to decapitate Tom Hardy's best friend, Sacha, and use his head to complete his creature mainly because he has 'a perfect nose'. What else could a master race of 'ZOMBIES require? Unfortunately Sacha doesn't quite rise to the occasion as expected and things turn progressively nastier. The film was originally shot in 3-D so expect handfuls of internal organs being thrust towards the camera and the gratuitous use of a boat hook.

I imagine it is no coincidence that The Rocky Horror Picture Show appeared two years after this film's release. They bare remarkable similarities with the Rocky Horror Show being a kind of Disneyfied, lightweight, musical, bastard offspring of Flesh For Frankenstein.

The camerawork and art direction are sumptuous as are so many Italian made films of this era. The pace is languid but never boring and the effects awful. However this film is still more entertaining, innovative, imaginative and watchable than the majority of horror movies released nowadays. Joe Dallesandro is an inspired piece of casting; I imagine it is entirely historically accurate that all Bosnian peasants spoke like Robert De Niro in Mean Streets. Not sure that the humour in the performances is intentional but it raises a good few laughs. This is a good attempt to out Hammer Hammer Horror and push the limits of what was playing in the local Odeon's and ABC's of that era. Expect necrophilia, incest and decapitation. Bizarre and hilarious. They don't make them like they used to but there is probably a reason for that.

-Graham Fletcher-Cook   Actor, Director, Producer.

As I was yet to be born during the Video Nasty controversy of the 1980's I can't give you a personal first-hand account of my experience with them but as a big horror fan, and movie fan in general, it is impossible for me not to know of and not to have felt the repercussions of the incident.

An unsurprising movement born out of conservatism, and really down to a matter of taste dressed up as a concern 'for the children', the outcry and attempt of banning of some horror films from this period, now looking back, seems almost ludicrous considering the quality and content of the films. Hearing stories of people having to buy them under the counter and of stores being raided like they were home to drugs and weapons seems almost comical. Now that most of these films are out on general release, easily picked up from high street film stores or online, you feel it really was a lot of fuss over nothing. My own experience with them has been in buying them from shops and happily watching them in the comfort of my own home. I also remember the DVD covers of films like *Cannibal Holocaust* and *Cannibal Ferox* proudly shouting that they were once banned in several countries, as my brother bought them in our local film shop, though not without a tut from my mother.

What is interesting is the legacy of the video nasty is now really more seen as a badge of honour and almost as a challenge. People now watch some of the so-called Nasties to see what the fuss was all about. Certainly, when compared to some of the films which are widely available these days, and available on general cinema release no less, the Video Nasties are tame by comparison. Violent films are still being made, this time made for wide box office release, such as Eli Roth's *Hostel* series, as well as being buried on the home video and download market. The Video Nasty is obviously an influence on many horror directors working today, such as with Eli Roth's new film *The Green Inferno* harking back and being a homage to films such as *Cannibal Ferox* and *Cannibal Holocaust*. Such a rarity it is now that it was quite the surprise when the film *A Serbian Film* was seized before its showing at British horror film festival FrightFest, an act which will have made it more infamous. It is very rare now that you will get an uprising of people trying to ban a general release horror film, though the Daily Mail does still try to drum up moral outrage from its frothing mouth every now and again. Tastes have since changed and the BBFC does a good job of policing such films with a clear head and professional eye.

The Video Nasty's have become more like the old Granddads of horror cinema, not so much famous for their outlandish content as for their slightly ropey creation. I have been to screenings of both *The Evil Dead* and *Zombie Flesh Eaters* where the audience have been whooping and laughing throughout, the audience together in enjoying them more for their dated acting, dialogue and scripts rather than being scared by them or disgusted by their gore.

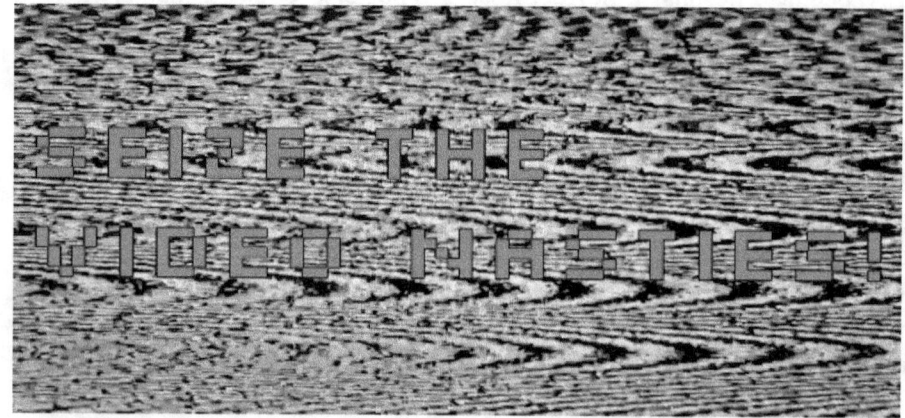

The Hollywood studios are now even trading on the infamy of Video Nasties to churn out their own remakes, titles that ride on the coattails of a horror title like it is a brand name. The recent release of an *Evil Dead* remake, surely the most high profile of the Video Nasty remakes, updated the violence but neglected to bring much of the charm of the original. It slid to a fairly easy gross of over $90 million by trading on its name, making it probably the most successful of these remakes. The 2010 *I Spit on your Grave* managed to get itself a sequel, creating another mediocre horror franchise, and a slightly uncomfortable one as its cover images seem to be selling it on rape and violence while also trying to arouse. *The Last House on the Left* has also had a slick and violent remake that will hardly stick in the memory. All these films come from companies knowing that they will get a slightly higher percentage of ticket sales than your average studio horror slasher just because of the ties with their namesake Nasty, and none of these films really had any particular effect on inciting moral outrage. The Video Nasty it seems has become a marketing tool and more of a historical horror artefact rather than a grubby stamp, frowned upon by those who like to spout moral outrage.

-Courtney Button   Writer.

The great "Satanic Panic" of the 80s made growing up in southern Illinois even more fun that you can probably imagine, and that's assuming you're the sort who finds paranoia and persecution complexes a laugh riot. By the time I was ten years old, I was certain that the devil was going to get me... if the Russians didn't beat him to it. There were strange rumblings on the playground, though. Kids talking in hushed and excited voices about a movie, but not a movie like anything we'd ever seen... a film about death. Real death. One of the kids, my friend Josh, swore that he had seen it. And that my uncle, who worked in the town's first (and only) video store, had been the one to show it to him. Thanks to the magic of guilt by association, the school bullies stopped picking on me almost overnight out of fear that my uncle, suddenly the town snuff peddler, would hunt them down and make Faces of Death 2. Though those movies ended up disappointing me (once I'd finally gotten up the nerve to watch them), I remain fascinated by the way that the unknown and the taboo can lure us. Whether it is the schoolyard whisperings over Faces of Death or the Internet outrage over A Serbian Film, it is clear that films can still push us, shock us, test our limits, and provoke intense feelings.

-Charles Colyott   Writer.

I am particularly fond of the Warhol FRANKENSTEIN (aka FLESH FOR FRANKENSTEIN) for many reasons. First, I've had the pleasure of seeing it several times in 3D, which puts the film's groundbreaking gore literally in your face. There are also hysterical performances by Udo Kier and others enhanced by the fact that they, with the exception of Joe Dallesandro were delivered phonetically. To know death, you must first fuck life in the gall bladder." Let's not forget the strong resemblance the lab set had on the later ROCKY HORROR PICTURE SHOW. "

Obviously, THE EVIL DEAD is an indie classic for its over-the top-gore and slapstick comedy. Are you detecting a pattern in what appeals to me?

One film that is not goofy like the first two is Tobe Hooper's THE FUNHOUSE is a dark and atmospheric little sleeper that stood out from the numerous slasher flicks of the day. A great John Beal score and disturbing, murderous sideshow mutant courtesy of Rick Baker are pluses.

There are many other titles on the list that have achieved a classic status - NIGHT OF THE LIVING DEAD, THE TEXAS CHAINSAW MASSACRE, THE HILLS HAVE EYES, FRIDAY THE 13TH, Carpenter's THE THING, PHANTASM, DEEP RED, SUSPIRIA, and even I SPIT ON YOUR GRAVE - which are must-sees for any horror fan, along with some entertainingly cheesy ones like the original TOOLBOX MURDERS, NIGHT OF THE BLOODY APES, DAWN OF THE MUMMY, and MAUSOLEUM, which also deserve a look.

-Kenneth J. Hall   Screenwriter of *Puppet Master, Dr. Alien, Virgin Hunters, Nightmare Sisters*.

Night of the Demon was my first taste of the forbidden Video Nasties, however this was actually before the video nasties even existed. It was a late night in 1983, I was about 11 years old and we were at a friend's house. They were the only people we knew who owned a brand new Betamax video recorder so for the first time you could really choose what films you wanted to watch. They had quite a few pirate videos and not all had been labeled. This sometimes made it a lucky dip as to what you might find. As we inserted tape after tape, we were treated to all manner of weird and wonderful, and not so wonderful movies. The type of movies you could never find on TV. The Hills have, eyes Friday the 13th, Jungle Burger etc. Then as we reached the end of the film we were watching, the picture flickered and fuzzed, followed by the distorted sound track of a film that had been partially taped over. As the tracking was adjusted, a huge hairy and rather frightening face loomed onto screen. The music kept speeding up then slowing down with a rather stomach churning sound. What followed was even more stomach churning. This hairy ape like creature started to rip, stab, burn, garrotte, and disembowel his way through everyone in the room. Just to add insult to injury, the creature then proceeded to whip the remaining unfortunates with their own intestines. This film was completely off the rails! As an eleven year old it completely blew me away. I couldn't get those images out of my mind. I had nightmares on and off for weeks but somehow I was fascinated by the extremes this film went to. Little by little, the thought of seeing another of these extreme movies scared and excited me at the same time. I had no idea what the film was called, but I knew I had to find out. A little while later the media frenzy over violent videos began and the police were confiscating these movies all over the country. My brother Howard and myself used to make regular trips to all the video libraries in town just to look at the graphic covers which promised violence and bloodshed on an unimaginable scale! Frustratingly we were too young to hire any of these films and we had to watch in dismay as the lurid video boxes disappeared.

About three years later, I came across a "for sale" advert in the classified section of a film magazine. The advert was for an original Zombie creeping flesh. I was excited as I had remembered the images on the video box all those years ago and was aware that this was not available to the public anymore. Just the images on the box had given me nightmares at the time so I was buzzing with excitement as to what the actual film might do. The fact that I wasn't even old enough to see it made this forbidden fruit that much more tempting.

On contacting the seller I stumbled on an underground network of dealers and enthusiasts trading in video nasties. I was immediately offered an original Nightmares in a damaged brain, which I had never even heard of but the title was as irresistible as an orphan choirboy to a catholic priest! I had to have it and sold anything I could to raise the cash for it.

I cut the DPP's list of 39 films, out of a newspaper and nailed it to my bedroom wall. I was literally salivating over that list of forbidden films: Driller Killer, I Spit on your Grave, The Gestapo's Last Orgy and of course Night of the Demon, (I had since learned the title after describing the scene to my new dealer friends). What type of sick and twisted filth was on this illegal list? I had no idea, but I was damn well going to find out! With the help of a couple of friends we set about hunting them down! This mission became an obsession and after several years of searching, not to mention spending most of my money, I had found all but 2 of them. The Beast in Heat proved almost impossible as many people had faked them with copied videos and photo copied covers. I wanted the real deal, complete with their original video covers.

It was clear that many of the films were very low budget, which got me thinking; maybe I could make my own video nasty! It didn't look too difficult, (I was very wrong on that point) then I too could create something to wow and excite an audience. Knowing how much impact these films had on me; the thought of playing in this arena was very exciting.

I suppose it really was the video nasties that shaped my career and set me off on the path to become a filmmaker.

-Jon Ford Writer, Director, Cinematographer: The Dead, The Dead 2.

Not being a particular lover of the kind of horror that was blacklisted under the term video nasties, my own take on this whole contentious sub strata of cinema is a little more philosophical. As a prepubescent child in the late 80s, I got the chance, courtesy of rather lax and indifferent video store counter staff to view lots of horror movies. We would convene at a friend's house, invariably whilst their parents were in the pub (which in the greater Glasgow area was a lot) and we would enjoy the thrill of underage movie exhibition. Of course the more violent, gory, or just downright profane the movie happened to be, the more kudos you won amongst your peers. And with pirate movies doing a roaring trade, the possession of a video nasty or simply knowing someone who had a copy of one became the video entertainment version of the search for the Holy Grail. From under the bed, came an invariably dreadful quality copy of a copy and we were soon on a cinematic rites of passage, nibbling at the filmic forbidden fruit. Of the ones I remember at the time, I found the exorcist impenetrable (I was *eight* for Christ's sake!), the Texas Chainsaw Massacre an anti climax (where was the massacre?!) and Zombie Flesh Eaters laughable - with the exception of the bit where the zombie starts munching on the shark. I admit I didn't read any kind of subtext Fulci may have been making about predatory nature in reverse, I think I was imagining how disturbing a David Attenborough show about marine wildlife would be with a reanimated carnivorous cadaver swimming around in the background.

So by the British Board of film classification and the saviour of the nation's morals, Mary Whitehouse's standards, I should have grown up into a demented, slavering creature of the night that makes bangles and baubles from my victims' appendages because I saw some of these things. I didn't and neither did anyone else I knew who had seen such films, even all of the original seventy-two, whether they seen them as an adult or a child. The hysterical, quasi religious reaction to these pictures deemed that they were almost a threat to the fabric of civilised society because not only did they risk people copycatting what they had seen but they would essentially drive us all into a degenerative, voyeuristic moral sludge, eschewing all the wholesome values of yesteryear. If I wanted to entertain this absurd argument I could bring up a crappy B horror film from the 80s, which seemed to be the kernel for far more unrest than any on the BBFC's list.

Even though the tone of the film was clearly tongue in cheek, nineteen eighty eight's Killer Klowns From Outer Space sparked off perhaps the most terrifying urban myth amongst children in the West Coast of Scotland during the period. Inspired by the events in the movie and children's natural coulrophobia, the story grew legs and took on various interpolations but the basics were a blue Transit van was going around primary schools filled with hell-born harlequins who would lure the children toward them with juggling and japery before slicing their mouths open with a butcher's knife and giving them a "Chelsea smile." Apocryphal isn't the right term... Utter bollocks would be closer to the mark but nonetheless at every school interval time you could hear the cry go up whenever a similar vehicle went past the gates. "It's the killer clowns!" And playgrounds the length of the central belt ran yellow with rivers of urine. Our primary school event sent us home with a newsletter warning of vigilance, thereby pouring several tankers worth of oil on the fire. So by the standards set out, didn't Killer Klowns cause a disturbance and a negative influence? Should that have been added to the list?

The BBFC always struck me as extremely out of touch and elitist with their stance on video nasties, gladly passing eighteen certificates to the works of Martin Scorsese and David Cronenbourg which often have a lot more visual gore and violence than say, the Texas chainsaw massacre. Their thinking seemed to be to me, that video nasties were generally aimed at working class young men, who weren't intelligent enough to view the more lurid works from esteemed artists such as those mentioned above but couldn't be relied upon not to mimic the blood soaked exploits in far less cerebral pictures like Driller Killer or I Spit On Your Grave. With the likes of Saw and Hostel ten a penny now, the social decline and copycat arguments can be easily refuted. As Kubrick once said, art or suggestion in general cannot change basic human nature. If you try and hypnotise someone to kill themselves, in the vast majority of cases, they won't do it... Just as most people who view Tenebrae won't run amok with an open razor.

Looking back with nostalgic fondness for the period, I smile when I consider that the entire campaign to morally cleanse the viewing habits of the British public actually had the reverse effect. Telling people, especially young people that they couldn't watch these movies immediately made everyone want to do just that. And it was generally these snobbish, patronising and condescending attitudes of the nanny state that I found a lot nastier than any video.

-David Magowan   Actor.

How I loved exploitation films. The first burst of adrenalin upon seeing the poster art, those publicity stills that energised the imagination, the long wait until someone's older brother got hold of a contraband VHS, the disappointment that your months of imagining had outdone the director's budget and ability. I waited thirty years to see "electrocuted worms take revenge on swampland man" movie Squirm. Thirty years of imagining Stygian lagoons of worms. Suffice to say, I was disappointed, very disappointed.

I became obsessed with horror movies when I was eight. At that time, I hankered to see the work of Val Lewton, James Whale and Freddie Francis. By the time we had a video recorder in our house (Betamax, as my father had been informed that was the future), the rumblings of censorship and minds being mangled by home video were making headlines. The nearest I had come to a nasty was Wes Craven's The Hills Have Eyes. My older sisters, by then certain I would grow up to be a serial killer, had bought it for me at a house clearance auction in Amersham.

It would be many years before I saw any of the actual films that made the DPP list.

I was in my 30s by the time I saw Last House on the Left, such a simple title, yet so haunting.

So much left to the imagination.

I had managed to get hold of an uncut copy via a continental friend as I was going to interview David Hess. About five minutes into the interview, he stopped, smiled, and said, "You've actually seen it!" By then, he had clearly got used to people building their interviews around hearsay. I have listened to his soundtrack, which contains some lovely and haunting songs, more than I have watched the film. I have no problem with the nastiness of it; I think if you are going to make a revenge film based around such horror, it isn't a bad thing if the audience feel queasy and wrong for watching it. What jarred most with me was the comedy, slapstick cops. I think Ingmar Bergman was correct in avoiding a couple of knockabout henchmen and a zany banjo for The Virgin Spring.

I have a fondness for Zombie Flesh Eaters, like much of Fulci's work, it is not a complete success, but there are dark and haunting qualities. The head shot while wrapped in hessian, or just the wind blowing and the emptiness of the island as Fabio Frizzi's music plays. And, most importantly, a shark versus zombie scene. One night, during the Laugharne festival in Wales, I sat with Graeme Garden at dinner and he spoke fondly of that scene. Would my pre-teen horror loving, comedy adoring self ever have imagined I would be talking sharks and zombies with a Goodie? A few days later, he told me had watched it again, and was disappointed to notice the shark's lack of teeth. Of all the directors on the nasties list, Fulci is my favourite. I think *The Beyond* - I know it was only *nearly* on the nasty list - is his closest to a classic work, with vivid, cold, and lonely hellish quality, and a devilish ending. While *The House by the Cemetery* has a ludicrous and illogical ending and way too many scenes where you just bellow, "stop standing still just waiting to be devoured, just run, or at least walk a bit faster".

My favourite of the nearly prosecuted films is "The Living Dead at Manchester Morgue". As a lover of Manchester, fetishist of bleak industrial dystopias, a lover of the Lake District, and admirer of zombies, this has it all.

-Robin Ince   Comedian/Writer.

MY RELATIONSHIP WITH VIDEO NASTIES

When I'm asked where my love of horror comes from, I generally cite two factors from my teenage years. The first was growing up in the Cold War, where it seemed likely that the air raid sirens would start blaring at any moment, announcing that we'd all got around four minutes left to live. The other – less frightening, but equally affecting – was the Video Nasties debacle.

I expect I'm similar to many other people who remember those days. Rather than making me critical of these frowned upon horror movies, all their removal from video store shelves did was make me want to watch them even more. They attained immediate cult status, regardless of quality. There were endless discussions in the school playground about this title and that title and the urban myths, which sprung up around them. Kids who'd seen any of the films in question were hailed as heroes. Others, like me, did whatever they could to get even the merest glimpse. I remember buying a paperback novelisation of THE INCREDIBLE MELTING MAN because it was the closest I could get to watching it, and staying up late watching the then newly launched Channel 4 for hours after closedown because we'd heard a private TV station based in Birmingham was planning to take over the airwaves and broadcast the EVIL DEAD. As it was, we were left with horror double bills on BBC 2 on Saturday nights (generally Hammer, Amicus and old Universal films). They were great, but we were still left wanting.

Equally clearly, I remember the buzz of excitement a decade or so later when the films in question finally started being made available. I'd just started work and I went to college every Monday in Birmingham city centre. Every week I'd return home with another of those titles I'd waited what felt like an eternity to see. And boy, were they worth the wait. There were plenty of duff movies in the mix, of course, but there were some real classics too.

Ultimately, though, as frustrating as it was, the Video Nasties bill seemed to me to have positive repercussions in the long run. Though we were deprived of these movies for far too long, the notoriety they gained through their banning hugely increased the public's awareness of them. Looking back all these years later, I find it really satisfying (and not a little amusing) to think how the legislation backfired for the censors, politicians and do-gooders.

-David Moody   Author of Autumn.

Chapter 7: Ban This Vile Filth

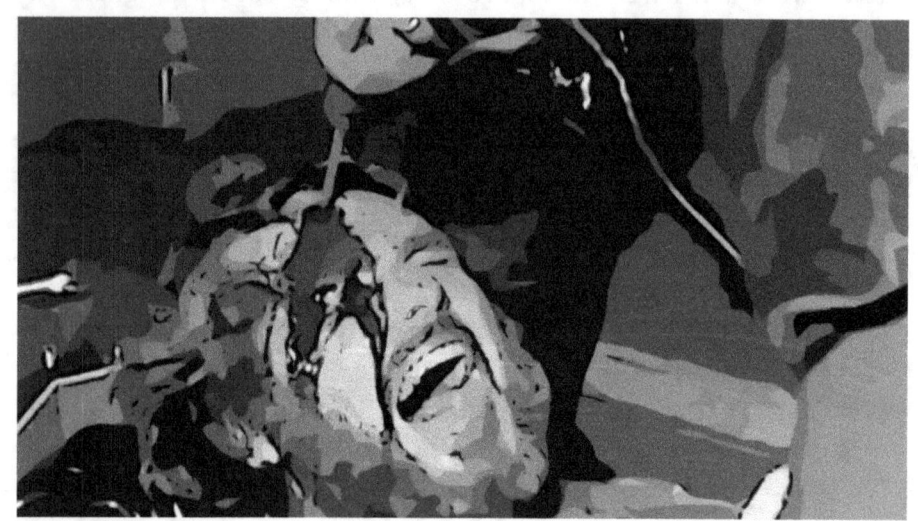

Censorship has been a disease that has been apparent since long before the 80s' video nasty epidemic. Folk had very thin skin back then, sex was something totally outlawed unless in the comfort of one's own boudoir and after wedding nuptials had been exchanged. Even then, you were still required to wrestle off a corset and unlock a chastity belt before you could actually embark on some good old lights-off missionary. Grue had no place back then either; the effect would be lost in translation in black & white and, again, prudish attitudes allowed not for anything resembling bloodletting.

It was the sixties when film censorship really reared its head. While peace-loving hippies were prancing about on acid, clad only in daisy chains and sowing their seeds at Woodstock, legislation was beginning to be put in place to halt the insurgence of such blasphemy. Of course, it was the 1980s when the shit really hit the fan in mid-oscillation as the tabloids decided that escalating violence was due to the upsurge in violent films hitting the marketplace with increasing regularity. Having laid the blame squarely on horror's doorstep, the police were called into action in a number of raids; whereby they seized copies of these immoral pieces of filth.

In 1983 the BBFC named and shamed the supposed ringleaders of exploitative cinema, banishing them to some ram-shackled warehouse where they watched them in privacy, whilst smoking all the cannabis they'd pillaged from the youth on their daily beat. It was all pretty shambolic to say the very least; highlighted by the fact *Tobe Hooper's* hardly blood-saturated **Funhouse** was one of the movies chastised, purely through clerical error, for sharing mantles with another, more deserving piece now known as **The Last House on Dead End Street.**

Poor hapless *David Grant* from Obsidian even served time for the distribution of *Roman Scavolini's* **Nightmares in a Damaged Brain,** It all amassed to one of the most ridiculous knee-jerk reactions ever seen and now, thirty years on, many of the renowned nasties are available uncensored with R rating.

Certain films have been held accountable for particular atrocities since, including **Child's Play 3** no less which, two years after its release in 1993, shouldered the blame for the murder of 2-year old *Jamie Bulger* at the hands of two pre-pubescent boys. **Child's Play 3?!** What next, **Bambi** getting blamed for an Amazon forest fire?!!!

-Keeper of the Crimson Quill (Rivers of Grue).

I suspect it's hard for horror fans these days to imagine the effect these films had on us when we were growing up.

Back in the day, whole weeks would be devoted to tracking down a hard-to-get-hold-of horror (let's not call them "Nasties" - they weren't all nasty; they were just horror films that got picked on politically), and the excitement and anticipation of going around your mate's house to watch *The Living Dead at The Manchester Morgue* or *The Beyond* would be unfathomable to today's horror fans when you can just fire up Netflix, browse Amazon, or even turn to the dark side of torrenting to get your kicks.

It was true event programming. People went to great lengths to get their mitts on these movies.

The news of a title being successfully procured would spread like wildfire without the aid of Twitter or Facebook. The excruciating countdown would then commence until the moment you all got together to not just watch these films, but also to talk about them, experience them, enjoy them.

I know I'm probably being over nostalgic; a lot of films are more sophisticated these days and we live in an era of digital delivery and availability, high turnover of releases, clever multi-channel marketing campaigns, remakes, sequels, homages, spin-offs...but maybe that's just it. Not easily being able to watch what you wanted, or having it taken away from you (as much as I disagreed with this) actually made the life of a horror fan way more interesting. We all had to become pre-internet aficionados if we were to survive.

A strange quality control developed along with the grapevine that informed us about these films. Everything was based on personal recommendations, so you'd know if something was great, or bad, or had that amazing scene with the...and the wait for your next title was almost as sweet as watching the film itself, (OK, sometimes a lot sweeter), but the point was it created a network; loose clubs of defiant horror fans who had to be proactive and get involved to carry on viewing. When you compare that idea to today's notion of films being transient, disposable files heavily marketed and consumed while commuting or multi-skilling, then forgotten like digested digital snacks, well, I guess I am nostalgic for the days of the Nasty (OK, there, I said it - if you can't bet 'em, join 'em).

For all the persecution and bombastic journalism around at the time, I still have fond memories of my mates and I talking about these films, watching them, and then talking about them more. I watched some duds, but I also saw some great banned movies that have stayed with me over the years and outlived many others that came later. I can remember listening to screams and power tool abuse on high volume as my parents watched these movies downstairs, whilst I was relegated to my bedroom (damn you school nights...), and Dad locking the offending VHS's in the boot of his car to keep them out of my reach. I remember my sister's face when she and her boyfriend came back from the video shop (it was a good one) with Faces of Death, instead of the slasher-thon she thought she was renting. I even remember a young Sam Raimi appearing in a Nottingham TV Studio on Central Weekend to defend The Evil Dead from rabid, crusading counsellors and a mob of angry viewers – none of whom had seen the film. He was quite rightly bemused, but hey, it was great publicity for those of us who wanted to see that kind of film.

More fuel for the fire – ta very much like.

So, all in all, my memories of growing up with "Nasties" were happy ones - nice ones. I still think it is hard for the current generation of horror fans to imagine what it was like to love horror back in the 80's if they weren't around then, but don't feel sorry for us. Though some of us had to clock up a few extra miles and head underground to get our movies, I think we enjoyed the ride.

-Leigh Dovey   Writer.

In 1978, I was laying in my bed, watching the black & white, hand-me-down TV, dozing off while trying to finish my homework. I remember hearing the narrator saying, "In 1968 George Romero brought us 'Night of the Living Dead'" I looked up and saw these undead ghouls bursting through the elevator doors and had nightmares all night long. To this day, I stand to the back of the elevator with slight apprehension of what's waiting for me as those doors slide open.

When I was in high school, 'Faces of Death' was like the Holy Grail of forbidden taboos. When someone managed to snag a copy from someone there would be these secret gatherings at someone's house to watch the harsh reality of the many ways a living thing can die. Invariably, 10 minutes into it, those with weak stomachs would start dropping out one by one. Those of us with the fortitude to watch every grisly minute to the end would come away feeling that we had just watched something that was better left unseen. Today in comparison, all one must do is type death, killed, or maimed into YouTube to be inundated with far worse images of reality. The unfortunate side effect of all of this, is that filmmakers are now forced to up the ante, in order to compete with reality to reach today's desensitized viewer and at times the artful craft of building fear, in a horror film, falls short.

The Evil Dead was another product of the great horror renaissance of the 80's. It gave us one more reason not to go into the woods for drinking and sexing it up. I'm pretty sure the tree rape scene scarred its fair share of young, impressionable campers. Films like 'The Evil Dead' really broke the horror genre's cherry in terms of notching the shock and terror factor up a notch, or twenty.

-Shawn Conn   Artist.

One of my earliest childhood memories is of my sitting in front of the television watching and episode of The Young Ones, where Rik, Neil, Vyvyan, and Mike are sitting down with a newly rented VHS player to watch a video nasty. I would later find myself ready to spend terribly similar nights with friends. Granted, they went uninterrupted by a killer vampire, claiming to be a driving instructor from Johannesburg, while the punk rock band The Damned sung their song, also titled Video Nasty (Yes, that happened on the show, too.) but the experience was non the less magical, in a gleefully demented way. We were death rockers, bohemians, and future film makers ourselves, beginning to understand that there were like-minded people out there, creating unconventional things, that got under people's skins, without studio approval or money. They had to think on their feet and be creative with what they had. We understood that if they could tell stories like this on screen, then we were free to do it, too.

We must not have been the only ones, because their influence can be felt in today's mainstream cinema. What is now the norm for audiences to thrill to in theaters today was once yesterday's contraband, thought to be enjoyed by the sick and undesirable social outcasts, who were really the rebels and pioneers of modern cinema.

-Christopher Moonlight   Moonlight Art Magazine.

Rape Me, My Friend
The Twisted Ethics of the Rape/Revenge Nasties.

It could be argued that four films were largely responsible for kick starting the whole media frenzy and the wave of video nasties protests in the media and public. SS Experiment Camp, Cannibal Holocaust, Driller Killer, and I Spit on your Grave. For it was these four films which regularly featured in news reports about the nasties, with politicians name-checking them at every possible occasion, along with their covers being pasted across every trash tabloid article on the subject. These four films also seemed to sum up the full spectrum of what the video nasties were about. Nazipolitation, nudity, gut munching cannibals, nudity, power tool killers, nudity, and rape (with added nudity). Although lacking the attention-grabbing title of the first three (even less so under its original title Day of the Woman), I Spit on your Grave made up for it with its DDP enticing front cover. Lurid but gorgeous yellow framing, reminiscent of the Italian giallo films, a tagline that read 'THIS WOMAN HAS JUST CUT, CHOPPED AND BURNED FOUR MEN BEYOND RECOGNITION' and a half naked woman (allegedly a young Demi Moore*) covered in cuts and holding a bloody knife. This was enough to get it seized and prosecuted at every possible occasion. That and the fact that it contained a nearly forty-minute rape sequence, shot in unflinching and graphic detail. A sequence, which has meant that, unlike many of the other video nasties, it is still unavailable in its full, uncut form in the U.K to this day **

The film stars Camille Keaton, niece of Buster Keaton (no, really) as Jennifer Hills. An aspiring writer, she leaves New York and heads out to the rural countryside, where she rents a small cottage in order to complete her first novel. Almost immediately she attracts the action of a few local low lives, Andy, Stanley, and Johnny at a local gas station. Later on, she meets Matthew, a simpleton, who brings her some shopping. She takes a sympathetic shine towards Matthew, but it later transpires he is involved with the other three degenerates. Then the following day they decide to attack her, first chasing her around the woods, before raping her, repeatedly (in what must be the longest rape sequence ever committed to celluloid.)

Leaving her for dead, they send Matthew back to finish the job, which he is unable to do. The following day the three other men see that she is still alive and subsequently beat up Matthew for failing to kill her. Jennifer then finds the strength to take her revenge, dispatching each guy in more and more shocking ways (most notably, the castration scene in the bath!) Director Meir Zarchi has claimed that the film was inspired by a true event. Driving through New York one day with his daughter, they witnessed a young woman crawling out of some bushes, naked and covered in blood. It transpired that she had been raped. He decided to take her to the police station, which he later regretted, as the officer in charge was more interested in interrogating the shocked and distraught woman instead of actually helping her. He later said that the officer was "not fit to wear the uniform" and wished he had taken her directly to hospital instead. Critic Roger Egbert gave the film two thumbs down calling it "a vile bag of garbage...without a shred of artistic distinction," adding "Attending it was one of the most depressing experiences of my life." It's this great bit of unwitting endorsement which helped the film break out of the 42 street flea pit cinemas and go on to be success it eventually became. Released over here around 1982/1983 via the Wizard video and Astra labels (the Wizard video now being the hardest to find, due to it being withdrawn at the time over copyright reasons) the film quickly caught the attention of the DDP and was single handily selected as one of the most extreme of the nasties and was the casualty of numerous court cases across the country. Meir Zarchi has always stated that the only real influences on his film was the 1972 film 'Deliverance' and Sam Peckinpah's 1971 'Straw Dogs', before adding that he never actually saw Wes Craven's debut feature 'Last House on the Left' (released the same year as 'Deliverance'), prior to starting work on 'I Spit on your Grave'. Even though both films follow a very similar narrative arch (a group of low life's commit a vicious rape before getting their comeuppance at either the hands of the victim or the victim's parents.)

'Last House on the left' follows two hippy teenagers, Mari, and Phyllis, as they plan to attend a rock concert. 'I think it's crazy', says Mari's dad, John, when hearing about the band called Bloodlust which they're going to see, 'All that blood and violence. I thought you were supposed to be the Love Generation'.

Straight away, Craven lays his hands on the table. The film's gonna be a conflicted clash between the left-wing hippies and the right-wing government sending out troops to fight in the increasingly unpopular war in Vietnam at the time of filming. Interestingly this film, and 'I Spit on your Grave' both have numerous references to the Vietnam War throughout their running times. 'I Spit on your Grave' has various shots of Jennifer hills, naked and bloody with a look of devastation and loss on her face. These shots echo the image of the Pulitzer Prize-winning photograph of Phan Thi Kim Phuc, best known as the Napalm Girl, running naked down the street after a Napalm attack during the Vietnam War. In 'Last House on the Left' we have the execution of Mari in the lake, where she is shot in the head, which Craven has admitted was directly influenced by the video of General Nguyen Ngoc Loan where he executed a Viet Cong prisoner by shooting him point blank in the head in Saigon.

Anyway, back to the plot of 'Last House on the Left'. Mari and Phyllis head out to buy some weed for the concert. They encounter Junior, who says he can fix them up with some. He leads them into his rundown apartment where they are trapped by Weasel, Sadie and Krug (the name later re-used by Craven for Freddy Krueger in his 1984 film 'A Nightmare on Elm Street') Things turn from bad to worse as the girls are abused before finally being taken out to the woods, raped and killed. The killers then take refuge in a nearby house when their car breaks down, unbeknown to them to belong to one of the murdered girls' parents. Slowly the truth is revealed to the parents who then take it upon themselves to enact callous and violent revenge. Strangely, whilst condemning 'I Spit on your Grave' Roger Ebert gave high praise to Craven's debut, giving it three and a half stars out of a possible four and saying that it had 'A Powerful narrative of sheer, unexpected terror'. The moment when Mari believes she has reached safety through a graveyard, when she sees the passing cars on a nearby road, only for Krug to suddenly appear with a machete is regarded as the first jump-scare of its type (to be used countless times in horror films later.) 'Last House on the Left' Producer Sean S Cunningham went on to direct the ever popular 'Friday the 13th' series, which Roger Ebert and his partner Gene Siskel spent an entire episode of their T.V show condemning, because they felt they made the audience sympathise with the killer.

What always struck me as different about the two films on first viewing was their overall cinematic look and texture (if there is in fact a phrase.) Basically, 'I Spit on your Grave' always felt much brighter and colourful in look (maybe in part to that bright yellow cover), whilst 'Last House on the Left' had a much more grubby and darker look. Also the camera moves very little in 'I Spit on your Grave', often coming to a complete standstill, whilst 'Last House on the Left' has an almost Cinéma Vérité feel, with the camera constantly moving to give it an authentic newsreel look. I must admit that it took a while for me to really appreciate 'Last House on the Left', initially dismissing the film as amateurish dreck, before coming to appreciate its deeper qualities. Ignoring all the silly slap stick with the two detectives, and overlooking the subpar acting quality of the two parents, 'Last House on the Left' is the far better of the two films, packing the most punch and feeling like a much more honest indictment to anti-violence during the trouble years that it was made. It was these deeper messages, which influenced by first feature 'Season of the Witch' ***

Made for very little, well frankly nothing, 'Season of the Witch' tells the story of the Blackwell's—and in particular, Alice Blackwell—who ends up being raped and killed by local vicar Michael Howdy in the small town of Maiden Hollow. The local villagers discover what he has done and enact swift and callous revenge, burning him at the stake like a 1700's witch. Despite taking influence from British folk horror films such as, most notably, 'The Wicker Man', 'Witchfinder General' and 'Blood on Satan's Claw', the main story arch if essentially a rape/revenge film in the vein of 'Last House on the Left'. A young girl (or girls) are raped and killed, the people close to them (either family or villagers) take violent revenge outside of the law and social values, before realising, at the climax, that they have gone too far and have become just as bad as the bad guy(s) which they were revenging.

In the 1970's this would have been a parable of the Vietnam War, in the 2000's it's the Iraq war. Sure there are bad people in the world, but killing them in a brutal and Neolithic fashion, without trial, won't elevate you above them. Maybe it will even make you worse than them as you know the difference between right and wrong, but you chose the path down which to travel. I was driving home from work one night, trying to figure out how best to finish by third feature 'Harvest of the Dead'. Although progressing, it was (and still is) progressing somewhat slowly due to numerous characters (read, actors) who all needed to be in the same location at once (somewhat difficult, as everyone's work schedule runs differently to each other.) I started thinking about how I could make a film with limited characters, a few easily obtained locations and very few props. My mind suddenly jumped back to the plot outline of 'I Spit on your Grave'. One main actress, three rapists, a few select locations. Suddenly the genesis of 'Blood will have Blood' was formed.

A young woman named Lydia Parker is on her way to spend a romantic weekend with her boyfriend out in the countryside. Her boyfriend, known only as David Moore (never seen or heard) is due to meet her in a couple of days. On her way to the rented cabin she encounters several lowlifes, Rick, and Tommy Webber, in a local pub. She dismisses them, only to come across Lucy in the middle of the road. She tells Lydia how she and her boyfriend were attacked out in the woods. Events start to twist and turn until Lydia becomes the attacker, leading to a dramatic climax where the tables have fully turned.

Filming has yet to commence, but the spirit of both 'I Spit on your Grave' and 'Last House on the Left' has influenced the script for 'Blood Will Have Blood' deeply. It's always hard to argue why you like something that other people find so abhorrent. Finding value in what others see as complete trash. But I respect these films in more ways than many other more respectable works of the time. To me these films reflect the moral and ethical values felt by the nation during the Vietnam War. At time when students peacefully protesting at Kent State University could be shot down by the government. The basic argument of any film dealing with revenge is to what point does the victim become the aggressor. Sure there are evil people out there, willing to do harm, but if you retaliate with more brute force and violence then what makes you the better man? As someone once said, 'If what we're doing in Indochina can be called right, then what is there left to be called wrong?' As the final image of Jennifer Hills staring blankly into the distance as she rides the speedboat to no destination in particular, or the shot of the police officer taking the chain saw from a shattered and devastated Collingwood shows, there are no winners. Like that ever-unpopular war, which continued to rage on despite all the bloodshed and loss of life, nothing was achieved, and no victory can be claimed. In a civilised society with law and order, simply taking matters into your own hands debases the whole human race and reduces us back to barbaric cave men. With our own Vietnam War still unresolved in Afghanistan as I type these words now, maybe the messages in these films should be heard by more people today. But then again, is revenge in a civilised society right or wrong? Who knows? (I sure as Hell don't.) I mean, getting pay back for an awful crime will always be justice in some sense, but how far is too far actually going? To what extent do we end up worse than the perpetrators of a crime? Maybe these films hold some sort of answer, or maybe not. Watching them you're left in no doubt that the perpetrators deserve what they get, but also that the victims end up morally and mentally ruined by the experience in the process. So these are the twisted ethics of these films. They provide no real definitive answers, and probably leave the viewer asking more questions. But hey, isn't that what great cinema is really about? Someone once said that 'films shouldn't entertain, they should scar' and these films have left me, and many others, with difficult and troubling scars. Still, it's better to feel something when watching a film, than nothing at all, like so many of the current films of today. But then again, they were only movies.

*Although never confirmed to actually be her, Demi Moore did make one of her first films via Charles Bands Empire Company called 'Parasite' in 1982. It was around this time that Charles Band started releasing various horror films via his Wizard video label in the U.S, including 'I Spit on your Grave', complete with that iconic front cover. So it's entirely possible that she was asked to pose for the shot.

** Cuts of 2 minutes and 54 seconds were required to pass as an 18 certificate when submitted to the BBFC back in 2010.

*** Worth noting that 'Last House on the Left' was based upon an early Ingmar Bergman film called 'The Virgin Spring'. This film was influenced by a Swedish ballad called 'Tores Daughter at Vange.' This poem is recited at the end of my feature 'Season of the Witch.'

-Peter Goddard   Writer, Director, Producer: Any Minute Now, Harvest of the Dead.

Lucio Fulci and the Curious Case of the Video Nasties

Lucio Fulci (1927-1996) spent the bulk of his career moving from one disparate genre to the next—he directed comedies, musicals, westerns, thrillers, sci-fi, even erotica. However, there is no denying that he attained lasting immortality (and notoriety!) for his excessively gory horror films. Fulci's fascination with the human body and how it could be dismembered probably had its origins in his background in medicine—he was on his way to becoming a doctor when he decided to chuck it in and go into movies instead—and this, coupled with his willingness to go where others feared to tread, resulted in his staging some of the most spectacular scenes of visceral mayhem in cinema history. When he came to direct *Zombie* (*Zombi 2*, 1979), he had no first-hand experience with making true-blue horror movies. His stylish *gialli* like *A Lizard in a Woman's Skin* (*Una lucertola con la pelle di donna*, 1971) and *The Psychic* (*Sette notte in nero*, 1977) incorporated some macabre elements, but they were basically rooted in reality. Zombie allowed him to cut loose and go for something much more extreme, but its success came at a cost: he would forever be seen as a rip-off artist, as the film was sold in Italy as a sequel to George A. Romero's *Dawn of the Dead* (1978), which was released there under the title of *Zombi* in a version re-edited by co-producer Dario Argento. Fulci's

willingness to go for broke with excess as well as his understanding that horror films needn't be focused on complex plots if they had the mood and atmosphere to entrance the viewer marked him out as a pandering hack who didn't know how to tell a coherent story.

No matter that he had spent the first part of his career directing films that were largely devoid of gore, or that his thrillers, for example, were exceedingly well-plotted. In the eyes of mainstream reviewers, Fulci became emblematic of everything that was wrong with modern horror; but to the fans, he became The Godfather of Gore. In being enshrined in this manner, the fans have done him a slight disservice, as this represents only one facet of his fascinating career—but in the context of this particular discussion, it's the part of his legacy that is most significant.

Zombie became the source of considerable controversy when it was released in 1979 into 1980. In the UK, it was subjected to numerous cuts by skittish censors. When the home video boom of the early 1980s took off, it became one of the infamous "Video Nasties." Readers interested in learning the full, convoluted back story of the "Video Nasty" debate and the films affected by it are encouraged to check out Jake West's exhaustive and definitive documentary *Video Nasties: The Definitive Guide* (2010) and its follow-up *Video Nasties: The Definitive Guide, Part 2* (2014). To recap the basics, however, here is a rundown of some salient points made in the documentaries: the whole sorry mess got underway thanks to staunchly conservative moral crusader Mary Whitehouse, who campaigned relentlessly against the availability of violent and sexually explicit videos on the grounds that they could warp impressionable minds. In 1982, Vipco Video, a UK-based outfit, brought a lot of heat on itself by taking out lurid, full-page ads for their release of Abel Ferrara's controversial *Driller Killer* (1979) on VHS. A short time later, another video outfit, Go Video, inflicted even further self-injury by bringing Mary Whitehouse's attention to their release of Ruggero Deodato's *Cannibal Holocaust* (1980); they had hoped that the ensuing controversy would help to sell copies, but instead it led to a crackdown on the sale of films deemed unfit by the British Board of Film Censors (BBFC). James Ferman, director of the BBFC from 1975-1999, decided to back Whitehouse, bowed to pressure from various special interest groups and devised the *Video Recordings Act 1984*, which decreed that all films for sale on cassette must be approved by the BBFC; films released without this classification would be impounded as obscene, and people who broke the law could face stiff financial penalties or even jail time. *Zombie* had secured an official "X" certificate for distribution in British theatres under the name *Zombie Flesh Eaters*, but nearly two minutes of gory thrills were removed in the bargain. When Vipco decided to play slick and release it on video in its fully uncut form, the film found itself on the list of "Video Nasty" targets. As censorship began to soften a bit, the film was ultimately released on video in the UK in 1992—but this, too, was the version passed for exhibition by the BBFC. The film was eventually removed from the official "Nasties" list sometime in 2005, at which point it cropped up on video in its intended form. Ultimately, the *Video Recordings Act 1984* was repealed and replaced by the comparatively liberal *Video Recordings Act 2010*.

Zombie was the first of Fulci's films to encounter this kind of difficulty in the UK, but it would not be the last: *The Beyond* and *The House by the Cemetery* would also land on the list, after having been cut for theatrical exhibition, while *The New York Ripper* found itself banned in *any* form for many years. For whatever reason, Fulci's other renowned gore title of the period, *City of the Living Dead* (*Paura nella città dei morti viventi*, 1980)

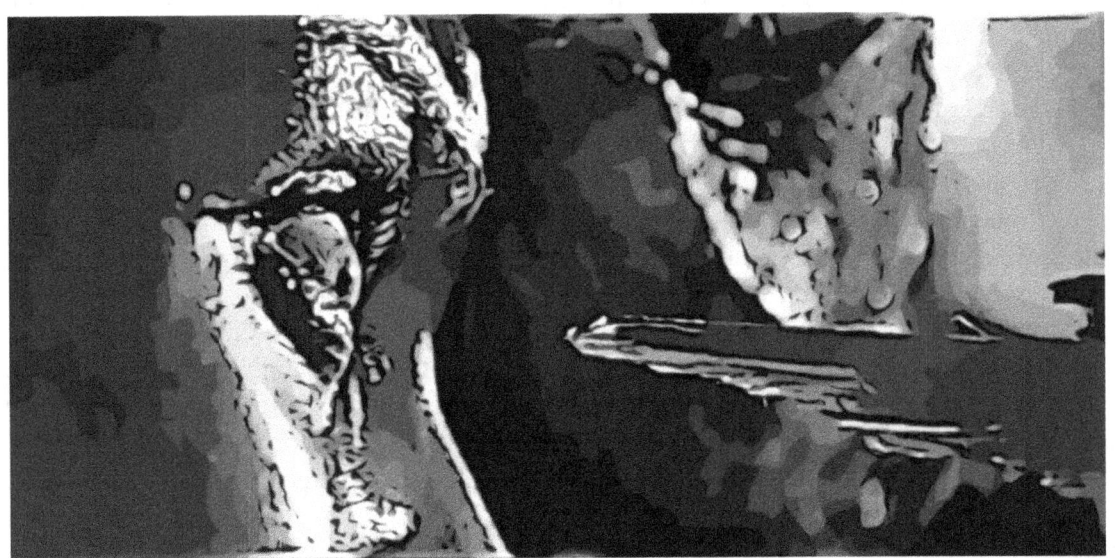

managed to escape the clutches of the official "Nasties" list. Legend has it that it was still confiscated from a few video shops due to its lurid cover art, but as it was not actually included on the list of films that were forbidden to be sold and/or rented, nothing ever came of these incidents.

Absurd as the furore over these so-called morally indecent films may have been, it seems likely that the moral finger pointing helped make the films more desirable among thrill-hungry genre buffs. Many of the films that ended up on the list quite simply weren't very good, but this can hardly be said of Fulci's films. They are done with a level of professionalism that is sorely lacking in the likes of, say, Aristide Massaccesi/Joe D'Amato's *Absurd* (*Rosso Sangue*, 1981) or Cesare Canevari's *The Gestapo's Last Orgy* (*L'ultimo orgia del III Reich*, 1977), for example. They are also genuinely effective horror films, staged with considerable skill and dripping with plenty of atmosphere. Like they best Italian genre films, they are also visually and aurally dynamic.

After *Zombie*, the next Fulci film to land on the list was *The Beyond* (*L'aldila*, 1981). The BBFC passed the film with an X rating, but demanded numerous cuts. It would later end up on the infamous "Video Nasties" list, but was ultimately released fully uncut to video in 2001. The same year's *The House by the Cemetery* (*Quella Villa Accanto al Cimitero*) encountered a similar fate: the censors permitted it to be shown, with some cuts, but it would later be subjected to stricter censorship before landing on the "Nasties" list of forbidden videos. The film was still being subjected to cuts as late as the early 2000s but was ultimately released fully uncut by Arrow Video in 2009.

The problems encountered by these films were nothing compared to what waited in store, however. To say that *The New York Ripper* (*Lo Squartatore di New York*, 1982) was greeted with controversy would be a major understatement. The British had already developed a queasy relationship with Fulci based on his recent horror films; it is probably fair to say that the BBFC held their breath every time a copy of his latest film came into their office. *Zombie*, *The Beyond* and *The House by the Cemetery* were certainly not beloved by the censors, but their excesses took place in a recognizably fantastic context; they were over-the-top and the stiff-backed censors were not amused, but they were *just barely* tolerable. *The New York Ripper* upped the ante considerably by adding in sleazy sex and, above all else, by setting the action in a more realistic context. As such, *The New York Ripper* proved to be too much for them to stomach. In the documentary *Video Nasties: The Definitive Guide, Part 2* (2014), Carol Topolski, a former examiner with the BBFC from 1983 to 1995, recalled seeing the film for the first time: "I saw a film with [BBFC director] Jim Ferman and two other senior colleagues, both of whom were women, called *The New York Ripper*. And it is simply the most damaging film I have ever seen in my whole life. It was simply a relentless catalogue of the eponymous antihero/villain cutting women up. And the filmmakers were feasting on what women's bodies looked like when they were cut up. At the end of that film, which was clearly never, *ever* going to be passed—there was no way that that level of unremitting sadistic attacks on women was ever going to be passed—at the end of the film, all four of us sat in the cinema, and three of us were quite quietly weeping, as we… actually, all of us went into Jim's office just to recover, because it was the most—it was being in the presence of a film which was gratifying a particular desire. I always thought that the difficulty for censors… the *question*, not difficulty, for censors is the dispiriting thing about seeing a film of that nature is not that it was made, because it could have been made and left in a cupboard, but that there was an audience for it. I think that says something about the viewing audience." Wow—quite a statement, no? Leaving aside Topolski's obvious right to hold and express her own opinion, the extreme sensitivity of her reaction to Fulci's film is indicative of the slippery slope of film censorship. Simply put, censors are human beings and they are in the position of passing a form of moral judgment over the films they are assessing. Ideally, people who do this job should possess the intelligence to be able to see past their own kneejerk reactions and understand the point the filmmaker is trying to make; even if they don't like the film, they should hopefully be able to comprehend that there is a place for confrontational cinema. *The New York Ripper* shows Fulci at his most abrasive. It's an unpleasant film. This is deliberate, not accidental. As such, to criticize it for being too unpleasant or by jumping to the conclusion that it is inherently misogynistic for depicting the crimes of a misogynist is to completely miss the point; indeed, the fact that the film proved to be so upsetting to the censors is proof of its effectiveness. There is a time and a place for restraint and good manners, but *The New York Ripper* is not that type of film. Sadly, Topolski and her cohorts at the BBFC used their position and power to ban the film outright in the UK for many years; it would not be permissible to sell or own a copy of the film in England until 2002, and even then its release would come with the built-in caveat of some edits during Daniela Doria's painfully protracted death scene.

Interestingly, it was never a part of the "Nasties" list, *per se*—its notoriety exceeded even that. It was, quite simply, a film that was illegal to show in any way, shape or form in the UK for decades. Fulci fans looking to complete their collection of the master's works had to tread very lightly when it came to trying to get their hands on a VHS and anybody caught trying to sell it would be in for a world of trouble. One is reminded of the furore which surrounded the original British release of Michael Powell's *Peeping Tom* (1960) and how one critic fumed that the film deserved to be thrown into the sewer—but that then even the stench would remain. Peeping Tom would ultimately undergo a major critical rehabilitation and be rightly embraced as a masterpiece, but people are still catching up with *The New York Ripper*. Those who appreciate it, however, recognize that there is more to it than meets the (bisected) eye.

Everything has its time and eventually the era of the "Video Nasty" came to well-deserved end. The films included on the list have mostly been granted certificates, which enable them to be screened in the UK, though a few of them have yet to be given official sanction to be shown fully uncut. In the years since the whole scandal has evaporated from public view, the debate over the "social responsibility" of the filmmaker continues to wage. For some, it's a question of what is moral and "proper," but the larger question remains: who makes these determinations? Surely not the squeamish types who were so utterly appalled by the films that were subjected to so much close scrutiny back in the day. Here as in so many areas, it really should boil down to a matter of individual choice—that is to see and enjoy these films if they choose to do so, and to also bypass and avoid them if they are of easily offended sensibilities. Lucio Fulci was not a man of such sensibilities, however, and his visceral approach to genre filmmaking continues to inspire generations of new artists.

-Troy Howarth   Author of *Splintered Visions: Lucio Fulci and His Films*, *The Haunted World of Mario Bava, Tome of Terror So Deadly, So Perverse: 50 Years of Italian Giallo Films* (Volumes 1 and 2 are available, with a third forthcoming), The upcoming *Real Depravities: The Films of Klaus Kinski*.

Chapter 8: The Final Cut, Censorship No More?

Britain, for some reason, had the great misfortune of being somewhat protected from the dangers of foreign cinema!

The BBFC cut—and even re-cut—footage, or even outright *banned* movies in Britain to protect British residents from (in their eyes at least), harmful and disturbing images that may have the power to corrupt; more often than not, it was horror films falling victim to the censors. The 1970's would be a challenging decade for censorship in Britain, but neither the censors nor the filmmakers could have predicted the influx of home video in the 1980s and just how much press and media attention both the BBFC and the video nasties would get! You do have to question just how much the BBFC's actions were in place to protect themselves; just imagine if they had not implemented such actions—with the huge amount of press surrounding them, there would have been repercussions. Plus, I don't think the BBFC's branch were ever skint from the early 80s onwards! It is not cheap to get your film even submitted for a rating!

Ironically, ten years later (just when we thought it was safe to set foot in the video shop), moral panic started all over again! This, from November 26th 1993, front page of The Sun newspaper: "For the sake of all your kids… burn your video nasty!" Around that time the terrible James Bulger murder, along with rumors of the killers' copycat style after watching Childs Play 3, moral panic exploded in the UK. Independent video stores started to burn every copy of Child's Play 3, with major chains even following suit by removing the title from the shelves. Although "Childs Play 2" and "Childs Play 3" were never officially banned after the sad death of James Bulger, yet again we saw another media frenzy, although it was reported the two young murderers had never even seen the film "Child's Play 3." It was the tabloid press picking up on the fact that one of the murder's fathers had rented the title, along with other video nasties. After the horrific incident and all the media frenzy surrounding it, video stockists refused to stock any of the "Child's Play" films in the UK.

An Inspector from the James Bulger case said: "If you are going to link this murder to a film you might as well link it to The Railway Children."

Apparently they picked a connection out of thin air with "Child's Play 3," in which Chucky has blue paint on him (killers threw blue paint on their victim, which they had stolen that day). The tabloid press picked up on The Hungerford Massacre in 1987, and the British press was filled with stories the killer was obsessed with "Rambo: First Blood." Later findings proved the killer didn't even own a VCR player and hadn't even seen the film.

Following on from the 1984 Video Recordings Act, 1994 saw the Criminal Justice Act in Britain; this piece of the controversial legislation gave the police yet more power to arrest and seize! Section VII of the Criminal Justice Act covering obscenity and pornography in videos even extended the power of the 1978 Protection of Children Act *and* the 1984 Video Recordings Act. The penalties for supplying unclassified videos were increased: they even included new clauses to restrict videos depicting techniques likely to be useful in the commission of offences. The BBFC, the designated authority, were given even greater powers—including being able to recall films for re-classification. Another addition to the Video Recordings Act was a new clause covering potential harm caused to potential viewers, or their behavior to society, which dealt with criminal behavior, illegal drugs, violent behavior/incidents, or human sexual activity. The harm element was triggered by the James Bulger case and a news report that followed, which stated that violent videos were capable of causing psychological damage to young and impressionable children.

It seems crazy to think that when the BBFC were making a decision on an 18-rated film, the potential harm element on children came into play, which made a mockery for any kind of need for certification. This followed a big change at the BBFC and films that were actually aimed at children; a decision for certification was only reached by a psychologist report and careful examination by the BBFC. Even 11 years later, in 1995, just after the second wave of media frenzy we saw a headline: "snuff film found in classroom." Underground film operations were selling video nasties to kids just like in the 1980s. The tapes ended up in schools, being passed around in playgrounds; I remember in the early 1990s carrying a rucksack full of VHS horror films, and my friends and I would trade titles, all excited to watch a video nasty.

1999 would mark a huge change in British censorship, with films such as "Irreversible" allowed an 18-certificate. Even "Baise-Moi" only received 10 seconds of cuts to be passed 18 in the UK, having been refused classification in Australia, and it was around that time the whiff of James Ferman and his BBFC heyday was all but a distant memory. The 90s were still a far cry from the video nasty moral panic we had once seen in Britain. James Furman was well known for delaying films for political reasons, and even his successor, Robin Duval, publically announced in 1998 future decisions regarding classifications would be reached as promptly as possible and films would no longer be delayed for political reasons.

-Tony Newton

In the slightly pre-Nasties era, I witnessed a super example of the pillars of society protecting the minds of the pathetic and ill-prepared public. After a three year stint in the army in Germany, I spent two weeks in England, living in a friend's little flat outside London. I noticed NIGHT OF THE LIVING DEAD was playing at some little neighbourhood theatre —Elephant & Castle, some place like that—and since I'd only read about the film, I decided to check it out. This was 1975, the movie was seven years old, long before it became a widespread "classic" by virtue of its public domain status and the fact that anyone with a print could go into the NOTLD bootleg business, but a couple years after a scathing Roger Ebert article in the conservative American magazine Reader's Digest. Ebert railed on about how this grim, grisly film was unsuitable for children, which, actually, makes sense. But the English censors circumvented any problems with the version I saw.

The cinema was about 25% filled, with no children in evidence, just adults with nothing else to do on a July afternoon. I liked the film, and could see where it'd been eviscerated, even without having seen the uncut version. The UK censor eliminated the entire sequence of the zombies chomping on the guts of the victims—not a frame of that remained. The little zombie girl's attack on her mother with a trowel was obviously clipped short. But other than that, the film played fine. It moved, Romero showed a steady hand, the performances were several strips above the usual indie movie level.

Therein lies an interesting conundrum. The film played fine without those scenes—establishing its mood of terror right away, tightening the screws one by one, adding elements, which hyped the mystery and the hopelessness. So were those scenes necessary in the first place? What, exactly, did those scenes add to the overall power of the movie, which was not already there? The answer was—not much.

Guarding the public morality is an iffy proposition. There are those who have always, will always, say that motion picture images imprint on the minds of viewers, and that horrific images will therefore cause horrific thoughts and deeds. Balderdash and poo-poo, gore lovers will say. But where do we get our views of society, or morality, of philosophy or love, of the sanctity of life or the importance of death? Some of this clearly does come from thoughts and images to which we've been exposed. If only one out of a million people who see a movie takes it unto themselves to copy a detailed menu of horror and replay it in real life, should we err on the side of the lucky 999,999 who didn't react that way?

Violent and/or effective horror movies have often been used as a scapegoat by those who take upon themselves the job of protecting the minds of the impressionable. As long ago as 1928, the attorney for an accused murderer in England blamed his client's insanity on him having seen the Lon Chaney vampire mystery London After Midnight. The jury apparently didn't buy the argument in that case, but within ten years the BBFC instigated the "H Certificate," presumably to prevent a generation of little kids from becoming a legion of Jacks & Jill's the Rippers (the original of whom, I believe, was not a regular cinema-goer.). A generation later, another defence lawyer in America tried the same tack, blaming his client's viewing of Psycho as the trigger for a murder spree that was nothing like Norman Bates' fun and games. He lost, too.

I have never read in any correspondence between, say, the BBFC's John Trevelyan and Hammer Films, which was not pleasant and business-like. A person like Trevelyan was not a bluenose and not unaware that selling movies was a business proposition, that the manufacturers needed something to sell—in Hammer's case, terror and sex. It was a constant push-pull between the BBFC and Wardour Street, but not impolite. Likewise, in the US, dealing the MPAA, which doles out theatrical ratings, is a negotiation process. "I'll trade you three 'damns' for one 'fuck,' and we'll remove the nipple shot if you let us keep the knife up the ass."

I have one second-hand anecdote about the ludicrous "censorship" of a slasher film I wrote in 1983, right smack dab in the era of Video Nasties: Blood Frenzy. It would not surprise me at all if the thing was on the official "Chuck this video in the rubbish bin" list in England at the time. I'd written a dozen or so adult films for a porn film maker named Hal Freeman, whose company Hollywood Video made what he called "Charmin' Cheapies,"—sex movies with a plot, shot in 3 or 4 days. His biggest seller had been a "couples" film I wrote, X-Factor (long before the comic book, or the game show—though they both did swipe Hal's logo!), which was shot on location in San Francisco as a "soft" erotic film with no actual sex scenes. As with gratuitous gore scenes, the movie played just fine (or even better) without them he actually was able to sell it to cable TV. He wanted to branch out from making smut to making generally acceptable ones. This inspired him to create a company offshoot for "mainstream" movies and videos, naming his secondary imprint Hollywood Family Video. Among the few things he made was a how-to educational primer Earthquake Safety, hosted by Shelley Duvall.

He hired me to rewrite a slasher script set in the California desert, then titled Danger—No Trespassing. I retitled it Blood Frenzy, anticipating that in quality it would end up somewhere between Herschel Lewis' Blood Feast on the one end and Hitchcock's Frenzy on the other. It was 10 Little Indians meets Friday the 13th in the desert, basically. I arranged for my friend John Goodwin to do the make-up special effects, and Hal treated the blood scenes like orgasms in a porn film, the splashier, the better. That drove John crazy, since he is of the "less is more" school. It was a two-week shoot, on 35mm, with a good crew and cast, including Lisa Loring (TV's original Wednesday on The Addams Family), John Clark (Lynn Redgrave's husband, whose own career went back to the Will Hay era), and Hank Garrett (memorable as the postman/hitman in Three Days of the Condor).

Blood spurted everywhere! A garden trowel gouged out a drunk's trachea, wiggling in the wound. A knife in giant close-up carving into another guy's throat. Yet another knife plunging in a Psycho-like montage into a third guy as blood cascaded out his mouth, shot up onto his face and shirt, and drenched the toy Jack in the Box he held. The Grand Guingol ending in a desert cave where the madwoman carves the cute blonde on a table and the killer's halfwit hulking brother drools happily, and the all-out screaming, ranting, wailing end with a grisly, protracted impalement. Yee-haw!

Hal Freeman was so proud and enthused about Blood Frenzy he wanted to push it as a theatrical film, but for that he needed to apply to the MPPA for a ratings certificate. He didn't get far. The board screened the film, and one member had issue not with the film, but with Freeman's production company name. "Hollywood FAMILY Video?!?!" the censor asked incredulously. "What the hell kind of family would watch a movie called Blood Frenzy?!?!?!"

I wasn't there, but I would've answered, "My family, sir. My grandma remembered Phantom of the Opera from when she was a child. My Mom and Dad saw The Thing when they were dating. My sisters and I saw Circus of Horrors and Horrors of the Black Museum when we were little kids, and we turned out just fine."

The MPPA refused to rate the film at all, not G, not GP or PG, not R, not even X. And you know what? It did just fine on video. It was in many respects a pretty clunky movie… but people liked the nasty parts.

-Ted Newsom   writer, director, producer and Actor.

My personal view on censorship in films is: If people can experience extreme murder, rape, and torture vicariously through watching a film, then there is a lesser chance that they will commit these acts themselves. Japan's homicide rate has been decreasing since the 1950's and I believe this is due to the Japanese people watching extremely gory films.

I would rather people watch films with extreme murder, rape, and torture rather than committing those acts themselves.

-John Borowski   Filmmaker.

I hadn't really dealt with censorship personally until my 3rd film, THE VIOLENT KIND, which premièred at the Sundance Film Festival. When the film was released we got a pretty hard R-rating here in the states, but little did I know the film was being chopped down for release in other countries. They way I found out is that our German distributor had called me about 6 months later with some exciting news -- They were preparing to release a super nice "special edition" DVD with a primo booklet, a couple bonus disks, all new artwork, etc.... And it was to contain the "uncut" version of the film. I responded with, *"what uncut version of the film?"* I quickly discovered that many countries had edited the film down to meet their rating requirements without our knowledge.

When I did THE THOMPSONS, the sequel to THE HAMILTONS, it was released in the UK before anywhere else (we also shot it in the UK). We had a brutal opening scene where two innocent backpackers are forced to strip down, have sex with each other, and then butchered. We fought hard to keep it in but the UK Film Board was not having it at all. We ended up having to chop it out. The full version of the movie is only available in a few countries, including the US. It's kind of hard to sit with the idea that most people don't get to see my work as I intended but rather what a rating system allows.

Back when I was a teenager, before the Internet, in South San Francisco, I had this friend Chad who always obtained these obscure VHS tapes of odd movies like OVER THE EDGE or CLASS OF 1984... Lots of teenage angst stuff. We would cut class, get high, and go watch whatever he could a hold of. One day he pulled out FACES OF DEATH and loaded into the VCR. You see nowadays you can pretty much research anything online and call its bluff. Back then -- it was what you just watched in front of you, your imagination, and Chad telling you how he supposedly got the tape on the black market. Now that I'm a horror director I pretty much have a hard time believing in most stuff but that day, after FACES OF DEATH, that feeling has always stuck with me.... Not really any of the gruesome stuff, but the fear, the excitement, that unknown. That's the stuff I try and put forth in my work till this day.

On one of my very first films, we were getting ready to advertise its official trailer for the theatrical run... But first we had to get the trailer rated for "general audiences." One of the notes we received back from MPAA was "the blood is too red." "Well, blood is red if I'm not mistaken," I replied. "Do you want us to remove all the blood? Which would be hard because it's a horror film..." "No," was the answer. "Just make the blood another color." I, being rather new to the industry at that time, started watching all the trailers for horror films I could find. "Wow, all that blood is brown!" We know it's blood, it's oozing out like blood... But it's just not red. Like changing the color somehow makes it less scary or violent. Which is the complete opposite of what most horror directors are trying to accomplish. Lesson quickly learned.

-Mitchell Altieri   Director (The Hamiltons/The Thompsons, Holy Ghost People).

It's a bit bittersweet that the releases of each of my films have been small enough thus far that I haven't had to deal yet with ratings or censorship. I believe if PROXY were to have played in one more city theatrically, we would have had to submit the film to the MPAA, which would definitely not have been a good thing.

I would say I'm influenced by almost every film on this list. Influences are peculiar things. In fact, I believe I've been influenced by everything I've ever seen, both consciously and subconsciously. What's interesting is how the influences filter through you. Sometimes you can learn more from watching a bad film than you can from a good one, because you see why or how something doesn't work.

I will say this; I've always admired filmmakers that take risks. That have a singular voice. Filmmakers that tackle dark and difficult subject matter, yet execute them in intelligent, unique, and beautiful ways. That is what I'm always striving for in my work.

-Zack Parker   Director of "Proxy" 2013.

Relaxation of Censorship: The New Nasties and the Changing Nature of Censorship

The relaxation of censorship in recent decades has led to the most horrific, abusive, depraved, violent, and twisted cinema in history being produced. With relative carte blanche, directors have pushed the envelope to exploding point, and from their warped experiments the New Extremism and Torture Porn genres have emerged. Movies that would have faced continental-wide bans in the 80's are now produced on a regular basis.

The French New Wave

Befitting a country that the Marquis de Sade called home, the French have been the vanguard for the recent tsunami of brain-destroying celluloid. Baise-Moi (2000 // Virginie Despentes & Coralie), meaning 'Fuck Me,' was a two-fingered salute to censorship, showing very real sex in the extremely unsettling manner of a rape. Playing out like a nightmarish version of Thelma and Louise, we follow Nadine (Karen Lancaume) and Manu (Raffaëla Anderson) on a violent revenge road-trip born out of drugs, gang rape, and murder. The movie was shot down by Malaysia and Singapore, and after a short run as a Rated R movie in Australia, was pulled. Except for a graphic penetration, which many countries sliced, its widespread release was fairly unharmed, although Hong Kong edited a full 155 seconds of it before letting it even approach a cinema.

Gasper Noe has emerged as both one of the most shockingly brutal and visually intense directors of the New French Wave, with his first three features being noted for their extreme qualities. The first, Seul Contre Tous (I Stand Alone - 1998), is an unrelentingly grim peek into the life of the miserable, isolated, and hateful man known as The Butcher, his struggles with both himself and employment, and the perpetual downs of his troubled life. Noe followed this with a piece of art so bleak that is has been said 'only a film fan could enjoy it' – Irreversible (2002). Told scene-by-scene in reverse chronological order, we begin with a trip into The Rectum, a sadomasochistic gay club which is portrayed as being a version of Hades composed of tight corridors and skewed red light. Following a man having his skull caved in with a fire extinguisher, the film extrapolates backwards in time to the inciting incident – an unbearably uncomfortable nine-minute rape scene, where the true horror lies in how random the event is; simply a matter of being in the wrong subway at the wrong time. In some ways the worst is yet to come, as the movie finishes with the woman (Monica Belluci) enjoying a summer afternoon on the grass, a vision of relaxed happiness, at the chronological beginning of the story.

Having pummelled our mind, Noe took something of a left turn with his next vision. The hyperpsychedelia of Enter The Void (2009) shows us both a Gods eye view of the joy and terror of our sins and depravities, and, for the uninitiated, takes us inside a hallucinogenic trip. This was an experimental piece of film that Noe had wanted to make for a while, and the success of Irreversible allowed him to get his teeth into it. Inspired both by his own drug experiences, and his musings on life and death, Enter the Void is an entirely first-person-perspective experience. Our protagonist, Oscar (Nathaniel Brown), is living in neon-saturated Tokyo, where he hangs around with dodgy friends and smokes DMT. Participating in a drug deal, Oscar is shot, dies on a toilet floor, and floats out of his body. He then follows, from a birds-eye view, the effects of his death on the people around him, most notably his sister (Paz de la Huerta). The film climaxes (literally) with Oscars point of view inside his sisters vagina while she has sex, and seems to suggest that his incorporeal participation in this leads to his rebirth.

The horror of the home invasion, of violence and terror within the assumed safety of our own houses, was a popular genre to explore in France and beyond. With its roots in the 60's and 70's with such classics as Wait Until Dark and Straw Dogs, the subgenre returned in force in the form of Michael Haneke's Funny Games (1997). Two young adults, scary because they don't seem deranged, play deadly psychological games with a family, for seemingly nothing more than trivial reasons. This cult Austrian movie was an inspiration for a host of French features, including the lethal horror of children gone bad in Ils (2006). It was Julien Maury and Alexandre Bustillo's combined effort on Inside (2007) however, that not only upped the bloodletting in every form, but also was lauded by critics and audiences alike.

Heavily pregnant Sarah (Alysson Paradis) is having one last calm evening alone at home, before planning to induce labour the following day. It is Christmas Eve, and in the night, a mysterious woman arrives and begins to threaten her, finally making her way into the house while Sarah is asleep. The danger extends to anybody who happens to arrive at the house during the course of the night, and various people do. The limiting location brings a sense of desperation and inescapability to the horror, and once the gore begins, it never lets up, and predominantly involves a large scissors.

Martyrs (2008 // Pascal Laugier), another home invasion flick of sorts, arrived as the French Extreme began to quieten down, and is the last of the (in)famous movies of this cinematic phase. Lucie (Mylène Jampanoï), who was mysteriously tortured as a child, enters a very normal household and murders everyone, claiming to her friend Anna (Morjana Alaoui) that these were the people responsible for her abused childhood. As Lucie tackles horrific hallucinations and unwinds more and more, Anna finds no evidence that this murdered family had any ulterior agenda – until she uncovers a secret door to a sterile basement, containing a woman with a metallic headpiece nailed to her skull. While the brutality of the film is extreme, Martyrs also borders on the metaphysical in places, and this gives it a unique position among its peers. The central concept behind the story is that through extreme suffering we may see beyond this life and into the next one. This sets up the difficult third act of the movie, but culminates in an intriguing ending that may or may not be philosophically nihilistic.

2002 to 2008 were the peak years of the French Extreme. Many of the filmmakers flourished, and off the critical acclaim that numerous films garnered, a number of French filmmakers were lured to Hollywood. Alexandre Aja's 2003 calling card was Haute Tension (High Tension/Switchblade Romance). With the lofty goal of out-doing any movie in terms of visceral gore, Aja's story is another of seeming randomness – while staying with the family of a friend, Marie hears someone come to the house in the middle of the night and begin to slay everybody in grisly fashion. The impact of Aja's gorefest led to Wes Craven enlisting his help on the remake of The Hills Have Eyes, and he has remained in North America ever since. Another French director to make the transition is Xavier Gens. His 2007 movie Frontier(s) was awash with nastiness, and secured him a position as director of Hitman and The Divide. Even Laugier has succumbed to the lure of the USA, with his follow-on movie from Martyrs being The Tall Man, a serial killer flick starring Jessica Biel.

Beyond Torture Porn – The New Extremism

It is unfair to attribute everything extreme in recent cinema to the French however.

For more mainstream audiences, it was probably Saw (2004 // James Wan) that is remembered as the opening shift in the horror genre towards a new plateau of nasty. Trapped in a room and handcuffed to a drainpipe, with a variety of clues and rusty hacksaws around, Cary Elwes is told he has to kill the person who is secured at the far wall. Unbeknownst to them, a series of events are occurring out in the world, where the maniac Jigsaw is putting people he has already judged as guilty through a variety of oft-lethal but always enlightening death traps.

The phenomenal success of Saw and its ilk was an eye-opener for executives and studio heads, and a proliferation of hard-core gore movies rolled into development and out of the cinema screen. There was money to be made here, and once gold had been sighted, the excavations began. Eli Roth's Hostel (2005) was the biggest name out the gate. All 70's exploitation, rolled up in the quality of the 00's, it was a big earner for Lions Gate Films, and softened the investors attitude to the genre further. Many studios began releasing 're-imaginings' – taking ultra-famous horror movies, such as The Texas Chainsaw Massacre, Nightmare on Elm Street, Friday the 13th, and painting them over with increased gore and tinted darkness. These moneymaking monsters were always desaturated and darkened, or hued over with off-colour yellows and reds. And they always made the money.

Elsewhere, in Europe and beyond, the genre was being pushed to its zenith. The Danish filmmaker Lars von Trier had established himself as a man who does not compromise on his vision, and entered the scene with thoroughly real depictions of misery. Significantly depressing films such as Breaking the Waves (1996) and Dancer in the Dark (2000) led the way to Antichrist (2009), where von Trier finally reached the bottom of the well of darkness, and any element of humanity disappeared.

Antichrist is set in a completely isolated cabin in the woodland, one that could have easily been the centrepiece for more light-hearted movies such as The Evil Dead or Cabin Fever. A couple (William Dafoe and Charlotte Gainsbourg, credited as 'He' and 'She') retreat to this grim location after their only son steps out of a high-rise window and dies. Their overwhelming grief and blame manifests first as difficult conversations and quirky behaviour, but slowly escalates into unparalleled sexual violence. Miraculously, it appeared uncut when released around the world, although von Trier did have two cuts ready for different audiences and distributions – a 'Catholic' edit, and a slightly longer, relatively uncut 'Protestant' one.

Further east, the Japanese have brought extreme cinema into their country and mixed it with their styles and sensibilities. The Guinea Pig Series from the 80's/90's set the tone, delivering a series of seven controversial horror movies, and towards the end of the 90's new directors were beginning to establish themselves. On the forefront of this was the acclaimed director Takashi Miike. In the heyday, Miike was a machine, sometimes churning out six or more films a year. His most famous, Audition (1999) and Ichi the Killer (2001), are known for the kinetic film-making, and for the extremes they are willing to go, something not often considered in relation to more Eastern countries. A quick glance at the needle/eyeball scene in Audition will settle any doubt in the matter.

Extremism reached its conclusion with A Serbian Film (2010). A cinematic provocation, it is not by any stretch an enjoyable film, and seems to exist solely to incite controversy and sicken audiences. Scenes depicting the rape of a new-born child, a mid-coital decapitation, and even a literal skull fucking, assault our senses and conceptions, but the movie is lost in its increasingly Looney Tunes ante-upping, and becomes a parody of itself. A Serbian Film was banned in Spain, Norway, Australia, New Zealand, Malaysia and Singapore. It faced a temporary ban in Brazil, and was released in Germany after 13 minutes had been removed (compared to 4 minutes in the UK and 5 minutes in the USA). The movie was seen to be violating laws left right and centre. And riding the crest of this wave came The Human Centipede 2.

The first Human Centipede (2009) had enjoyed a lot of controversy for its central concept – three people are sown together, lips to anus, in order to create a single digestive system. It was slammed critically, but made an instant cult name for itself, and allowed director Tom Six to make the sequel. The Human Centipede 2 (2011) was designed to make the first film seem subtle and manageable, and taking a page out of A Serbian Film's book, Six aimed high. Or low, as it is. Very, very low.

Obsessed with The Human Centipede, mentally scarred and grimly perverted Martin Lomax (Laurence R. Harvey) decides that he can do better, and, over the course of the story, works his way towards creating a 12 person centipede using random victims. This involves, but is not limited to, teeth smashed out with hammers, masturbating with sandpaper, tendon severing, baby crushing, involuntary scatology, and lots and lots of staples.

The BBFC declared outright that the film was potentially a breach of the Obscene Publications Act, and refused to budge from their decision until Tom Six personally complained in an open letter to Empire Magazine. Relenting (somewhat) from their decision, The Human Centipede 2 was finally released with two and a half minutes edited out. The classification review in Australia resulted in only 30 seconds lost, but in New Zealand it faced a total ban.

Indeed, it seems that the lethal cocktail of A Serbian Movie, The Human Centipede 2, and a variety of others, had pushed the genre as far as it was capable of going, and the Extreme Movie has since entered a lull phase. The Saw series, while still generating profit, has undeniably trundled downhill, and is now a shadow of its former, and more critically acclaimed, early days. The money machine has moved on to new pastures, and while intense midnight movies are still being made on a regular basis, none have the personality or profit, which the uncompromising earlier ones had.

The Changing Nature of Censorship

The BBFC's take on the proliferation of video nasties may be questionable, but there is a consistency within it. Its judgments fell clearly into the realms of sex and violence, with the occasional nod to drugs that they felt warranted illegalisation. But in our current international climate, things are not as black and white. The unsettling cinema of the New Extremism would have been locked up and buried thirty years ago, but these movies are now churned out on a regular, monthly basis. Not only are these productions encountering less resistance, but they are also seeing unprecedented returns. It is increasingly becoming reasons of a cultural or political nature that sees movies banned entirely.

We still live in a diverse world, where there is a growing number of cultural conflicts. In this environment, and where pretty much any film about anything can be made, nations are safeguarding their borders by blocking parodies and artistic statements. There are very few comedies on the BBFC Video Nasty list, but if you look at recent censorship decisions, a large number are directed towards this genre. While the South Park Movie (1997) not being distributed in Iraq would not come as a surprise to anyone who saw it, films such as The Simpsons Movie (2007) has been denied in Myanmar based on the skin colour of its characters (yellow), while Zoolander (2001) was slammed down in Iran for allegedly promoting a homosexual lifestyle.

Movies these days are also increasingly likely to be dumped for religious reasoning, rather than because someone has a reverse-bear trap sown on to their face. Even the excruciatingly unpleasant Antichrist is shown nearly everywhere with Catherine's clitoral self-mutilation intact. Monty Python's Life of Brian (1979) does intentionally provoke and may have been banned in Ireland and Norway, but on the other hand Darren Aronofsky's blockbuster Noah (2014) has been prohibited from screening in China, Egypt, Indonesia, and much of the Middle East, despite the fact that it has no chainsaw murders or interspecies gang rape in its entire 138 minute running time.

Incredibly, despite the wide variety of mutilations and abuse harboured by today's cinema, it is a man from Hammersmith, in West London, who has generated some of the most vocal international complaint this side of the millennium. Sacha Baron Cohen, also known as Borat, Bruno, and Ali G, has faced off, and ripped the piss out of, numerous countries in his career. Borat (2006, full title – Borat: Cultural Learnings of America for Make Benefit Glorious Nation of Kazakhstan) was successfully blocked in 2006 by the Khazk government, while in Ukraine, Brüno (2009) was forbidden due to its "offensive language and homosexual scenes". The Dictator (2012) was banned in Tajikistan, Turkmenistan, and Kazakhstan, and lost a full 12 minutes of screen time (as much as A Serbian Film was trimmed in Germany) in order to play in Uzbekistan.

Teddy-bear American comedian Seth Rogen seems to be an epicentre for further international controversy. Trinidad, Tobago, Malaysia and Thailand refused to show Zack and Miri Make A Porno (2008), and even in its home country in was banned in the state of Utah. The same year, Rogen starred in The Pineapple Express, a stoner buddy comedy that had an emphasis on yoga, which irked the Islamic state of Malaysia due to the view of yoga being a distraction from true faith. The Interview (2014), a comedy where two journalists are sent to assassinate the supreme leader of North Korean, Kim Jong-un, understandably upset the leaders of the Democratic People's Republic.

Avatar (2009) was pulled from cinemas in China, possibly for the politically charged themes of the suppressed lower class rising up against the property developers. Bruce Almighty (2003) faced the wrath of Egypt for the scene when Jim Carry uses Gods powers to make Jennifer Aniston's breasts bigger. And The Da Vinci Code (2006), which suggests that Jesus may have actually had sex at some point, received a boycotting from the Vatican City, the Faroe Islands, and Peru, and was totally banned in Egypt, Lebanon, Jordan, Pakistan, Samoa, and Sri Lanka.

With brutally violent movies available to anyone with enough motivation or over a certain age, and hardly any act of pornography considered too extreme, the profit margin on sex and violence will keep them in our lives for a long time to come. But it seems that the expression of ideas is what causes the most controversy, and which will face the toughest barriers, now and in the future.

-Stephen Wright   Writer/Filmmaker.

Censorship: Where we are Today...

The Video Recordings Act of 1984 was simply the most overt step towards state censorship that has been made in modern politics in this country, at least until recently. At the time the Conservative government also made such censorious steps as censoring the voices of the IRA spokesmen in Sinn Fein whilst allowing their words to be heard. They fully understood the power of censorship and were more than happy to use it.

The political opposition with all too few exceptions were unwilling to stand up for freedom of speech at the time and those who did were heckled, hounded and derided. The VRA was such a knee jerk piece of legislation that was forcibly rammed through parliament so fast that its very enactment was botched. In late 2009 it was discovered that the legislation violated European commerce laws in that it negatively affected commerce from within the European Union. By banning the films and requiring them to go through the censor board this meant that a product that could otherwise be sold freely throughout Europe had to go through an artificial barrier in order to get into the country, if indeed it was of course not simply banned by the BBFC. Because of this oversight the legislation that had allowed the arrest and prosecution of not just the 'unscrupulous' video dealers but of many legitimate distributors and rental outlets was in fact unenforceable. This however did not stop the government denying, albeit not definitively, any right to appeal from any victims of the enforcement of this...

The department [For Culture, Media and Sport] said it had received legal advice that people who had been prosecuted and convicted would be unable to overturn their convictions or seek compensation. However, it is possible that those who were convicted may mount legal challenges as they were, in effect, prosecuted under an act that should not have been enforced.

http://www.guardian.co.uk/uk/2009/aug/25/video-piracy-damages-1984-act

The upshot of this was that convictions had been made, property had been seized, business and reputations had been destroyed and tainted by criminal proceedings that should never have taken place not simply because they were morally dubious and politically despicable, but because the process itself was illegal. All for the sake of a political movement that at its heart was not about doing the right thing.

The Video Recordings Act was in 2010 revoked and then reinstated verbatim, this time with the right names being signed on the right lines, at least as far as we can tell. The fact that state censorship, and that is what it is, was finally officially passed with barely a column inch being written about it in any of the news papers speaks volumes of how complacent we have become about the idea that the government should have a hand in the censorship of our cinema.

Some heart should be taken in the fact that they have relatively little influence in the process these days though, at least until a convenient moral outrage is linked to a particular title (see True Romance, Reservoir Dogs, Natural Born killers etc.) but the net interference by ministers seems to be fairly minimal for the most part. The BBFC also have changed significantly in the years following the VRA's handing of the proverbial golden egg to them back in 1984.

Since the days when the political arena was raging about sexually explicit films being allowed even in the R18 category (reserved for retail in only licensed sex shops) there have been a few examples of films that have managed to gain respectable 18 certificates because of the context of that material i.e. it being part of a complete and adult discussion of sex and sexual behaviour. What a long way from the days when David

Cronenberg's study of the extremities of sexual behaviour, Crash, or the comically ridiculous soft core antics of Basic Instinct would offend when now we can watch the likes of The Idiots, Ai No Corrida and the entirely explicit Nine Songs which all include actual sex as part of the film.

Despite this apparent leniency we find the BBFC are still here and still doing their jobs, which mean that of course censorship is still going on.

R18 still remains the most heavily censored rating, certainly the most strictly controlled and that's a category designed for a very narrow market who will these days prefer the anonymity of the internet to supply their demand.

Of course even in the mainstream there have decisions to ban films. The horror genre particularly gets the most notable bans with in previous years there being bans of the 'August Underground films' Murder Set Pieces, The American indie horror The Bunny Game, and the Japanese so-called 'Torture Porn' feature Grotesque. It still is the case that the BBFC are particularly squeamish about the combination of sex and violence, Grotesque certainly crossed that line with the sexual fervour with which the torturer carries out his work. Probably not useful to the defence of the film was the mad man inducing the captive girl to a particularly spectacular wet orgasm. Again with another example the dividing line between sex and violence was blurred with Adam Rehmeier's rape nightmare The Bunny Game. It's the perceived eroticisation of violent and non-consensual sex that proved the sticking point as it's protagonist kidnaps and sexually brutalises his victim. The banning of films these days is thankfully very rare. Even during John Trevelyan's stint as secretary of the BBFC (1959-1971) which saw an unprecedented level of cinematic bans it was around 12 a year on average, this was less than one percent of the films examined that were refused classification.

There has of late been a more considered approach be the BBFC though certain flavours of film such as the previously mentioned ones still cause angst. One film in particular that caused significant ructions was Srdjan Spasojevic's hugely controversial A Serbian Film.

A Serbian Film follows the story of Milosh, a retired porn actor of some note who is invited to return to work to star in a "more artistic" project by a mysterious director. It quickly becomes obvious there is a reason for the mystery, as the porn turns darker - with children being thrown into the mix in various roles (mostly observing). Milosh refuses to work any more, but is drugged and made to get on with making the film against his will.

A Serbian Film is certainly a difficult film to justify; it uses an awful lot of suggestion to make you think you've seen things you may not have actually seen, and there are times when it is disturbingly explicit. However, it's the idea of what's going on that is particularly irksome for the BBFC more than anything, anything that is other than the involvement of children though no accusations have been levelled regarding the production, which was apparently very careful to keep the children away from anything inappropriate. In reality, during the Frightfest film festival, as the film was being prepared to screen, the BBFC demanded 39 cuts to be made, which was fairly major. The local council refused to allow the film to be shown without BBFC approval and the festival organisers refused to show a cut version (though they did show a cut version of the I Spit on your Grave remake). The fact that the BBFC passed it at all, even in a cut form was surprising in many regards however a rather ominous revisit of the nasties days came about after A Serbian Film was released on DVD. Northampton Police received a complaint from an anonymous member of the public which resulted in a Blockbuster store being raided and its copies of A Serbian Film being seized from the shelves; the police claim one copy was taken, other sources say all. Bearing in mind that these DVD's all carried the BBFC certificates it does beg some explanation as to why the police felt the need to carry out such a dramatic and draconian action, which I would imagine was terrifying and upsetting to the staff of the shop. Blockbuster withdrew all copies at this point and closed links to the film on its website. More importantly the action called into question the position of the BBFC. If a film carrying a BBFC certificate was liable to being scooped off the shelves by the police at any point then what point was there to the VRA? To those with an interest in the 'nasties' period it was a brief peek back to the time when the police were free to rifle through peoples personal property in the name of decency.

The Video Recordings Act brought in an unimaginable level of film censorship most specifically because of the VRA's consideration of the home environment which forces the BBFC to consider the fact that not all adults are necessarily responsible to lock unsuitable material away. While this may seem a reasonable concern it has not been established that this is in fact a major problem, or indeed that films deemed suitable for the cinema would be harmful to children in the first place. Considering there are practical and more demonstrable risks to other age restricted items being in the house, i.e. alcohol, pharmaceuticals, potential weaponry such as knives or of course tobacco amongst others, and none of these things requires special legislation to mitigate their potential use in the hands of children beyond the point of sale it seems odd that films should be specifically targeted when all of the above have actual rather than anecdotal evidence of what bad can happen as a result of their misuse. The potential for harm from film is at best hazy and it always seems to be just one element amongst many in a criminal life (an element that may be symptomatic rather than causal.

With the VRA having been eventually legalised after the embarrassing discovery of its 25-year illegitimacy the government have moved on from film somewhat. Now it's the Internet that has come under scrutiny and the cycle of censorious behaviour begins again with its familiar overtones and subject matters. David Cameron announced his intention to block pornography on the Internet in a speech that rang with echoes of the nasties scare.

"Today, I am going to tread into territory that can be hard for our society to confront that is frankly difficult for politicians to talk about but that I believe we need to address as a matter of urgency.

I want to talk about the internet the impact it is having on the innocence of our children how online pornography is corroding childhood and how, in the darkest corners of the internet, there are things going on that are a direct danger to our children, and that must be stamped out.

I'm not making this speech because I want to moralise or scaremonger, but because I feel profoundly as a politician, and as a father, that the time for action has come.

This is, quite simply, about how we protect our children and their innocence."

http://www.politics.co.uk/comment-analysis/2013/07/22/david-cameron-s-porn-speech-in-full

Now let's substitute a few words....

Today, I am going to tread into territory that can be hard for our society to confront that is frankly difficult for politicians to talk about but that I believe we need to address as a matter of urgency. I want to talk about *video **horror***, the impact it is having on the innocence of our children how *video violence* is corroding childhood and how, in the darkest corners of ***our*** *living rooms*, there are things going on that are a direct danger to our children, and that must be stamped out.

I'm not making this speech because I want to moralise or scaremonger, but because I feel profoundly as a politician, and as a father, that the time for action has come.

This is, quite simply, about how we protect our children and their innocence.

The familiar keywords are once again present and the breadth of what PM David Cameron is proposing is being smuggled in under the radar. When one looks at the reports following this speech that expand upon the scope of the 'porn block' it becomes astoundingly obvious that this is not at all about porn, porn is simply the public face of the proposal. Included in the default block will be pornography, violent material, extremist and terrorist related content, anorexia and eating disorder websites, suicide related websites, alcohol, smoking, web forums, esoteric material and web blocking circumvention tools. A brief glance at this list and all may seem fine though when you consider that within those sites there have already been sites identified as being either informational or of the kind that provides help and advice to people affected by these issues that may be blocked to those, people who need it most and things seem less comfortable. Also, as the mobile Internet companies have already demonstrated, many sites have already been blocked including some that are political, not extremist mind you, and some that are simply businesses. There is a serious concern about what will be blocked as part of an automated system because historically this has proved to be unreliable at best and censorious at worst. How these black lists will work is at this point an unknown and there are many important questions about how it will work.

Will we be able to examine the black lists? Who will be responsible for overseeing them? Will there be a means of appeal and will it be independent? How will those affected be able to tell that they are on this list? Will those affected be compensated for loss of earnings if they are mistakenly blocked by the filter?

Apart from this selection of issues there are other concerns such as the approach of making the filter 'Opt out'. This setting up of a default censorship is odious and unethical to begin with particularly when you take into mind the intrusions into our privacy by our governments of late. In the wake of terrifying and scandalous levels of privacy invasion, particularly by the US and UK government, the likes of which George Orwell would have baulked at, we find ourselves in a situation where our governments are trying desperately to control the Internet and everything that happens on it. The familiar language of security and child protection and protection from perverts/terrorists have come flooding back into the political arena with all the fear-mongering and urgency that always accompanies such drives. All of this is very familiar, it's the same old song remixed to a tune re-mastered to fit the net. With the battle for copyright protection still raging in a war being waged by studios and distributors, a war that has seen indiscriminate and dirty tactics being used, and with the blatant corporate buyout of our governments there is a situation now where the government want to hand the net to those that pay them. This cannot be allowed to happen. The language of censorship is back and to anyone with a knowledge of the history of previous battles it's very clear what is going on. This is why the nasties scare is such an important piece of history, it's all there, it's history that has surfaced time and time again and it is history that illuminates what is going on now.

In this post 9/11 world, terror and national security have become the excuse for censorship along with the usual suspects of paedophiles, childhood innocence and crime and an excuse is exactly what it is.

-Glenn Criddle   Writer/Critic.

When Henry Met Mick: Misguided Censorship in Australia

Australia has a long and proud tradition of censorship. Perhaps this is part of the problem of being an isolated island so far from the rest of the West. Or perhaps it is because we are such a young nation our leaders believe they need to mollycoddle its citizens.

Early bushranger films, initially a staple of the burgeoning local film scene, were banned for fear of inciting similar criminal acts in the population, according to Rebecca Harkins-Cross in a 2008 *Film Ink* article. In 1929 Australia followed Britain's lead by banning D. H. Lawrence's novel *Lady Chatterley's Lover* due to its depictions of sex. Expurgated editions were eventually released but controversy raged in the '60s when the original text was again submitted, only to be banned once more. It took until 1965 for the novel to finally be allowed in full, in a move that pioneered some relaxing of the censorship laws for books (although Bret Easton Ellis's *American Psycho* was still famously sealed in plastic like some biohazard). However films and other forms of cultural expression continued to be refused classification over the years—and still are, as witnessed by the recent banning of the films *Found, Father's Day*, and the video game *South Park: The Stick of Truth* (which was forced to cut a pivotal and satirical anal probe scene that was described as "sexual violence", the creators replacing it with a cartoon of a crying koala).

Once the Office of Film and Literature Classification refuses to classify a film it cannot be distributed or obtained in Australia (and many horror fans were raided in the 1980s and 1990s if suspected of having such material), whereas in the United States objectionable films are often released uncut with an X rating, and even if the Motion Picture Association of America refuses classification the film can still be released, though it will suffer from reduced access to distribution.

Often the Censorship Board instead requests cuts to a film to make it more palatable for the Australian audience. I would argue this can have a converse effect of the intention to protect its citizens from the nastiness of filmed violence, particularly if it muddies the intention of the filmmakers and sanitizes the confrontational effect of some films.

Henry: Portrait of a Serial Killer (directed by John McNaughton), although made in 1985, was eventually only released in the US in 1990 initially with an X rating and then an UR (unrated) rating. The MPAA told the filmmakers no combination of cuts would allow an R rating, a decision that fueled the call for the NC-17 rating in the States. However the UK's distributor Electric Pictures pre-empted the British Board of Film Classification's reaction by cutting 62 seconds of what they thought were the more extreme scenes of violence without McNaughton's approval, mostly of a harrowing family massacre scene. When the film was submitted for video in 1992, rather than this theatrical version being passed BBFC director James Ferman himself intervened and ordered 113 seconds in total cut, reducing the family massacre scene almost to nothing, and targeting other sections of the film.

In doing so, the board missed the point of the movie. McNaughton had been given a brief by his producers to create an exploitation movie after funding for various documentaries had fallen through. What he turned in was instead a searing exposé not only examining the potential sociopath lurking behind the placid face of the Everyman, but a work that implicated the viewer in the voyeurism of screen murder. The film expressly does this in the family massacre scene, which the two lead characters Henry (Michael Rooker) and Otis (Tom Towles) film. At first we experience the events through the camera's viewfinder along with the killers, continuing and expanding upon the time-honored slasher tradition of witnessing the murder through the point-of-view of the killer (pioneered by John Carpenter's *Halloween*). However we pan out to reveal we're watching this footage on television alongside Henry and Otis sprawled on a couch some time after the murders, in one of the most brilliant critiques of the modern horror audience and its usually dissociated voyeurism of onscreen death. Toning down the violence of this scene and reducing its length (indeed to virtual non-existence in the widely-distributed video release) nullifies its impact. Rather than confronting the audience with extreme violence that is uncomfortable and intimate and realistic and then further questioning our consumption of such images by the sleight-of-hand of the television reveal, instead it becomes just another murder that happens somewhere off-screen before the story continues. The audience is not forced to question their complicity in the glorification and consumption of murder, and so the central theme of the movie is lost.

In Australia the distributors Dendy submitted *Henry* to the Australian Film and Censorship Board in 1992, which refused classification on the grounds it was "indecent." Upon appeal to the Film and Literature Board of Review the Board noted their conflict in upholding its ban, identifying that the film indeed had artistic merit. Yet it couldn't resist a snide comment in its summation, stating, "some American and English critics, not necessarily the most esteemed, have called it a masterpiece." Roger Ebert hailed the film, arguing it deals "honestly with its subject matter, instead of trying to sugar-coat violence as most 'slasher' films do." *The Village Voice* proclaimed it film of the year. Even the staunchly conservative Australian critic David Stratton (who, along with a one-time champion of the fight against censorship Margaret Pomeranz, famously refused to review *Wolf Creek 2* on the ABC show *At The Movies*, stating in a later dismissive piece for *The Australian* "this is not the place to discuss the worldwide appeal of torture-porn and extreme screen violence") submitted a letter accompanying the *Henry* submission, declaring "I can't imagine it being in the least bit stimulating." Hardly lightweight reviewers. Yet despite this the FLBR took the lead of the BBFC and suggested a re-edit along the lines of the UK release and resubmission. Eventually the film was released theatrically with 90 seconds missing, the most in the world. And so Australian audiences were denied the film in its entirety, and the opportunity to make up their own minds about whether it is indeed indecent.

Similarly in Australia 2014's *Wolf Creek 2* faced an indirect form of censorship, and also suffered from re-editing of a key scene. At the end of the first act one of the lead characters—rather than being our strong protagonist leading us through the film in their efforts to escape, as we might assume—is instead beheaded before our eyes. This was intended to be as confronting as possible, and the opposite of the gothic 'pleasure of terror' (which arguably some horror movies revel in). In fact, when writing the scene I'd imagined it shown in one continuous take without cutaways or edits for special effects interjections (perhaps through CGI as with the unforgettable head-stomping scene in *Irreversible*). For me it would be an echo of freelancer Nick Berg's beheading in Iraq in 2004, which marked one of the first filmed deaths to be widely distributed on the internet (presaging the spate of ISIS beheadings that coincidently coincided with *Wolf Creek 2*'s release). The footage of Berg was so powerful because for many it was the first time witnessing a death play out before their eyes. Here a man went from a living, breathing, talking sentient being to a piece of degraded meat. To nothing. That anyone could do this to another human was and is unfathomable. In *Wolf Creek 2* the death of Rutger (Philippe Klaus) was supposed to be as confronting as this—true horror, in the sense of creating a lasting sense of dread that stays beyond the viewing (for that is the definition of horror, not a moment of exciting terror or thrill of the hoary "roller coaster ride" that excites with its flippant and non-consequential blood and guts, but a lasting dread that changes the world of the viewer, and which should be the underlying impulse of all horror). Here is a character we have spent the entire film with so far, the protector of his girlfriend Katarina (Shannon Ashlyn), who we should hopefully be emotionally attached to, and that should seem a worthy opponent to the film's villain, Mick Taylor (John Jarratt). But, like Janet Leigh in *Psycho* the German couple are a red herring that give way to the film's real protagonist: the passing British backpacker Paul Hammersmith (Ryan Corr). And so their deaths should be just as surprising and shocking. The beheading would show this in the most extreme and matter-of-fact way possible. Although the continuous single shot became only a pipe dream, director Greg McLean did not shy away from our intention, filming the scene as viscerally and explicitly as possible, including the full trauma experienced by girlfriend Kata—for she cannot escape the full horror of the events, so why should the audience be able to?

Although the first *Wolf Creek* became the highest-grossing R-rated ever in Australia, in the month prior to *Wolf Creek 2*'s release in Australia it was decided by the film's distributors Village Roadshow that the film needed an MA15+ cut to reach a wider audience. The scene of the beheading of Rutger and his subsequent no-holds barred butchering (because Mick is a pig shooter, and would see the butchering of humans as no different) were reduced. Rather than the confronting and still almost edit-free vision of Rutger's neck being sawed and his head detaching from his body—a shot that had people groaning and walking out during test screenings—instead we only see the throat being slashed (unfortunately, a common enough image in horror films) and then the aftermath of the head being dropped on the ground accompanied by a Mick quip (a more jokey line than that in the original version). The scene arguably loses some of its power and certainly no longer has the intended impact of making the audience experience an almost unadulterated depiction of a beheading. In fact, it possibly becomes too comedic with the addition of the line of dialogue, and again it just becomes another death that happens more or less off-screen. The film itself, without such shocking moments of confronting realistic violence, loses some of its shifts of tone and instead becomes more an action movie.

Such omissions of the more extreme moments of violence in the film (in addition, some finger-grinding was 'cut' from the quiz scene at the end of the film) may well have had the intended result of the distributor in strengthening the film's appeal to a broader audience. The film was widely promoted by Roadshow on billboards and even television, and subsequently smashed its way into number one at the box office in its first week, almost unheard-of for a local horror film. At the time of writing the film is still the second highest-grossing Australian film of 2014, so perhaps the move was justified—for film is of course a compromised art that must generate money. At a promotional screening in Adelaide just prior to release grandmothers in the audience came up afterwards to say how much they'd surprisingly liked it. However, some horror fans felt the movie lacked some of the confrontational horror of the first *Wolf Creek* (even though it was *still* more explicit, even in its cut version), not knowing the film's intended form until it was eventually released in full on Blu-ray in Australia as a 'Director's Cut' edition.

In the US and UK the film was released wholly uncut.

This became then an example not so much of censorship by the ratings board (as the edits pre-empted their response), but one of catering for market forces. Unfortunately the resulting film lost the intended power of the beheading scene, just as the sanitizing of *Henry*'s filmed family massacre scene obfuscated its critique of the reception of filmed violence. And it further highlights the problem of outside forces placing moral restrictions on art.

Evan Williams, the then chairman of the FLBR, states in the 1991-1992 Report on Activities that the Review Board's starting point when approaching *Henry* "has been the view adopted by the Chief Censor and enunciated in the classification guidelines that adults in a free society should be at liberty, subject to certain agreed constraints, to see, hear and read what they please." This is the first line of the Classification Code, in fact, but the rub has always been the problem of 'agreed constraints.' A free society's citizens are *never* free to consume any material, but are in fact subject to the moralities and predilections of the current ruling State. Harkins-Cross notes that when Don Chipp took over the Customs portfolio in 1969 he inherited a system that had only two classification categories: General Exhibition and Not Recommended for Children. So effectively adults were being treated the same as kids (a situation some would argue hasn't changed). "I inherited a censorship system which was secretive, archaic and illogical," Chipp writes in his autobiography. "It falsely imposed on the nation the standards of people with massive sexual hang-ups and obsessions."

In their initial banning of the movie *Found* in 2012 (it was subsequently released with cuts) the Classification Board's report justifies the ban by noting "the Guidelines state that films will be refused classification if they contain gratuitous, exploitative or offensive depictions of violence with a very high degree of impact or which are excessively frequent, prolonged or detailed". With *Henry*, the board notes that Dendy in their submission argued "the film in no way glamorized its violent events or its central character, and indeed provoked suitable feelings of horror and revulsion […] Although the subject matter was disturbing, there was no attempt to sensationalise it or to render it alluring or even entertaining in any conventional way." And yet while the board seemed to implicitly agree with this it still requested cuts. If the scene is not salacious or exploitative, and there's a valid artistic reason for the level of violence, then why censor it?

Treating all depicted forms of violence or sexualized violence the same—as objectionable to the sensibilities of the audience and therefore in need of suppression—is a generalized reaction that is not always appropriate, if ever. While there might be some forms of expression that contain criminal acts—such as pedophilia or bestiality—that should arguably indeed be restricted, arbitrarily and inconsistently imposing an assumed set of values on the community as a whole is troublesome and belies the stated assumption that a free society should be able to make up its own mind about certain material or avoid it if necessary.

An added danger is that when cuts are forced on artworks, as they were with *Henry* and *Wolf Creek 2*, they change the nature of the film. Scenes which are intentionally non-exploitative, non-salacious, and which force the audience on the back foot with their extreme nature and which encourage the questioning of the viewer's role in consuming such violence, or are at least integral elements of the storyline, instead become neutered and sanitized.

And in doing so censorship may actually let the audience off the hook.

-Aaron Sterns Screenwriter.

Combat Shock in the 90s.

One of my first experiences as a filmmaker with censorship was in 1990. I was invited to Splatter fest at the Scala Theatre in London with COMBAT SHOCK. A lot of the really strong horror films of the day were banned in England by the British Board of Film Censorship; you couldn't buy or rent many genre films on VHS or see them in theatres. But if there was a film festival running, the films would be allowed to screen as part of the festival. So I was invited along with John McNaughton and Roy Frumkes, Scotti Spiegel, Greg Nicotero and a few others to screen our films and talk about them afterward.

I wasn't used to having an audience for my film because it had pretty much been rejected by every festival that I entered it into; but to be fair, these were mainstream or indie festivals and they just couldn't stomach the darkness and the harshness of the film. At market screenings for film festival programmers CS was sure to clear the room. One scene in particular never failed to create an exodus: The coat hangar scene. I would stand in the back of the theater and watch people walk out throughout the film, one or two at a time—I never took it personally, I knew what I'd made was not for everyone. But after the coat hanger scene half the audience would get up and leave (well, I did take it a little personally, but I kept it to myself). Anyway, back at Splatter fest, I was having lunch with Scotti Spiegel at a small restaurant, and then we were going to the theatre for the screening of CS. As we're walking to the theater there was a long line on the street; it looked like a rock concert. I remember thinking, Damn, London has a lot of freaks - just like NYC! You can see of course where this is going. It was the line for Splatter fest and I couldn't believe these people were there to see my film. After the screening I met a couple from Amsterdam who took the train that morning to come to London. They told me they'd screened my film 12 times—there were many VSH bootleg copies out there, which didn't bother me at all because I wanted people to see the film. Anyway, this couple told me they came all the way from Amsterdam to finally see the film in color -. I was completely confused. But the film *IS* in color, I told them. They told me the film had been banned in the Netherlands and their bootleg VHS copy had been copied and recopied so many times that the film was in Black and White. That's when it hit me how starved the genre audience was for the films we love, and also how ridiculous censorship is.

It seems like the dark ages now when we look back on it, but at the time, you really had to be tenacious to find and screen films that you wanted to see. One last story. Shortly after CS had been released on VHS I got a call one night from a guy living in Finland. How he found my number I don't know, but don't fuck with the Finns; they'll find you. Anyway, this guy called me up angry; he just had to tell me about the outrage that had taken place. He told me my film CS had gotten a release in Finland, but the film ended when Frankie Dunlan goes home to his apartment after being on the street all day long. They simply cut off the last 15 minutes of the film. Gone. As if it never existed. Needless to say, I was also really angry after hearing this, but there was nothing you could do back then. To be fair, Lloyd Kaufman at Troma was a huge supporter of the film - he loved it! He didn't want to cut one frame, but as they made distribution deals with other countries, every country could cut the film as they saw fit, to satisfy local community boards and censors. Those bastards.

It seems like today we can see just about anything we want whenever we want. But this convenience comes with a cost. It's cost us that thrill of finding something rare and hard-to-get, of searching a film out and holding it in your hand, or finding a midnight screening three hours away by bus. It took effort to hunt out great films in their original form, uncut and very rarely screened.

There was something rebellious about that too. It was breaking the rules. A private "Fuck You" to Authority. Damn, I hope we never stop telling Authority to fuck off.

-Buddy Giovinazzo   Director "Combat Shock".

My Proudest Moment: Being Banned

In 1992, I wrote and associate produced "Return of the Living Dead 3." One day after the movie was released, I visited Brian Yuzna, the director, who had a big smile on his face as he showed me a letter that the distributor had received from South Africa. At the time, South Africa was in the final throes of apartheid, one of the most egregious examples of racism and violence against an indigenous population. The letter from the censors in South Africa took it upon themselves to ban our little zombie film for being morally reprehensible. The letter stated that the government committee had "never been subjected to such evil violence." Wow... My jaw dropped. It was surreal. Our film was set in a fairy tale world in which people come back from the dead. Obviously pure fiction. For the ruling to come from a government that had perpetrated real horrific violence on their own citizens seemed preposterous. Fortunately, the zombie genre has flourished and body mutilation is widely recognized as a fictional element totally accepted when it comes to the living dead.

-John Penney   Writer, Director.

Hate the Censor

Film censorship in Britain in the 1980s and 1990s was a total farce. We have since moved on from there, and things seem that little better in regards to the censorship of films within Britain as a whole. It seems like a very long time ago, but those draconian days will forever haunt every single video nasty collector and fan of horror VHS nasties.

The video nasty era was a part of history in Britain. It actually happened! As much as I hate censorship and detest the BBFC in the 80s and 90s, I secretly loved the challenge of trying to track down VHS video nasties and banned VHS titles, the thrill of the hunt, the excitement watching every single film, the unity between collectors, the feeling of living on the edge of society—depraved enough to watch so-called filth and rebelling against the system. Video nasties introduced me to underground horror, and since the 1980s, I've been obsessed with finding obscure VHS titles like "Nekromantik" and the "Guinea Pig" films and trying to own every shot-on-video horror film in existence.

I don't think we are ever going to experience a time like the video nasty scandal again, unless strict regulations are enforced on the Internet (which I believe could actually happen in the future).

Most of my VHS collection at the time consisted of a blank VHS tape or sell-through carton VHS tape with a strip of Sellotape placed over the tab so you could record over the original film. I would record copies of video nasties—most of which were second-generation copies already (or bootlegs). I made lists of all the VHS titles I was hunting down—some copied from magazines doing an expose on video nasties and even articles in newspapers at the time. I recall one list had over 200 titles, which was main video nasty list plus other films from the section 3 banned list.

As soon as the BBFC was set up as the governing body and the implementation of the Video Recordings Act 1984 rating system was introduced, official records of the section 2 and section 3 DPP lists were destroyed by the courts. I have tried contacting the courts themselves, but they say they kept no log of either of the lists on file.

It was hard to actually know what titles were on each list and what titles were banned at the time. Long before the Internet and IMDB, it was simply word of mouth; I remember trying to track down many films that didn't actually exist or weren't actually what they appeared to be.

I always assumed films like "The Texas Chain Saw Massacre," "Xtro," and "Zombie Holocaust" were on the main video nasty list and not on the section 3 list—if you'd have asked me at the time, I would have argued the toss for days!

My dream list consisted of well over two hundred VHS nasties—mainly titles which are now featured on a mix of the old section 2 and 3 hit list: 99% horror films and a few experimental art films that were doing the rounds on VHS at the time. My nasty list featured tons of titles refused classification by the BBFC, such as "The Class of 1984," "Back in Action," "Sadomania," "Silent Night Deadly Night 2," as well as trying to find uncut versions of films like "Rosemary's Killer," "The Evil Dead," and cult zombie movies.

What list these films originated on didn't matter; all that mattered to me was I got to see the films in their full, uncut glory and perhaps even to own a copy (or even a bootleg copy) of each on VHS so I could watch and re-watch them over and over again!

If you were lucky enough at the time to have seen a film like "The Texas Chainsaw Massacre," "Faces of Death," "I spit on Your Grave," or "Cannibal Holocaust," it was like a badge of honor! You could talk about the films to people who hadn't seen them, and even make up parts that didn't exist to scare them! Every film from the video nasty list was deemed to be *too real*—you actually thought you were watching real snuff films and, with the copies being sometimes truly bad, almost black and white, it could well have been real—it could have been anything you were watching!

In the late 80s, we used to use the term video nasty as a more general term. In the 1980s and 1990s, so many films were banned in the UK, we would try to get the nastiest, most gruesome horror films legally available. Sadly, that often meant renting films like "Ghoulies," "Zone Troopers," "The Video Dead," or "C.H.U.D," which weren't video nasties at all (still really cool VHS horror films though!).

I miss the days of walking out of a collectors' trade fair with a VHS nasty hidden under my jumper or stuck down my jeans in case the police knew I had a banned VHS tape on me; the likelihood was pretty slim, but you never knew for sure. It was a very exciting time to be a horror film fan and VHS collector!

VHS is the only true way to watch a video nasty—do try to make sure it's a first generation copy though, even they look clear as day compared to the bootlegs in the 80s and 90s. Blu-Ray is far to clear and crisp, and you don't feel like you are watching a true exploitation film with the picture that pristine; the special effects look so much better on VHS—no one wants to see high definition bad effects or puppet strings!

VHS… even the word sends shivers of excitement down my spine. I'm instantly transported back to the 80s heyday when VHS was the media of not so much choice, but the only way we could view films at home.

My walls were filled with big box VHS tapes from the video rental stores, my walls were full of VHS rental posters, and as I look at my office walls now… to be honest, not much has changed!

I still adore VHS as much as I did when I was a youngster, and VHS still has the power to excite me and nothing is better than hunting for a title or getting a VHS tape on my wanted list through the post! It is much harder to track down VHS tapes now, as everyone is capitalising on the popularity of VHS cassettes. Serious collectors pay a high premium just to have a certain tape in their collection. Video nasties are the highest priced of all VHS tapes, often are selling in the hundreds and thousands; I've seen full collections of the 39 list of banned VHS titles going for five thousand pounds and upwards!

Much like our parents and grandparents with their china ornaments and trinkets, these are our generations' antiques. There are only a certain amount of the tapes in existence, as the police destroyed many of the originals. Those that survived the early draconian days of the1980s had to survive being sent packing to the tip when VHS gave way to DVD and 99% of collectors gave up VHS to collect the new media. Then factor in many of the copies left are covered in mould due to being kept in garages and lofts… so, if you are lucky enough to have an original copy of one of the video nasties without mould and in good condition, you are very lucky indeed!

VHS… the large casing, the magnetic tape, the reels, it's a piece of heaven. I love everything about VHS, from the look to the feel. For me, there is nothing better than a big-box ex-rental VHS tape: VHS films in all their glory, just as I first laid eyes on them in the video store in the early 1980s.

As well as my continued hunt for video nasties (a hunt that would continue into my late thirties and beyond into my forties), I started to collect ex-rental videotapes. Those are the original VHS tapes that stood proud on the shelves of the video store. I didn't want the sell-through VHS tapes that anyone could buy, I wanted tapes that had some of the magic, and the big-box videos with bigger cover art, bolder pictures, and the cassette that had lived within. They had been used by hundreds of customers, bringing that bit of magic into everyone's homes. The cassettes were hard-core (not hard-core porn), like the SAS of videotapes—cassettes made to last.

Censorship is a word synonymous with the UK.

In Britain, we have always had Big Brother watching over us, deciding what is appropriate for our viewing pleasure. The ridiculous decisions made by governing bodies throughout the years are laughable, especially so when you look back at the decisions made by the censors. If a film contained strong nudity, sexual violence, or two people of the same sex involved in sexual acts on-screen, the film would be doomed from the get-go. Britain in the 1980s and 1990s had the harshest censorship system in the world. The tiny islands' occupants didn't take kindly to the censorship thrust upon them—of course, there were councils and MPs and groups that agreed with the harsh censorship, but the majority of the general public didn't. With the implementation of the Video Recordings Act and the head of the BBFC, James Ferman, we were doomed from the very start. Just when we thought the video nasty fiasco and the banning of many horror-related titles could get any worse, it did! James Ferman and the BBFC had even more power to govern what we could or couldn't watch. I could almost picture Ferman sitting next to me on the sofa nodding his head every time I rented a VHS tape complete with a rating sticker, or wanting to smack the smug git (Radio One DJ, Simon Bates) who appeared at the start of every official VHS tape saying: "Whenever you rent or buy a video, you need to be sure that it's suitable for the audience."

Mary Whitehouse still managed to ruin 1980's VHS for home viewing when she managed to implement a claim making sure any classification decisions should have special regard to the likelihood of those video works being viewed in the family home. That, in turn makes no sense at all for implementing a rating system; if they were going to judge them based upon children having access to home video, surely it should be up to the parents to enforce their own law and not allow their children to watch an 18 or 15-cert.

As crazy as it sounds, I doubt I would have the love for video nasties and banned films if it wasn't for a majority of them being banned; the hunt was always the best thing for me. Although the BBFC may seem more relaxed now, we do still have one of the harshest censorship governing bodies in the western world; there are still a number of films deemed by the BBFC too outrageous and morally corrupt for British viewers, so a feint foul whiff of yesteryear does still exist.

The following films have been banned in Britain over the last few decades.

Love Camp 7
1969

Directed by Lee Frost

Love Camp 7 is the longest running film the BBFC have held a ban for. Lee Frost is the director who also brought us "Chain Gang Women".

Love Camp 7 shows no sign of getting a UK release—the film was re-submitted in 2002, but got rejected for a home video release. The BBFC have states the film has been rejected as many of the scenes feature sexual violence. The BBFC prohibits scenes which erotize, or indeed *endorse*, sexual assault. Love Camp 7 is an official VHS Nasty!

Women in Cellblock 9
1977

Directed by Jess Franco

Jess Franco makes the hit list once again!

Women in Cellblock 9 is *still* banned in the UK. The Swiss offering was outright banned because one of the actresses was only 16 when she filmed scenes including some violent sexual assault. In 2004, the film was re-submitted for classification—but was instantly rejected!

Mickey
1992
Directed by Dennis Dimster

Currently still banned in the UK. In 1992, the trailer was given an 18-certificate, but later the film was outright banned in 1996. The film was banned because of its theme, which focuses on a child as a killer. The BBFC and psychiatrists believed children who viewed the film may act violently—bear in mind this was very close to the horrific James Bulger murder.

Traces of Death
1993
Directed by Damon Fox

This film is still banned in Britain. It's very similar to The Faces of Death franchise as it shows death scenes. This gruesome offering was outright banned. In 2005, the BBFC stated the film had no journalistic, educational, or other justifying content for the images shown.

Crash
1996
Directed by David Cronenberg

Once again, the British media where in full swing around this controversial film. However, this time the BBFC didn't have a problem with it. The film was passed uncut for British cinema, but the London film Festival (1996) refused to show the film without cuts being made. Crash's distributor had refused to make cuts before the West End screening, or specifically for the London Film Festival, and thus the film was effectively banned in Westminster/ Leicester Square area.

Silent Night Deadly Night Part 2
1987
Directed by Lee Harry

The film was rejected for video release in the UK.

I think it's rather strange for this bizarre, camp romp of a horror film to be banned. It just seems to pass off as yet another teen-style, stalk-and-slash offering.

The BBFC rejected the film because of three scenes: The killing of a woman whose breasts are exposed, the killing of a couple during sex, and the continued pursuit to kill a woman with her breasts exposed.

The original distributor refused to make cuts the BBFC suggested to gain a certificate—since then the film has remained banned in the UK.

Murder Set Pieces
2004
Directed by Nick Palumbo

The film is banned to this day; this gruesome gore and sexual violence fest was outright banned in the UK.

The BBFC rejected the film because of its strong themes of sexual violence throughout and it potentially breaking UK obscenity laws.

My Daughter's a Cocksucker
2006

Directed by Bobbi Rinaldi

No surprise at all—the title alone is a big no-no for the BBFC!

The film is banned in the UK due to its strong irrumatio (thrusting of the penis into the mouth or throat or between the legs, breasts, feet or thighs) and other sexual scenes.

This incest-themed porn offering was a dead cert for the banned film list!

The Texas Vibrator Massacre
2008
Directed by Rob Rotton

This film is banned to this day. Okay, so no surprises here, judging by the title alone! This take off of The Texas Chainsaw Massacre and early 70s horror slashers is a porn horror film. It was rejected for classification in the UK for its eroticized sexual violence and incestuous sex between a brother and sister onscreen. No big surprise it's banned!

Lost in the Hood
2009
Directed by Edward James

Outright banned to this day in the UK.

This film is basically a gay porn film, which focuses on men being abducted, tortured, and raped throughout. The film was banned by the BBFC because of the high volume of graphic and eroticized sexual violence. The BBFC had a long running history of censoring both sexual violence and gay sex scenes, so this film was doomed from the get-go!

NF713
2009
Directed by China Hamilton

NF713 was banned in the UK, and still is to this day.

NF713 is basically a torture porn film, which revolves around a female victim being interrogated, sexually assaulted, and tortured. The harshness and terror the victim goes through, both mentally and physically, is relentless. The BBFC banned the film because its primary purpose was judged too sexually arousing to the viewer at the sight of women being sexually humiliated, tortured, and abused.

Grotesque
2009
Directed by Koji Shiraishi

This film was banned in 2009

This torture porn, almost snuff-style, offering from Japan has caused controversy across the globe and is banned in most countries—but surprisingly not in Japan! The BBFC banned this film because it lacked context or any purpose behind its gruesome content.

The Human Centipede Part 2: [The Full Sequence]
2011
Directed by Tom Six

In 2011, the film was originally banned for strong, explicit sexual violence, graphic forced defecation, and potential obscenity. It was the film's content and theme the BBFC disapproved of, even though the first film in the series was not deemed a problem (the theme was of a mad doctor doing medical experiments). For Part 2, the BBFC were worried we saw the events unfold from the point of view of the protagonist. On 6th Oct 2011, the film was given an 18-certificate with 32 cuts in total—two minutes and 37 seconds!

The Bunny Game
2011
Directed by Adam Reheiher
Outright banned in the UK. This film focuses on a prostitute called Bunny, who is kidnapped by a psycho truck driver that puts Bunny through copious amounts of physical and sexual abuse. This film was banned by the BBFC because of extreme levels of sexual violence throughout the film.

Hate Crime
2013
Directed by James Cullen Bressack
Banned in 2015 for its video-on-demand release. This film features Nazis invading and terrorizing a Jewish family home. The BBFC outright banned "Hate Crime" because it focuses on the terrorization, mutilation, physical and sexual abuse, and murder of the members of a Jewish family by Neo Nazi thugs who invade their home. The BBFC did consider the film for cuts, but due to the fact unacceptable content was continuous throughout the film, they could not. "Hate Crime" is a very good film, and does tread new ground, albeit with touchy subject matter. The following was stated by the BBFC: "Hate Crime" focuses on physical and sexual abuse, aggravated by racist incentives, which means that to issue a certification to this work—even to adults—would be inconsistent with the board's guild, would risk potential harm, and would be unacceptable to broad public opinion."

It is going to be very interesting to see what the future holds for censorship in Britain and across the globe. It just feels to relaxed at present, but I'm stockpiling copies of films just in case; it's like we are Doomsday preppers in my house, only with VHS tapes, horror films, and exploitation classics!

Forget the food and water, we must save the most important things first: VHS!

I have visions of all films stored in the cloud being censored at some point; people just don't seem to own physical media anymore. If there is a way "they" can control what we watch over the Internet, they are sure to enforce it in the near future!

-Tony Newton

Chapter 9: VHS Memories
The Growth of Movie Censorship

Since the dawn of its invention, Horror films have been the subject of cruel and unfair censorship. A beautiful painting of a woman in the nude isn't given an "R"/"18" rating. Yet, if a film contains an image of a nude woman it will be. They are both forms of art, so what gives? Why is one OK and not the other? Back in the 60's is when movie censorship started to become commonplace. "Psycho" had several frames removed during the infamous "shower sequence" as well as a brief few seconds of Marion Crane in her bra. The movie as a whole is pretty "PG"/"GP" by today's standards, but at the time, studios felt the imagery was too "explicit" for mainstream audiences.

Today, you can rent a movie like "The Human Centipede" at Redbox or Amazon...fully uncensored. You can show nudity on basic cable. You can use swear words in modern Police or Hospital Dramas. It's a different world now, but it was a long uphill battle to get here and we still have a ways to go. Probably the most notorious instance of movie censorship occurred during what would become the "Video Nasties" era. While the U.S. dealt with only getting heavily censored versions of "Tenebrae" (released Stateside as "Unsane") and "Last House On The Left", Britain flat out banned the sale or rental of certain titles, as they actually believed it contributed to criminal acts and human indecency.

Video Store Owners were arrested if caught selling something like "Faces of Death" and entire video inventories had been seized by authorities. Many youngsters had to get their Horror fix either on a bootleg import from the States or Japan, or just had to suffer through a usually even further censored version of a movie than what everyone else got. The BBFC (Britain's version of the MPAA) had successfully controlled what Horror films where available there for a long time. Since the Internet and movie downloading started to boom, that era began to drift away as there now was no real way to fully control the content it's citizens could see.

During the "Video Nasties" days, it scared a lot of filmmakers and Rental Store Owners into not wanting to take any risks. Many films became tamer in the genre, in fear of a Retailer refusing to carry it. It sent a rift through the scene and the U.S. began applying similar rules to other genres like "Thrillers" and "Sex Comedies". It became really taboo to show a female's gentials for a period of about 15 years from the late 80s and most of the 90s. Notably "Basic Instinct" and "Showgirls," both faced visual censorship during their more explicit moments. Nothing more distracting than a "blur" over Sharon Stone's vagina.

Today we have the ability to view most films the way they were intended. With "Director's Cuts" and "Unrated" versions being the new fad over the last decade, many studios actually encourage the filmmakers to make more explicit versions as they better understand the market now and how pointless censorship was in the first place. Horror films don't cause violent crime. If anything, I believe they help pacify many of the weirdoes out there.

Television has a ways to still go, but we are much further than we were during the 80's "Video Nasty" days. You can no longer get arrested for selling or renting a particular Horror film, and the boundaries of what can be shown have certainly grown. With an almost "anything goes" mentality with Horror films today, it will be interesting to see what the future holds for the genre and how far it can really be taken, and hopefully television follows suit.-

Dustin Ferguson Filmmaker.

Surely more has been written about the Video Nasties than copies of the Bible have been sold. Being American, I can't accurately speak about this often documented phenomenon in the UK... but can make a comparison to my experience with a censorious celluloid crusade at home that, despite discouraging young viewers from "getting filthy", ultimately had a positive effect in the end; a positive that was possibly felt in Great Britain as well.

Many great things came out of the 1980s. It was a fantastic era to grow up in. Pop culture blossomed and bloomed to such a degree, it retains a vibrancy even today. One such aspect of that devout decade that made it worth remembering was the home video boom; movies of various sizes and quality were clogging video store shelves across the country. The aisles themselves were similarly stopped up by eager patrons curious of what was on these tapes; their only inclination being often deceptively lurid box art that either fit the tape snugly; or an instant attention-getter in a big box or clamshell case. I remember one local video store; it wasn't uncommon to find a customer sitting in a lawn chair awaiting the return of a new arrival.

Now, any cheaply made piece of crap could get a chance with the renter's dollar as easily as the most polished Hollywood product. This was the one method by which six-figure financed exploitation could successfully compete with Tinsel town blockbusters. Drive-in low-budgeters and the most depraved exploitation could now be seen by a bigger audience than the regional, theatrical one they may have enjoyed under any number of titles. However, one man's trash is another man's treasure... and a great many of these "crap" films were most certainly treasures.

In other countries—like Great Britain—these prized videocassettes were coveted not totally for their content, but the fact that it became illegal to see or own them. 72 films were deemed obscene by the Director of Public Prosecutions after the VRA (Video Recording Act) was implemented in 1984. Of the 72 titles, 33 were successfully prosecuted to be in violation of the Obscene Publications Act of 1959. To be in possession of any of these "nasty" movies meant you were breaking the law; said tapes would be confiscated and destroyed (surely a few among the cassette crusading constabulary kept some of the tapes for themselves?).

This sort of moral outrage eventually occurred in America, but it was nowhere near as serious since you couldn't get arrested for having a copy of Abel Ferrara's THE DRILLER KILLER (1979) on your person. About the worst that could happen to you was that your parents might send you to bed without supper; or become perturbed that their child may need a psychiatric evaluation.

While Britain's government was taking the place of the parent, in America, the studios were more concerned with how much of their revenue was being depleted by VCR owners copying their tapes. In Britain's early 80s, you might become a murderous, foaming-at-the-mouth sadist for watching extreme violence at home; in America's early 80s, your crime is merely copying it—possibly watching it multiple times and loaning it out to friends. Following the lead of the British, it would be a few more years before the American youth would be in danger of moral corruptness due to their viewing habits.

Still, morality is not a bad thing. It's only natural that responsible adults are going to be interested in what their child or children are being exposed to. Akin to the Delinquent fear of the 1950s, it was no longer rock and roll music causing the decline of youth, but the scourge of blood and gore on video rental tapes (later to include violent video games and even Bugs Bunny cartoons).

Adults keeping their kids on a leash is only going to make them remove it when the parents aren't looking. This protective mindset can be taken to alarming extremes as in the Video Nasties Era; yet this mass exposure brought notoriety to films that likely never attained it during their theatrical runs... the irony being that a lot of them didn't deserve it.

Back in America, my mother was very protective as to what she would allow me to see. I wasn't even allowed to see CONAN THE BARBARIAN (1982). I remember she and her sister and her boyfriend were watching it downstairs in the den one evening. I stealthily descended the stairs to the opening of the doorway to listen to the clashing blades and utterances of "Crom!" Any time I heard footsteps towards the stairs I'd use ninja-like skills, darting fleet-footed up the steps and down the hall into my room, feigning being asleep.

Another time I effortlessly slipped my hands into my dad's VHS cabinet and, much like a jewel thief in any of your finer heist pictures, came away with his copy of FRIDY THE 13TH PART 2 (1981); descending the stairs to the den, placing the tape inside the VCR, and scaring myself witless in the darkness, a blanket half covering my face. When the film was over, I was nearly too scared to leave the sofa to turn on the lights! Still, it was an adrenaline-rushing experience—not only being scared, but also viewing something that would guarantee me a punishment in the form of a scolding or a spanking... maybe both. Mind you, I still had to return the tape to the cabinet undetected.

Once my parents divorced in 1983, all bets were off and I could finally view things I couldn't have seen otherwise; although my father was curious as to why I'd want to see something like THE TEXAS CHAIN SAW MASSACRE (1974) when Media Home Entertainment released it in 1984. Prior to that, as noted above, I had to sneak to see that which was forbidden. Horror movies were my 'Tree of Knowledge'; having began with Universal Horrors at a very young age, graduating to giant monsters and British horror on television, such sanguinary sights as Fulci's ZOMBIE (1979) and American slasher pictures were a natural progression for genre intake to my young eyes at that time.

Granted, a fateful renting of the Thriller Video release of MAKE THEM DIE SLOWLY (CANNIBAL FEROX [1981]) put me right back to square one when I carelessly watched the picture right in front of my grandparents.

I imagine this same feeling of obtaining forbidden fruit was felt by British genre fans during the controversial days of the Video Nasties. You always want what you cannot have. This was my reasoning for seeing the above-mentioned MAKE THEM DIE SLOWLY. Aside from the sleazy, unrestrained artwork, what really caught my attention was the "banned in 31 countries" tagline; that alone set off my repugnance radar. Umberto Lenzi's cannibal classic was now at the top of the must-see list.

I became acutely aware of the Nasties in 1986. This awareness was in the book, Horror Films by Nigel Andrews (Gallery Books, 1985). Reading about this movement of cinematic banishment, paired with the colorfully descriptive writings of guys like the late Chas Balun in Fangoria magazine, fueled my fascination with extreme gore even more. Since I was, at this time, allowed to enter video stores and pick what I wanted unattended, I would rent the most grotesque tapes imaginable. I'd already seen a double feature of BLOOD FEAST (1963) and PIECES (1983) after school one particularly soul-shocking afternoon, so the search was on for more dissolute delights. No place in town catered to my sadistic nature as The Video Station, a small video shop that was the bumper crop of trash; a veritable treasure trove of exploitation par excellence.

It was there that I rented MAKE THEM DIE SLOWLY. That day I added Herschell Gordon Lewis's THE WIZARD OF GORE (1970) to make it a double. My grandfather never even bothered asking me what I had rented. Naturally, he had no idea such movies even existed. It was bad timing on my part as to when I chose to watch the former. My grandparents were in such shock witnessing John Morghen torture and maim a defenseless Portuguese, they quickly became interested in my reading and viewing habits. Things escalated when my uncle recorded a 20/20 segment hosted by Barbra Walters and Hugh Downs titled, "VCR Horrors". We all sat around the TV and watched it on a Saturday afternoon. Walters opens with: "Horror movies-- mutilation, decapitation, torture... does that sound entertaining? More blood than a blood bank! Have we got your attention? Well you may be sickened. But what about your kids? They seem to love every moment of today's horror films; movies that by comparison, make FRANKENSTEIN seem cute and cuddly. If you find this disturbing, just wait, because there is a whole other dimension".

This 15+ minute segment is a historic moment in network television; it's the only time stomach-turners like BLOODSUCKING FREAKS (1976) and CANNIBAL FEROX (1981) will ever be glimpsed on prime time TV. For the latter title, you get to see Italian actor, John Morghen (Giovanni Lombardo Radice) have the top of his head lopped off as a room-full of cringing women sit aghast at what they're witnessing. The segment narrator asks, "How did it get to this? What happened to old-fashioned horror?" Nothing happened to it; it was supplanted by a then all-new level of sadism that has since gone about as far as it can go. In the narrator's defense, a return of the aforementioned "old-fashioned horror" is warranted.

The larger picture being painted with this news report was that horror movies were possibly linked to violent crime. The nonchalant attitude kids had towards the visualization of gruesome acts (the ages on this program were between 10-17) was somehow going to turn them into raving maniacs prone to misogyny and murder.

With gore being in the spotlight both here and abroad in the 1980s, crimes committed by youngsters were reportedly due to the viewing of slasher movies and, in one such example of extreme cinema, the infamous FACES OF DEATH (1978). David E. Metcalf, a 19-year-old senior in Beckville, Texas, was arrested after murdering 18-year-old Theresa Ann Downing when they left a graduation party. In his High School yearbook, FACES OF DEATH was listed as his favorite movie. FACES was a mostly fake documentary portending to show actual death on-camera. The popular series has since been exposed as a fraud (although there are real deaths seen—the sort you'd see in high school about the dangers of driving irresponsibly), but back then, it was passed off as the real thing.

Over in Britain, it wasn't just horror movies that was horrifying the censors, it was action pictures like RAMBO III (1988). The previous year, the Hungerford Massacre set off film classification alarms after Michael Robert Ryan went on a shooting spree killing 16 people (17 including himself). Tabloids were quick to jump on unsubstantiated claims that the disturbed man was inspired by the Rambo movies and had a collection of Soldier of Fortune magazines, among other things.

There was legitimate reason to be concerned, or to question the why; although it should be obvious that a movie can't make you go out and kill. There is something already wrong with a person. One can speculate that visuals may trigger something deep within a disturbed person's psyche, but a movie can't command you to commit murder; if anything, seeing violent imagery is a release from the all-too real brutality and stress of day-to-day living. I do know that when I see a cheeseburger commercial I can be coerced to go out and buy one... but not kill a man over it.

Granted, I'd be hesitant to let my kids watch gory horror movies; I'd most likely take my mother's approach... and hope that they would do as I did and see them when I wasn't looking.

After viewing this episode of 20/20, it was decided something must be done to save me from the depravities of Amazonian cannibals, hockey masked killers, and demons summoned from mysterious tape recorders left behind in isolated cabins in the woods.

I was very much into art, and my taste in film spilled over into my drawings. I also had a large collection of Fangoria magazines and posters all over my walls and ceiling. Much like the video confiscation in the UK, so went my magazine and poster collections; my drawings were taken, and two recent book purchases I made with my allowance—Chas Balun's Horror Holocaust and The Gore Score—were taken and burned; even my audio cassette soundtrack of THE TEXAS CHAINSAW MASSACRE 2 was taken away—a relative convincing my grandparents that, "when he listens to the music he can visualize the violence in the movie". What was ironic about all this was that I was likewise fascinated with swords and knives from my interest in all things Conan the Barbarian; so this love of fantasy and swords and sorcery was misconstrued for some sort of Michael Myers syndrome.

These were sad days in my young life, although it didn't last for a great length of time. Rules were relaxed and I eventually got my Fangoria collection returned and slipped back into seeing "nasties" again. Years later, many of the Video Nasties would receive their DVD due, many of them uncut; and others gaining a release, but shorn of some of the violence.

Looking back, if there hadn't been a banning body many of these examples of artistic expression would likely never have received as much notoriety. Fans would have eventually seen them, but the decades-long fascination wouldn't be as palpable or as long lasting. Look at the numerous documentaries—particularly in the United Kingdom—about film censorship. Not only are the channels airing them (or digital mediums containing them as extras) making money, but yet again, the films are thrust back into the spotlight... again accruing revenue as fans plop down their cash for the shiny new Blu-ray/DVD combo special edition with a bumper crop of extras; said extras keeping the stars and filmmakers fresh in the public conscious; so everyone wins in some way.

Without the Video Nasties scare, or the nationwide concern of nervous parents in America, we wouldn't be talking about, nor glamorizing these movies over 30 years later... and beyond.

-Brian Bankston Writer.

How Star Video Stripped the Nasties of Their Power (In a Good Way)

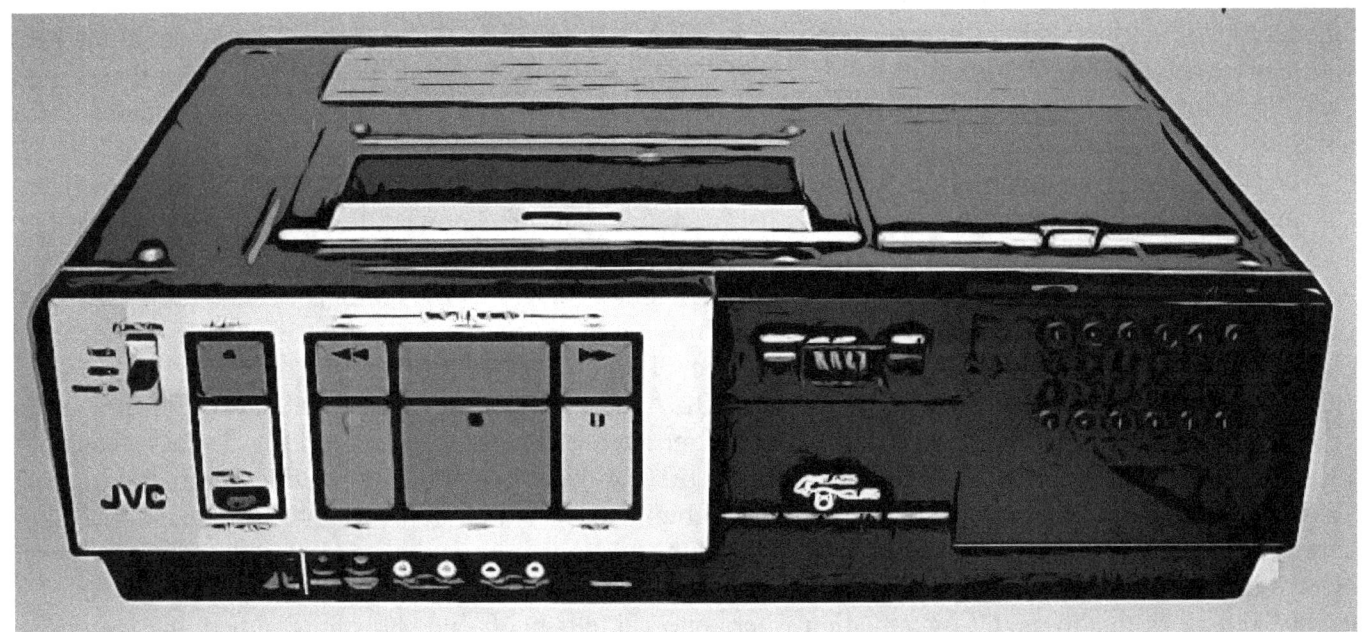

Rural Ohio had the greatest video store no one has ever heard of. It wasn't an epic retro genre tribute like the few surviving stores today. It most certainly wasn't part of a corporate chain with 100 copies of The Avengers being crammed down your throat by a uniformed fella who has only seen the films on the wall that cost more than 40 million to make. It wasn't glossy, though it was far from a hole in the wall. It simply... just... was.

The first of its kind in my area, Star Video was a matter of fact video rental joint that became for a time, a local entertainment Mecca. The enthusiastic owner Mark was one hell of a guy, he cut the kids deals, the regulars were friends, and had there been an Avengers in 1983, he wouldn't have crammed it down my throat because he actually knew what I was really there for already. There were other video stores that popped up, but under Mark's reign as VHS commander and chief, there was never a doubt from both my child aged self, and my movie centric father, that THIS store had the goods, and all of them. Not a title slipped through the cracks, good and bad, oversized boxes, clamshell boxes, cheap economical cardboard boxes, all adorned with the (mostly) striking kind of art that screamed, "Rent me! I'm the best damn flick on the shelf! I won't let you down!" While many of them DID let us down, it wasn't so much the act of watching them as it was the act of browsing what seemed like an infinite amount of those varied in sizes covers for the perfect few to kill a Sunday afternoon.

What the hell does this have to do with controversial movies that were banned you may be asking? Mark carried all of them. But it wasn't so much that he carried them, it was HOW he carried them. Boxes that proudly proclaimed "BANNED in 46 countries!" would be sitting loud and proud next to "Romancing the Stone" on the new release rack, and the horror section a variable what's what of the genre, no title left out, all tapes equal in their alphabetized section.

The Sunday Star Video ritual went simply as so; Dad caroused a little more than me, and mostly shot the shit with the owner, as dads are apt to do. Part of me thinks he did this just so my little self could take his time soaking in the lurid artwork and carefully making my limited amount of selections carefully. See my pops did the great favor of explaining that movies were fake, especially horror films. So with all the being afraid of movies taken care of, he worried a lot less, and I enjoyed a lot more. There was no place outside home I loved more than Star Video, and my Pops knew it. Did I finally get the courage to take that oversized "Gates of Hell" box up to the counter? Or did I dare investigate "The Evil Dead"? This Evil Dead thing must be cool, it's rarely ever in, and that box is practically smacking me in the face to rent it. What I didn't know in my child like, rose-tinted video store view of the world was that there were places that this video box couldn't smack anyone at all. For those privy to this kind of forbidden cinema, the open availability of such a controversial title, hiding in plain sight on Star Videos shelves, surely a rare find, but not to me, it was just like the store itself… just there. The other pop up rental joints surely didn't have these pictures; let alone hanging out next to the likes of "Return of the Jedi". That was honestly my first tiny-brained indication that something was up. That according to the world at large, not all horror films were created as equal as the alphabetization of Star Video had led me to believe.

Luckily, it's always been easier for an unrated cut of a film in the States, and Gorgon video sure knew that in their day. We didn't have a video nasties list of course, but unbeknownst to me, the films on that list had developed reputations, large reputations, and ones that in most cases the film and its content could never live up to. But we had the option of carrying them on our shelves, sadly though, most didn't. It was these erroneous reputations that made the pop ups skittish. What moral outrage would besiege their tiny storefront if they carried "I Spit on Your Grave"? Not Star Video, "I Spit…" just sort of hung out there next to some studio picture like there was nothing special about it at all. As I grew older and was made aware of the nasties by Fangoria and the like, it sunk in. Obtaining every movie on that list had been no big deal. Because of Star Video's confidence in its customer to pick the right title for them, or not pick a title for that matter, renting the Evil Dead (if it was actually there) was simply no big deal. It had no context other than that which the box presented to me. Each films reputation had been stripped from its plastic reels and only the film itself was left. It was up to the film to terrify me with no reputation speaking on its behalf.

I liken all of this to the classic situation where one kid tells his friend shots hurt so bad, it's just the worst thing in the world (this is also popular of older siblings I'm told) SO when little Jenny gets her first shot, it's awful, it's the worst thing in the damn world and she's pretty sure they were going to take the whole arm. So Jenny in turn tells HER friends or younger siblings how AWFUL it was, and we can all see how that cycle works. Now imagine little Tammy has no clue that shots are somehow the work of devil worshipping mad scientist doctors who crave the tears of freshly shot given children. Nope, she knows she's getting a shot, that's all. She maybe even has that cool nurse that distracts you whilst poking you. Hell, in that case, Tammy may not have felt much of anything. She takes away the experience exactly how it plays out, good or bad, but certainly not in any of the severity that poor Jenny had to endure. Tammy will invariably tell her friends it was no big deal, and even if it did pinch a little, chances are she got some reward, and her friends will see the worth in the reward as well. Such as how the first name basis customers got to experience the nasties. Sometimes we got a reward, like I did when I fell in love with Evil Dead, or sometimes we got a pinch, but either way we walked away and knew exactly what the actual film itself had given us, not some fear mongered distortion of the truth.

I will always be thankful for my pops taking me to that little video store every Sunday, and for believing in me to pick titles so freely. But had Mark and Star Video not allowed me the opportunity to view so many titles so freely, without censor, I wouldn't be the film maker and cinema lover I am today. Whether someone likes the work I do or not, I love doing it, and that gang traces all the way back to the video store shelves of the greatest video store no one ever heard of.

-Dustin Austen Filmmaker.

The first time I saw *The Amityville Horror* it was a VHS double feature with *Last House on the Left* and I was nine. I don't remember much about Last House, but Amityville scared the hell out of me. It didn't help that I had cousins who told me that it was real and was happening at my Grandmother's house. When I saw

Last House again years later, I wondered why that movie made no impression on me, but Amityville haunted my dreams. Part of it I'm sure has to do with my cousins tormenting me. That kept the movie fresh in my mind and convinced me I'd go to my Grandmother's basement and find a hell room behind her stone wall. Most of it I believe has to do with my nine-year-old self focusing on and accepting the supernatural horror and blocking out the horror of what man can do to a fellow human being. To this day I prefer watching spooky ghost stories that make me turn all the lights on at night instead of movies that depict the worst of humanity. I appreciate the Last House-type movies and do think that they have their place, but I'd rather be spooked than horrified. I believe that is why a lot of these movies can be banned. It's not so much the specific violence that occurs but how the movie tells us that it is possible that a person can do something horrific to another person and feel nothing. That is the most petrifying feeling in the world.

-Amy Lynn Best   Actress.

I've always been a fan of horror films – one of my earliest memories was staying up late to watch The Satanic Rites of Dracula on the TV in my bedroom when I was about ten years old. It scared the shit out of me but from that moment I was hooked on horror and have been ever since. I remember squeezing into a friend's bedroom when I was about fourteen to watch The Evil Dead on Betamax on a tiny portable TV with about six other eager teenagers because we heard it had been banned, but it wasn't really until I arrived at Leeds University as a student in 1988 that I really discovered the 'Video Nasty' at a Film Collectors' Fair. Amongst dusty old back issues of film magazines and old cinema quad posters, a couple of stalls had boxes of VHS tapes, all with lurid photocopied covers and exciting titles like Anthropophagus the Beast and Nightmare in a Damaged Brain. I'd never seen anything like them before so taking a chance (there was no IMDB back then to check reviews or synopses) I bought two films: Herschell Gordon Lewis's Blood Feast and Ruggero Deodato's Cannibal Holocaust, partly because of the cover art and partly because it claimed to be banned in over 50 countries around the world. Those two films opened up a world of horror that I never knew existed and over the next few years I made it my mission to track down and watch every video nasty on the list (something which I'm proud to say I did before I left university). Having seen all the films prosecuted by the DPP at the time (both successfully and unsuccessfully), only a few have stood the test of time, but none ever had the gut-wrenching impact that 'Cannibal Holocaust' did. Over the years I've replaced my VHS copy for DVD and most recently Blu-ray (ironically now available uncut in the UK) – something that I've only done with a handful of titles, which shows how important the film has been to me. For me the success of Cannibal Holocaust is a combination of many things – a strong script, great cinematography, an amazing score by the legendary Riz Ortolani and brave performances from a cast who were literally put through hell. The found-footage approach to the film seems commonplace today but at the time it was fresh and unexpected; playing like a documentary, the shocking content of the film seemed all the more real. Deodato's decision to shoot in the Amazonian rainforest with indigenous tribes also added depth and realism to the film and while it has frequently been described as a horror film or exploitation movie, it is also a scathing social commentary. Cannibal Holocaust will always be notorious for its controversial animal killings and graphic violence but if you look beyond this, there is an intelligent, thought-provoking piece of cinema that is still relevant today. I recently had the pleasure of meeting director Ruggero Deodato and interviewing him for a rare cinema screening of the film and it was fascinating to hear him talk about the making of the film and all the controversy it attracted on its release (and beyond). No other 'Video Nasty' can claim to have had such an impact or influence on modern cinema and for this reason, it's still one of my all time favourite films.

-Martin Grund   Leeds International Film Festival.

I've always enjoyed watching horror films of all shapes and sizes, but there are some that truly stand out to me. Nosferatu, Symphony of Horrors, takes the prize, for instance, for being the only film that has ever given me nightmares, and I have a vivid memory of waking up, sweating, convinced that Count Orlok was standing in my doorway, holding up that menacingly crooked hand of his... Jump to the later incarnations of Dracula, and, for me, the most memorable was Frank Langella's interpretation of the black count as well as, of course, Gary Oldman's. Bram Stoker's Dracula and Interview with the Vampire are the two vampiric epics that I most enjoy simply for their visual richness: Who can forget the bone-white and crimson of The Bloofer Lady or Louisiana's eyelid-batting stone statues! And from the sublime to the ridiculous: a film that had a huge effect on me when I was all of nine years old was The Haunted House of Horror although I've since heard that it's actually the height of camp! Other disturbing – and clinging – visuals include rattlers launching themselves out of cupboards in Race with the Devil, flies on windows in The Amityville Horror and, of course, the chilling 360 head spin from The Exorcist!

-Maria Olsen   Actor/Producer MOnsterworks66.

My first encounter with a film on VHS on a holiday in a jungle resort in Malaysia in 1981, the film in question changed my life Hammer films 'The Legend of the 7 Golden Vampires', a blood and boob soaked eye-opener playing in the lobby of the hotel, while my parents sipped on cocktails and left me to be baby sat by this new medium. That night my head was filled with feverish nightmares and the following morning I got to experience real blood sucking creatures first hand, when we were attacked by thousands of leeches on a jungle walk!

Seeing my parents covered in blood bursting leeches as they smothered them in salt could have freaked me out for life. Luckily my fertile imagination lapped it up! Shortly after that I watched the Planet of the Apes Gorilla attack sequence at a kids party on 8mm, the reel was only 8/9min long. When the sequence finished I realised half the kids had burst into tears, but I wanted more!

It was another two years before I was able to get my dirty mitts on an actual VHS recorder when my parents brought home a reconditioned ex-rental top-loading monster with huge diving board function switches. We had had a colour TV for about six months and already seen a few hammer horror films and the terrifying 'Invasion of the Body Snatchers' 1978

But now everything was about to change…it started with the weekly escorted visit to our new local video shop, filled with amazing posters and big chunky display boards filled with beautiful big boxes as far as the eye could see. You have to realise that early 80s Britain was a pretty drab colourless place and the crazy colourful posters on ever release were completely captivating. In the end the shop had had a pretty average collection, but my parents letting me pick at least one title a week and of course my choice was always sci-fi/fantasy/action or horror!

Then I discovered that the local florist also had a video hire section in their shop, everyone and their mother was throwing to together a selection of videos to rent in those days. They only had a quarter of the selection of the first shop, but pretty much their entire catalogue was exploitation! When they realised my parents were cool with me watching pretty much anything they suggested a film called the Evil Dead. The Evil Dead was withdrawn at that time due to the whole video nasties debacle, but they had an uncut pre cert under the counter, which they eventually did me a copy of. Sadly the florist went bust and I had to search elsewhere for the gorier films that I was now obsessed with and luckily discovered that the local Saturday second hand junk market had not one, but three video stalls.

That's where the collecting bug kicked in as started picking up all kinds of really cool and crazy films for £3.00 or a £1.50 swap. Censorship in the UK just got worse and worse, but luckily there were already thousands upon thousands of pre-certs being dumped onto the second-hand market.

I managed to get hold of a second VCR, which I could hook up to the family VCR when they weren't looking. Slowly, I built my collection of bootleg tapes photocopying the covers and colouring them in to try to, mostly unsuccessfully, replicate the original lurid colours. As prices went down I mostly picked up original ex rentals from the local market and started postal trading with other collectors. Everyone had their own handmade catalogues to choose from, and some collectors already seemed to have everything! By now the VHS sell through revolution had gone into full swing and it was finally possible to buy brand new tapes including new releases for less than £15. Unfortunately censorship was at its most insane during the late VHS days and very few VHS sell through a were worth getting if they contained any kind of gore or sexual scenario as they would have been shredded and sterile. Even today I don't have much affection for sell through tapes. Laser discs, way too expensive, and VCDs, not very available in the UK, came and went, but I was still a VHS faithful, until one day a chance visit to a record shop in Amsterdam revealed all the classic Lucio Fulci Zombie films and 'Cannibal Ferox' uncut on a newish medium...DVD! I was hooked! Although I've never fallen out of love with the pleasure of putting on a tape, my serious VHS were over from that day. Today the hunt is not about seeing an uncut mythical gore epic in English, it's about the best print, sound and going deeper and deeper into the Weird and obscure. Nothing will ever beat the early thrill of having a 6th generation uncut VHS copy of 'Zombie Flesheaters' in my grubby hands and re-watching 4 times in a row!

-Merlyn Roberts   Writer/Filmmaker.

The Snake Sacrifice

When I was growing up, my mother bought Zenith brand TV's and appliances from our local Zenith retailer. She was a single mom with one grown-up kid and one little runt (me) still running around, so she liked buying from small stores- places where she knew and could trust the owner.

Our Zenith TV was one of those big box cabinet deals that sat on the floor and let you put a tea service or lava lamp or a booze bar or whatever you liked on top, like it was just another piece of living room furniture- one you plugged in and stared at for hours. I don't remember what, if anything, my mom chose to ornament the top of our television with before we got our VCR (also Zenith brand, of course) in 1984, but I remember the evening my mom called me downstairs and I saw the man installing (yes, there was a guy who would come and *install*) this amazing rectangular silver box. Suddenly I could watch everything from *Gremlins* and *First Blood* to the *Charlie Brown Christmas Special* whenever I wanted to, while lying on the tan low pile carpet of my own living room. This device was magical and came into my life at just the moment when I was starting to put aside action figures and Lego's, and looking for more sophisticated things to waste my time on.

There was a drug store about a mile down the road which had an impressively wide selection of movies to chose from, and at the rental counter (such was the boom of this new home video industry that they actually had installed their own separate rental counter) the middle-aged lady in the blue apron never concerned herself about an elementary school kid renting titles like *I Spit on your Grave* and *Lucio* Fulci's *City of the Living Dead* (which bore the slightly-more ominous title *The Gates of Hell* back in those days). Practically every day during that all-too-short summer of 1984, squeezed in between the yearly trip up at Lake Heritage and the despised but requisite soccer camp, I'd hike down Sleepy Hollow Rd. and rent two or three movies for forty-nine cents apiece (plus tax), then hurry back home with the tapes in their unmarked bulky clear plastic shell containers under one skinny arm. The whole way I would be terrified that one of the older kids in the neighborhood who frequently picked on me would catch me and steal them, and my mom would have to pay the replacement fine- which in those days before consumer video collecting took off would have been a pricey tab.

Again it was just my mom and me at home, and when it came to my more dangerous rental choices like *Shogun Assassin* or *Texas Chainsaw Massacre*, I was smart. I'd always rent at least one family-friendly selection when I went to the store: something like *TRON* or *Superman III*. That way I had something to put on top of the stack of tapes sitting on the TV if my mom happened to notice the label. For the more gnarly selections, I'd wait until she was out playing cards with friends or running errands or at least in the kitchen cooking dinner or talking to the neighbor lady before popping them in. We had a big picture window in the front of the living room so usually I'd catch a glimpse of her coming back inside- enough time to hit STOP or jump up and switch the TV dial back to regular cable. But just like anything else, you're always lucky- until you aren't.

It wasn't something wretchedly lurid that shut down my video watching privileges that summer. It wasn't *House on the Edge of the Park* or *Gestapo's Last Orgy* or anything. It wasn't even one of those films like *Evil Dead* that at the time were considered outrageous or in bad taste, but thanks to the years and changing sensibilities are now considered pretty tame in retrospect.

No, it was *Conan the* friggin' *Barbarian* that got me busted.

At that age I'd read neither Robert E. Howard's books nor the Marvel comics based on them. My very first introduction to the character was when my mom took a friend and I to see *E.T.* a year or two before. I remember pausing upon seeing the poster for John Milius' movie adaptation in the dim lobby. The image was a primal thing: a feral and dangerous depiction of this titanic tower of a man, with a gorgeous and intimidating blonde Valkyrie crouched on one knee at his feet- not in subservience, but as though she was prepared to spring forward into action should a little pipsqueak like me stare into her steely eyes for a moment too long. The two bronzed figures stood out against a haunted background of lurid reds and deep blacks, and atop it all floated a gilded logo bearing the title, even the letters of which were being run through with a skull-hilted broadsword. That poster by Renato Casaro promised everything a boy travelling the bumpy road towards puberty could hope for in a film: violence, gore, swordfights and scantily-clad women. My mom wasn't having ANY of that junk, of course. So at the time I was stuck watching a little cross-dressing prune of an alien waddle around bumping into the furniture and trying to get his wrinkly ass back home, and could only imagine the mayhem and debauchery I was missing out on.

But now it was two years later and thanks to home video, the paradigm had changed. Now I could watch this amazing movie I'd been prohibited from seeing in the theater. Barbarians. Sex. Death. All for my personal viewing pleasure in the comfort of our living room. All I had to do was hike two miles to the store and back in oppressively humid summer heat—and of course pick a prudent time to watch it so as to be sure of privacy.

I remember it was during the day. Probably the afternoon. I don't remember what else I'd rented but it might have been *Monty Python and the Holy Grail*. I don't remember what my mom was doing either. Perhaps in my eagerness to enjoy my long-withheld barbarian gore fantasy breastiganza, I'd been incautious.

Conan did not disappoint. The protracted period I'd spent waiting to see it was well worth it: this movie was AMAZING. There were decapitations within MINUTES of the credits. Those opening credits were mainly shots of a sword on FIRE. There was a great wheel where condemned men dug furrows in the sand as they pushed it endlessly. And there were gladiator fights and boobs and hungry wolves and sexy witches and more boobs. I was barely through the first act of the film and I was already sure that- aside from *Star Wars* and *Raiders of the Lost Ark*, of course—this was the most amazing movie my eager young eyes had ever absorbed. This was no candy ass kiddies' fantasy flick. This was obviously something much more mature and profound.

I was forty minutes in. This was one hundred percent awesome. Conan and his partner, Subotai, had met the beautiful, dangerous Valeria while sneaking into the Snake Worshippers' temple. They'd climbed the side and roped down into the bowels of the building to find a white-robed cult gathered around a deep pit. A bearded leader had emerged and beckoned an attractive young woman forward. Below I now saw that a GIANT FRIGGIN' SNAKE was coiled at the bottom of the pit, waiting and blinking its slit-pupiled eyes. The young woman stepped towards the pit in complete obeisance and paused at the precipice a moment to allow two other female cult members to remove her robes. In a few magical seconds she was standing there in nothing but a kind-of weird white loincloth/diaper thing but that didn't matter because there were breasts and she was actually going to jump in there and *let* the snake eat her. That complex concept blew my ten-year old mind. The movie had taken a dramatic step up in my opinion. It could only get better from here.

And that's when I heard my mom's voice from behind me:

"What… are… you… watching…?"

I'd been completely absorbed. I hadn't heard her coming. My neck almost broke I spun around so fast. There was my mom standing in the doorway to the living room staring dumfounded at what was happening on the screen of her Zenith. Ten minutes earlier and all she would have seen was an oiled-up Austrian running through the desert. But she hadn't come in ten minutes ago. No, she'd picked this exact moment to come into the room and tell me something. The timing was almost perfect in its awfulness. My mom had already been older when she'd had me. She'd bought the TV to watch the news and *Lawrence Welk* and *M*A*S*H**. She wasn't a total square or anything- she enjoyed the *Dirty Harry* movies and loved seeing the bad guys pay at the end. But the image playing on the TV screen right now was something I don't think she could even process. The overtly-Freudian juxtaposition of the half-naked lady and the serpent was twisted in such a primal way, I think she was stuck somewhere between being completely confused and totally horrified- those two feelings both quickly giving way to anger.

Thinking back, there were probably several better responses I could have given to her question that the one I chose at the time. If I'd had a few more years and a little more maturity, maybe I could have explained the context of the scene to her. If I'd been better read on mythology and pulp literature back then I could have possibly described the anthropological significance of this kind of scenario. But I was ten and when my mother asked me what I was watching the only response I could think of was:

"Nothing…"

Well that answer didn't exactly satisfy Martha Towns, and within moments my tape had been stopped and ejected, reinserted into its case and would soon be on its way back to the drugstore in her purse. My solo renting privileges were revoked for the rest of the summer. All my tapes had to be approved by her at the time of renting. I was in the movie rental gulag. But the days and weeks moved on and, as was always the way, her anger gradually subsided. Soon I was back in school for fifth grade and there were other things to focus on.

I know it wasn't too long before I eventually managed to see the rest of *Conan the Barbarian*, but I don't exactly recall when or where. It was probably at a friend's house. When watching it the second time, having now passed the point in the film where I'd previously been cut off and upon getting to the temple orgy scene, I *do* remember thinking to myself: *well at least she didn't walk in during THIS*.

Now it's thirty years later, and in the intervening decades I've read many of Robert Howard's original 1930's *Conan* stories as well as some of his other voluminous writings. I know much more about the tragic life and all-too-early death of this talented but tortured author. I've become a devotee of the work of Frank Frazetta, whose depictions of the titular Barbarian set the standard not only for the character, but also for how fantasy is supposed to look. I've collected many of the *Savage Sword of Conan* comics from the 70's, and I once got to meet its brilliant artist John Buscema, whose brush breathed sinuous life into the Cimmerian warrior's adventures. Yet apart from all those incarnations, John Milius' 1982 film remains one of my favorite depictions of the character. The film is a kind of cipher to me: one that begs repeated scrutiny, like some stupefying magic trick. It's simultaneously scary and fun. Amusing yet sincere. Violent, but also poignant.

Today in a film world brimming with CGI fantasy environments and photorealistic digital effects, it remains visually stunning in its simplicity. Yes, some of the special effects haven't aged incredibly well, but others (like the foreground city miniatures) remain as impressively believable as ever. Except for young Conan learning about the riddle of steel from his father, the first ten minutes of the film are practically dialogue free, filled only by the pounding of horse's hooves, the screams of men and women, the clash of steel, and Basil Poledouris' incredibly sensuous and soaring score. It's as close to Wagner as Hollywood ever came.

But more than all this, what's really enjoyable to me is just how dangerously irresponsible the movie feels when you're watching it: there's this vague terror in being wholly at the mercy of a mad storyteller for the next two hours- the feeling that this man at the helm, like Conan himself, does NOT have either your delicate sensibilities nor your best interests at heart. You're his captive and you must resign yourself to being a witness to the bestial violence of this ancient world being depicted on screen, as well as its primordial beauty and heartache. The film is at once juvenile and yet possessed of a sagest wisdom that should not comfortably co-exist, but which, thanks to Milius' sublime skill as a storyteller, find a perfect balance on the massive juggernaut shoulders of the films' title character.

My mom's been gone for a few years now. I doubt after a time she even remembered that afternoon. Thinking back I'm thankful that watching that snake sacrifice scene was the *worst* thing she ever walked in on me doing. I'm sure I was annoyed at the time that she didn't understand that I could HANDLE seeing this kind of thing, but that kind of upset vanishes over time and the incident has now become a story I enjoy telling people when I talk about growing up with her- one that in its own way perfectly epitomizes our relationship, as well as that unique moment in early home video.

And just for the record, seeing *Conan* at that impressionable young age didn't warp me. I didn't grow up to be a sexual deviant or a serial murderer or anything. I'm a fully functional member of society. Okay yes I make horror movies for a living, and yes, many of those films feature scenes of bare breasted women—but none of those characters have EVER been fed to a giant snake in my films, so obviously watching that scene when I was ten had no effect on me whatsoever.

Revisiting my love of this mad tale has made me want to pop in my DVD and watch it again tonight. Or maybe I'll just stream it. Either way, the bullies won't be able to take it from me anymore.

-Jim Towns   Filmmaker.

"Hello, my name is Talky Tina., and I'm going to kill you…"

November 1st, 1963, the 126th episode of Twilight Zone, "Living Doll," featured a demonic toy that gave birth to an entire sub-genre of horror films: Child's Play, Puppet Master, Magic, The Conjuring and countless others. All of these films were born from the seminal episode directed by my father, Richard C. Sarafian, a respected filmmaker who was best known for the cult car chase hit of 1971, Vanishing Point. My name is Tedi Sarafian, the youngest of five. I have recently directed my first horror film, Altergeist, coming out October 15th, 2014. I am also the writer of the cult comic film, Tank Girl, and I co-wrote *Terminator 3: Rise of The Machines*.

Many nights I spoke with my father about "Living Doll." He told me that when he was a child what scared him the most was what shouldn't be scary. A mother's smile… that suddenly turns evil. Or a father's pat on the back… while in his other hand is a knife. My father had a tremendous imagination. When the things we rely on for safety and comfort turn against us, where do we run? Who do we trust? That is what scared my father the most. "Talky Tina" embraced this concept. A child's favorite toy… that is demonic. My father felt no need to cosmetically alter the doll. He didn't need to give it a scary face. For my father, the more Talky Tina looked like a common toy, the kind that populated every bedroom across the globe, the more he could invade the psyche of the audience and twist their perception of reality.

My father would often ask me, "What is evil?" I wasn't quite sure why he posed this question, but we would consider the answer for many hours over countless games of backgammon, which I rarely won as my father slammed down the thick wooden chips on an old walnut backgammon board laden with pearly inlays.

He played with authority and fire, sometimes yelling out "Yah-Lah!" as he flung the miniature dice like a craps player on a hot roll. He never hesitated with his play. Like Bobby Fischer, he was moves ahead. His only focus was intimidation. And he intimidated. But all of this was in good fun. My father was 270 pounds of pure charisma, had a kind heart, and was the best storyteller on the face of the planet. He exuded love and the competition was always in good fun. When I was in my teens, my answer to his question was simplistic, "Evil is everything that isn't God." But as the years passed, my answers grew more complex and I began adopting my mother's view. I'll pause here and tell you about my mother, Helen "Joan" Altman, her brother was the famous director Robert B. Altman (M*A*S*H). My father and "Uncle Bob" did not get along. But that's a whole other story. My father described Joan as mercurial, a contrarian. This definitely rubbed off on me as I entered my twenties. "Evil is needed," I explained to my dad. In a world where duality stands before us like a cosmic professor, we need 'evil' to teach us 'good.' "So is evil good, or bad?" My father questioned. My reply was uncertain.

We discussed the characters in "Living Doll." We have the mother, Annabelle, a divorcee who recently married Erich, played by my father's dear friend, Telly Savalas. And finally, we have Annabelle's daughter, Christie, who does not get along with her new stepfather. Erich does not have the skill set to be a good father, which is indicative of his own toxic childhood. Ah, the perfect recipe for drama, a common family dynamic, to which many could relate, and a common and seemingly harmless doll. My father asked me if I thought the doll was evil, or if Christie was. "Why would Christie be evil?" I asked. "She's just a girl who is being mistreated by Erich, who was a disturbed and angry man." So he challenged me to create a scenario where Christie was the evil one. Okay, I see where this is going. The girl manifested the doll to kill Erich because he was mean to her. "So Christie is a witch?" my father enquired. "Now create a scenario where Annabelle is the evil one." My answer: Annabelle didn't like the way Erich was treating her daughter, so she bought an evil doll to kill him. And although she acted innocent, her intent was well masked. Annabelle is the twisted one! I continued, "Or perhaps, the doll is really evil." My father continued prodding me as he bounced the backgammon chips across table, slapping them loudly onto the walnut, rolling doubles and playing so fast that I made mistake after mistake. Then he barked at me, "If the doll is evil, why would it save Christie from Erich's borderline personality disorder? Wow, big words. Had to look that up. It's when a person suffers a mental condition where they are turbulent, unstable, and fly off the handle at any given time. "Why wouldn't the doll simply kill the entire family if it was evil?" He interrogated. I wasn't sure what the answer was. I began guessing. I was unfocused. And so was my backgammon. I was losing. I couldn't roll the dice for shit. I was coming apart at the seams. So I threw in the towel, "Okay, I give up." I muttered, "What's the answer?" My father blasted me, "The answer is you're lazy, you lack conviction, you lack the authority that you will need, if you ever wanted to be a director." Okay, he knew how to get my goat. And that pissed me off. So I set the board up for another game, fisted the dice and threw them down. 6 and a 4, that makes a door. A slammed down the chips and danced them into position. "Evil is good!" I sang out. "Okay, why?" My father asked with his patented smirk, half bathed in menace, the other half in love. "Because it makes us look at ourselves. It challenges us to be strong. Like this game of backgammon… you play like the devil. You yell at me, slam down the checkers and burst out in your victory laugh when you make a great play. And I want to kill you like Talky Tina, I'm so angry. This was all very sarcastic, of course. "But I know, the only way I can beat you, is if I put some fire in my game!"

I'm going to pause here for another moment and say this about my father. He had this bookie who lived next door - a short, stocky Guido of a slime bucket. But the dude was an excellent backgammon player. My father beat the bookie out of tens of thousands, which he never got paid. My father would play against Greek tycoons on their own yachts and humiliate them. So beating the Goliath at backgammon took David's sling. I knew this, oh, too well. "The doll is not evil, nor is it good." Within the doll exists duality. Within each character exists duality." Where did that come from? I wondered. I don't know, but I liked the sound of it. I rolled double sixes and danced my checkers, chips, and pieces, whatever the hell they're called across the board. Now I felt hot. I was onto something. And I knew it by the look on my father's face. I kept barking at him. "That's the key! You must know the duality of each character. And within that, lies truth. "Wrong answer," he said while flaming a new Marlboro light. What the F&^%$!? I thought I had it. "But you were close." My father grinned warmly. Okay, okay, okay! My heart was racing. The game, awfully close. Either could win. But I had to stay tough. STAY TOUGH! Don't let this Armenian genius win one more game, Tedi! DO NOT! Duality; let's get back to that word. "Let's," my father said, while exhaling a cloud of smoke. Oh, I hated it when he smoked, because soon after, he would reach for his inhaler. No matter how many times I told him to quit…

I looked down at the board. We were picking up our chips now. He was one chip ahead. Shit, shit, shit. I needed doubles to win. I had three rolls left to do it. I rolled the dice. No luck. He rolled, picked up two. I rolled again. Still no luck! He rolled, picked up two. I needed doubles. I scooped up the miniature dice, gazed at my father with fire in my eyes and lion-growled in desperate retaliation… "YAH-LAH!" Double fours! The blood drained from his face. I grabbed the last stack of checkers, slammed them down so hard on the other side of the board, I nearly broke it in half. I won! I WON!!! "What is evil? You want to know what evil is?" I drilled him with a look as he casually ashed his cigarette, and I told him the answer. And I could see in his eyes, brimming with a look that only a proud father could provide, that I understood what "Living Doll" was really about. And I knew that I was right. Oh, I was right. But I'm not going to tell you. If you don't know, then I encourage you watch the episode again and look closely. It will be like looking into a mirror. I promise…

-Tedi Sarafian   Filmmaker.

A few weeks ago, I got a DVD copy of Nekromantik 1 & 2 through the post. My AD who was around at the time couldn't figure out why I was so damn excited. So I ran upstairs. Went through my VHS collection, got the old tattered blank covered VHS, it's only reminder of content as in a dymo strip with "NECROMANTIK 1 & 2" on it. I brought it down to him and said, "THIS! This is why I'm so excited!"

Being a few year younger than me he had missed the whole video nasty era. Nowadays, with everything pirated and on instant download, if the government try to ban you from watching something you just hop online, but back in the day…well, that was a different story. You spent months trawling the backstreets of Camden market, gaining confidence from the sellers to try and convince them to let you (at the time being a 14 year old boy) buy a banned, pirated x rated video nasty. So I waffled on at him for ages, sounding like a right old git with my tales of how hard it was (but you know, secretly loving the fact you had to work for the privilege of watching such sought after films) and after he looked so bored he wanted to quit, I just sat back in quiet reflection of that special time of my life. You see, the video nasty era was a very special time for me. Growing up on Hammer Horror and old Vincent Price films, as gory as they may be, I had never witnessed anything in terms of brutality in film past the camp era of cloaks, castles and over acted mad scientist. I think the film that got me was (and I'm guessing here as it's been well over 20 years since I last saw it) was a film called Summer School(?). The film in itself was an 80's comedy, but there were these two horror fans in it that were obsessed with a film called "The Texas Chainsaw Massacre". Well needless to say my little mind was blown right open. Just the name sent shivers down my pubescent spine. Then to find it was banned in England…well, the Holy Grail had just been named. From that moment on I was obsessed, every article. I could find, every mention in any magazine (remember there was no internet around then, not even dialup) or book retrospective, posters, the lot. I had to have or read them all. I even managed to find a comic book adaptation of Leatherface: The Texas Chainsaw Massacre part 3. My little geek mind JUST EXPLODED! And remember, this was when horror comics (in England especially) where like gold dust - not like now. So I know what happens in the third one panel by panel, but still have not seen either of the first two films. Oh I know scene for scene via a trashcan retrospective I picked up at Forbidden Planet for 5.99, but bar the clips shown on TV on a 80's comedy and a 5 second clip of Dennis Hopper I saw once in a documentary I had seen no actual full screen footage of any of the alleged carnage and horror that I so desperately craved.

That was until, that fateful day, of after spending several months searching, we finally managed to find someone who was willing to sell us a copy of my beloved film THE TEXAS CHAINSAW MASACRE! Ever been looking forward to something so much that your hands are shaking? Well, that was me, VHS in hand, parents out of the house I sat down to reach what I was sure was going to be the movie experience of my life.

The picture quality was shocking, no matter how much a wrestled with the tracking, the sound was crackly and there were times where I just plain didn't know what the hell was going on. But I'll be damned if it wasn't one of the most awesome things I had ever seen.

That tape must have been through more viewings than any other film I have had prior or since. So you can imagine my joy when they finally stopped acting like arses and released the video nasties onto DVD and my beloved The Texas Chainsaw Massacre onto the cinema screen. I now own that film on VHS, DVD and am just waiting for Arrow Video to do something as glorious with it as they have with part 2. I even had the cinema stump for several years, only losing it via one of my many house moves. I have (of course) tracked down all of the other films upon their release, and for the most part found them a very mixed bag. But the era did give me a great appreciation for pushing boundaries, censorship and the art of tracking down truly great films that are worth the watch.

-Dan Brownlie Director, Brand-B Corporation.

I've always longed for underground cinema. I remember at a young age looking through all the titles available at the local video store, where I spent a lot of time as a youngster, looking for the strangest options I could find. The usual Hollywood offerings that boasted twenty copies that would later be sold off as previously viewed never did much for me. I preferred the titles that sounded like there might be more explicit adult content and darker themes. I actually think at one point I rented every single title I could in our little small town video store. But there was an itch that demanded to be obeyed.

This coincided with my adolescence and making day trips on my own into the city downtown. Back in those days, Granville Street was not the outdoor mall of franchise shops that it is now. It was street that had been the heart of Theatre Row in the 40s and 50s and by that point had fallen from grace and housed a number of porn shops, jack shacks, used books stores and a host of crust punks and street kids.

It was here that I found the culture I had been looking for. Walking into the old punk stores that always smelled of Nag Champa incense and sold concert posters, studded accessories, body jewellery and hair dye, underground icons I had not yet met peered down at me from the walls. The Divine brandishing her gun from Pink Flamingos, Bettie Page giving a winsome smile as she was trussed in bondage, and Coop devil girls giving me the eye.

A few of these places sold, along with these treasures, old VHS tapes of films you weren't going to find in a suburban video store. The ones they didn't have, I asked about. Prior to Internet searches that gave instant gratification of information, these video nasties were not just the prize of obtaining and watching the film itself, but also the very hunt to find out about them in the first place. By collecting flyers heaped by promoters at the doors of these shops, I found screenings, specialty video stores, and festivals that catered to my exotic tastes. Not yet old enough to buy alcohol or vote, I instead spent my time trying to find these events. It was there I found kindred spirits who were also interested in the genre and were my white rabbits that

I chased merrily down the video nasty rabbit hole to a wonderland of debauched film. Cutie nudies, Noir, exploitation film sub genres too numerous to name weren't just something of my imagination, they were now real and in my grasp.

It has fuelled a lifelong obsession, and I'm forever grateful when I still come across a new gem at a flea market or used video store. This obsession continues and now, as an actress, I'm happy to be contributing to something that so richly influenced my life. I like to think, and this might be hugely egotistical of me to say, but I truly hope my work will one day influence other young women to go out and look for the strange and unusual as well. It might not happen next week, it might not be for a few decades…but hopefully the slow burn lights someone else's fire and burns just as brightly for them as these films lit the way for me.

-Tristan Risk Little Miss Risk Actress.

Chapter 10: Prosecuted Video Nasties

Welcome to the world of the video nasty with this intricate look at some of the most shocking, bizarre and damn scary films in history. Prepare for Giallo slashers, exploitation gems, Euro sleaze, sexploitation Hell - or indeed Heaven! And much more, as we open the gates of Hell into the realm of the video nasty!

Find out if they were really are as nasty as Mary Whitehouse thought they were!

Absurd

Also known as: "Rosso Sangue", "Anthropophagous 2", " "Zombie 6:Monster Hunter", "Horrible", "Rosso Sangue" and "The Grim Reaper 2" Year of release: 1981 Writer: George Eastman as John Cart

Director: Joe D'Amato as Peter Newton

R rating 90 min -Italy

Main cast: George Eastman (Mikos Stenopolis) Annie Belle (Emily) Charles Borromel (Sgt. Engleman) Katya Berger (Katia Bennet) Kasimir Berger (willy Bennett) Hanja Kochansky (Mrs.Bennett).

Video Distributed by: MEDUSA

Originally released uncut by Medusa on VHS. The theatrical release gained an 18 rating with 2m 32s cut in 1983. Then the film was withdrawn post certification. Absurd was released in the United States fully uncut and unrated in 2009 as the title "Horrible" at present the film is part of 88 films Italian restoration project which means the film will be restored and brought on in the near future in 2k.

The uncut version finally passed through British censors in 2016 and finally passed in Britain and available in its full, uncut glory.

Absurd was prosecuted. The film is available uncut from 88 Films on Blu-ray.

Plot:

Absurd tells the story of Mikos, the virtually invincible man who is subjected to scientific experimentation at the hands of the church. We follow his transformation into a crazed psychopathic murderer who is pursued by a priest hell-bent on his destruction. There are disastrous results as the priest's intentions don't go to plan and there's an unexpected twist of fate as the priest discovers that Mikos isn't as easy to dispose of as he first thought.

Appraisal:

Absurd could have been so much more! It's by no means the worst addition to the video nasty list, but it certainly falls short of what it could have been. It does receive criticism and it's definitely not one of the most popular of the video nasties, but is hard not to like this slice of very nasty pie. Joe D'Amato's somewhat of a sequel to "Anthropophagus" has all the makings of a B-movie Halloween love child. Absurd's stand out scenes are Mikos' disembowelling on the railings closely followed by hypodermic needles being inserted into someone's eye (be warned it's not an easy watch)! Oh, and you may not want to bake a lasagne in the oven either after watching this movie! Absurd has its own place in horror film history, deserved mainly because of its inclusion in the banned film list. This films prosecution only served to add press and exposure to the title. George Eastman is a total wrecking machine as the psycho killer! No one stands a chance against him, but it's Eastman's creative methods of killing people that makes this film worth watching. You know what's in store when you watch a D'amato film, copious amounts of blood washed down with a torrent of gore, shocks and surprises with exception to the ending which you could see coming a mile away. This low budget gore offering makes a great contribution to the list though it's somewhat lacking in suspense, a vital ingredient to any horror film, but to its credit there are fantastically unique methods of killing used in the film, no CGI effects here just buckets and buckets of blood!

In 1982 the VHS of "Absurd" was originally released uncut but this was short-lived. Absurd had its theatrical release in 1983 having 2 minutes and 32 seconds cut from the film. "Absurd" was later withdrawn and the theatrical cut version was released on VHS but the film still found its way into the video nasty hall of fame!

-Tony Newton

I found this a fun popcorn flick to watch. It reminded me a lot of John Carpenter's Halloween, very similar storylines but Absurd is not as good, but does excel in the gore factor, although I don't believe Halloween needed the gore as it had the fantastic atmosphere where as Absurd needs the gore as that is the appealing thing about seeing this - the creative and shocking death scenes, my favourite being the saw through the head!

I also used to save all my pocket money just so at the weekends I could go to the local shopping centre and hit the videos stores to buy new tapes. I loved collecting the Manga VHS's, especially The Guyver & Angel Cop series, and there was one particular feature film I wanted from Manga but was rated 18 and I was only 12, however I did persuade my Nan to take my pocket money and purchase it for me! That beauty of a film was Wicked City, a movie never to be forgot!

-Jason Impey   Filmmaker.

Anthropophagous

Also known as: "The Anthropophagous Beast", "Anthropophagous: The Beast", "Antropofago", "The Grim Reaper", "Man Beast", "Man-Eater", "Gomia" and "The Savage Island".

Year of release: 1980. **Writer**: Joe D'Amato, George Eastman **Director**: Joe D'Amato

R Rating, 90 Minutes, Italy

Tagline: "It's not fear that tears you apart…it's him!"

Main cast: Tisa Farrow (Julie), Saverio Vallone (Andy), Serena Grandi (Maggie), Margaret Mazzantini (Henriette), Mark Bodin (Daniel), Bob Larson (Arnold). Distributed by: Video Film Promotions

Anthropophagous was originally distributed uncut by Video Film Promotions in 1983. The VHS version in its cut form was later distributed by Video Shack. In 2002 the film resurfaced as "The Grim Reaper", this version was severely cut and was the US R rated version but did get passed by the BBFC in 2015 a fully uncut version of "Anthropophagus was released by 88 films. Anthropophagous was prosecuted.

Plot:

In this cult horror film a group of terrorists visit a Greek island to discover that the occupants have been devoured by the survivor of a shipwreck who has seemingly developed a taste for human flesh after murdering and eating his own family at sea. Members of the group slowly fall victim to the crazed cannibal psychopath. Will anyone survive the evil clutches of this bloodthirsty cannibal?

Appraisal:

Anthropophagous provides a generous helping of blood, shocks and carnage. The director gives his own stamp or seal of death with this no holds barred shocker. This film contains some scenes, which are quite disturbing to watch, none more so than the psycho killer devouring the fetus of an infant direct from its mother's womb! Aargh! That scene stands out and is as distressing to watch now as it was back then, in fact probably more so now when you're watching in glorious HD, those cracks, lines and bad tracking did come in handy at times and this was most definitely one of them! You can see why this film was banned and prosecuted that scene alone turns my stomach and that's when I knew it was coming! For someone viewing this for the first time "good luck!" don't order a Chinese takeout beforehand! Anthropophagous begins at a good pace with a couple falling prey to the killer but half way through when we get to the monster reveal it seems to deflate, had the director kept up the pace of the film and given viewers a continual feeling of unease and anticipation it may have been a better film. The film stars include Tisa Farrow star of Lucio Fulci's Zombie Flesh Eaters, Tisa Farrow is the sister of Mia, Tisa took to acting shortly after Mia Farrow's success with her first leading film role of Rosemary's Baby. Tisa retired from acting after her ten year run in 1980 where she played Jane in Antonii Margheriti's The Last Hunter alternatively known as Hunter of the Apocalypse her last film would be Anthropophagus. This film does have some very shocking moments, and is in some places is hard to watch not just for the hammy acting and low budget but also for truly groundbreaking horror. Joe D'Amato's Anthropophagus is a far cry from his porn/erotica features, anyone expecting Emmanuelle style exploitation film will be in for a nasty shock. If you haven't already seen "Anthropophagous," this should be on your to do list!

-Tony Newton

This is another good video nasty. You can't beat George Eastman chasing you around an island trying to kill you! I actually have a full size original poster of this great film hung on display in my bedroom! I think this film certainly has an unbelievable ending that to me is very fun and just nuts - how I like it!

-Jason Impey   Filmmaker.

Most films like this were rumored to have a scene in that was too shocking to mention, and if you could get your hands on an uncut copy it was like gold. In this case it was a cannibal monster devouring an unborn baby, hence it making the banned 39 original DPP list.It's really not a great film at all, really not worth ploughing through to watch the infamous scene.

-John Thomson   Actor/Comedian.

For those in the know, the name Joe D'Amato will bring to mind certain things. Mostly impure and terrifying things. Some involving horses, cannibals and Tom Selleck look-alikes with genital warts (see *Erotic Nights of the Living Dead* if you wish to learn more about that reference). The voyeuristic director had an illustrious and evocative career, directing Spaghetti Westerns, Barbarian Movies, Swashbucklers and obscure Fantasy, but he is arguably best known for his collaborations with the captivating Laura Gemser.

The aforementioned collaborations largely consisted of D'Amato's vision of the *Emmanuelle* movies (a soft-core French series of 'Erotic Thrillers'), in which he pushed the envelopes of taste, decency and in some cases legality. He used these films as a springboard for some seriously disturbing imagery, in particular *Emmanuelle in America* (1977), *Emmanuelle and the Last Cannibals* (1977) and *Emmanuelle and the White Slave Trade* (1978). The forays into horror territory led almost sequentially into *Anthropophagus: The Beast*, his first straight up horror movie.

Anthropophagy is the act of eating human flesh, which may give some indication to the motivations of the monster, which the title refers to. The monster (played by George Eastman) is, in fact, very human. A man driven to madness after being stranded at sea and forced to eat his wife and child, he now preys on the inhabitants of a lonely Greek island. The island now lies practically deserted, until a few visitors become unwittingly stranded upon it.

One of the refreshing things about *Anthropophagus* is the use of adults as opposed to teenagers for the main roles. The dubbing is so horrendous that it is difficult to decipher if their acting skills are any good, but very few people watch this type of movie for impressive displays of thespian ability. The actual premise takes a long time to set up, with the beast not actually gracing our screens for approximately 50 minutes, and so we are left to familiarise ourselves with the (rather dislikeable) collection of holidaymakers.

As with all Italian horrors of a certain age, the soundtrack is fantastic; with this one is provided by Marcello Giombini. There is an electronic, synthesizer heavy barrage at every possible moment and it only adds to the charm of the overall feature. The prolonged build up only serves to add extra tension and atmosphere to later scenes in which people begin to get picked off. There are some fantastic moments of comedy relief (one with a kitten on a piano which proceeds to play spooky music being a personal favourite) but once the blood begins to flow, I imagine that only the sickest amongst you will get any chuckles.

The scene which undoubtedly caused the most furore and earned this movie a place on the DPP Video Nasties list was one in which Eastman strangles a woman who is very heavily pregnant, removes the foetus with his bare hands and proceeds to eat is while it is still attached to the umbilical cord after the mother has died. All of this occurs in plain view of her fatally injured but agonisingly aware husband. D'Amato used a skinned rabbit as the foetus but the effect is startlingly effective and on a second or third generation VHS would have easily made it appear to be the snuff film, which the censors believed it to be.

The climactic finale, which includes a brutal evisceration and self-cannibalism, also raised a few eyebrows, but the viewer is left replaying the previous grisly moment over and over in their mind long after the credits roll. It is interesting that in his somewhat sequel to *Anthropophagus*, *Absurd* Eastman reprises his role as Nikos and his guts fall out of him at the beginning of that movie as he gets impaled on a railing.

It's a movie with flaws and positives in almost equal merit, whilst being far from a classic it certainly holds an important place within the Video Nasties cannon and is most deserving of at least one viewing for any discerning horror fan. The effects lose some of their impact on a crystal clear DVD version however, even though the scenes which once evoked terror and shock may now inspire little more than a cynical, altogether knowing sneer, there are remnants of a dingier, grottier movie. D'Amato tread similar ground when he made *Porno Holocaust* (1981), but you don't want to go down that road, trust me, I've been there.

-Colin McCracken   Writer.

Axe

Also known as: "Lisa", "Lisa", "Lisa" and "California Axe Massacre".
Year of release: 1977
Writer: Frederick R. Friedel
Director: Frederick R. Friedel
R rating, 65 mins, USA
Tagline: "Total terror – you'll be scared to breath…!"
Main cast: Leslie Lee (Lisa), Jack Canon (Steele), Ray Green (Lomax), Frederick R. Friedel (Billy), Douglas Powers (Grandfather), Frank Jones (Aubrey).
Distributed by: Video Releasing Organisation

Axe was originally distributed in its uncut form by Video Releasing Organisation in 1982. In 1999 the film was released as "California Axe Massacre" with 19 seconds of cuts made by the BBFC. Released on DVD by ILC as "Axe" in its uncut form by the BBFC in 2006. Axe was prosecuted.

Plot:
Axe is another of the sinister revenge movies from the Video Nasty list. The film follows a group of psychopaths attempting to escape the clutches of the law; these sadistic psychopaths wreak havoc amongst a small town and soon discover an isolated farmhouse where the occupants (a young girl named Lisa and her disabled Grandfather) are tormented at the hands of these psychos. With their house occupied by these maniacs Lisa takes revenge into her own hands…

Appraisal:
Axe is often compared to "The Last House on the Left", with the rape scene being the only reason basically the film got banned. "Axe" is not excessively gory or graphic. I felt that Axe was a great low budget film and does have elements of gore and shock factors, which every horror film needs! It's rumored that the cover of the video sleeve alone led to its short-lived inclusion on the DPP list amongst other banned films. Axe builds the suspense well although it loses momentum in parts but the graphic murders that take place in the film clearly make up for the pacing. Axe is a low budget movie though the acting and atmospherics delivered throughout this film set the whole film up nicely. Axe has deservedly procured cult like status as an exploitation flick and provides a great example of what filmmaking on a budget can be. Coming in at around 70 minutes "Axe" is one of the shorter films on the list and in parts leaves you wanting more gore, this film has a great soundtrack and doesn't disappoint. Axe does stand the test of time if only for the elements of mystery surrounding it. Every time I watch this film I have hours of conversations "What Happened there?" "Is that because she?" ... I just love films where it's not all a closed book, it's leaves unanswered questions that play on your mind long after you have viewed it! Axe had its theatrical release under the title "California Axe Massacre" in 1982, which had around 3 minutes of footage cut. Artsy and shrouded with mystery, what's not to love about Axe!? Friedel's debut feature film Axe is a gem of a movie. On the outset a low budget affair but the deeper you delve you discover a thought provoking cult classic with a haunting score which holds its own against any of today's generic horror releases.

-Tony Newton

I had no idea Axe, or Lisa, Lisa, as I originally titled it, would make history. It was made to play in drive-in theaters, which generally play for a week and then disappear. We shot it in 8 and 1/2 days with almost no money. We could afford so little film that we used almost every foot we shot in the movie, and some of the shots even twice. I was actually using the movie as my way of learning how to make a movie because I never went to film school. My inspiration for the movie was probably "Repulsion", Polanski's film about a beautiful but unstable girl who is pushed to the brink by unwanted male attention and ends up killing in rather violent fashion. I lost touch with the film after it was initially distributed and only found out that it been released on video in England in 2006 when Stephen Thrower contacted me about including it in "Nightmare USA". It was only then that I found out it was banned in England and put on the Video Nasty List, which is shocking because most of the violent moments are played off screen. I was very surprised and gratified to find out that the film still had fans after all these years. David Gregory, who was the original video distributor in England, will be releasing AXE on Blu-ray in March through Severin Films. That there's still an audience for this film after all these years is quite amazing and wonderful. Especially since we were just a bunch of kids who were excited to just to be making a movie.

-Frederick R. Friedel   Writer and Director of "Axe".

The premise of Axe is a simple one; three hoods on the run take refuge in a house, which is occupied by a young girl caring for her invalid grandfather. With the exception of two other scenes, the majority of the movie takes place in and around the house. What was probably a budgetary decision actually adds a great deal of atmospheric tension within the movie, also greatly increasing the aesthetic creativity, which was needed to maintain interest within such claustrophobic settings.

The aforementioned criminals, dressed sharply in business suits (arguably a partial influence on the costume design for *Reservoir Dogs*, especially given the juxtaposition of the men's appearance and the unspeakable nature of their deeds) who are waiting in the apartment of a man whom they believe has informed on them. It is revealed that he is a cross dresser named Aubrey. One of the men (Billy) seems slightly more reluctant to involve himself with the violence that ensues upon Aubrey's return. Lomax and Steele, however, have no issues with dispensing sadism and misery upon everyone their path crosses. Aubrey is beaten, burnt and eventually bludgeoned to death. It is after this that the men decide they should get themselves out of sight for a while.

Their journey takes them through a convenience store, where a homely shop assistant is subjected to a series of humiliating and potentially fatal ordeals. We are then brought to the centre stage, an old farmhouse where Lisa (Leslie Lee) is preparing food. There are elements of distance and a troubled mind which give her character extra resonance onscreen. She consistently hums tunelessly, and her emotions do not seem to fluctuate at any stage in the movie. This is by no means a criticism; the effect from her stoic and unnerving performance is both haunting and eerie and brings a unique element to an otherwise formulaic movie.

While the gore filled scenes in *Axe* are scant and often superfluous, it would appear that there were other factors involved which upset the DPP. While it was never actually alluded to in the movie, the video box claimed that Lisa was only 13, which would make the actions and events contained in the movie abhorrent and unsupportable. There is, however, no mention of Lisa's age contained in the dialogue and the actress playing her is clearly in her early to mid-twenties. The objections did seem to be tonally based, especially a seemingly innocuous scene involving a decapitated chicken being left upon the kitchen sink. This was one scene, which the censors had a particular problem with. Go figure.

Frederick R Friedel is only accredited with one other movie, which is known as *Date with A Kidnapper*, which also starred Jack Canon (Steele). The short running time and the gritty camerawork and general aura of the movie suggest either a lucky accident or a failed attempt at Arthouse. There are a great deal of creative shots and some of the developments within the story do come as a surprise. Lee's performance as Lisa ties the whole thing together, with her unflinching and distant stare dominating the time she is onscreen.

There are aspects of surrealism, including a possibly imagined scene involving a snake, as well as a laugh out loud finale regarding some peculiar tasting tomato soup.

It's an altogether unpleasant affair, yet not one that would warrant being outlawed. One can only assume from what little information is available on the subject that it was the distributors claim that Lisa was so young, combined with the realistic, nasty tone of the movie that led them to place it upon the banned list, as opposed to any one particular scene. I was, admittedly, taken in by the pseudo Arthouse approach to a home invasion movie and remained interested until the altogether infantile conclusion.

-Colin McCracken   Writer.

The Beast in Heat

Also known as: "La Bestia in Calore" and "S.S. Hell Camp".
Year of release: 1977
Writers: Lorenzo Artale, Luigi Batzella
Director: Luigi Batzella
Italy
Tagline: "Horrifying experiences in the last days of the S.S."
Main cast: Macha Magall (Dr. Ellen Kratsch), Gino Turini (Drago), Edilio Kim (Capt. Hardinghauser), Xiro Papas (Lupo), Salvatore Baccaro (The Beast).
Distributed by: JVI

The Beast in Heat was originally distributed by JVI, released uncut on VHS in 1982 and is still banned in the UK even to this day. A US was version released in 2004 on DVD R1 in its uncut and unrated form. The Beast in Heat was prosecuted.

Plot:
The Beast in Heat is set in a fictionalised prisoner of war camp in occupied Europe during World War II. This film follows the depravity, torture and sadistic exploitation subjected to female prisoners of war when the barbarous Nazi, Doctor Kratsch unleashes the half man, half beast mutant (Played by Sal Boris) that was the product of genetic experimentation to create a 'Master Race'. It's through this violent caged beast that Doctor Kratch satisfies her own savage sexual desires! Features exploitation of the most obvious kind!

Appraisal:
The Beast in Heat is a full on exploitation feast; yes the film is somewhat offensive but also an all-round piece of cult horror entertainment. Any film that turns a hairy beast of a man into a crazy psycho rapist through Nazi experiment is at the very least intriguing to watch. The Beast in Heat features psycho/voyeuristic Nazi's, cringe worthy acting and awkward sex scenes ... okay, that was an understatement extremely awkward and not sexy at all! The acting over the top acting is so far over the top that they're hanging off the fucking cliff, its most certainly not one of the better titles on the list but engaging none the less. The Beast in Heat offers a bizarre mix of exploitation merged with some serious undertones of War; it's an odd coupling. The film never really knows exactly what it is except a cash-in to make a buck, it's entertaining but it's viewed in a serious light. The Beast in Heat was one of the hardest VHS tapes to track down, I never managed to unearth an original copy on VHS, only a blank tape to tape copy with a custom hand written label which is a shame because I love the original cover art with the beast poised ready to clutch the scantily clad woman. The Beast in Heat is a fun watch in a very strange way, it will keep you entertained to say the least, grab a pack of beers, spin this, watch with your mates and you will have a blast!

-Tony Newton

The Ilsa movies have a lot to answer for. Dyanne Thorne and her eponymous dominatrix S.S. Officer caused such a sensation in 1975 with Ilsa: She Wolf of the S.S. that those industrious Italians were in like a shot to capitalise with a vast range of Nazisploitation flicks. Taste and decency really went out the window with these ones, and close to the very bottom of the barrel, clinging to the edge like something you'd find in a neglected public toilet is *The Beast in Heat*. However, there's something captivating about this one that belies the sheer abhorrence of the subject matter. This is mostly to do with the fact that it contains so many hilarious shortcomings that it's almost impossible to be actually offended by it.

Directed by Ivan Katansky (AKA Luigi Batzella), this is nothing shy of a garbled mess of stock footage, scenes from one of the director's other movies (*When The Bell Rings* AKA: *Quandosuona la campana*) and several prolonged shots of the most unconvincing torture scenes ever committed to film.

On paper the movie sounds particularly shocking. A crazed Nazi Doctor and high standing Officer in the S.S. (Macha Magall) genetically creates a Neanderthal / Homo sapiens hybrid which she feeds on mind-altering, powerful aphrodisiacs. The sex-crazed beast is then provided with endless amounts of female prisoners for him to pummel into extinction.

The mixture of Nazi fetishism and the semi-bestial nature of the main concepts would surely revolt the most liberal of cinemagoers, but this was not where the main offences lie. The beast in question is played by a rotund comedy actor by the name of Sal Boris (AKA: Salvatore Baccaro). The bizarre choices which led them to make absolutely no effort whatsoever to alter his appearance simply left him looking like a fat, naked Italian man in a cage. His incessant huffing and puffing, and endless face pulling become nothing shy of hypnotically dreadful. The other bizarre thing is how minimal his screen time is, given that he is the alleged subject of the movie.

Instead, we are taken through a ridiculous array of incredibly dull sub-pots in which lots of people argue unconvincingly and at great length. There is a storyline involving a resistance movement within a village, a town whore's relationship with a Nazi officer, and a few other ones that don't warrant mentioning. The overall sensation elicited of one of exasperation and masochistic endurance. When a friend gave it to me first, he described it as a really bad spaghetti western; he wasn't far wrong.

Some light relief comes in the form of the torture scenes (which I know sounds like a terrible thing to say, but they really have to be seen to be believed). This includes fingernails being removed to the meekest pleas of "Ow, stop that, you're hurting me". The filmmakers also painted some guinea pigs black in a feeble attempt to pass them off as rats. The scene in which a girl flails around in faux terror, covered in terribly fake blood whilst two of these cute little critters plod around harmlessly on her stomach is one of the funniest moments I have witnessed as part of this Video Nasties marathon. There are some truly bizarre ideas contained within, especially a questionable segment in which the beast rips out a clump of his victim's pubic hair and proceeds to eat it.

There is absolutely nothing to be gained from suffering through *The Beast in Heat*. It is drastically caught between wanting to be a shocking exploitation flick and a war drama. Neither of these elements work particularly well and it very quickly becomes an ordeal to make it through the running time. For serious completists, fans of men with hairy backs and Nazi fetishists only.

-Colin McCracken   writer.

Despite being intercut with some standard Macaroni Combat filler noise, The Beast in Heat is, in effect, a slightly oddball addition to the Nazisploitation wave that plays on a familiar Nazi Boudoir theme. Even the obligatory Ilsa type figure is present. Where Dyanne Thorne's Ilsa references infamous concentration camp wife Ilse Koch, in The Beast in Heat Macha Magall, from Bruno Mattei's Private House of the SS, plays the similarly titled Dr. Ellen Kratsch. In The Beast in Heat, Dr. Ellen puts politically undesirable women through their sexual paces with a number of "scientific" trials before they are allowed to meet "The Beast". Played by "Sal Boris", this so-called Beast is less beast and more of a squat, hairy, Luciano-Pigozzi-headed Ron Jeremy figure in a Luis Guzmán fright mask. Before the ladies get to play with this furry ball of unadulterated miniature man-sex they must first endure some time in a clear plastic bubbly-water tank.

They must also be psychological tortured by some guinea pigs that have been painted black in order to resemble, erm, black guinea pigs! Because, as with an infamous scene in Turkey's Captain America and Santo vs. Spider-Man, we are supposed to believe these particular guinea pigs are in fact rats. But, in truth, they just look like the black guinea pigs that they are not supposed to be. However, black guinea pigs are not especially scary. So this could, at best, be considered as a form of tickle-torture for the restrained would-be lovers of The Beast. Oh, and there is a little fingernail removal to be endured too. Sadly, in practice, this effect is so poorly realised as to put it right up there with the fluffy threat of guinea pig tickle-torture. Of course viewers are supposed to believe that The Beast represents some rampant overpowering sexuality that can strike fear into women in a way that bubbly water and black guinea pigs never could. That he can, apparently, shag them to death! However, an unfortunate camera angle reveals the beastly todger to be remarkably unexceptional for such a mutant human-monkey-hybrid killer sex monster. The Beast, we learn, is all too human. He is also flaccid. This is confirmed as viewers are given a brief glimpse of the floppy pecker of the titular monster as he swings it about in a futile act of non-threatening, aerial frottage.

Oh, the horror! Indeed, fingernails, non-consensual bubble bathing and rodents aside, the enduring image of the Beast in Heat is that of the rampant, mutant sex monster swinging his willy about in a rattling, Tiswas-style prop cage as it threatens to come apart at the hinges. The Beast grimaces, splutters and growls. He defies his own gag-reflex by munching on a bunch of pubes. He also froths and gurns into a fish-eye lens to emphasise his depravity. Yet, in its desire to upset, the film far too easily lapses into parody. Indeed, far from being shocking, The Beast in Heat is a little ray of unintentionally comic sunshine. Not least because of the occasional blooper. For example, in an attempt to convey the awesome scale and power of the NAZI regime, the viewer is invited to dwell upon a giant Swastika as it glistens in the sun. However, the impact of this scene proves to be somewhat blunted by the shadow of crew and camera that is cast, like a dark cloud of incompetence, upon the symbol of hate. Of course the humourless minds and puffed up, purple faced, pinstripe suits and blue rinsed biddies that made up the great and the good of the British establishment did not see the funny side of any of this. Maybe it was the portrayal of an extreme right wing ideology as sexually degenerate that got the Thatcherite cilices rattling in horror? Indeed, with Gestapo's Last Orgy, SS Experiment Camp and Love Camp 7 all making the list, the recurring theme of right wing perverts comes up time and again. However, even given this context, it is surprising that The Beast in Heat found its way onto their stupid nasties list at all.

-Nigel Maskell   Writer.

Blood Bath

Also known as "Reazione a Catena", "Twitch of the Death Nerve" and "A Bay of Blood",
Year of release: 1971
Writers: Franco Barberi, Mario Bava.
Director: Mario Bava
R rating, 84 mins, Italy
Tagline: "The second movie rated "V" for Violence."
Main cast: Claudine Auer (Renata), Luigi Pistilli (Albert), Claudio Camaso (Simon), Anna Maria Rosati (Laura), Chris Avram (Frank), Leopoldo Trieste (Paolo).
Distributed by: Hokushin

In 1972 the original theatrical release was refused certification by the BBFC. "Blood Bath" was originally distributed by Hokushin in its uncut form in 1983. This film was later released on VHS in 1994 with 43 seconds of cuts made by the BBFC. It was not until 2010 that Arrow released the uncut version as the BBFC finally allowed the film to be seen in full. Blood Bath was prosecuted and included on the official DPP list of banned films.

Plot:
Mario Bava's giallo Blood Bath more commonly known as "A Bay of Blood" tells the story of an heiress (Federica) who is brutally murdered by her husband (Donati) in order to inherit her fortune, but when Donati is also murdered it soon becomes apparent that her wealth has many benefactors all eager to inherit ownership of the Bay. Murders continue in the interest of gaining Federica's money as well as ownership of the Bay and its surrounding land. Who will survive? Who will inherit the Bay?

Appraisal:
This influential almost giallo-esque slasher feast of a film gives enough blood, murders and suspense throughout to warrant your attention.
"They came to play, they stayed to die…"
The Italian maestro Mario Bava directs this nasty and shocking classic; the godfather of the slasher Mario Bava was obviously a huge inspiration to horror and slasher filmmakers. This 1971 horror movie is considered Mario Bava's most violent film and another controversial classic that has been given the gift of immortality by being added to the list of the damned "The Video Nasty hit list!" When you consider this film was made in 1971 this really is a clear inspiration for the wave of slasher films that came along in the late 1970's and early 1980's. Initially this film was distributed by Hallmark releasing co who changed the title to "Carnage" and tried a repeat of their bizarre advertising used for the film "Mark of the Devil" stating that the film was rated V for violence! This was an unsuccessful campaign, which was withdrawn, and then later in 1972 the film was again released this time entitled "Twitch of the Death Nerve". Mario Bava's Blood Bath is a classic slasher film, a true masterpiece. This is definitely Bava's most violent work and notoriously his most controversial it certainly doesn't hold back on gore, shocks or scares and is an amazing horror film on so many different levels. The release of Blood Bath was greeted by many critics with disgust and disappointment, it was ahead of its time and played a crucial role in the slasher genre, with huge body counts the film is one of the reasons slasher films became successful. This gore masterpiece has obviously influenced countless filmmakers and modern films such as "Scream", "I Know What You Did Last Summer", "Urban Legend", as well as films from the video nasty era such as "The Burning", "Just Before Dawn", and "Friday the 13th". In "Friday the 13th" pt2 it's easy to see the homage being made to Bava's masterpiece with two of the death sequences

including the Impalement of a couple having sex! Bava's classic will continue to be loved as new audiences appreciate this Italian classic! A Bay of Blood goes by many different titles, even pre-release the titles kept changing: "The Odor of Flesh", "Thus do we Live to be Evil", "Before the Fact".

It was released initially as "The Ecology of Crime" but due to the films poor performance it was renamed "Chain Reaction" and later renamed "A Bay of Blood" but in the UK will be most associated with the title "Blood Bath". This is a gory horror film, which does not disappoint.

-Tony Newton

A late career renaissance with an alternate title like 'Twitch of the Death Nerve' became a true tent pole of influence in the macabre circus of Italian Horror. Its cinematic ring master Mario Bava directed some of the industries masterpieces from 'Black Sunday' (1960) which re-ignited the career of horror femme fatale Barbara Steele, 'The Girl Who Knew Too Much' (1963) a compactly produced Giallo after various prototypes by other directors lacked the operant charm and subtle humor of Bava's work, and 1964's' 'Blood and Black Lace' a kaleidoscopic murder mystery with more mood lighting than a jazz festival.

Mario Bava is arguably the father of modern Italian horror – born In Sanremo, Italy (1914) his career was somewhat overshadowed in the mainstream by the likes of art house directors like Pier Paolo Pasolini, Michelangelo Antonioni and Federico Fellini. Bava, was considered by some as a filmmaker whose greatest achievements were the echoes of influence in other filmmakers' work – the likes of Martin Scorsese have admitted a Bava influence on his use of stark primary colour in films. This influence on directors at the time caused a schism in 1960's cinema – the blood red imagery painted with broad strokes across Roger Corman's Edgar Allen Poe series of films versus those who attempted instead to be more influenced by the operatic representation of violence.

Bava had been lured to a deal with American International Pictures with a mixed degree of success. Spy nostalgia such as 'Dr. Goldfoot and the 'S' Bomb' (1966) starring Vincent Price and pop star turned pub quiz question Fabian failed to capture the magic of the Italian maestro. More successful attempts at a more commercial mid Atlantic market such as 'Danger Diabolik' (1968) under the intense Stewardship of Dino De Laurentiis were more artistically pleasing although still not commercially successful in the US. The good looks of leading man John Phillip Law (recently a green screen Angel in 'Barbarella' with Jane Fonda), recent Bond Villain Adolfo Celi, and more beautiful women than plot holes (just about) could not appeal to the U.S market – it was deemed too childish for adults (with a 'Batman' esque vibe – the original show of which was deemed too tired and retired the same year) and too adult for children - Marisa Mell's roll around in dollar bills swirls with doe eyed Italian eroticism.

Bava films had often been re-edited, re-dubbed, and re-scored for the American market – often to the frustration of the director and generations of fans. Several have an AIP instated Les Baxter score and 'Black Sabbath' (1963) – a film where one famous band got its name... Black Sabbath had a lesbian subplot ironed out to not ruffle conservative feathers. Homosexuality was considered a 'mental illness' by the American Psychology Association up until 1972!

'Twitch of the Death Nerve', 'Blood Bath', or 'Bay of Blood' as it was predominantly known in the UK is to many the last great hurrah of Bava's career and feels like one last stab (pun intended) at challenging perceived moral decency – a pressure cooker of quiet rage in a world that was boiling over as the Vietnam war escalated. At the 1971 Avoriaz Film Festival, Christopher Lee who had started on Bava's erotically tinged Hammer Horror like 'Whip and the Body' (1963) attended a screening and was apparently disgusted.

This particular zeitgeist is examined superbly in Wes Craven's 'Last House on the Left' (1972) – but it is his collaborator Sean S. Cunningham's 'Friday the 13th' (1980) that bares the closest link to Bava's work.

Watching 'Bay of Blood' today it is impossible to shake the similarity to the Crystal Lake shenanigans, which gave us Kevin Bacon before he was mugging it to camera trying to sell us 4G. Cunningham has always noted a debt to the business success of 'Halloween' (1978) on his movie but has rarely commented on 'A Bay of Blood' – perhaps he had not seen it at the time, although it did run as a double bill with 'Last House on the Left' in some parts of the U.S.

In the film, an elderly heiress played by Italian screen legend Isa Miranda is brutally murdered in the opening scene – shocking to audiences as Miranda was a big star at the time – a move that checkmates Janet Leigh's murder in 'Psycho'. The opening long sequence without dialogue feels like a gradual transgression between the horror of old and something much more ferocious. Tip toeing around spoilers there is soon a struggle for her fortunes with real estate agent Frank Ventura (Chris Avram) and his lover Laura (Anna Maria Rosati) plotting to take possession of the bay.

Soon we have more red herrings than a Grimsby fish market with a cameo from the world's most pessimistic looking octopus – albeit a cephalopod that found short lived fame on some of the movies posters for no apparent reason. Rumours of a failed jazz combo with Squiddly Diddly are yet unconfirmed at the time of publishing. However soon a troupe of randy teenagers arrive in a dune buggy lead by Brigitte Skay, an actress who had made a decent career in lacy-racy dramas to make the Mediterranean blood boil. If that wasn't enough former Bond girl Claudine Auger and 1958 Miss World Runner Up is added to the mix.

The mix soon forms into an all-out murder spree which surrounds the lake with the teenagers staying in a dilapidated building in one leafy nook and the relatives and friends of the heiress nearby all suddenly disappearing (occasionally re-appearing with a collection of house hold objects intertwined with their essential areas). It is easy to lose track of the plot – Italian horrors often neglect plot points for ambience or bloody bombast: Lucio Fulci's 'Living Dead Trilogy', although, excellent fun is a testament to this theory. Dario Argento's work at times feels like he is reaching for something slightly out of grasp – although not fully aware of what is on the top cinematic shelf.

Perhaps the presence of these two titans of Italian horror nudged Bava towards extending his 57-year-old arm more towards the tin of red paint more frequently. In terms of a career path 'Bay of Blood' feels like a cinematic late mid-life crisis with a slightly tetchy and edgy atmosphere – perhaps he should have kept the dune buggy. Dario Argento had ushered in a new generation of Italian horror with his first movie 'Bird with the Crystal Plumage' that mixed populist slasher spectacle with art house aesthetics and stars – the likes of Antonioni favourite David Hemmings, Warhol luvvie Udo Kier, and acting legend Alida Valli were soon queuing to be in his films. Fulci had not yet hit full stride with his marathons of maggots but had recently raised his head above the parapet of the gates of horror hell with 'Lizard in a Woman's Skin' (1971).

A Bay of Blood does feel like a timepiece of that era – the amber like handheld woodlands sequences and the fact everyone is dressed like they are from a Carpenters tribute act adds a sense of nostalgia. Perhaps this is part of its charm, the slasher genre in America that followed in the 1980's is often blighted with budgetary aesthetics such as 16mm prints blown up to 35mm creating a grainy image. This style is perfect for urban gritty slices of sleaze such as Frank Henenlotters 'Basketcase' (1982), but for more forest bound affairs it robs the natural beauty of the scenery. The re-appraisal of Bava's work can largely be drawn to key individuals such as the likes of critics such as Italian horror experts Alan Jones and Tim Lucas but also to the spate of excellent remastered re-releases of the films from Anchor Bay in the US and Arrow Video in the UK. Trying to get hold of a decent print of Bava classics such as 'Kill Baby Kill' (1966) and Bava's hugely influential sci-fi opus 'Planet of the Vampires' (1965) has always been a challenge – the latter a film that Dan O'Bannon cites as a major influence on his and Ronald Shusett's screenplay for 'Alien' (1979). As films become more seen they gain potential oxygen for credibility – the resurgence of Alfred Hitchcock's 'Vertigo' (1958) to being considered the greatest movie ever made in a Sight and Sound pole is a testament to this fact.

'Bay of Blood' suffered for a long time due to a lack of a decent print and also a lack of a release at all in the UK after being rejected for a cinema release by the BBFC in 1972 under the title of 'Blood Bath' and ended up as one of the original 39 "video nasties" in the UK. Several versions of the film circulated on the black market – a financially viable piracy chain that flowed from more liberal minded countries such as the Netherlands. However, a jaunty pirate (not of the Jack Sparrow kind) would be faced with different versions of the film. On initial release in Italy the film was titled 'Ecologia del delitto' ("The Ecology of Crime") – which sounds like part of a Green Party manifesto pledge on corporate greed but let's consider previously considered titles of the production - Odore di carne ("The Odor of Flesh") Cosi Imparano a Fare I Cattivi ("Thus do we live to be evil") sound like hokum parodies that the late 1980's would churn out.

The English language dub has different names for the teenage characters and completely different dialogue in certain sequences – although this is extremely common as Italian cinema has a long history of not recording audio on set arcing back to Mussolini's paranoid state control of cultural production in fascist Italy. This diverse collection of versions of the film on the market raises certain questions as to the notion of a finished cultural product – fans of Romero's 'Dawn of the Dead' (1978), Sam Peckinpah's 'Pat Garrett and Billy the Kid (1973), and Sam Fuller's 'The Big Red One' (1979) know too well of a film in flux with different versions available grasping for the attention of the public. Incidentally, Fuller's war epic starring gravel voiced whisper Lee Marvin was seized by the police as they felt that 'The Big Red One' was a different form of adult entertainment.

The home video market with VHS, DVD & Blu-Ray at first seemed to democratise the consumption of media products but the purposeful production now of alternate cuts and extended additions has created a certain ambivalence to the idea of a movie as a work of art. To reassure you that horror and art can find a shared dwelling place put on a copy of any of Bava's masterpieces, and if you put on 'Bay of Blood' prepare yourself for one of the greatest film endings in cinema history.

-Marc Wright   Writer/Lecturer.

"Mario Bava's Bay of Blood is an outstanding little horror film and should never have been a Video Nasty. This moody and bizarre slasher is very obviously the inspiration for many more well known sadistic horror offerings. Bava's stylish out-of-body-experience is a one-of-a-kind giallo. Bay of Blood is a film that marches to the beat of its own drummer. It's difficult to get a grip on the proceedings as the plot is like a mirage. Where is this all going? There are moments of absurdity and dreamlike beauty. Odd, whimsical and deranged, Bay of Blood sure has its share of violent outbursts. Nothing matches the deliciously macabre opening sequence murder for sheer craftsmanship and ingenuity in the art of staging a creative death scene. It must be seen to be believed. I always felt that Visiting Hours was a bit underrated and didn't deserve to be on the list. The complete opposite of Bay of Blood in terms of style and atmosphere; it looks flat, like a made-for-TV project and lacks mystery and depth. Still, Visiting Hours is suspenseful and taut and delivers some occasional chills. It also contains a very disturbing portrait of a cold-blooded murderer. Here Michael Ironside, the telepathic grim reaper from Cronenberg's classic Scanners, is supremely creepy as the serial killer terrorized by ugly childhood abuse memories. I always liked Lee Grant, and in Visiting Hours she's gutsy and intense. Plus it looks like she just wandered off the set of Damien Omen 2, one of my favorites. This below-the-radar and unjustly maligned slasher is definitely worth checking out."

-Dante Tomaselli   Writer, Director, Producer, musical artist.

Blood Feast

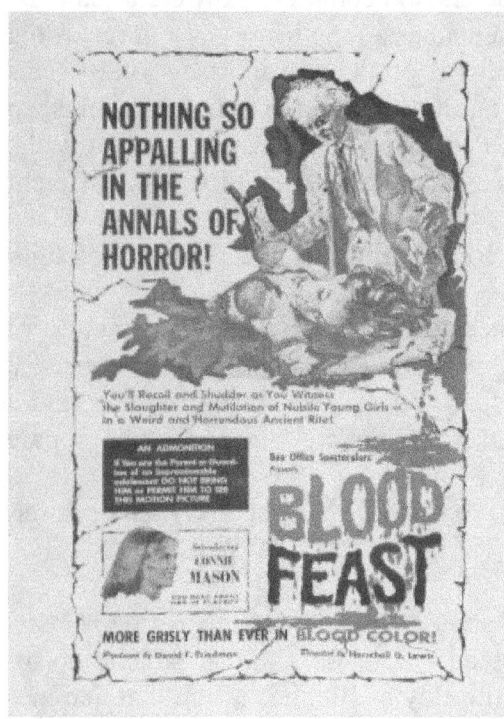

Also known as "Egyptian Blood Feast" and "Feast of Flesh".
Year of release: 1963
Writer: Allison Louise Downe
Director: Herschell Gordon Lewis
Unrated 67 mins. USA

Tagline: "A weird, grisly ancient rite horrendously brought to life in blood color."

Main cast: William Kerwin (Det. Pete Thornton), Mal Arnold (Fuad Ramses), Connie Mason (Suzette Fremont), Lyn Bolton (Mrs. Dorothy Fremont), Scott H. Hall (Police Captain Frank), Christy Foushee (Toni Calvert).

Distributed by: Astra

Blood Feast was originally distributed by Astra in 1982. In 2001 Tartan Video released the film passed by the BBFC with 23 seconds of cuts. In 2005 the BBFC passed it uncut, and the DVD was released by Odeon. Blood Feast was prosecuted and included on the official DPP list of banned films.

Plot:
In Herschell Gordon Lewis's classic horror film Blood Feast, Psycho killer Fuad Ramses is hired as a caterer by Mrs. Fremont, he suggests an authentic Egyptian feast at which he plans to bring an ancient goddess of good and evil back to life by creating the perfect woman, using the body parts of his victims. His plan involves Mrs. Fremont's daughter being slaughtered as the final sacrifice in order to bring goddess Ishtar back to life, will Fuad be stopped in time?

Appraisal:
Blood Feast is a superb film that was way ahead of its time. Directed by the godfather of gore himself Herschell Gordon Lewis where he earns the crown for having the oldest title on the DPP list.

I'm one of those people who adore Herschell Gordon Lewis's work, his films are amazing in my eyes, so you may get a slightly biased review here. Why "Bloodfeast" gets a bad rap is beyond me. "Bloodfeast" is the oldest film on the list here but one of the best, it's a low budget offering which stands out as a groundbreaking film that has obviously inspired filmmakers from around the globe. I love the way that the low budget is never hidden, but more rammed down the viewers throat! This film is stunning, especially when you consider the year it was made and even more incredible are the rumors that the film took a mere 7-9 days to actually film and with no named actors! Though they did capitalize on the fact that actress Connie Mason (Playboy model) featured in the movie, so much so that they advertised the feature with "Introducing Connie Mason, you saw her in Playboy, adult horror!"

The remake of "BloodFeast" is out now, I'm not a huge fan of remakes but I would love to see what they do with it and hope they manage to keep the feel of a true Herschell Gordon Lewis film.

-Tony Newton

Directed by Herschel Gordon Lewis "Blood Feast" tells the story of psychopathic caterer Fuad Ramses played by Mal Arnold. Our wide-eyed (disturbingly large browed) villain is hired to cater the dinner party of Mrs. Freemont's daughter, with his own unique culinary flair he begins preparations for the perfect dish, collecting additions for his feast of blood as he hacks the limbs from numerous beautiful young innocents and harvests their organs for an extravagant cannibal feast as part of an ancient ritual to resurrect the Egyptian goddess Ishtar.

In this 1963 all you can stomach gore-fest the screen quite literally oozes blood. From the outset "Blood Feast's" cheesy charm draws the viewer deep into the depths of its gory depravity. Yes, it's hilarious, the makeshift gore effects are completely unconvincing, the acting's tragic, the dialogue cringe-worthy and there's a continual deluge of lack-lustre camera work teamed with an ultra-simplistic music score but "Blood Feast" succeeded in what it set out to do at the time which was to shock its audience with unrelenting gore, pioneering the splatter genre.

Herschell Gordon Lewis imagined up a new genre of horror with this film, "Blood Feast" is the splatter film's very first offering and that in itself sets this film apart from others of its kind. It's not for its artistic merit that "Blood Feast" has earned its place in horror film history but for the sheer genius of "Godfather of Horror" Herschell Gordon Lewis as he redefines the horror genre with this one-of-a-kind splatterfest. On a modest budget of just $25,000 Herschell Gordon Lewis set out to break new ground with his depiction of on-screen gore, he wanted to make a movie which would shock its audience (even issuing vomit bags to movie goers as a marketing ploy) and this gore-fest doesn't disappoint!

Despite (and because of) its quirks "Blood Feast" has achieved cult status, it's certainly not shocking by today's standards but remains a rare and entertaining piece of ground breaking horror history.

-Kerry Newton   Writer.

Blood Rites

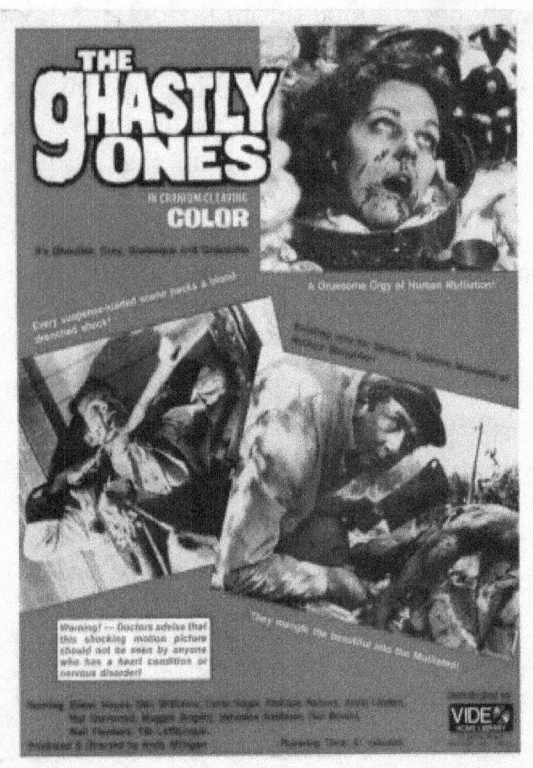

Also known as "The Ghastly Ones" and "Blood Orgy".
Year of release: 1968
Writers: Andy Milligan and Hal Sherwood.
Director: Andy Milligan
Unrated 81 mins. USA
Tagline: "Mad creatures of the night existing only for sensual sadistic moments of human slaughter!"
Main cast: Veronica Radburn (Martha), Maggie Rogers (Hattie), Hal Borske (Colin Trask), Anne Linden (Vicky), Fib LaBlaque (Rich), Carol Vogel (Liz).
Distributed by: Scorpio
Originally distributed by Scorpio in 1983. The only available copy of the film is an unrated and uncut R1 US DVD released by Image in 2004. The Ghastly Ones was prosecuted and included on the official DPP list of banned films.

Plot:
Blood Rites sees a group of 3 sisters and their respective husbands summoned to a reading of their fathers will, at his request the couples are forced to spend 3 days in his remote Victorian house with staff Martha, Hattie and Colin before receiving their inheritance. Severed heads are accidently served for dinner and the couples begin being murdered one by one but just who is the killer? And who will claim their father's inheritance?

Appraisal:
I'm a fan of low budget films and a huge lover of B movies, but for some reason this just didn't hit the spot for me. I actually enjoyed the film after a recent viewing as I did when I watched it for the first time as a teenager though on first viewing I was expecting a lot more from the film, you always got that feeling of disappointment if any of the video nasties didn't deliver or live up to their expectations. This film is dreadful; it feels as if you're watching a really bad live play finding yourself wanting to inconspicuously edge out of your seat and straight out of the theatre. The best way to enjoy this film is to turn down the volume and play your favourite rock opera at least this way you'll be getting some enjoyment and maybe, just maybe you could trick your brain into liking this film! This film contains nudity and some seriously bad effects, but we don't see much in the way of gore. There aren't many things I thank the BBFC for but banning this film is definitely one of them. Blood Rites is all over the place. Murders, naked flesh and a plot twist still can't save this film. There are low budget films then there's "The Ghastly Ones", this film sets the bar for bad films, the bad acting ruins what could have been a good idea just very poorly executed, to sum up this film really is GHASTLY!
-Tony Newton

Bloody Moon

Also known as: "Die Sage des Todes".
Year of release: 1981
Writer: ErichTomek
Director: Jesús Franco
X rated 90 mins. West Germany, Spain

Tagline: "Don't panic…it only happens once in a ….Bloody Moon"

Main cast: Olivia Pascal (Angela), Christoph Moosbrugger (Alvarao), Nadja Gerganoff (Manuela), Alexander Waechter (Miguel), Jasmin Losensky (Inga), Corinna Drews (Laura).

Distributed by: Interlight

Bloody Moon was originally distributed by Interlight in both cut and uncut versions on VHS video. There's also a release by Video Classics. In 1993 the BBFC cut 1.20 seconds and Vipco released the VHS of this film. In 2008 Severin released a DVD in its uncut form with the cuts wavered by the BBFC.

Bloody Moon was prosecuted and included on the official DPP list of banned films.

Plot:
In Jesús Franco's 80's slasher a disfigured young man(Miguel) is released from a mental asylum after a stabbing incident five years earlier and his attempts to rekindle his incestuous relationship with his sister are rebuffed he begins stalking International Youth-Club Boarding School of Languages student Angela. When Angela's friends begin being murdered one by one Angela desperately tries to convince those around her that the murderer is after her!

Appraisal:
Bloody Moon see's Jesús Franco at his finest! This 1981 film has an almost Giallo quality to it. Bloody Moon is well worth a watch, it's full of innuendos, though some of the dialogue leaves a lot to be desired, but it's saved by fantastic scenes—including decapitation by a gigantic saw. The laughable effects, like the huge bolder falling, actually serve to make the film entertaining. The cinematography is great throughout, the whole movie feels almost Dario Argento-esque! There's a scene in which a woman's nipple is severed (never a good site!) and of course there's the typical supply of bare flesh expected from a video nasty. Some original murders take place in this successor to the teen slasher films, which are now produced by the bucket load. This full on slasher horror offering from cult movie director Jesús Franco is a welcome change to Franco's other work, whatever Jesús Franco did here it just worked, this is one of Franco's best films. "Bloody Moon" is an inspiration to the stalk and slash genre we see today and has stood the test of time with its Innovative kills and laugh out loud moments "Bloody Moon" makes for an all around great cult horror movie viewing experience!
-Tony Newton

The Burning

Also known as: "Cropsy".
Year of release: 1981
Writers: Harvey Weinstein and Tony Maylam
Director: Tony Maylam
R rating 91 mins. USA, Canada
Tagline: "Today is not Friday the 13th. But if you see this movie alone…you'll never be the same again!"

Main cast: Brian Matthews (Todd), Leah Ayres (Michelle), Brian Backer (Alfred), Larry Joshua (Glazer), Jason Alexander (Dave), Ned Eisenberg (Eddy).
Distributed by: Thorn EMI

Originally distributed by Thorn EMI. In 1992 Thorn EMI released an uncut version of the film with 19 seconds of cuts made by the BFFC. In 2002 Vipco released an uncut DVD of the film with BBFC finally releasing an uncut version. The Burning was prosecuted and included on the official DPP list of banned films.

Plot:
The Burning tells the story of an ex-summer camp caretaker (Cropsy) who was badly disfigured during a prank, which went horribly wrong when he was badly burned. After being discharged from hospital Cropsy returns to camp and is hell bent on taking revenge on the teenagers who initiated the prank, which led to his life of torment. These unlucky campers come face to face with shear wielding maniac Cropsy; will there be any survivors?

Appraisal:
The Burning is a classic 1980's slasher which is not dissimilar to "Friday the 13th" both of the films are two of my favourite slasher films of all time. Tom Savini provided make up special effects here and for "Friday the 13th" and for far too many horror features to list in this paragraph. The film does hold up well and is an enjoyable watch, so much so that it joins my annual Halloween horrorathon. Look out for a young Jason Alexander and Holly Hunter in the film. Director and writer Tony Maylam does a great job but unfortunately didn't seem to direct a lot after this film.

The Burning is a most welcome addition to the DPP list for horror fans but obviously not for the distributors of the movie at the time. Now we just sit back and wait for Hollywood to do a bad job of re-making this classic horror movie, which is only a matter of time. There are lots of slasher films out there and most aren't that great, but "The Burning" is one of the very few classic 80s slasher films that does deliver in all areas.

This classic slasher is everything you would expect from a 1980's stalk n' slash flick. In my opinion the fact Cropsy the psycho killer doesn't wear a mask makes this even more effective and scary, Cropsy's mask is his own face, which was burnt by an evil prankster. This film is a cult slasher, sleaze offering which is very enjoyable and will stand the test of time.

The Burning or as I like to call it "The Banning" did suffer at the hands of the censors. The film was originally cut then released uncut and later banned outright, it was then released with cuts and eventually released uncut. The film was uncut for its z rated theatrical release, it's not until you watch the uncut version in all its glory that you notice just how good Tom Savini's effects are. The scene with the killer on the raft hacking fingers off and puncturing the throat with gardening shears is done so well and is very effective, especially for the time.

The Burning was released in 1982 by Thorn EMI, Thorn unknowingly released the uncut version of the film which was soon replaced with the cut version though there were rumors of high street video stores keeping the uncut version for sale or rental. Later, in October 1983 the film was outright banned and joined the video nasty time capsule.

The Burning is just fantastic! It really is a must watch for all horror film fans!

I've yet to find a horror fan who doesn't like "The Burning" it will remain the guilty pleasure of horror fans for years to come!

-Tony Newton

There are two great joys of The Burning. One is seeing Jason Alexander aka George Costanza of Seinfeld as a summer camp frat fool, the other is the Rick Wakeman soundtrack. I bought this on vinyl for 50 pence at the first HMV sale I went to, and I still adore it. Listening to the title track, as played on the album; you can't help but imagine an elf dancing much like Spinal Tap's Stonehenge.

-Robin Ince   Writer/Comedian.

The Burning is nothing short of a joyful surprise. Even by the end of the title sequence, the hopes are high as many of the names involved went on to be big players in the movie industry. It was one of the first movies to be produced by Miramax, with the original story being accredited to Bob Weinstein, with production duties falling upon his brother Harvey. The cinematic entrepreneurs were clearly intent on capitalising upon the rise of teen slasher movies, which were prevalent at the time, going so far as to draft in *Friday 13th* makeup artist and special effects maestro Tom Savini.

The score was created by Rick Wakeman, who does a fantastic job of providing not just a wonderful accompaniment to the movie, but a superb standalone album as well. *The Burning* features the onscreen debuts of several actors who would come very well known, including Holly Hunter (*The Piano*), Jason Alexander (*Seinfeld*) and Fisher Stevens (*Hackers / Short Circuit*). The result of knowing these faces so well does create a minor distraction from time to time as you do find yourself pausing occasionally to comment something on the lines of *"Oh wow, look how young they were"*.

The story itself is an age old one, but delivered with confidence and to great success. At a summer camp in 1976 a group of teens decide to play a prank on the sadistic and alcoholic Cropsy, one of the employees. The prank goes horribly wrong and Cropsy is engulfed in flame (with the stuntman's fire repellent suit being entirely visible). He is sent to a burns unit for the next five years where even the nurses are terrified of his grisly appearance. He is finally released and the first thing he does is to butcher a prostitute, before making his way to another summer camp to have his revenge.

The camp provides the filmmakers with all the excuses that they need for a variety of shower scenes, skinny-dipping and various other acts of adolescent promiscuity. After a few red herrings the murders begin and the terror soon spreads throughout the previously idyllic woodland setting.

In terms of advanced narrative, there is not a whole lot of originality on offer, but that doesn't affect the impact which the movie has. Even though the teens are ousted one by one in an almost direct retelling of *Friday 13th*, or *Bay of Blood*, there is still something, which makes this movie worthy of recommendation. The goofy humour and knowing ridiculousness of the whole affair are almost regularly alluded to by the filmmakers. An elaborate multiple death frenzy involving some gardening shears and a succession of impalements and gashes seems to have been the main bone of contention for the DPP when this film was picked up.

Originally released by Thorn-EMI, it was cleared of obscenity and went on to be released in a slightly edited form afterwards. The final revelation of the perpetrator does, unfortunately, cause more giggles than gasps. Savini reportedly only had a few days in which to construct the makeup for Cropsy, which is why he looks slightly more mutated than burnt. It is Savini's work, however, which creates the anchor for the rest of the movie, with severed limbs and gallons of blood awash on the screen throughout.

The Burning, whilst not particularly evil, is certainly a gruesome delight. The soundtrack is definitely its most killer asset, and it certainly helped to set the template for the onslaught of slasher flicks, which followed in its wake.

-Colin McCracken   Writer.

While Jason was the king of the campsite killing, he wasn't out there all alone. Cropsy (check out a recent documentary on this true American urban legend) was a summer camp caretaker burnt to insanity by a group of young campers. Five years later he is out of the hospital and out for revenge. Is it as polished as Voorhees vehicles? No. But just like Friday it had a major star making a first appearance. No, not Kevin Footloose Bacon but Holly Hunter. The music by Rick Wakeman is 80s slick (make of that what you will) and of course Tom Savini is in the effects mix. This film scared the living bejesus out of me. Even now one scene sticks in my head. The new campers (and there are always new campers) gather around the fire on the first night and the tale of Cropsy is told. At the mention of his iconic shears, they appear out of the darkness between two of the kids and snap silently shut before vanishing again into the black night. There were no sequels. There will be no re-imagining. There doesn't need to be. The Burning is what The Burning is. Of its time. Creepy. Scary. With some real 'jumps' throughout. What sets it aside was that in the UK an uncut version was released on video. Although compared to today's torture porn norm, the contentious scenes were nothing to write home about, but back then they were enough for The Burning to receive the tag of being a Video Nasty.

-Craig jones   Writer/Author.

When VHS finally replaced Betamax in our house in 1989, it was as if a previously unseen world opened up to me when I went to Video Magic, my local video store, in my hometown of Port Moody, British Columbia. In 1990, when I was seventeen, I got my own membership card and was able to rent movies on my own, and having that laminated yellow piece of plastic in my wallet gave me more of a sense of independence than I felt throughout my twenties.

No longer restricted to the hinterlands of the store's shrinking Beta section, I finally was able to wander throughout the entire store, and I started with the Horror section. With my eyes and my mind overloaded by the rush of new titles that had previously been unavailable to me, because of Beta and also my mother, I began the process of going down my mental list of unseen films, one title at a time, and one of the first videos I rented was *The Burning*.

Filmed in 1980, just weeks after the release of *Friday the 13th*, and released in 1981, *The Burning* is the best and most well-known of the post-*Friday the 13th* summer camp slasher films, but I was virtually unaware of the film's pedigree when I rented the film for the first time on a Friday morning in the summer of 1990, the summer before I entered my senior year of high school.

Terrified of the new school year, and gripped by agoraphobic paralysis, leaving my house and walking down the hill to the video store was a big adventure for me, especially without being seen by someone I knew, a difficult feat given that Port Moody was still a small town back then. Nowadays, Video Magic is long gone, Port Moody has been overrun by construction and condominiums, and I don't know anyone who lives here anymore.

Why did I pick *The Burning*? A few years earlier, I'd heard people at elementary school mention the film, so I knew the title, but I was really motivated to see the film when I read a review in *Fangoria* that praised the film's cheerful decadence, and how it served as an emblem of the slasher crazy era of the early 80s, a time when, and I quote the *Fangoria* review from memory, "everyone and their sister was making slasher movies."

That was all I knew about *The Burning* at that point, although I dimly recall noting that *The Burning* was the first production from Miramax Films, the once fledgling production entity that was just beginning to flourish in the late 80s. I also recognized several faces and names in the cast, especially Jason Alexander, Brian Backer of *Fast Times at Ridgemont High* fame, Holly Hunter, and Fisher Stevens, several years before they became famous.

The real marquee name in the film, of course, was effects expert Tom Savini, fresh off of his triumph in *Friday the 13th*. I didn't know that Miramax boss Harvey Weinstein had recruited Savini to work on *The Burning* after Weinstein saw *Friday the 13th*, or that Savini was later sent out to promote the film, but I sure recognized Savini's handiwork in the film.

I watched *The Burning* that first time while I was sitting on the living-room carpet, against the glare of the sun that shot through the living-room curtains, the appearance of which always made me depressed that I was inside, but not on that day. When I'd picked up the video box for *The Burning*, I was surprised when I looked at the back cover and saw a list of review quotes, praising the film in terms of its execution, its shock value and its emphasis on suspense. I hadn't yet read Leonard Maltin's review, where he rated the film a Bomb.

What I saw in the film was a synthesis of all of the slasher movie conventions that I'd already long memorized at that point in my life, but had never seen presented in such merciless, swift, unapologetic fashion. A character is disfigured and plots revenge. Check. Summer camp setting. Check. There's a group of camp counsellors, who are either so loathsome you're begging for them to be killed, or so goody-goody that you want them to be killed just for the sake of variety. Check. They're all killed one by one save for a few pure-hearted survivors, one of whom discovers the killer's lair and eventually kills the freak, known as Cropsy in the film.

Seeing those conventions unfold so crudely and being able to rattle them off on my fingers was a lot of fun back then and made me feel smart, a feeling I never had at school. The most fun I had watching *The Burning* was in the sequence when the counsellors are riding along in a canoe and are attacked by Cropsy, who rises out of a seemingly abandoned canoe and proceeds to chop digits with his trademark shears. I hadn't seen that before.

I rented the film again in the 90s, but without the element of surprise, both in terms of the film itself and my discovery of it, I couldn't bring myself to watch it again, much as I wanted to. In 2009, I bought the special edition DVD, which was informative but which I found very depressing, making me wish I was back in the summer of 1990, seventeen years old, when most of my life story was still unwritten.

-David Grove   Author of *Jamie Lee Curtis*: Scream Queen and *On Location in Blairstown*: The Making of Friday the 13th.

It's been a very long time since seeing a video nasty, so I had to revisit the genre to review these films. Growing up in the VHS period, I came across these movies accidentally when browsing through a family members pirate-video collection, and would watch them when no one was around...regardless to say that these VHS versions weren't of the greatest quality, thus it made for a more 'nasty' viewing. So, watching these movies again, this time viewed from Blu-ray versions, was an improved blast from the past.

I watched this movie a lot between the age of 10 and 15, due to having access to a poor quality pirate VHS copy, where I'd even tell friends about the movie, and try to give them the opportunity to see it, too. So watching it again many years later – in higher quality – it was great to see why it had appeal back then.

The Burning has great characters and decent dynamics between them, and, an interesting enough story so that it doesn't have to lower itself to desperation elements such as masses of nudity and over-the-top gore – the nudity is tasteful and hot, and, the death scenes are quick and effective.

One thing I wasn't aware of when I was younger is that the movie is a product of Harvey Weinstein chain, I'm sure he was less than pleased when the film was banned in the UK.

-Shaun Troke   Filmmaker.

I never went to Summer Camp. The closest I got was a three-day stay at a camp during elementary school for a program called R.O.E. (Resident Outdoor Education).... MEATBALLS (1979) was one of my favorite Billy Murray comedies; I even had the movie tie-in from the School's book club. A summer camp is the perfect setting for a slasher film, as Sean S. Cunningham was to discover the following year. Time to put to rest a wrong about THE BURNING (1981), which many reviews claim....this film was not a rip off of

FRIDAY THE 13TH, as Harvey Weinstein of Miramax registered his treatment (called THE CROPSY MURDERS) of THE BURNING before Cunningham's movie was released. The film was not the hit FRIDAY THE 13TH was, but it is a well-made horror flick with a cast that was better than most of these types of movies. Jason Alexander (Seinfeld), Fisher Stevens (SHORT CIRCUIT, SHORT CIRCUIT 2) and Holly Hunter (BROADCAST NEWS, RAISING ARIZONA) were just a few to go on to bigger and better things. Brian Backer (FAST TIMES AT RIDEMONT HIGH) is the film's FINAL GUY instead of the usual final girl. Larry Joshua is Glazer, the bully, who torments him. The movie begins with a group of kids at Camp Blackfoot playing a prank on caretaker Cropsy (Lou David), which backfires. Cropsy is burned and spends the next five years trying not to look like a deep-fried monster. The skin grafts fail and Cropsy finds, much to his displeasure, that even hookers won't have anything to do with him. Cropsy kills the prostitute and heads over to Camp Stonewater (Camp Blackfoot was closed after the fire) to work out his frustrations with a pair of garden shears. Tom Savini, who did the effects for FRIDAY THE 13TH, works his gory magic, especially on the infamous raft scene where our crispy maniac dispatches a raft full of unsuspecting teens in brutal fashion. THE BURNING was one of the first Video Nasties, banned from the U.K. because it would traumatize the kiddies who might rent it from the video stores. It was a long time coming to DVD, not making its American debut until the fall of 2007. Scream Factory released it on Blu-Ray in 2013.

-David Brown   Writer.

Cannibal Apocalypse

Also known as "Apocalypse Domani" and "Invasion of the Flesh Hunters"
Year of release: 1980
Writers: Antonio Margheriti and Dardano Sacchetti
Director: Antonio Margheriti
R rating 96 mins. Italy, Spain
Tagline: "In the jungle, or in the city, still they must EAT!"
Main cast: John Saxon (Norman Hopper), Elizabeth Turner (Jane Hopper), Giovanni Lombardo Radice (Charlie Bukowski), Cinzia De Carolis (Mary), Tony King (Tom Thompson), Wallace Wilkinson (Captain McCoy).
Distributed by: Replay
Originally distributed by Replay in 1982. In 2010 the film was released by Cinema Club on DVD with 2 seconds of cuts from the BBFC. Cannibal Apocalypse was prosecuted and included on the official DPP list of banned films.

Plot:
Released back into society from a psychiatric institution following a horrifying experience at a Vietnam prisoner of war camp in which their former friends were forced to turn to cannibalism.
"Who will survive the Cannibal Apocalypse?"

Appraisal:
Vietnam veterans Norman Hopper (played by cult favorite John Saxon) and Charlie Bukowski Giovanni Lombardo Radice wreak havoc when their cannibalistic desires and lust for blood take over as the deadly virus they brought back with them turns their victims into flesh hungry cannibals This zombie pandemic style film has strong undertones of PTSD suffering, this alone provides an original take on the genre. This cannibal offering does seem to lack gore somewhat but doesn't disappoint as an enjoyable and unique horror film, John Saxon is on fine form in this cult cannibal zombie flick.

This 1980's horror flick does seems to get a bad rap for some unknown reason. Cannibal Apocalypse is an obvious cash in on George Romero's "Dawn of the Dead", and other late 70's Italian zombie features. Mixing the popular Vietnam War elements with the even more popular cannibal genre was a clusterfuck of cleverness and a great way to pull in viewers. The Vietnam scenes only last a few minutes and work really well, the idea for the film alone is fantastic. Vietnam war veteran brings home a contagion virus, which turns people into rabid cannibals when bitten.

The film does tick all the boxes for me, yes it's low budget but I'm a sucker for Italian horror films and "Cannibal Apocalypse" is no exception. This cannibal zombie-esque film is a fresh take on the genre, the mix works really well. John Saxon stole the show here, as ever, his presence as usual dominates the screen. Giovanni Lomabrado Radice was fantastic as Charlie Bukowski everything about his performance just radiates a true Vietnam vet with a hunger for flesh.

My favourite scene is Charlie watching a Vietnam war movie at the cinema whilst a young couple make out, he proceeds to bite a chunk out of the woman's neck It's so wrong, but I love the use of showing the war film and in a strange way an aftermath that effects soldiers with PTSD.

I think "Cannibal Apocalypse" was a clever way of raising awareness of the post trauma soldiers experienced from the Vietnam War; a new and original way to bring awareness to PTSD. This is definitely one to watch, don't expect a standard cannibal horror film, it's far from that but a unique and original twist on a few genres which just seems to work. Was this the inspiration for "28 Days Later"?...who knows?

-Tony Newton

Cannibal Ferox

Also known as "Make Them Die Slowly".
Year of release: 1981
Writer: Umberto Lenzi
Director: Umberto Lenzi
Unrated 93 mins. Italy

Tagline: "They raped and killed his sister while he watched helplessly. Now it's his turn to make them die slowly."

Main cast: Giovanni Lombardo Radice (Mike Logan), Lorraine De Selle (Gloria Davis), Danilo Mattei (Rudy Davis), Zora Kerova (Pat Johnson), Walter Lucchini (Joe Costolani), Fiamma Maglione (Myrna Stenn).

Distributed by: Replay

Originally distributed on VHS by Replay in its uncut form. There were 2 versions on VHS in the early 80's the uncut one and a cut version, cut by 6.51 seconds, this was unofficially cut by the BBFC, both versions were prosecuted. In 2000 an extra 6 seconds were added to the ordinary cut 6.51 seconds version but was passed for UK viewing. In 2006, Aquarius distributed an uncut, unrated version. Cannibal Ferox finally saw a new cut in 2018 with a shameless limited Blu-ray release that was Passed 18 for strong bloody violence and gore featuring previous cuts waived but still missing 1:55s of BBFC compulsory animal cruelty scenes cut. Cannibal Ferox was prosecuted and included on the official DPP list of banned films.

Plot:
In New York City Gloria works on a dissertation, which aims to disprove the myth of Amazonian cannibal tribes. They head to the jungle but become abandoned in the Amazonian forest when their car becomes stuck in the mud leaving them stranded in the jungle for the night, it's here that the group meet up with jewel smugglers Mike and Joe who are heavily under the influence of drugs, when one of the drug crazed jewel thieves shoots a member of the Indio tribe the tribe revert back to their cannibalistic ways and begin to exact their revenge on the unwanted inhabitants. Will there be any survivors?

Appraisal:
Cannibal Ferox put the nasty in video nasty! Animal cruelty in any way, shape or form turns my stomach, but in most cases its nothing that you wouldn't see in an animal documentary nowadays and it's very effective against the backdrop of the other killings on screen. The soundtrack is incredibly powerful and builds tension nicely, the music parallels killings or a brutal attack, which is a nice touch and adds to the atmospherics of the film! "Cannibal Ferox" is undoubtedly one of the best films on the list, the acting is faultless and the storyline believable as you could imagine something like this actually happening.

This film provides chills and scares and still manages to shock audiences today, which is no mean feat especially with the shit people are watching on the Internet nowadays. Cannibal Ferox stands out as one of the most shocking titles on the DPP list and as a very innovative and creative piece of cinema. This has to be one of director Umberto Lenzi's finest pieces of work.

I love this film as much today as I did watching it through partially closed eyes all those years ago, this film is a total classic and a masterpiece of cult horror cinema!

Cannibal Ferox has a feel all of its own! The film is a heart pounding, visceral treat, a non-stop hell ride that the viewer goes on from the very start building to a fantastic climax at the end!

If you haven't seen "Cannibal Ferox" where have you been hiding? If you have, dig out that old VHS copy and let Umberto Lenzi and the magnetic tape work its magic once again!.

-Tony Newton

Two sisters, along with their friend Pat, travel into the Paraguayan Rain Forest to prove cannibalism in the modern world is a myth. The group meet Mike, a sleazy New York drug dealer, and his friend Joe, who have been partying it up in South America, whilst trying to attain a massive score. Joe becomes seriously injured, and that night, while the group is asleep, one of the sisters goes missing. Joe reveals that it was he and Mike who incensed and subsequently triggered the ferocity of a local tribe, while using them to find drugs and emeralds. After this, the entire group is captured. Several scenes of graphic mutilation follow. This is another of the better-known cannibal films and, like many of its contemporaries, it fell afoul of censors worldwide. It was eventually banned in 31 countries, and marks Umberto Lenzi's third trip to the jungle to make a cannibal film. With an infectious soundtrack and some truly shocking sequences, this is one of the nastiest and best of the bunch.

-David Bond

The fun you can have with this film is unbelievable. It has some of the best dialogue ever! I
believe they discovered the word 'twat' on set! This has some mean gore and you can see strong similarities between this one and Cannibal Holocaust - although I slightly prefer Cannibal Holocaust this is still well worth a watch if you love your classic Italian cannibal movies! Giovanni Lombardo Radice aka John Morghen makes this a truly thrilling and fun film to watch, his character added a real exploitation charm - it's almost the cherry on top.

-Jason Impey   Filmmaker.

Classic exploitative gratuitous genital mutilation. Breasts through hooks and a penis removed and eaten by a vengeful tribal chief. Drug fuelled gratuitous violence. Just say no in my opinion.

-John Thomson   Actor/Comedian.

The damning aspect of that opening quote is the fact that it succinctly represented the views of the sneering Daily Mail reading middle-classes. It was also delivered by the epitome of what they embody – a stuffy segment of society, out of touch and unwilling to escape the utopian Island mentality they immerse themselves in.

This nasty era level of censorship and outrage has always existed. Take Memoirs of a Woman of Pleasure (aka Fanny Hill), written by the author John Cleland and published in 1748. Considered the first erotic novel in the English language, its publication saw Cleland arrested for obscenity while the book itself has been banned, seized and smuggled around countries throughout its history. Sound familiar?

Art exists to connect with our primal feelings. The medium in which it's presented is irrelevant – art, literature, poetry or film. It should never be censored because all that represents is the more powerful members of society attempting to control what common people are permitted to watch, read or view. As James Ferman (BBFC director 1975-99) damningly said ""It's alright for you middle-class cineastes to see this film, but what would happen if a factory worker from Manchester happened to see it?".

After establishing my general disdain for censorship of any kind, I have to say I find Cannibal Ferox thoroughly grim and disgusting. In fact, after watching it three times in short succession I really don't think I could bear to look at it again anytime soon. Having said that, Cannibal Ferox IS a fascinating piece of filmmaking and – forgive the cliché – is a product of its time. In 1980 the cult Italian director Ruggero Deodato released perhaps the most infamous video nasty of all – Cannibal Holocaust. Its worldwide notoriety is stuff of legend with classic tales such as the film being seized by the Italian courts, Deodato arrested on grounds of obscenity then later charged with murdering several actors on camera. Irrespective of this insanity, such controversy (not to mention iconic artwork) ensured that the film was a massive success on video worldwide, so much so that Italian film producers immediately requested more of the same.

Umberto Lenzi at the start of the 1980s was a well-established Italian director whose career had managed to successfully move in time with the various genres that his homeland specialized in. From sword and sandal epics like Samson and the Slave Queen (1963) to Euro spy with cheese like 008: Operation Exterminate (1965), Lenzi proved that he could adapt to any style of picture. He shot a Spaghetti Western with Pistol for a Hundred Coffins (1968), and a Gialli in Seven Blood-Stained Orchids (1972), but his directorial ability was best showcased in the Poliziotteschi movies he shot in the 70s such as Milano Rovente (1973), Almost Human (1974) and The Manhunt (1975).

"I'm ashamed of this movie. It's not fantasy, it's reality. There's a political side (to it). It's a bit Fascist in the deepest sense" - Giovanni Lombardo Radice

By the time Cannibal Ferox came around, Lenzi already had previous with this niche horror sub-genre. In fact some have even said that he started the Italian cannibal craze with the release of The Man from Deep River in 1972 – a grisly little flick starring Me Me Lai and Ivan Rassimov. Ferox begins in New York City in the wake of a heroin trafficking scheme gone wrong where we meet Lt. Rizzo (ironically played by Robert Kerman, the lead in Cannibal Holocaust) who is on the lookout for 'Mike', the key suspect in this drug deal who appears to have skipped town. Without much in the way of cohesive narrative we then find ourselves introduced to Gloria (Lorraine de Selle), Rudy (Danile Mattei) and Pat (Zora Kerova) who are on the way into the jungle for the purpose of completing Gloria's doctoral thesis which claims cannibalism doesn't exist. Soon after their arrival into the tropical South American location they run into the fugitive Mike (Giovanni Lombardo Radice) who along with his friend Joe (Walter Lucchini) states that they have just escaped the clutches of some cannibals – cue some gratuitous mastication!

"The following feature is one of the most violent films ever made. There are at least two-dozen scenes of barbaric torture and sadistic cruelty graphically shown. If the presentation of disgusting and repulsive subject matter upsets you, please do not view this film."

The above quote is the first thing you see when you watch Cannibal Ferox. As with any scaremongering warning that finds itself either adorning the video sleeve or the film itself, it's a ploy I've always treated with a great deal of cynicism. With Ferox though it's actually damningly accurate with the words 'disgusting' and 'repulsive' being the ones that most succinctly describe this grim natured piece of filmmaking. The animal cruelty in the film I find far worse than Cannibal Holocaust. There a coati being (very slowly) strangled by a snake with the camera staying fixed on it as it squeals in pain. Radice states that the Italian crew stopped and refused to film any more of the scene until the animal was aided to safety. Elsewhere we have a monkey being attacked by a jaguar, an iguana fending off a snake, a live turtle having its head and legs chopped off and a crocodile being killed and eaten by natives. It's grim viewing, and while some of the contemporary nasties have seemed to mellow with age as some make-up effects become somewhat outdated, these scenes from Ferox retain the same vomit-inducing ferocity as back when it was originally released. It's not just the animal cruelty that repulses the viewer either. Nightmarish scenes litter the movie such as a woman being hung up with meat hooks inserted into her breasts, Radice's character having his penis chopped off with a machete (then eaten), and also the top of his skull sliced off and his brains scooped out by natives.

What makes the animal cruelty worse though is Lenzi's apparent lack of contrition as he looks back on it. He states "I think a lot of this movie. I wasn't sure before now, but I find it very professional". Even during these barbaric scenes he seems to view them with an air of nonchalance, which is in direct opposition to Giovanni Lombardo Radice who you can almost sense squirming as he watches the picture. "We should have been forbidden to do things like this" he says during one of the films' most notorious sequences. Even during the shoot he states how he refused to perform certain acts like killing a pig despite Lenzi's dogged insistence.

There's an irony in Radice saying things like this as in the film his character is an absolute horror of a man. He's arrogantly misogynistic as he refers to the women as "twats", he's always on coke and he also kills a native woman with a remorseless arrogance that makes him a thoroughly reprehensible individual. Conversely in real life Radice is a gentleman and he looks back on Ferox as a big mistake in his career. He was a classically trained actor who preferred the stage to the screen, and he dismisses Lenzi's film at any given opportunity – "what you're saying is shit, what you're doing is shit, but you have to be serious". He's never been afraid to dismiss Lenzi's ability either and once said that "these types of Italian directors were not renowned for working with actors".

Cannibal Ferox was released on home video in the UK in 1982 by Replay Video in an uncut pre-cert version that ran to just over 89 minutes. Needless to say it was listed as a video nasty in July 1983, with the cut version having a whopping 6 minutes and 51 seconds removed from it. It was resubmitted to the BBFC in 2001 by Gold's in a pre-cut version (the same 6:51 removed) only to have another six seconds cut due to the sight of a small animal on the end of a rope banging against the side of a jeep. In America it was released uncut in 2006 on the Grindhouse Releasing label, which is the edition that this writer used to catch an in-depth glance over the last few weeks.

Critically Cannibal Ferox pales quite starkly in relation to Cannibal Holocaust, with the latter being a far more accomplished production. The fact that recently Ruggero Deodato did a special director's cut removing all the animal cruelty speaks volumes towards how he views what is contained in his infamous film. Ferox meanwhile remains as gratuitous as always. The narrative is very haphazardly plotted while the characters don't engage you as much as the perilous situation needs them to. Perhaps Gloria comes closest to achieving some affinity with the audience, but the others leave you cold – and as I mentioned earlier the character of Mike is surely one of the most repellent committed to celluloid. Upon its release the horror press condemned it, and in this subsequent passage of time it's fared no better. Cinema Crazed call it "clunky and tedious" while DVD Talk say it's "poorly made".

Personally speaking, I first caught Cannibal Ferox on Vipco VHS many years ago as I educated myself about just what video nasties were. At the time (and in cut form) it seemed fun, and it also was a badge of honour to a young horror viewer having sat through such an infamous film. Revisiting the film (uncut) in 2014 it's striking just how poor it is. I endured the animal cruelty on the first viewing but each subsequent time after that I had to turn away. It's a needless, offensive ploy to simply give the film a shock value. It's succeeded in many ways in that 33 years after its release we're still talking about this movie, and admittedly as a historical document it does have a place in the legacy of envelope pushing horror films. It's not to be celebrated though, nor is it to be fawned over – and you can't help but think if it didn't attract the attention of an over-zealous BBFC whether it would simply just be consigned to a footnote in Italian horror history, a place where it's probably best abandoned.

-Dave Wain   Writer: Zombiehamster.

What a terrible little gem of a film. Murdered natives, a lopped off penis, and a gouged out eyeball… everything needed for a romantic comedy… in Hell. This film features some of the roughest scenes in its particular genre. There is, at least, a bit of justice in the film, as the main antagonist gets what he deserves (the aforementioned penis lopping) in the end. Even if it looks as fake as can be, the eating of it really seals the deal for me. In many ways, this film is every bit as brutal as Cannibal Holocaust, but it never seemed as dirty to me for whatever reason. It is a mean spirited film for sure, but I think it is nowhere near as bleak and its characters nowhere near as irredeemable as those in Cannibal Holocaust. There is also a stronger storyline in place here, to be sure. The cannibal film as a whole is something I can't say I've ever been a fan of, yet I'm always drawn in and curious about the levels of depravity the filmmakers will lower themselves to. Another honorable mention in this genre is the uncut version of *Mountain of The Cannibal God*.

-Brian Steward   Artist/Fangoria Magazine, GoreZone Magazine, Delirium Magazine.

Cannibal Holocaust

Year of release: 1980
Writer: Gianfranco Clerici
Director: Ruggero Deodato
Unrated 95 mins. Italy
Tagline: Savage! Terrifying! True!
Main cast: Robert Kerman (Harold Monroe), Francesca Ciardi (Faye Daniels), Perry Pirkanen (Jack Anders), Luca Barbareschi (Marc Tomaso), Salvatore Basile (Chaco Losojos), Carl Gabriel Yorke (Alan Yates).
Distributed by: Go-Video

In 2001 the film was released with 5.44 seconds removed by the BBFC. This film still has 15 seconds of footage cut for its UK release but is available in a director's edition with less animal violence still with 15 seconds cut distributed by Shameless DVD 2011.

Plot:
In Cannibal Holocaust Professor Harold Monroe travels to the rain forests of South American search of a missing documentary crew. Whilst amongst the Yanomamo tribe he discovers the remains of the documentary crew along with their reels of film, what happens next questions just who the cannibals really are as the reels show atrocities the documentary crew themselves inflicted on the tribe before the cannibals ultimate vengeance.

Appraisal:
This famous prosecuted nasty... is very nasty indeed! Ruggero Deodato was famously inspired to make Cannibal Holocaust after speaking with his son about a recent viewing of news coverage on terrorism following the Red Brigades in Italy and how the media could stage certain aspects on news.

Ruggero Deodato learned his craft under the wing of Italian director Roberto Rosselini also working as an assistant director on Sergio Corbucci's "Django" during his career. Ruggero Deodato has his own unique style of filmmaking and is not afraid to think outside of the box, with "Cannibal Holocaust" he annihilated the box and pretty much took a shit on it!

Where do you start with this masterpiece? Okay I'm going to bitch about animal cruelty but this film is the utter dogs bollocks! I love it with a passion! I still have a really bad third generation VHS copy of this, yeah it's bad, it's not worth the magnetic tape it's on, it's got the start of something more evil than any video nasty, mold-forming, but it was that very tape that put the fear in me!

This is Ruggero Deodato's most controversial film and one of the most controversial films of all time. Cannibal holocaust very cleverly intertwines supposed discovered documentary footage of the original party and their fate along with the standard horror movie fair! This film was not only very well marketed but it seemed marketing was at the forefront when they wrote the script. This film is the best found footage movie ever made, it's obvious to see why it made it to the video nasty list as "Cannibal Holocaust" paved the way for films of this genre being the first ever found footage film of its kind.

Cannibal Holocaust contains a lot of scenes of animal cruelty, which are real, or at least I think they are all real (the scene with the turtle turn my stomach even now!). For me animal cruelty ruins many cannibal films, that` aside "Cannibal Holocaust" is a very original and gory horror film that is on a level all of it's own.

This type of documentary style gory cannibal film wasn't new for Italian cinema including the Classic "Mono Cane" 1962. Cannibal Holocaust pulls it out of the bag and remakes the bag (with human flesh). Cannibal Holocaust created an experience of its own. I remember initially watching Cannibal Holocaust on a bootleg VHS video and not knowing if it was real or not, I think the film being banned added both to the film and the whole viewing experience.

Imagine if "Paranormal Activity" or "The Blair Witch Project" not only had the found footage thing going for it, but had also been banned and copies passed around the underground film circuit.

Ruggero Deodato was actually tried in court on suspicion that he actually killed the cast of his film "Cannibal Holocaust" it was not until he bought along the actors themselves into court that he was cleared, though Ruggero Deodato was actually fired for the use of animal cruelty.

This film has to win the prize for the most controversial of all the films on the DPP list and one of the most controversial horror film ever made. The first of the found footage genre that no one can seem to emulate in the right way. Everything about this film is so unique and so cleverly put together, this is how you make a horror film, this is the bar setter!

Cannibal Holocaust is one of, if not the best horror movie of all time. This ground breaker is hands down the most shocking and disturbing film on the Video Nasty hit list, but one of the best without a doubt, it certainly leaves you thinking and questioning everything. This film is not for the casual horror film fan and be prepared to enter a different kind of hell here, full of shocks and disturbing scenes. I've never watched the uncut version without squinting or going to make a cup of tea when certain parts are coming up!

Cannibal Holocaust does feature Genuine footage of animals being killed on screen, thus leading to Ruggero Deodato and co being found guilty by the court for obscenity and animal cruelty which features in the film. Ruggero Deodato is one of my favorite directors of all time, but if you're not a fan of "Cannibal Holocaust" at least give the soundtrack a spin, Riz Ortolani's score is superb and compliments the film perfectly.

The stand out scenes are the rape which is both brutal and horrific to watch, the woman being mutilated by a tribesman for infidelity and the turtle scene, even to this day I can't re-watch that scene, once was enough for me! I always fast forward straight past that scene, but bring on the human carnage and total horror that is Cannibal Holocaust! A true video nasty for sure!

-Tony Newton

Cannibal Holocaust has been the most difficult film of my career, definitely the most watched (and this should also explain something about the strong choices of the audience), and certainly the most abused and the most complicated to manage in the chaos of hypocrisy cultural and respectable. My generation grew up after the war, when the campaign was alive and living cultural traditions and established certain rites. For example, the death of the pig was just a party in the country world, this rite being planned for time and all attended (including children) to the violent sacrifice of the beast which was slaughtered and bled to death. Then there was the incident of the transformation of the cocks in capons, pigeons that were drowned because they remain the tenderest meat, and many baby kittens were chosen and then drowned in the river because they were, as they say, limited. We grew up in the cultural normality of these violent events. Then I have to say that "Cannibal Holocaust" is now thirty years old, and I had behind me is still fresh in my youth, my rural experience. In life, beyond all, shows like this, even the most obscene cruelty and truth, are still going on today in slaughterhouses, for example, or by the laws still in force, which still recognize the scientific value of vivisection on defenseless animals. "I do not regret anything", but the culture, the one that I express, has always been against a violent reality. And "Cannibal Holocaust", made with all the trappings of truth, even the most heinous, was and remains a film against the violence of the complaint, and not a splatter, but unfortunately still not be interpreted in the correct way. "Cannibal Holocaust", in particular, has not speculated, because life in the Amazon, where the film was shot, had daily violent situations, such as those described in the film, with absolute normality. We shot with a sketchy screenplay, I was in places and filming, I sent the material to Milan to Mifed (the most important film market in the world), and there it was bought by countries around the world unseen. The producer from Rome repeated, "filming Ruggero runs as you can and send the movies. I met his wife at a festival of Joe Dante's; she did not want to believe I was the director of a film as bad as "Cannibal Holocaust."

"Why, you do not have a pierced tongue and on the lashes, you do not have blue hair and orange, or tattoos?" I asked the lady just amazed Dante. The French call me "Monsieur Cannibal," and I like it.

-Ruggero Deodato   Director of "Cannibal Holocaust".

Where do you start and what can you say about this epic monster of a movie! Well I believe that this is actually a very relevant and intellectual film. It has a very strong clear message about society and the world we live in, it is almost too clever for its own good as it mocks what it actually is itself! It is certainly not for the squeamish, and is a very hard and shocking view, however it is an absolute amazing piece of filmmaking and is the granddad of found footage films. The story is told it a fantastic manner and the film is not scared to make such a bold in your face statement. Once seen - never forgotten. Everything about this motion picture is haunting, the visuals, the story and the score, and together they make a truly unforgettable cinematic experience.

-Jason Impey   Filmmaker.

No overview of the 'video nasty' phenomena would be complete without careful consideration of what many consider to be not one of the most provocative entries in the core group of criminalized titles to appear on the original banned list but a title that remains, quite simply, one of the most infamous horror movies ever made.

Ruggero Deodato began his long and chequered career as first assistant to Roberto Rossellini, though few could have guessed to what ends his grounding in neo-realism would lead. His masterwork concerns four Americans who set out for a remote corner of the Amazon known as the 'green inferno' to document the last tribes to practice cannibalism. Months later, a second expedition follows and succeeds in retrieving the unexposed footage shot by the missing explorers, the film cans left unopened by the superstitious natives who believe they contain 'evil spirits'. In a plot device borrowed to lesser effect by 'THE BLAIR WITCH PROJECT' (1999) and virtually every other 'found footage' film that followed in it's wake, what follows purports to be the unedited rushes charting the explorers' demise. The 'twist' in the tale comes with the revelation that the atrocities have been committed not by stone age 'savages' but by the film makers themselves in their rapacious quest for sensational footage. By the time the locals turn on the documentary crew in the last reel, their fate is richly deserved.

While the self-reflexive structure serves as an apt metaphor for Western exploitation of the third world, the apparent critique of the brutal methods employed by the fictional crew offers a copper bottomed excuse for Deodato to duplicate their actions, committing to camera a series of scenes utterly beyond the pale of acceptable civilized human conduct in what amounts to – if not a crime against cinema – then at the very least one of the most morally reprehensible motion pictures ever made and an enduring monument to mankind's capacity for evil. The compelling performances from a largely unfamiliar cast, the weirdly romantic score by Riz Ortolani, and the sheer virtuosity of Deodato's camerawork only add to the outrage. After all, these are acts committed by sophisticated artists fully aware of their implications.

Deodato has yet to make good on his repeated threats to helm a sequel, despite the slew of cheesy imitations that continue to follow in Holocaust's wake. As Robert Kerman's phony anthropologist puts it: "I wonder who the real cannibals are?"

-Richard Stanley   Writer and Director Hardware/The Island of Dr. Moreau.

Munroe, a New York anthropologist, is hired by network executives to venture into the Amazon to rescue a documentary team. He trades a tape recorder with a local tribe and participates in a cannibal ritual in order to obtain the last two film reels of the missing filmmakers… and those reels contain shocking footage revealing the ultimate fate of the first team. Munroe then returns to New York to screen the reels for the network executives, and the audiences sees this footage for the first time. It shows the documentary crew were in South America making a follow-up to their controversial film *The Last Road To Hell*, the footage of which is shown to Munroe (which disgusts him), and includes actual execution footage from Africa and Southeast Asia. *Cannibal Holocaust* is considered the father of the "Found Footage" genre, as well as the pinnacle of the cannibal genre. Director Deodato himself makes a brief cameo in the picture, which he made after suffering from a prolonged bout of depression. The most talked-about moment of the film, sadly, does not exist: the infamous "piranha scene" was deeply problematic, and ended up being sold for its weight in silver: Deodato said all the outtakes and extra footage were sold off and ended up as demitasse spoons! This bit of info was revealed to me by Deodato himself over dinner one night (no, it wasn't turtle soup). The director's motivation for making the film was largely driven by his disdain for the lack of journalistic integrity in Italy in the late 70's during a period of intense civil unrest. A vital and significant film which contains a great deal of political and social commentary, *Cannibal Holocaust* transcends the genre, offering far more than gory shock value.

-David Bond

The first time I saw Cannibal Holocaust, I felt like I needed to pressure spray the filth out of my brain. I remember seeing it later in life when horror had already gotten to be a staple for me. Somehow, after having seen years of horror and gore, Ruggero Deodato still managed to make me cringe. It wasn't just the animal violence or the rape and carnage specifically. I think, for me it was just the overall hateful intent of the film that really got me. I swore off the film and thought I was done with it.

Oddly enough, years later, after meeting Deodato, I actually ended up doing a licensed poster for the film and releasing it with my horror movie poster series and as a centerfold in the newly resurrected GoreZone Magazine. I guess I finally gave in to the dark side.

I still can't say I like the film, but I think I understand it more now. I do own a copy that I never watch. I still haven't warmed up to it enough that I pop some popcorn and curl up on the couch with it on a rainy day.

-Brian Steward   Artist.

A surprisingly good film in the fact that it is one of the first originators of "Found footage " some of the effects are particularly good and realistic particularly a "Native" impaled to a stake.
 There are some completely unnecessary scenes of animal cruelty like a piglet being shot and a turtle being torn apart.
I feel the interesting thing about this film is that the "monsters" in the film are the journalists and that was something director Ruggero Deodato wanted to convey. Definitely worth a watch as probably the best of the cannibal films of the period.
Trivia- second most popular film to "ET" that year in Japan!!

-John Thomson   Actor/Comedian.

Cannibal Holocaust. WOW. I have so much to say about this film. Not only did it have a brilliant score but it also has the distinction of being one of the only films that almost made me Vomit. I was watching the film when I was about fifteen, I always spent a ton of my free time hunting down the nastiest stuff I could find. I have always found violence in film interesting and comical at times. I love blood and gore. The more realistic the better, however onscreen violence has never disturbed me, that is, until I watched Cannibal Holocaust; I guess I learned something about myself while watching this movie. Harm humans on screen and I will laugh or smile or enjoy the shit out of the movie. Harm an animal on screen and I will almost throw up. The scene in this film where they are killing the turtle is so hard for me to watch or even talk about. I am getting sick now just thinking about it and typing about it. Having been a vegetarian for seven years after going fishing for the first time as a young lad, this film reinvigorated my distaste for violence against animals. It begs the question why are we more accepting of onscreen violence against our fellow man vs. an animal. It's also has continued to haunt me ever since. Brilliant film, and I understand why some banned this one, especially because it was really the first ever found footage style film. It also had the people who played the actors in the film disappear for a few years so people seeing it would think they were dead. Brilliant marketing.

-James Cullen Bressack   Director of Blood Lake, Hate Crime, and Pernicious.

Probably the most notorious and well known of all the Video Nasties is Ruggero Deodato's Cannibal Holocaust, a survival horror movie well ahead of its time, and to this day remains one of the most shocking films ever put to video.

In July 1983 Cannibal Holocaust was removed from UK shelves as a Video Nasty, and remained banned, even though Go-Video had already pre-cut the film for their February 1982 release. It wasn't until July 2001, almost twenty years later, that the film was released, although cut by 5:44 minutes! It was Shameless who released the film again in 2012, with all the violence and animal cruelty pretty much restored, with only 15 seconds of cuts. The director himself released his own edit for Shameless Video, reducing the animal cruelty but restoring all the human violence, and this version was released without any further cuts, and is the director's preferred version. However, if you want to see the fully uncut version (there are a number of versions out there claiming to be fully uncut) then you need to buy the Region One Grindhouse Deluxe Two Disk Edition. Regardless of what anyone tells you, this is the truest version of the film, completely uncut.

Italian born Ruggero Deodato was one of the first of the Italian horror directors to re-kick start the Cannibal film craze of the late 70's and early 80's, after Umberto Lenzi's early film The Man From Deep River (1972). It was his own Cannibal World AKA Jungle Holocaust (1977), which influenced other director's to make films such as Cannibal Ferox (1981). Throughout the Video Nasties scare, it seemed any film with the word Cannibal in it got itself banned: Cannibal Ferox, Cannibal Man, and Cannibal Apocalypse to name a few, but for me, Cannibal Holocaust is the best and most frightening out of the lot.

There is no doubt that Cannibal Holocaust caused controversy, from the real life animal killings to the rumours of the film being an actual snuff movie. Not many films can have such an impact that the director was actually arrested and jailed for ten days on charges of murder and animal cruelty, but Deodato went through just that. His film, Cannibal Holocaust, notorious as it was, was incredibly successful before being banned just about everywhere. It was the second highest grossing film in Japan when released, second only to E.T, and it is claimed the film has so far made $200 million worldwide in both cinema and DVD sales. There is no question that when people discuss Video Nasties, Cannibal Holocaust will get a mention, and rightly so. The film is a vile, vicious but brilliant piece of work, and even with today's gore hungry horrors, you are unlikely to see anything quite as shocking as this.

However, for all it's bad reputation and notoriety, the film is actually incredibly well made and, in my opinion, one of the greatest horror movies of all time. To still have a hold over modern horror in that it influenced the entire found footage genre (no one has yet matched it) and pretty much every cannibal horror released will get compared to it (again, none have even come close to its brilliance), like it or not, Cannibal Holocaust is a very important film and one of the most important and influential horrors of all time. The fact Deodato was arrested and facing murder charges is testament to the films brilliance and realism. In fact, he was in so much trouble he had to ask his producer to get his cast of actors, killed off in the film, to fly to Italy to prove they were still alive! Initially, Deodato had asked his cast to lay low for a year after the film to give the impression they had actually died, but in desperation he had to get them back.

Another part of the film he had to prove was fake in court was the native girl on a stick, which was believed to be real. The effect was created by having the girl sit in a bicycle seat and placing a piece of wood in her mouth while she looked up, to give the impression of being impaled, the actress had to recreate this in court to prove it was fake!

Documentaries, known as Mondo, were available around these times which had filmmakers filming so-called Cannibals and other bizarre aspects of human nature, often getting their subjects to act up for the camera to boost ratings. It is believed that Cannibal Holocaust was Deodato's answer to those filmmakers, and it was also the fact he witnessed his son watching violence on the news, which influenced him to make such a film.

Cannibal Holocaust is a work of art, a work of genius as a crew of rescuers head into the Amazon Jungle to try a find a documentary film crew who went there to film and study the Cannibal tribes. They haven't been heard from in a long time, and we follow the rescue team, eventually finding the leftover cameras and then presenting the videos to a TV network, who plan to show the original expedition. However, as they watch what happened to the documentary film crew scenes of violence and disgust appear on screen for us all to see.

The film opens with gentle, tranquil music that is a million miles from the horrors that follow, but is testament to the great Italian horrors of that era, and we then dive straight in to a news real explaining about the explorers and who they were. The rescuers then head into the jungle and do their best not to upset any of the local tribes. Our first real scene of violence comes as we bear witness to a native girl being brutally beaten and raped with a large rock. Some of the rescuers want to help, however one of them says not to interfere as it is a tribal ritual. It is a shocking and violent scene that still holds up today as a sickening act, and one that has been copied numerous times - but never bettered. If you haven't seen the film before, it is here where you suddenly realise just how real and how frightening this film really is. The brilliance of these early Cannibal films was the use of Jungle tribes, making it all seem far more believable to the point you actually begin to question if this is in-fact real.

Now you must remember that back then, 'found footage' horror had never been heard of, so as we watch the tapes of the doomed explorers unfold, we can only assume it is real. Even by today's standards, it is very difficult to see what is fake and what's not. Granted there are a few minor issues in certain camera angles, but for the majority this is flawless: the hand held camera being done right and done effectively and it is totally believable. It is no wonder people thought this was a snuff film, and watching the film now and based on its merits and authenticity, there is no doubt that thirty years ago this would have caused absolute blind panic among those who watched it. To this day I am staggered at how well this film is put together and presented.

In the film the researches kill and cut open a live turtle, something which the actors look to be enjoying, however once the camera's stopped filming they were disgusted in what they were doing. Most of the film crew tried to get Deodato to stop the animal cruelty, but he stated legally they could do it based on where they were filming. However, looking back, Deodato has expressed his regret in his actions. The scene was made up by the researchers as a homage to the infamous Mondo films where scenes were often staged to boost viewings. Animals are used not only to disgust, but also to frighten as one scene involves a horrific giant spider resting on the shoulder of one of the girls, and later on a snake bite leads the way to a vicious and barbaric chopping off of a cameraman's leg as he his then left to die. The most unsettling part is the madness in the guy's eyes as he raises his machete and chops away, again the special effects are flawless.

The researchers soon find the village where the previous expedition were heading, and in probably the worst image of animal cruelty, we witness the natives slice off the top of a monkeys head. The plan here was for the special effects guys to then replace the monkey's head with a fake one in order for the natives to eat a fake pink goo made to look like brains. The native's refused, claiming monkey's brains were a delicacy to them!

Most found footage films look for impact in the final shot, and they all learnt that from Deodato, the master. The final shot, the finale, blimey the whole damn film will leave a lasting, chilling impression and is impossible to forget. Cannibal Holocaust is without doubt not only one of the greatest horrors ever made, but also one of the greatest films of all time. Now, I don't mean this simply for its shock value, but also for its attention to detail, its superb acting, breath-taking scenery, flawless special effects and true and real horror, which delivers maximum impact. Like it or not, you cannot deny the staggering power of this film, and even now, thirty years on, filmmakers are still learning from Deodato's genius and that in itself is worthy of the your respect. Cannibal Holocaust is, and always will be the Daddy of the Video Nasty era, one of the most shocking and influential films ever made, and a film that not only warrants but demands respect.

-Matt Wavish   Writer.

I hate to be cliché and count myself as yet another person that feels like they have something to say about Cannibal Holocaust. Believe me, I get it. It's cruel, and shocking, and it birthed the found footage sub-genre. All that aside, I have to mention that I came to this film late in my horror movie game. I thought I'd seen all there was to see. And I'd done plenty of reading on the film before I was even able to track a copy of it down. But when I finally did and loaded that baby into my DVD player, I watched in open-mouthed surprise at what was unfolding.

Even though the acting is borderline abysmal and the dubbing is what you'd expect from an Italian film shot in the jungles of South America, there came a point where I found it necessary to pause the movie, take a minute to collect my thoughts, and do an Internet search to double check that the film I was watching didn't actually consist of real found footage.

The place I paused was directly after the infamous woman on a spike scene, and the effect was so convincing that I had to find out whether or not it was real before I could carry on. And if it wasn't real then I needed to know how it was done.

I learned that Deodato had to face the same question in court and showed how it was pulled off in front of a judge. That was all I needed to know. I resumed the film, no less stymied by what I was watching, but comforted by the fact that it was for the most part, fiction.

-Mark Miller   Writer, Director, Producer, Seraphim Films.

The 7th of February 1980 may not hold significance for many people, but for Ruggero Deodato it would shape both the rest of his life, and his career as a filmmaker. It was on this day that *Cannibal Holocaust* was released upon the world, and cinema would never be the same again. The sensation that surrounded it caused delight amongst cinemagoers, particularly aficionados of the grindhouse circuit, and the film became incredibly popular and lucrative; but the powers that be found it abhorrent and convinced that it was representative of actual criminal acts. Deodato would spend the following three years pleading his case in the courts. Originally pulled in on an archaic law which prohibited all scenes of animal cruelty onscreen in Italy (a measure put in place to stem the popularity of bullfighting), he soon found himself being charged with the murders of the performers involved. A contract which the director had drafted for the principal actors all stated that they disappear from the public eye for one year after filming. This was done with the intention of adding to the perceived authenticity of the movie, but with the case becoming more intense, and a prison sentence looking inevitable, Deodato was forced to call in all of those involved to verify that they were, in fact, still in existence.

The situation was further propelled into infamy by the statement from a British policeman who declared that he had 'seen an actual snuff movie and its name was *Cannibal Holocaust*'. Due to the fact that there were no regulations in regards to film classification in the UK at the time, this was one of the incendiary forces behind the introduction of the DPP 'Video Nasties' list, and so the hunt began. The documentary style of the film was created to satirize the exploitative Mondo scene of the time, as well as making a wry and acerbic stab at the methods of western journalism. The intended subtleties of these motivations were greatly overlooked by the authorities, as the carnage and mayhem portrayed onscreen was like that of which they had never seen before.

Cannibal Holocaust is accredited with many things, one of them being the invention of the 'found footage' horror movie. The story charts the South American expedition of journalists led by Alan Yates (Gabriel Yorke), his girlfriend Faye Daniels (Francesca Ciardi) and two crew members / cameramen; Jack Anders (Perry Pirkanen) and Mark Tomaso (Luca Giorgio Barbareschi). Their intention was to make a film entitled *The Green Inferno*, which was to capitalize on their success after their previous documentary *The Last Road to Hell*, a brutal and horrific examination of African rebellion and dictatorship. Their disappearance whilst filming the movie causes the TV station that is funding it to call in Professor Harold Monroe to investigate. Monroe is played by Robert Kerman – a prolific '70's porn star, known as R. Bolla, in one of his major non-adult movie roles. Kerman, who had several on set altercations with Deodato, is one of the most powerful elements of the film. He leads a team into the Amazon to trace the whereabouts of the missing crew.

Cannibal Holocaust is a film of two distinct halves, the first being Monroe's investigation and the second is the footage belonging to Yeats' crew, which he discovers in a rather grisly fashion. When he encounters the Yanomamö for the first time, they are skeptical and it takes cautious steps to win their favour (including a very clever trick with a tape recorder). He manages to do so and they allow him to leave with the film stock.

Back in New York, the TV executives reveal their plan to release the footage. They play Monroe sections of *Last Road to Hell* and inform him that their methods of documentary making were not always the most scrupulous. This spurns him on to examine the tapes, which leads us into the second, and significantly more horrifying, section of the movie.

What is shown in the Yeats footage is truly barbaric, savage and cruel, but the perpetrators are not the cannibal tribes. The actions of the crew are reprehensible; they perform acts of rape, violence and disrespect against the tribes and did nothing but plead for their grisly fate. The rough camerawork serves to add to the Mondo style, which Deodato was satirizing, with gruesome scenes of animal mutilation juxtaposed with acts of dissection, amputation, impalement and assault upon the human cast members. The director claims that all the animals that were killed onscreen were used as food and shared with the natives, but this does not make it any less harrowing to sit through.

The emphasis is on the impact, which westerners have on indigenous societies and it is not a complimentary portrait. In one particular section, Yeats and his crew rape a young tribal girl, who is brutally executed by her own people for the shame, which the attack has brought upon her and her family. Yeats then fawns in mock repulsion as he discovers her body, feigning that he is utterly confounded as to why the tribe would do something like this. The impalement is shown in such graphic detail (with the pole seemingly entering the girl's groin and coming out of her mouth) that no one could attest to how *Cannibal Holocaust* couldn't be a snuff film. The truth finally materialized that the girl was sitting on a bicycle seat which was placed on top of a small pole, she then balanced a piece of light balsa wood in her mouth and a few gallons of fake blood were poured over her to hide all of the tell-tale signs. The effect is astounding, iconic and remains one of the most chilling images in 20th Century horror.

The visceral nature of the movie is accentuated by one of the most haunting scores in memory, provided by Riz Ortolani, with an unforgettable title theme, which, upon future listens, will forever evoke the accompanying images as clear as if they were taking place before your very eyes. What really sets *Cannibal Holocaust* apart from the rest of the Video Nasties (because some of them are truly awful) is that it is an exceptionally well-made movie. It might not be anything resembling subtle, with the social commentary practically spelt out for the viewer, but its professional and highly stylized cinematography and structure remain wholly admirable to this day. Deodato has claimed that he was suffering from a serious bout of depression at the time when he made the movie. He attests the motivation behind it to the exploitative coverage of terrorism on television at the time and wanted to expose this. He had journeyed into the realm of the cannibal movie four years earlier in *Last Cannibal World*, but it was a far less effective feature.

As grotesque, unpleasant and genuinely disturbing as *Cannibal Holocaust* is, it remains an inarguable classic. There is an ugly beauty to this movie, which is representative of so much in the world; the environment portrayed is so harsh, yet equally fragile. It's one of the few examples of a film, which is equally gratifying and gruelling, not in its savagery, but in its execution. It's a testament to just how good a genre picture can be. The reason for this being that it shows that every one of us, and our so-called 'civilized society,' are the greatest monsters of all. To finish on Monroe's final line in the movie; "I wonder who the real cannibals are?'"

-Colin McCracken   Writer.

The Cannibal Man

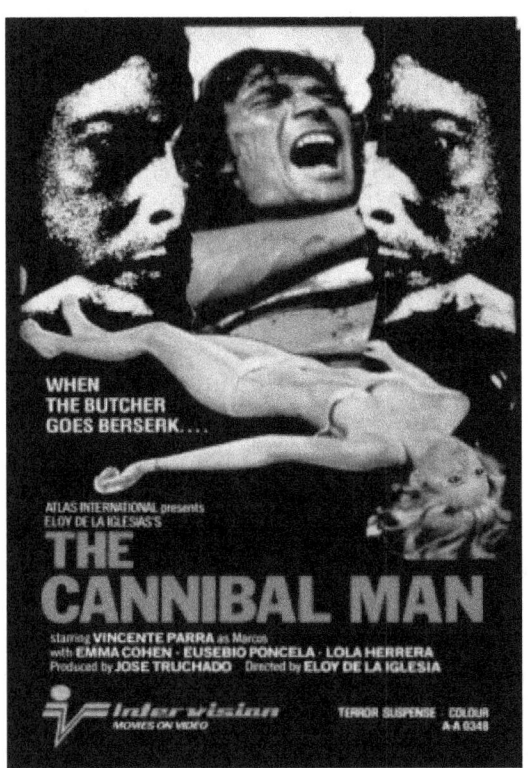

Also known as "La Semana del Asesino".
Year of release: 1973
Writer: Eloy de la Iglesia
Director: Eloy de la Iglesia
R Rated 98 mins. Spain
Tagline: "When the butcher goes berserk...."

Main cast: Vicente Parra (Marcos), Emma Cohen (Paula), Eusebio Poncela (Nestor), Charly Bravo (Esteban), Fernando Sanchez Polack (Senor Ambrosio), Goyo Lebrero (Taxista).

Distributed by: Intervision

In 1993 Redemption released a version on VHS with 3 seconds cut by the BBFC. Available on DVD by Blue Underground in its uncut unrated form R1 US release. The Cannibal Man was prosecuted.

Plot:
In Cannibal Man Slaughterhouse worker Marco's life takes a serious downward spiral when he accidently kills a taxi driver, his appetite for murder is insatiable following the murder of the only witness to his crime. One by one the death toll rises as people become suspicious of his actions and meet a grisly end with the victims being disposed of and packaged for human consumption!

Appraisal:
Eloy de la Iglesia's gore, shock, extreme horror piece is an enjoyable crazy unsettling film which keeps you engrossed and strangely wanting more throughout! This low budget offering from Spain is often overlooked or mostly forgotten but do yourself a favor if you have let this one slip through your fingers, make time for a viewing!

This film was made in the early 1970's but does hold its own down to the overall atmospherics and production of the movie. I was pleasantly surprised by "The Cannibal Man", on paper it shouldn't work but the superb performances provided by the actors and gloomy ambience result in this unique little gem of a horror movie!

The idea of the film is amazing, Marcos Vincente Parra accidently kills a truck driver and the whole film goes from there, he goes on an uncontrollable killing frenzy to avoid ending up in jail.

It's all very bizarre, you can't help but keep on watching?.

-Tony Newton

Surrealism, homoerotic subplots and post dictatorial tension all simmer in Eloy de la Iglesia's The Cannibal Man'.

When Spain was under the dictatorship of General Francisco Franco, who ruled the country from 1939 until his death in 1975, censorship was an everyday fact of life. The secret police and associated informants meant that people went about their everyday business in constant fear and were always under the watchful eye of everyone that surrounded them. It is this level of paranoia and claustrophobic tension which is addressed in Eloy de la Iglesia's *La Semana del Aasesino* or as it was known in the UK; *Cannibal Man*.

Vicente Parra plays Marcos, a conflicted young man whose days are spent in the gut-wrenching environment of a slaughterhouse. He works as a lowly paid drone on the killing floor of a soup factory. As the movie opens, the bloody death throes of cattle fill the screen as they are hoisted, bled out and sent along the production line. As this occurs Marcos casually chews upon a sandwich, an indication of the nonchalance, which he presents in the face of violence throughout the remainder of the feature.

His life is that of mundane squalor, he lives in a dilapidated area of the city and his girlfriend Paola refuses to reveal her relationship with him to her parents until he acquires a better paying job. This is one of the first allusions made towards the inherent class structure, which existed in the fallout of Franco's dictatorship. There is a towering block of apartments overlooking Marco's and from the upper echelons it transpires that he is being surreptitiously observed. Marco and Paola are taking a cab ride home and start to get fairly intimate when the driver takes great offense ("I'm a married man") and gets into a heated argument with Marco which progresses into an altercation that culminates with Marco bashing his head in with a rock.

Back in the perceived safety of his apartment, Marco and Paola continue where they left off, but in a post-coital expression of regret, Paola insists that they confess their crime. Marco assures her that the police would never listen to a man as poor as he is, implying that the corruption in Spain at the time favoured the rich, as it often tends to do. What happens next triggers every subsequent action in the movie; Marco leans in to kiss his lover passionately, casually lifting his hands to her neck he proceeds to strangle her. He carefully lays the body on the bed and becomes even more withdrawn.

As the movie progresses there are several other people who fall foul of Marco, who does not really seem to have any major motive or plan. His apathy and confusion grow and he develops a bizarre relationship with Nestor (who is the man who has been watching him). This blossoms into a strange mutual dependency, with hints at a homoerotic subtext. The two spend more time together, and become increasingly drawn into their respective worlds, each of which contains its own clandestine elements.

The portrayal of life in this part of Spain at the time is one of division, unhappiness and unfairness. Marco leads an existence in which he is doomed to failure. Even when he is promoted at the factory, his co-workers turn against him. The bodies begin to build up in his bedroom and he finds himself left with no other option than to begin transporting pieces of them into the factory to add to the soup mix. This action is the only possible explanation as to why the movie was given the moniker of *Cannibal Man*, as there are no other references or allusions to flesh eating in the movie.

It was probably due to the title that the movie ended up on the DPP list, being wrongly thrown in with the Italian shockers of the tribal Cannibal / Mondo genre. The film suffers from some technical and budgetary limitations, but this only adds to the grindhouse aesthetic. The socio-political commentary which lies just underneath the surface, and the hinted subtext of Marco's battle with his own sexual motivations makes this an interesting psychological examination, which is absolutely full of metaphor and suggestion. There's enough gore to keep the horror hounds happy, but *Cannibal Man* offers an added layer of surrealistic intellect that is absent from so much contemporary genre.

-Colin McCracken   Writer.

Slaughterhouse worker Marcos takes his girlfriend out for the night and while making out with her in the back of a taxi gets booted out by the driver mid journey. When Marcos refuses to pay the cabbie for his unfinished work the driver attacks them but is then killed by Marcos in an act of self-defence. Wanting to keep the incident secret fearing his social status will earn him a harsh sentence he finds his upper class girlfriend insists otherwise, so she has to die. Family and friends turn up asking questions they one by one follow in the dead girlfriends footsteps and rapidly the dead Spaniard storage that was a bedroom fills up while becoming less than delightfully fragrant.

Attempting to dispose of the skeletons in his closet he makes use of his works facilities but the spiral continues with more bodies piling up and fewer friends being left to help him break the deadly cycle.

Cannibal Man is probably one of the most misleading titles since 'Snuff'. There is only a suggestion of unintentional cannibalism by a very minor character who didn't know better, besides that not a jot of anthropophagic action is to be found, not even a nibble. The story itself is heavily allegorical and it has to be said that only the most sheltered viewer this would remain oblivious to this for more than half an hour at best. Essentially running as a coming out story, the initial murder serves as the 'dirty little secret' that Marcos brutally acts to bury, and when his girl friend states her intention to go to the police Marcos firstly tries to persuade her not to, fearing his social status would result in unusually harsh treatment at the hands of the authorities.

As person after person lines up, trying to force Marco to own up they all meet the same fate. There is one exception to this though, a man who lives in the ivory towers that dwarfs the rather squalid villa that Marcos lives in. Nestor befriends Marcos and is a somewhat calming influence never pressuring him to reveal his secret though gently encouraging him. It's this relationship that is central to what the film is trying to do, which is to present an analogy for coming out. Although Marcos is superficially presented as being straight the film provides clues ranging from subtler moments such as his dialogue when he is under threat from others through to the blatantly homoerotic swimming scene. Though it's never made entirely clear as to whether he's fully gay or bisexual, not that that really matters particularly, the character is clearly suffering because of having to carry his secret, which he defends with deadly force.

A class issue is brought up here which is illustrated not only with Marcos, his blue collar job and his near poverty lifestyle Marcos clearly believes his position is more tenuous because of his social standing and this is counterpointed by Nestor. Nestor is clearly a member of the upper classes. He lives in the luxury towers high above the likes of Marcos and the authority figures treat him with respect when they find out where he lives. Its seems from this that the concern is not only one of coming out but also that of a particular difficulty for the working class to do so.

It becomes clear there's a fear of the authorities with the rather fascist look and conduct of the police from the badges to the requirement for identification to be produced on demand, this is not a film that reflects a favourable light on those authority figures.

Throughout the film the dialogue between Nestor and Marcos is barely allegorical in nature. It's to the point that the conversation they have can be transferred directly word for word to relate to them discussing the situation of their sexuality. It's not subtle about what it's talking about and although the script avoids literally stating its intentions it's not exactly covert either. How the viewer will perceive this film will depend largely on their familiarity and comfort with gay issues because if that aspect is ignored or not understood then the film will be entirely too much talking and a very, very plain story interspersed with a few murders and a curiously close relationship with a rather over familiar man thrown into the mix.

Looking at the film in context of the gay issues it addresses finds a seemingly heartfelt exploration of the subject that is angry and passionate whilst stopping short of being hysterical or overly vicious, it does however take some understandable frustration and fear and project it through Marcos in his acts of violence. Cannibal Man is not a film that will be enjoyed by everyone although the things it explores are important and interesting enough in my opinion for a wider audience to see rather than being limited to the community it's primarily aimed at. While it's not exactly the most exciting film in the list it does at least have some thoughtfulness and heart behind it, which makes it worth checking out.

-Glenn Criddle   Writer/Critic.

Not many horror films from the 70s and 80s are political. *The Cannibal Man*, a Spanish film from 1972, however, is, albeit covertly. Focusing on a butcher who, through an unfortunate series of events, becomes a serial killer, *The Cannibal Man* serves as a subtle, satirical send-up of life in Spain under Fascist leader Francisco Franco (who ruled from 1936 to 1975). More than a string of gruesome images, *The Cannibal Man* is a statement, an expression of political dissidence at a time and place where political dissidence got you into trouble. We should *all* applaud the courage of director Eloy de la Iglesia.

-Joseph Rubas   Writer/Author.

Devil Hunter

Also known as "El Canibal", "The Devil Hunter"
Year of release: 1980
Writer: Julian Esteban
Director: Jesús Franco
Unrated 102 mins. Spain, France, West Germany
Tagline: "Hunted, raped and tormented out of her mind…"
Main cast: Ursula Buchfellner (Laura Crawford), Al Cliver (Peter Weston), Antonio Mayans (Jack), Antonio de Cabo (Thomas), Bertrand Altmann (The Devil), Gisela Hahn (Jane).
Distributed by: Cinehollywood

In 2008 Severin released the film titled "El Cannibal" in its uncut form with cuts wavered by the BBFC. Devil Hunter was prosecuted.

Plot:
Peter Weston is hired to travel to the jungles of South America in order to rescue model Laura Crawford who is being held hostage by a tribe of cannibals. This tribe plans to sacrifice the model to their "Devil God". Will Peter get the beautiful Laura Crawford out alive or will she be sacrificed to the tribes bug-eyed "Devil God"?

Appraisal:
Jesús Franco directs Devil Hunter, but it's certainly not his finest work. I'm not sure how much of the blame can be accredited to the over-dubbed voices and somewhat crummy plot. "Devil Hunter" isn't one of the best films on the DPP list but it's certainly not the worst, it's a tough watch and at times pretty laughable, but between the bad audio dubbing this film does have a few surprises and it keeps you watching, Devil Hunter could have been so much better with a bigger budget. You do get the Franco stamp of bare-skinned heroines, and women being abused and some strange FX to say the least, the FX are anything but special here.

Devil Hunter has an crazy, nightmarish tone to it, it does feel dated and somewhat lackluster and after watching the movie you feel almost drunk on Jess Franco and couldn't watch another of his movies for a while. Devil Hunter was obviously banned due to the sheer volume of nudity and gore displayed throughout. The VHS cover of the film is one of the less disturbing featured on the list and pictures the Hunter with gun in hand ready to take on his enemies or anyone else that may stand in his way.

-Tony Newton

Don't Go in the Woods

Also known as "Don't Go In the Woods...Alone!"
Year of release: 1981
Writer: Garth Eliassen
Director: James Bryan
R rated 82 mins. USA
Tagline: "Everyone has nightmares about the ugliest way to die."
Main cast: Jack McClelland (Peter), Mary Gail Artz (Ingrid), James P. Hayden (Craig), Angie Brown (Joanne), Ken Carter (Sheriff), David Barth (Deputy Benson).
Distributed by: VRO
IN 2007 the film was released in its uncut form on DVD in the UK passed by the BBFC with a certificate of 15. Don't Go in the Woods was prosecuted.

Plot:
This is a tale of four backpackers whose relaxing weekend in the wilderness soon turns into a nightmare as a crazed huntsman lurking in the woods begins murdering tourists. The local sheriff begins to investigate the disappearances and attempts to hunt down the lunatic bloodthirsty wild man waiting in the wilderness.

Appraisal:
Another of the very popular "Don't Go" entitled horror films featured on the DPP list, I went through a spate of collecting any VHS that started with "Don't Go", there's a fair few titles to collect though they're mostly dire!
Don't Go in the Woods is a contender for one of the worst films on the DPP list, It's a film I don't really revisit as there's nothing much to offer here for fans of horror or gore or even a good storyline!
The whole production is pretty amateurish from start to finish and fails to deliver on any level. The most alarming part of the film is not the poor acting or plot but the child holding an axe, and that says something about the film! It's not scary but you can help but think he's going to hurt himself any minute!
This film features over enthusiastic acting, it's not purposely humorous but you can't help but laugh out loud at this movie. The most hilarious scenes of the film have to be those in which a wheelchair bound victim meets an unruly demise. To its credit there are plenty of murders and unexpected twists to keep you engaged though the best part of Don't Go in the Woods is without doubt the VHS cover itself, I'd be happy with the cover and a blank VHS inside.
The silver and black VRO release featuring a knife alongside the bloodied face of a woman is awesome. This iconic video sleeve is the 1980's you can almost hear Devo playing whilst looking at it. Don't Go in the Woods was prosecuted and was released in 2007 with a 15 rating. Maybe 15 year olds weren't ready for this then but after being exposed to the Internet for years it's the equivalent of a young adult show nowadays.
The film was released out on DVD by Code Red in 2006.

-Tony Newton

The Driller Killer

Year of release: 1979
Writer: Nicholas St. John
Director: Abel Ferrara
Unrated 94 mins. USA

Tagline: "The blood runs in rivers…and the drill keeps tearing through flesh and bone."

Main cast: Abel Ferrara (Reno Miller), Carolyn Marz (Carol Slaughter), Baybi Day (Pamela), Harry Schultz (Dalton Briggs), Alan Wynroth (Al the Landlord), Maria Helhoski (The Nun).

Distributed by: Originally distributed by Vipco in 1999 a cut version of the film with 54 seconds of cuts. In 2002 ILC Prime released the full, uncut version of the film passed by the BBFC.

Plot:
The Driller Killer sees an American artist as he struggles to complete his masterpiece, juggling finances and a punk bands incessant practicing in the building where he lives and the relationship with his girlfriend and her lesbian lover his world slowly unravels. Reno's daily life begins to take its toll as he slowly loses his mind and takes to the streets to unleash his growing anger as he cracks!

Appraisal:
The Driller Killer poster and VHS sleeve are just as iconic as the film itself, the shocking poster featuring a drill being driven into someone's head was just too much not to get attention from do-gooding arseholes!.

Abel Ferrara does an excellent job with his debut film breaking away from the porn industry.

In Abel Ferra's debut he plays an artist struggling to finish his masterpiece, he finally goes over the edge and into his own personal hell as his world seems crumble around him. This grimy, sleaze-fest is on the money and creates a similar atmosphere to "Maniacs". "The Driller killer" is a cult horror film, which any film fan will have heard of at some stage in their life.

The Driller Killer is another top film from the DPP list, it contains countless murders which all involve the dreaded drill! This film gave me nightmares before I'd even seen it! I'd heard the gruesome stories (which were actually much worse than the film itself).

The Driller Killer is gritty; in fact America hasn't looked so dark on film since "Taxi Driver" and later "Bad Lieutenant". Punk rock, thrills, spills and all out carnage all play a part in this tragic story of a man lost. The Driller Killer is a dark horror, which at times is almost trying to be too clever for its own good leaving the viewer wanting more.

I never did like DIY and don't own a drill of any kind thanks to The Driller Killer, well that's my excuse anyway!

The Driller Killer is a very good horror film of its time. Personally, I love this film; it's a melancholic film, which leaves you with a curious empathy for its central character.

Don't expect jumps, hillbillies or cannibalism but as the title suggest do expect a drill and an almost voyeuristic slice of classic horror.

The Driller Killer was prosecuted. It was further released in 1999 with 54 seconds of cuts. The film was re-released fully uncut in 2002 in the UK.

Do Vipco regret taking out that full-page advert in movie magazines?. I think not...

-Tony Newton

Under the guise of Jimmy Laine, Abel Ferrara plays Reno Miller, a struggling New York City artist who co-habits with two girls; Carol Slaughter (Carolyn Marz) and her lover, Pamela (Baybi Day). The three exist in a life of squalor and borderline starvation. Reno becomes increasingly frustrated with the pressure that mounts upon him in the form of utility bills and everyday costs. He is working on what he feels is his masterpiece and these everyday occurrences seem only to irk and annoy him with increasing intensity.

He is also beginning to be plagued by nightmarish visions, which gradually begin to dissolve both his sanity and grip on reality. Driven to desperate measures to release his anger and his hatred of what he describes as the degenerates and bums that litter the streets.

The Driller Killer is not only significant as an Arthouse piece but is also the definitive punk rock horror movie. Ferrara manages to encapsulate the gritty feel of New York in a manner, which has rarely been seen since. It excels even Andy Warhol's efforts in the overblown *Chelsea Girls* (1966) and becomes more akin to the filthy and seedy world that inhabits the lyrics of The Velvet Underground.

Harry Schultz II plays Dalton, Reno's art dealer who refuses him another advance on his next piece, stating that he has already paid for his girlfriend's most recent abortion amongst other things. This pushes him close to the edge but the turning point comes when a pretentious no wave band called The Roosters take up residence in a neighbouring apartment. Fronted by the preposterous Tony Coca Cola (in a thinly veiled representation of bands such as the New York Dolls and Television) their endless rehearsals and hipster posturing cause Reno to take to the streets.

After seeing an advertisement for a portable electrical power tool generator called a Portapak, Reno arms himself with a drill and, in the darkened hours of the New York night, begins disposing of those whom he sees as nothing but a scourge on society. His anger festers as The Roosters begin to attain critical acclaim and a lucrative record deal, whilst his latest efforts are greeted with disgust and scorn by Dalton.

The Driller Killer stands out as one of the highlights of the Video Nasties list. It is an uncomfortable watch at times, but only in the realistic and hard-hitting realities of city life and artistic frustration, which it portrays. There is an inescapable feeling of claustrophobia in Reno's breakdown and we not only feel empathy for him, but also at times, almost share his rage at the unfair and arbitrary nature of the art and cultural world, which has rejected him almost in direct favour of fashionistas and pretenders.

The film declares in the opening title card that it should be played loud and indeed it should. A glimpse into the long sanitised backstreets of New York City, *The Driller Killer* now serves as much as a period piece as it does a genre feature.

-Colin McCracken   Writer.

Horror movies, especially those made on shoestring budgets in the 70s and 80s, get a bad rap. "Serious" reviewers (snooty intellectuals, all of them) say those types of movies were made simply to showcase gratuitous amounts of blood and, sometimes, nudity.

They couldn't be more wrong. Sure, there *were* a lot of those, but there were also movies like Driller Killer, a surprisingly cerebral art house effort chronicling an artist's descent into madness. In this offering from Abel Ferrara released in 1979, we find a struggling artist (Reno Miller) unable to pay his bills. Disgusted at the deplorable state of the city (New York was a cesspool back then...not the gleaming tourist Mecca it is today), Miller embarks on a brutal campaign to rid the world of hobos and transients. Featuring more than its fair share of violence, Driller Killer was more than a blood flick. It was a commentary on contemporary urban decay and the madness it spawns. Employing many revolutionary film techniques, Driller Killer deserves a place at the table of great underground cinema.

-Joseph Rubas   Writer/Author.

Evilspeak

Year of release: 1981
Writer: Joseph Garofalo
Director: Eric Weston
R rated 89 mins. USA
Tagline: "Remember the little kid you used to pick on? Well, he's a big boy now."

Main cast: Clint Howard (Stanley Coopersmith), R.G Armstrong (Sarge), Joe Cortese (Reverend Jameson), Claude Earl Jones (Coach), Haywood Nelson (Kowalski), Don Stark (Bubba).

Distributed by: Originally distributed by Videospace. In 1987 Horror Classics released a cut version of the film with 3.34 cuts made by the BBFC. In 2004 Anchor bay released the full uncut version with previous cuts wavered by the BBFC.

Plot:
Clint Howard plays the role of outcast Military cadet Stanley Coopersmith. Stanley struggles at the Military Training Academy as he's tormented by bullies who make his life a living hell; that is, until one day, he discovers a mysterious book. Translating the books text using his computer Stanley unleashes demons when he to summons a satanic high priest to exact revenge on his tormentors.

Appraisal:
This dark doorway into Stanley's world is welcome and well received although this film does receive its fair share of criticism but Clint Howard is on top form (not since "Gentle Ben" has Howard's face been so welcoming).

Evilspeak is an essential addition to any horror collection as the idea was somewhat new at the time and very different from other offerings on the DPP list. The soundtrack has its obvious "Omen" inspired terrifying tunes. "Evilspeak" has aged very well but you can't summon up demons with a Smartphone, an 80s big screen PC is the only way to go, just try to find one of those old monitors now, it's impossible, they knew something we didn't. "Evilspeak" was quite popular with geeks before it was popular to be a geek, which is probably why I enjoyed the film.

Evilspeak is a total gem of a film that has gained cult status around the globe, I love "Evilspeak" and must watch this film at least once a year, I love everything about it!

Many people who have been bullied at some stage in their life can relate to this film the only thing missing is the book and the ability to summon demons! to kill real bullies!

I still have the big box VHS video complete with pull out poster, which video stockists would use to promote the movie, I love the cover it screams horror in the 1980's!

Evilspeak was prosecuted and further released on VHS in 1987 with 3 minutes 34 seconds of cuts, it wasn't released uncut until 2004 by the BBFC.

-Tony Newton

When I first read the script written by Joe Garofalo it was called "The Foundling". The narrative was about bullying. It's effects on Coopersmith and his ultimate revenge. He conjures the devil and creates an unholy alliance. But to do that he must use ancient chants and prayers dedicated to summoning demons and especially the Devil. He does this when he finds the monk's (Esteban) black magic and satanic "how-to book". This is what Coopersmith does. He speaks to the demons. The Devil. Spouting the secrets of evil divination. *Evilspeak*.

Joe has a great sense for the bizarre and the dark side, which I found entertaining and fresh.

But I also felt the narrative needed a bump. I've always been a techy (that terminology was yet to be born in 1980) and what I saw was an evolving technology called the personal computer. I was fascinated by the idea. And I knew about the new company called Apple that was doing exciting things with these computers. Creating a user interface that had great potential. and I wanted to use it as the tool for Coopersmith to communicate with the dark side. Joe agreed and we followed that narrative path.

I met Clint when he came in to audition. My first thought that he was perfect for the part. He had the acting chops and the look for the character. If someone was created from spare parts, Clint sure was. It was a very demanding role both emotionally and physically and Clint proved he was up to the task.

A fan base side story. Anton LaVey was an unexpected addition to the film's fan base.

I guess Evil is in the eye of the beholder. Coopersmith had nowhere left to turn. Even the chaplain at the academy couldn't and wouldn't come to his rescue. I never intended to give the devil a hero turn. He just was the opportunist when Coopersmith called. Evil has a way of doing that.

As far as the video nasty controversy, it was amazing and curious thing when I heard about it. A U.K. law to ban my film. Wow! Hard to believe then and even now. Considering it was just a film. A fiction. Of course, there were financial implications that I didn't find amusing. A whole market had been taken away. That didn't go over well. The UK was the last place I expected that to happen. I had received an MPAA X rating here which in some ways was more understandable. And that was a crazy thing. I've always though the film was a victim of a double standard. The clout of a studio vs. the independent filmmaker.

As a citizen of the world I abhor the concept of censorship. We live with it every day in one form or another. From wearing the politically correct cloth to the always frightening thought of control by outside forces. The religious, government and groups that want to deliver their message to others while controlling thought and expression. The world news will tell us all we need to know on the subject. But there censorship runs rampant.

Because of this Evilspeak suffered. There were more cuts that you'd find in a butcher shop. It started with the MPAA demanding cuts. Then TV and syndication. The domestic distributor considering the running time too long. The number of worldwide distributors wanted their requirements fulfilled. Time and content.

The cherry on the top was the U.K. ban.

After a while you lose control even if you ever fantasied you had any. Most filmmakers can understand that. I don't think there ever will be a "true" director's cut. But we're as close as we'll ever be.

I wanted to explore the arriving of cutting edge technology with the film. The problem was , which really didn't realize at the time, was that I was working in an analogue world. The digital hadn't arrived into the film world. It would for another twenty years.

As beautiful as film is it had it limitations when working with effects. Analogue meant everything had to be done practical. In-camera. And that was a great challenge. From the early decapitation of the girl to the mayhem at the end. Nothing existed in the film world to create that other that ingenuity and smoke and mirrors (literally). Today's young filmmakers can hardly begin to imagine that.

I've been fortunate enough to transition from film to digital. But there have been many casualties along the way.

One story, that fans are familiar with, I'd like to share was the church where the final mayhem unfolds. I wanted to reach as high as I could with production values. I didn't just want four walls, a cross and a few pews to represent the chapel. It was a challenge with our budget.

The person up to that challenge was Kathy Petty, our production coordinator. She went scouting with a vengeance. Even though it wasn't her job. She had a great commitment to the film.

Lo and behold, she travelled into what is now the Howard Hughes Parkway. The city was preparing to build it and a long strip of homes and businesses were being demolished. This included a church. She found it. It was basically a crack house in the middle of a very dangerous area. How she got in and out alive is still a wonder to me. But Kathy was fearless. The city gave us unfettered use. They didn't care what we did. And, boy, did we do stuff. Fire and brimstone.

The art department did the show biz refurbishment. From the still intact marble floors to the dressing of pews and statuary. They built a raised pulpit with a life-size Jesus on the cross above it. The altar had a thirty-foot cross dominating it. Stained glass replaced on the blown out windows. It was an incredible feat for a small budget film. And of course, Jesus on the cross that comes to life. More fodder for the video nasty boys.

Word got around the neighborhood. One day the church's previous minister dropped in and saw what we had done. He dropped to his knees and with clasped hands declared, "Praise the Lord, my church is back!"

The next day we dug a tunnel under the altar where the devil's pigs appear and Coopersmith floats up behind them. A large explosion follows that sent a forty-foot fireball into the ceiling. It rolled towards camera and we had to abandon them and flee. They kept rolling and captured the action. Jesus on the cross and the pulpit were burned to ashes. Pews were burned. Statuary was smashed. And the stained glass windows exploded.

I felt bad for the minister. He never knew what our intentions were. I didn't have the heart to tell him.

Even with all the tampering Evilspeak was a financial success and still enjoys a fan following for which I'm very proud. We were #1 in the box office when we opened. Sold well foreign. The VHS sales and rentals were spectacular. The film did worldwide over $10M. And this is before DVD or cable. And a theater ticket in the U.S. was $2. Years later it was released on DVD, then Blu-ray. It keeps rolling along.

Evilspeak was a Carrie gender spin and Clint created a memorable character.

I'm always asked about a remake and I consider it from time to time. Listen, I'm still around and keeping up with the latest and greatest. 1981 it was "do it practical" on set. And we did. Things can be done to enhance the narrative and production of Evilspeak that we couldn't even imagine back then. And as a practical matter it would make sense financially given the number of fans that want to see a remake and the new ones it would attract.

-Eric Weston   Director of "Evilspeak".

I was never sure if this was supposed to read "Evil speak" or Evil's peak. Featuring Clint(the kid in Gentle Ben) Howard. Who has one of those faces that never cease to fascinate me, like Michael J. Pollard.

I really love this film and it was one I just rented despite being banned uncut. Classic bullied student embraces Satan for revenge purposes. Murderous satanic pigs and some really original deaths make for a decent film with good effects, proper acting and what seems like a half decent budget. Well worth a watch as an introduction to cybersatanism!

-John Thomson   Actor/Comedian.

Expose

Also known as "House on Straw Hill" and "Trauma".
Year of release: 1976
Writer: James Kenelm Clarke
Director: James Kenelm Clarke
X rated 82 mins. UK
Tagline: "She'll take your breath away…your life is next."
Main cast: Udo Kier (Paul Martin), Linda Hayden (Linda), Fiona Richmond (Suzanne), Patsy Smart (Mrs. Aston), Karl Howman (Small youth), Vic Armstrong (Big Youth).
Distributed by: Intervision
In 1997 the film was released with 51 seconds cut by the BBFC.

Plot:
Paul Martin has writers block and buckles under the pressure to write his new novel. When he enlists the help of his secretary he is initially unaware of the vendetta she has against him. The film constant visions and dream-like state provides mystery and suspense throughout building to a climatic ending.

Appraisal:
Expose aka "The House on Straw Hill" aka "Trauma" is the only UK offering to achieve "video nasty" status in the moral panic that plagued the home video industry in the 1980's! Udo Kier appears again in a banned video nasty, only this time as a writer who is plagued by much bigger problems than running out of ink for his typewriter. Udo Kier, as always has a huge on screen presence as he undertakes the role of English novelist Paul Martin but its Linda Hayden (Linda) who really steals the show here.

It's well documented that Linda Hayden regretted her decision to star in "Expose" which is understandable when you consider that it earned its title as a notorious sleaze fest.

Masturbation, weird sex fetishes and rape scenes are the only reason that this film is on the DPP list. "Expose" feels like a Hammer House of Horror hour-long episode from the suspense and horror series and leaves you thinking well beyond the tape stopping in the VCR player.

Expose was prosecuted, the only version that is available in the UK now is rated 18 and heavily cut including a violent rape scene and spoiler alert…Suzanna's death.

-Tony Newton

This sexploitation offering was banned in the UK for 30 years, originally sparking controversy as it teetered the fine line between erotic thriller and pornography, it's due to an abundance of graphic sex and violence that it was considered too nasty for its audience by the BBFC.

In "Expose" cult icon Udo Kier (flesh for Frankenstein) makes a frankly brilliant portrayal of egotistical, unhinged writer Paul Martin. After securing a best-selling novel he succumbs to the pressures of penning his second masterpiece. In an attempt to overcome writer's block Paul retreats to a remote country house on straw hill with girlfriend Suzanne played by British sex symbol Fiona Richmond.

It's here in this remote country setting that live-in secretary Linda (played by Linda Hayden) is hired, her rebuffs to the his advances create a sexual tension as her motives are revealed.

The author becomes plagued with guilt, his paranoid hallucinations intensify as the truth unfolds and we discover that the content of Paul Martin's best-selling novel was actually stolen from Linda's husband resulting in his suicide. Paul is responsible for the death of Linda's husband and she's out for revenge!

"Expose" features rape, murder, lesbianism and masturbation a plenty; it's pure, unadulterated sexually charged exploitation from the mind of writer/director James Kenhelm Clarke. It provides eerie, unsettling and voyeuristic atmospherics throughout, focusing on the somewhat hopelessness of the characters in this desperate isolation.

The picturesque location is breathtaking, the seclusion stunning, all of which allows for complete uninterrupted character development in this rural entrapment, throwing the audience deep into a claustrophobic nightmare of isolation.

Udo Kier plays the character of Paul Martin well although the dubbing does throw the film kind of off kilter. We see throughout the film that author Paul Martin is a control freak with a capacity for violence, he's a dominant man with some disturbing characteristics (donning surgical gloves during sex). Linda Hayden's performance is also outstanding, she's believable in the character as she transitions from doe-eyed innocent to gun wielding, vengeful antagonist on screen. Unfortunately although well portrayed by the actors neither our misogynistic protagonist Paul Martin nor his vengeful good girl gone bad secretary Linda are likeable characters (even Linda's killing spree draws little empathy due to her complete lack of likeability)

"Expose" is a straightforward revenge film, beautifully shot and visually stunning, the plot's there but it's predictable, feels drawn out in parts and lacks momentum, it's difficult to tell if it's the dubbing that sets it off balance or the random lingering shots of strange objects but there's something out of place. It's nightmarish, it's mysterious, yet it's tame by today's standards. It certainly provides ample nudity and exploitation, violence and bloodshed though it's execution incorporates a sly undertone of humour and it's for this reason that it's somewhat surprising that "Expose" was so heavily censored by the BBFC.

A deeply oppressive piano synth score works well to build the atmospheric tension and considering the low budget of the film the spattering of gore featured is well executed. "Expose" is both bizarre and eccentric at times, there's an underlying sleaze tone to the film with elements obviously inspired by "Psycho" and "Straw Dogs" though it feels a little hollow and diluted. "Expose" is definitely worth a watch (if you can get hold of a copy) but despite its place on the video nasty list modern day viewers may be disappointed that this notorious sleaze fest falls short of its scandalous reputation but when all's said and done "Expose" is an unsettling, obscure offering, a gruesome erotic thriller which will meet your pure exploitation expectations!

-Kerry Newton   Writer.

Faces of Death

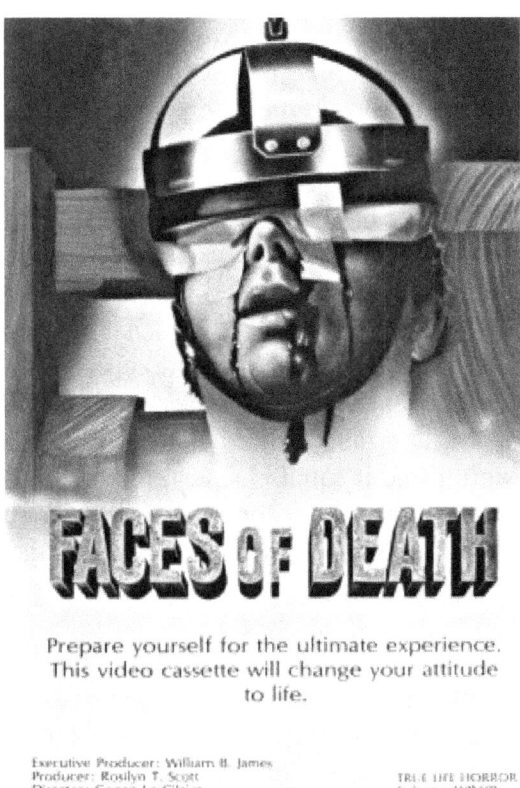

Year of release: 1978
Writer: Alan Black
Director: John Alan Schwartz as Conan LeCilaire
Unrated 105 mins. USA
Tagline: "Banned in 46 countries."
Main cast: Michael Carr (Dr. Francis B. Gross)
Distributed by: Atlantis Video Productions.

Even the original VHS release had around 32 minutes of footage cut. In 2003 this film was released with 2.19 seconds cut by the BBFC. This film is available in an uncut and unrated version in the US.

Plot:
Faces of Death is a documentary style film hosted by coroner Dr. Francis B. Gross, Faces of death features a large collection of deaths on screen, the film boasts being banned in 46 countries worldwide, The film focuses on the many faces of people dying in a number of very different way!

This Mondo style documentary mixes real death footage cleverly with fake staged deaths, including footage of horrific accidents and executions.

Appraisal:
This Mondo nightmare brought to you by John Alan Schwartz aka Conan LeCilaire and narrated by Dr. Francis B. Gross is a total mind fuck from start to finish! This film is both brutal and sickening and will leave you with a bitter aftertaste in your mouth. Faces of Death is a Mondo nightmare , the film is laid out like a real documentary with Charles B, Gross uncovering gruesome deaths from across the globe. This shockumentary, a rather original take on the video nasty with obvious hints to the godfather of the shockumentary 1962's "Mondo Cane". This is a non-stop journey into death itself, this vomit inducing feature film is a mix of real death scenes and fake scenes, well the jury is still out, some people say it does feature real deaths and most say that all the scenes from the film are staged all in all whether is the case it adds to the film and the sleazy feel to it, you feel like you are a voyeur watching something you shouldn't be watching.

Faces of Death does what it says on the tin, this film follows faces of death in a pseudo-documentary style slice of death. This film features grotesque real footage intermingled with faked scenes narrated by fictional consultant Dr. Francis B. Gross (Michael Carr) in an overall pretty disturbing offering featuring rituals, executions, monkey torture and orgies! This is definitely the most repulsive of all the video nasties and makes you feel well... nasty! I hate censorship, but you can see why in the early 80's this film was banned, It's sick and even at the time when I first got my hands on this film I just thought why would people actually watch this for entertainment, it just doesn't make sense to me. Faces of Death stayed with me, for good and bad the film is an inspiration to me, the no holds barred approach at the horror genre that we see here is both very clever and innovative filmmaking and marketing. Faces of Death makes me feel physically sick to this very day, it did the first time I watched it on a grainy old bootleg copy and does now with its high res picture, I think somewhat worse! Faces of Death is an important movie, it's a staple of its time, I still have the original VHS copy on my shelf to this day. Faces of Death is a shockumentary, and it certainly delivers on the shocks! I think what really freaked me out as a kid watching this movie is that I couldn't figure out what was real and what was actually fake in the playground it was rumoured everything in this movie was real, I was so damn nervous watching this film for the first time, I think I walked out the room at least three times as I thought I was going to be sick. I have always been a gore hound, but this out of all the Video Nasties did the job; it shocked me, it scared me, and it scarred me! Is Faces a Death a documentary, a Mondo movie, an experimental film, an art film? Is Faces of Death the best horror movie of all time? I'm yet to answer the above questions, but what I do know is for all its sins, it's a stand out horror film from the video nasty list, that is pure horror and terror rolled into one, it was ahead of its time it was a film that wasn't afraid to take risks. The film spawned may a sequel but no other in the series had the exposure that the original had being on the infamous video nasty hit list Faces of Death is a new in era of nasty, it's a cult horror movie that does need a warning sticker on the cover!

It's rumored that many death scenes are real including the questionable monkey brain feast or cauliflower with red dye?. This film is a hard watch, a voyeuristic slice of death. The animal deaths are a hard watch especially the scene with the seal. A combination of known fake and real footage make this Mondo classic one of the hardest to watch on the DPP list. This so-called documentary on death feature comes to life with narration by actor Michael Carr. At the time this film was perceived to be far worse than it actually is, in fact now, if you watch a news special on how meat gets to your plate you would find it equal in squeal factor.

Faces of Death does seem to have survived the test of time, it worked back then, but for a teenager today it would feel like an untimely drop in the fiber optic broadband connection. teenagers have seen far worse than this online but the youth in the early 80's certainly weren't ready for Faces of Death! The film features home footage style and super 8 video clips. On its release in the early 80's it had already been cut by over 30 minutes though was still included on the DPP list. There is a cut version with 2 minutes and 19 seconds removed (mainly a dog fight scene and monkey head bashing). "Faces of Death" was prosecuted, there have been another 5 films made in the series but only for European viewers eyes. This was one of the most talked about films in the school yard, if you hadn't seen it you were a pussy, there were tales of people vomiting watching it, even a rumor of someone having a heart attack and dying of shock due to the nature of the film though you have to factor into that the wild imaginations of school kids.

Besides "Cannibal Holocaust" this was one of my most memorable experiences of film as a child, I can vividly recall feeling sick to my stomach in anticipation as I loaded the VHS into the player! There was an unsettling feeling to it, a voyeuristic element that just seemed so wrong. At the time "Faces of Death" was shocking and some of those shocks still hold up today but with the internet nowadays you'll find a lot worse by accident or an unwelcoming post from a friend on a social networking website before it's censored by the powers that be!

This rather tasteless shockumentary does leave a rather bitter aftertaste in the mouth after viewing, the use of surgical procedures, airplane crashes, autopsies, and super 8 home video style footage is very effective.

Faces of Death is not a traditional horror film but the film is maybe the most horrific on the video nasty banned list!

Death is real we can all relate to it, we are all scared of death, This is what makes Faces of Death so damn scary! The message that death can strike at anytime, anywhere is conveyed really well, "Faces of Death" is the stuff of nightmares and the use of the grim reaper on the cover was one smart move, it really sums the whole film up perfectly!

I'd opt for a re-watch of an 80's slasher with a masked killer or exploitation film any day of the week, re-visiting Faces of Death after 20 odd years I have come to the conclusion that I will certainly not be watching the film for at least 20 more! and that'll be too soon! Not a great choice for a date movie, Faces of Death and Chill or Kill...just wouldn't work!

-Tony Newton

Standing as the most famous of the death 'documentaries' Faces of Death provoked a wave of disgust and protest amongst not only the usual suspects of Mary Whitehouse and the festival of light and ambitious politicians but from a wider range of the populace who had never seen the film but were none the less concerned by stories that this film that reportedly exhibited real death in many forms.

Such a subject was always likely to garner a reaction especially considering the general public's lack of understanding or knowledge of the conventions of Mondo films.

Faces of Death is really a typical Mondo film in almost all respects, its subject matter is typically more narrow though more morose than that of its predecessors such as Mondo Cane. The divergence of sex and violence in Mondo movies was clearly signposted by the arrival of Faces and the most notable examples from this point on stand in either camp and less frequently both.

The film opens with open-heart surgery being performed in a piece of semi theatrical filming (there is a POV shot looking up from the heart up at the surgeons) and leads us via morgue and autopsy footage until me meet our narrator. The odd looking 'Pathologist' Francis B Gross introduces us to the justification for this movie. This film is his exploration into the subject of death in its many forms, an exploration that has taken him around the world.

This is merely exposition though, Dr Gross is a fairly odd character and isn't very convincing and the theatrics of this film are obvious from the start despite some of the real footage we have just seen. From the outset we can see clear adhesion to the conventions of Mondo. We have the narrator who attempts to put the things we see into some context, we have a loose concept for why these things have been collected in the form of a journey of sorts and we're promised a trip around the world satisfying the travelogue element. We also of course see the combination of forgery and reality.

The theatrics of this film are heightened by the occasionally over sentimental and pseudo informative commentary and the almost always inappropriate choice of music that mocks the footage (old McDonald had a farm plays over the scene of the beheading of a chicken by a farmer's wife).

Without going into every scene it becomes fairly obvious when you know how films are constructed which scenes are reconstructions as the makers would have it, fakes as the cynics would have it, and which scenes are genuine. In common with the examples of the Italian horror films that made the nasties list, the animal death tends to real. The restaurant scene featuring a meal of live monkey brains however, arguably one of the most cited example of the barbarity of this film is in fact a fake. This scene and the dogfight were cut from the film prior to its eventual UK DVD release

Other notable scenes are again recreated, the gassing and electrocution are obviously fake; you can't record such events in the USA even with the consent of the victim. The Dixieland jazz soundtrack as the electric chair victim is strapped down and electrocuted somehow seems a little disrespectful. it is worth noting of course that most Mondo films accompany their most disgusting scenes with the most outrageously inappropriate music. This does have the effect of watering down the impact somewhat and I wonder if this is deliberate so as to not entirely alienate the audience of the time.

Speaking of the audience, It is worth noting that is seems that this film was originally destined for the Japanese market, one thing that this and other Mondo death films have in common are a remarkable aversion to sex or nudity as is illustrated by the diligent blurring or covering of the private areas of naked corpses. This prohibition of nudity while anything goes in the violence stakes, was as I understand it, a peculiarity of the Japanese market at the time, though it doesn't seem to be as much of an issue these days. It's interesting to note that even the extremely repellent 'Traces of Death' seems, remarkably, to adhere to this convention of no genitalia on view.

But, back to faces. Near the end of the film following a particularly gory segment of the remains of people after traffic accidents culminating in the aftermath of a plane crash in an urban, then after a brief excursion into life after death we have a birth scene followed by a montage of saccharin baby images, and as is obligatory with the best that Mondo has to offer we are treated to a cheesefest song called 'life'. This is presumably to act as a 'sorbet' of sorts. Funny enough it does distract you at least from the awfulness of some of the images we have been witness to.

Anything that is 'real' in relation to human tragedy in this film is usually sourced from news reels and the like, the animal death is most probably stock footage and the rest is by and large recreation. This last category makes up the majority of this film. The blurring of reality and fiction certainly makes this film more effective in its aim and surprisingly, as cynical and insincere as it is it still is not entirely damnable. There are a few moments that seem to resonate with a modicum of meaning, such as the abattoir footage, it's a fact of life and folks should know where their food comes from, and it is often a good thing to confront the taboo of death. It only has a limited success but hey this is Mondo and deep thought is only a secondary concern.

Anecdotally I remember the air of morbid curiosity that surrounded this particular film very well. It was something that one would approach with a certain trepidation and nervousness, its very viewing was almost akin to watching pornography though its effect was not one of titillation but that of an ordeal that one had to push through, the feeling of having survived it unharmed was quite exhilarating although this was tempered by a feeling of being somewhat dirtied by it, I had seen something that had been deliberately and earnestly hidden from me.

The supposed 'reality' of the film was one of its most impacting weapons. Other films had portrayed similar contents, granted not necessarily in as concentrated a form but perhaps too much higher production standards. But the very idea that this was for real instantly elevated its impact from cheap special effect to a moment of life or death with the gravitas that naturally commands. Combining the authentic footage along side the fake somehow made the fake seem as bad or worse than the real. The real of course almost always being of much lower film quality with it being grainier and harder to see meaning that the fake with its higher production values can be hyper real with its glorious close ups and higher quality images.

So what can be said for this film? What we can say about this film is that it is as awful as it is compelling. Is it the trash that the tabloids would have us believe? I don't think so. I feel that Mondo as a genre, of which this film stands as a prime example, plays the perfect exploitation game. It sucks you in with the promise of reality but more often than not doesn't deliver on that promise.

Even when the footage is in fact as honest and real as it can be, whatever that can mean in film terms, there is still a voyeuristic spin on it but in these regards Faces of Death is no different to other Mondo examples. Indeed the various media still churn out contemporary equivalents and the reporting media and public continue to swallow the bait, hook line and sinker, buying in at the first opportunity.

This film at least attempts to contextualise the content, however shallow the attempt is. This is something that some of the later films in this sub genre don't even bother to attempt (I'm talking to you 'traces of death') and despite it's morose tone it really doesn't actually contain anything I could honestly call obscene. When it comes down to it there are films of a similar nature that do the job more effectively but in the catalogue of these movies, this really isn't as bad as some would make out. Certainly you can see similar footage on the late night news on a fairly regular basis. At the time it was released it was rather more of a gut punch than it is these days but even so it still manages to be repellent and fascinating at the same time. Compared to others in its immediate genre it stands out as one of the better offerings, certainly it is the definitive example, but also because considering how upsetting the subject can be this film actually didn't leave me feeling too bad. The negative feelings I'd associate with this kind of material seem to evaporate surprisingly quickly and it's almost liberating to have gotten through it unscathed.

I would not recommend this to those who are squeamish or easily upset but if you have a strong stomach and can cope with the excesses this film contains then by all means watch it, especially with a mind as to what exactly it really is as opposed to what it has been reported to be.

-Glenn Criddle   Writer/Critic.

To have seen this film when I was growing up was like a badge of honour as at the time this was the only film to feature "real" deaths. Rumours about "Snuff" abounded, but were quickly quashed. When I first saw this film I was under the impression that everything I was witnessing was real. So when a copy came into my possession there was an equal 'horror' of whether or not I should actually view it.

When I eventually did I was genuinely shocked. Imagine American audiences seeing The Blair witch Project without knowing any hype.

Knowing what I know now, some of this film is faked, but there were specific scenes that stayed with me particularly the monkey's brains and the real autopsy at the beginning.

In my red-blooded teens I had the appetite for films like this , but now as the father of a young family that appetite has definitely waned. There are some quite grim aspects to this film and it's definitely not for the anaemic

There are also several sequels to this as the Japanese have a real desire for this kind of thing and made money over there.

-John Thomson   Actor/Comedian.

I actually can't recall watching a single horror film as a kid let alone a 'video nasty'. I remember hearing about them. *Faces of Death* was like the Boogeyman of cinema; does it exist? How do I find it? Am I safe if I watch it? Will my soul survive it if my body does not? I remember going into video stores searching for it on the walls, though terrified with the idea of finding it. Asking the clerks at the counters about it, store after store, city after city, as if it were some old folk tale I'd heard. Or maybe I just thought that I had asked them, as if even asking about this film was too much of a terrifying idea. Or worse than terrifying - simply wrong. I'd be damned to hell for speaking of and wondering about such vile pieces of cinema. I'm not sure what sparked my curiosity so much. I probably wouldn't have dared to watch it had I ever found it. I remember my childhood being flooded with nightmares after accidentally seeing any kind of terror on screen, real or not (even true crime mysteries on TV made me check my bed a hundred times before attempting to go to sleep). After going to the drive-in one night to see my favorite kind of cinema, the latest Jean-Claude Van Damme action flick, I was left scarred for years, shit stained of monkeys and dolls. The drive-in theatre we frequently attended was the Winnetka. It had eight screens. This particular night the screen next to ours was playing some kind of horror film with monkeys and dolls, or it must have been a monkey doll. I was terrified,and just wanted my action hero and flying jump split kicks. But I could not, just could not look away from that other screen. Even without the sound of it, just those images, made me nearly wet myself. That's my first real memory of a horror film. Other than that my dad says that the first movie he took me to I was pulled out screaming and crying during the first trailer (that of a John Carpenter film). He brought me back in when the film began and I was glued to the screen of whatever the actual movie was. So, I had an instant love for film, despite my traumatic experience minutes early. And I continued to love action films and steer clear of horror, especially after the drive-in incident. But I couldn't help the curiosity of *Faces of Death*. And I've still never seen it. Nor do I have any desire to. And yet I've now made multiple faux-snuff films myself, and still don't care much for watching any gruesome deaths on screen. Go figure.

-Shane Ryan   Writer, Producer, Director: *Amateur Porn Star Killer* series & the Alyssa Bustamante inspired picture, *My Name is 'A' by anonymous*, and creator of the anthology *Faces of Snuff*).

I remember being in high school, and going to visit family in New York. A buddy of mine, who is now one of my partner's in Raven Banner Entertainment, asked me to find Faces of Death in a video store, and bring it back for him. I think it may have been banned in Canada. So we grabbed it for him, but before we came back we watched it. I wouldn't necessarily say I enjoyed it, but I remember it being a far different experience than the average horror film. Back then, not being able to tell what was real or fake within the video, made the experience of just watching the most frightening aspect. Some of it was schlock, but some segments felt real enough that it felt I shouldn't be watching. Like a car accident, you can't turn away from. Back home, everyone wanted to see the video, if nothing else, just so they could say they had watched. It was one of the first films I remember that almost felt like a right of passage to me. From then on memories I have of my youth are often tied to the horror films I was watching.

-James Fler   Raven Banner Entertainment.

My earliest horror memories go back to the days when my middle sister and our friends would be over at my house watching some of the greatest horror films ever created. Films like "Friday the 13th" (which will be discussed in another essay), "Nightmare on Elm Street", "The Evil Dead", "House" and many more would be alive in the darkness of a room with pre-teen kids attempting to rage against the adult machine by watching these films and not believing that it would affect them. Well, I'm sorry to say it did and for me this film has been both a blessing and curse. These films all made an impact on me but my first ever horror film that I saw has never left me and impacted the way I view horror films. It was one of those films that my friends said, "I Dare You to Watch"! This film was John Alan Schwartz's super-8 movie of death, "Faces of Death".

Released in November of 1978, this near $450,000 film would gross nearly thirty-five million dollars and spawned multiple sequels being banned in over 40 countries earning its cult status to fans for generations. It featured under two hours of a mockumentary with narration showcasing pain, torture, disaster, dying, belief, and death in countries around the world. "Faces of Death" offered examples that varied throughout the film from natural disasters to slaughterhouses to napalm to torture to car accidents to animal killings and more! Each sequence was more graphic, disturbing, blunt, visceral, and real than the next one and nothing that I had seen at my tender age of eight. Watching the film several times over the years and owning a copy of it, most of the deaths are lost on me now blending together in a sick and jaded stew that floats in my head.

You may ask, why then does this film stick with you and has had this effect on you for so many years? Simple, I truly believe that "Faces of Death" changed who I was as a person and my mentality towards all that is horror. As a fan, nothing really shocks, surprises or scares me as it did before. No… this film changed my perspective on all that is horror and desensitize me a great deal.

One scene however has stayed with me showing the true power of film over the years. The scene is based on the foundation of luxury and taste as the narrator discusses a special delicacy for a group in a restaurant. Viewing these events and happenings in a dark room before me watching on my tube television a group now sits around a table with a locking ring in the center. The waiter puts a monkey into a circle locking it in place with a very blunt snap. The monkey fights to be free, making shrieking noises and violent movements being watched by the group around the table. A moment goes by and with use of blunt instrument, the monkey is smacked on the head until the skull is cracked open and the delicacy of "Monkey's Brains" is ready to scoop out of its lifeless body and skull. With each scoop and taste, the customers continue with their conversation, mannerisms and lives going about an evening of dining with no care in the world about another one of the faces of death.

That scene has never left me and changed a part of me. Many people will say "Faces of Death" is garbage or filth or a waste of film but I say it is diverse, disturbing and filmmaking that changed who I was as a person and a fan! To me, that is what a quality film is supposed to do. It makes you remember, stays with you and changes you as a fan. John Alan Schwartz did that for me and I thank him for those experiences that sent me down that dark path to the horror and the world I love today.

-Jay K   (The Horror Happens Radio Show).

Fight for Your Life

Also known as "Hostage", "Stayin' Alive".
Year of release: 1977
Writer: Straw Weisman
Director: Robert A. Endelson
R rated 82 mins. USA
Tagline: "There is no greater violence than a father's revenge for the rape of his daughter."
Main cast: Robert Judd (Ted Turner), Catherine Peppers (Mrs. Turner), Lela Small (Grandma Turner), Yvonne Ross (Corrie Turner), Reggie Rock Bythewood (Floyd Turner), Ramon Saunders (Val Turner).
Distributed by: Originally distributed by Vision On. This film is still banned in the UK even after all these year and is available in an uncut and unrated version in the US.

Plot:
Fight For Your Life is a Blaxploitation film, which features a trio of escaped convicts who wreak havoc in a small town as their attempt at a liquor store robbery goes awry. The racist trio take a black minister and his family hostage and subject them to brutal, savage and humiliating torture before the tables are turned as the minister regains the upper hand and takes revenge on the his tormentors.

Appraisal:
Fight for Your Life doesn't just provide the usual gore and rape scenes just for the hell of it, this film covers genuine issues of racism. For the late 1970's this film is a very underrated little gem.
It's a difficult watch as you find yourself connecting with the characters and rooting for the bad guys to get their comeuppance. William Sanderson (better known as J.F. Sebastian) in Ridley Scott's "Blade Runner" is on fire in this film, his awkwardness is perfect to believably portray this evil onscreen thug, he has a slime-bag creepiness to him as he plays Kane, the red neck with no rules!
Fight for Your Life does receive bad press; it's ultimately a low budget film which could have been better. I think this is a great action thriller, a true Blaxploitation horror, which is well worth watching. If you are a fan of films like "The Last House on the Left," you are in for a no holds barred exploitation treat.

-Tony Newton

While nearly all the most notorious of the so-called nasties have to some extent been critically redeemed, *Fight for Your Life* seems doomed for the moment to stay out there in the dark. It's frequently disparaged as a racist film, which would be the case if the film endorsed the racism it displays. In my observation it does nothing of the kind. It's an unacknowledged variation on *The Desperate Hours*, in both versions of which a middle-class family is held hostage at home by escaped convicts. *Fight for Your Life* makes the family black and adds virulent racism in the person of the gang's ringleader, played with unnerving conviction by William Sanderson (*Blade Runner*'s J. F. Sebastian).

Like the *Desperate Hours* films, it tests how far the family will be driven before they're forced to fight back, but puts more pressure on them by making the father (Robert Judd) a preacher who believes in peace and the rest of the family equally devout Christians. The film is certainly exploitative, but in the way common to many other 70s films, it uses these elements to address serious issues. Crucially, it shows only as much as it needs to show, and much of the violence is reticently presented, sometimes even off screen. The vengeful finale reportedly brought black American audiences to their feet in celebration, and I'd be surprised if anyone except a racist could resist the emotional release. It's significant that the original trailer described the film as "a saga of extraordinary courage that will leave you cheering". While this too is a simplification, it demonstrates that there's more to *Fight for Your Life* than its grubby reputation. It's overdue for reappraisal.

-Ramsey Campbell   Author, Writer: The Face That Must Die, Cold Print, The Grin of the Dark.

Robert A. Endelson's *Fight for Your Life* is a notable entry upon the Video Nasties list for several reasons. It features the big screen debut of the highly underrated actor William Sanderson (Deadwood, Blade Runner), it was the only Blaxploitation title to make it onto the list and also is was the only title to be lifted for language and tonal content as opposed to cinematic violence.

This is not to say that the movie is free of blood; not by any means. There are several shocking moments in which a young child has his skull pummelled in by a rock, a savage and brutal gang rape of a girl within earshot of her family and, in what is possibly the most alarming scene, a gun is placed to the head of a baby.

The movie begins with the escape of three convicts who we soon learn are both despicable in nature and highly dangerous. They steal the car of a pimp, who has just been abusing one of his girls, before making their way into the countryside, intent on fleeing to Canada. The trio of Jessie Lee Kane (Sanderson), Chino (Daniel Faraldo) and Ling (Peter Yoshida) represent an oddly diverse mix, given Kane's overt racist and bigoted outlook, but this will be the first of many of the film's slightly conflictive commentaries on the issues of racism.

They hold up a liquor store and in doing so manage to kill the clerk, leaving his baby in her high chair as they flee with the only customer, a young African American girl named Corrie Turner (Yvonne Ross) who had stopped by to pick up some wine for a family gathering. They demand to be brought to her house whereupon they subject all present to an incredibly abusive and reprehensible home invasion.

The Turner family are a very well scripted group of strong individual characters. The father (Ted: Robert Judd) is a pacifist preacher who believes in a peaceful way of life, whilst his wife and mother have a slightly more cynical and suspect view of outsiders (whites). Connie is still best friends with a white girl named Karen (Bonnie Martin), who was once engaged to her brother (who it transpires was killed in a tragic car accident). The youngest brother Floyd is a pre-teen who idolises Muhammad Ali and yells of 'Black Power', much to his grandmother's approval and his father's disdain.

This rather fragmented mix of sociological viewpoints is one of the movie's cleverest turns with regard to script and storyline. The inherent racism that exists in the Turner family is mirrored by the disgusting and repulsive forms of racist taunts and abuses, which Kane bestows upon them whilst they are under his capture. The derisive and insulting nature of the way in which he treats the family is difficult to watch and would undoubtedly unsettle even more people now than it did in 1977, but it would be too easy to dismiss this movie as an exploitative piece of sadism. There are some exceptionally poignant and relevant issues raised in relation to class, abuse, familial beliefs and world views.

The example of Floyd's relationship with the local Sherriff's son is a perfect one. For them their skin colour is irrelevant, no matter what Floyd's seemingly radical outbursts around the dinner table might otherwise suggest. There is also the possibility that Kane represents a lot more than a lone character, that he is indicative of a dying world, one in which power and brutality were once able to control an entire section of society, but are now steadily becoming the weak and out-dated minority.

The turnaround comes when Ted and his family regain control over their captors and seek to avenge the wrongs, which are carried out upon them. This is an entirely necessary plot development as otherwise it would leave the movie as a crass piece of highly racist and repugnant cinema. Some may argue that the revenge is short-lived and in no way reciprocates the ills which the Turners have suffered in the preceding 60 minutes, but this argument could also be placed against movies such as *I Spit on your Grave* (1978) in which greater focus is placed on the initial wrongdoings than on the subsequent vengeance.

Fight for Your Life has been largely lambasted by critics and remains unavailable in the UK to this day, with a release seeming highly unlikely at any point in the near future. I personally feel that this is a shame, as it means that the censors are still focusing on all the wrong elements of the movie. Such actions of outlawing this film are merely branding the movie as a racist feature, which places the emphasis only on the words and deeds of Kane. This is a shame, for there are a lot of questions being asked by the filmmakers. Admittedly, they are handled in a rather ramshackle and unsubtle manner, but I would most definitely advise that you watch this movie to make a decision for yourself. It is a tense, well crafted, if marginally flawed piece of cinema which does not deserve to be hidden away forever, and as repugnant as Kane's character may be, Sanderson gives a marvellous performance and it serves as a fine indication of his potential and talent.

-Colin McCracken   Writer.

Most of the Video Nasties were horror films. FIGHT FOR YOUR LIFE (aka STAYIN' ALIVE) was a 1977 exploitation film that earned its spot on the banned list with incendiary racial content. Not that there isn't violence in the movie, but other than the brutal killing of a child with a rock, it isn't anything audiences had not seen in plenty of other films that never made the list. The movie centers on a trio of convicts, led by Jessie Lee Kane (William Sanderson), a redneck with a hatred of blacks. Kane breaks out during a transport of prisoners with a Hispanic named Chino and a dangerously insane Chinaman named Ling. After stealing a pimp's Mercury, they decide to make a run for the Canadian border, but they take the daughter of a church deacon hostage after a liquor store robbery, and then her entire family as well. Kane torments Ted Turner (Robert Judd) by making him dance, sing and beating him unconscious with his own bible. Various humiliations follow, including the three convicts taking turns raping Turner's daughter. The grinning Ling disposes of the white girlfriend of the Turner's late son by tossing her over a waterfall and then the youngest son Floyd's friend by bashing him in the head with a rock. Turns out the kid is son of the Police Captain, who is helping Lieutenant "Rulebook" Reilly (David Cargill) track down the escaped convicts. The film shows Reilly several times being a stickler for the law and the rules, so that his allowing the family to have their vengeance (once they turn the tables on their captors) will be cheered by the audience. Two different trailers were issued...one catering to white audiences and the other to black audiences, and I can imagine what it must have been like to sit on a screening with black audiences as Kane and his cohorts are given their just deserts after all the terrible things the trio did to the Turner family. There is never any doubt that the filmmakers side with the victimized blacks and not with the racist Kane, and it is notable that his cohorts are not white as well, so that Kane becomes the laser focus of the audience hatred and, of course, his is the final showdown with the father, who just decided that "Turn the other cheek" is not all that is cracked up to be when dealing with scum like Kane. When Blue Underground finally released this on DVD, William Sanderson, embarrassed by the film, refused to participate in the extras. He certainly played up the role, however, gleefully pointing a gun at a crying toddler during the liquor store robbery and even pulling the trigger, but laughing at Chino how he pulled one on him cause he knew the gun was empty, having empty the remaining bullet in the store owner moments before. Kane even attempts to hang Turner's wife at on point for punishment when several family members pull knives on him. Despite its low budget and uneven acting, this is an entertaining "worm turns" revenge flick worth checking out.

-David Brown   Writer.

Flesh for Frankenstein

Also known as "Andy Warhol's Frankenstein".
Year of release: 1973
Writer : Paul Morrissey
Directors: Paul Morrissey and Antonio Margheriti
R rating 95 minutes US, France, Italy
Tagline: "We dare you to see..."
Main Cast: Udo Kier (Baron Frankenstein) Monique Van Vooren (Baroness Katrin Frankenstein) Joe Dallesandro (Nicholas the stable boy) Arno Juerging (Otto) Dalila Di Lazzaro (Female Monster) Srdjan Zelenovic (Sacha male monster).
Distributed by: Video Gems

The original theatrical release was distributed by Video Gems; the release was cut by around 8 minutes. In 1981 the uncut version was distributed in the UK. Late in 1982 Vipco distributed the original cut theatrical version on VHS. First Independent also released a version in 1996 on VHS, which had been cut by the BBFC by around 1 minute. The film did not surface uncut again until 2006 when it was released fully uncut by Tartan DVD in the UK.

Plot:
Baron Frankenstein should have an idyllic lifestyle with his wife and two children but instead he decides to create the Serbian super race starting with the perfect man and woman with help from his assistant Otto. Disastrous results occur as Baron Frankenstein's greed and lust takeover leading to a bloodbath as Baron Frankenstein struggles to control the monsters he has brought to life.

Appraisal:
This film is also known as Andy Warhol's Frankenstein, the film itself is produced by Andy Warhol among others; it was Andy Warhol's involvement, or should I say at least namesake that gave the film the exposure it deserved. "Flesh for Frankenstein" was presented in a space-vision 3D process debuting in cinemas across the globe including, Australia, Sweden and London. The use of 3D gave the impression that the film was gorier than it actually was, most notably the disembowelment scene with guts and entrails thrusting towards the audience and the scene in which children are attacked by bats, seemingly permeating the screen toward the audience. The film was initially X rated then later cut to 93 minutes and received an R rating in the US. The film is now available on DVD in its uncut form. The first time I watched "Flesh for Frankenstein" was on a bootleg VHS, the copy was actually cut and a far cry from the original version though it could have been a bad bootleg edition. I was thrilled to find that "Flesh for Frankenstein" was part of the channel 4's 3D week in November 2009 and as an added bonus it was the uncut version! Channel 4's 3D week also featured "Friday the 13th part 3". Udo Kier is such an underrated actor he is on nothing but top form here as the Baron Frankenstein whose soul we see fall apart onscreen. The gore is plentiful but blends in well, this whole film feels like you're watching a Hammer Horror film with unlimited gore and nudity, grand costumes and sets, it's a treat from start to finish. Paul Morrissey's/Andy Warhol's take on Frankenstein does actually work, it's always risky when fucking with the formula. The only problem I have with the film it when you view it in 2D the film doesn't work so well as it was originally made for 3D viewing. The 3D scenes stand out and it feels like everything including waving guts and bats at the camera just detracts from the film itself which when you watch in 3D you actually get a more pleasurable experience. I'm not a big fan of 3D and have only seen a few films at the cinema in 3D or in screenings in theatres "Jaws", "A Nightmare on Elm Street"

and "Friday the 13th part 3". I don't by in to today's modern 3D headaches and had to walk out on "Avatar" for being a headache inducing film in more ways than one.

If you haven't seen "Flesh for Frankenstein" and it's your first viewing of the film try to get a chance to see it in 3D.

I remember the Vipco release on VHS, it was a standout cover depicting the mad scientist complete with lightening surrounding the Baron who was impaled with guts on the end of the stick.

Flesh for Frankenstein was prosecuted.

An asset to anyone's horror collection.

Most notable line in the film.

"To know death, Otto, you have to fuck life in the gallbladder"
–Baron Frankenstein
-Tony Newton

The very fact that this was a "forbidden fruit" was exactly why I sought it out with two friends one night when I was growing up. It was playing on Cannery Row in Monterey, California, the heart of Steinbeck country. It was a small theater that was screening it in glorious 3D against an actual silver lenticular screen. The film has stretches that are slow and certainly by today's standards, glacially so, but for me at the time it delivered exactly what it promised. Intertwining sex and body gore (and gallbladders) with re-animation and obsession made for a kind of X-rated giddiness in which I felt I was an accomplice to an inside joke. By the time entrails were dangling inches away from my face I was giggling out loud. Most of the fun came the next day when I could actually tell other friends that I had seen it. All in all, it still gets a big thumbs up from me more for the tone and audacity than for anything else.

-John Penney   Writer: The Return of the Living Dead 3/Director: Hellgate.

Paul Morrissey(b.1938) was a regular creative collaborator with Andy Warhol, working on some of the movies, which helped to manipulate the enigmatic artist's vision into cinematic form. Whilst history has finally allowed Morrissey to take the deserved credit for the films he made, it is unlikely that they will ever be independently referenced without somehow being associated with Warhol, regardless of his creative input (which by all accounts is pretty minimal).

With the likes of *Flesh* (1968), *Trash* (1970) and *Heat* (1972)Morrissey created highly eroticised, gritty, yet surreal examinations of sexuality and the darker elements of life in New York and L.A. at the time. Often put together with little to no budgets, most of his movies from that period were shot at weekends over the course of a few months. These films also assisted in launching the career of Joe Dallesandro, a teenage runaway who would go on to become a sexual icon for both men and women for decades afterwards(as well as later featuring as the infamous crotch on the cover of The Rolling Stones' *Sticky Fingers* album and The Smiths' eponymous debut).

Morrissey and Dallesandro went to Italy to create two very unique interpretations of Gothic horror classics in the form of *Flesh for Frankenstein* (1973) and *Blood for Dracula* (1974). The use of 3D for the release of *Frankenstein* allowed the filmmakers to play extensively with the gore, taking full advantage of the entrails and body parts, which they had hurtling out of the screen. Avid watchers of Morrissey's material will already be familiar with Dallesandro's body parts hurtling towards the screen, but the context is somewhat different in this case.

Udo Kier (at his absolute finest) plays the erratic Baron Frankenstein, offering one of the most genuinely demented interpretations of the doctor to date. His insanity is only surpassed by his sexual desire and, in his cloud of madness, seeks to create the perfect couple. The Baroness Katrin Frankenstein is an abandoned, sexually unfulfilled wife (and, incidentally, the Doctor's sister) played with eerie dominance by Monique van Vooren. Her husband, lost in his work and assisted by the hapless Otto (Arno Juerging) is in the process of creating the perfect couple, so as to forward the development of the ultimate 'Serbian Race'. This particular element offers possible analysis into underlying commentary on the ideals of eugenics and selective breeding, which add an unsettling resonance to the movie.

Dallesandro plays a noble stable boy, reminiscent of a character from a steamy, bodice-ripping novel. Frankenstein and Otto observe him in a brothel, ("Two girls, one man? He must be very powerful. Look at his head!") and set designs upon him to serve as the male breeding specimen. The Baroness demands that he also be used for her own sexual gratification and in conjunction after finding him in a compromising position with a local girl. The Doctor utilises the, as of yet un-reanimated, female for his own perverse desires (one scene which caused particular affront to some involved, not only copulation with the corpse, but simultaneous investigative probing into its open wounds). That sequence also spawned the unforgettable line; "To know death, Otto, you have to fuck life in the gall bladder!"

Flesh For Frankenstein is beautifully shot and not without intentional (and unintentional) humour, all of which is complimented greatly by Claudio Gizzi's delicate and graceful score. I would love to have had the opportunity to witness it in the cinema, in its original 3D print, as all of my encounters with the film were from VHS copies. It is definitely a worthy acquisition for Frankenstein completists, Warhol fans, or the simply curious. Warhol's name was, essentially, just attached to the project to boost sales, for he had little (if anything) to do with the actual film itself. The gore is particularly well presented for the time and, rubber bats aside, the overall special effects are well constructed and would have definitely been highly shocking for the casual cinemagoer in the early 1970's.

-Colin McCracken   Writer.

David Bond: Can you tell me why your father was listed as second unit Director for Andy Warhol's Frankenstein?

While some Italian prints reportedly give second unit director Antonio Margheriti credit as director of the film, Udo Kier has stated that Antonio Margheriti had nothing to do with directing the film. Udo Kier stated that he and the other cast members received direction only from Morrissey, and noted that he never saw Margheriti on the set.

Edoardo Margheriti:

In that film I know that Antonio Margheriti was in charge of the 3D shooting, due to his technical experience.. He was shooting all the shots in 3D of Frankenstein and in that film he also directs some sequences with the two little kids doing experiments... those scenes were added to the film after principal photography to be able to edit the film. Paul Morrisey and Andy Warhol were working without a script, inventing day by day with the Actors. Carlo Ponti was afraid of it and asked Antonio to help take care of the 3D affects.

-Edoardo Margheriti   Writer, Director, Producer.

Forest of Fear

Also known as "Toxic Zombies" and "Bloodeaters".
Year of release: 1980
Writer: Charles McCrann
Director: Charles McCrann
R rated 89 mins. USA
Tagline: "Nothing prepared the world for the horror…"
Main cast: Charles McCrann (Tom Cole), Beverly Shapiro (Polly Cole), Dennis Helfend (Hermit), Kevin Hanlon (Jimmy), Judith Brown (Amy), Pat Kellis (Mother).
Distributed by Monte Video. This film has no UK release but is available in an unrated and uncut US version.

Plot:
Forest of Fear see's zombies in yes you guessed it a forest! Hippies are poisoned after their illegal drug plantation is dusted with the chemical Dromax by a passing airplane following instructions from the Government. The drug farmers turn into flesh-eating zombie-like creatures whilst an innocent family desperately try to find a safe route out of the forest and away from the ensuing terror.

Appraisal:
This film is just okay, it's not groundbreaking but in fact more soul crushing for the viewer. Forest of Fear has a ridiculously low budget which is reflected in most aspects of the film none more so than the acting which consequently leaves a lot to be desired.

The cinematography throughout feels low grade and the film overall has dated badly. All things considered this wouldn't be one of my first recommendations from the video nasty list, not by a long shot. On paper the premise of the film has potential but that's as far as it goes I'm afraid. It's a fun watch if you have a few friends over for a laugh out loud movie, in fact you would need to be stoned to watch the film, which is quite ironic.

In my opinion this film could have been so much more if it weren't for the constraints of its all but non-existent budget, I think I smell a remake on the horizon! or is that just the feint whiff of the weed in the air?

-Tony Newton

I find it hard to believe that this came out in 1980. It must have felt dated even when it was first released. Either this was shelved for a number of years, or it was directed by someone trying very hard to make something the 'kids' might like. The gore is cheesy, the acting is non-existent, and the plot is just plain lame.

We open on what appears to be a group of hunters stalking and gunning down a hippie in the middle of the woods. As it turns out, the 'hunters' in question are feds. You can tell by their lack of anything resembling federal identification. The hippie in question is one of many marijuana farmers. And when the farmers find their downed colleague, they take their bloody revenge on the feds. As a result, "The Government" decides to spray the crops with a deadly toxin that turns the farmers into zombies when exposed to it that dangerous Devil Weed. The film that plays out as a result is laughable.

If Richard Nixon remade Reefer Madness it would look a lot like this film.

In a way, it's classic sci-fi, with its static 2-Shot cutaways to 'government headquarters' and its bat-shit insane social 'message.' It's hard to believe the DPP had a problem with this film. If anything, it comes off as pro-government and is so lacking in entertainment that it comes off like a poorly made industrial training film.

When all is said and done, this could be one of the worst films that made the Video Nasty list. And that's saying something.

-Mark Miller   Writer, Director, Producer: Seraphim Films.

The Gestapo's Last Orgy

Also known as "L'ultimate Orgia del III Reich", "Last Orgy of the Third Reich" and "Caligula Reincarnated as Hitler"
Year of release: 1977
Writer: Cesare Canevari
Directors: Cesare Canevari and Antonio Lucarella
X rated 81 mins. Italy
Tagline: "The sickest entry in the Nazisploitation genre!"
Main cast: Adriano Micantoni (Commandant Conrad Von Starker), Daniela Poggi (Lise Cohen), Maristella Greco (Alma), Fulvio Ricciardi, Antiniska Nemour, Caterina Barbero.
Distributed by: Originally distributed by VFP. The film is still banned in Britain but is available in an uncut and unrated US R1 release.

Plot:
Gestapo's Last Orgy is a Nazisploitation film. This film sees Lise Cohen flashback to the point in her life when she was taken to a women's prisoner of war camp at which she endured unspeakable terror at the hands of her tormentor Conrad Van Stark who is now her lover!

Appraisal:
The Gestapo's Last Orgy is actually a serious take on the Nazisploitation genre film and doesn't hold back on the full-on torture, sex, and yes, you guessed it - more sex! It's disturbing to watch in places including (but not limited to) the cannibalism. It's certainly a unique take on the genre and as such is definitely worth a watch. On the first viewing I expected a more fun film and more horror but this certainly isn't that! This is a far from the usual naziploitation offerings, of course it still involves the typically sadistic, twisted and unsettling acts of crazed Nazi's but "The Gestapo's Last Orgy" does have a more serious undertone which highlights the perversions of the Nazi's and the realities of their treatment of female Jewish prisoners. This film finds the Nazis eating human flesh, which left me questioning: did they actually do this?

The film's pacing is incredibly slow in parts to the point where at times it's easy to forget you're watching a video nasty. The Gestapo's Last Orgy is the "Schindlers List" of Nazi exploitation: no Oscars here, but it does leave you feeling uncomfortable and with a bitter aftertaste.

-Tony Newton

The House by the Cemetery

Also known as "Quella Villa Accanto al Cimitero."
Year of release: 1981
Writers: Elisa Briganti and Lucio Fulci
Director: Lucio Fulci
Unrated 87 mins. Italy
Tagline: "Past and present collide in a vortex of fear!"
Main cast: Catriona MacColl (Lucy Boyle), Paolo Malco (Dr. Norman Boyle), Ania Pieroni (Ann), Giovanni Frezza (Bob Boyle), Silvia Collatina (Mae Freudstein), Dagmar Lassander (Laura Gittleson).
Distributed by: Originally distributed by Videomedia. In 1988 Elephant Video released a cut version of the film with 4.45 seconds of cuts by the BBFC. In 2009 Arrow released a fully uncut version of the film passed by the BBFC.

Plot:
Lucio Fulci's classic The House by the Cemetery follows new residents Dr. Norman Boyle, his family and babysitter as strange and terrifying things begin to occur in their new family home. These strange goings on occur as Dr. Norman Boyle is researching Dr. Freudstein, a job his predecessor apparently committed suicide whilst working on and Dr. Boyle's son befriends Mae, a mysterious girl whom can only be seen by him. What dark secrets lurk inside the house by the cemetery?

Appraisal:
The House by the Cemetery delivers on so many levels, it has scares, shocks, plot twists and supernatural components to it. Since "The Omen" Children have never been portrayed in a way that is so unnerving as they are in this film, they're creepy as hell! Ania Pieroni plays the role of Ann the babysitter and appears both effortless and faultless in the role. Paolo Malco plays the character very convincingly with an almost comfortable approach as Doctor Norman Boyle, the beard and glasses suit the character well and the actor's child-like charm shines through in this role. The House by the Cemetery is a great all-rounder, it provides the viewer with psychological horror, shocks, a small amount of gore plus a crazy dream-like sequence and doesn't seem to have dated too badly either. Fulci captures a certain feel with this film and at times leaves you as the viewer almost making your own mind up, not dissimilar to those classic choose your own adventure books. The House by the Cemetery is often snubbed due to the fact that a similar film "The Beyond" (another classic from the DPP banned list) is a much better film overall. The House by the Cemetery was prosecuted.
-Tony Newton

There is a sticker that's bound to adorn the accessories of nearly every convention-dwelling horror obsessive you'll meet. It's black, approaching bumper sticker size and, next to its iconic image from the 1979 undead classic, *Zombie*, touts the exclamation: "FULCI LIVES!" Two of these bad boys grace my own water bottle and keyboard case with their presence, and they loom over genre-philia at large like a specter, beckoning enthusiasts to visit or revisit the prolific filmography of the man whom the sticker makes mention. That man, Lucio Fulci: written off as a hack with delusions of aesthetic grandeur by just as many *giallo* purists as those who deem his unchecked gore fixation key to the mastery of his domain. In the realm of Video Nasties, Fulci's 1981 supernatural exploitationer, *The House by the Cemetery*, stands as a curious case of a film that, after its initial United Kingdom ban in 1984, has lived and died and lived again during its journey from rabidly cut mid-'80s home video release to restoration in its unholy, original form.

With the luxury of viewing Fulci's director's cut of *The House by the Cemetery* comes the burden of frustration over how it could have been allowed to be seen any other way. To break into outrage in response to the BBFC's objections to the film's various bodily mutilations and its killer, Dr. Freudstein's, (Giovanni De Nava) unconventional use of a fireplace poker is to overstate the obviousness of the token anti-censorship stance. But then, the art of 'getting' Fulci is one of knowing that Fulci doesn't 'get' art devoid of overstatement — or, at the very least, of knowing that the graphic violence of his films begets an obviated art of its own. As do the rest of his finest works, *The House by the Cemetery* steeps itself in the pulpy, pleasurable trappings of amplified wooden floor creaks, ghostly moans that weave in and out of punchy synthesizer riffs, and gargantuan keys that seem to exist only to be *heard* in their dogged efforts to pry open rusty locked doors. And just as Fulci milks these tropes to convey the sonic spookiness of their literal existence, so too does he hang his camera on geysers of blood, severed heads and stabbed throats to divorce them from narrative context and foreground them as 'just scary,' without explanation.

The House by the Cemetery exists in some aesthetic purgatory in which traditional Gothicism, the stylization of Fulci's Italian contemporaries (chiefly, Dario Argento and Mario Bava) and the director's fetishization of blood-letting 'money-shots' all hold its efforts to attain a singular identity hostage. It is with great irony, then, that a retroactive look at the film makes clear that its amorphousness renders its specificity. That the BBFC would forbid it to see the light of day is perhaps a direct mode of response to the film's exploitive encroachment on British Gothic Horror's prestigious, hallowed grounds. Consider: does our knowledge of the film's censorship-related history make the on-screen cemetery to which the title refers its own metaphor? Indeed, this corpse-filled space can be easily understood as a burial ground for the polite Gothic horror titles of the British old guard, which, in the wake of the proliferation of Fulci and others, has been desecrated with gory glee. In the wake of its ban, release, and re-release(s), the smoke has cleared, the dust has settled and *The House by the Cemetery* has effectively, (if only momentarily) laid conservative (British) conceptions of Gothic tropes to rest. And Fulci, meanwhile… Well, Fulci lives.

-Max Weinstein   Writer, Editorial Director MovieMaker Magazine.

The House on the Edge of the Park

Also known as "La Casa Sperduta Nel Parco"
Year of release: 1980
Writers: Gianfranco Clerici and Vincenzo Mannino
Director: Ruggero Deodato
Unrated: 79 minutes, Italy
Tagline: "David Hess … star of "Last House on the Left" is loose again … Don't go in the park."
Main cast: David Hess (Alex), Annie Bell (Lisa), Christian Borromeo (Tom), Giovanni Lombardo Radice (Ricky), Marie Claude Joseph (Glenda), Gabriele Di Giulio (Howard).
Distributed by: Originally distributed by Skyline. In 2011 Shameless released a cut version of the film with 43 seconds cut by the BBFC. Available uncut and unrated in the US R1.

Plot:
The House on the Edge of the Park follows a psycho degenerate mechanic (Alex) whose spare time is spent stalking the streets of New York. Alex tortures and rapes women for his own entertainment. Alex and his simple friend Ricky are invited to an upper class party, when Alex's straight razor comes out the torture, mayhem and horror continues.

Appraisal:
In Ruggero Deodato's cult horror offering, The House on the Edge of the Park, we encounter a rather explicit, sleazy horror, which centers on psycho rapist David Hess and his friend Giovani Lombardo of "Cannibal Ferox" fame. This film is often swept under the carpet but this exploitation gem is one that is not to be missed! David Hess of "The Last House on the Left" fame is fantastic throughout the film and portrays a very frightening and realistic villain. "The house on the Edge of the Park" is a sick, twisted and disturbing film, it features a harrowing rape scene even before the initial credits have rolled so you know what you are in for! When Hess and Lombardo find themselves guests at a party in the company of the rich upper-class things go from fun to frantic as they bring the party to an abrupt end by taking the guests hostage and brutally attacking and raping them. The music score is a full on Disco Funk frenzy. Lombardo has a manic psycho quality though there's a naivety to his performance alongside Hess' strong psycho portrayal. It's well worth checking out this often-overlooked classic slice of nastiness. I just love this film and give it a watch at least once a year!
Pure exploitation gold!

-Tony Newton

Think of every home invasion movie you've ever seen. Now combine all of those films and multiply their intensity by 10 and you're beginning to understand what kind of film you're dealing with.
The House on the Edge of the Park was directed by Ruggero "More Rape" Deodato, so you know, going in, that something special is about to take place.
The film borrows from The Last House on the Left so heavily that it even has David Hess in it. Hess, who should be played by Ken Marino if they ever make a biopic about him, is here doing what he does best: portraying a scumbag guido with a penchant for non-consensual intercourse.

The film opens with Hess driving and making eyes at a woman he's spotted on the road next to him. As the tender ballad "Sweetly. Oh Sweetly" caresses our ears, we see Hess swerve out in front of her so that she has to stop her car. He then gets out of his car and has his way with her before slashing her to death with a straight razor. And that's just the first 5 minutes.

But, lest you think the The House on the Edge of the Park is all shock factor and no story, you should know that there is a plot afoot here, and it takes such a hard left turn at the end it almost gives the viewer whiplash.

Once our obligatory opening is out of the way, we move into the film proper. It follows our scumbag guido, Alex (Hess, Natch) and his tweaker friend, Ricky, (played with zany zeal by Giovani Lombardo Radice) who, I think, run a parking garage. Two young, attractive yuppies (who must have been the visual inspiration for the violent youths in 2013s The Purge) pull into said garage and strike up a conversation with Alex and Ricky. It turns out that the yuppies are on their way to a party and through some forced dialogue, Alex and Ricky end up going to the party with them. This is where the real fun begins.

The second Alex and Ricky arrive at the posh residence (the titular house on said edge of park, which is really just an expansive backyard, it would seem) they meet the attendants of the party and find themselves on the receiving end of laughter. To be sure, the partygoers are not laughing WITH Alex and Ricky, they're laughing AT them. What they don't know is that Alex and Ricky aren't the kind of people you should laugh at.

After watching the yuppies laugh at Ricky's high-energy shenanigans, having his clothes stolen, and watching Ricky lose at poker, Alex decides he's had enough and declares, "Now we're gonna have some fun with these cunts."

And here's where the movie earns its place in the Video Nasty pantheon. The bulk of the action takes place as Alex and Ricky hold the party-goers hostage, piss on them, slash at them with the aforementioned straight razor, and repeatedly tear the clothes off of all of the women at various points throughout the film.

But through all its brutality, the HOUSE has a benign lyricism that belies its subject matter. There is, of course, that soft, misty ballad, "Sweetly, oh Sweetly." It keeps showing up at only the most violent of sequences. But that's just one of the many gently laced melodies found within in the film. Even HOUSE's second (!) rape scene is cut to a tender acoustic instrumental arrangement.

But, after a good 70 minutes of torturing everyone in the house, Ricky, out of the blue, decides he's had enough and steps in between Alex, mid-slash, as he lays into one of the guests. Ricky gets a gut full of straight razor and falls to the floor. He dies in Alex's arms, that haunting instrumental dirge playing him off this mortal coil. Apparently he was a very sensitive soul.

And while Alex looses cries of, "Ricky. Why did you make me do it? Why'd you turn against me? I didn't want to hurt you," our main yuppie pulls out a gun and shoots Alex in the chest, but not before explaining to him that all of this was one big setup. He reveals that he is the brother of the woman Hess raped and killed at the start of the film. "And you fell for it, faggot," says our yuppie.

It seems like there are easier ways to get revenge. He could have at least pulled the gun out sooner. But maybe he's a sadist and preferred to have his face smashed in for an hour before drawing on Alex.

Regardless, our partygoers get a real kick out of dispatching Alex. They each take turns shooting him. And eventually he falls into the swimming pool and lies there, face down, bleeding out, as that aforementioned gentle ballad rises in volume once more. Apparently, his arc is complete. He lived as he died. Sweetly. Oh Sweetly.

-Mark Miller   Writer, Director, Producer: Seraphim Films.

I Spit on Your Grave

Also known as "Day of the Woman".
Year of release: 1978
Writer: Meir Zarchi
Director: Meir Zarchi
X rated 101 mins. USA
Tagline: "More devastating than Deliverance!"
Main cast: Camille Keaton (Jennifer), Eron Tabor (Johnny), Richard Pace (Matthew), Anthony Nichols (Stanley), Gunter Kleemann (Andy), Alexis Magnotti (Attendant's wife).
Distributed by: Originally distributed by Wizard Video. In 2001 the film was released on DVD with 7.02 seconds cut by the BBFC. In 2010 a cut with only 2.54 seconds missing was passed by the BBFC. It's available uncut and unrated in R1 US DVD.

Plot:
I Spit on Your Grave tells the story of Jennifer Hills, a young lady and aspiring writer who escapes to a cabin in the country in order to work on her novel. Jennifer receives the unwanted attention of a local barbarous group of hillbillies who attack and brutally rape her. Victim Jennifer soon turns the tables as one by one she then seeks revenge on each of her attackers.

Appraisal:
I Spit on Your Grave is one of the most popular and well-known titles on the DPP list and caused quite a stir at the time. The controversy surrounding the film attracted bigger audiences; the hype was caused mainly by the scene featuring a man's penis being severed (which is, in my view the punishment every single rapist should receive in real life). I Spit on Your Grave is an extreme revenge movie, you root for the girl to exact bloody revenge on each of her vial attackers. The film is a disturbing tale which both shocks and terrifies its audience. I Spit on Your Grave doesn't seem dated and still stands up as a classic horror film, which has inspired many horror filmmakers across the globe. I Spit on Your Grave, Cannibal Holocaust and Faces of Death are up there as the poster children films from the banned movie era, there is no poster as iconic as the young innocent teen with ripped underwear clutching a knife, it was such a simple poster/video sleeve yet so effective. I remember seeing the original poster in the video store surrounded by bright yellow borders drawing you in, once again there was so much hype surrounding this cult classic horror film that you always remember where you were the first time you saw "I Spit on Your Grave". I remember sneaking downstairs nervously, late one night to watch it without my parents knowing, with an enormous feeling of apprehension that I was watching something that felt very wrong indeed. The acting from Camille Keaton is faultless; this movie is a true video nasty.

Women are strong and Camille Keaton shows that you don't mess with women.

-Tony Newton

Jennifer Hills is a writer from the city who rents a small cabin near the Housatonic River seeking the peace and isolation necessary to finish writing her book. It all goes wrong, however, when she attracts the attention of a few local men (the only denizens of Kent, Connecticut we are allowed to meet, as a matter of fact) who spend close to half of the film raping and abusing her. Five men, over three different encounters, sexually assault and abuse Jennifer for forty-five minutes of the movie before entrusting the mentally enfeebled Matthew to murder her. He doesn't, and so begins Jennifer's physical recovery and path of revenge.

When I was a teenager there were a few infamous films whose acquisition was paramount. Among the movies my friends and I absolutely HAD to get our hands on, this was close to top of the list. What put it there was partially due to Roger Ebert's reaction that I SPIT was one of the most reprehensible films he'd ever seen. He went so far as to call it a "vile bag of garbage" and commented as much on the reaction of the audience to the rape as much as he did on the movie itself. But it wasn't the rape my friends and I were interested in as much as the revenge, particularly, the bathtub scene. See, among boys of a certain age, the rape in the film might have initially been titillating, until it drags on so long as to be discomforting, and finally numbing, bordering on boring. Zarchi sets up the final act of the movie by doubling and then tripling down on the insults heaped on the unfortunate Ms. Hills. There can be no mistake that she is perfectly justified in going on a brutal mutilation and murder spree. I don't know if it was Zarchi's intent to make the sexual assault go on so long that anyone who started out being amused or entertained would have to sit fully with her character and confront his own culpability as an observer (Zarchi has spent an awful lot of time over the years defending his work by claiming it's a feminist fable, when in reality the sexual assaults in the picture are lurid, if not prurient), but that's how it feels on a re-watch now. But like I said, when my friends and I were talking about what we'd heard about this movie, it wasn't the rape we spoke of--it was the guy who gets his dick cut off in the tub! Although the premise that gets Jennifer in the bathtub with her attacker is ridiculous by modern imagining (maybe it was seen differently in the 70s), the scene itself is impactful because the camera doesn't turn away. Just like in the assaults against her, this scene is filmed with a documentary sterility that confronts the viewer as it lingers. We, of course, were all clutching our wedding tackle, groaning at the worst conceivable nightmare a boy could imagine.

Is I SPIT ON YOUR GRAVE a good film or even a watchable one? No. But it is two things: 1) it is exceedingly confrontational and discomforting (if you're at all human), and 2) clearly an inspiration to scores of other filmmakers in the rape-revenge genre.

-Bracken MacLeod   Writer, Horror Author.

What a great title! This is a late 1970's revenge flick with very bold subject matter. Not just another rape/revenge movie...this is the rape revenge movie. It was banned for a while and I question if that was due to the rape scenes or was it that they did not want women to get ideas and commit acts of revenge such as this. Not all victims just take what is dished out to them. Some like to take matters into their own hands and dish it out cold. I think part of the controversy was because she used her sexuality to lure the rapists so she could have her vengeance, good for her. I hope she was able to get her writing done after all that.

I hear some people don't like this movie due to the length and relentless rape scene. Well, this was done so the viewer would know and experience what Jenny went through. I've heard some people refer to the rape scene as pornographic. It is not meant to be sexy. Again it is so you the watcher of the movie will fully understand the devastating acts she had to live through. Not everyone has been raped, so not everyone knows what the victim of this type crime has to deal with. There are reasons why she ended up castrating a dude. If you don't view the rape you don't have a reason behind the R&R. Otherwise with no rape it would just be a movie about a woman serial killer.

-Lilith Stabs   Horror Actress.

THE MAKING OF "SAVAGE VENGEANCE"
I spit on your grave 2 - Unofficial Sequel

For better or worse, SAVAGE VENGEANCE has earned the most notorious reputation of the two dozen or so movies I've directed. Since its production in 1988, SAVAGE VENGEANCE has gone from despised to scandalous to now something of a cult oddity. And of all the movies I've made since the 80's, it's the one I'm most asked about.

It wasn't supposed to be that way. Of the three movies I worked on in 1988, SAVAGE VENGEANCE was by far the cheapest… an ultra low budget follow-up to a much bigger Camille Keaton movie with six times the shooting days and 100 times the budget! But today that bigger film is virtually forgotten while interest in SAVAGE VENGEANCE shows no signs of waning.

The long and winding road that lead to Camille Keaton and I to making SAVAGE VENGEANCE in rural Tennessee locations actually started the previous year in Los Angeles. And it all started with my friend, Rodney.

Rodney was a free-lance actor who paid the bills as a cabin attendant on Amtrak's LA to Seattle route - fluffing pillows and bringing drinks for the stressed-out train travelers. He had done a few days on my current project, CANNIBAL HOOKERS, and was full of ideas how he could help with my next production.

CANNIBAL HOOKERS had just wrapped when I got a call from a very excited Rodney. I'd barely picked up the phone when he blurted out, "How'd you like Camille Keaton in your next movie?"

I was sceptical but kept listening. How could RODNEY of all people know Camille Keaton? I only knew her as the star of I SPIT ON YOUR GRAVE - a film I'd seen ten years earlier at Murfreesboro, Tennessee's Marlboro Drive-In, but knew she was a huge horror star. . . in part thanks to a vicious, misguided attack piece from film critic Roger Ebert.

"A vile bag of garbage" is how Ebert began his review, not mentioning that the film had been made under the empowering shooting title of DAY OF THE ROMAN. Ebert also failed to mention that Keaton had been mentored by ROMEO AND JULIET director Franco Zeffirelli during her short career in Italian films, was a friend of multi-Oscar winner Federico Fellini and had starred in a film scored by no less then acclaimed composer Ennio Morricone.

Instead, Ebert vented on and on. . .little realizing he words were transforming an obscure revenge thriller into a "must see" sensation. "It is a film so sick, reprehensible and contemptible," Ebert raged, "I can hardly believe it's playing in respectable theatres." Yes it was, Mr. Ebert. And making Camille Keaton a bigger star every day!

None of my previous film had featured a celebrity of Camille Keaton's name value. The closest I came on CANNIBAL HOOKERS was hiring Jocelyn Lew, the sometime girlfriend of Marlon Brando's son, Christian Brando. Jocelyn had just co-starred in a movie with Klaus Kinski but - luckily for me - she appeared in CANNIBAL HOOKERS for the same pay rate as the other actors - next to nothing!

But CAMILLE KEATON - this was an ENTIRELY different matter. I would need a real budget to work with her. The buzz from I SPIT ON YOUR GRAVE was still going strong and Camille has recently co-starred with no less than DIAMONDS ARE FOREVER star Jill St. John in the prison drama THE CONCRETE JUNGLE. But then Rodney told me something I could scarcely believe.

"She works with me at Amtrak," Rodney said casually.

"With YOU?" I asked incredulously. "At AMTRAK?? What does she DO?"

"The same thing I do!" Fluffs pillows. Brings snacks to passengers. We do the LA to Seattle route every week!"

What Rodney was telling me was that Camille Keaton was paying the bills as a TRAIN STEWARDESS. I couldn't believe it and instantly concluded he was lying. . .just testing me to see how gullible I was. But I played along.

"Okay," I said. "Can I meet her then?"

"Sure," Rodney replied. "I'll tell her we're coming over!"

So that was that. Rodney had called my bluff. If this was a con, it was one slick, flawlessly executed con. Rodney's voice hadn't betrayed the slightest hesitation. He said he worked with Camille Keaton on Amtrak and. . . I think I BELIEVED him!!

The next day, I found myself standing next to Rodney as he knocked on the door of a modest Los Angeles apartment. The door swung open and. . .it was HER. CAMILLE KEATON in the flesh! Her hair was shorter than I'd last seen in I SPIT ON YOUR GRAVE but there was no mistaking that face. . .that frankly beautiful face. I was about to meet Camille Keaton because. . . Rodney had been telling me the TRUTH!!

Once inside, Camille happily gave me a quick tour of her apartment. There was a huge stuffed animal on a shelf - a gift from CHILDREN SHOULDN'T PLAY WITH DEAD THINGS star Alan Ormsby. In a corner were two side-by-side 35mm film cans. The contents, Camille told me, was a complete print of her Italian film WHAT HAVE YOU DONE TO SOLANGE, the film with that beautiful Morricone score. And framed on one wall was an Italian poster for TRAGIC CEREMONY, a film I was soon to learn Camille has starred in for legendary Italian director Riccardo Freda, the man who guided Barbara Steele through THE HORRIBLE DR. HITCHCOCK.

Camille verified everything Rodney had told me about her. Yes, she was really working with him for Amtrak. Yes, she was a cabin attendant just like Rodney, earning a regular paycheck between acting jobs. I didn't realize then just how scare acting work had become for Camille. Since making I SPIT ON YOUR GRAVE in the late 70's she had only appeared in two films, THE CONCRETE JUNGLE and a cameo role in the zombie/martial arts epic RAW FORCE. Her name hadn't even appeared on the RAW FORCE posters. . .Cameron Mitchell was that film's top billed celebrity.

So I knew what I had to do. I wanted to correct this situation and put Camille back in front of a movie camera. Every horror fan knew her name but she was on the sidelines while other actresses scored all the work. That had to change! But I wouldn't have the budget to hire Camille until CANNIBAL HOOKERS was edited and licensed for distribution.

Rodney and I said our goodbyes and I promised to stay in touch with Camille, letting her know when I would be ready to have her star in one of my movies. The words "FIND A MOVIE FOR CAMILLE" lit up in blazing neon in my mind - a constant, everyday reminder of what I had to do.

Within a year I accomplished that goal. TWICE actually…. with two back-to-back films for Camille to star in. But not in Los Angeles where she lived. Instead, I would find the producer who made it all possible in my Tennessee hometown.

Richard Wayne Martin - "Rick" to his friends - was actually a Los Angeles native. He's been a car dealer with a profitable limo business on the side. And he owned property. LOTS of property. Rick and his family had hardly resettled in Tennessee when Rick began buying up rental properties – homes, apartment buildings - and drawing a monthly cash income from his holdings. Now Rick was flush and he knew exactly what he wanted to spent a nice chunk of his savings on. He wanted to make a movie. And he wanted ME to help.

Rick has a ready-to-go script for his dream project titled NO JUSTICE. Rick told me he'd written it during his limo services days in LA. It was a redneck revenge tale with an evil major, a corrupt sheriff and a good-hearted preacher. Rick was saving the preacher role for himself. But he needed a preacher's wife! And I knew exactly whom we should get.

But Rick wanted at least two celebrities in NO JUSTICE and he'd never heard of Camille Keaton. So I went into FULL-TILT sales pitch mode. I told him how I SPIT ON YOUR GRAVE had made her an overnight sensation. How she was an international name who would be an asset to the worldwide licensing of NO JUSTICE. Rick was sold!

But Rick insisted we also needed a MALE star. Someone with much more of a household name. At least Rick was smart enough not to aim too high. He was budgeting $350,000 - more than a quarter million bucks -

for his dream movie, but knew that wouldn't impress major stars of the day like Robert Redford or Jack Nicholson. We had to be REALISTIC, Rick said, and get somebody we could afford. I wholeheartedly agreed but was underwhelmed by his first suggestion.

Rick wanted CHARLES NAPIER - not exactly a household name but a respected character actor. I mainly knew Napier from his Russ Meyer turns in SUPER VIXENS and BEYOND THE VALLEY OF THE DOLLS. Napier was still a couple years away from the smash success of THE SILENCE OF THE LAMBS - his most recent credit was a Fred Olen Ray monster mash called DEEP SPACE. Anyway, Rick got Napier's number from the Screen Actor's Guild and made his pitch. Napier wasn't impressed. We'd have to keep looking.

That's when I spoke up. Just a few years earlier I'd interviewed Camille's RAW FORCE co-star Cameron Mitchell for a national film magazine. I'd kept Mitchell's home number - even lending it to Fred Olen Ray when he was casting THE TOMB. I told Rick I could easily score us Cameron Mitchell - a genuine 50's star who'd worked with John Wayne, Marlon Brando and Marilyn Monroe. And Mitchell was still a hot name - just a few years earlier he'd made the critical favorite MY FAVORITE YEAR with Peter O'Toole. And EVERYONE remembered his long-running western series THE HIGH CHAPARRAL. Rick was convinced. I made the call and Mitchell quickly came on board. Possibly because I said the five magic words every actor loves to hear. "We'll pay you in CASH!"

So we had our stars. . .Camille Keaton and Cameron Mitchell. Rick didn't even hesitate when I quoted Camille's asking price. I called Ms. Keaton and told her I'd landed her the female lead in a 35mm theatrical feature film. It was frankly more than I'd imagined possible and it all came together so quickly. I had planned to hire Camille for a $10,000 quickie made with licensing funds from CANNIBAL HOOKERS. Now she was starring in a theatrical feature with a $350,000 budget. Things were looking up! And that's when I had an idea.

If ONE new Camille Keaton movie was good, wouldn't TWO new Camille Keaton movies be better? I was getting a pretty nice salary for my work as Production Manager and supporting actor in NO JUSTICE. What if I used that money to fund a second movie we'd make back-to-back with Rick's movie. Of course, the second movie would have a fraction of the budget of NO JUSTICE. It would have to be shot on fuzzy three-quarter inch video. . .not pristine 35mm film stock. But Camille would be paid the exact same salary on both films…to the penny...and I reasoned that was all that mattered. What could go wrong?

So NO JUSTICE wrapped, Camille flew home to LA., and I instantly set to work on our "second" film's script with the generic title of SAVAGE VENGEANCE. It would be a DEATH WISH style movie with Camille as a vigilante detective unleashing outrageous violence against criminals.

A few weeks later Camille flew to Atlanta to spend a week with her retired parents and I came down to update her on my progress. I also brought Camille a video copy of WHAT HAVE YOU DONE TO SOLANGE since she had no way to watch her 35mm print. Together we all sat in her parent's living room.- Camille, her parents and I - as we watched a young Camille bicycle under the film's opening credits and the hypnotic strains of Morricone.

But a few days later- back in my hometown of Cookeville, Tennessee - I made the call I've regretted ever since. I had enough money to shoot this shoestring quickie. I had the licensing bucks from CANNIBAL HOOKERS plus my salary from NO JUSTICE. But a little padding in the budget couldn't hurt. . .could it? And I knew just where to get it.

Mel Lieberman was a Canadian video distributor. His amusingly named company LETTUCE ENTERTAIN YOU had been the north-of-the-border distributor for CANNIBAL HOOKERS, paying a five grand flat fee for the Canadian rights upon delivery of the elements needed for mass video duplication. But NOW I was doing a movie with a real celebrity so. . .would he be interested in Canadian rights? And paying part of that licensing fee UP FRONT?

Lieberman agreed but he had conditions . . .LOTS of conditions. We could keep the title' he loved SAVAGE VENGEANCE. But the plot was all wrong. Lieberman wanted a movie that more directly cashed in on the I SPIT ON YOUR GRAVE phenomena. The more I talked to him on the phone, the more it became apparent EXACTLY what he wanted. Lieberman wanted me to make an unofficial SEQUEL to I SPIT ON YOUR GRAVE.

Those were Lieberman's terms. He assured me his company had top lawyers and there would be no copyright problems. And who was I to disagree with him? This was the man who'd made a small fortune taking an obscure porn loop starring a young Sylvester Stallone and releasing it with the catchy moniker ITALIAN STALLONE. It became a sensation and made Lieberman one of Canada's most successful video distributors.

But Lieberman's funds would only represent about 20 percent of our budget - not enough for him to be calling the shots. Of course, he promised more money on delivery and his company WAS a powerhouse in video distribution. When I'd licensed DEMON QUEEN to Mogul Video I'd been bitterly disappointed that the tape barely made a dent in U.S. video stores. I'd checked DOZENS of shops before finally finding one lone copy of DEMON QUEEN in Nashville.

But it was a very different story with CANNIBAL HOOKERS. Lieberman's company did a saturation campaign with the landscape of mom 'n pop owned video stores of the late 80's. This was before the advent of national chains like Blockbuster and Hollywood Video. To distribute his tapes, Lieberman placed full-page ads in the trade magazines mailed free to every independent video store in the U.S. and Canada. And he worked the media like a maestro. There was a half page ad in VARIETY - the trade bible of the entertainment industry - where Lieberman extolled his own marketing genius in taking a title like CANNIBAL HOOKERS and getting multiple copies of the shelves of every video store from Vancouver to Miami. Even the Los Angeles Times was game - they put a CANNIBAL HOOKERS article right next to one about the new Warren Beatty film. Working with Lieberman was like having a video distributor and a top Hollywood press agent all in one neat package!

That's the MAIN reason I wanted to do business with Lieberman again. I wanted my movies to be SEEN - to be EVERYWHERE. What's the point of making a straight-to-video film if it doesn't go straight to every video store? Lieberman gave his films a prime spot on the shelves of virtually every video store I explored. . .and I wanted that again for SAVAGE VENGEANCE.

I brought in my favorite make-up effects man, Rick Gonzales, who'd worked with me on DEMON QUEEN and SCREAM DREAM, to do the key effects scenes. I also brought in Barney Griner, the no frills cinematographer of SCREAM DREAM, to shoot on his three-quarter inch video camera. He wasn't that great but the price was right. Then I started lining up locations. A country music club was happy to let me film their performers. I secured a VERY scary house in the middle of nowhere decked out with animal skulls and skins on nearly every square foot of wall space. I'd used this house for SCREAM DREAM and the owners were happy to have us back a second time. And I booked the same grocery store where I'd taken Cameron Mitchell to lunch during the NO JUSTICE shoot - that's where my character would meet Camille for the first time. Oh yes, I was ACTING in this thing too!

One of our key locations needed no negotiations or special permission. I wanted to shoot a major rape scene and chainsaw murder at the Cummins. Falls area - a local waterfall on private land, which locals could visit with no restrictions. Now it's become a spruced up State Park, but in 1988 it was an unmarked hiking trail leading to a 75-foot tall waterfall with a long list of casualties. It seemed like once every year or two, a chopper was dispatched to airlift visitors who fell from the falls' slippery rocks. The lucky ones had broken necks and backs. Camille was going to attacked on a bluff extending out an easy 150 feet in mid-air, looking down - WAY DOWN - on the TOP of Cumming's Falls. Who says I don't think big?

Then the big day finally came. Camille was flying into to Nashville International Airport, just as she had three months earlier for NO JUSTICE. I was there bright and early to pick her up and we drove to her hotel. . .mostly in uncomfortable silence. Something was different. Camille has been informed of Lieberman's changes to the film's story - his demand that I completely rewrite the script to his specifications - and she wasn't happy about it. Only much later did I learn exactly HOW unhappy Camille was with the film's new plotline. She was no longer a lone wolf detective - now it was the basic rape and revenge story. I should have cut ties with Lieberman right then and there, gone back to my original script and everything would have been fine. But he'd sent his advance money and - for better or worse - we were in business together. Lieberman had only been the distributor on CANNIBAL HOOKERS. Now he was the Executive Producer and we worked for him.

So we filmed for a few days but the tension was too thick to ignore . . .I sensed impending disaster around every corner. What if Camille WALKED and left me with a half-finished film? Lieberman would demand his money back and SAVAGE VENGEANCE would be unreleasable. I quickly shuffled the shooting schedule to do all the most important scenes first - ESPECIALLY the ending where she shoots me in the groin - leaving me to a slow death. Camille actually seemed to ENJOY filming that scene. I tried to stay positive and we plodded on. Soon all the key, most important scenes were in the can. If Camille walked NOW the film could survive.

And that's exactly what happened. One morning Camille simply didn't show up for work. I made some calls and found she had called a cab to pick her up from the local hotel I booked her into. But before she left, Camille made a call to Lieberman to vent about his script changes and the film's new direction. Lieberman panicked and stopped payment on his check. Now we hadn't just lost our actress - we'd lost our Executive Producer and distributor. But in a way, I was glad. With Lieberman out of the picture, I was free from his constant phone calls - micro-managing every aspect of the shoot from Toronto. I could find a new distributor, I figured. There was just a one bit of unfinished business.

Camille had shot all of her crucial scenes except ONE. There was a major kill scene where she chainsaws the head of her main rapist. We used a body double for Camille and shot the scene - focusing on the gore and simply not showing the killer's face. It actually kind of worked and even made the scene even a little creepier. Plus this was our standout effects scene - Rick Gonzales had fabricated a duplicate of actor Phil Newman's head and face, then stuffed it with blood bags and raw meat. There results are pretty much the highlight of the movie.

So SAVAGE VENGEANCE was finally in the can. Now what to do with it? I didn't have a distributor - I would have to shop it from scratch to any likely company I could find. But then I found a NEW executive producer - someone willing to invest four times as much as Lieberman gave me if I would make a BRAND NEW movie with them.

But they wanted nothing to do with SAVAGE VENGEANCE so I pitched them an idea called VAMPIRE COP and they loved it. Their only condition was I write a small role for their redheaded teenage daughter. Done and DONE! I was in business on VAMPIRE COP while the master tapes of SAVAGE VENGEANCE gathered dust on a shelf.

1989 flew by without a second thought to SAVAGE VENGEANCE. I'd finished it but was a little embarrassed by what we'd done. Even by MY low standards it was a pretty weak movie, I thought. Would anybody WANT it? Plus Camille made it very clear we couldn't use her name on the video store or opening credits. She had been fined by the Screen Actors Guild for acting in the non-union NO JUSTICE and said that couldn't happen again. So I focused on VAMPIRE COP and put SAVAGE VENGEANCE in the back of my mind. . .WAY back.

Before the end of 1989, NO JUSTICE opened simultaneously in Nashville and Cookeville with the two (and ONLY two) 35mm prints Rick Martin struck from his negative. It played four weeks straight in Cookeville and outperformed a current John Candy hit called UNCLE BUCK. We were all amazed! As for VAMPIRE COP, the shooting continued into 1990 and finally finished with a flurry of new, hastily written scenes to shoot. Our main stars were Mal Arnold from BLOOD FEAST and Melissa Moore from SCREAM DREAM. I thought a distributor would snatch it up quickly and I was right.

It wasn't until 1992 that a deal was finally struck to unleash SAVAGE VENGEANCE on the world. A little L.A. company called Magnum Video wanted it for a package of four films to release under the umbrella title I WILL DANCE ON YOUR GRAVE. Therefore, SAVAGE VENGEANCE was retitled I WILL DANCE ON YOUR GRAVE: SAVAGE VENGEANCE. The other three films included my own CANNIBAL HOOKERS - making its official U.S. video debut, and Tim Ritter's KILLING Spree, a film I had helped cast.

I wasn't thrilled with this deal but it was all I thought SAVAGE VENGEANCE deserved. I was even LESS happy with the distributor completely overhauled my opening credits and spelled SAVAGE VENGEANCE as "SAVAGE VENGENCE." Dozens of reviewers picked up on this faux pas and accused me of being an idiot who couldn't spell the word "VENGEANCE." Gee. . .thanks a lot, Magnum!

Soon SAVAGE VENGEANCE was popping up in video stores - including shops in my own small town. I stopped by one, pointed to SAVAGE VENGEANCE on the shelf, and informed the store manager that myself and my friends had made that film. What I got in return was a serious tongue lashing of epic proportions. "That's not a movie… that's a piece of TRASH!" I was informed. "I actually WARN customers not to rent it. And who's going to pay me back for the money I've spent on it?"

What could I say? I muttered a weak, "Well, thanks!" and made a hasty exit. I stopped looking for video stores that carried SAVAGE VENGEANCE after that. Maybe some films are better left unseen.

I was frankly amazed a few years ago when MASSACRE VIDEO approached me about re-releasing SAVAGE VENGEANCE. Did I REALLY want a new generation of fans to see it? Not really, but Massacre had done an amazing job re-releasing my first film, DEMON QUEEN, so why not give them a go? Camille even agreed to do a new interview for this release. We filmed it at a restaurant in Atlanta - just around the corner from the same movie theatre where we saw Tom Cruise in COCKTAIL together - during that brief, happy period after NO JUSTICE and before SAVAGE VENGEANCE. Things have a way of coming full circle and now I could finally close the book on SAVAGE VENGEANCE.

The irony is that NO JUSTICE - for all the money Rick Martin spent on it - is now virtually impossible to find. I uploaded some of Camille's best clips to YouTube but the full film had never had an official U.S. DVD release. Martin licensed it for international sales but never struck a U.S. deal. Now he's gone and the two 35mm prints are presumably rotting away in the storage building he left his wife and daughter.

As for YOU. . .if you've never seen SAVAGE VENGEANCE and are considering it. . .I would say. . . DON'T. Some movies are better imagined or read about than actually WATCHED. Check out one of my better movies. . .DEADLY RUN, COMPELLING EVIDENCE, CHAINSAW CHEERLEADERS. . .even CANNIBAL HOOKERS.

They're not classics but - then again - they don't make me cringe like SAVAGE VENGEANCE.

               -Donald Farmer Director of "Savage Vengeance".

Pictures below courtesy Donald Farmer on set. (Savage Vengeance)

Island of Death

Also known as "Ta Pedhia Tou Dhiavolou", "Devils in Mykonos" and "A Craving for Lust."
Year of release: 1976
Writer: Nico Mastorakis
Director: Nico Mastorakis
Banned 108 mins. Greece
Tagline: "The lucky ones simply got their brains blown out."
Main cast: Robert Behling (Christopher), Jane Lyle (Celia), Jessica Dublin (Patricia), Gerard Gonalons (Foster), Jannice McConnell (Leslie), Ray Richardson.
Distributed by: AVI

In 1987 this film tried to sneak its way back onto the shelves as the newly re-named "Psycho Killer 2" but this was also rejected by the BBFC even though the version submitted was heavily cut. In 2010 the full uncut version was released by Arrow with previous cuts wavered by the BBFC.

Plot:
Christopher and Celia's Mykonos vacations take a dark turn when the British couple spread fear throughout the inhabitants of the island with a bloodbath of violence, sex, murder and sadism. A British detective is called in to catch the couple but can anyone stop the perverse twisted couple from killing and is anybody safe from the judgment of these holidaymakers?

Appraisal:
When a British couple holiday at Mykonos it's not all sun and sea but instead sex, sleaze and deviant psychopaths.

This low budget sleaze exploitation offering is somewhat of a cult film. Island of Death is a rather bizarre video nasty, as the psychopathic lead is actually on a crazy crusade to rid the island of perversions; Christopher, though is more perverse than any of the islands inhabitants, as he begins his quest of death and ridding the unclean of their sins. This film does have strong Christian references and very unsettling scenes including bestiality and incest and an array of perversions. This exploitation classic is an all round solid film that feels somewhat dated now but is still an entertaining watch. I do have a soft spot for this video nasty from yesteryear, it's so wrong, but something a bit different to get your teeth into!

-Tony Newton

Mastorakis had one intention and one alone when making this grubby little movie. Having been suitably impressed by Tobe Hooper's **The Texas Chain Saw Massacre** and even more so by the money which is recouped, he set out to make a film even more unsavoury and grab himself some Benjamin Franklins on the quick. Hurriedly he cobbled together a rough script and cut every corner imaginable attempting to get his film made. It wasn't so much a labor of love as it was one of lust …lust for the almighty buck. He even cast himself as it saved him a whopping $80. Skinflint or genius? Deranged reprobate or merely naive? Having shared the inimitable experience of **Island of Death** twice in my lifetime I would have to say a little of both.

It starts as little more than an advertisement for the Greek tourist board as vacationing British couple Christopher *(Robert Behling)* and Celia *(Jane Lyle)* step off the boat in an idyllic coastal town in Mykonos.

The first ten minutes involve the snapping of many photos as they soak in the summer rays and slip into their espadrilles. However, have you ever heard the term "not how it looked in the brochure?" It turns out that this picturesque paradise is more of a haven of excess than anything else and is heaving with feckless bohemians, reckless sexual abandon, blatant homosexuality, partner swapping, and drug abuse. Needless to say, the pair are somewhat bemused.

The moment when Christopher calls his mother back in London while unloading his creamy sailors in Celia's starboard, we get the sense that the elevator stops a good few floors from the summit and our worst fears are realized as the town goat bleats its morning welcome. What better way to start the day than with a spot of bestiality followed up with some ritualistic slaughter? On the **Island of Death** every goat is a goal and it doesn't take much convincing before Celia joins in with the shenanigans. The couple embark on a rampage of sorts; cleansing this backward town, defiling, and slaughtering anyone they see fit.

Anyone searching for a thread to hang their hat on will be left wanting as there is no great science to Mastorakis' approach. He's only looking to mortify his audience and those expecting hidden subtext won't find it here. It's a grimy little film for damned sure but, from a technical standpoint, it's actually fairly decent. *Nikos Gardelis'* slick cinematography makes the most of some stunning landscapes and it has an almost hypnotic charm. Maybe that is, in part, due to the fact that we haven't the vaguest idea what kind of debauchery lays in wait around the corner. But by hook or by crook, it nabs us when we're least expecting it.

The performances are uniformly terrible and dialogue beyond laughable, while the score by *Nikos Lavranos* is memorable for precisely the wrong reasons but, try as I do to object to the rubble that is **Island of Death,** I just can't bring myself to be too hard on it. The censors had a field day of course and Mastorakis' film was swiftly trimmed of fifteen minutes of content when submitted for classification in 1976 under the mantle **A Craving for Lust.** The director was desperate to get his picture out there and, in 1987, three years after it was branded as a video nasty and removed from circulation, he attempted to slip under the radar under the more ambiguous title **Psychic Killer 2.** As one would imagine, his plan was foiled; it was all going well until the goat sex. *Arrow Video* to the rescue and it is now available in all its uncut glory. But don't thank them just yet.

Your enjoyment of **Island of Death** hinges on three factors. Firstly, your ability to overlook certain flaws. Under no circumstances should this be regarded as anything more than low-rent trash. Secondly, your willingness to step outside your comfort zone and allow it to wash over you with its low tide. Being sickened is par for the course and human depravity in any form should not make for a comforting experience. Should you choose to stand atop your soapbox then the view will be disconcerting I assure you. Finally, your contempt of goats. If, like Keeper, you have a fondness for lamb cutlets, then Billy need never have died in vain. As for the whole sorry goat molestation thing, well the less said about that the better but in Christopher's defense I think it's a dry hump. On the plus side, at least Mastorakis saved another eighty bucks. Meanwhile, the goat received some remuneration for services rendered so no harm, no foul right Nico?

Island of Death is Potentially the most politically incorrect film of all time. **Island of Death** takes a suspiciously hedonistic approach to the tackling the following … misogyny, crucifixion, sexual violation, extreme sadism, homophobia, and features golden showers, a dash of flatulence and a smattering of bestiality. The kills, somewhat lame by current standards, are nothing if not inventive. Death comes to us all in turn, but I would imagine our wish lists would negate to facilitate any of these ominous beauties. Death by aerosol flamethrower, death by decapitation via bulldozer, death by paint consumption, death by being dangled from the wing of a plane in mid-flight, not to mention blasé stalwarts such as sword, scythe, and handgun. For the record, no goats were harmed in the making of **Island of Death,** although one of them now walks with a distinct limp and a perma-grin on its face.

-Keeper of the Crimson Quill (Rivers of Grue).

The Last House on the Left

Year of release: 1972
Writer: Wes Craven
Director: Wes Craven
X rated 64 mins. USA
Tagline "Mari, 17, is dying. Even for her the worst is yet to come."
Main cast: Sandra Peabody (Mari Collingwood), Lucy Grantham (Phyllis Stone), David Hess (Krug Stillo), Fred J, Lincoln (Fred 'Weasel' Podowski), Jeramie Rain (Sadie), Marc Sheffler (Junior Stillo).
Distributed by: Replay

This film was banned on its cinematic release in 1974, released in 1982 and banned in 1983. The film was turned down again by the BBFC in 2001. It was not until 2008 that the BBFC released it officially in its uncut form. Before this the film was turned down by the BBFC in 2001 and released cut in 2002.

Plot:

The Last House on the Left finds two teenage girls going to a rock concert for a birthday treat! The band called "Bloodlust" gives a hint to what happens next. The two girls, desperate to smoke some weed manage to score some from some a group of seedy looking men. The girls end up at the drug dealer's house where the terror begins…

Appraisal:

The Last House on the Left, the Wes Craven classic, is just that… a cult VHS nasty which has aged as well as a true malt whisky. This film is loosely based on Ingmar Bergman's "The Virgin Spring". This horror/thriller has characters you can actually feel for, the girls and their families are good, wholesome folk, and it's for this reason that the film is so much more disturbing, and the fact that the bad guys are so disgustingly mind numbingly fucked up that this works perfectly. I can't imagine The Last House on the Left without David Hess he was an amazing actor who knew how to bring the crazy and boy did he bring it in this one!

The Last House on the Left has influenced many of the films we have today, when you consider that this film was made over 40 years ago you appreciate it all the more, as with "the Texas Chainsaw Massacre" this is a groundbreaking movie all round.

The Last House on the Left" is brimming with suspense (edge of your seat stuff); psychopathic rapists are always a deadly enemy on screen!

The rape and murder scenes are uncomfortable to watch as you root for the good guys to prevail. Revenge films are always interesting as you put yourself in the shoes of the victim and go on a journey with them.

Wes Craven wanted to show the masses how violence effects people, he was a war protestor and the film's release came at a time in history shrouded by the Vietnam war and civil rights movement. "The Last House on the Left" in a way is a protest movie in itself; Wes Craven did a great job of showing the effects of violence and bringing this to everyone's attention in a brutal way of storytelling! The film was controversial to say the least.

Rape revenge thrillers seemed to be on an all time high with many directors jumping on the band wagon with films like "Straw Dogs", "Death Weekend", "I Spit on Your Grave", 1973's Thriller: "A Cruel Picture", "Death Wish", "Lipstick", "The Violator", "Pigs" and "Wild Riders" although rape revenge seemed to peak in the 1970's and cause a large wave of controversy to follow the genre. The 1980's did have a few classics, which tried to resurrect the genre such as "The House on the Edge of the Park", "MS.45","Extremeties" and "Sudden Impact".

Although this genre was seemingly unfamiliar at the time, director Ingmar Bergman broke ground with his controversial film "The Virgin Spring" the tale of rape revenge set in medieval Sweden, the film itself won best foreign language film in 1961 at the Academy awards and was almost certainly the inspiration for Wes Craven's "The Last House on the Left" and the whole rape revenge film genre!

Wes Craven famously said-

"Horror films don't create fear. They release it".

"I like to address the fears of my culture. I believe it's good to face the enemy, for the enemy is fear."

The film's alternative tagline-marketing ploy was just amazing...

"To avoid fainting,
keep repeating
'It's only a movie
... only a movie
... only a movie
... only a movie
... only a movie
... only a movie
... only a movie...'"
-Tony Newton

This is early 70s raw Wes Craven and is a great horror classic. I personally enjoy a good revenge plot and this movie indeed qualifies. In short girls are raped, tortured and killed. The trio of rapists get what they so deserve in the end. I've heard some complain about the rapes scenes depicted in the film. If you don't show the rapes and violence then it would be all sugarcoated goodness and there would be no need for these criminals to get what they got coming to them. They end up in the hands of the rightfully vengeance seeking parents.

The cops deserve a mention since they are more than amusing, but then there are some out there quite like this. Trust me you don't want to encounter them. It could lead to a truly frightening time.

I've also heard some complaints that the music was not appropriate. Listen to some of the music set in today's horror flicks; of course it is not appropriate....that is the whole point.

Some horror fans don't seem to appreciate the revenge flicks so if there are not a monsters, zombies', gore or supernatural beings in general they seem to hate it. I think these folks have never been through anything much in life. So they can't understand the whole concept of what enduring violence or rape is. How deeply it affects the human condition and how that might make you seek revenge. If they only knew then they might thoroughly enjoy the justice achieved by these so called psychotic heroes in this and other films like it.

The genre of horror deals with subject matter that could easily get banned by the powers that be.

-Lilith Stabs Horror Actress.

My love for Wes Craven's THE LAST HOUSE ON THE LEFT is astronomical. It's my second favorite film of all time, right behind John Carpenter's HALLOWEEN, and it's a film that I find myself revisiting quite regularly.

Telling the story of three brutally vicious criminals trying to elude being caught, THE LAST HOUSE ON THE LEFT doesn't pull a single punch, giving you as a viewer, a piece of cinema that you're unable to look away from, not matter how much you might want to. When the criminals (and the son of the gang's leader, Krug) come across two young girls wanting to score some pot, the film's nightmare of a journey begins, leading into some of the most visually intense scenes in film history. After kidnapping, raping and murdering both girls, the gang pretends to be a family looking for a place to stay for the night, and the house that they end up at, just happens to be the house of one of the murdered girls' family. After discovering that the people staying at their house raped and killed their daughter, the film's protagonists, Mr. and Mrs. Collingwood, decide to turn the tables on the insane trio and exact some pretty gnarly revenge, with everything from throat-cutting, to biting off one of their penises.

What's so great about this film, and a lot of Craven's work, is how on the surface it might seem like a straight up horror film, but in reality, there's a lot more going on within the film. A response to the Vietnam War and how the media was portraying it, Craven made THE LAST HOUSE ON THE LEFT a film that absolutely refuses to turn away, even when the most repulsive acts are done to the victims of Krug, Weasel and Sadie. Also under examination, is the idea of Mr. and Mrs. becoming the very thing they're fighting. When the film ends, the married protagonists have brutally murdered the film's villains and in ways that one can never forget. Having chain sawed, cut and killed the villains, there is still no going back to how things were before their daughter was murdered, and despite exacting revenge, their daughter is still dead. It's a spectacular and very unnerving look at revenge and how nothing is really changed by exacting it.

-Jerry Smith Editor in Chief/Writer Icons of Fright.

The Last House on the Left: An Appreciation for Craven's 1972 Shocker

Even in its compromised form, Wes Craven's *The Last House on the Left* is a sucker punch of a film. And it was in a compromised form that I first saw it, thanks to Anchor Bay's extra-stuffed DVD which, censorial issues aside, was an honorable effort to give justice to a masterpiece of terror.

For better or worse, I missed out on the video nasties fallout of the 80s, having been born in 1994. My interest in horror films was developing around the time that once-banned titles were finally being issued on UK DVD. I must've been twelve when I finally saw *Last House* so I saw it several years later than *The Evil Dead* and *The Driller Killer*, but although I'd seen my fair share of notorious films by that point, Wes Craven's debut still managed to live up to my expectations. It was one of the nasties I'd most wanted to see and it was every bit as grimy and unrelenting as its reputation suggested. Chest carving or no chest carving...

Naturally the uncut version was at the top of my mental 'must see' list and when Metrodome released the Ultimate Edition in late 2008, it was a day one purchase. Of course, its uncut status was a surprise in itself. Apparently a lot can change in five years because while the 2003 DVD was a product of the BBFC's misinformed belief that the film could cause harm to viewers, the 2008 DVD was fully uncut (or at least as uncut as it could be, given that the version widely available is still missing footage). I could finally see the prop intestines torn from Phyllis' twitching body and it made the gritty, documentary-like murder scene all the more savage and unsettling.

Unfortunately I seem to be in the minority when I sing the film praises. The film's notoriety overshadows its worth as a genuinely great film, so much so that it seems all modern audiences can do is mock the low production values and David Hess' surprisingly upbeat soundtrack (which makes a lovely addition to my vinyl collection). For all the discussion about the film's violence – which is undeniably effective – it's often forgotten just how subtle and realistic the characterisation is.

There's no black-and-white 'heroes versus villains' going on here. As despicable as Krug and company are, there's no denying that they're also very human, evidenced by the scene in which, following the rape of Mari Collingwood, they exchange looks of disgust with each other and literally try to wipe the blood away from their hands. We see enough of these characters early in the film to understand that they're a warped family of sorts – a family of molesters and murderers, of course, but a family nonetheless.

Also at the forefront of the film's understated humanity is the relationship between Mari and Phyllis. The scene in which the two girls are forced to strip is touching as well as disturbing, thanks to Phyllis' insistence to her friend Mari that it's just the two of them there… "no-one else." Much of Phyllis' actions in the film's middle act consist of her striving to protect her friend. Tragically it's something that her friend's stuck-up parents (Mari's mother makes it clear early on that she doesn't trust Phyllis Stone) will never know.

It's possibly this area most of all in which the original triumphs over its remake. The characters in the 2009 version are devoid of soul, two-dimensional incarnations of the ones in Craven's original script. We see too little of Phyllis – or rather Paige as she's named in the remake – prior to her death to really care about her and Mari isn't much better. The remake exchanges genuine characterisation for backstory, assuming that a subplot concerning the death of Mari's brother will add depth. It doesn't and it ultimately feels tacked-on.

The same goes for Krug and company. They were likeable as well as reprehensible in the original film, easy to hate but also charismatic and fascinating to watch. The remake reduces them to clear-cut villains with no grey areas in which to sink your teeth into. Submitting yourself to the 2009 'reimagining' proves to be a dull experience, further underlining the problem with many of today's horror remakes: they're boosting the production values but forgetting entirely about the heart and soul of the film.

Yes, the original was primitive in its filmmaking and it's not entirely successful in certain aspects, but isn't that part of the beauty of it? It's a rough, raw piece of work, spawned at a time in which cinema demanded something hard-hitting. As much as the film is labelled an exploitation flick, Wes Craven's claim that he approached the film from an intellectual viewpoint seems legitimate. There's obvious social commentary running throughout, from its depiction of the hippy culture to the conflict of classes. Craven stated that he wanted to create a film as unpleasant as the war footage that was often broadcast on the news at the time. Death is presented in all its ugliness: long and agonising. As much as she fights to survive, Phyllis is reduced to a disembowelled corpse, left lifeless in the woods while her severed arm is presented like a trophy to her devastated friend.

The level of hate for David Hess' bipolar soundtrack is borderline hyperbolic. Contrary to popular belief, bright and cheery music is not being played whilst the girls are being butchered. There is the tongue-in-cheek 'Sadie and Krug' song that plays whilst Krug and company are driving away with the girls in the trunk, but bear in mind that we're seeing things from their perspective at this precise moment. They're oblivious to the girls and are instead fuelling their energies into discussing Sigmund Freud and the Grand Canyon. When the film takes a darker turn within the woods, as does the music. The appropriately titled 'The Chase' drums up suspense magnificently as Phyllis evades her attackers, and 'Phyllis Spills Her Guts' is haunting. Let's not forget the brilliance of 'Now You're All Alone.'

Those tracks that are considerably more upbeat tend to appear between the scenes of mayhem, a backdrop for the comedic moments with the two cops. It's possible that the film would work better without such moments – they're easily the weakest point of the film – but the jarring contrast does heighten the sense of dread and make the horror sequences all the more alarming. *Last House* is more honest than most horror films in that it displays the most trivial instants of life directly alongside its final, whimpering moments.

For all its faults, Wes Craven's 1972 debut is nonetheless a compelling contribution to the horror genre, still as brutal and uncompromising now as it was over forty years ago. Not only is it one of my favourite horror films but it's also one of my favourite films - full stop. It is a flawed masterpiece, which I will continue to defend with as much passion as I can possibly summon. Now pop in that Blu-ray and revisit the film in all its gritty, grainy and gory glory. "All that blood and violence… I thought you were supposed to be the love generation?"

-Dale white   Writer.

Love Camp 7

Year of release: 1969
Writer: Bob Cresse
Director: Lee Frost
Banned 94 minutes USA
Tagline: "A place of total despair. All the youthful beauty of Europe enslaved with for the pleasure of the 3rd Reich."
Main cast: Bob Cresse (Commandant), Maria Lease (WAC Lt. Linda Harman), Kathy Williams (WAC Lt. Grace Freeman), Bruce Kimball (Sgt. Klaus Muller), John Alderman (Robert Calais), Rodger Steel (Erich Von Hamer).
Distributed by: Market
Still banned in the UK the film was turned down for classification by the BBFC in 2002. The film is available uncut and unrated in the US.

Plot:
Set in World War two, Love Camp 7 sees two female American officers sent undercover to a Nazi prisoner of war camp set up for the Nazi soldiers on the front line. The Americans are sent in to gather top-secret information from one of the inmates (A former scientist). When their efforts to escape the camp fail the girls suffer the same fate as their inmates.

Appraisal:
In this cult Nazisploitation film we see a Nazi brothel Love Camp 7, the women are there for one reason only to get there clothes off and to please the soldiers, this film is bound around the poor unfortunate women who for one reason or another end up being used as sex slaves (Including two female officers going under-cover in more ways than one).

This is not one of the greatest Nazisploitation films out there, this is more of a full on exploitation film, full of women subjected to sexual assault and abuse.

"Love Camp 7" being banned for so long was a good thing as it's actually quite a dreary film with a down beat tone. Once again you are forced to realize that we're just a few decades ahead of the real Nazi torturing and that to me is the scariest thing about this movie.

-Tony Newton

Love Camp 7 opens with some stock footage. It's The Houses of Parliament kids! This means, of course, that our film opens in London. It is worth noting that these are the same Houses of Parliament that, during the early 80s, shamefully thought that, under the influence of the National Viewers' and Listeners' Association, it would be appropriate to legislate for taste. This was under the reactionary standard of a pointless moral crusade. Indeed, at the hands of these guardians of the greater good, the term video nasty was born. So, over this period there were a total of 39 films that were prosecuted. Love Camp 7 was one of the 39. Still, in the subsequent decades, a lot of water has passed under Westminster Bridge. One by one, many of these formerly banned titles have been re-classified. Sadly, Love Camp 7 was not among those that have been allowed a release. It is still banned in Britain. Indeed, when it was re-submitted for consideration in 2002, it was, once again, rejected for release. The board cited the "numerous scenes of women prisoners being abused, tortured and humiliated by their Nazi captors" as a reason for rejection. The censors clarified the law on this subject when they stated that the film was in contravention of "the Board's strict policy on depictions of sexual violence, which prohibits scenes that eroticise or endorse sexual assault". However, such an interpretation of the content of this film is risible. But it seems that, as far as the government is concerned, we can't be allowed to have a film about Nazis that is too sleazy! After all, what would happen if people saw the regime as being depicted as slightly degenerate? Luckily for us all, the British establishment was at hand to preserve the cinematic integrity of Nazis. So, they not only banned Love Camp 7, but also SS Experiment Camp and SS Hell Camp too. Having said that, British censors, in the name of public decency, also banned a Bigfoot movie. So, what was it about Love Camp 7 that made the establishment rattle its cilices in terror? Could it be, for example, the graphic sex? Despite the stated reasons from the censors, the answer is probably not. After all, the film doesn't feature any real sex. It has a sexual theme, but here it is strictly a simulated depiction of sex. However, the comfort women, occasionally, appear to be having too good a time. That would certainly be an issue, but, nevertheless, it is all so tame by today's standards. Because the film itself is barely even soft-core. Sure, the girls who feature in the film engage in a bit of topless groping. However it's mostly grunts, moans and clinches while the camera flails around wildly to convey the mayhem of raucous orgies. Indeed, as Bob Cresse's David Brent-esque, scenery-chewing, Nazi camp commandant states during the film: "I cannot guarantee you that you will love Love Camp Seven but I can guarantee that you will love in Love Camp Seven." Maybe it's the violence? Again this is a possibility, but the film is not especially violent either. After all, it offers nothing that hasn't been seen a hundred-and-one time or more in the Women in Prison genre. So it's medical check-ups, hose-downs, cruel and unusual punishments, some brief nudity and light frottage. Even the combination of the two themes, sex and violence, can be found in titles that have been allowed a certificate. Night Train Murders, for example. Who could argue with that? The BBFC, that's who! Yet, despite the current status of the film in Britain, Love Camp 7 is merely low-rent schlock that is very much in the spirit of the Cinema of Transgression Manifesto. It is a film that exists in that grand tradition of hucksterism and showmanship that goes right back to the days when films used to tour as fairground attractions. It should be appreciated as such. Even appeals to authenticity should be seen in this light. After all, throughout the history of cinema there have been attempts to offer the "real deal" for the sake of sensationalism. Early ethnographic documentary films such as Harry Schenck's Beyond Bengal did this. For, even though the film depicted what was claimed to be a scientific expedition into the uncharted east, it was actually filmed in Florida. Reefer Madness and Sex Madness also went down the same sensationalism-as-authenticity route when it offered the promise of a look at public morals when they are placed under the microscope. In Germany The Schoolgirl Reports tried similar. All these films, in their own way, offered sensationalism in the name of "authenticity". Love Camp 7 tries to do this too. So, Love Camp 7 features an earnest documentary-style voiceover. There are also some black and white stills accompanying the credits. It also makes use of natural lighting and some documentary style camerawork. So, even though the film is accompanied by a dramatic score throughout, it is all done in the name of offering the viewer the chance of experiencing the real deal. But, even then, it is all far from shocking. Sure Love Camp 7 gets a little violent towards the end and a prisoner sticking a corkscrew in the neck of a Nazi guard is hardly the best advertisement for passive resistance. However, just like the Beast in Heat, the film is surely too silly to be taken that seriously by anyone beyond the seat of power. Nevertheless, anyone who takes an interest in exploitation cinema should really make a point of going out of their way to see Love Camp 7. Because, what Lee Frost has directed here is one of the key films in the history of genre film. It is a forerunner to the Nazisploitation boudoir cycle that was popularised with the likes of Salon Kitty, Red Nights of the Gestapo and other, similar, titles.

-Nigel Maskell Writer.

Madhouse

Also known as "There Was a Little Girl" and "And When She Was Bad".
Year of release: 1981
Writer: Ovidio G. Assonitis
Director: Ovidio G. Assontis
Rated 18 Italy
Tagline: "Julia thinks she lives alone… she doesn't!"
Main cast: Trish Everly (Julia Sullivan), Michael MacRae (Sam Edwards), Dennis Robertson (Father James), Morgan Most (Helen), Allsion Biggers (Mary Sullivan), Edith Ivey (Amantha Beauregard).
Distributed by: Medusa
In 2004 the film was released fully uncut and passed 18 by the BBFC.

Plot:
Julia a young Georgia teacher if children with disabilities, has bizarre flashbacks of her childhood, in which she succumbs to the abuse from her twin sister Mary.
Julia meets up with her twin sister Mary, the bitter and twisted sister who has the ability of controlling dogs for torture and torment unleashes an onslaught of terror on her sister and some unsuspecting victims.

Appraisal:
Madhouse follows a pair of twins, one good, one evil. Julia is the good-natured sister and Mary, the evil twin subjects her sister Julia to a torrent of abuse and torture, she suffers from a rare disease/skin condition and is institutionalized in an insane asylum. Mary has the ability to control canines and after leaving the hospital the dogs begin attacking people with gory results including one man's retaliation whilst equipped with a power drill, which as a standalone scene had the capability to raise the eyebrows of the censors. "Madhouse" has supernatural qualities but they fail to save this film, which is mediocre at best. Even Riz Ortolani's (of Cannibal Holocaust fame) musical score couldn't save this film and just seems underappreciated here.

The cinematography is good and there's an overall dark ambience to the entire picture. By no means is this a film to skip, if you haven't caught "Madhouse" yet watch it, but it's not got the appeal for repeated viewing. This may not help for me as the first time I ever saw "Madhouse" was on tape-to-tape (probably 7th generation copy) and all I remember is how dark this film was, it was barely viewable and trying to see anyone was virtually impossible. The truth of the matter is that the brutal Rottweiler killings freaked me out, especially as our Rottweiler would sleep on my bed at night!
-Tony Newton

Mardi Gras Massacre

Also known as "Emisario del Terror"
Year of release: 1978
Writer: Jack Weis
Director: Jack Weis
X rated 97 mins. USA
Tagline: "Everyone is celebrating nobody hears the screams of the victims for the sacrifice."
Main cast: Curt Dawson (Sgt. Frank Hebert), Gwen Arment (Sherry), William Metzo (John), Laura Misch Owens (Shirley Anderson). Cathryn Lacey (Disco Girl 1), Nancy Dancer (Disco Girl 2).
Distributed by: Goldstar
This film is still banned in the UK but an uncut and unrated version is available in the US.

Plot:
Mardi Gras Massacre sees a welding mask wearing psychotic killer named John, he's sacrificing prostitutes in New Orleans during the Mardi Gras festival. He continues making these sacrifices to Coatla, the Aztec goddess, in exchange for his own immortality. Police attempt to capture the person responsible for these ritualistic murders but will they be successful in their hunt?

Appraisal:
Mardi Gras Massacre isn't one of the best from the DPP list in fact it's probably one of the worst offerings here. The acting is hammy and ridiculously over the top, I'd be surprised if any of the actors had ever participated in a single acting lesson, in fact the actor who plays the lead role of the serial killer delivers his lines so slowly it's laughable.

Mardi Gras Massacre is a low-budget film; it does have a smattering of disturbing scenes (disregarding the acting and production) though some of the sacrificial scenes do seem a bit drawn out.

Overall this film contains massive plot holes, is poorly edited and features some of the worst acting performances I've ever seen but despite this it does have a certain ambience to it and is a homage to HG Lewis's work.

Mardi Gras Massacre is definitely a laugh out loud film! You actually end up thinking why the hell was this on the banned film list? I love the cover art for the film, so that is its saving grace for me.

-Tony Newton

Nightmares in a Damaged Brain

Also known as: "Nightmare", "Nightmare in a Damaged Brain".
Year of release: 1981
Writer: Romano Scavolini
Director: Romano Scavolini
Unrated 97 mins. USA, Italy
Tagline: "The dream you can't escape ALIVE!"
Main Cast: Baird Stafford (George Tatum), Sharon Smith (Susan Temper), C.J Cooke (C.J Temper), Mik Cribben (Bob Rosen), Danny Ronan (Kathy the babysitter), John L Watkins (Man with cigar).
Distributed by: Oppidan
In 2002 the cut version passed 18 by the BBFC.

Plot:
After sexually mutilating a family George is treated with innovative drug therapy at a psychiatric hospital, believing him to be cured George is released back into society, but far from cured George's psychotic mania rears its ugly head as he goes on a violent killing spree. In this grueling slasher movie, no one's safe!

Appraisal:
Nightmares in a Damaged Brain AKA "Nightmare in a Damaged Brain", and "Nightmare" I prefer the title Nightmares in a Damaged Brain as when I think of "Nightmare" I think of the cult classic kids ITV series from the 80's/90's, I was obsessed with that TV show and filled endless VHS tapes with episodes, the film is far from that!. This is a crazy horror movie (no pun intended). I remember the first time I saw the film it was a poster that caught my attention because it had written in bold writing "If you were terrified by Dawn of the Dead and Friday the 13th you must see Nightmare", it was this that outraged Tom Savini as his FX helped bring both "Dawn of the Dead" and "Friday the 13th" to life. Tom Savini sued to remove his name from the cover and promotional materials stating that he was responsible for the FX. I think Tom Savini was a consultant for certain parts of the effects scenes, most notably some of the hatchet scenes that appear throughout the movie. Nightmares in a Damaged Brain has been given a lot of bad press and although it does feel dated, it wasn't filmed on a massive budget. Most of the acting leaves a lot to be desired the main character George (played by actor Baird Stafford) gives a brilliant performance in this movie, one that is both captivating and terrifying.

The film has many different twists and turns and some interesting moments to say the least, it weaves seedy moments, gritty horror, nudity and family viewing into one, the whole feel of the film reminds me of the horror classic "Peeping Tom". It could have been better but it's still an enjoyable film with an obvious nod to secret government testing.

There are some stand out gore scenes here, none more so than the picture on the back of the VHS sleeve of a woman's decapitated head surrounded by blood, guts and body parts. This low budget offering does deliver on many levels! Nightmare in a Damaged Brain was prosecuted.

-Tony Newton

Of all the Nasties, Italian director Roman Scavolini's Nightmares In a Damaged Brain is, along with fellow countryman Ruggero Deodato's Cannibal Holocaust, one of the most genuinely affecting. Though the likes of Tenebrae, The Burning, and the Fulci triptych of Zombie Flesh Eaters, House By the Cemetery, and The

Beyond all remain potent jolters, by and large most of them are more liable to provoke unintentional laughs than spine-scraping frissons. They're tosh; tawdrily entertaining clag gross-outs, even something as mean-spirited as Cannibal Ferox, which veers dangerously close to camp thanks to the eminently watchable scene chewing of perennial victim John Morghen (or Giovani Lombardo Radice, to give the spaghetti splat regular his real name).

The Director of Public Prosecutions and the eyes of the law seemed to think so too: On February 3rd 1984, the man responsible for distributing the film on British tape, World of Video 2000 boss David Hamilton Grant, was sentenced to eighteen months at her majesty's pleasure (though later reduced to twelve) for being "in possession of over two-hundred copies of an obscene article for publication for gain". Grant was issuing cassettes one whole minute longer than the official BBFC-approved theatrical release. It didn't matter that it was still a compromised version, the victim of all the same censorious snips as the R-rated US print, and *still* shorn of just under ten minutes of expository bumf; sixty additional seconds, after all, was more than enough time to destroy the moral fabric of British society...

Crazy, but trivia hawks should note that, in the expanded Grant universe, it's barely a footnote. The self-style King of Sexploitation, the rest of entrepreneurial porn don Grant's personal saga is even stranger; a convoluted web that - if former sports presenter turned conspiracy theorist David Icke is to be believed anyway - involves Grant faking his own death at the hands of an alleged contract killing, and his position as a major player in a high-reaching international paedophile ring. It's a mythos as suitably disturbing as Nightmares In a Damaged Brain itself.

Baird Stafford (whose only other screen credit is Scavolini's 1985 'Nam action pic Dog Tags) gives a terrific performance as George Tatum; a dangerous schizophrenic wrongly deemed cured and released back into the seedy New York City streets. Plagued by violent recurring dreams, Tatum sets off on a bloodthirsty journey back to his family home in Florida, to a house now occupied by single mother Susan (the perfunctory Sharon Smith) and her three children. Edging ever closer, Tatum's homicidal mania increases; a plot point mirrored by the increasingly worrying penchant Susan's super-brat young son CJ (blonde moppet CJ Cooke) has for sadistic practical jokes. Soon, all is set for the inevitable confrontation; a frightening and distressing final act in which Tatum and CJ's past, present and future entwine with claret-soaked consequences...

At its core, Nightmares In a Damaged Brain is a slasher movie. Inspired by an article, which alleged to the CIA's use of mental patients in mind-altering pharmacological experiments, and originally scripted under the more esoteric title of "Dark Game", Scavolini's whopping 167-page script was - according to trash film guru Lee Christian, who helped curate the extras for Code Red DVD's 30th Anniversary Edition – very different. "It wasn't really the same movie," Christian once told me. "It's been a long time since I read [the original script], but as I recall, it was a little more centred around CJ."

Though a handful of ideas remain - the notion of whether Tatum's pills are helping or making him even worse, most teasingly of all - Scavolini's more thoughtful intentions of crafting a truly subversive thriller are marred considerably by his over-reliance on clunky slice n' dice cliché. Empty false scares and the usual uninspired killer-on-the-loose histrionics plague the narrative; bizarre considering just how vocal Scavolini is about his disdain for the genre and its by-the-numbers approach. "I don't watch horror films; they don't interest me," he's arrogantly exclaimed. "If I do, it's twice or triple speed because I immediately know everything. I immediately understand what the mechanisms are."*

Beneath its low-end schlock trappings though, there lurks a provocative and distinctly adult horror movie; a striking, gut-punching cocktail of mental disintegration, neglect and the long-term repercussions of extreme violence. Flawed in its execution, yes, but it's powerful stuff; certainly more so than your usual body count flick anyway.

Nightmares In a Damaged Brain is more Repulsion than Friday the 13th; a proto Henry: Portrait of a Serial Killer-style bracket occupied by the likes of Don't Go In the House, Visiting Hours and Bill Lustig's Maniac. Its immediate peers, they too are character-based frighteners; grindhouse dissections of the psychological make-up of murder.

Alluding to both Halloween and The Shining, it's Nightmares In a Damaged Brain's final stretch that is the most effective, with Tatum pursuing CJ through the house, clad in the same creepy old man mask that CJ had previously used in a prank (one that looks remarkably like Sid Haig...) and wielding a claw hammer. It's long, lingering and luridly drawn out; a hyper-real assault sequence with CJ messily fighting off his assailant before Scavolini pieces together the mystery of Tatum's frightening visions in a graphic flashback - a refreshing twist on the "you have sex, you die" maxim. Here, fucking is no longer just punishable with violent death by masked maniac but the reason said maniac is totally cuckoo in the first place; sex as homicidal catalyst. It's Scavolini's most satisfying and fully realised concept, a notion established during Tatum's frothy-mouthed meltdown at a XXX peepshow earlier in the film.

The ending itself packs an emotive punch too; a grim coda, albeit one that doesn't make a whole heap of sense the more you think about it. Seasoned narrative detectives will likely spot it a mile off too, though it's really more sickeningly inevitable than predictable.

Its status as a Nasty aside, Nightmares In a Damaged Brain is perhaps best known for the controversy that surrounds its squirty make up effects; the long and the short of it being whether legendary gore wizard Tom Savini was responsible for them or not. Despite his credit as Special Effects Director and his name being used in the film's American marketing campaign ("From the man who terrified you in Dawn of the Dead and Friday the 13th!" screamed the poster), Savini himself vehemently denies any sort of involvement, other than in a technical advisory capacity. "They keep using my name and I did not do the effects on that piece of shit," he firmly told author Christian Sellers back in 2007. "The guy who did do the effects, Lester Loraine, killed himself. He was a friend and they gave him no credit but tried to steal my name to promote this trash."**

Scavolini's version of events, of course, is grossly different, the bottom line being that Savini was a much more active participant than he'd care to admit. It's hard not to deny the similarities between Nightmares In a Damaged Brain's effects and Savini's stuff too; they may be a little cruder than the watershed, artery-splitting money shots in The Prowler et al, but they certainly have enough of Savini's trademark, bright red gush behind them - a little more so than what one of the film's confirmed effects guys Ed French (later of Sleepaway Camp, The Stuff and Rejuvenator) puts down to Savini serving simply as "splatter coach".**

What's more, it's hard not to deny that Savini was actually pretty hands-on from a production photo readily in circulation showing him giving young actor Scott Praetorius (Young George) a crash course in axe handling. Very odd, considering Savini once stated that, as he was working on George Romero's Creepshow at the time, he'd never even set foot on Scavolini's set...

Regardless, Nightmares In a Damaged remains a minor classic of sorts. It's naff in spots and incredibly rough around the edges in others, but with a quiet, unspoken influence on the more introspective strain of extreme skin crawlers that have emerged in the last half-dozen years or so - its legacy of brutality that can be felt in the acclaimed likes of Pascal Laugier's Martyrs and Adam Wingard's A Horrible Way to Die - Nightmares In a Damaged Brain is an essential, must-see slab of down and dirty cult horror. Seek it out or just pay it another visit; you'll be glad you did.

* *As explained in the ninety minute interview with him on the Code Red DVD*
* * *Taken from Scavolini vs. Savini: Nightmare In a Damaged Brain by Christian Sellers, originally published on retroslashers.net. Used by permission, with thanks to the author. Read the brilliant full article here: http://retroslashers.net/scavolini-vs-savini-nightmare-in-a-damaged-brain/*

-Matty Budrewicz   writer.

This is not actually a movie that I can watch now, due to how unsettling it still manages to be, after all these years. However, its influence is as palpable today, in modern thrillers as its vivid and graphic images ever were. At its foundation it is the story of a murderer who cannot separate his sexual impulses from his violent ones, stemming from the fact that as a young boy, his rage at his father's infidelity was so great, that he decapitates his mistress while she rode him - as he orgasmed. We see from flashbacks that the image of her stump of a neck, spurting blood, has forever taken the place of an ejaculating penis, from that point on. Yes, I'd imagine that it would be hard to argue such a movie not being band, but the truth is, that this is a real issue in the modern world of serial killers. After Nightmares came out, other dared to follow suit. Alan Moore penned his character Rorschach, a brutal "super-hero" whose origin story featured his childhood life with his prostitute mother. Later pop star Jennifer Lopez would try to psychoanalyze a serial murderer with similar sexual issues, in the movie Cell.

-Christopher Moonlight   Moonlight Art Magazine.

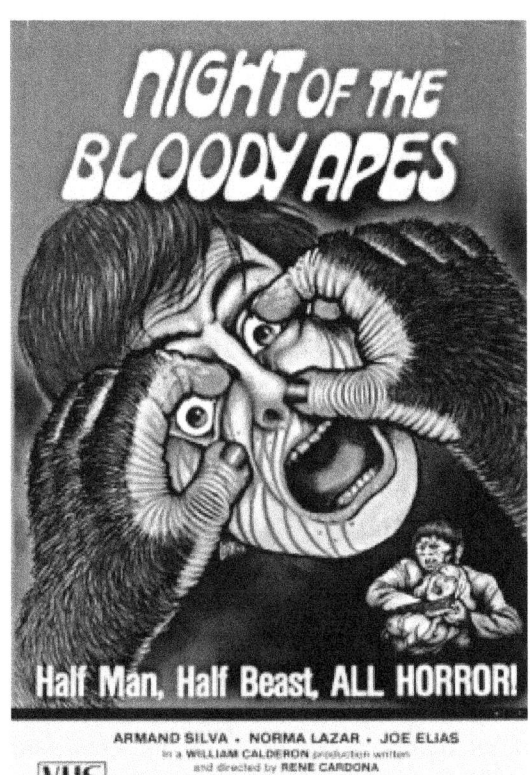

Night of the Bloody Apes

Also known as: "La Horripilante Bestia Humana"
Year of release: 1969
Writer: Rene Cardona Jr, Rene Cardona
Director: Rene Cardona, Jerald Intrator
R Rated
Tagline: "They rip, they claw, they tear you to pieces!"
Main cast: Jose Elias Moreno (Dr. Krallman), Carlos Lopez Moctezuma (Goyo), Armando Silvestre (Lt. Arturo Martinez), Norma Lazareno (Lucy Osorio), Agustin Matinez Solares (Julio Krallman), Javier Rizo.
Distributed by: Iver Film Services
In 2012 a full, uncut version was passed by the BBFC for DVD.

Plot:
This 1969 offering Night of the Bloody Apes begins with a wrestling match that ends in tragedy. Cut to mad scientist Dr Krallman's son who is terminally ill with leukaemia and in an attempt to save his son Dr Krallmanoperates on him substituting his heart with that of a gorillas with the help of his sidekick Goyo, things turn sour when his mutated then son then goes on a bloody rampage!

Appraisal:
Night of the Bloody Apes is an insane horror movie, this cult Mexican film procured an early entry on the DPP List.

Made in the late 1960's "Night of the Bloody Apes" is somewhat dated, the premise alone of a human having a heart transplant from an orang-utan, after surgery the man ends up acting like an ape! This film does have hammer-esque qualities and does feel like you are watching a bad Frankenstein- knock off with a little gore and nudity thrown in just for the hell of it!

The director is not a fan of continuity but for all its bad qualities it's a fun B-style movie, no scares, but a truly bizarre Mexican horror film. This is a good addition to the DPP list but feels very tame nowadays.

-Tony Newton

If there ever were a cure for melancholy, it would have to be cheap Mexican exploitation flicks. With origins stretching back to the thirties when the set's of *Tod Browning's* **Dracula** was used afterhours to shoot a Spanish language version of the same production for the Latino market. Twenty years later filmmakers saw an increasing demand for cheap fare during the mid fifties as Mexico found itself in a time of political uncertainty. Calamities within the Mexican film industry led to the production of loads of low-budget films at minimal costs something that demanded filmmakers to be more creative than they had needed to be previously.

It's from those times of low budget, cheap production, and quick and dirty tricks, that screenwriters and directors like *Ramón Obón, Rafael Baledón,* the brothers *Alfredo and Abel Salazar, René Cardona, Chano Urueta, Miguel M. Delgado, Alfredo B. Crevenna* and the great *Fernando Méndez* came to their full exploitative potential. *Méndez* stunning El Vampiro *(The Vampire)* 1957 became something of a surprise smash hit generating a huge demand for native genre fare. Although El Vampiro didn't reach English-speaking soil until the late sixties when *K. Gordon Murray* took it under his wings and dubbed it into an

English language version – like a multitude of Mexican films he Americanized under the same time period. It's also told that *Christopher Lee* claimed that *Méndez* El Vampiro was seen by the heads at Hammer studios and left an important impression on them. Something that allegedly was one of the influences upon the genesis of the glossy gothic style of horror that exploded upon the world with Hammers 1958 classic Horror of Dracula.

But back to Mexico; gothic horrors and Mexican folklore themed films soon gave way to another favoured pastime, Wrestling. Televised Lucha Libre bouts where suddenly deemed vulgar and banned by the government as to "protect underage viewers". In a genius move, they simply shifted into the cinemas and showcased their exploits there instead – hence many Lucha Libre movies being bookended with lead characters engaging in wrestling matches. After a few films of fighting each other, gothic horror and Mexican folklore seeped back in and Lucha Libre genre and legends such as *Santo, Blue Demon* and *Mil Mascaras* started taking on Aztec mummies, Dracula, Frankenstein, Wolfmen and even had a couple of encounters with Martian invaders. Within this niche also came the Luchadora, the Female Wrestler; a sexier, cooler sub-niche, in which *Loretta Velázquez* and her character "Gloria Venus" was the undefeated queen of Mexican exploitation cinema.

If there was a king of the genre it was undoubtedly writer, actor, director *René Cardona*! Personally responsible for a good half dozen or more Luchadoras films, *Cardona* probably did more for the Mexican female action hero than any other director with his successful string of Luchadora flicks, including the initial **Las Luchadoras vs. el Médecino Asesino** *(Doctor of Doom)* 1962, cult favourite La Mujer Muriciélago *(Bat Woman)*, 1967 and La Horripilante Bestia Human *(Night of the Bloody Apes)* 1969, which even ended up on the infamous British Video Nasties list of prosecuted titles.

Two seemingly parallel stories set the stage for this sinister gem of Mexican exploitation cinema. One path follows Lieutenant Arturo Martinez [*Armando Silvestre*] and his Luchadora girlfriend Lucy Ossorio [*Norma Lazareno* who also starred in *Cardona's* Superviventes de los Andes *(Survive)* 1976 alongside legend *Hugo Stiglitz*], and her story of nursing a bad conscious after tossing her opponent Elena Gomez [*Noelia Noel*] out of the wrestling ring, hence putting her in hospital in a serious condition. If nothing else, it brings some neat girl fight scenes to the movie and Lazareno sports a spiffy red cat/devil outfit with mask and all. The other path follows renown, but heavily frustrated Professor Krallman [*José Elías Moreno*, who starred as The Ogre in *Roberto Rodriguez's* Caperucita y Pulgracito Contra los Monstros (*Tom Thumb and Little Red Riding Hood*) 1962] as he conducts depraved experiments on primates in a desperate attempt to cure his son's deadly disease.

Transplanting the heart of a gorilla he and his henchman have stolen from a zoo – showcased through wonderful gorilla suits and authentic gory surgery footage, which most likely is the only reason the movie ended up on the nasties list to start with - Professor Krallman and assistant Goyo [*Carlos Lòpez Moctezuma*] operate on his son Julio [*Agustin Martinez Solares*]. But despite the ape heart transplant being a success, Julio soon transforms into a grotesquely apelike beast, another hideous monster makeup face job for former professional wrestler *Gerardo Zepeda*! Breaking out of the Professor's secret basement laboratory, which for some reason has a penthouse window, the beast escapes into the night, stalks his prey and strikes in bloody sexual frenzy!

Called to the scene of the brutal murder, Lt. Arturo finds himself facing one of the most bizarre cases of his career. This is where the two paths come together into one main narrative. Arturo is on the case, racing against time to stop the beast man from committing further crimes! Things get worse when Professor Krallman – who incidentally performed the life saving brain surgery on Elena after Lucy chucked her out of the ring during the opening fight - kidnaps the still lethargic Elena from hospital with the intention of removing the gorillas heart and putting hers into the body of the beast as to save him from the transmutation which turns him into the manic ape beast. Cue more real gory stock footage, and Oh do I enjoy scenes of medical mumbo jumbo blurted out to give the illusion of being authentic, and Night of the Bloody Apes delivers it en masse.

I love how the *Cardona's*, yes both Father and son *René Cardona Jr.,* (who went on to enjoy a great career as an exploitation filmmaker himself) came together and co-wrote the script to this one, as they did occasionally, creating such delightful empathy for both sides of the piece whilst they set this one up. Basically it's a remake of *Cardona Sr's* earlier film Doctor of Doom, which also starred Armando Silvestre and Gerardo Zepeda in similar roles they hold in Night of the Bloody Apes.

Even though it's wasted, empathy for *Lazareno's* Lucy Ossorio is created because she's a fighter, but a fighter with a heart, who has terrible remorse when putting her opponent in hospital. It's what we call character dimension in the storytelling world. She struggles with the following fights as the guilt is heavy to carry, and Silvestre does his best to console her trying his outmost to keep her fighting spirits up. Unfortunately it really leads to nothing, but acts more as a semi sub-plot to weave in *Silvestre* and *Moreno's* characters.

Krallman is a delightful character, a cocktail of doing wrong for the cause of good. He's the saver of lives as Elena's brain surgeon, but also a mad professor, a constant evil in Mexican horror cinema, who conducts vile tests in his secret home laboratory, taking innocent lives for scientific experiments. But the complexity of his deeds and their reason is an exciting one. We can judge him for the crimes he commits, but we can also respect the reasons why he committed them… It's a classic case of doing wrong for good, once again, that all-important character dimension. Interestingly enough, even the beast has some basic emotions beyond hate and lust. He shows empathy for his creator/father when Krallman falls and bashes himself unconscious. He even picks him up and gently places him on his bed in the aftermath! Awww, the Monster man loves his Dad!

Being made in the midst of the degeneration of Mexican exploitation cinemas Golden age, it's pretty fair to say that the movie more or less runs on routine. Although it does manage to squeeze in plentiful cheap effects, throat rippings, decapitations, and a surprising amount of nudity as the Beast rapes and mutilates his way through the night. And not forgetting the number of times Lt. Martinez calls Lucy, only to catch her standing in, or leaving the shower! She must easily be the most squeaky clean Luchadora ever; all this keeps this movie a splendid late entry into the sub niche and it's main genre. Where the previous Luchadora films had focused on the female characters, Night of the Bloody Apes focuses more on the Professor and his qualms with playing God – there's a Prometheus story in there if there ever was one, and the climax definitely nods it's head at *Whale's* infamous censored "I know what it feels like to *be* God!" moment from **Frankenstein** 1931. Instead the Wrestling acts more as a lure to pull audiences in and before you know it *Lazareno's* Lucy Ossorio is reduced to nothing more but eye candy and has no real part of the movies climactic last act.

René Cardona's La Horripilante Bestia Humana, is back from the land of the censors, freed from the stigmata of being labelled a "nasty" and finally accessible to anyone who's up for some wholehearted Luchadora fun and monster mayhem madness.

-Jason Meredith   Writer, Producer, Film distributor at Last Exit Entertainment.

Night of the Demon

Year of release: 1980
Writer: Jim L. Ball, Mike Williams
Director: James C. Wasson
R rated
Tagline: "An evil mutation embarks on a wave of brutal butchery."
Main cast: Michael Cutt (Prof. Nugent), Joy Allen, Bob Collins, Jody Lazarus, Rick Fields, Michael Lang.
Distributed by: Vipco
In 1994 Vipco released a version with 1.41 seconds of BBFC cuts, this is the only UK available release but an uncut and unrated US version is available.

Plot:
When Professor Nugent takes his students on an expedition in the search for Bigfoot they get more than they bargained for when they stumble upon a black magic ritual. In this James Wasson outing the students explore Bigfoot territory and uncover the sordid truth before the yeti like creature tearing limbs from their sockets. Just what is the truth behind the legend that is Bigfoot?

Appraisal:
Night of the Demon contains some out there scenes including genitals and entrails being ripped from the unlucky victims. This film is well worth a watch in its uncut form but sadly falls short in its edited version. No, this is not high art but its the simplicity of this movie that makes it viewable.

This is a rather bizarre entry on the DPP list, an all out gloriously explicit monster mash-up. A group of students and their Professor get more than they bargained for when they embark on a mission to track down Bigfoot!

This is one crazy film, which is strangely enjoyable. There is a stand out scene in which a man's junk is ripped off by the hand of the beast! That scene alone is enough to make any man squirm. This is not one of the goriest films within the Bigfoot genre, but it would make Harry and the Henderson's think twice about inviting a Sasquatch into their family home!

This is all out Bigfootspolitation, a genre that has yet to explode! You are in for blood, guts, shocks and nudity in this low budget movie, it does have the usual bad acting but all this gets pushed to the back as we watch the Sasquatch cause mayhem and carnage. A very entertaining film which does have some original death scenes.

Definitely worth a watch for exploitation fans!

-Tony Newton

I actually own this film on its original, nearly impossible to find, VCII VHS imprint. Back in the late '90s and early '00s, I used to sell VHS tapes on eBay. I'd watch everything I bought before I sold it, holding on to the occasional gem. When this crossed my path, I couldn't part with it.

For my money, this is the quintessential Bigfoot horror film. Anything else pales in comparison to this monumentally bizarre experience. The movie starts with a middle-aged camper sitting around a campfire, in the daytime mind you, being stalked by Bigfoot. This is where we get out first glimpse of "Bigfoot vision." Any time we're in Bigfoot's POV, the image on screen is cropped by a red frame leaving a circle in the middle of the shot where there's no effect whatsoever. Apparently Bigfoot is a Cyclops with a degenerative eye condition.

However, I digress. Completely unprovoked, Bigfoot attacks the camper and tears off his arm. The man falls to his death and bleeds out. As the blood begins to pool the camera zeroes in and lingers on maybe the single greatest shot in all of the Video Nasty catalogue. As the blood flows, we soon realize that it's pouring into Bigfoot's footprint. When the deep, substantial print is filled with a footprint shaped blood pool, the title comes at us in red: "NIGHT OF THE DEMON." Possibly the strangest, and most confusing title for a Bigfoot film. Ever. But presumably it comes from the fucked-out story that presents itself late in the film when we meet a mute hermit woman, living alone in a cabin, at the top of Bigfoot Mountain. But I'm getting ahead of myself...

Let's get to the meat of the - ahem - story.

We fade in on a hospital room and meet Professor Nugent who, having just regained consciousness, lies on a hospital bed, his face covered in bandages. He tells the many doctors surrounding him how he found himself in this terrible condition.

Here we enter the first of many, many, many flashbacks.

The catalyst for the film comes in the discovery of a Patterson-Gimlin style piece of footage in which bigfoot crosses the screen of a camper's 8MM camera, but in this version, that familiar loping gait occurs only after two unwitting campers have been slaughtered directly on film.

Professor Nugent is screening the footage in question for his class. And, directly after seeing two campers disemboweled on film, the professor and his students decide the best idea is for them to head out in the direction of where the film footage was found to see if they can't locate Bigfoot themselves. Capital idea!

They college kids head up the mountain, by boat for some reason, and begin pestering the locals for answers and clues to Bigfoot's whereabouts.

The small town Sheriff disapproves. We know this because we see him smoking a cigarette while looking at them. And then he never shows up again. How's that for a payoff?

After a long day of harassing strangers, the university crew sets up camp. They all sit around a campfire as Professor Nugent tells them stories of Bigfoot killing people in increasingly violent ways.

One of the best concerns a motorcyclist who came to the woods seemingly just to have a smoke and pee. In the middle of urinating, he gets his dick ripped off by Bigfoot.

Thanks for the story, Professor! Sweet dreams, everyone!

Later on, we get into even stranger territory when the gang discovers that the townsfolk just might worship Bigfoot. In a Dark Secret of Harvest Home twist, the Uni Kids spot the townsfolk laying a nude woman on an alter that sits in front of a man-made effigy of Bigfoot.

Our gang fire some shots (because they brought guns) and scare the townsfolk away, spilling gasoline and lighting the place on fire in the process. When one of the students laments the fact that this will start a forest fire, they're met with the reply, "This is their territory. Let them worry about it. We're not equipped to handle it." What exactly is going on here? Are these people environmentalists? Are they cryptozoologists? Or just sociopaths?

The next day their boats have of course gone missing, leaving them stranded. And it would appear that they've landed on Bigfoot's radar as well because he's now taken to picking them off one by one, which they don't seem particularly bothered by.

After one of the men dies and another is attacked, someone remarks, "Maybe he's just trying to scare us," to which another member of the party replies, "Then why did he kill one of us?" I love the smell of fresh dialogue.

That night, Nugent tells them another ripping yarn about the time Bigfoot killed a farmer with his own axe, and then a pair of Girl Scouts that got lost in the woods. He concludes by saying "Bigfoot's not playing games any more. Maybe next time he won't be happy just to scare us." But...he's already killed...never mind.

As I mentioned earlier, the title seemingly makes no sense. But an argument could be made that the title references the climax when our "heroes" find a cabin at the top of the mountain inhabited by a catatonic old woman who I reckon survives on oxygen alone.

Absolutely no questions are asked as Professor Nugent hypnotizes the woman (yes, you read that right) into sharing her life story with everyone.

Apparently, she was raped by Bigfoot after her father cast her out of her home for being a sinner. Welp, Bigfoot (a demon in daddy's eyes) knocks her up, she carries the baby to term (we see it in all its half-human, half-Bigfoot bloody afterbirth glory - where's that prop, I ask you???), and she wakes from hypnosis, screaming, "Don't kill my baby!"

That's when Bigfoot breaks in and kills everyone except Nugent whose face he seems content to melt on a piping hot stove.

That's the end of our tale. We're mercilessly back in present day with Nugent in the hospital bed. Having finished his story, the doctors conclude that he's insane. They're not wrong.

The film remains one of the Crown Jewels of my VHS collection.

-Mark Miller   Writer, Director, Producer, Seraphim Films.

Snuff

Also known as: "Slaughter"
Year of release: 1976
Writers: Michael Findlay, Roberta Findlay, A. Bochin
Directors: Michael Findlay, Roberta Findlay, Horacio Fredriksson
X rated
Tagline "The bloodiest thing that ever happened in front of a camera!!!"
Main cast: Margarita Amuchastegui (Angelica), Ana Carro (Ana), Liliana Fernandez Blanco (Suzanna), Michael Findlay (Detective), Roberta Findlay (Carmela), Alfredo Iglesias (Horst's father).
Distributed by: Astra
The original Asra release was cancelled though many bootlegs being produced. In 2003 the film was passed uncut but this version was never distributed. Snuff is available uncut and unrated in the US.
No UK release

Plot:
Snuff follows a cult hippie motorcycle gang leader who goes by the name of Satan, he leads his gang into a downward spiral torturing and murdering anyone who gets in their way, when the director yells cut the murders continue, but are these murders real or staged?

Appraisal:
Snuff had so much hype surrounding it in the 1980's, there were talks of the film actually being a real Snuff film and containing actual deaths captured on film. I was actually slightly hesitant the first time I watched this movie but the hype was unfounded as Snuff (the movie) proved to be pretty underwhelming and the characters are really quite irritating. The films working title is rumored to be "Slaughter". "Snuff" must have had genius distributors who changed the name of the film to "Snuff" and later even shot the final scene of the film. The only good part in the film is where they kill a cast member, that scene alone is really exceptional and very effective on screen, they really pulled off the effects with the hand and guts especially considering the budget they had to work with. For controversy "Snuff" gets a 5/5, there's no arguing that but it received so much attention and hype that it certainly doesn't live up to the expectations in fact the whole film is a flop. The ending was magic you forget the entire film that you've just watched and just remember those last few moments that stay with you! The ending could have been added to anything and it would seem better than it actually is! It's really strange on the first watch all those decades ago the film had so much impact, but now the video nasty mirror has been shattered the film is just another low budget affair that has secured a place in cult film history. I watched "Snuff" with my son who couldn't even manage to break eye contact with his Smartphone for even a few minutes during the film, it really hit home how all those years ago this film had such an impact but in this day and age it just doesn't hit the mark! All that said "Snuff" holds a very dark space in my psyche from being pushed with force into the back of my seat and feeling just that little bit sick and thrust into the voyeuristic seedy underworld of what I truly believed I was watching a snuff movie, What the hell did we just watch! Was it real? That was the first thing I said! In the days before the Internet and watching a banned copy, you really didn't know what the fuck you did just watch! People actually believed that Snuff was a real snuff film in the 1980's rumors hit an all time high, the film itself (working title "Slaughter") was far from the myth and cult following that surrounds the film today.

Sa-tan is the leader of a gang of motor cycling crazies who go around killing people, "Slaughter" was basically a Charles Manson style cult knock off movie. The film was released but didn't deserve great recognition it got. Snuff is full of legend and folklore and helped put the nasty in video nasty!

The ending alone is worth a watch, a true clever masterpiece distribution stunt!

All hail VHS!

-Tony Newton

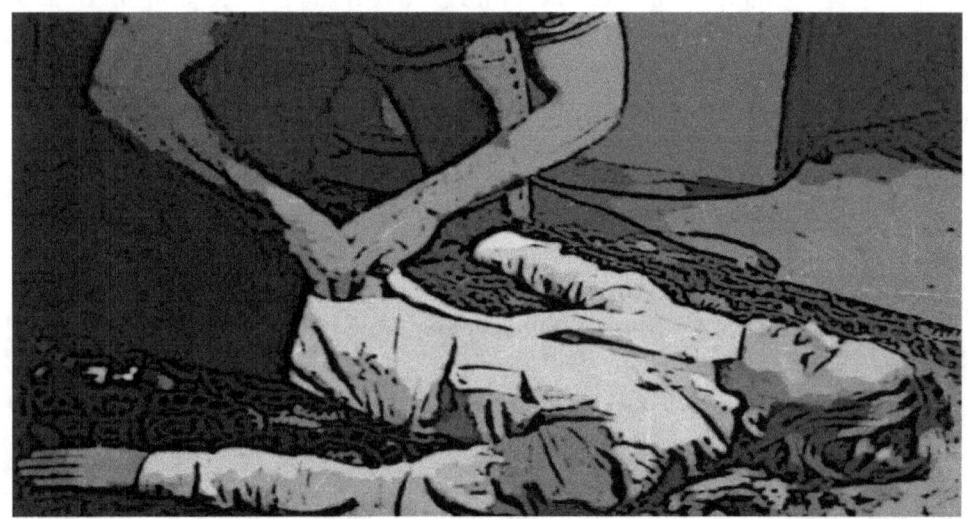

If ever a film defined a genre, then Snuff was the movie that set the tone for the Video Nasty. It wasn't the first (The Manson Family it is claimed have that macabre trophy to add to their notoriety although 1960's Peeping Tom appears to be the first fictional snuff movie) and it certainly wasn't the best but any film that results in a police investigation to check that an actress still walked amongst the living was sure to have its own celluloid infamy.

Made in South America initially as a low budget slasher called Slaughter, an extra scene was added to the end where the documentary makers turn on one of the crew and end her life on screen. Or so the producers wanted the world to believe. How many people searched out the banned tape because of that urban legend is hard to guess but it certainly added to the look of glee on my brothers' faces when they brought it home from the pub one Friday night. This was the only one they wouldn't let me watch but they told me all about it and I just had to see it. I was around fourteen or fifteen so when the rest of the family were out on the Saturday afternoon, watch it I did in broad daylight. Surely it couldn't be real? I didn't sleep for a week. The mockumentary/ found footage style has been done with bigger budgets and more engaging storylines (I think of the Belgian dark comedy Man Bites Dog as a reference point here) but there was never an talk of the actors actually dying. Because of the grainy nature of the tape it looked far too real. You know that no one is truly dying in Eli Roth's Hostel. Mike Myers didn't actually chop people up and Freddie never got into Mister Depp's dreams but could a little known South American actress just disappear. Maybe. Because as the tagline says, it's the film that could only be made in South America… where life is CHEAP.

By the time I actually saw the film, it had been exposed as a fake but that didn't stop the myth still perpetuating. This wasn't an on screen accident taking a life like in Mad Max 2. This was the intentional murder of a human being to sell movie tickets. It turns out that no one would go to such lengths to fill a movie theatre. Yet.

-Craig Jones   Author.

The Making Of One Of The Most Notorious Exploitation Movies Of All Time.

<u>WARNING:</u> You are about to see scenes of a film said to be the most controversial in the history of motion pictures. The movie they said could never be shown...in fact, you have read the headlines across the newspapers of this country and the world, and you have heard the news...This is the movie that could only have been made in South America where life is cheap...It will shock you and astound you...it is not meant for

weak hearts...or weak stomachs...Because of the highly controversial and violent nature of this movie we are only able to show you some selected, edited scenes at this time...but the COMPLETE, UNEXPURAGTED, UNEDITED, UNCENSORED version will be coming soon to this theatre...

Ladies and Gentlemen, the bloodiest thing that ever happened in front of a camera....

SNUFF

So begins the outrageous and over-the-top U.S. trailer for one of the most infamous of the Video Nasties. A film with the shocking premise that someone was actually murdered on camera during it's making. But was it actually real?

I first heard of the term Video Nasty at the tender age of 10. I had recently become obsessed with horror movies finding a stash of my dads' old VHS tapes with titles such as Re-animator, From Beyond, Halloween, The Thing, The Evil Dead 1 & 2, Tenebrae, Dawn Of The Dead, Day Of The Dead and many others. I started to frequent the video shop looking for the names of my favorite directors in the credits or my favourite makeup artist such as Tom Savini, Rob Bottin, Rick Baker or Screaming Mad George.

So it was around this time that my dad opened up the newspaper only to see an advertisement for *Zombie Flesh Eaters*, which had just been re-released on VHS by Vipco. He mentioned it to me and said that I might want to check it out as it was one of the original Video Nasties.

"Video Nasties? " I thought to myself. "What the hell is a Video Nasty?"

Little did I know that one movie would send me on a quest to seek out these Video Nasties. I was determined to see every damned one of them. And I was even more motivated by the fact the tapes being re-released by Vipco were actually BBFC censored versions.

Screw that, I thought to myself, I wanted to see the complete uncut versions. I wanted to see all the blood and gore that they had to offer.

So it was during this search for the elusive uncut tapes of each of the nasties that I first heard about the film *Snuff*. Usually the name was said in hushed tones and just the simple title "Snuff "had an ominous ring to it.

Snuff also started to be associated with other titles I was searching for at that time such as *Cannibal Holocaust* and *Faces Of Death*.

So what exactly is Snuff and where did this term originate?

The first time Snuff is mentioned in the context of an actual murder captured on camera is in Ed Sanders book *The Family: The Story Of Charles Manson's Dune Buggy Attack Battalion.*

In the book Sanders claims that the Manson family were rumoured to have made "brutality" films" or as he would later have it "snuff" films. And so the term snuff entered into the popular culture.

During the time of the Manson murders and the subsequent trial a number of exploitation filmmakers jumped on the bandwagon and started to produce their own projects centred on the Manson case.

One of these films was called *Slaughter* which was directed by the husband and wife film making team Michael and Roberta Findlay who had made a host of sexploitation pictures like *The Curse Of Her Flesh* and *The Kiss Of Her Flesh* and the ultra low budget horror picture *Shriek Of The Mutilated*.

Slaughter was filmed in Argentina with no sound as the cast was made up with native Argentineans who spoke no English. Michael Findlay even took on a couple of roles, dubbing the character of Max Marsh and playing a Detective. Roberta Findlay also dubbed the voice of the character Carmela.

The story of *Slaughter* centres on a Manson like cult leader called Satan and his group of biker chick disciples.

When a sexy American actress called Terry London appears on the scene to make a new movie the cult set their sights on her and murder and mayhem ensue.

When Allan Shackleton of Monarch Releasing saw the finished *Slaughter* he knew that he had a pretty poor product on his hands so the movie was promptly shelved.

The movie languished there for many years until a series of Mondo films were released.

Many of these Mondo films claimed to depict actual scenes of real death captured on camera. Some actually did show such scenes, usually culled from newsreel footage deemed to gruesome to show on TV but most of the time on closer inspection such scenes were obvious fakes.

Around the mid 70s Mondo documentaries such as *Brutes And Savages* and *Savage Man...Savage Beast* had captured the interested of the public.

It was then that Allan Shackleton, inspired by this new public interest in atrocity footage decided on an idea that would turn a poorly made and inept piece of work like *Slaughter* into one of the most notorious exploitation movies of all time.

Shackleton scrubbed all mention of the name *Slaughter* and got rid of all the credits. He then rented out porn producer Carter Stevens New York studio and hired director Simon Nuchtern (*Savage Dawn* [1985]) to film some additional footage that he would then splice onto the end of *Slaughter*.

The Findlay's movie ends with one of the female cultist plunging a knife into the pregnant Terry London. This scene then cuts to the new footage produced by Shackleton.

The new scenes opens on a shot of what we're meant to take as the set on which this last sequence was filmed. We see a bed and couple of actresses that only vaguely resemble the two that we've just seen. Surrounding them is the usual paraphernalia of a film production and various members of the crew.

The "director" then ushers over a female "production assistant" and we hear him whisper: "That was dynamite. That was a gory scene and it really turned me on."

The PA replies: "It turned *me* on to."

The director then moves her over to the bed and the two start kissing and fondling each other.

The female PA suddenly gets disturbed by the fact there is a camera crew still filming.

"What are you doing? Are you filming this? They're filming it!" she exclaims and then starts struggling, trying desperately to free herself from the demented directors grip.

The director then produces a knife and proceeds to slash her across the chest. Bright red "blood" oozes from the wound.

Reaching into his back pocket the director produces a pair of pliers and snips off one of the girls' fingers. The girl screams. Bright red blood seeps into the bed sheets.

"One of you guys come around and help me, will you?" the director orders, a maniacal grin on his face.

An electric saw is now brought into play, the whirring blade slicing through the girl's wrist, severing her hand.

With that done the director now plunges the knife into the PA's stomach. The girl coughs up blood and then goes silent.

The director slices the blade downwards and then reaches into the gaping wound pulling out a handful of entrails.

He raises the dripping pile guts into the air and screams.

Freeze frame. The screen blurs. Flickering leader tape and then blackness.

"Shit...shit...we ran out of film."

"Did you get it?...Did you get it all?"

"Yeah, we got it all."

"Let's get outta here".

There is the sound of breathing. The film ends.

For today's jaded horror movie fans this scene will be obvious for what it is. A complete fake!

If you were watching closely during these scenes of apparent butchery, you would have noticed that after the female PA's finger is snipped off it suddenly and magically reappears when the scene cuts to a new camera angle.

But such obvious fakery didn't stop some of the audience back in the 70's from believing it was actually real.

When released into the cinema the film sparked a storm of protest. It was even rumoured that Allan Shackleton himself had called in anonymously to newspapers and feminists groups to tip them off. This would ensure that the film was picketed at many theatres in which it was playing and proved that there is no such thing as bad publicity as audiences flocked to see "The Movie They Said Could Never Be Shown."

TV crews turned up to film women's rights groups chanting " Stop Snuff Now!"

In Denver, Colorado, feminists organized a mass telephone campaign in order to urge a local theatre to not show the film.

Snuff even prompted a month long police investigation. The actress who played the "murder victim" was found and interviewed.

Robert M. Morgenthau, the district attorney for Manhattan, prompted by a deluge of complaints and petitions had to hold a press conference where he stated that the on screen murder depicted in Snuff was hoax: " It is nothing more than conventional trick photography as is evident to anyone that has seen the movie."

Shackleton. Yep. They don't make 'em like *Snuff* anymore.

This all begs the question.

Do snuff movies actually exist?

Despite intensive F.B.I investigations no actual snuff movies have ever been found.

There have been a number of high profile murder cases in which the killers filmed themselves killing or dismembering their victims but these can't be classed as "Snuff Movies" as the films were never intended for sale.

Documentaries such as *Faces Of Death* and *Death Scenes* have been accused of being snuff films by the tabloid press despite the fact that many of the scenes are either fake or have been culled from news reel footage showing car crash victims, crime scenes or war atrocities.

Cannibal Holocaust was even called into question as being a "Snuff Movie" despite the fact that the actors actually show up in a number of different films after it was made.

During the period in which these so called video nasties where being demonised as the cause of all societies problems a scene from Joe D'Amato's *Anthropophagous The Beast* was shown on the nightly news as an alleged scene from a "Snuff Movie".

Other films frequently cited as "Snuff Movies" are two episodes from the Japanese *Guinea Pig* series: *The Devils Experiment and Flower Of Flesh And Blood*.

Actor Charlie Sheen was so disturbed after seeing *Guinea Pig: Flower Of Flesh And Blood* that he contacted the F.B.I.

Flower Of Flesh And Blood follows a demented Samurai who kidnaps a girl, ties her to a bed and then for the remaining 45 minutes proceeds to slowly dismember her.

The entire *Guinea Pig* series can now be purchased off Amazon and *Flower Of Flesh And Blood* comes bundled with a making of documentary showing the viewer how the gruesome make up effects work was done.

During my travels through the video underground searching for video nasties I've spoken with a number of people who were absolutely adamant that the original *I Spit On Your Grave* was real and that the people involved were actually killed.

Now with only a few clicks on the Internet you can find grisly beheading videos, suicides, and crime scene photos. All real. All extremely disturbing.

So has the Internet now made "Snuff Movies" extinct?

There are plenty of crazy people in the world and, who knows, there might be actual snuff films out there somewhere.

Maybe those brutality movies rumoured to have been made by the Manson Family are still out there buried in the desert just waiting to be discovered.

For more info on snuff films I would highly recommend the book *KILLING FOR CULTURE: An Illustrated History Of Death Film From Mondo To Snuff* by David Kerekes & David Slater

SNUFF can also be purchased in a pristine uncut special edition Blu-ray or DVD from blue-underground.

-Chris Yardley   Filmmaker.

SS Experiment Camp

Also known as: "SS Experiment Love Camp" and "Lager SSadis Kastrat Kommandantur".
Year of release: 1976
Writer: Sergio Chiusi, Sergio Garrone
Director: Sergio Garrone
Rated 18
Tagline: "Sex experiments in pursuit of a better tomorrow!"
Main cast: Mircha Carven (Helmut), Paolo Corazzi (Mirelle), Giorgio Cerioni (Col. Von Kleiben), Giovanna Mainardi, Serafino Profumo (The Sergeant), Attilio Dottesio (Dr. Steiner).
Distributed by: GO Video
In 2005 the film was passed uncut by the BBFC and was available from 2006 onwards on DVD.

Plot:
SS Experiment Camp sees women sent to a Nazi Von Kleiben's secret experimental prisoner of war camp, where the women are selected to be sex toys for the troops. These women are experimented on by a Jewish surgeon as part of a breeding study. The inmates are then farmed out to a local whorehouse, where the girls are tortured and murdered, and there are terrible consequences afoot when one of the troops falls in love with an inmate from within the camp.

Appraisal:
Yet another Nazisploitation film on the infamous DPP list. This is one of the more popular of the Nazisploitation films from the list. SS Experiment Camp is full on exploitation and just like most of the Nazisploitation films it's once again women who are being exploited on screen.

This lurid, sleazefest is anything but sexy as we follow the twisted, evil minds of the SS as they embark on a sex frenzy on the female prisoners of a World War 2 Nazi camp.

This film does seem less serious than most of the other Nazi films and at times has a camp and almost comedic feel. The stand out scene is the so-called testicular transplant where a guard's bollocks get cut off!

Apart from orgies and a small amount of torture this film plays like a soft core, low budget porn film, it just won't hit the spot for most horror lovers!

-Tony Newton

Tenebrae

Also known as: "Tenebre" and "Unsane."
Year of release: 1982
Writer: Dario Argento
Director: Dario Argento
X-rated
Tagline: "Terror beyond belief!"
Main cast: Anthony Franciosa (Peter Neal), Christian Borromeo (Gianni), Mirella D'Angelo (Tilde), Veronica Lario (Jane McKerrow), Ania Pieroni (Elsa Manni), Eva Robins (Girl on beach).
Distributed by: Videomedia
In 2003 the film was released in the UK in its full glory with previous cuts removed by the BBFC.

Plot:
In this Dario Argento classic a novelist (Peter Neal) from the United States of America is stalked by a psycho serial killer in Rome, who is obsessed by Neal's work, the killer not only harasses the author but also uses his work as an inspiration for murder. No one is off limits in Dario Argento's Tenebrae!

Appraisal:
Dario Argento's Tenebrae is one of those films that you don't expect to be part of the video nasty list. The film is a classic horror piece that has been a source of inspiration and will continue to influence filmmakers for decades to come. Tenebrae is one of my favourite giallo films of all-time , it has a great musical score, paces the suspense and is very well shot by Dario Argento. Tenebrae is a must watch film and easily one of Dario Argento's best. Until recently this film was never released and consequently didn't receive the attention it deserved. This 1982 film by master of horror Dario Argento finds a writer in Rome who is stalked by a psycho serial killer! The killer goes on a killing frenzy using the writer's novels for inspiration and killing people who are in some way associated with the authors work. This film is a giallo classic and as such the killer is complete with leather gloves, it's a true masterpiece from start to finish. The film delivers on many levels including gory kills, stalking psychos and a crazy violent killer, Tenebrae is a great example of true horror. This is one of Dario Argento's most shocking films and one of the later giallo films which pays homage to his own earlier works with gore, nudity and scares throughout and the fantastic building of eerie atmospherics. This who done it horror hell ride will have you guessing at the killers identity, providing shocks and scares along the way. Tenebrae is a very stylish horror/thriller, which does deliver, and in my opinion is one of the best films Dario Argento has ever made though it is sometimes overshadowed by films like "Suspiria". We're left guessing as to the identity of the killer right up until the end of the film - it's an outright nut job, who takes photographs of his own crime scenes and enjoys the voyeuristic aspect of watching his victims suffer. This is pure giallo heaven and is a must in every horror fans collection, all this and a killer soundtrack!
This is giallo at its finest! Pure gialli heaven!

-Tony Newton

After the majesty of Suspiria, I rented a lot of Argento's work. Tenebrae is probably my second favourite work by the auteur, though it's been a while since I've seen it, so whether it stands the test of time, who knows...? Just one image stands out for me: the scene where the hapless victim gets both hands cut off and sprays copious amounts of blood up against a pristine white wall in a massive arc. A great Argento set piece in a period of movies designed around set pieces... But what imagery. And sometimes that's all it takes.

-Charlie Adlard   The Walking Dead Comic Artist.

The Werewolf and the Yeti

Also known as: "La Maldicion de la Bestia" and "Night of the Howling Beast".
Year of release: 1975
Writer: Paul Naschy
Director: Miguel Iglesias
R rated
Tagline: "Two bloodthirsty beasts in deadly combat."
Main cast: Paul Naschy (Waldemar Daninsky), Mercedes Molina (Sylvia Lacombe), Silvia Solar (Wandesa), Gil Vidal (Larry Talbot), Luis Induni (Sekkar Khan), Josep Castillo Escalano (Prof Lacombe).
Distributed by: Canon
There has not been a further release of this film but a USRI unrated and uncut version exists.

Plot:
The Werewolf and the Yeti follows Waldemar (a great adventurer) who joins a group on an expedition (led by Professor Lacombe) to the Himalayas in search of the yeti. Waldemar is captured by a pair of sex-starved cannibals in the mountains and when he's bitten by one of these cannibalistic nymphs he transforms into a werewolf like creature.

Appraisal:
The Werewolf and the Yeti is a tongue in cheek hammer-esque horror film full of werewolves and female cannibals residing in caves. The Werewolf and the Yeti hasn't really dated well, it's quite a difficult watch and in some parts there's actually no better word for it than boring! What a carry on!

This 1973 film belongs on the "Carry On" film list not on the banned film list, It's one of the stranger entries here, it has laugh out loud effects and the only screaming you'll do when you watch this film at the TV.

This is a bizarre low budget film, which has not aged well, at the time the appeal might have been there but it's certainly not nowadays.

The one saving grace to "The Werewolf and the Yeti" has to be the musical score, it's by far the creepiest part of the entire film.

Paul Naschy actually does a decent job in this film especially considering what he had to work within this lackluster horror. The first version I saw was cut to high hell though there were rumors of an uncut version featuring a lot more gore and I did later see a slightly different version but even the additional gore couldn't save this film, no scares for me here!

The Werewolf and the Yeti was prosecuted and is yet to be released in the UK.

-Tony Newton

There is no doubt that filmmaking on a tight budget can present a whole series of challenges. However, by operating within limited means, many of these challenges can be met through the ingenuity of the would-be filmmaker and by the utilisation of whatever tools happen to be at hand. So, unable to travel? No problem! Thanks to the magic of stock footage a film can be set absolutely anywhere in the world. Cannot afford a composer and orchestra? Then again, no problem! The application of carefully selected, appropriate library music can help to set the desired tone. However, opening a film with a shot of London's Houses of Parliament to the sound of Scotland the Brave being squeaked out on the bagpipes is geographically illiterate and, quite frankly, bonkers! But, since this is a Paul Naschy horror film, you can be absolutely certain that the nonsense will not end there. Indeed, The Werewolf and the Yeti is nuts. It is a perfect example of wildly hyperactive, genre transcending filmmaking. All on a shoestring budget. The Werewolf and the Yeti was the eighth occasion, out of thirteen, that Paul Naschy played the werewolf, Waldemar Daninsky. Indeed this was, pretty much, a career defining character for the Spanish, classic horror obsessive. He would follow the likes of Frankenstein's Bloody Terror, Dracula vs. Frankenstein and Dr. Jekyll vs. the Werewolf by taking the whole show, yet again, on the road. This time Waldemar would be visiting the Himalayas and, as the title suggests, there will be a yeti. However, the expedition goes pear-shaped from the outset and Waldemar finds himself separated from his entourage. He is lost, alone and hungry. Luckily, in a clearing in the forest, he notices a the golden light of a grotto.

It is lit with some delightful Bava-esque gels. Desperate, and in need of rest, Waldermar investigates. As he enters the cave he discovers that it is a temple. While he is contemplating the scene, he is confronted by a woman. She is one of two, chosen, female guardians of the shrine. It is here, at this point, that the film starts to get a little busy. With his energy deserting him, Waldemar collapses upon the floor. In his stupor he dreams that he is having sex with one of the two women. However, when he wakes, he discovers his two beautiful hostesses snacking upon on a rubbery human arm. Naturally, as would be expected, this leads to a confrontation. Things snowball and Waldermar winds up killing the two women by stabbing them with an arrow. But, this is not before one of the two has bitten Waldemar. You see, as it turns out, the women are werewolves. Now, so is Waldemar toooooooooo wooooooooooo. Ahem, sorry! Anyhow, this is all in the space of a couple of minutes. It is clear that Naschy is an absolute whirlwind of creative ideas. With an almost childlike and feverish enthusiasm for classic horror, he simply continues, throughout, to throw everything, but the kitchen sink, at this story. Over the space of ninety minutes the Universal Wolfman influenced creature kills random people from his party, rescues others, mostly the girls, gets captured by bandit leader Sekkar Khan and finds himself chained up by an Elvira-alike Himalayan Ilsa type dominatrix, who is played by Silvia Solar. He escapes and ultimately goes toe-to-toe with the Yeti that was promised in the title. Meanwhile, there are gun battles, impaling, whippings, bitings, beatings, some skinning, an attempted rape, some chaining, more whipping, and a bit of machete action. There is even a sort of "women in prison" segment. Of course all this is done on the cheap. So, stock footage aside, it all feels like it was filmed in Spain. Which it was! So, each time this movie comes up for air, we get to see the lovely Mercedes Molina, aka Grace Mills, enjoying the, ahem, diverse climate of the Mediterranean countryside. She gets to spend some time walking among golden fallen leaves, or snow, while enjoying the beautiful, autumn and winter countryside. You see, the film occasionally plays peekaboo with the snow. It puts in the occasional appearance as the film veers between looking vaguely Alpine and autumnally Iberian. Also, putting in an appearance is the mesmerising Verónica Miriel. Her role here, in the expedition, seems to be ill defined. Mostly it consists of coming along for the ride, looking very nice and getting captured. More central to the premise is an Einstein-like professor, played by Josep Castillo Escalona. He lends the whole enterprise an air of pseudoscientific authority. While it is all enjoyable enough, the British government, in an act of craziness that rivals anything shown in this film, branded The Werewolf and the Yeti as a Video Nasty. However, this is one that fans of Hammer and its ilk should seek out.

It also has to be recommended to anyone who has a fondness for oddball European cinema of the 70s. After all, there is nothing especially nasty here. It's simply a classic horror monster, a few dissolve transformations and some creative use of blood-knives.

-Nigel Maskell   Writer.

Zombie Flesh Eaters

Also known as: "Zombie", "Zombie 2", "Island of the Flesh-Eaters", "Island of the Living Dead".
Year of release: 1979
Writer: Elisa Briganti
Director: Lucio Fulci
R-rated
Tagline: "When the Earth spits out the dead… they will return to tear the flesh of the living."
Main Cast: Tisa Farrow (Anne Bowles), Ian McCulloch (Peter West), Richard Johnson (Dr. Menard), Al Cliver (Brian Hull), Auretta Gay (Susan Barrett), Stefania D'Amario (Menard's Nurse).
Re-released in 1992 with 1 minute 46 seconds cut.
Released again in 1999 with 23 seconds cut.
Released uncut in 2005.
Distributed by: Vipco

Plot:
Zombie Flesh Eaters is also known as "Zombie 2" an unofficial sequel to George A Romero's "Dawn of the Dead". Police discover a zombie on board a boat on the coast of New York, journalist Peter West boards the boat in search of clues and is pointed in the direction of a tropical island named Matool. After arriving on the tropical island he discovers that the dead have begun to walk and a zombie pandemic has taken over the island!

Appraisal:
Zombie Flesh Eaters is an amazing film; in fact it's one of the all time favorite zombie films. This is one of Lucio Fulci's greatest films, which gave the director the attention he really did deserve. This film has a great steady pace to it, there's ample gore and even features a shark attacking a zombie and biting his arm off! If you are a fan of zombie films then you will love this film, although it didn't seem that the UK censors did! Zombie Flesh Eaters has a some fantastic scenes of a woman's eye being gouged from her head, which is cut in many formats. There's plenty of blood and gore in this film and it's packed with horror and suspense but we wouldn't expect anything less from the master of horror. The original screenplay was entitled "Nightmare Island (Island of the Living Dead) and had a happier ending with the virus being contained rather than the dark ending that we all know and love! In the UK Zombie Flesh Eaters was given an X rating and even then the film was cut slightly, consequently the British public never got the chance to enjoy the gruesome gore on the big screen until later. Vipco released a strong uncut version, which sealed its fate forever as a video nasty, Vipco released the same strong uncut version on VHS and it's one of my favourite films of all time. Zombie Flesh Eaters pays homage to "Dawn of the Dead" making the most of riding the wave of "Dawn of the Dead's" success. It's a stand out film in its own right, "Zombie Flesh Eaters" was more popular than "Dawn of the Dead" having said that in the 1980's in the UK there were a lot more VHS copies of "Zombie Flesh Eaters" in circulation than "Dawn of the Dead", this was the only reason! Lucio Fulci's Zombie Flesh Eaters is an amazing thrill ride for viewers and horror film fans alike. This is a masterpiece! Lucio Fulci went on to make classic horror films like "The Beyond", "House by the Cemetery", "The New York Ripper" all of which are immortalized in the video nasty hall of fame. Lucio Fulci also went on to direct "Zombie 3" in 1988 along with Bruno Mattei and Claudio Fragasso. Lucio Fulci worked on well over 80 films, mostly in the role of

director. Fucli is a master of the horror genre breaking the rules and inventing and creating his own path along the way, he has been an inspiration to filmmakers and continues to inspire generation after generation.

-Tony Newton

In 1980, I was living just outside of Toronto, Ontario. My dad would take me to the local newsstand to get comics, but that year was special; for 8 months I stopped reading *Famous Monsters*, and instead, my spending money went to something new: *Fangoria* magazine. Issue 8 had excited me with its cover – that month, it was Lucio Fulci's *Zombie* (as it was known in North America). That night, I just stared at the images over and over. (This moment would also be the birth of my love for Charles band's videotape label Wizard Home Video. But I digress…) I was only 10 at the time, and it would be 4 years before I actually got to see this film… one night in 1984, at a sleepover with friends, I would finally see *Zombi 2* (the film's European title, since George Romero's classic *Dawn of the Dead* was titled *Zombi* in Europe). After that, I discovered more, including the films of Dario Argento and Lucio Fulci. But that night, my love affair with Fulci's films began. The plot of *Zombi 2* was much simpler that Romero's *Dawn* – it depicted a zombie uprising on the small Caribbean island of Matul. The daughter of a missing scientist, with a reporter in tow, journeys to the small island after her father's abandoned boat washes ashore in New York City.

As a 14-year-old, this film was mainly about two things: the notorious "eye gouging" scene (my favorite for many years, until I finally saw Luis Bunuel & Salvador Dali's *Un Chien Andalou* two years later), and, of course, the "zombie vs. shark" scene (most interesting because the shark's trainer was forced at the last moment to play the zombie). As I got older, I got to read more about the film, and met some of the people involved in it – including Enzo Castelliari, who revealed having been the original director of the film, but he left early during development.

The two best stories I know about the production of the film include an incident involving one of the zombie performers walking into CBGB – the NYC club which was once ground zero for the American punk movement – wearing full FX makeup. No one batted an eye, and he drank there most of the night! The other story is a little strange: During the scene where Fulci plays the editor of the newspaper, notorious FOX mogul Rupert Murdoch reportedly kicked everyone out of the office they were using.

I hope next time you watch this film (titled *Zombie Flesh Eaters* in the UK), you'll think a little about the strange and wild road that is the production of a horror film… and how loyal fans are born in this genre!

-David Bond

Made by Italian maestro of the low budget, gory Italian horror film, Lucio Fulci, *Zombie Flesh Eaters* is a film, like a lot of the Video Nasties, that time has not been kind to. Though that is not to say that it doesn't have a certain amount of merit and enjoyment to give.

After a mysteriously empty, well not quite, boat drifts towards a city, the daughter of its former owner and a journalist travel to an island to find out what happened to the boat's owner.

Along the way they pick up two other travelling companions and together they reach the island that is succumbing to a zombie plague.

Zombie Flesh Eaters is certainly an enjoyable film but perhaps not for the reasons originally intended and is really best watched with a group of friends. It suffers from quite a bit of poor dialogue, acting and lapses of sense while also fighting the limitations of its budget. Also there is a crop of pointless nudity that is quite common in films such as this from the late 70's and early 80's. Quite a bit of your enjoyment will be taken up with laughing at the film rather than being scared by it.

However, it is one of the better zombie movies of this time for zombie make up. The zombies do actually look like they are rotting and crusty, with a liberal use of worms to add to the effect. Also the notorious eye-piercing scene is not for the faint hearted and can still produce a wince. The film's high point though is a zombie fight with a shark, which occurs completely underwater, that I still have no idea how they actually managed to pull off. It is one of the greatest zombie scenes in zombie cinema. The last twenty minutes are also a lot of fun, with a zombie fighting denouement that is full of Molotov cocktails and slow moving zombie action and the film ends with a sense of impending doom as the main characters listen to an interrupted radio broadcast and the film ends with its shot signalling the spread of the zombie plague. The music is also particularly good, with a main synth theme that will stick in your head, courtesy of Fabio Frizzi.

A still very enjoyable film, even if that enjoyment is more because of the accidental comedy than any real horror, but it still has a few aspects that really stand up today. It is a classic entry in to the zombie horror genre.

-Courtney Button Writer.

A tremendous success upon release, George A. Romero's Dawn of the Dead found itself most popular in Italy, where it was released under the title *Zombi*. In the months and years following, a virtual army of Italian filmmakers released their own zombie movies in hopes of cashing in on the craze. Known for low production values and extremely liberal amounts of gore, many of these are lost to varying forms of obscurity today. A few, however, stand above the rest.

Often hailed by fans and critics alike as the best Italian zombie film ever made, *Zombie* (1980) is certainly the most well-known, owing largely to its wide availability; released internationally, it became hugely successful in Europe, and has been rereleased on home video no less than four times by different distributors, most namely by Anchor Bay in 1998.

Released as *Zombi II* in Italy (though branded as a sequel to *Dawn*, the films are entirely unrelated) *Zombie* revitalized the lulling career of director Lucio Fulci and turned him, almost overnight, into a horror icon. It was banned in many countries due to its shocking violence, though it circulated in the UK for several years uncut before being deemed a "Video Nasty" by the conservative government.

Summary: A small group of people visiting a remote tropical island where the dead walk are caught up in the most terrifying series of events ever committed to celluloid.

Earlier, I said that Zombie is largely successful because it's been released so many times. That's no accident. Fulci was a cinematic genius, and what might have become a forgettable grindhouse gore-fest in less capable hands is, here, a tight, suspenseful, and genuinely terrifying movie. The special effects department also deserves a nod; working with a small budget, they managed to craft the most grotesquely beautiful zombies to ever shamble across a screen. They look, legitimately, like human bodies that have been decomposing in the ground. In Dawn of the Dead, the zombies are...fresher. Here, they're horrible, and that's what really puts this one over the top. In a good way, of course.

-Joseph Rubas Author.

A shark, some zombies. New York, circa some grainy 70s stock footage, where a seemingly abandoned ship drifts spookily through the harbour, out of control and unstoppable. Luckily, the local (seemingly French from the boat's flag) harbour patrol's two best men are sent to investigate. Arriving on board in a flurry of Action Slacks and sideburns the brave officers find that the ship is deserted, or so it seems until the fattest bastard zombie you will ever see shambles out of the hold moaning and dribbling as he goes. Though how the fuck he managed to hide aboard such a little boat is never explain, I mean even if you discount his size, he still must stink worse than your gran after the retirement home Xmas party. Anyways back to the action. Refusing to show his ID (though not ashamed to flaunt his terrifying man-tits) our rotund rotter kills one of the patrolmen with a nasty bite to the throat and a quick stroke of the balls before the other, less dead cop shoots him in the face causing him to flop overboard faster than Natalie Wood before sinking straight to the bottom.

Seeing as stuff like this doesn't usually happen in the Big Apple, NYPD's finest decide to get in touch with the boat owner's daughter, the delectable Ms. Ann Bowles (Tisa, genre superstar, ex taxicab driver and sister of Mia, Farrow) in order to question her regarding the scary fat cannibal bloke, find out who styles her hair and ask the whereabouts of her missing dad.

Pleased that someone appreciates the effort she puts into looking so good but surprised to hear her dad is missing (close family eh?) Ann, concerned not only about his welfare but her huge inheritance too, returns to the ship that very night to search for clues and stuff but what she finds on board is far more exciting. And considerably sexier than anything we've seen so far. Please welcome ace reporter and all round stud Italian horror movie hero, the scarily comb-overed, yet still cool as fuck, Peter West (the man, the myth, the legend that is Sir Ian McCulloch). West has found a letter written to Ann from her father (told you he was a good reporter, well it's either that or he's broken into her mail box, which frankly is the last box of Farrow's I'd want to break), which tells of a mysterious disease that is ravaging his home on the mysterious island of Matool and that he may never leave alive. Ann, now very worried about her inheritance (you can tell by her quivering lip), and Peter, interested in the story (and in Ann), decide to travel together to the island to discover the truth.

Being too tight to get their own boat, the dynamic duo hitch a ride with a couple of hip American tourists, the swoonsome beefcake Bryan (the fantastically furry chinned Cliver) and his shapely wife Susan (Auretta 'Brillantina Rock' Gay- can this cast get any better?), who are enjoying a pleasant sailing holiday. By sailing holiday I mean Cliver stands around looking rugged in a shirt that's about three sizes too small whilst Gay spends her days busying herself scuba diving in nothing but a pair of flimsy, fanny revealing pants and a pink flowery swimming cap. We are indeed in cinematic heaven.

It's during one such dive that possibly the greatest scene ever committed to celluloid occurs when the positively pneumatic Susan is attacked by a terrifying Tiger Shark. Susan wiggles her huge arse and sticks her breasts out towards the camera in fright as the fairly ferocious fish swims around thinking "Check the hat". But that's not the best bit, you see just when it looks like it's going to eat her whole (you know the punch line) a zombie pops up from behind a clump of undersea fauna and tries to bite the beast on the arse. The shark, that is, not Susan. The ensuing spectacle of watching a stuntman attempt to punch out a shark will stay with you forever and is probably one of the reasons that cinema exists in the first place. Pant-wettingly exciting.

Eventually the intrepid party arrive on the shores of Matool and are approached by what looks like a gang of drunken tramps. On closer inspection though they discover that they are, in fact an ARMY OF ZOMBIE FLESH EATERS!

As in, they're zombies that eat flesh, not just a group of sick fetishists that only feast on the flesh of zombies. Though in retrospect the title does kinda give it away. Unsurprisingly our heroes leg it up the beach (to be honest it's more a leisurely jog up the beach seeing as zombies aren't that quick).

After stopping for a rest, being chased, stopping for another rest, and being chased again, a pal of Anne's dad, the enigmatic Dr Menard (a very angry Johnson) turns up in a jeep and offers them all safe haven at his house. Menard is convinced that the mysterious plague ravaging the island is also responsible for the dead rising from their graves. Peter West nods sagely and adjusts his hair whilst the others look on, Susan in a particularly toothish manner usually seen only on rabbits.

Now it's a race against time as Menard struggles to find a cure, Peter and Bryan struggle over who's the more alpha male, Ann struggles to find her father's whereabouts, Susan struggles to keep her kit on and Menard's sexily stern wife Paola struggles to finish her shower before a zombie pierces her eye on a large shard of splintered wood....

Will they survive the terrifying attack of the zombie flesh eaters and will horror cinema ever be the same again?

What can you possibly say about this film, probably one of the finest genre movies ever made, that hasn't been said a thousand times before?

And sometimes even by people that saw it on release?

Planned to cash-in on the huge success of George A Romero's global (and cultural) phenomenon Dawn Of The Dead (AKA Zombies: Dawn Of The Dead, Zombi), Zombie Flesh Eaters – or Zombi 2 as it was known in Italy, see what they did there? - is one of those rare beasts that transcends its humble origins and now sits as an equal to the film that 'inspired' it.

Filmed around New York and Haiti (sometimes even with permits), the exotic locations adding a stark otherworldly air to the proceedings with the island of Matool, all dust storms and barren decayed buildings cleverly mirroring the colours used in the zombie make-up. The dead being as much a part of the island as the beach and sands; a stark contrast to the vivid greens of the jungle scenes.

Also on show is Fulci's predilection for using the "crash zoom" as a shorthand way to heighten the audience's reaction to scenes of horror and gore. Sometimes overused in his later movies, this (his) signature effect serves him well when it comes to the sheer horror of the decaying army slowly lumbering towards our heroes; never have zombies looked so hideous or repellent, bloated and muck encrusted with gaping wounds, tore flesh and dead eye sockets writhing with maggots. Something that I'm used to after living in Glasgow for so long, especially when you've navigated Sauchiehall Street after an Old Firm game. Nasty.

Back to the movie though and more importantly its cast which is, quite frankly magnificent, featuring the ultimate team of the grumpy Scotsman McCulloch, whining waif Farrow and the manly Cliver, all mainstays of the Italian horror genre and all never better than onscreen here. Plus when you add the Rubenesque form of one (oh go on then, two) hit wooden wonder Auretta Gay and her much needed gratuitous nudity to the mix, wobbling about in a pair of her mums pants as she desperately trying not to chafe her nipples on her oxygen tanks you know you're in the presence of a director of rare genius. Behind the camera too, Fulci is served well by his crew, from screenwriter Walter Patriarca's cut to the bone script to the unforgettable make up effects from Giovanni Corridori and his team the entire film is a perfect example of what happens on those rare occasions when everything just clicks.

And the blood splattered icing on the offal filled cake?

Fabio Frizzi's minimalist score that for the first time in zombie movie history gives the undead their own dread theme music in much the same way John Williams' Jaws score gave the shark its own musical motif. Simple, brutal and relentless, Frizzi's mix of minimalist synth coupled with a subtle hint of Gregorian chants must rank as one of the most perfect film scores from one of the world's most under-rated – outside of genre fans – composers of all time.

Track it down then track down Frizzi's other works if you need convincing, you can thank me later.

Most importantly though is the reason for the films longevity, whereas many Italian movies of the time were content to rip-off - sorry, pay homage to - current Hollywood trends (Starcrash, Ator The fighting Eagle, Hercules, any film featuring Fred Williamson in leather fighting bike-riding mutants), Fulci only really takes the zombie 'concept' from George A Romero – and it must be said, the jungle setting and Voodoo hoodoo from the granddaddy of them all I Walked With A Zombie – and uses these ideas as a springboard to send us kicking and screaming into a much darker, much grimmer and much less comedic vision of the undead than its American counterpart.

Romero's critique of consumerism and Fulci's full throttle gory boys own adventure are flip sides of the same corpse clutched coin yet sadly outside the horror genre only one is celebrated by mainstream critics.

Let's make it our aim to change this criminal oversight over the next year.

Now who's with me?

-Ash Loydon   Artist, Illustrator, writer.

Chapter 11: Non-Prosecuted Films

The Beyond

Also known as "E Tu Vivrai Nel Terrore! L'Aldila" and "Seven Doors of Death"
Year of release: 1981
Writer: Dardano Sacchetti
Director: Lucio Fulci
X rated 87 mins. Italy
Tagline: "The seven dreaded getaways to hell are concealed in seven cursed places...and from the day the gates of hell are opened, the dead will walk the Earth."
Main cast: Catriona MacColl (Liza Merril), David Warbeck (Dr. John McCabe), Cinzia Monreale (Emily), Antoine Saint-John (Schweick), Veronica Lazar (Martha), Anthony Flees (Larry).
Re-released in 1987 with 2 minutes cut.
Released again in 2001 uncut
Distributed by: Vampix

This film was released on VHS in its cut form. The film was originally cut for its theatrical release and 1.39 seconds were cut by the BBFC in 1981. Elephant Video released the same cut version in 1987 Vipco later released the same version in 1992. It was not until 2002 that the uncut version finally made its way on to the shelves on DVD with the cuts removed by the BBFC.

Plot:
Lucio Fulci's classic The Beyond takes inspiration from Michael Winner's "The Sentinel" with the storyline being centered on a hotel, which in its darkest depths holds a gateway to hell, the horror begins when the new owner decides to restore the hotel to its former glory. When the renovations begin terrifying occurrences happen including the disappearance of a plumber and a nasty fall from the decorator.

Appraisal:
This is one of Fulci's best pieces of work, the film is enjoyable from start to finish. Horror fans of all genres will enjoy this film. Fulci provides blood, guts and zombie-like creatures a plenty whilst capturing the tense and somewhat claustrophobic atmosphere well. The Beyond was not prosecuted, in 1987 "The Beyond" was released with 2 minutes of footage cut and later released fully uncut in 2001. Note to anyone thinking of building on land: Make sure the plot is not on one of the seventh gates of hell! Fulci creates a great atmosphere here and plays on the squeamishness we all have for our eyes. This film is pure horror heaven, a classic, which gets improves with every watch! I love the musical score, use of effects and cinematography this film is not just a visceral nightmare but in a strange way a complete mind fuck that plays with your own fears, cleverly dishing out shocks and scares along the way.

-Tony Newton

Where to start with Lucio Fulci? Where to start with The Beyond? Both have been a massive part of my life for so long I tend to just assume that everyone else has the same level of familiarity with both the director and his masterpiece. *Zombi 2* (Better known as *Zombie Flesh Eaters*) may have garnered more notoriety with its infamous eye-gouging scene, but *The Beyond* contains sufficient ocular trauma to keep even the most bloodthirsty gorehound satisfied. Eyes were always a focal point for Fulci, his cinematography always rested on elaborate and aesthetically challenging physical surroundings juxtaposed with intense close ups on the eyes of his leading ladies. Dario Argento uses similar techniques, but Fulci emphasises them in his own unique way.

The Louisiana setting for *The Beyond* couldn't be more perfect, the film drips as much sweat and southern discomfort as it does blood, but there is so much more on offer here than the standard horror film would normally contain. Fulci was an astute and innovative artist, with great respect and knowledge of the surrealist movements of the early 20th century. His movies are often sporadic and occasionally non-sequitur, but with *The Beyond* he took it to another level. It is as frantic and disconnected as a nightmare in places, vivid but beautiful in its own particular world of violent deaths and demons.

An initial lynching of a suspected heretic throws us into a burning title sequence accompanied by a hypnotic score courtesy of the horrendously underrated Fabio Frizzi. From this point on, the viewer is left on their own to piece together a consistent narrative and plot amongst the eye gouging, acid baths, exploding heads and rubber spiders that bathe the screen in their scarlet hue. The late David Warbeck is wonderful as a sceptical Dr. John McCabe, who befriends Liza Merril, the heiress of a hotel (played by regular Fulci collaborator by Catriona MacColl). It is not long before a sequence of mysterious deaths and catastrophes arouse suspicion of the true nature of the building in which she intends to make her new home.

The Beyond is not so much a zombie movie, but a playfully surreal haunted house movie with the occasional zombie thrown in for good measure. It was upon the studio's insistence (following the success of *House by the Cemetery* and *City of the Living Dead*) that Fulci reluctantly added the zombie element to the picture. This explains the detached feeling that one may experience during the hospital scenes later in the film.

Poetic, sumptuous, violent and daft, *The Beyond* has everything. The horrendous dubbing only adds charm to the picture and anyone who complains about it is definitely missing the point. Fulci makes his own traditional Hitchcock style cameo as a librarian before the infamous spider scene and it's always a thrill to see the auteur making his mark upon the screen.

Brandished like one of the seven cursed gateways, *The Beyond* is an untouchable piece of Italian Horror history and is more than worthy of both your time and many repeated viewings afterwards.

-Colin McCracken   Writer.

This is my second favourite zombie film, the first being Zombie Flesh Eaters. Lucio Fulci brings us another fantastic gore fest with some great horror moments in this quite bizarre yet very intriguing movie. It is shot beautifully, has a bit of fun cheesiness about it but also some absolute stand out to die for moments. My personal favourite scene would have to be Joe the plumber coming out of the bathtub.

-Jason Impey   Filmmaker.

One of the more famous films in this list, The Beyond is considered by many to be Lucio Fulchi's opus. At the start of the film, there's quite a gruesome scene of a pussy old corpse coming off of his place, which was nailed to the wall. In a flashback scene, we see that he was beaten to death in a New Orleans hotel (if memory serves right) for possessing the Book of Ebon. This hotel is one of the seven doors of death, which was also explored in Fulchi's The City of the Living Dead and The House by the Cemetery.

Catriona MacColl plays a woman who inherits this hotel a few generations later, and she finds out that things are pretty fucked up. She meets a blind psychic woman named Emily, and things only get weirder. Tarantulas attack, zombies lumber after people, and... then there's the purgatory of an ending. If you haven't seen this film, you owe it to yourself to watch it!

-Izzy Lee   Filmmaker.

The Bogey Man

Also known as "The Boogeyman"
Year of release: 1980
Writer: Ulli Lommel and Suzanna Love
Director: Ulli Lommel
R rated 82 mins. USA
Tagline: "The most terrifying nightmare of childhood is about to return!"
Main cast: Suzanna Love (Lacey), Ron James (Jake), John Carradine (Dr. Warren), Nicholas Love (Willy), Raymond Boyden (Kevin), Felicite Morgan (Aunt Helen).
Distributed by: Vipco
In 1992 Vipco released the VHS with 44 seconds by the BBFC. In 1999 the film was released on DVD alongside "The Devonsville Terror" by Anchor Bay R1 US release uncut. In 2000 a full uncut version was released with the cuts wavered.

Plot:
In this quietly sinister 1980's slasher offering, siblings Lacey and her mute brother Willy receive a letter from their dying mother requesting to see them 20 years after murdering her abusive lover, it's then that terror begins. An evil spirit is released when a mirror is smashed and when a bloody rampage and a quest for revenge ensues will good ultimately prevail over evil?

Appraisal:
The Bogey Man is a classic 80's horror, the film hasn't dated too badly and still stands out today. It doesn't feature gore for gore's sake, which makes a change for those featured in the DPP list.
Characters Lacy and Willy are played by real life brother and sister and consequently have great chemistry in the film. This film takes elements from "The Exorcist," "Amityville Horror," and even "Halloween," it's entertaining and a must-watch from the DPP list.
The Bogey Man was released with 44 seconds cut in 1992 and finally released uncut in 2000.
This film is a refreshing change to the slasher genre and does have some interesting scenes, which are shocking and reminiscent of "The Exorcist" and John Carpenters "Halloween". The sequel "Revenge of the Boogeyman" was released in 1983 and "Return of the Bogey Man in 1993.
The Bogey Man was not released in its full, uncut version until 2001.

-Tony Newton

To talk about *The Boogeyman*, you really have to talk about the force of nature that is its creator, Ulli Lommel. What words can truly summarize a man who, on the first day of meeting legendary director Rainer Werner Fassbinder, gave him his car. A man who sang with Elvis. Who went to the United States to become a member of Andy Warhol's Factory. A man who, when he looked at you, could tell everything about you by the shoes you wore. I'm very lucky to call Ulli a very close friend. So for me, *The Boogeyman* is so much more than one of the most iconic slashers of the 1980s. While others will debate its artistic and cinematic merit, I'll leave you with just two pieces of trivia to add to your horror knowledge: First, the film was edited in Los Angeles, and during that time its editing bay was visited countless times by William s Burroughs, Andy Warhol and Orson Welles. Some nights they just watched, sometimes they edited; sometimes it was just a wild party… but most of the time during these long nights, they just offered advice to a fellow artist. Second,

The Boogeyman went on to became one of the most profitable franchises in horror history. Horror has afforded me a lot of great moments... but learning, drinking and making films with this man are some of my favorites.

-David Bond

Ulli Lommel on the making of "The Boogeyman"

On the weekends, Andy Warhol would also appear. Of course he found everything just "beautiful" and "magic." So this was the ideal location to edit my horror film "Boogeyman."

The continuous screaming of the victims in the film drew Burroughs attention and after a few days he knocked on the door, wondering what on earth I was doing. He sat down next to me at the editing table and soon was offering the coolest ideas on how I could edit the film. In the process he used the word "fuck" dozens of times every minute in every possible variation. "Fuck this" and "fuck that", "fucking great!" and "Fucking awful!" "Fuck me" and "Fuck you!" The scene on the Potomac River, in which a teenager gets killed in his car, he wanted to turn into a "fucking masterpiece."

The following twelve nights Burroughs took over the direction of the editing, with occasional guest appearances by Warhol. Andy still found everything "perfect" and "beautiful", but he confided over breakfast that he was only having nightmares. He asked if I could please return to New York. In his opinion the LA climate was not healthy for me.

He would get totally stoned, kick back with me in my cutting room and then work on editing horror scenes. He was always rearranging his favorite scene, the one in which a teenager gives his girlfriend a deadly kiss in his car. The Boogeyman had just stuck a grill skewer through his neck from behind and the skewer was sticking out his mouth - half ridiculous and half insane.

"That's how every kiss should end!" Burroughs would say.

Burroughs replayed this scene almost infinitely. Again and again the spirit of the Boogeyman would shove the girl into the death kiss. The skewer became a gruesome phallic symbol of an ill-advised camping trip on the Potomac.

The infamous skewer scene in Boogeyman is one that horror fans remember with enthusiasm even today, thirty years later. I have William Burroughs to thank for that. This beanpole spirit in the wrinkled suit with a little hat and glasses looked like a small town bookseller from the 50s, and not like some Punk-Fuck-Beat-Smack Superstar.

We worked the whole night through. On the next morning, as Burroughs fell asleep at the cutting table, for the first time I had the feeling that this "Boogeyman" could be a hit. And so it was. In August 19980 "Boogeyman" opened in 80 theaters in New York. It became the most successful horror film of that year. Shot for only $300,000, it grossed $25 million worldwide. Unfortunately, I only saw a small part of the profits. Several distributors disappeared in the night along with millions in proceeds and were never seen again. The Boogeyman had struck again.

-Ulli Lommel 2010

Over the past decade *Ulli Lommel* has become known as one of the most inept film-makers of our generation, a modern-day *Ed Wood* if you like. In 2005 I had the distinct displeasure of watching his woefully abysmal Zombie Nation, which was utterly bereft of quality, and would have been inclined to agree with popular consensus at that point. However, his directorial career has spread across five decades, and afforded him the opportunity to rub noses with such greats as *Donald Pleasence, Tony Curtis, Andy Warhol,* and even *Russ Meyer* so there have been positives. Admittedly his later works are largely vilified, and rightly so, but every dog has its day, even one afflicted with rabies.

Shortly after The Boogey Man was released at the turn of the 80s, it became embroiled in the video nasty debate and, in 1984, was placed on the DPP's 33-strong second list of films deemed inappropriate for public consumption and whisked from video store shelves faster than you could say pariah. While never actually successfully prosecuted, it made a name for itself, so much so that its appalling sequel from 1983, Revenge of The Boogey Man, which was little more than a shameless retread comprising over fifty percent regurgitated footage, was also banished. Over thirty years later it is affectionately remembered and Keeper, for one, is culpable of possessing something of a soft spot for it.

Innovation clearly wasn't of any great concern to Lommel and, within the first ten minutes, it states its intent. *John Carpenter's* influence is evident, from the title itself, to the opening static shot of a house which bears more than a passing resemblance to the old Myers homestead, and its set-up which features a small child stabbing his mother's lover to death in a scene pulled directly from Halloween, it's clear that Carpenter was a huge source of motivation to Lommel although that is where any similarities end. Similarly, The Exorcist also receives a clear nod of reverence, and he also borrows shamelessly from *William Friedkin's* masterpiece as the film wears on.

Having said that, the film which closest resembles The Boogey Man in terms of overall theme and foreboding Southern Gothic atmosphere is *James W. Robertson's* vastly underrated Superstition from two years later and the parallels are there for all to see. Like Robertson's film there are numerous slasher leanings but, what is most notable is the supernatural element and similarly mean-spirited approach. An underlying sense of dread serves it best, along with a glorious synthesized score courtesy of *Tim Krog,* the likes of which just don't get made anymore. Despite such spikes in quality, it's best revisited with rose-tinted spectacles firmly in place, particularly when it comes to dialogue and performances. One distinct plus would be the appearance of *John Carradine,* although he had the astute sense to get in and get out in the same day of shooting.

Still traumatized by the events of twenty years prior, whereby Willy's sibling Lacey slaughters their mother's abusive lover whilst bathing in her own reflection, the pair continue to pay psychological penance for their actions. Lacey suffers from particularly lurid and vicious dreams whereas her brother has been mute since that very night. Hilariously, his nearest and dearest appear to have forgotten his vow of silence as they spend the entire duration making one-way conversation with Willy. After unwittingly releasing our malevolent spirit by shattering a mirror, their ten years of bad luck commences. This has particularly foul repercussions for their loved ones and any fringe players as the pent-up evil spreads faster than an outbreak of head lice at a *Justin Bieber* concert.

The main reason for watching The Boogey Man was always its kills and I shall get to them in turn during my post-appraisal wind down. However, it has more going for it than it may have appeared initially. Visually it ranges wildly from shambolic to reasonably masterful and Lommel's directorial style is as uneven as the film itself. Having said this, its numerous laughably inept moments are largely forgivable given the era, while certain lasting imagery still possesses an exclusive nostalgic charm even now. Lommel saturates his lens in vivid primary colors and an airborne mirror shard lodges itself into our hippocampus both effortlessly and effectively. Likewise, the glimmer of a steel blade as it prepares to perforate still sticks in my mind all these years later. Married with Krog's goosebump-encouraging score, it makes for a mildly unsettling experience.

Scoring a film such as Lommel's The Boogey Man is somewhat troublesome. On one hand it is likely that, have you not shared in its guilty pleasures previously, you will find it painful to sit through. However, for those already initiated, it has matured surprisingly well with age. Sure the performances range from good to shockingly bad and it's a muddled mess of gargantuan proportions, but it knows what it is that its core audience craves and delivers with kindness. With gory kills, often tinged with black humor, a soundtrack to kill for, brisk pace, and optical confectionary at every turn, it can never be accused of being miserly. So many films of its epoch, particularly those that landed themselves in hot water with the censors, are long-in-the-tooth now but I'm pleased as punch to report that its one list The Boogey Man doesn't populate.

-Keeper of the Crimson Quill   (Rivers of Grue)

Cannibal Terror

Also known as "Terreur Cannibale".
Year of release: 1980
Writer: Julio Perez Tabernero and H.L Rostaine.
Director: Alain Deruelle and Oliver Mathot
Unrated 93 mins. Spain, France
Tagline: "Gut munching gore hounds."
Main cast: Silvia Solar (Madame Danville), Gerard Lemaire, Pamela Stanford (Manuela), Olivier Mathot (Monsieur Danville), Bertrand Altmann, Stan Hamilton.
Distributed by: Modern Films
Originally distributed by Modern Films. In 2003 International Trading released an uncut version with cuts wavered by the BBFC.
Cannibal Terror wasn't prosecuted, It was released uncut until 2003.

Plot:
Cannibal Terror is one of the many cannibal films on the DPP list.
Criminals Mario and Roberto turn to kidnapping a young girl and hide out in the jungle with their victim. The tables are turned on the criminals as the bloodthirsty cannibals living in the jungle rear their ugly heads and the victim's parents are informed of her whereabouts.

Appraisal:
The first time I watched this film, I watched through the barely parted fingers of my hands, I was about 12 years old and the premise alone freaked the hell out of me. A friend of mine told me that this was one of those snuff movies, I couldn't make out the bad effects through my fingers, I had memories of a visceral treat, unrelenting and harsh gore though looking back I think I may have missed my Horlicks the night before as the film is lacking on all of the above elements, in fact I had to check it was the same film! The effect of my recent re-watch of the film was a headache, I felt like I was doing a challenge to sit through the full film, It's a shame, I'm a lover of the cannibal horror genre if executed correctly!

Cannibal Terror surely only earned its place on the video nasty list because it had the word cannibal in the title. If you like bad Spanish films, dire effects, cannibalism and hammy acting you're in for a treat, if not you're fucked! Watch closely and you can see that this was filmed around the same time as Jess Franco's "Cannibals" which he directed for Eurocine, the film features the same sets, the same extras and the same bad stock footage. Both films were made in the same year 1980 and were obviously rushed out to cash in on the booming indie horror film market explosion, capitalizing on the VHS home rentals market. The superior film is Jess Franco's "Cannibals" without a doubt.

Cannibal Terror is all over the place, it could have been a good film if it had a bigger budget, the scenes of rape are as disturbing as they are bad. The weak plot and slicing and dicing of footage randomly makes the whole film hard to follow and a very uneasy watch, at which point you're actually pleased to see anyone eaten by cannibals and wish it was the director being eaten alive.

-Tony Newton

There's an unmistakable whiff of *eau de Jess Franco* surrounding Cannibal Terror. Unbelievably, however, the producers found a director just as inept in Alain Deruelle. The man responsible for such edifying spectacles such as *Festival Porno* and *Orgies pour nymphomanes* gives us possibly the worst film ever made. The cannibal genre has perhaps only produced one important work, Ruggero Deodato's *Cannibal Holocaust*. Among the casual racism and unconvincing prosthetics, there lurks a work of considerable impact and power. *Terror*, on the other hand, is a work of unremitting shittiness.

In a film like this, plot is meaningless. All that is needed is a perfunctory storyline to get the protagonists into cannibal country, preferably with a few offal-spilling moments and some tits to spice things up a little. Whereas most cannibal films use an expedition-gone-terribly-wrong plot device, at least *Terror* goes the extra mile to give us a needlessly convoluted kidnap-goes-totally-awry plot instead, which is nice. What follows is so stupefying badly done that words cannot fully describe it. I'll have a go anyway, though. That this film was banned in the UK as a video nasty makes me want to renounce my citizenship and move to somewhere good, like North Korea.

Actors wander around in a Quaaludes daze, struggling not to look directly into the camera, and failing miserably not to appear embarrassed. The kidnapped little girl, the most irritating child actor ever seen until Macaulay Culkin crawled out of Michael Jackson's love nest, is dragged to a place deep in an unnamed South American country. This South American country appears to be Spain. The cannibals themselves, who appear to live five minutes from a main road, are, to a man, Europeans in Adam Ant-style face paint, and wield sticks topped with plastic skulls. Their fantastic native dancing, much of which is looped and shown several times, proves once and for all that white boys got rhythm. Witness them openly laughing into the camera as they shake their sticks around a feeble campfire with Red Indian-style chanting playing on the soundtrack. Special mention must be made to the two sex case-types who watch the chief dismember a Kate Bush look-a-like whose Jeep overheats too close to the cannibal camp. Their self-conscious shimmying and nervous glances towards the camera give a scene, which the filmmakers presumably meant to be horrifying, a real air of farce and total incompetence.

Anyone committed enough to sit through this tripe will be rewarded by the sight of a sturdy-thighed woman in a white cocktail dress and matching shoes slogging through the 'jungle', the feeblest death-by-arrow scene ever, a respectable businessman calling a border guard a cunt, people tied to poles, Tarzan-style and a rape scene which could not have been more ineffectively done than if one of the watching monkeys had filmed it. Some scenes seem to have drifted onto the celluloid of their own volition: several times, a native attempts to steal one of the stern-faced-arms-folded chief's bones from his pile. Why? On the guy's second try at bone snatching the cameraman's attention is obviously elsewhere (possibly on the nearby topless native girl), and completely misses the attempt. His hurried downwards pan shows nothing but the chief's feet.

This film is shit - total, unmitigated shit. That's why I've watched it more than any Cannibal film, and enjoyed it every single, shameful time. Franco's films leave me cold and, poor as they invariably are, they do border on the competent occasionally. Although *Cannibal Terror* shares some footage and actors with Franco's *Mondo Cannibale*, the sheer effrontery of producing a film this shambolic is endearing. There are no saving graces: acting, production values, plot? Nope, it has none. It's still great though.

-Rich Flannagan   Writer.

Contamination

Also known as "*Alien Contamination*", "*Toxic Spawn*", and "*Alien Arrives on Earth*"

Year of release: 1980
Writer: Luigi Cozzi and Erich Tomek
Director: Luigi Cozzi
R rated 84 mins. Italy, West Germany
Tagline: "A new plague on Earth will come from the stars!"
Main cast: Ian McCulloch (Cmdr, Ian Hubbard), Louise Marleau (Col. Stella Holmes), Marino Mase (NYPD Lt. Tony Aris), Siegfried Rauch (Hamilton), Gisela Hahn (Perla de la Cruz), Carlo De Mejo (Agent Young).
Distributed by: Originally distributed by VIP.
IN 2004 Anchor Bay released a fully uncut version of the film in the UKK passed by the BBFC with a 15 certificate.
Contamination was not prosecuted and was not released uncut until 2004 when it received a 15 rating.

Plot:
Contamination begins with an empty ship discovered at New York Harbor, when the police investigate the ship they discover green alien eggs and the remains of the former crew on board. The police enlist the help of an ex-astronaut turned detective to attempt to discover the source of these alien eggs/pods.

Appraisal:
It's obvious to see how much the director of this film liked the film "Alien". Contamination is another welcome sci-fi horror on the DPP list, it doesn't have a big budget, the plot could've been better but has exploding eggs! The first time I saw this film complete with big moustaches (the film not me!) I think I tried not to like it just because of its "Alien" connection.

But since initially watching Contamination in the 80s for the first time I adore this movie for so many reasons! I have since watched this cult horror on VHS about 30 times! It's got a charm all of its own!

It's easy to see how Contamination could have been seen as a copy of Alien. Strange as it seems this film in its uncut form is actually a very entertaining watch and overall a great video nasty for the sci-fi horror fan.

They were at least trying here with effects, music and the overall feel of the movie. Contamination is easily one of the best foreign sci-fi films of the early 80', to be fair there weren't that many ... well, good ones anyway.

-Tony Newton

In 1979, *Ridley Scott* birthed unto the world **Alien,** a film that is still regarded as the template for sci-fi horror over thirty-five years later. It went on to enjoy massive worldwide success and leagues of low-budget filmmakers began to rub their hands together excitedly at the prospect of emulating its global success on just a fraction of the budget. Some of the better examples of this in action were *Bruce D. Clark's* **Galaxy of Terror** and *Allan Holzman's* **Forbidden World** from the *Roger Corman* stable, and *William Malone's* **Titan Find.** However, word travelled fast and, before long, the Italians had formulated their own attack plan.

With *Dario Argento, Lucio Fulci, Umberto Lenzi, Bruno Mattei,* and *Lamberto Bava* leading the charge, it was an exciting time for Italian cinema and Fulci's **Zombi 2** was understandably turning heads the world over. *Luigi Cozzi* wanted in and had already been responsible for sci-fi fantasy **Starcrash** in 1978, a film that enjoyed moderate success and put his name on the map. Having watched Alien, he decided to give the world his own interstellar horror flick and set out to make **Contamination** with the very best of reasoning - being to earn the almighty buck and ride this new wave before it inevitably came crashing down. His was one of two Italian efforts to emerge in 1980, with *Ciro Ippolito's* **Alien 2: On Earth** also doing the rounds about the same time. However, where Ippolito's wonderful B-grade schlockfest disappeared without trace, Cozzi's effort gained considerable infamy.

It surfaced in the UK in 1982 after receiving nearly three minutes of cuts and was promptly banned in October 1983 and placed on the DPP's video nasty list a few months later. After unsuccessful attempts to prosecute, it was dropped from the naughty list in 1985 and, thirty years on, is available fully uncut with a 15 certificate. It's hard to decipher just what all of the fuss was about but it provides additional evidence of how misguided the censors were as they pressed the panic button amidst national outcry.

The film's production company was based in the same offices responsible for **Zombi 2** thus it appeared a no-brainer to Cozzi to attempt at hiring the exact same cast. He failed in his bid but did manage to accost *Ian McCulloch*, while plans to include *Caroline Munro* a second time fell flat due to producer *Claudio Mancini's* stipulation that he cast an older actress. Actually, Mancini proved to be his nemesis (and our worst nightmare) as he insisted on Cozzi focusing more on James Bond-style elements in an endeavor to gain wider appeal.

To rub marinara in his deepening abrasions, he also vetoed the director's plan to use stop-motion for the alien organism at the film's close and demanded that animatronics be used. As a result, The Cyclops was barely functional and had to be manipulated by stagehands with rapid jump cuts being used to paper over the cracks. The deluded suit then conjured up the moniker **Contamination: Alien on Earth** for release in certain regions, which sparked mass confusion, given the parallels to Ippolito's title, so it was swiftly shortened to simply **Contamination.** Personally, I preferred another of its working titles, **Toxic Spawn,** but **Contamination** works for me also. Nevertheless, what a fucking douchebag!

Budgetary constraints also left Cozzi hamstrung and any hopes to set his movie in space were quashed, thus the Earth became his playground and he brought the aliens to us instead. How delightfully thoughtful. It started, much like **Zombi 2,** with a massive sea vessel drifting into New York Harbor, seemingly devoid of life. A crew were dispatched to investigate the ship and discovered a most ominous cargo, tucked away beneath the coffee beans. After likening these gooey green ova to avocados, they soon rued their inquisitive nature as a number of the orbs burst in their sorry faces, coating them in flesh-dissolving gunk. An unsolicited facemask turned out to be the least of their concerns as contact with the eggs provoked rapid inflammation within their stomachs causing them to explode from the inside out like primed pimples.

As far as openers are concerned, **Contamination** had itself something of a doozy but it is here that Mancini's meddling ways became evident as it settled into a sedate pace for the next hour or so as it struggled to build up the same head of steam a second time. The espionage sub-plot was borderline dull and it was left to McCulloch to liven things up with lines of Brie dialogue such as "I looked at Hamilton – and he was, his eyes, he was beginning to… Hamilton… HAMILTON!" followed by a priceless dramatic sound bite.

As well as a number of glaring plot holes, there was also a considerable amount of padding with instances of supposed tension dragging on far too long, pointless travelogue scenes, and precious little in the way of exploding chests or melted away faces. Fuck James Bond and his shaken Martinis, we wanted to see some splatter, and it all felt contaminated by its overly pernickety producer's insistence that it play to entirely the wrong demographic. Watching any spaghetti horror from the period meant accepting particular realities, any fan of Fulci would be required to overlook a lack of coherent narrative, and it mattered not as his work delivered on many other levels. Cozzi's film was occasionally borderline lackluster and that proved a far more bitter pill to swallow.

In that respect, it fell short of **Alien 2: On Earth** in my estimations, at least where the fun factor was concerned. However, it wasn't all bad, by a long chalk. *Goblin* provided the score, which is never a negative and, whilst not one of their better compositions, it assisted in creating a moody atmosphere. In addition, by the final third, **Contamination** ceased dragging its heels and offered pay-off for our perseverance, albeit a tad preposterous. Should you possess a book of Sudoku and a crate of cheap industrial strength lager, then knock yourselves out as amidst numerous troughs lay a number of notable peaks. However, you'll be needing those rose-tinted spectacles and perhaps even a shot of adrenaline or three to make it through 95 minutes. -Keeper of the Crimson Quill (Rivers of Grue)

Dead and Buried

Year of release: 1981
Writer: Jeff Millar and Alex Stern
Director: Gary Sherman
R rating 94 mins. USA
Tagline: "The writers of Alien… bring a new terror to Earth."
Main cast: James Farentino (Sheriff Dan Gillis), Melody Anderson (Janet Gillis), Jack Albertson (Willian G. Dobbs), Dennis Redfield (Ron), Nancy Locke (Linda), Lisa Blount (Girl on the beach).
Distributed by: Thorn EMI.
Originally distributed by Thorn EMI. In 1990 the Video Collection released a cut version with 30 seconds of cuts by the BBFC. In 1999 the film was released uncut by Polygram with previous BBFC cuts wavered.

Plot:
The supreme horror "Dead and Buried" is set in the small American town of Potter Bluff where the local towns folk have their own unique way of dealing with unwanted tourists. Who is murdering the tourists? The town's sheriff becomes suspicious as the death toll rises and things slowly go from bad to worse when corpses of dead tourists appear to come back to life!

Appraisal:
Director Gary Sherman does a great job of making the audience feel uneasy from the very opening scene of the film. "Dead and Buried" is a slice of 80's horror film heaven in which we are exposed to re-animated corpses and a passion for undead flesh that Dr Frankenstein would be proud of!

Dead and Buried features an appearance from horror favourite Robert England (Freddy Krueger) and enough gore to keep all horror fans glued to their seats, a timeless classic that is slowly gaining a cult following from the banned DPP video nasty list.

Dead and Buried was not prosecuted and the film was released with around 30 seconds cut in 1990 and finally released uncut in 1999.

Gary Sherman's film is a cult smash that just doesn't date. Dead and Buried had a larger budget than many on the DPP list and it really shows here. This film features the great Stan Winston special effects, which stand out in the film, an obvious reason why "Dead and Buried" was caught up in the banned horror film frenzy. This is one of the best films on the DPP list; it's crazy to think a film of this caliber getting banned.

-Tony Newton

The banning of Dead and Buried in the UK was something that came as quite a surprise to me.

It had been close to a decade earlier that Death Line debuted in London, a film that contained a hundred times more reasons for censors to object. Violence. Cannibalism. Very pointed political satire. Just to mention a few of its attributes. But, except for the Daily Mail in a scathing review aimed at Review Board and Rank, the distributor, no one called for that film to be kept from the public. Unlike Death Line, "Dead and Buried" was meant to be much more a general audience entertainment piece, a very tongue-in-cheek dark comedy... so the reasoning behind its being chosen to be banned, even all these years later, continues to elude me.

-Gary Sherman   Director: "Dead and Buried".

A creepy, frequently forgotten gem from the early 80's, DEAD AND BURIED boasts a surprising wealth of behind-the-scenes talent. With a screenplay by Dan O'Bannon and Ronald Shussett (fresh from their success with ALIEN) and directed by Gary Sherman (who had previously made the equally effective and equally forgotten chiller DEATH LINE), it's an atmospheric thriller that, due to several large plot and logic holes, just misses the mark. But what it lacks in common sense, it more than makes up for with some outstanding gore effects (courtesy of the late legend Stan Winston in an early credit).

A series of unprovoked, brutal murders rock the small coastal town of Potters Bluff. The sheriff of the small, uncomfortably tight-knit community (played by James Farentino), struggles to piece together the clues and solve the crimes, steadily becoming aware that everyone knows more about what's happening than he does. Other performances of note come from Melody Anderson (best remembered as Dale Arden from 1980's FLASH GORDON) and a young Robert Englund in an underused supporting role, demonstrating flashes of the menace he later brought to NIGHTMARE ON ELM STREET's Freddy Kruger. The show is comprehensively stolen, however, by US TV veteran Jack Albertson as Dobbs, the town mortician, who harbours a terrible dark secret.

Sherman and his cast do a good job of conveying the mode and tone of the village and its inhabitants and it genuinely feels like somewhere you wouldn't want to visit (and I should know – my in-laws live on the east coast and I've been to more than my fair share of 'local shops for local people'). The film plays out like a bizarre hybrid of THE STEPFORD WIVES and NIGHT OF THE LIVING DEAD, with Winston's gore effects being more than worth the price of admission alone (the time-lapse scene where Dodds lovingly strips down and rebuilds a hitch-hikers crushed face being a particular highlight). Suspend your disbelief and stick with DEAD AND BURIED through to the wonderful denouement. It's a well-made and unfairly overlooked film.

-David Moody   Author of Autumn.

Death Trap

Also known as "Eaten Alive" and "Starlight Slaughter".
Year of release: 1977
Writer: Alvin L. Fast and Mohammed Rustam
Director: Tobe Hooper
R rating 91 mins. USA
Tagline: "You check in alive….but check out dead!"
Main cast: Neville Brand (Judd), Mel Ferrer (Harvey Wood), Carolyn Jones (Miss Hattie), Marilyn Burns (Faye), William Finley (Roy), Stuart Whitman (Sheriff Martin).
Distributed by: VCL.
Originally distributed by VCL.
In 1992 Vipco released a version of the film again on VHS with 25 seconds cut by the BBFC. In 2000 Vipco released a fully uncut version with the BBFC wavered previous cuts.

Plot:
Tobe Hooper's second film on the DPP list is a far cry from the classic "The Texas Chain saw Massacre". A psychotic redneck begins murdering anyone who gets in the way of his beloved hotel business; you'd be scared to leave a bad review on trip advisor! The psychotic killer feeds his victims' bodies to his only companion, a crocodile that lives in a nearby swamp!

Appraisal:
This low budget affair is rumored to be based on a true story, and you thought Basil Faulty was bad at managing a hotel! This film provides exactly what you'd expect from a low budget horror, but not what you'd expect from master of horror Tobe Hooper! It's not Tobe Hooper's finest hour by a long shot or even a long shot with a bucket on your head. The film doesn't stand the test of time and the acting is hammy at best... But I can't help to secretly love this film, it's watch for comfort, it's so bad it's good! Not high art, but not the worst on the list either! a guilty pleasure from a master of horror! Don't forget it's hard not to judge this film against in my eyes one of the best horror films ever made "The Texas Chain saw Massacre".

-Tony Newton

The name Tobe Hooper has become synonymous with blood-curdling shocks and gut-wrenching gore, so it's easy to forget that his first feature – the inimitable Texas Chain Saw Massacre – was a largely bloodless affair. Not so with his sophomore offering, Death Trap AKA Eaten Alive AKA Horror Hotel AKA Starlight Slaughter AKA Crocodile Conundrum (at least one of those is made up).

As so-called video nasties go – a term infamously coined by someone who'd never watched one – Death Trap is pretty rough. Adapting a grainy, lurid quality akin to Texas Chain Saw, the film takes place in a dilapidated motel in the middle of nowhere, which is operated by the clearly mental Judd (played with wild-eyed abandon by Neville Brand). Of course, why anyone would want to stay there is beyond comprehension, especially as there is a giant crocodile lurking in the adjoining swamp.

Currently holding an 18% approval rating on Rotten Tomatoes, and a 5.4/10 on IMDb, Death Trap wasn't received particularly well upon its release and has since faded into obscurity (aside from a particular group of cult followers). It's easy to understand why. A nasty, relentlessly loud, very tough watch, in spite of its relatively short running time, the film features a shitload of violence towards its female characters, litres of joke-shop blood and some seriously dodgy wigs.

Arguably the biggest talking point nowadays is the addition of one Robert Englund, in one of his earliest roles. He stars as a horny young buck named, er, Buck, who as Tarantino "paid homage to" in Kill Bill, really likes to fuck. Funnily enough, Buck is the most likeable character and his death – also the lengthiest and gruesome – is the only one that elicits any kind of sympathy. Go figure.

Texas Chain Saw alum Marilyn Burns returns as a girl who, once again, runs around screaming a lot, but considering she doesn't have woodland to get lost in this time around, she mostly goes around in circles. Halloween's Kyle Richards – currently a Real Housewife and perpetuator of too-long hair – features as a resourceful little girl who cries too much and sadly does not perish when really she should.

The croc itself doesn't get much of a starring role, popping its unconvincing head in and out of the frame here and there, before slinking back under the murky surface. Hooper may have been trying to recreate the Jaws effect, but an abundance of dry ice, some screeching violins and a clearly intentional lack of lighting do not an ambience make – nor do they compensate for a lack of believable creature SFX.

Hooper takes part credit for the intrusive, headache-inducing score, alongside William Bell who was also responsible for that of Texas Chain Saw 1 and 2. Here, Bell throws caution to the wind, undercutting every attempt at tension. It almost sounds like the score to a low-budget sci-fi flick, with a weird organ pummelling away underneath everything. Brand's performance as Judd caters to this quite well, even though his hair does most of the acting. Constantly muttering to himself, with his face shrouded in darkness throughout, the hotel owner/operator is the definition of a creepy old man – he even has a big ol' swastika draped over his favourite chair, just to drive the point home.

He has a gumball machine on his reception desk though, so he can't be all bad. Also, he seems shocked by his own murders so perhaps there were originally layers to the character that were left on the cutting room floor in favour of more scythe-swinging action. The farming tool is his weapon of choice, because this is Texas. The entire film is set at night, but the hotel is bathed in an eerie, red glow, which only further serves to highlight the fact that nobody would stay there. Characters go missing for long periods of time, but nobody worries until it's too late. Women are consistently left alone, before being revealed as utterly unable to take care of themselves when things go to hell.

Although everyone screams themselves hoarse throughout – aside from when delivering the painfully bad dialogue – nobody makes a noise while being, as the title suggests, eaten alive apart from Buck. Constant radio noise in the background alludes to Texas Chain Saw, but here it's more jarring than creepy. Suffice to say, there isn't much atmosphere, and the "scares" are created mostly by the unconvincing croc, whose appetite is damn near insatiable, or Judd being, well, Judd.

Death Trap wasn't prosecuted under the Obscene Publications Act, but it didn't receive an uncut release until 2000 (it was originally released with 25 seconds cut in 1992). Considering the film utilises, among other things, drug use, nudity, attempted anal rape, a significant amount of violence against women, swearing, and a shit tonne of bloody violence, it's bizarre that it was considered tamer than almost forty other films.

This is especially interesting given that The Funhouse, also by Hooper, was wrongfully prosecuted as a video nasty a few years after its release. Most claim that the film was mistaken for The Last House On Dead End Street, which also went by the title The Fun House, while The Texas Chain Saw Massacre was itself banned from theatrical release in 1975, in spite of the fact it contains very little gore.

Considering that, nowadays, films such as Hostel and the stomach-churning Saw series have passed through the BBFC's filter to enjoy massive box office success, it's almost unthinkable that something as tame as Death Trap could be regarded as having the potential to "deprave and corrupt" an unsuspecting audience.

In fact, the only recent horror films to have fallen foul of modern "censorship", for want of a better word, are those that really straddle the exploitation line. For example, the often unfairly derided A Serbian Film – widely denounced because of one, particularly gruesome sequence – or The Human Centipede 2, which is laughably rubbish and not nearly as clever or as disturbing as its predecessor, and which found its audience in the home viewing market (it had two minutes and thirty-seven seconds cut by order of the BBFC).

Similarly, and somewhat bizarrely, Hostel Part II was once cited in the House Of Commons as an example of a film where screenshots could become illegal to possess. This was in reference to a recently-passed law criminalising possession of extreme pornography – what this has to do with Eli Roth's gory, yet otherwise restrained, sequel to his hit torture porn flick is unclear. Surely a screenshot of three people attached mouth-to-anus is more demoralising and offensive, not to mention arguably more pornographic?

Although the legacy of video nasties is evident, Death Trap is one of the least noteworthy of its kind, and for good reason. In a modern context, the most obvious comparisons could be made to big budget creature features such as the Lake Placid series – which thankfully utilised a more authentic-looking croc, at least at first – or Adam Green's Hatchet trilogy, which set the action in a swamp that looked, somewhat purposefully, like a set.

It's easy to speculate as to why the idea of video nasties, and their impact on an easily-compromised youth, became such a cause for concern when it did. The video market was still an unregulated, burgeoning, area and one which the powers that be didn't quite understand yet. The so-called nasties were also an easy target. The press noticed early on that the growth of such features, and the independent market which catered to, and often created, them, could have a negative impact on mainstream establishments, such as Sky, which was still in its infancy. Whatever the reasoning behind it, in most cases – particularly with the most famous video nasty, The Evil Dead – the level of scorn aimed at these features was utterly unjustified.

More often than not, the films were being judged almost as propaganda, meant to incite hatred and violence. At one point, the infamous Mary Whitehouse even described video as the "biggest threat" to life in the UK, which is ludicrous even considering how many terrible things have happened in the wake of such protestations, many of which are unfairly attributed to video games/horror movies/Marilyn Manson. Death Trap is perhaps one of the best examples of this misunderstanding as, although it's a nasty film and it looks like shit, it isn't particularly gruesome or disturbing. It's also unlikely that it'll encourage anyone to pick up a scythe and lay waste to those around them, before feeding victims to a giant crocodile.

The majority of cuts were made to video nasties because of real-life animal cruelty or excessive violence to women – Death Trap boasts plenty of the latter, but the term "excessive" is of course open to interpretation. Nasty, rough and very odd, Death Trap is a schlocky affair, which tries desperately to pass itself off as a Southern Gothic nightmare. It thinks of itself as far worse than it actually is, and in a lot of ways, that's why it was considered to be part of this most illustrious group. Nasty it most definitely is, but as video nasties go, Death Trap is probably lucky to even get a mention alongside so much other "filth". If it wasn't on the infamous List, or if Hooper and Englund's names weren't stamped on it, it's doubtful we'd even still discuss it nowadays.

-Joey Keogh   Writer.

Almost every existing analysis of Death Trap aka *Eaten Alive* chastises Tobe Hooper for trying to remake *The Texas Chainsaw Massacre* (1974) with this tale of backwater madness and murders on the bayou. The truth is that a great deal of the responsibility fell upon producers Marty Rustam and Alvin Fast. They were the Hollywood bigwigs who enticed Hooper into making his first big budget feature. The story was theirs and, apparently, they also caused a great deal of difficulty for the young director throughout the production. Kim Henkel was the co-writer of TCM and he was drafted in to assist with the rewrites of *Eaten Alive*.

The story was originally based on another Texas serial killer known as The Alligator Man (Joe Ball), who killed up to twenty women, feeding their bodies to a small collection of 'gators which he kept in a specially made pond. The alligators in *Eaten Alive* are changed to a singular mysterious African crocodile, which is kept by an unhinged, peg legged hotel owner named Judd (Played by Neville Brand). He is an emotionally unstable war veteran who looks like the product of an unholy union between Stephen King and Steve Earle. Judd insists that his Croc will never die, but part of this stipulation seems to be reliant upon supplying him with a regular supply of (human) meat.

Thankfully, running a hotel in the middle of nowhere far from prying eyes allows Judd to scythe his way through the customers with astounding regularity. The nearest town is a strange place filled with colourful caricatures of dim-witted yokels and confederate wastrels. The local brothel is run by the original Morticia Addams herself, Carolyn Jones, in an almost unrecognisable role as Miss Hattie. It is rumoured that Jones took over the directorial duties from Hooper after he abandoned the project completely, with three weeks of filming left. This wouldn't be a complete stretch as at one time, Jones was married to the highly esteemed producer Aaron Spelling and so had more business savvy and working knowledge of the industry than most starlets. She sadly died of cancer just six years after filming Eaten Alive, one of her scant movie roles of the 70's.

Also featuring in the movie was a young man named Robert Englund, who would go on to become a Hooper regular, featuring in many of his subsequent features, such as *Night Terrors* (1993) and *The Mangler (*1995). Marilyn Burns also made her return to Hooper's lens. The last time we saw her she was screaming, sweating and bloodied, escaping from an infuriated Leatherface in the back of a pickup truck. She plays the mother of a young girl who is positively terrorised for the duration of the movie, from the point when she arrives when her little dog Snoopy is eaten by the croc, to when she has Judd chase her through the crawl space under the house later on.

Technically, the film has neither the stark appeal of TCM nor the lavish claustrophobia of Hooper's subsequent *Funhouse* (1981). This is partially down to the studio setting, which looks incredibly cheap and shoddy. The lighting ranges from playfully experimental (bathing the screen in vivid oranges and reds for long periods of time) to the irritating (shadows and smoke clouds obscuring what is actually taking place and almost prohibiting the action from being witnessed). The sound doesn't echo the repetitive terror that was exuded in TCM and primarily consists of layers of screaming placed on top of each other, the effect of which is grating after a few minutes and unfortunately lasts for most of the running time.

Those minor faults aside, it remains an enjoyable romp. There is no way that it can be taken as anything else than a cartoonish foray into camp terror, as opposed to the acid infused surrealism of its predecessor. It is hard to know if what we are left with was even Hooper's overall vision and so it must be taken at face value. Rubber crocodiles and balsa wood sets aside, this makes for a highly entertaining midnight movie.

-Colin McCracken   Writer.

Deep River Savages

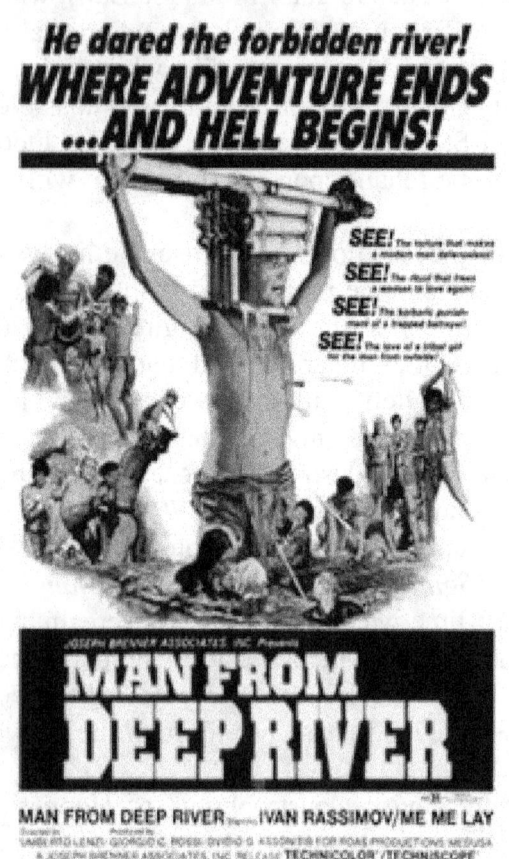

Also known as "Il Paese del Sesso Selvaggio", "Man From Deep River" and "Sacrifice"
Year of release: 1972
Writers: Francesco Barilli and Massimo D'Avak
Director: Umberto Lenzi
Not Rated 93 mins. Italy
Tagline: "See! The ritual that frees a woman to love again!"
Main cast: Ivan Rassimov (John Bradley), Me Me Lai (Maraya), Prasitsak Singhara (Taima), Sulallewan Suxantant (Karen), Ong Ard (Lahuna), Prapas Chindang (Chuan).
Distributed by: Derann.
Originally distributed by Derann.
In 2003 the film was passed for distribution in the UK with 3.45 seconds cut. Uncut and unrated US versions are available.

Plot:
Umberto Lenzi godfather of the jungle cannibal movement gives us "Deep River Savages" in which a photographer is captured in the rain forests of Thailand by a primitive tribe, after some time in the hands of the tribe he becomes one of them and marries the chief's daughter. The former photographer goes on to defend the tribe when savage cannibals attack!

Appraisal:
This is Umberto Lenzi's earlier cannibal film. "Cannibal Ferox" is nothing short of a masterpiece; it's a starting point into the Mondo style genre and a building block for "Cannibal Ferox"! In my eyes this is a quality film which offers an a typical take on the cannibal genre.

I watched "Cannibal Ferox" first so it really set a precedent for me; it's hard not to have high expectations after that! Apart from a small amount of cannibalism and yes, you guessed it animal cruelty, this film which is an obvious remake of the Richard Harris film "A Man Called Horse" doesn't hit the horror or video nasty spot for me. Deep River Savages is actually a decent film, at times you don't think you're watching a video nasty.

Deep River Savages is the story of a prisoner in a tribe being both integrated and accepted, with a love story throughout. The acting is great; Me Me Lai's performance is outstanding.

Deep River Savages is an all round well directed and shot film, which has great production and visuals, it's not for the hardcore horror fan, but well worth checking out.

-Tony Newton

John Bradley (Ivan Rassimov) is a handsome young British photographer on assignment to photograph wildlife in the rain forest of Thailand. One night, after watching a boxing match, he accidentally kills an unknown man in self-defence. Fearing the authorities, Bradley flees the scene in great haste; the next morning, along with a guide he canoes deep into the forest. John awakens to find his guide has been killed, and that he has been captured by a native tribe. He is left hanging in a large fishing net for days, dehydrated and starving. During this time the chief's daughter Maraya (Me Me Lai) becomes infatuated with him and helps him try to escape. The title and theme of the film were largely based on Elliot Silverstein's 1970 classic A Man Called Horse, starring Richard Harris. Lenzi goes so far in his "homage" to replicate certain scenes from that film shot for shot.

-David Bond

Delirium

Also known as "Psycho Puppet" and "Le Foto de Giolia"
Year of release: 1979
Writer: Peter Maris and Richard Yalem
Director: Peter Maris
Unrated 90 mins. USA
Main cast: Turk Cekovsky (Paul Dollinger), Debi Chaney (Susan Norcross) Terry TenBroek (Larry Mead).
Distributed by: VTC.
Originally distributed by VTC. IN 1987 global sales video released a cut version of the film called psycho puppet.

Plot:
When an ex-soldier is hired by local right-wingers to be a vigilante gun for hire, the streets become total carnage. He was supposed to clean up the criminals and street people, but he freaks out and starts killing off everybody!

Appraisal:
This 1979 horror also known as "Psycho Puppet" sees a Vietnam war veteran with a weakness for the female form hired to clean up the streets. Things go from bad to worse as the ex-veteran goes haywire, taking to the streets to embark bloody carnage on his victims. "Delirium" joins others on the list taking on the issue of posttraumatic stress. These films weren't made too long after Vietnam and many people had personal experience from relatives and friends (not that this film was a personal experience). The start of this film sees Charlie as a psycho killer but changes pace and direction abruptly.

Delirium as another bizarre entry on the list and once again we see a film of two halves, posttraumatic stress disorder complete with Vietnam flashbacks.

This psycho killer offering is certainly unique and the first half of the film has some great standout scenes, spoiler Charles's death was a surprise, I didn't see coming that early on!

I loved the mix of vigilante style with the psycho element although the low, if not ultra low budget stands out a mile. Delirium is a real mix; you even get car chases and shoot-outs, kills and gore. It's a crazy little film, which doesn't quite know what it wants to be.

-Tony Newton

Don't Go in the House

Year of release: 1979
Writer: Joe Masefield and Joseph Ellison
Director: Joseph Ellison
R rated 82 mins. USA
Tagline: "….Threshold into terror."
Main cast: Dan Grimaldi (Donny Kohler), Charles Bonet (Ben), Bill Ricci (Vito), Robert Osth (Bobby Tuttle), Dennis M. Hunter (Worker), John Hedberg (Worker).
Distributed by: Arcade
In 1987 the film was released with 3.05 seconds of cuts made. In 2012 Arrow released an uncut version of the film with the BBFC wavering previous cuts.

Plot:
Donny Kohler was abused as a child by his sadistic, psychopathic mother; his horrific upbringing molded him into the twisted killer he is today. When Donny discovers that his mother has passed on he loses his grip on reality and struggles to cope. He replicates the torture he suffered at his mother's hands only far worse as he murders young female victims, who he lures back to his lair.

Appraisal:
Don't go In the House is one of my favourite Don't Go series feature films on the DPP list, if not my overall favourite. This horror thriller borrows elements from "Psycho" complete with his mums decomposing body and a man boy who never really grew up and kept a firm grasp on his mother's apron strings (he wasn't just grasping he was holding on for dear life). "Don't go into the House" is a good film with a chilling feel to it.

Don't Go in the House wasn't prosecuted, the film was released with 3 minutes and 7 seconds cut in 1987 and wasn't passed uncut until 2011. It's hard to see why "Don't Go in the House" was actually banned, there aren't many kills in the film and the effects used with the woman burning are so unrealistic. The dodgy effects don't detract from this classic film, you know you're watching a good film when the silence of anticipation lingers in the air, "Don't Go in the Woods" does just that and leaves you wanting more every time.

Donny the child-like psycho killer carries the physical scars on his arms from childhood abuse at the hands of his mother along with the mental scars from the whole ordeal. Donny played by Dan Grimaldi does a great job portraying the child-like, cold-blooded killer.

This film combines "Saturday Night Fever" and "Psycho" with a disco-esque soundtrack and the scene in which Donny throws a lit candle into a girl's face, setting her hair alight.

-Tony Newton

A psychopathic mama's boy, abused as a child by the woman who gave birth to him, stalks and murders young women. The loner, plagued by voices in his head that urge him to kill, saves "trophies" of his comely victims in his creepy abode. In the end, the dead girls come back to life and exact their revenge…

If you guessed that this short synopsis comes from William Lustig's *Maniac*, you're right. But it's also the basic storyline of director Joseph Ellison's largely forgotten and underappreciated Video Nasty *Don't Go in the House*, which came out nearly a year before Lustig's notorious bloodbath. Likewise, *Don't Go in the*

House was produced right at the *start* of the 1980s slasher boom. It was so overlooked that you won't even discover a mention of the movie in many of the major American filmbooks covering the slasher subgenre. Gorehound bible *Fangoria*, which I joined as an editor in 1985, barely wrote a word about *Don't Go in the House* when the film began its release in the US in early 1980. In the last few years, however, *Don't Go in the House* has begun winning a little well-deserved recognition for being one of the better entries in the first great slasher wave. Much credit goes to Stephen Thrower's exhaustive *Nightmare USA: The Untold Story of Exploitation Independents* (FAB Press) for living up to its subtitle and finally shedding a (burning) light on *Don't Go in the House* in 2007. *Don't Go in the House*'s fan roster, which boasts none other than Quentin Tarantino, continues to grow.

The film opens at an incineration plant where the socially awkward Donald ("Donny") Kohler (Dan Grimaldi in his screen debut) does the 9 to 5. When Donny fails to come to the aid of a co-worker who accidentally catches on fire, he is viciously berated by his supervisor. Donny then heads to his secluded old house, one of the creepiest homes since the Bates' place went on the market. Speaking of Hitchcock's *Psycho*, much of *Don't Go in the House* mimics Hitchcock's *Psycho* template fairly closely. Like Norman, Donny is a pathetic, emotionally stunted loner who lives under his mother's torturous thumb. And when the old hag (Ruth Dardick) eventually croaks, it unleashes Donny's unbridled id. Donny's childhood emerges as a casebook study of abuse. As a kid, Mother held his arms over a hot stove, scarring him physically and emotionally. When Mom exits the picture, an amusing scene of adolescent regression follows and shows Donny literally jumping for joy. He then begins his wave of terror, compelled to strike out at the female race that failed to nurture him as a youngster. Abuse begets abuse, a theme that *Don't Go in the House* will return to again and again.

Donny finds victim number one toiling late in a flower shop, the lovely Kathy (Johanna Brushay), who he cons into going home with him. He promptly clocks the young lady on the head, and when we next see her, she's dangling naked from her wrists in a cold-blue steel room. A door swings open and there's Donny, standing in a bulky asbestos suit. He pours gasoline over the mewling girl, then points a long flamethrower directly at her—and us—and lets it rip. Coming in at the 27-minute mark, this jaw-dropping moment arrives as the movie's most shocking setpiece and the scene in which the film's Video Nasty labeling, most likely, stems from. Nothing that comes after will match the brutality, explicitness and sheer horror of that initial casualty's fiery demise. Later we will witness Donny pick up a few more victims along the way, be tormented by the walking rotting corpse of his mother and flip out in a disco.

Besides *Psycho*, *Don't Go in the House*'s other sprinkled inspirations include 1974's *Texas Chainsaw Massacre* (Donny's greeting in the kill room echoes Leatherface maiden entrance) and 1976's *Carrie* (Donny's midpoint nightmare moment on the beach with his grasping victims swipes *Carrie*'s kicker at the end). I once assumed that the filmmakers derived Donny's weapon of choice from another of that era's grindhouse classics, James Glickenhaus' *The Exterminator*, but, as in the case of *Maniac*, *Don't Go in the House* opened months before that vigilante movie. However, I bet 1977's *Saturday Night Fever* played on the screenwriters' minds when they scripted *Don't Go in the House*; one could easily imagine the film's characters hanging with Tony Manero and company at their favorite Brooklyn discotheque, and Donny's ultimate downfall is sparked during the film's extended disco scene.

Critics have derided *Don't Go in the House* as being misogynistic, a complaint with no merit. Besides the fact that we only see Donny kill one lady, the movie was produced and co-written by a woman (Ellen Hammill, the director's wife), edited by a woman (Jane Kurson), and many of the other major crew slots, from assistant director to art director, were held by women. Ellison, Hammill and co-writer Joseph Masefield were more concerned with making a subtle statement on the dangers of child abuse with their film than slashing sexy girls, as we watch in the flashbacks of little Donny's original trauma and in three additional "throwaway bits." These understated scenes, mostly occurring in the background of other shots, depict mean mothers haranguing their kids, including a final boy at the denouement poised to carry on the now-deceased Donny's terrible legacy.

Production-wise, *Don't Go in the House* sports a gritty slickness that belies its low budget, quite an accomplishment for novice moviemakers. Shot on 35mm, *Don't Go in the House* captures the dual motifs of hot (Donny's pyromaniac hobby and his day job at the plant) and cold (his all-steel murder room, his unheated decrepit house, the desolate beach and wharf) quite well. It's no surprise that director of photography Oliver Wood graduated to such major efforts as the first three *Bourne* films. Likewise, editor Kurson later cut such Hollywood pictures as *Beetlejuice*. Composer Richard Einhorn also scored exploitation favorites like *Shock Waves*, *The Prowler* and *Eyes of a Stranger*.

Of the cast, only lead Grimaldi managed to continue his acting career in a noticeable way. For years, Grimaldi played "quiet" mobster Patsy Parisi on cable hit *The Sopranos*. Unfortunately, the husband and wife team of Ellison and Hammill never worked on any additional fright films. With slasher remakes all the rage these days and DVD and Blu-ray digging up old '70s-'80s chestnuts, perhaps interest in *Don't Go in the House* will reignite as well.

-Tony Timpone

**A longer version of this essay appeared as the liner Notes to Arrow's* Don't Go in the House *DVD.*

Tony Timpone served as FANGORIA editor-in-chief from 1987-2010 before moving on to manage the company's Video on Demand and DVD divisions.

Don't Go In The House is an American movie from 1980, which became infamous for one particular scene which remains both brutal and shocking even when viewed today. In a specially constructed fireproof room a woman hangs naked and in chains. She struggles to try and loosen the attachments but she is held steadfast, vulnerable and at the mercy of her captor. The door opens and our movie's protagonist Donny Kohler (Dan Grimaldi) walks in wearing a flame retardant suit. Without uttering a word he walks up to his victim and douses her in gasoline. He then retreats to the other side of the room and ignites a flamethrower, engulfing the woman in a blistering inferno as she writhes and screams in agony. The explicit nature of this scene is unusual for an American movie in that the full frontal nudity is more prominent and emphasised than in standard R-Rated movies and the sadism is equally glorified. Upon learning that the film was originally filmed with a European market in mind, it begins to make far more sense.

Donny (Dan Grimaldi) is a man who has spent his entire life under the manipulative domination of his mother. Flashbacks portray a deranged and paranoid matriarch who physically and mentally tortured her son. The verbal and physical abuse extends to her holding a young Donny's arms over a gas stove, causing scars, which run far deeper than the malformed tissue his body is now adorned with. As an adult, Donny works in a waste incineration plant and as a co-worker is horrifically injured in an accidental breakout of fire, his inability to save or assist his colleague leads him to be aggressively chastised by his boss. In a petulant rage, he is offered solace and companionship by his friend, Bob (Robert Osth), something he rejects under the obligation of caring for his mother who he says is ailing and frail.

When Donny returns to the house, he finds that his mother has died during the day. In a contemplative state, he begins to act like a child whose parents have left him alone, playing his vinyl records loud and smoking inside the house. He begins to toy with his mother's corpse, burning parts of it and as he does so, internalised voices begin to speak to him.

The parallels to other, more successful, movies are inevitable. There is a huge section of the story which is borrowed from Alfred Hitchcock's *Psycho* (1960) and there are also heavy comparisons which can be made to Tobe Hooper's *The Texas Chainsaw Massacre*(1974). These aspects aside, *Don't Go In The House* is an exceptional movie, strangely balancing a bizarre interpretation of a man's descent into madness, balanced with some horrific and haunting imagery. Whilst nothing that happens subsequent to the aforementioned execution of Donny's first victim manages to have the same impact, the remainder of the film manages to both maintain and command attention throughout.

There are elements of humour as blackened as the corpses which are kept in Donny's attic. The remnants of the bodies are all sat in chairs upstairs and Donny is regularly abused and haunted by them as they maintain the control and manipulative restraints upon him that they did when they were alive. Donny seems greatly intimidated by women; by their beauty, their power and their very existence. Because of this *Don't Go In the House* removes itself from the traditional misogynist elements that usually propel the murderers in similar movies. The writers make a strong attempt to contextualise and explain the reasons behind Donny's actions. They are not justified, of course, but they are at least clarified and examined in more depth than a great deal of movies attempt to do and for that reason alone the movie stands somewhat apart from its contemporaries.

The film is flawed in the areas in which it tries too hard to emulate the formula of its predecessors, but where it succeeds it does so with gusto. It remains an incredibly worthwhile acquisition and the humorous elements resonate well when juxtaposed with the genuinely disturbing nature of the initial murder. Grimaldi never rose to any further cinematic success, but he did have somewhat of resurgence in his later career when he landed the dual roles of Philly and Patsy Parisi in the hit HBO show *The Sopranos*.

The DPP's attention was most definitely drawn by the provocative and intentionally shocking cover art which resulted in the movie being banned outright in the UK. It was released in France under the slight misnomer of *Pyromaniac* and in the US as *The Burning*, but is not to be confused with the fabulous 1981 slasher movie by Tony Maylam of the same name. *Don't Go In The House* is definitely worth rooting out as it is an oftentimes overlooked instalment into the horror genre, it's also got one of the best soundtracks of any of the Video Nasties.

-Colin McCracken   Writer.

Don't Go Near the Park

Year of release: 1979
Writer: Linwood Chase and Lawrence David Foldes
Director: Lawrence David Foldes
R rated 83 mins. USA
Tagline: "They were cursed to eternal life at the cost of their souls!"
Main cast: Aldo Ray (Taft), Meeno Peluce (Nick), Tammy Taylor (Bondi), Barbara Bain (Patty), Robert Gribbin (Mark), Linnea Quigley (Bondi's mother).
Distributed by: Home Video Productions
In 2006 Anchor Bay released an uncut version of the film passed by the BBFC.

Plot:
Don't Go Near the Park tells the story of tribe members Gar and Tre, these tribe members live cannibalistic and incestuous lives. Gar and Tre are tortured souls who will suffer an eternal life, they feed on defenseless victims feasting on their intestines in order to maintain their eternal youth. What will happen when an investigative reporter discovers their existence?

Appraisal:
Don't go Near the Park is yet another film that should have been thrust into the abyss of bad horror movies, the room 101 of trash cinema, but instead was granted longevity by being a part of the video nasty banned film entries.
Director Laurence David Foldes who also directed "Night Force" starring the Exorcists Linda Blair only directed a handful of films after watching this and you can see why!
Don't go Near the Park should be just another low budget flick which fell short of the bar, I certainly wouldn't be re-watching this film now if it wasn't a Video Nasty, and I love trash cinema!
Even the use of nudity including a young Linnea Quigley fails miserably at saving this shockingly bad horror offering. There's cannibalism, incest and a really strange sleazy feel to "Don't Go Near the Park" and it deals with some rather strange situations with young children, this is a car crash of a movie on every level, the acting, the whole production including the music score and the editing which is terrible. I wish I could be teleported back to a time before I had seen this film!
The film has comical elements whether they are meant to be is out for review, this film does not age well. There are some uncomfortable bits, I found myself in fits of uncontrollable laughter a lot while watching it with a beer buddy; it's a laugh-out-loud movie, but not high art by a long shot. "Don't go Near the Park" was not prosecuted, the film was released uncut in 2006. The best part of the movie is the end!

-Tony Newton

Don't Look in the Basement

Also known as "The Forgotten"
Year of release: 1973
Writer: Tim Pope
Director: S.F Brownrigg
R-rated
Tagline: "Not recommended for persons over 30!"
Main cast: Bill McGhee (Sam), Jessie Lee Fulton (Jane St. Claire), Robert Dracup (Ray Daniels), Harryette Warren (Jennifer D, Michael Harvey (Dr. Stephens), Jessie Kirby (Danny).
Distributed by: Derann
In 2005 Stax DVD released an uncut version of the film passed by the BBFC.

Plot:
Don't Look in the Basement tells the story of Nurse Charlotte Beale who begins a new job at the Stephens Sanitarium. The young nurse enters the isolated asylum to be greeted by menacing and somewhat terrifying patients. The nurse realizes all is not what it seems to be as she discovers that the patients are acting out there urges as a sordid kind of therapy.

Appraisal:
I'm a huge fan of films set in mental institutions, they work well as a great backdrop in films, "One flew Over the Cuckoo's Nest" is a piece of art, growing up in the 80's one of my favorite comedy films was "The Dream Team" starring Michael Keaton pure comedy gold, another great 80's comedy that never left my VCR was Crazy People with Dudley Moore and Daryl Hannah, I remember watching "Don't look in the Basement" directly after I rented the comedy films! And it was something very different indeed, "Don't Look in Basement" does get a lot of shit, people seem to always hate this movie, but I seem to still get some enjoyment from it, maybe it's my fascination with insane asylums, or watching the Amicus classic "Asylum" as a 9 year old on a portable black and white TV in my bedroom and giving me nightmares for weeks. This is an eerie film with twists and turns, though the main twist a five year old could see coming a mile off, the patients in the film are genuinely creepy, the film could have been a lot more gorier and had more scares throughout, once again the film itself wasn't that bad it just wasn't that nasty to warrant itself a place on the video nasty list!

I always had high expectations of any film on the DPP list! Considering when the film was made the film holds up against newer horror titles. The films claustrophobic feel connects well from the screen to the viewer, the film is slow and at times feels somewhat repetitive in nature, The films trailer is so good one of my favorite horror film trailers the trailer makes the film seem so much better than the film actually is! Give the trailer a watch first then spin this crazy little film!

-Tony Newton

The Evil Dead

Year of release: 1981
Writer: Sam Raimi
Director: Sam Raimi
Rated NC-17 85 mins. USA
Tagline: "They got up on the wrong side of the grave."
Main cast: Bruce Campbell (Ash), Ellen Sandweiss (Cheryl), Richard DeManincor (Scott), Betsy Baker (Linda), Theresa Tilly (Shelly), Phillip A. Gillis (Fake Shemp).
Distributed by: Palace Video
In 1990 a version of the film was released with 1.5 seconds of cuts. In 2001 Anchor Bay released a full, uncut version of the film passed by the BBFC.

Plot:
When a close knit group of five university students travel to a remote cabin in the woods, they inadvertently unleash evil spirits when they stumble across a human flesh bound book (The Necronomicon) in the cellar of the cabin, they transcribe the text leaving the hero, Ash (Bruce Campbell) to save the day. Battling for survival, can anyone stop these demonic spirits?

Appraisal:
This film is the stuff of schoolyard legends to me The Evil Dead wasn't just a film, but pure evil, long before the film The Ring was a twinkle in its creators mind. The Evil Dead sparked teenagers to tell tall tales relating to this film, there were rumors of people watching the film throwing up, having heart attacks and even dying the next day or week after watching it, of course none of this was true though the odd person may have been sick watching it but that no doubt may have been the mix of beers and a late night kebab, This was one of the first horror films I ever saw we watched this altogether as a family, and apart from not being able to sleep that night I remember my mum putting the video in the car overnight before the it's trip back to the video store just in case the evil from the film would somehow get to us through the tape itself, this action alone scared me more as if my mum thought this it must be real! Sam Raimi breaks new ground here with this cult classic masterpiece, a true contender for the best film on the DPP video nasty list. This is an all out rollercoaster ride with fingernails embedded on the seats and blood on the hand rail!

Sam Raimi's film direction was ground breaking for the time, and it still holds its own today. Raimi creates an eerie atmosphere with good actors. The film was an instant best seller on VHS, the poster art work is as classic as the film itself, easily one of the most popular of the titles on the list even if the DPP list never existed the film would be up there as a true horror classic. This film had another 2 films in the trilogy made and spawned a not too dreadful remake. The original working title for the film was "The Book of the Dead" but I'm glad it was changed to "The Evil Dead" because at five years old when I watched the film it was pure Evil!

After the problem distributors had with "The Evil Dead," and it's addition on the Video Nasty list, upon receiving news that "The Evil Dead" had not been prosecuted in court and the film had applied for a certification following The Video Recordings Act, they issued a new sleeve for "The Evil Dead." The actual sleeve was exactly the same, but it had a bold in black on silver "Not guilty - The Evil Dead is back", BBFC certification applied for. Not only was it a "fuck you" to the system and the BBFC, the courts and police but because of the issues this was sent out to retailers to swap over and put in place of the original sleeve, though a lot of stockists were spooked due to all the hassle with the film and decided not to stock it. I have seen the sleeve with "Not Guilty" change hands for over £350!

VHS NASTY: THE VIDEO NASTIES

-Tony Newton

In a desolate cabin in the woods, just outside Morristown Tennessee, a young girl named Clara lived happily with her parents. It was sometime in the 1930s and one night, when there was a fierce and relentless storm, Clara's parents were brutally murdered in their own home. The girl escaped this grisly fate and managed to seek shelter in the town. It was said that from that day forth, whenever there would be a storm of equal strength and power, Clara would wander from the Morristown Manor Rest Home back into the forest in an attempt to get home.

So the story goes. This is not in any way a part of the narrative outline for *The Evil Dead*, but an urban legend that was attached to the infamous cabin, which would become home to the crew for three long, arduous and grueling months in the winter of 1979. Director Sam Raimi (who had just turned 20 years old), his leading man Bruce Campbell and special effects wizard Tom Sullivan made the considerable journey from Detroit, Michigan with a van full of basic equipment, a crew of unknowns and a vision.

There was a significant amount of preliminary work, which went into *The Evil Dead*. Raimi had spent a great deal of his formative years making Super 8 movies, putting on amateur dramatic productions and practicing magic tricks. All of these skills would be utilised in full over the course of filming and added the elements, which created one of the most exhilarating, original and memorable horror movies of all time. The mixture of EC Comics terror and Three Stooges style slapstick combined with a youthful exuberance and a willingness to experiment were also considerable factors in the unique and visceral end product.

It all started with a short film called *Within The Woods*. This 30-minute piece was used to showcase to potential investors. This was a time long before Kickstarter and so it literally involved selling the movie door to door. The team would approach local businessmen; dentists, shop owners and lawyers. They even had an investment brochure legally drafted, one which clearly stated: *'Warning: The securities offered by this document are highly speculative, will have no market and should be considered only by an investor who has no plans to resell the security, and fully and adequately understands the risks involved and can afford to lose his entire investment!'*

Even with the apparent lack of belief in the movies financial potential, they still managed to raise the $150,000 that they needed to make a start. The decision was made that it would be a non-union picture and so SAG actors were not permitted to be a part of the movie (one actress tried under a pseudonym and was found out). They recruited from the amateur scene, people who wanted to become union members but who lacked the relevant experience to do so. Remember, with the Screen Actors Guild, you can't become a member until you get experience and you can't get experience if you're not a member. Raimi offered the local hopefuls a way out of this predicament.

It wasn't always their intention to schlep everything halfway across northern America. They had spent months scouting locations, it just so happened that the only agency to show them any interest was the Tennessee Film Commission. They even paid a visit to the set one day during filming, convinced that some big budget affair was taking place. When they found a group of young twentysomethings running around the woods covered in blood and makeup, with limbs strewn everywhere, they promptly left them to it.

Over the course of the three-month shoot, the cast and crew were subjected to freezes, theft, and hillbillies. None of them found it easy, but the majority found it enjoyable and a few found their experiences life changing. *The Evil Dead* took over a year to find a studio and a distributor, but when Palace Pictures, along with the might of Hollywood mogul Ivan Shapiro took the movie to Cannes, everything changed. Reports that Steven King, the master of horror fiction himself, was cowering behind his seat whilst watching the picture are notorious, but unconfirmed. King did, however, give the movie his ultimate seal of approval in the much referenced strapline "Evil Dead is the most ferociously horror film of the year". All of a sudden, the gang from Detroit found themselves the subject of the attention of the entire world. Magazines came calling for interviews, word spread about this exciting new movie and *The Evil Dead* was cemented in the annals of horror from then on.

The film itself stands up remarkably well today. The highly stylised camerawork is the result of the comic book styling, extensive storyboards by Raimi himself, quick shots and experimentation. Cameras were taped to Raimi's hands as he was pushed through murky swamps with smoke machines churning out atmospheric mist on all sides (and in one event malfunctioning and almost burning the entire forest down). He held onto the roof of a moving van to get shots, created rudimentary Steadicams and even attached cameras to Vaseline smeared boards. It was this creativeness and determination to achieve the aesthetic that existed in the mind of the young director that helped to form the inimitable look of *The Evil Dead*.

The film features literally buckets of gore. The unsuspecting holidaymakers unwittingly discover The Necronomicon, a book inked in human blood and bound in human skin. Its contents hold the power of raising evil spirits, which descend upon the house and plague its inhabitants. Time is frozen and all hope for mankind rests on Ash (Bruce Campbell), whose matinee idol looks and incessant hamming it up for the camera created one of the most endearing and iconic roles in horror movie history.

Raimi went on to achieve Hollywood success and is now a major league player. Campbell became king of the B-Movies and now resides in a regular slot on the highly entertaining TV show *Burn Notice*. Ash and his adventures were given two more cinematic instalments, an off Broadway musical and a video game, but whatever merits they did have never lived up to the wonderment that is this movie.

It was an unusual title for inclusion on the DPP Video Nasties list, due to the cartoonish nature of the violence. This is indicative of the arbitrary nature of the haul on horror, which happened in the UK in the early 1980s. Possible reasons for complaint are a scene in which Ellen Sandweiss is raped by tree branches and an excruciatingly painful moment in which a pencil is introduced to an ankle by a malevolent demon.

The Evil Dead is one of the rare movies, which I feel I will always revisit. The charm, skill and wonder on display are almost unrivalled and nothing will ever take that joy away from me. Chances are you have seen this movie many times already, but on the off chance you haven't, get a high quality copy, turn off all the lights, the computer and your phone and take a journey into a masterpiece.

-Colin McCracken   Writer.

The Evil Dead – Gritty, low budget splatter with style. This movie charm comes from how lightning-in-a-bottle perfect every aspect of the production came together, making it the ultimate template for aspiring genre filmmakers. It proves that ingenuity, perseverance, and reckless endangerment of your lead can lead to a classic, regardless of budget. This is the movie that got me hooked on horror and hooked on the hell that is low-budget filmmaking. The idea of going out to a run-down cabin with your friends to throw blood around and make a nutso movie will always be the ultimate adventure to, thanks to The Evil Dead.

-Steven Kostanski   Astron–6.

Growing up, my uncle would regularly get tapes from Blockbuster, make copies, then return them, he had this gigantic bootleg video collection that took up a whole living room. The "off-limits" section was easy to access, of course, so one night my cousin popped open the locked closet and introduced me to the most ghetto VHS double-copied, scanlined POS version of The Evil Dead you've ever seen. If you watch the film now, frankly, it's just not all that frightening, but MAN, the ambition, the charm, the vision is all still there. In a FIRST FILM! If you look at my very first films they're complete garbage, but Raimi somehow made something that even today, despite its ham-factor, despite its lo-fi effects and cheesy, well, everything, you can see something so singular and so weirdly perfect in its imperfection. We should all hope we can keep our voice the way that Raimi does.

-Aaron Moorhead   Screenwriter/Director.

Although I am just an observer of this film, not having participated in it, I think it is particularly important to the horror genre. It has a certain "tongue in cheek" tone that is unique to the genre. Without a film like this, I think we would not have the inspiration to experiment within genre, try for some dark humor. To what degree, matters not, but without some dark humor, a film I did participate in THE DEVIL'S REJECTS (which did have MP AA ratings issues) would not be the same film. So I give "The EVIL DEAD" credit for excelling in the "campy" humor category.

-Lew Temple   Actor.

By far one of the most unique and outside of the box-like horror films of all time, Sam Raimi's THE EVIL DEAD is a perfect example of a filmmaker not letting a lack of a big budget hinder his vision. Whatever the film might have lacked in said budget, it made up with some of the most inventive and intense scene committed to film.

While the second and third films in the EVIL DEAD series went for more of a horror slapstick angle, the original film didn't focus on that approach, instead giving fans one hell of a ride. It's an almost jokeless movie, relying more on tension, atmosphere and some downright gory sequences to win the viewer over, and it's almost impossible not to feel bad for each of the characters involved in the film, as each of them is slowly taken over by the evil in which they foolishly unleashed. It's no surprise that film was infamously banned in some countries, as it's full of decapitation, tree rape, and has enough gore and blood to fill multiple movies, let alone just one.

It's one of the movies that I hold very close to my heart, and when taking on challenges or artistic endeavors that seem too ambitious to be created within whatever confines in front of me, I've always used Raimi's classic as a catalyst to embrace those confines and do my best to overcome them.

-Jerry Smith   Editor in Chief/Writer Icons of Fright.

I distinctly remember a school friends "outing" to the local video store [which, at the time, was just one of those many newsagents that had diversified into an upstairs video counter] and came away with the above film. I think I'd already heard about it and its notoriety, but I wasn't prepared for how genuinely scary it was, as we all crowded into one of the school's form rooms to watch the movie. That's what I remember most about the first time I saw the Evil Dead - that communal gathering to be scared witless... It worked.

-Charlie Adlard   The Walking Dead Comic Artist.

So much has been said of *The Evil Dead* over the years that to review it again here could only come across as boring and repetitive. So, instead, let me simply say this; when I first saw *The Evil Dead* (on a bad DVD transfer, in which the full moon seen in so many classic shots looked like a postcard tacked into the top-right corner of the frame) it touched me.

It touched me deep.

With a sharpened 2B pencil.

The Evil Dead is where '80s horror truly began. Not with Jason (or should I say Pamela?) Voorhees's enormous machete, or with Freddy Krueger's knife-fingered glove; *The Evil Dead* showed horror fans, future horror filmmakers and the world at large just exactly what being a horror movie is all about.

It's about being confronting; disturbing people from their delusions of a sensible universe ruled over by a well-adjusted God. It's about showing things on celluloid that no man was ever meant to see.

It's about showing a distraught, grieving man forced to hack his dead girlfriend's head off with the blade of a shovel because she simply *refuses to stay dead*.

There's a reason why us horror movie fans are considered by the general populace to be weirdoes, freaks, even perverts. It's because our iconic heroes are sadistic, murdering bastards. We cheer when Jason hacks off a limb, we grin and pump our fists in the air when Freddy says "Bitch!" and crushes a young girl's head with a

TV set. And, when a rotting zombie takes a bite out of a naked Italian girl's neck, we laugh and grab another slice of pizza.

But with *The Evil Dead*, the horror genre was finally given a real hero to root for. A hero named Ash.

Someone we can point to and say; "See! Not all of our heroes are murderers, rapists and cannibals!"

Who else could stay alive through three movies and countless spin-off comics, only growing more wise-assed and cynical with each step of his journey?

Ash.

So, if Ash truly is horror's first iconic hero, then *The Evil Dead* is more than just a gleeful chunk of cinematic carnage…

It's a superhero origin story.

-Joe Ramshaw   Writer.

An amazing exercise in low budget, one location film making, the original Evil Dead could be considered "the little horror movie that could." Plagued with money problems, actor availability issues, and all the challenges that come with having to shoot around them, the now A list director Sam Raimi still managed to pull together every available resource to make a fun, scary horror flick that incorporated all the best elements from films like The Exorcist and Night Of The Living Dead, and wrapped them in his own original style. If George Romero was the one to light the reactionary torch to Roger Corman's Gothic tales, by introducing his own brand of indie shock cinema to the Saturday matinees, then Raimi was the one to transcend it, with his innovative camera work, practical effects, and crazy fast paced story telling, that took just the right amount of seriousness out of the mix, and set the tone for what would later become the backyard indie movement. Evil Dead 2 would later follow as a sort of quasi remake that upped the anti, with a bigger budget and even more craziness, but the original will always stand as testament to how the creative spirit can help a movie stand tall, in spite of its flaws. It will forever be the original cabin in the woods, flick.

-Christopher Moonlight   Moonlight Art Magazine.

Growing up in the 80's gave birth to some thrilling viewings of horror films I consider on the vanguard of originality. The Evil Dead was one of them when you consider how the film introduces the Necronomicon: book of the dead to its audience. Five friends come up to a deserted cabin and all get possessed after the book is found there and opened – via a tape recorder translating its contents.

For me, the film is a no holds barred gore-fest – a real gut puncher in terms of the nasty effects of being possessed by demons. I think most of the scenes of demon possession are relentless – shocking even when you are forced to watch the friends fall one by one to some of the most ghastly and primitive ways a demonic presence can take over your body.

I remember watching this film for the first time with my eyes bulging wide and mouth fully agape. I couldn't stop starring at it and it had me transfixed to the TV screen because the level of violence satiated a growing need I had as a young gore hound. Thinking back now, this was the film that initiated me into the 80's - and loving gore and horror at the movies. The Evil Dead also became a guilty pleasure every time out because I actually cared for the five friends and to watch them go through this horrendous ordeal sickens my sense of decency – but at the same time I couldn't stop watching!

-Kenneth Gallant   Editor-In-Chief: Horror Metal Sounds.

The nasty that I remember with fondness was The Evil Dead. I remember going to the local video store – totally underage, seeing this grey badly photocopied cover on the shelf next to Evil Dead 2. Being 6ft 2" as a teenager generally helped these situations! I took it to the counter and realized the fella behind the counter already had it on. I remember absolutely shitting myself as I put the cover on the counter. "You up for this?" I responded "Yes" in my gruffest voice – was charged a couple of quid and off I went to watch it with a friend in a top-loader Ferguson video recorder.

Clearly a third or 4th generation copy, I remember really being sucked into the movie from the beginning. Even distorted the sound was as creepy as hell. The tree rape sequence combined the slightly horny with the insanely grotesque and as the cellar door opened revealing THAT horrendous face – me and my buddy had by now totally lost it! The film absolutely rocked – after watching that, Evil Dead 2 just simply didn't cut it. Bruce Campbell however was a total legend from that point!!!

-Andy Soar   Art Director Haunted: After Dark Magazine.

The first time I watched The Evil Dead I was 13, and I truly fell in love with horror. From the low budget special effects, which still hold up so many years later, to the start of Bruce Campbell's acting career, the whole film is perfect anytime viewing. Best with a group of friends and beer, to be honest.

Of course the storyline is a simple 'trapped in the woods, Deadites coming to get you', and the acting at times could be called ropey but there's so much more to it. The film may have gripped me from that first scene, but the love that was put into the making of the film also draws me to it. The fundraising, the drive to keep making a film on a tiny budget, the hard work put in to those special effects? It's all a part of the magic of the film.

It may be low budget make up but the Deadites are still creepy and the jumps were there to get you. Bruce Campbell shot to b-movie stardom on the back of The Evil Dead and is king of the genre, and the film lives on in the fans hearts. Its humour, brutal terror and fun storyline all work well and keep you gripped until the end. Innovative ways of moving the camera, and Sam Raimi's inventive ways to torture Bruce Campbell have helped shape and change the way the future generations of directors would shoot their films. After watching The Evil Dead I ended up finding more horror films to watch and became a huge fan of the horror genre, it is one that takes you away from reality. We all enjoy being scared and that's what the horror genre provides for us, a little escape from reality, but where we can enjoy being scared, but turn it off if it get too much. My love of the film has led me to Las Vegas where I watched Evil Dead The Musical, which is a must see by the way, the film never feels old to me, I will happily sit down and watch this film anytime - any day! Groovy.

-Sian Richter   Writer.

Frozen Scream

Year of release: 1975
Writer: Doug Ferrin and Celeste Hammond
Director: Frank Roach
Tagline: "A real chiller!"
Main cast: Renee Harmon (Lil Stanhope), Lynne Kocol (Ann Girard), Wolf Muser (Tom Girard), Thomas McGowan (Kevin McGuire), Wayne Liebman (Father O'Brien), Lee James (Sven Johnsson).
Distributed by: Home Video Productions
This film is still banned in the UK but is available in a German release including English subtitles.

Plot:
When crazy scientists Sven Johnsson and his trusty sidekick Lil Stanhope experiment to create immortality with cryogenics they discover the secret in the form of the walking dead resulting in the dead rising as zombie–like creatures. But, when test subject Tom Girard disappears, his wife a gets a little too close to the truth.

Appraisal:
Frozen Scream follows a woman trying to track down her husband. Mad scientists turning the living, into zombie-like beings…
Stop!
That film actually sounds good to me. I'd give it a watch, but never a re-watch, if I hadn't seen it already; the premise is better than the film itself.
Frozen Scream is car crash viewing, so bad you want to tear your own eyes out! And, the music score is just as bad. The film is all over the place both in terms of the direction, production, and writing.
How this film made it to the DPP list is a mystery, I assume "Frozen Scream" was added to the list because it's zombie-related. Frozen Scream was not prosecuted and has yet to be released in the UK.
Thank you BBFC you finally got something right.
Frozen Scream is hands down the best contender for the worst film on the banned list.

-Tony Newton

The Funhouse

Year of release: 1981
Writer: Lawrence Block
Director: Tobe Hooper
R rated 80 mins. USA
Tagline: "Pay to get in. Pray to get out!"
Main cast: Eizabeth Burridge (Amy Harper), Shawn Carson (Joey Harper), Jeanne Austin (Mrs. Harper), Jack McDermott (Mr. Harper), Cooper Huckabee (Buzz Dawson), Largo Woodruff (Liz).
Distributed by: CIC
In 1987 a cut version was passed by the BBFC. In 2007 the film was released uncut with a BBFC rating of 15 certificate.

Plot:
The Funhouse follows two young couples who organize a double date at a mysterious carnival. The film centers around these four teenagers who become trapped inside the carnivals funhouse, when they witness a murder at the hands of a gruesomely deformed masked man dressed as Frankenstein they all too soon find themselves in terrible danger.

Appraisal:
Tobe Hooper's Fun House is a classic 1980's horror stalk n' slash film, this video nasty has an almost cult following to it and it's easy to see why.

You should always listen your parents when they tell you not to go the carnival, as the teenagers in "The Funhouse" sadly discover. Spending the night in The Funhouse sounds creepy at the best of times but especially so when a family of freaks are out for blood, can you survive the fun house? "The Funhouse" is Tobe Hooper's biggest budget feature and shows a greater use of filming equipment and increased experience. The Funhouse is a well-made film full of carnival freaks and scares. The actual writing of the film could have been better as many of the plotlines don't actually go anywhere, I expected "The Funhouse 2" to be on the horizon after the first watch of the film and the atmosphere created by Tobe Hooper in this film is incredible and it appears that Rob Zombie has paid homage to the film in "House of 1000 Corpses" and almost certainly in The Texas Chainsaw Massacre.

There's lots of controversy surrounding the inclusion of "The Funhouse" on the DPP list as although this film is somewhat disturbing on a psychological level it definitely falls short on blood and gore and should in my opinion never have been included on the banned film list. At the time there were rumors the BBFC banned this film due to the fact that Tobe Hooper's "Texas Chain Saw Massacre" was banned from cinemas and Tobe Hooper had another title "Death Trap" on the list. The Funhouse video cover features a hair lip, fanged creature whereas the main video released by CIC depicts a clown with an axe coming out of what appears to be a jack in the box. The Funhouse is an all round good fun standard horror film, which doesn't really belong on the infamous DPP list. This movie sticks out like a sore thumb for being like most 80's general release horror movies. There are more jumps than gore here and personally I don't think that this film got banned for the scary jump factor.

Funhouse is an all-round good fun standard horror film that does not belong on the infamous DPP list, this film stands out like a sore thumb for being like most 80's general release horror films. There are more jumps than gore here and I don't think it was banned for the scary/ jump factor.

-Tony Newton

I love The Funhouse. I think it's the best thing Tobe Hooper made after The Texas Chainsaw Massacre. The creepy carnival sets are great, and the denizens of the carnival are too. In a short scene, William Finely is broad but a lot of fun as the flask-nipping Marco the Magnificent with his little staking act. Sylvia Miles' Madame Zena has a cheesiness that veers unexpectedly into menace when she gets pissed off and the crystal ball rumbles back to her on the table. Cooper Huckabee is the real star; his performances are outstanding. The multiple roles as three different barkers add a subtle weirdness to the proceedings. The kids are better than adequate and the one the counts the most, Elizabeth Berridge is excellent. The story setup is a great one- four kids hop off their little carnival cars during their ride through the spook house, intending the spend the night there. But when they witness a murder things turn inexorably down that dark hallway at the end of which is a genuine monster. The design of the monster's face is brilliant, hideous and very well done. Only in a few shots does its immobility slightly hinder the illusion. The extra touches like the creepy old "God is watching you" woman and the recurring Frankenstein and Bride of Frankenstein imagery foreshadow events well. It's a very simple story but told well with atmosphere galore. The haunting music is perfect as well. Three or four inbred twisted thumbs up for The Funhouse.

-Pete Von Sholly   Horror Artist.

When I first saw Funhouse I was terrified of the monster, it took me years to re-watch it and while I am no longer scared of the monster I can almost see why my 12-year-old self was! But now I personally can't see why it was almost banned its fairly tame compared to the other films that were banned at the time maybe there was a confusion with Last House on Dead End Street aka The Fun House?

Anyway I digress, back to the original Funhouse, I love how scattered throughout the film there are mini tributes to other horror films through the character of Joey. And I love that Kevin Conway played several characters in the film, this adds to that freaky feel and slightly to that creepy carnie effect. The idea of using what should be innocent fun at a carnival, and that there really are monsters in the freak show will put you on edge slightly.

So re-watching, yeah it isn't super scary and you almost feel sorry for the monster there are some great ideas I just wished they had pushed further, made it scarier and what I thought it had been when I was younger.

There is a novelization of the film, written by Dean Koontz, which adds to the back story of the characters. And while sneaking into a funhouse and staying the night might sound like a good idea, after this film I'd say that's a no. Maybe this film is the reason I've avoided funhouses at carnivals?

-Sian Richter   Writer/Horror Fan.

Human Experiments

Year of release: 1979
Writers: Gregory Goodell and Richard Rothstein
Director: Gregory Goodell
R rated 82 mins. USA
Tagline: "The victims: Young female inmates."
Main cast: Linda Haynes (Rachel Foster), Geoffrey Lewis (Doctor Hans R. Kline), Ellen Travolta (Mover), Lurene Tuttle (Granny), Mercedes Shirley (Warden Weber), Darlene Craviotto (Rita).
Distributed by: Jaguar
This film has not shown any sign of surfacing and has not been released since.

Plot:
When a country singer is wrongly accused of the murder of four strangers she is sentenced to life imprisonment and placed in a correctional facility where she is introduced to the prison psychiatrist Dr Hans Kline who has a somewhat unorthodox approach to rehabilitation. She finds herself victim to the Dr Hans who uses shock therapy as a trial of new medical science.

Appraisal:
Human Experiments is an okay film, this is another on the video nasty hit list that gets a bad rap but has somewhat of a cult following because of its exploitation qualities. Wrongly accused Rachel Foster's character is very likable so you instantly connect and feel sorry for her as you join her for the ride of terror she is about to face in this women's prison. Linda Haynes who plays the character of Rachel is on fine form and can hold her own, she's up there with the best of the scream queens with her blood curdling scream. Actor Geoffrey Lewis plays the sick and twisted doctor and also gives a Stella performance. I found this film to be a bit of a gem once you polished the dirt off. Well worth a watch, some good twists along the way.

It's a crazy one, but not a shocker. No need to reach for the complimentary sick bag with this one - save that for Cannibal Holocaust!

-Tony Newton

I Miss You, Hugs and Kisses

Also known as "Drop Dead, Dearest".
Year of release: 1978
Writer: Murray Markowitz
Director: Murray Markowitz
Rated 18
Tagline: "A bizarre love, a strange death."
Main cast: Elke Sommer (Magdalene Kruschen), Donald Pilon (Charles Kuuschen), Chuck Shamata (Gershen Isen), George Touliatos (Tibor Zanopek), Cindy Girling (Pauline Corte), George Chuvalo (George Weiller).
Distributed by: Intercity
In 1986 Heron released the film as "Drop Dead Dearest" with 1.06 cuts by the BBFC. As it stands there is no full uncut available in the UK.

Plot:
I Miss You Hugs and Kisses is based on a real life 1973 Canadian murder case. When beautiful model (Magdalene) is brutally murdered and her body discovered by her wealthy husband Charles. A media frenzy begins. Charles has motive, but is he really responsible for bludgeoning his wife to death?

Appraisal:
This Canadian video nasty that was also known as "Drop Dead Dearest" is an actual true story, a strange addition on this list, in fact this film stands out as why the hell is it here on this list to begin with. The time capsule that is the video nasties preserved forever in a twisted exploitation cask soaked in blood and brains and rotting remains. Does not welcome this title, the film is a dated slow paced offering that is neither entertaining nor out there providing gore, scares, shocks or suspense. This film should be on a daytime true movie station and even if it was you would not bother to watch it. This film stars Elk Sommer as the main star, Elke Sommer most famously starred in "Carry On Behind" this only adds to the film being literally a farce. The film has flashbacks and is a film that has a small amount of gore and nudity; once again, this can't save the slow-paced, TV movie feel to it, no scares, no shocks, no repeated viewing from me!

This film was famously only on the official video nasty list for a few months before it was removed, and dropped like a rotten egg!

-Tony Newton

It's beyond me how this movie made it onto the Video Nasty roster. It's like a glorified Lifetime movie.

The entire film is a trial, which tells the story of a marriage that started out perfectly, and then went horribly wrong, as they do in melodramas of this nature. The scenes from the marriage play out in flashbacks throughout the film as evidence is brought up in the courtroom.

And, true to lifetime form, the villainous husband, even ends up in prison. The last shot of the film is him, in full, heavily aged makeup rotting in his cell, filled with, we assume, remorse. It just doesn't pay to be a man...

Truth be told, this might be a rare example where censorship seems to work in favor for a film. Around the third act the movie becomes uncharacteristically violent and gratuitous, to the degree that it's almost as though we're watching a different film in the last 30 minutes. Perhaps the filmmakers realized the movie was completely lifeless and decided to spice it up. Whatever the case, it didn't help. The stark contrast of the Love

Story feel of the first two acts, compared to the Goodfellas vibe of the last act, just comes off jumbled and tonally uncomfortable.

The murder scenes are over the top and feature Day-Glo blood clotted onto sheets, and hair, and any other surface nearby. That being said, aside from a few splashes of blood and the occasional nip slip, this could easily air on TV today.

But If you want a real Video Nasty, you should probably look elsewhere.

-Mark Miller   Seraphim Films.

Inferno

Year of release: 1980
Writer: Dario Argento
Director: Dario Argento
R rated 102 mins. Italy
Tagline: "Terror that's hotter than hell!"
Main cast: Leigh McCloskey (Mark Elliot), Irene Miracle (Rose Elliot), Eleonora Giorgi (Sara), Daria Nicolodi (Elise Stallone Van Adler), Sacha Pitoeff (Kazanian), Alida Valli (Carol, the caretaker).
Distributed by: Originally distributed by 20th Century Fox.
In 1987 a release surfaced with 28 seconds cut. In 1993 a release came out with only 20 seconds cut. In 2010 Arrow released a full, uncut version with the BBFC cuts wavered.

Plot:
Rose Ellis' research into The Three Mothers lands her in a creepy bookshop where the owner loans her a very special book, it's through the book that she gains the knowledge that Mater Tenebrarum (the mother of shadows) once occupied her building, her brother Mark heads over to New York to investigate but the death toll is rising, will anyone live to discover the truth of Mater Tenebrarum?

Appraisal:
Dario Argento's Inferno is a giallo classic from the true master of the genre. This is a Dario Argento classic Italian 1980's horror flick through and through, that shows Argento's talent of perfectly. The cinematography is nothing but stunning, bright, vivid and bold. This film has a dream like quality to it and does lend itself to being best watched on the best way possible not on a 2nd generation VHS copy from the banned era as I watched this film for the first time. This is another of the three mother series of Argento, which Argento was obviously inspired by Thomas de Quincey's "Susperia De Profundis". This second offering is full of blood and gore and features ground breaking shocks and effects, which stand out on screen. This is a very underrated film, which is often swept under the carpet, but this film is not to be missed. This is a frightening and somewhat terrifying film that provides all you want from a horror movie. The clever lighting and camera work brings a dream like quality to this masterpiece. My favourite scene is Rose in the water where she finds herself face to face with a corpse. This film is an inspiration to filmmakers across the globe and for me stands out as one of his best pieces of work nest to Suspria.

-Tony Newton

1980's Italian supernatural horror "Inferno" is the second offering of "The Three Mothers" trilogy created from the beautifully twisted and wonderfully macabre mind of Dario Argento.

After reading alchemical architect Verelli's "The Three Mothers" (actually sisters of evil who rule the world with sorrow tears and darkness) young poet Rose (played by Irene Miracle) becomes convinced that her apartment building is home to one of the three mothers, as she begins to investigate she discovers an underwater chamber in the depths of the apartment building, meanwhile Rose's brother (college student Mark) promptly heads back to New York after receiving a disturbing letter from his sister.

"Dario Argento raised the bar with his perfectly crafted masterpiece "Suspiria" giving "Inferno" a lot to live up to.

"Inferno" delivers Argento's trademark breath-taking visual brilliance, the use of colour is awe-inspiring, the camera angles and unique style are effective in creating the films dreamlike ambience, with the viewer becoming lost in the films unrelenting fear "Inferno" is a savage and blood-thirsty offering in its own right.

That being said there are certain elements to the film, which fail to live up to expectations one of which is the sub-par acting (it's a bit hit and miss) and rigid dialogue. It's also frustratingly lacking in storyline and with a pretty incohesive, disjointed plot and underdeveloped characters; it's difficult to empathize with such hollow characters when they meet their bloody demise.

Despite its plot holes "Inferno" features gnarly, unique ways to die (one character is clawed to death by cats, another nibbled to death by rats), it's visually stunning, breath taking, and impressive on many levels. It's a bloodthirsty yet uniquely elegant offering and Argento's trademark visual artistic brilliance delivers overall.

Keith Emerson's rock opera score adds a whole other layer to the film; it's hauntingly spine-chilling, fear-inducing, and gives an extra dynamic to the film.

There are few directors who can deliver such intense horror as well as Argento unfortunately this film is let down by haphazard, fragmented narrative, hit or miss acting and a complete lack of cohesive plot, that said "Inferno" is so visually striking and impressive that it's easy to forgive its flaws but unfortunately this film is destined to live in the depths of the shadows of "Susperia". In my view it will always fall short in comparison but as a standalone film delivers.

-Kerry Newton   Writer.

The Killer Nun

Also known as "Suor Omicidi"
Writers: Giulio Berruti and Enzo Gallo
Director: Giulio Berruti
Rated 18 85 mins. Italy
Tagline: "From the secret files of the Vatican!"
Main cast: Anita Ekberg (Sister Gertrude), Paola Morra (Sister Mathieu), Alida Valli (Mother Superior), Massimo Serato (Dr. Poirret), Daniele Dublino (Director), Lou Castel (Peter).
Distributed by: Techno Film
In 1993 a version was released by Redemption cut by 13 seconds. In 2006 Shameless released the full uncut version with previous cuts wavered by the BBFC.

Plot:
Killer Nun is based on the true story of a killer nun! This Nunsploitation flick finds Anita Ekberg in the role of Sister Gertrude, whose life we see fall apart on screen. After the successful removal of a brain tumor, Sister Gertrude becomes addicted to painkillers (including morphine; self-medicating her psychotic behavior puts her patients and fellow staff in danger!

Appraisal:
Giulio Berruti's cult classic Nunsploitation nasty The Killer Nun is a bizarre film to say the least, but does deliver the goods albeit at a very slow pace, the film has an almost giallo quality to it, La Dolce Vita's sex symbol Anita Ekberg if fantastic in role of Sister Gertrude.

This film is not that gory but plays more on the psychological elements, which works well throughout, although we have to wait for kills but when they come they are brutally delivered.

There are twists and turns and a trip into the mind of a killer nun, overall it's quite a strange one but enjoyable. This film has a strong religious undertone, which makes you feel uncomfortable when you throw sex and violence into the mix, though it works well within the context of the storyline here. I think the only other film I had seen about nuns was The Sound of Music and I was surprised and the lack of singing and the lack of clothes the nuns were wearing! This film feels slow in parts but it is well worth watching it through to the end., this film has dated quite badly, But still manages to hold your attention and is something a little different from most of the offerings on the video nasty list.

The film as an eerie creepiness to it and some bizarre visuals wrapped together with a very creepy score.
-Tony Newton

As well as changing the face of the whole home video industry, the Video Nasty saga's burst of moral panic and outrage also helped a few lesser known horror titles escape from the realms of obscurity; pushing them out into the stratosphere of cult movie fandom for decades to come.

The majority of titles were notably banned for violence and assorted misogynistic acts, such as graphic depictions of rape, torture and general sexual deviancy. Giulio Berruti's Killer Nun meanwhile adds another to its cap, one which is still a very controversial topic to this day: blasphemy.

Much like its Nazisploitation counterpart, Nunsploitation was central to the rise of nasty fame, both sub-genres flourishing in a richly populated market that supposedly would exploit and corrupt the working class folk of 80s Great Britain. In typical class segregation and political elitism, some of the early Nunsploitation films condemned for home viewing within a Nasty-type bracket actually received acclaim from the upper-class, art-house scene – Ken Russell's The Devils (1971) and Walerian Borowczyk's Behind Convent Walls (1978) most notably.

Many Nunsploitation films would be set in a medieval/cathedral setting, usually including a sadistic mother superior with a penchant for flaying nubile Catholic nuns as she attempts to purify the flesh – a novel way for the 70s soft-core audience to witness a little more masochism than they were used to. It was a similar set up to the women in prison mantra: young women exploited and helpless, all the while giving in to sin, with varying degrees of pleasure after initial reluctance.

Killer Nun thrust aging Swedish sex siren and La Dolce Vita starlet Anita Ekberg – the main reason film fans flocked to screenings to see more of the beautiful actress in more ways than one- into a world of degradation and desperation. The sexual antics are a tool for her to achieve what she wants and is in full swing throughout. Couple this with her need for drugs, a slope of insanity makes Killer Nun a beautifully filmed Nunsploitaion picture; yet the film hasn't aged well and suffers like much of ilk to a now modern-day tameness.

Based upon a true story about a Nun working in a geriatric hospital, Sister Gertrude suffered with an addiction to morphine (due to cancer) and relentlessly killed patients, robbing them in the process to fund her morphine addiction. Taking out her own frustrations on her patients she becomes the antithesis of the veil and her religious duties, seen by Baba Yaga director Berruti whom then crafted and exploited the story as the basis for this film after seeing potential in the brutality of the crime.

An excellent, delirious score supplements the carnage and is a highlight of the film offering an almost dreamlike status to the murder sequences, which fits in well with the morphine thematic. During a scene where a patient is thrown from a window the repetitive pulsing sound-scape makes the sequence far more effective than it deserved adding surrealism and panic with a minimal yet aggressive sound structure; Kubrick would be proud.

Ekberg herself is noted in an interview from 2006 as taking the role as "the psyche of the nun appealed to her and was a deviation from the Dolce Vita clones that [she] was only getting offered at the time". Her descent into addiction, madness and lust is well played throughout. She is convincing in the seductress part of the role as well as the addictive junkie personality, merging the two persona's well and garnering both viewer sympathy and repulsion in the process. At heart this is a tale of a woman screaming out for help in a world, which has unfair preconceptions about her and the life she chose to lead, both religiously and as a drug abuser/sexual deviant. It's weirdly deep for a film of this ilk.

The supporting cast will be familiar to many a die hard Italian horror fanatic; roles from Suspiria's (1977) Alida Valli and Nunsploitation mainstay Paola Morra help proceedings along nicely. Killer Nun is by no means a great film but it offers enough charm, flair and scope to merit a viewing. The lesbian love interest, Sister Mathieu, plays well against Gertrude as she rebukes her advances while being meticulous and cruel, and she is deftly handled by Morra.

Upon release Killer Nun was banned in Italy and later in 1983 was banned in the United Kingdom and, to this day, the film remains banned in Iceland. The original poster art also came under scrutiny as the suggestion depiction of a nun performing a sex act was deemed unsuitable and was amended into a subtler affair with a silhouette of Morra looking into Ekberg's seductive gaze.

The religious iconography is also another moot point, this could have essentially been the same film with Gertrude being in any position of uniform and not a nun; would it have still attracted the intended audience? For the most part yes, but Killer Nun rides the coattails of Catholicism focusing on the purity of religion using it as a tool for dissection and deviation sure to ruffle a few feathers and excite a few others in the process.

Its also undoubtedly on this list because of the connotation of the title alone; if it would have been given a release under its original language title, Suor Omicidim would the DPP have clocked it? The widespread panic and attacks by name association alone helped fuel the Video Nasty fire. Nunsploitation fans are grateful to her for rescuing this title from video.

Nunsploitation expert Nigel Wingrove submitted the film to the BBFC again in 1993 as part of his aptly titled side label Salvation, an offshoot of Redemption films. Redemption were oft victims of the heavy handed clout of Mary Whitehouse and her fear mongering lynch mob; Wingrove was granted a VHS release with 13 seconds of footage omitted.

Removing two notable scenes of violence; the first a Needle in an eye sequence, the latter a depiction of Surgery on a skull, which looks terribly, dated upon viewing now. It is interesting to note than there are actually very few cuts compared to some of the more notorious titles on this list and that both cuts, although excessive were used to enhance the story not done for extra shocks.

The film is now available uncut in the UK from Shameless Screen Entertainment which resubmitted the film in 2006. Shameless have re-instated the cut footage from an Italian print – one which has never been dubbed into English – and this is an excellent way for people to witness the cut footage for the first time, although it does become a little distracting to have a tiny section of the film in Italian instead of using the whole Italian source. Presumably a full Italian print was unavailable or the print not of sufficient standard. Germany and USA also have fully uncut versions from Koch Media and Blue Underground respectively.

Killer Nun: perfect Saturday night viewing, before church on Sunday!

-Mark Pidgeon   Writer.

Late Night Trains

Also known as "L'Ultimo Treno Della Notte"
Year of release: 1975
Writer: Roberto Infascelli, Rentao Izzo
Director: Aldo Lado
R rated 94 mins. Italy
Tagline: "You can tell yourself it's only a movie- but it won't help."
Main cast: Flavio Bucci (Blackie), Macha Meril (Lady on the train), Gianfranco Dr Grassi (Curly), Enrico Maria Salerno (Prof. Giulio Stradi), Marina Berti (Laura Stradi), Franco Fabrizi (Peverted train passenger).
Distributed by: Originally distributed by Video Warehouse International, this version was cut. Later in 1981 Cinehollywood released a full, uncut version of the film titled "Night Train Murders". In 2008 the film was released fully uncut as "Night train Murders" and passed by the BBFC with an 18 certificate.

Plot:
In director Aldo Lado's film Late Night Trains we see two young students (Margaret and Lisa) board a train to visit Lisa's parents for Christmas break but the trip doesn't go to plan when a couple of psychotic criminals and a sex crazed woman strike terror into their innocent victims.

Appraisal:
The film is hard to get hold of but it's well worth hunting it down. This video nasty feels very similar to "The Last House on the Left" but that's not a bad thing at all.
I thought this film was great, a little lost gem, that truly does not get the attention it deserves for some reason, the film just seems to slip under the radar maybe because tracking a copy down on VHS was nearly impossible while getting hold of a bootleg driller killer or I spit on your gave was as easy as hell. I love films centered on trains. No, I'm not a trainspotter, but everyone who has ridden on a train knows how annoying it is when you're pestered by a drunk, a gang of youths, or people constantly going past you to the toilet. Plus, I never liked the ticket inspector; he would always show up just as I start to nod off. However, these guys had far worse than the old guy with a ticket punch. Being on an almost-deserted train is eerie at the best of times, let alone when there are psychos stalking you!
This film feels like "The Lady Vanishes" and "The Last House on the Left" morphed together. It's creepy, eerie, shockingly violent and disturbing at the same time! Seek this one out - it's well worth a watch.
This film in the UK was banned from the start. It was first rejected for its initial cinema certification in 1976 by the good old BBFC, then landed headfirst on the nasties list!

-Tony Newton

The Living Dead at the Manchester Morgue

Also known as "Let Sleeping Corpses Lie", "Non Si Deve Profanare il Sonno dei Morti" and "Don't Open the Window".
Year of release: 1974
Writer: Sandro Continenza and Marcello Coscia
Director: Jorge Grau
R rated 85 mins. Italy, Spain
Tagline: "Whatever's out there will wait!"
Main cast: Cristina Galbo (Edna), Ray Lovelock (George), Arthur Kennedy (The Inspector), Aldo Massasso (Kinsey), Giorgio Trestini (Craig), Roberto Posse (Benson).
Distributed by: VIP

In 1985 a version of the film surfaced, this was the pre cut theatrical version which the BBFC demanded an extra 26 seconds of cuts. In 2002 a version of the film entitled "Let Sleeping Dogs Lie" / "The Living Dead at Manchester Morgue" was released with all previous cuts wavered by the BBFC.

Plot:
A Policeman is on chase of two young hippies George and Edna; he believes them to have committed multiple murders in the area. Unbeknownst to him the real culprits of the murders are actually the dead who have come back to life after being exposed to radiation used by the department of agriculture in the area, it's a race to stop these blood thirsty zombies with George and Edna as humanity's only hope.

Appraisal:
The Living Dead at Manchester Morgue is another zombie entry on the DPP list. This is a classic horror film that once again doesn't get the attention it deserves. This doesn't date and really does stand out even today as a really cool zombie movie. This film has a great twist, we find the dead themselves are the evil killers. Don't use chemical pesticides or you may turn into a zombie, it's hard to think this film is over 40 years old, why don't we make them like we used to!

The Living Dead at Manchester Morgue is set in Manchester and has that hammer-esque feel to it like most British horror films of the 70's, and feels like it could have been the best ever episode from the Hammer TV series. The film's original title "Let Sleeping Corpses Lie" suits the film much better! It is also known as "Don't Open the Window" in America. The film works well with the British backdrop of old police cars and buildings of course there's a classic British antique shop surely an inspiration for zombie comedy flick "Shaun of the Dead"

Lovejoy as a zombie would have been the bollocks, but he was to come much later!

-Tony Newton

The Living Dead at Manchester Morgue, also known as Let Sleeping Corpses Lie, is still as fantastic fucking film. It's one of my favorite zombie films, and it was made well before zombies made their way into pop culture. For Christ sakes, I was called a Satanist for seeking out titles like this one when I was growing up. Now small children dress up as zombies, and everything is cool. Amazing.

The Living Dead at Manchester Morgue was directed by Jorge Grau, who made something really special: an excellent horror film with a social message. A couple is framed for murder and chased by cops out into the countryside, where a certain pesticide and earth-pounding machine is raising the dead. This film is one of the

few that managed to scare me when I saw it, and still gives me the willies, a very, very hard feat. It's an unsung masterpiece of horror and suspense. I think I'll watch it again this week. The Blu-ray is beautiful.
-Izzy Lee Filmmaker.

While some might name DAWN OF THE DEAD or Romero's classic NIGHT OF THE LIVING DEAD as their all time favorite zombie film, my personal favorite has always been THE LIVING DEAD AT MANCHESTER MORGUE. I've seen this film quite a few times over the years and love it more every time I see it. Filled with moody music and atmosphere and cast with dark and complex characters, THE LIVING DEAD AT MANCHESTER MORGUE is one of those obscure gems that no zombie fan should go without seeing, but most probably haven't seen.

Ray Lovelock (that can't be his real name, can it?) plays George, a hip, beatnik man about town/museum curator transporting a rare sculpture across the English countryside on his motorcycle. While stopping for gas, George's bike is hit by Edna's car in a gas station. George rather brashly encourages Edna to give him a lift while his bike is getting fixed and the two become uneasy travelling buddies for the rest of the film, both needing to get to their destinations in a hurry. But wouldn't you know it, the Department of Agriculture is testing a new pesticide which not only kills bugs dead, but it turns dead humans alive and buggy as well. Though it's not in his destination, George is convinced to go with Edna to visit her sister before heading to his client. Both find themselves in the middle of a police investigation as Edna's sister is suspected of murdering her husband, though he was actually killed by a zombie. Convoluted? Sure, but this movie is too much fun to give a care.

Director Jorge Grau paces the film perfectly as the traveling couple slowly realize what's going on before the authorities do. Grau smartly directs a script worked on by multiple folks, all of whom probably have seen their fair share of fright flicks, as this film does have some golden standards in terms of frightful scenarios. Scenes reminiscent of both GATES OF HELL and NIGHT OF THE LIVING DEAD are prominently featured throughout the film. The first time we see a zombie is straight out of the opening cemetery scene in NOTLD, as a lone zombie shambles towards our fearless couple. But this is more than just a knock-off. Grau overlaps shots of jolly old England with factory smoke stacks, heaps of garbage, and smoking manhole covers in the beginning to ring the point home that there is an environmental statement being made here. While most of Romero's zombie fests leave the cause of the undead hordes ambiguous, it's made clear here that the giant machine used by the government is the cause of all of this zombie apocalypse business. Grau not only peppers in a message, but is able to handle the rather complex plot without losing focus, while pulling off some truly frightening scenes of zombie attacks (the initial attack scene by a river is really well done, as is the final zombie massacre at the titular morgue and a middle section where our couple is trapped in a mausoleum). Grau doesn't forget to give gorehounds something to dine on as he lingers on the guts in order to display some gruesome moments of feasting and shredding of victims' bodies.

THE LIVING DEAD AT MANCHESTER MORGUE is one of those classic fright films that some may scoff at from the name or the somewhat hokey DVD cover art, but once seen, you're sure to be a fan. It's got a police investigator who is too busy being grumpy at the "long haired kids with faggoty clothes" to notice that there's a zombie apocalypse going on, a the wide-eyed heroin shooting sister who is tormented by her pervy photographer husband, and a dripping wet vagrant zombie who looks a bit like an unkempt and water-logged Adrian Brody. THE LIVING DEAD AT MANCHESTER MORGUE is filled with the stuff that makes watching old horror fun and a cut above your run of the mill zombie film. The effects are gory as hell. The music is funky. And there are scenes of zombie mayhem that you'll never forget. Though other films were more influential, THE LIVING DEAD AT MANCHESTER MORGUE is a zombie movie that you won't forget.

-Mark L. Miller   Writer.

An antique dealer plans to spend a quiet weekend in the countryside, but finds his plans shattered when a young woman accidentally crashes into his motorbike at a gas station. Edna (Cristina Galbó) offers George (Ray Lovelock) a ride to his destination, but on the way plans are changed once again and he ends up taking her to her visit her sister who lives in the countryside instead. After taking wrong route they stop to farmyard to ask for directions. A stranger wanders up from the river and towards the car. A stranger who has been dead for a month!

Jorge Grau's excellent "Undead" flick (I'll be saying undead from here on, as nobody in the movie ever utters the word zombie. But we all know that they are zombies don't we!) Let Sleeping Corpses Lie, with all of its many alternative titles is a great piece of horror cinema, and one of my personal favourites of the genre. Following in the wake of the groundbreaking Night of the Living Dead, it's possibly one of the finest entries into the sub-genre brought to recognition by George A. Romero in 1969. Luckily it's one of those Italian-Spanish coproduction's that relies more on story than gut munching effects that dominated the later wave of the zombie genre. Not that those movies are bad, quite the opposite, the apocalyptic world of the flesh eater is a tantalising one to say the least. But story will always conquer special effects when it comes to surviving the tests of time.

In the early 70s producer EdMondo Amati, (producer of such greats like Fulci's A Lizard in a Woman's Skin 1971, One on Top of the Other 1969, Alberto De Martino's The Antichrist 1974 and Antonio Margheriti's Cannibal Apocalypse 1980) decided that he needed to get in on the zombie niche after Romero's movie became a hit in Europe. In Spain he found his perfect candidate, the young Jorge Grau. Grau had a solid background in movies, not the horror genre per say, but a majority of his works had elements of the fantastic in them and had received overall fine reception amongst fans and critics. Amati approached him with the question "Do you like Night of the Living Dead?", a movie which Grau indeed was a fan of. But Grau had been trying as hard as he could to get his Ceremonia Sangrienta 1973 (aka The Legend of Blood Castle) off the ground since 1964, when he first heard of the Countess Bathory legend during a film festival in Czechoslovakia. Timing was off and Grau was fully dedicated to his future film, so the two could not collaborate on the project Amati was trying to pitch. Some years later, after the completion of Ceremonia Sangrienta, Amati once again approached Grau with the script penned by Sandro Continenza, asking if he still liked Night of the Living Dead. Giving Grau a free hand to change the script and take the time he needed to make it more realistic, the two started their relationship. A relationship that would end up seeing Let Sleeping Corpses Lie becoming fact, instead of just an ambition by Amati.

Made in an time before realistic gore exploded onto screens with movies like George A. Romero's Dawn of the Dead 1978, Andrea Bianchi's Nights of Terror 1981, Marino Girolami's eclectic Cannibal/Zombie hybrid Zombie Holocaust 1980 and Lucio Fulci's mother of all Euro Zombie flicks, Zombi2 1979, Grau chooses, much like Romero, to rely more on the realism and everyday drama of the people caught up in this strange new world, rather than focusing on the specific gut-munching and reigning chaos of a zombie infested landscape.

Let sleeping Corpses Lie tells a pretty straight forward story, George [the fantastic Ray Lovelock] sets out for a weekend in the countryside, getting away fro the stress of inner-city life, which is made quite obvious during the start of the movie as citizens walk aimlessly, staring blankly as they await busses in the heavy trafficked core of modern civilization. People are seen wearing facemasks to avoid breathing in toxic fumes, and the further George gets out of town on his motorbike - cross cut with images of fuming industrial towers, urban decay, dead birds - the imagery lightens up and instead of tight shots of decay, we start seeing wide shots of open country, fresh air and swaying fields. George is getting closer to his safe haven away from the deterioration of inner city life, but when he stops at a petrol station to fill up his bike, Edna accidentally crashes into him. Guilt-ridden Edna [Cristina Galbó, star of Massimo Dallamano's What Have You Done to Solange? 1972 and Luigi Cozzi's top notch Giallo The Killer Must Kill Again 1975, who also won the best actress award for her part in this movie at the 1974 Sitges film festival] offers to drive him to his destination. But they end up going the wrong way, into the middle of nowhere. George gets out at a nearby farm to ask for directions and two important storylines are introduced. The ecological cause of the forthcoming outbreak is established, which has George make a clear political statement. "Don't mess around with Mother Nature." No sooner has he said this when Edna has her first encounter with the undead, as Guthrie [Fernando Hilbeck], a local tramp tries to attacks her. Edna manages to evade him and runs up to the farmhouse, but George and the farmer can't believe what Edna tells them, and laugh off the shocking experience she just had. Guthrie couldn't possibly have attacked her; he died almost a month ago.

A subplot with Edna's sister Katie [Jeanine Mestre] is set in motion. Katie, a recovering drug addict has been forced out into the countryside by her husband Martin, [José Lifante] and Edna is on the way there to convince Katie to sign into a rehab programme and get of the drugs once and for all. But she just can't seem to stay of the smack, and as she secretly prepares to shoot up in the barn, she finds herself alone in the darkness face to face with Guthrie! This encounter leads up to the death of Martin and it's at this point of the movie that the real antagonist makes his entry, the Inspector portrayed with bravura by Arthur Kennedy. The Inspector quickly makes his mind up that these city folks, these damned hippies with their longhair and drugs, are the real culprits and that they must have killed Martin, not the fantasy figure that Katie claims murdered him. Now The Inspector is a cop who always gets his man. We can understand that from the way he moves, talks and acts. He isn't afraid to go out on a limb to bust a case, and his loyal men are loyally standing by, ready to act on his every call. Just watch as he lays pressure on Katie, trying to make her confess, not giving a damn that she just watched her husband get killed.

The movie moves forward as George and Edna try to figure out the whereabouts of Guthrie as both sisters now claim he is the real killer After an infant, unexplainably in a fit of rage, bites George at the nearby hospital he takes Dr Duffield [Vincente Vega] back to the farm where scientists explain the strange experiments they are conducting in the fields outside the village. Using ultrasonic radiation they are fighting off insects and bugs, who when hearing the noises the strange machine makes go insane and kill each other instead of eating the crops. Really it's a modified combine harvester, but it looks believable, and it gives a possible reason for the dead rising from their tombs.

George and Edna's quest leads them to a crypt under the village church, and low and behold, they find him, the undead Guthrie. This is followed by a wonderfully long sequence where they battle their way out of the underground tomb chased by several more undead that Guthrie wakes up by wiping blood on their foreheads. Once again their success in the horror narrative is their damnation in the drama narrative as the Inspector, arriving at the cemetery, finds the officer he sent out to trail the suspects gutted… and three burned corpses too. The undead, dead once again.

Finally they all gather for a splendid ending with several shocking moments back at the local hospital as the movie comes to its climax, with a bang to say the least. In some ways the ending is kind of silly, but at the same time it's the ending we always wanted for Ben [Duane Jones] in the movie that inspired this one to start with, Night of the Living Dead. Even though the special effects by Gianetto De Rossi are quite restrained, I'm sure that in 1974 they where quite shocking. Even the masterpiece from the other side of the Atlantic, Tobe Hooper's The Texas Chain Saw Massacre, made the same year, isn't' as visually spectacular as this movie is.

Non Si Deve Porfanare il Sonno Dei Morti is a wonderful time capsule of De Rossi's realistic effect wizardry just a few years before he really took it to the limit in those splendid Italian genre pieces.

Symbolism and negative counterparts play an important part in Grau's movie. During the very start of the movie we see a fertility stature the symbol of life, a few moments later the camera focuses on a haunting painting which look like a strange blend of the iconic atomic bomb mushroom and a harrowed face of a dead person. Also in a wider perspective it's somewhat ironic to start a movie that ends on such a down note with a symbol of life. The struggle for human survival is conquered, not by the monsters, but by humans themselves. The Cops, who are supposed to be the good guys, turn out to be the bad guys. It's all wonderfully sinister isn't it, and one can only imagine the degree of social criticism Grau brought into the movie here, as the idea that the police force represents Franco and his dictatorship over the people of Spain isn't too far from bay.

Much like The Exorcist 1973, Jaws 1975, and the Swedish hit Let the Right One In 2008, it's the realism of the drama that makes the movie work. The movie is set in a real world and is actually more of a drama with horror themes and elements. Also, it's the very ordinary characters who help drive the movie forth. George is a simple antique dealer who only wants' to get to his rural house in the countryside, to get away from the hectic tempo of the inner city. Edna is an everyday woman on her way to visit her sister who also lives in the countryside. There are no superpowers at play here, no secret army training, no suitcases full of weapons, just two regular people in the middle of a terrifying scenario. It's the simple choices that they make that make them believable characters. Running for their lives, fighting monsters as a last call of action, much like you and I would do.

The explanation for the undead coming back to life is also quite reasonable, and in many ways a critical standing point. The human element is to blame. It's not a freak of nature, but our own need to control our environment. An ecological theme that points out how we are to blame for our own downfall, much like in Romero's Crazies 1973 or Jean Rollin's Grapes of Death 1978. It works because we can relate to it, much like we still relate to discussions concerning the environment today. It's easier to swallow than radiation from outer space isn't it?

One of the more sophisticated tools used by Grau in *Let Sleeping Corpses Lie*, is that George is a sceptic. It's not until half the movie has passed that George actually believes that the dead have come back in to existence, and from then on starts fighting with his life at stake. This is a cunning device as we slowly grow into identification with George as he grows into the believer. His scepticism is the same as ours, there can't really be monsters, but as he changes and develops as a character we go along for the ride with him and he bring us into the story. As he comes to terms of the reality of monsters, so do we.

All of these splendid storytelling tools are used to crate a magnificent movie that forty years later still makes it a really disturbing, believable, engaging and highly entertaining movie. A masterpiece of the horror genre, to say the least. A definitive must see movie for any fan of early European Zombie Horror.

Finally, a word on Giuliano Sorgini's excellent soundtrack. It's honestly one of the most impressive scores conceived for an Italian/Spanish genre movie of that era, because where it starts out as a rock, funky, jazz thing so typical of the Italian movie scene at the time, it quickly degenerates into a terrifying mixture of primitive growling and guttural sounds which are really disturbing and go perfectly with the images of the undead feasting on the bleeding flesh of mankind. Great stuff, perhaps not as priggish as Goblin or as melodic as the Fabio Frizzi and Alexander Blonkensteiner tunes of the later wave of gut-munchers, but definitely a disturbing soundtrack for a fascinating movie.

-Jason Meredith   Writer, producer, film distributor.

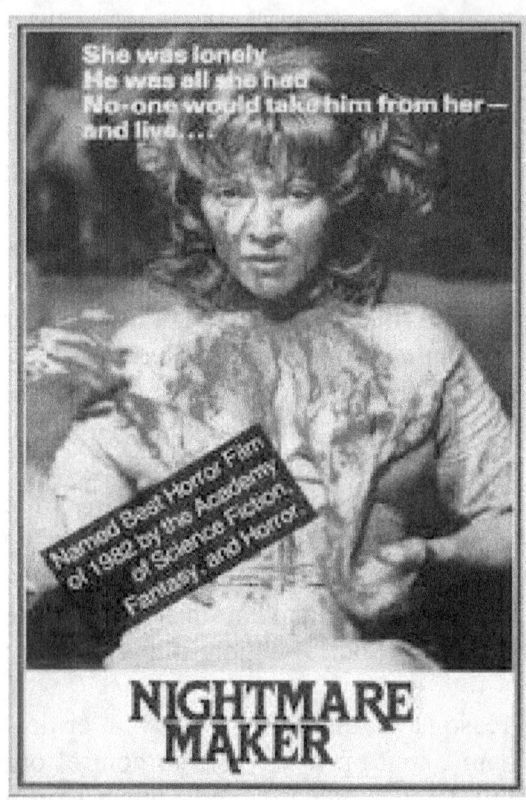

Nightmare Maker

Also known as "Night Warning" and "Butcher, Baker, Nightmare Maker".
Year of release: 1982
Writers: Steve Briemer and Alan Jay Gluekman
Director: William Asher
R rated 96 mins. USA
Tagline: "A haunting rhyme for bedtime."
Main cast: Jimmy McNichol (Billy Lynch), Susan Tyrrell (Chryl Roberts), Bo Svenson (Detective Joe Carlson), Marcia Lewis (Margie), Julia Duffy (Julia), Britt Leach (Sgt. Cook).
Distributed by: Atlantis
The film is still banned in the UK and was released certified in 1987 even with cuts made.

Plot:
Billy Lynch has been raised by his overbearing Aunt Cheryl following the death of his parents fourteen years earlier. Billy is offered a scholarship and a chance to make a life for himself away from his aunt but this news tips Cheryl over the edge bringing her violent, psychotic nature to the forefront. Cheryl will do anything to stop Billy from leaving her and when she murders the man she has falsely accused of rape the police detective believes that Billy is to blame.

Appraisal:
In this classic video nasty offering we see an aunt go to drastic lengths to gain custody of her niece, this film touches on homophobia and incest and delves into just how far some people will go for love. This strange tale is a very different film than any other on the nasty list. This feels like a TV movie gone on an acid trip into psycho destruction, but it does has its charm for some reason this is a crazy watch that make that sucks you in until the end! I can't see why this film belongs on the banned films list at all, ok there are a few death scenes and rather bizarre ones (heads chopped off and a machete to the stomach is never fun), though all this feels like an x rated True movie, definitely one of the more bizarre titles on the list and something very different indeed!.

-Tony Newton

Possession

Also known as "Night the Screaming Stops"
Year of release: 1982
Writer: Andrzej Żuławski
Director: Andrzej Żuławski
R rated 124 mins. France, West Germany
Tagline: "Murder. Evil. Infidelity. Madness."
Main cast: Isabelle Adjani (Anna), Sam Neill (Mark), Margit Cartensen (Margit Gluckmeister), Heinz Bennet (Heinrich), Johanna Hofer (Heinrich's mother), Carl Duering (Detective).
Distributed by: VTC
In 1999 an uncut version was released passed by the BBFC.

Plot:
When Anna played by (Isabelle Adjani) reveals to her husband, Mark played by the devil himself, well not literally but the (Omen 2) star(Sam Neill), that she has been having an affair, she quickly decides to leave her family behind. Mark hires a PI to follow her every move. Slowly, Anna descends into total madness, and it's clear she is hiding a much darker secret.

Appraisal:
Possession is yet another underrated gem of a movie, Wow, this is a trip of a film that just exudes class and style with heart throughout! This film sees a strange relationship between a spy and his wife. This is a trip into absurdity and the perverse world of monsters all at once. This 1981 film is a welcoming addition to the standard horror fare on the nasty list, it's unlike any other video nasty. No other film touches on monsters and demons that's for sure and this film wins the prize for the most arguments on screen, and some bizarre horror sequences. This film stars Sam Neill and Isabelle Adjani, both stars are great in the role and as we watch Isabelle Adjani's world fall apart and descend into madness. This film does find itself being compared to Lars Von Trier's 2009 film "Antichrist", with both films dealing with many of the same issues on screen, marital problems and self mutilation in one form or another. This is a very clever and underrated film that has shocks and leaves you thinking. Check out this masterpiece if you haven't already.

A stunning visceral experience that you won't forget; be sure to check out writer and Director Andrej Żuławski's other films, I'm a huge fan of everything the man does.

-Tony Newton

For much of the 1980s, Starburst and Fangoria were my only sources of horror-related news. One issue I remember particularly vividly featured picture of a bizarre-tentacled creature from Polish director Andrzej Zulawski's 1981 movie, POSSESSION.

Sam Neill and Isabelle Adjani star as a married couple, Mark and Anna, who live in West Berlin with their young son. Mark returns home after a work posting and discovers that Anna is leaving him, though she insists there is no one else involved. Mark leaves the marital home, only to return some days later to find his son alone and uncared for. Mark takes a phone call from a man called Heinrich who purports to be Anna's lover, who says she is with him. Mark meets his son's teacher (also played by Adjani) who, whilst identical, appears to be the antithesis of his wife: calm and dependable. After Anna returns to the flat and mutilates herself with an electric carving knife, Mark employs a private detective who follows her to a squalid apartment she shares with… well, I'm not going to tell you who or what she shares the apartment with – you should discover it for yourself.

POSSESSION is an astonishing film. It defies description and is, at times, harrowing viewing. Beautifully made, Zulawski makes excellent use of his West Berlin locations, even featuring the wall, which divided the city and its people back then. Special effects are used sparingly and are provided by Carlo Rambaldi, the genius responsible for creating Spielberg's ET as well as the xenomorph from ALIEN and the creatures from David Lynch's DUNE amongst others. An eerie electronic score by the director adds to the uneasy vibe, which permeates the movie.

But the real triumph of the film is Isabelle Adjani's dual performance. She's remarkable, the focus of every scene she appears in, and it's easy to see why this performance earned her the best actress award at Cannes in 1981. Of particular note is a startlingly physical sequence where she suffers a miscarriage in a subway. Really astonishing.

Looking back at this film now, it's easy to see why the BBFC categorised it as a video nasty. It's unpleasant viewing for sure, but it stands head and shoulders above most of the other 70+ films, which were banned at the time. It's a remarkable movie, very hard to describe (which is why I've made little attempt to do so here). Reminiscent of Lynch's ERASERHEAD and early Cronenberg, POSSESSION is highly recommended.

-David Moody   Author of Autumn.

Arthouse goes to the Grindhouse: The Censorship and rebirth of Andrzej Żuławski's *Possession*

When we think of the phrase Video Nasty, the films that immediately come to mind are those of a very specific ilk. Slasher, Splatter, Cannibal, and Zombie films are not only the most prevalent but have also become the most notorious—and have, no doubt, garnered the biggest fanatics. At a certain point, you can even argue that Video Nasty became a selling point for specific films; a sort of guarantee your dollar is met with gratuitous gore. Amongst a sea of gore-filled goodies, however, are a few titles that don't quite fit the mold. Principal among these titles is Andrzej Żuławski's 1981 film, *Possession*. Following a state-imposed exile from Polish filmmaking, and written amidst a disastrous divorce, Possession is, at its core, both an intimate portrayal of the mysterious forces that drive a wedge into love, as well as, a scathing indictment of the tyrannical control of communism. It is also a film—as Żuławski famously remembers pitching it—about "a woman who fucks an octopus;" to which we can further amend by adding that the Octopus is actually a creature who she in fact births. Sprinkle in vaguely blasphemous elements and graphic violence and it is not hard to see why *Possession* fell under the puritanical reign of the Video Recordings Act. It wasn't, however, only in the UK that the film was the victim of censorship. While it would take ten years for the film to receive distribution in the UK—after a limited theatrical release—, perhaps the biggest blow for *Possession* was the alternative form of censorship it was subjected to in the United States. For, in the US, it was not censored for being too graphic, blasphemous, or sexually perverse, it was censored for failing to adhere to generic conventions.

Believe it or not, *Possession*'s first US distribution was through an erotic distribution company called Limelight International. In order to sell the film to the grindhouse circuit, the company truncated the film's length from 123 to 81 minutes, going as far to even re-order the events of the film so that it adhered to the tropes of a monster-possession style horror film. This had a profound effect on the film and it would take nearly thirty years for the film to receive an uncut release in America. One can only hypothesis the disastrous effect this had on the American reception. Admittedly, even in its 123-minute runtime, the film offers a complex viewing experience, challenging viewers to engage with it, but it is also a film that is deceivingly simple. For example, while countless essays have been penned over the significance of the mysterious pink-socked agent, Żuławski has discussed in interviews that this strange inclusion was a jab at the desire for Westernizing fashion trends in Eastern Europe. Still, in spite of Żuławski's own beliefs, there just is no simple way to describe *Possession;* it is just a film that must be seen.

In a recent article I wrote for Diabolique Magazine, I discussed the film in relation to its themes of pregnancy horror and radical feminism. In this light, the film has many striking similarities to David

Cronenberg's *The Brood*, but *Possession* is not—as the original US distributors would have liked it to be—strict horror or reducible to any one analysis. Like cancer, *Possession* is a in a state of perpetual growth; subject yourself to five simultaneous viewings and you'll have five different interpretations. Like Żuławski's other films, the film's reality is built upon a foundation of madness, behavior is not dictated by rational human emotions. *Possession* breaks down verisimilitude and creates its own logic, a fact that leads us to Tom Huddleston's apt assessment that, "*Possession* may be the only film in existence which is itself mad…its not the characters who are possessed, but the film itself."[5] A rumination on identity and freedom under Soviet Control, an penetrating portrait of a decaying marriage, a religious allegory, a backlash against patriarchal control of female bodies, or a bloody and disturbing creature feature-slasher hybrid—regardless of how you view *Possession*, it is a film that has overcome opposition, defied censorship, and one in which remains every bit as relevant today as it did on its release in 1981. With everything stacked up against it that could have forced the film to fade into the cracks of cinematic obscurity, it is a testament to the power of the film that *Possession* has persevered.

Joe Yanick   Writer.

Pranks

Also known as "The Dorm That Dripped Blood" and "Il Paese del Sesso Selvaggio".
Year of release: 1982
Writers: Stephen Carpenter and Jeffrey Obrow
Director: Stephen Carpenter and Jeffrey Obrow
R-rated 104 mins. USA
Tagline: "When the kidding stops… the killing starts."
Main cast: Laurie Lapinski (Joanne Murray), Stephen Sachs (Craig), David Snow (Brian), Pamela Holland (Patti), Dennis Ely (Bobby Lee Tremble), Woody Roll (John Hemmit).
Distributed by: Canon
In 1992 a cut version with 10 seconds cut was released and this still remains the only uncut, an uncut and unrated US version is available R1 DVD.

Plot:
This 80's slasher begins on the eve of Christmas vacation in a condemned college dormitory with a group of students helping to clear and close down the dorm ready to be demolished. Friends Joanne, Patty, Brian and Craig are all alone in this derelict building when they discover that there is a crazed psychopath on the loose. He picks them off one by one, murdering them in inventive and gruesome ways.

Appraisal:
This early stalk n' slash offering is often overlooked, Being a slasher fan I was looking forward to seeing this video nasty from the DPP list, like most people I use the rule of the three, "Halloween", "The Burning" and "Friday the 13th" as the bench mark for slasher films. Pranks isn't as good as any of those three, but it does have its charm. This film does have a low budget feel to it, but what it lacks in budget it makes up for in kills, (though the kills are not always seen on screen), including someone burnt alive in an incinerator, a girl being boiled alive, a drill to the head and throat cut with cheese wire, these are just a few of the clever and original ways the psycho starts to use to kill his victims, in this fun nonstop stalk and slash movie. This film was also known as "The Dorm That Dripped Blood," I preferred the "Dorm That Dripped Blood" poster with the silhouette of the killer with a knife in his hand dripping with blood.
For slasher movie fans - be sure to check this one out!

-Tony Newton

This was the very first feature film I ever worked on and it will always have a special place in my heart. I started as a grip the day we were shooting the scene where we rolled over Daphne Zuniga's head in the parking garage at UCLA. Mathew Mungle seemed like a magician to me with his special make up effects. It was a real thrill to watch him work.
My career as a grip lasted for about an hour before I dropped one of the lights and it smashed to pieces- It was obvious I was not cut out to do that job and I was offered a chance to work in the editing room. I loved it. I was teamed with Earl Ghaffari (now a music editor: "Frozen" "Wreck it Ralph" "Tangled") We became the sound effects crew. With a very small budget, we went to the store, bought raw chicken, carrots, celery and anything we could to create fleshy sounds. We had a blast recording the sounds and cutting them in. It was a real labor of love.

I was so close to the film and the fun of making it, that I never gave it a second thought that it might be considered too strong for a general audience. The first clue came at the cast screening at the Avco theaters in Westwood. The pale look on people's faces as they walked out threw me. Later, when we needed to cut it down to get an R rating from the MPAA, we ended up making some trims to the drill in the head shots, and the baseball bat beating scene as well as a few other gore shots that we lingered on too long. It played in the U.S. in general theatrical release without much attention, so I was puzzled when it was banned in the U.K.

-John Penney   Writer/Filmmaker.

Prisoner of the Cannibal God

known as "The Mountain of the Cannibal God", "Slave of the Cannibal God" and "La Montagna del dio Cannibale".
Year of release: 1978
Writer: Cesare Frugoni
Director: Sergio Martino
Banned 99mins. Italy
Tagline: "Their cult was death…Their lust was for blood!"
Main cast: Ursula Andress (Susan Stevenson), Stacey Keach (Professor Edward Foster), Claudio Cassinelli (Manolo), Antonio Marsina (Arthur Weisser), Franco Fantasia (father Moses), Lanfranco Spinola (Consul Burns).

Distributed by: Originally distributed by Hokushin. In 2001 a version of the film was released with 2.06 seconds of cuts and passed by the BBFC this is the only version in the UK but an uncut and unrated version is available in R1 US format.

Plot:
Susan Stevenson and her brother Arthur enlist the help of professor Edward Foster in the search for Susan's anthropologist husband Henry who went missing whilst on an expedition to a mysterious island in Papua New Guinea. The terror begins as the group discover that the island is inhabited with flesh-hungry cannibals!

Appraisal:
This cult classic features (yet again) strange and deadly dealings with cannibals, this time Sergio Martino directs and the film starring (James Bond's own) Ursula Andress who stands out for her looks alone and the cherry on the cake she is a fantastic actress, she also appears in the Hammer Horror classic (She). Alongside Ursula Andress, Stacey Keach plays Edward Foster and is awesome in this movie! Susan (Ursula Andress) is on a mission with her brother looking for her husband who is missing! Keach helps them and they end up in the jungle, what follows are the three of them encountering the natives and are taken prisoner by merciless cannibals. The film features the usual animal cruelty, cannibalism, nudity, this is full on exploitation film that is always overlooked among the classic cannibal films although the film seems to have gained more recognition of late, it is a good film and has a sufficient storyline. The film is set up to shock the viewer but although it does shock it does this whilst being entertaining along the way, well worth a spin on good old VHS.

-Tony Newton

The memory of the movie is now far away. I remember it as a life experience and professional and very important, especially for the difficulties to make it happen, especially when shooting in Malaysia, where the sets were really difficult to reach. The cave's final scene was shot on a mountain with a vertical drop of 300 meters, and in conditions of hot weather and humidity.

I had to return from the jungle with a canoe, because the inability to restart a small plane landed in a small sitting airport of ETBA inside the area, but no roads with only the path of a river.

Ursula Andress and Claudio Cassinelli proved not only good actors but also great collaborators.

-Sergio Martino   Director Mountain of the Cannibal God.

A brother and sister (Claudio Cassinelli and Ursula Andress respectively) search for her missing husband on an uncharted island in New Guinea. Along with the help of their guide (Stacy Keach), it's revealed during their search that the real reason they are on this island is to find uranium deposits. Martino had huge aspirations for this film – which became an expensive and ambitious project, with a special credit even given for Ms. Andress' wardrobe designer. The outlandish plot and aforementioned cinematic ambition enabled the film to stand out from its contemporaries.

-David Bond

Revenge of the Bogeyman

Also known as "Revenge of the Boogey Man", "Boogeyman II".
Year of release: 1983
Writers: Suzanna Love, Ulli Lommel and Bruce Pearn as Bruce Starr
Directors: Bruce Pearn as Bruce Starr, Ulli Lommel - uncredited
R rated 79 mins. USA
Main cast: Suzanna Love (Lacey), Ulli Lommel (Mickey Lombard), Shannah Hall (Bonnie Lombard), Shoto Von Douglas (Joseph), Bob Rosenfarb (Bernie), Rhonda Aldrich (Cynthia).
Distributed by: VTC
In 2003 the directors cut a slightly different version was passed by the BBFC uncut.

Plot:
Revenge of the Bogey Man is the sequel to "The Boogey Man." The horror hiding deep inside the mirror, the Boogeyman has returned! When Lacey visits her friend Bonnie in Los Angeles, she brings with her the one remaining shard of glass from the mirror. When the butler, Joseph, gets his hands on it, the Boogey Man returns to kill them all.

Appraisal:
In Revenge of the Boogey Man, Lacey moves to Hollywood along with pieces of her doomed, broken mirror. It's in Hollywood that they attempt to make a film documenting her experiences. What we get here is far from what we should have! The first film is so far superior to this offering, that is does not even fall into the same category. The effects aren't great and the acting is appalling, this low budget film could have been so much more!. Revenge of the Boogeyman replays so much footage from the first "Bogeyman" film and Ulli Lommel should have gone with Paramount Pictures to make a better film, as this independent film is obviously made with a smaller budget than the original! and could have been so much better!

Fans of the first film will be disappointed here, mainly due the sheer volume of footage from the original film, If you haven't seen the original Boogeyman, be sure to watch that one first and not this one!

-Tony Newton

The Slayer

Also known as "Nightmare Island"
Year of release: 1982
Writers: J.S Cardone and Bill Ewing
Director: J.S Cardone
R rated 80 mins. USA
Tagline: "Is it a nightmare? Or is it….The Slayer?"
Main cast: Sarah Kendall (Kay), Frederick Flynn (Eric), Carol Kottenbrook (Brooke), Alan McRae (David), Michael Holmes (Marsh), Sandy Simpson (Norman).
Distributed by: Vipco
In 2001 an uncut version was passed by the BBFC, available in the UK.

Plot:
In The Slayer, Kay suffers with strange and disturbing nightmares, so when siblings Kay and Eric go on vacation with friends David and Brooke it should be the perfect getaway but instead the holiday on a secluded island turns into an horrific and barbaric ordeal as Kay begins to see her friends murdered one by one and the murders start to come true!

Appraisal:
The Slayer is also known as "Nightmare Island." The dream-like universe within The Slayer is very clever, and the ending of the film was superb, blurring the lines of reality and dreams. I love this tagline "Is it a nightmare or is the Slayer?"

I think The Slayer should have received more attention than it got at the time and definitely more today, as it definitely deserves more.

Some vacations turn out to be a nightmare, well for these siblings and their partners it did!

This film is a strange one, there are some creative kills in this slasher-esque offering, including a fish in a person's neck then whisked off to sea and of course the shocking pitchfork scene with the pitchfork exiting a woman's breasts. This film has an eerie atmosphere and the dream killer the stuff of nightmares is reminiscent of the later Freddy Krueger from the "Nightmare on Elm Street" films, though you would welcome Freddy Krueger to liven up this very slow offering, it makes a change not having teens but instead thirty something's. This film has a slow pace throughout, but a unique ending to say the least Not one of the greatest horrors, once again a superb idea which in some parts is poorly executed, with a bigger budget this film would have been amazing, though it's still a cracking film throughout.

-Tony Newton

Terror Eyes

Also known as "Night School"
Year of release: 1981
Writers: Ruth Avergon
Director: Ken Hughes
R rated 88 mins. USA
Tagline:
"A is for Apple B is for Bed C is for Co-ed D is for Dead F is for Failing to keep your head!"

Main cast: Leonard Mann (Lt. Judd Austin), Rachel Ward (Eleanor Adjai), Drew Snyder (Vincent Millett), Joseph R. Sicari (Taj), Nicholas Cairis (Gus), Karen MacDonald (Carol).

Distributed by: Guild

In 1987 Guild re-released this film, this time the BBFC made 1.16 seconds of cuts to the film, this is the only version available in the UK but the uncut and unrated version is available on R1 US DVD.

Plot:
In this 1981 slasher, the city of Boston is plagued by a leather-clad, crash-helmet-wearing, deranged psychopath, who commits a series of gruesome decapitations. The police believe the murders to be ritualistic and close in on the killer, but the suspect is arrested and the murders continue. Will the detective close the net on the true killer?

Appraisal:
Terror Eyes is a strange little slasher offering, this film seems to always get bad press and hated on by critics. It's a great stalk and slash film but doesn't age very well. I love this movie, I think the films charm is everything that is wrong with the film itself, including some choice dialogue from the detective and certain things, which are never explained. This film is like an adult version of Scooby Doo, complete with the killers reveal at the end.

Terror Eyes also known as "Night School" which to me had the better title and poster, sees a girl who attends yes you guessed right... night school, and is terrorized by a psychopathic killer who wears a black helmet and leather gloves, oh and loves nothing more than to decapitate his victims. This film comes complete with a Norman Bates-esque shower montage but there is no kill, but what follows is a bizarre body painting love scene.

This film has giallo qualities to it complete with the black leather gloves though this killer looks more like Street Hawk from the 80's TV show. This is an enjoyable slasher film but not the best, it feels dated but still entertaining.

-Tony Newton

The Toolbox Murders

Also known as "Der Killer Mit Bohr-Maschine"
Year of release: 1978
Writer: Neva Friedenn and Robert Easter
Director: Dennis Donnelly
R rated 93 mins. USA
Tagline: "Bit by bit…By bit he carved a nightmare!"
Main cast: Cameron Mitchell (Vance Kingsley), Pamelyn Ferdin (Laurie Ballard), Wesley Eure (Kent Kingsley), Nicholas Beauvy (Joey Ballard), Tim Donnelly (Detective Jamison), Aneta Corsaut (Joanne Ballard).
Distributed by: Hokushin

In 2000 this film was released with 1.45 seconds of cuts by the BBFC. This is the only version about in the UK but an unrated and uncut version is available R1 US DVD. The VHS or so called Two VHS released in the early 80s are very collectable as there are around 3 different versions, a version cut by 6 minutes, a version cut by 2 minutes and there's rumored to be a uncut version too.

Plot:
In L.A a ski-masked lunatic wreaks havoc on the beautiful young tenants of an apartment complex. This maniac is using the tools from his toolbox as murder weapons! The killer abducts Laurie and his sick and twisted intentions are revealed but will the cops figure out whom the killer is before he strikes again?

Appraisal:
Some video nasties need no introduction; this is one of them!
The Toolbox Murders was one of the first video nasties I ever watched on good old VHS! It was Creepy and messed up then and still is today!
In this classic slasher we see a masked killer who uses some very creative ways in which to kill his victims using work tools, that in itself is such a great premise for a film, who wouldn't want to watch that!
This film is a slice of exploitation sleaze but at its best, this is one of my favourites from the DPP list. The film does not pretend to be anything but a full on kill for kills sake affair and in this case killing young attractive women, then the film takes a strange turn into a kidnapping sort of drama film for the second half, which I really liked the first time I watched the film, this really stood out to me as something very different and a bit of an original slant on the horror genre at the time. During the second act where the killers mask comes off and the kidnapper takes his victim the young girl Laurie prisoner. this is acted out very well, Cameron Mitchell is very good at portraying the psycho complete with lollypop sucking and mind fucking performance that has as creepiness to it! Although we are spoon-fed the plot and even when we are meant to know the killers identity you would have to be insane not to realize it. That aside, this is a great exploitation film with original kills and does leave you feeling a little bit dirty. This film is a true classic and delivers one of the better films on the DPP list. This film lacks humor in many ways for me it's actually what makes the film stand out as a true nasty! Even today the subject of kidnapping a 15-year-old girl alone is fucked up, Big Time!
Tobe Hooper remade this with Angela Bettis, it was a very good remake but did lack some of the original qualities, which made this film sleazy and dark in all the right places.

-Tony Newton

Unhinged

Year of release: 1982
Writer: Don Gronquist and Reagan Ramsey
Director: Don Gronquist
Unrated 79 mins. USA
Tagline: "The nightmare begins when you wake up."
Main cast: Laurel Munson (Terry Morgan), Janet Penner (Marion Penrose), Sara Ansley (Nancy Paulson), Virginia Settle (Mrs. Penrose), John Morrison (Norman Barnes), Barbara Lusch (Gloria).
Distributed by: Avatar
In 2005 the film was released from its ban and a US R1 DVD was released at the time and now an R2 DVD is available of this film.

Plot:
Unhinged starts off in a similar vein to "The Last House on the Left" with a group of girls (Terry, Nancy and Gloria) on their way to a festival, the girls are involved in a car accident and find themselves non-paying guests at an elderly ladies home. Will the girls pay for their stay? They do in this film!

Appraisal:
This classic film delivers on certain aspects, more on twists and not much else, there are shocks but truthfully you see them coming a mile off. This video nasty seems to drag on and doesn't offer much in the way of gore or even murders. Once again what were they thinking banning this one? Although the film is slow the acting is quite bad for some reason this film is still an okay watch and quite memorable decades on, it does have a creepiness to it. "Unhinged" was banned in the UK, but it seems rather bizarre as there is nothing too harsh here, it's a very forgettable early 80s horror offering, there are so many early 80s horror films which are well worth re-watching more than this title. As a youngster the film did have a strange creepiness to it that really freaked me out, over time the film has lost its ability to have any effect on me which is crazy as I still love those Garbage Pail Kids cards and eat far too much candy, something's never change, not all things age well!

This is no vintage claret!

-Tony Newton

Visiting Hours

Also known as "Get Well Soon"
Year of release: 1981
Writer: Brian Taggert
Director: Jean-Claude Lord
R rated 105 mins. Canada
Tagline: "There is no known cure…for Murder!"
Distributed by: CBS FOX
In 1986 the cut of the film was released, the film still has 1.10 seconds of UK cuts made by the BBFC but is available uncut and unrated in the US RIDVD.
In 2006 Anchor bay released the film.
Main cast: Michael Ironside (Colt Hawker), Lee Grant (Deborah Ballin), Linda Purl (Sheila Munroe), William Shatner (Gary Baylor), Lenore Zann (Lisa), Harvey Atkin (Vinnie Bradshaw).
Re-released in 1986 with 1 minute cut.

Plot:
Michael Ironside plays a crazed psycho killer who attacks a journalist Deborah Ballin. Things don't go to plan as he discovers he didn't actually kill her. He tracks Deborah down and, as she lays in her hospital bed, he attempts to finish the job once and for all. This movie features Star Trek's William Shatner.

Appraisal:
This movie is a classic 1980's thriller horror film that builds suspense throughout. Ironside's screen presence as always saves the day here! This film should definitely not have been put on the DPP list, it's not overly gory and although it's scary in parts it has the feel and production of a TV movie. This film wasn't prosecuted and still appeared on the list, which is strange because the video released was the same as the cut cinema release. This is one of the higher budget films on the nasty list, but just goes to show that a bigger budget doesn't always mean a better film. In 1989 the uncut version appeared on ITV, which resulted in many complaints and censorship by the broadcasting standards council, as this version had not been cleared for video release.

I remember watching it when it aired on ITV late in 1989, I remember the creepy feel to it and I think this was on the day before "The Eyes of Laura Mars" which was on the same channel. TV in the late 80's was packed with horror thrillers in some form or the other albeit mostly cut for TV! They used to cut swear words out of films like "Beverly Hills Cop" and a lot of nudity and sex scenes from films, I think the British were only aloud to see Barbara Windsor's breasts in Carry on Camping, that was about as bad as it got, I still wonder if her breasts had some secret government hidden subliminal message in them, like a form of Clockwork Orange! no wonder I was on a continues hunt for extreme video nasties!

-Tony Newton

If there's one thing that really snags the pubes in my zipper it is censorship. In particular, the whole sorry "video nasty" debacle of 1984 gets my blood boiling over. Amidst a national outcry from enraged parents, fanatical religious organizations, and the typically misguided British tabloid press, politicians passed a new law that identified any supposedly obscene films and brought them swiftly to justice. Of the 72 films proposed as morally repugnant, just over half were successfully prosecuted. However, the DPP got it all so woefully wrong that often films were banished with little to no reasoning. Case in point; one distinctly nondescript offender, **Cannibal Man,** was banned for its name alone while *Tobe Hooper's* **The Funhouse** made the list purely through clerical error as it shared its title with *Roger Watkins'* **Last House on Dead End Street** which was also released under the same title.

I get that the market needed some sort of legislation in place to prevent these films falling into the wrong hands as, up until then, it had been unregulated. As a parent myself, it would be irresponsible stating otherwise. What rattles my cage most is the inconsistency shown as certain films were made an example of while other more mean-spirited works like **Maniac, The Prowler and The New York Ripper,** despite also being seized by police during raids, never officially made the shortlist. One inclusion, which dumbfounds me to this very day, is *Jean-Claude Lord's* **Visiting Hours.** Originally passed with cuts for cinema, it was then named and shamed, before eventually being released with approximately one minute cut in 1986. All this while being relatively bloodless. Hilariously, it later aired on television totally uncut in 1989 after, you guessed it, another clerical error. Shameful.

Visiting Hours was the first English language film from French-Canadian director Lord **(The Vindicator, Mindfield)** and marked the first of two instances where he worked alongside *Michael Ironside.* The studio responsible for *David Cronenberg's* **Scanners** had been so impressed with the actor's portrayal of Darryl Revok that they suggested him for the role of the similarly unhinged Cole Hawker and that most definitely wasn't a clerical error. Ironside broke his ankle on the first day of filming, thus the limp he carried towards the end of the film was entirely authentic.

The first example of Lord going against slasher convention was his choice to make the killer of the piece known to the audience from the very offset. There wasn't an abundance of P.O.V. shots, leather gloved hands, or tacky masks, and instead Hawker had a penchant for his mom's tacky costume jewellery and sported kinky leather vests as he went about his foul business. Ordinarily, this would appear something of a bum steer as it should have robbed Hawker of any mystery. However, what we weren't made privy to, was the madness which existed inside that glorious pulsating cranium and his enigmatic performance hinted at just how cluttered a locale that was. Let's not forget the kind of migraine this man could encourage through mind bullets alone.

Cole was a pure vessel of vitriolic rage and misogyny with curled snarling lips and a look of cold, passionless, malice in his eyes. While never explained why he garnered an inexplicable hatred towards women, it was hinted on occasion that he had suffered a torrid upbringing, and this was responsible for his contempt towards the fairer sex. Ironside played him to perfection, proving without reasonable doubt, that he is one of the finest character actors of our generation or any other come to think of it. So much of the success of **Visiting Hours** was simply down to him while none of the blame could be left on his doorstep for any of its numerous shortcomings.

After taking exception to feminist activist Deborah Ballin (an assured *Lee Grant*), after her appearance on a TV talk show, Hawker tracked her down and attempted to snuff her out. Having failed, she was admitted to the County General Hospital and he acquired himself some scrubs to continue tormenting her further. However, where *Rick Rosenthal's* excellent **Halloween II** was predisposed with coming good on its promise of a bloated body count, this played out more like a made-for-TV thriller, albeit a well-constructed one. It even pulled in *William Shatner* for a frankly pointless hammed-up cameo as Deborah's unhelpful boss, presumably to locate the knock-off Shatner mask that Michael Myers had pilfered years earlier. Wrong hospital, Bill; you may have traveled where no man had gone before, but geography clearly wasn't your major.

Visiting Hours was solid and well played overall, but the performance of Ironside was single-handedly responsible for keeping us on the edge of our seats and not dropping off in their comfy confines. Certain long drawn-out scenes of Hawker stalking his female victims wrung every last droplet of tension out of *Brian Taggert's* screenplay but wouldn't have resonated had it not been for his formidable presence. It wasn't half bad, despite being fifteen minutes overlong and needlessly padded out, but I'll tell you another thing it wasn't…a freaking video nasty. On the plus side, any infamy garnered has helped this decent Canadian tax shelter feature from vaporizing entirely but don't go expecting splatter as it was strictly a nil by mouth affair.

-Keeper of the Crimson Quill (Rivers of Grue)

There is no shortage of irony in branding *Visiting Hours* (1982) a Video Nasty. Not only quite tame in comparison to fellow victims of the UK banning spree, here is a slasher film whose main conceit is actually about the suppression of violence, specifically domestic abuse. The proof is in the plot: Deborah Ballin (Lee Grant), a stalwart feminist news anchor, struggles for media visibility of so-called battered women, posing both as a symbol of empowerment and the ultimate threat to The Man, portrayed here as psychopath Colt Hawker (Michael Ironside), whose endgame is to pacify such toughened voices through murder. Hawker's stalk and slash motif is a sleazy twist on the rote formula with his phallic switchblades, a mother-blaming back story of familial abuse, and, most of all, a camera to photograph his victims in the throes of their demise. Thus, the film's gaze is not on tantalizing sex scenes or stupid teenagers smoking dope, but on bruises, bloody noses and sweaty brows soaked in fear. It is about exposure, figuratively to the abuse Ballin combats and literally through a killer's shutter that makes misogynistic violence and feminine pain a twistedly timeless art. By its finale, *Visiting Hours* is a disquieting picture hampered only by languid pacing and William Shatner doing William Shatner. A few memorable gore effects evidences its place in the Nasty canon, but its censure only ignores that some horror films' screams of terror can in fact be cries for justice.

-Aaron Eischeid   Filmmaker/Author.

I'm not going to lie, I just watched this again because it was on this list. I remember seeing when I was a kid, but it really did not stand out at all in my memory. For the life of me I can't understand why it would have been banned at all, it didn't push the limits like The Hills Have Eyes, or Last House on the Left, unless there was another cut originally. It did feel unique though, for a slasher type film from the early 80's. The characters were interesting in that the female role was much different then the average horror flick of the time. Lee Grants character was unique in that she was such a strong female character. Not only does she incur the killer's wrath for defending an abused woman on her television show, but also then later in the film she physically defends Nurse Munroe from the killer on her own. Munroe herself is a strong female character as well, but she does shift somewhat to the more typical female role seen in these types of films. Her being protected and saved by Grants character does give the film an interesting spin though.

At the end of the day if nothing else, any time spent watching Michael Ironside in a film, is time very well spent!

-James Fler   Raven Banner Entertainment

The Witch Who Came From the Sea

Year of release: 1976
Writer: Robert Thom
Director: Matt Cimber
R rated 83 mins. USA
Tagline: "Molly really knows how to cut men down to size!!"
Main cast: Millie Perkins (Molly), Lonny Chapman (Long John), Vanessa Brown (Cathy), Peggy Feury (Doris), Jean Pierre Camps (Tadd), Mark Livingston (Tripoli).
Distributed by: VTC
The film was later released in 2006 uncut and passed by the BBFC.

Plot:
Molly tries to suppress the memories of abuse by her alcoholic father; she now works as a waitress in a bar on the Californian coast. Her father's abuse has taken its toll on Molly as she's now a dysfunctional and sadistic young woman who invites men back to her home to take revenge on them for the exploitation she suffered at the hands of her father.

Appraisal:
The Witch Who Came From the Sea is nothing like I expected the film to be from my initial glance at the cover art whilst wandering the isles of the video store. I expected to return home with some fucked up supernatural horror film like The Witchfinder General - the cover alone scared the shit out of me, and already I thought I knew just what to expect from the film. The Witch Who Came From The Sea sees actress Millie Perkins take on the role of Molly a psychologically disturbed 30 something woman struggling to deal with the repressed memories and emotions of the childhood abuse subjected upon her at the hands of her sea captain father. This film earns its place on the video nasty list largely due to its controversial storyline, this sexually charged rape revenge-esque offering is something very far removed from the likes of I Spit on Your Grave or The Last House on the Left. The film offers a comparatively subtle use of gore by today's standards yet the hallucinogenic, twisted glimpses into the world of this mentally scared murderess make the film disturbingly powerful with the ability to leave your skin crawling Molly develops an obsession with TV personalities (celebrity worship ahead of its time), as she struggles to differentiate between fantasy and reality we feel the pain of her tormented soul as she spirals into a castration murder spree in a bid to avenge the abuse inflicted upon her in a maze of dream-like sequences intertwined with childhood recollections. Overall The Witch Who Came From The Sea is a great watch, and I would recommend it to anyone! It takes some time to build the characters and unravels at a sometimes too-slow pace, but the almost dreamlike sequences cover this up well. The film contains some seriously dodgy camera angles and

consists of a highly disjointed narrative but… but... and there is a but… there's just something mesmerizing about the accompaniment of Hershel Burke Gilbert's nagging eerie score which sits perfectly alongside the film. The Witch Who Came From the Sea is unlike any other offering from the Video Nasty list, its fragmented construction, haunting atmospherics, muggy, bleak settings, and sheer bizarreness set it apart from anything else. It's unique, it's certainly out there, it doesn't shy away from its controversial theme, it's weird in a good way and one of those films that's guaranteed to get under your skin. Watch out for the quiet ones! They always have something to -hide!

-Tony Newton

Women Behind Bars

Also known as "Des Diamants Pour L'Enfer".
Year of release: 1975
Writer: Marius Lesoeur
Director: Jesús Franco
Unrated 75 mins. France, Belgium
Tagline: "99 women behind bars without men!"
Main cast: Lina Romay (Shirley Fields), Martine Stedil (Martine), Nathalie Chape, Roger Darton (Milton Warren), Ronald Weiss (Carlo de Bries), Denis Torre (Jailer).
No UK release.
Distributed by: GO Video
This film has not been re-released in the UK but is available in its uncut and unrated form on a RI US DVD.

Plot:
Jesús Franco's classic prison heist romp Women Behind Bars sees a diamond heist go terribly wrong. Shirley Fields shoots and kills her jewel thief boyfriend. Whilst she's in prison she becomes the subject of torture and interrogation as her attackers attempt to discover the hidden jewels.

Appraisal:
Master of controversy Jesús Franco's unleashes his trademark film style, which usually consisted of sex, nudity, torture and violence.

Jesús Franco's Women Behind Bars features Jesús Franco as a gangster! This alone is worth a watch! This prison exploitation offering is risqué to say the least. The film features gratuitous torture of women, which unfolds on-screen throughout the film.

Women Behind Bars stars Lina Romay who is no stranger to exploitation films and always demands you full attention on screen, Lina was famously married to director Jesús Franco, Lina Romay sadly passed away in 2012 at the very young age of 57 and sadly Jesús Franco died a year after Lina in 2013.

You can easily see why the BBFC had issues with the title as they seemed to have a problem with a lot of Franco's work. I can imagine every time they saw the name Jesús Franco or one of his aliases they used to say "Aargh... not again!" Or words to that effect.

The film itself is watchable but by no means great. I have to give credit where its due the film does focus on the heist and not as much as you would expect in the way of nudity as the title would suggest, yes the film features lots of nudity, lesbianism and scenes of torture, but these things are not just thrown in for the sake of it, they actually follow the plot of the film.

All in all Women Behind Bars is worth checking out, it feels a bit dated, but is a decent offering from Jesús Franco but certainly not his finest by a long shot!

-Tony Newton

Zombie Creeping Flesh

Also known as "Hell of the Living Dead" and "Virus", "Night of the Zombies", "Apocalipsis Canibal"
Year of release: 1981
Writer: Claudio Fragasso and Jose Maria Cunilles
Director: Bruno Mattei and Claudio Fragasso
Unrated 101 mins. Italy, Spain
Tagline: "They eat the living!"
Main cast: Margit Evelyn Newton (Lia Rousseau), Franco Garofalo (Zantoro), Selan Karay (Vincent), Jose Gras (Lt. Mike London), Gabriel Renom (Pierre), Josep Lluis Fonoll (Osborne).
Released uncut in 2002.
Distributed by: "Hell of the Living Dead" came out as a double feature on Blu-ray in October 2014, this comes unrated and in its uncut form from Blue Underground. "Hell of the Living Dead" was released as "Zombie Creeping Flesh" in the UK and was cut for the UK cinema release. It was not until 2002 that "Hell of the Living Dead" was first released uncut and unbanned.

Plot:
A four man group of elite swat soldiers head to a chemical research laboratory in Papua New Guinea, when all contact with the lab is lost, the group are under the impression that it has been taken over by terrorists, but when they reach the facility they discover that things are far worse than they could have imagined as the they're greeted by hordes of zombies!

Appraisal:
In this classic zombie horror film reporter Lia Rousseau (Margit Evelyn Newton) and her boyfriend end up fighting the undead with a commando unit in the New Guinea jungle. Director Bruno Mattei uses the name Vincent Dawn, I can only assume he's paying homage to George Romero's "Dawn of the Dead", the whole film has obviously been loosely based on "Dawn of the Dead".

Zombie Creeping Flesh is often compared to "Dawn of the Dead" not a comparison of the quality of the films but the soundtracks are comparatively similar and also the general ambience of the both films with the swat team and a comedy-esque feel to the film it's hard to take the film seriously, though it's obvious that the director is trying to send out a hidden message about the treatment of people in third world countries, which in itself is a good thing!

The zombies are the up side to this film, they look good but even great zombies can't save this film. Zombie Creeping Flesh is a weaker offering for this genre of film, but I have a huge soft spot for it, Margit Evelyn Newton is great in the film, the video sleeve cover really freaked me out as a kid it was one of those covers you could not put on the shelf unless you didn't want to sleep!, just the sight of those heads in a row was freaky as hell. It's well worth a watch for all zombie enthusiasts and most will find it entertaining. Even the director uses a pseudonym (Bruno Mattei uses the name Vincent Dawn), which should have been Vincent Dawn of Dead. The film is a far cry from the director's earlier work, which is almost soft-core porn - like his movie "The True Story of the Nun of Monza", hailed as the first Nunsploitation film.

Zombie Creeping Flesh wasn't prosecuted and was released uncut in 2002.

When the film was released it was heavily cut but it's rumored that the reason behind this was actually the length of the film as well as scenes of violence.

-Tony Newton

Many years have passed now since the filming of Zombie Creeping Flesh, but I have great memories of this film. We had a close-knit crew.

It was very early on in my career and was a great responsibility, as I was the lead actress. Rehearsing before shooting, The two Spanish actors were wonderful. Very cute; Bruno Mattei was very professional. I remember I was smoking a lot, My first semi nude was traumatic, I did remove all my clothes. I was very uncomfortable, and I think you can also see this in the film. The make-up FX in the film were exceptional.

-Margit Newton   Actress/ Lia Rousseau in "Zombie Creeping Flesh".

Once upon a time, I was a horror movie junkie. In fact, growing up, guys like Freddy Krueger and Leatherface were my heroes. Especially Freddy. Hell, I used to hold Nightmare on Elm Street movie marathons dressed up in a Freddy Halloween costume. And when I didn't have a plastic Freddy glove, I gutted markers and put the hallow plastic tubes on my fingers instead. Over the years, though, I stopped getting my horror from Hollywood and started getting it from New York...the major publishers. Books, I mean.

Recently, however, I started watching horror again, mainly free movies posted to YouTube. One of the horror movies I've seen lately is Zombie Creeping Flesh, also known as Night of the Zombies and City of the Living Dead.

Directed by Bruno Mattei, ZCF is one of those grand old Italian zombie movies heavy on gore and light (even lacking) in everything else. But like most good low-budget horror films, it builds a palpable sense of dread and horror throughout.

The story is original enough. A crack team of Commandos set off on a journey to a tropical locale, where a government research center has gone offline, worrying the higher-ups. Of course, the staff has been turned into zombies, and soon, the entire jungle is crawling with the living dead.

More so than any other early 80s Italian zombie flick, ZCF owes a huge debt to George A. Romero's Dawn of the Dead. I believe ZCF even used some of Dawn's soundtrack.

Regardless, Zombie Creeping Flesh is one of my favorites, mainly for the funky, low-tech special effects.

Sometimes, it's better than Hollywood.

-Joseph Rubas Author

Chapter 12: VIDEO NASTIES
The DPP Section 3 List!

The following films were all in some way associated with the Video Nasty scandal most of the titles featured on the section 3 list of films that were banned and destroyed in the UK. The DPP section 3 list of banned VHS videos are a list films that were banned in the 1980's, under section 3 of the Obscene Publications Act, many of the titles on the section 3 list were rumored to be on the section 2 video nasty list at one time or the other and caused a lot of confusion to stockist's and people trying to hunt down these tapes. The section 3 list of films, none of which of these titles were prosecuted but the films had a similar fate to the section 2 titles. The section 3 titles were confiscated and destroyed by the authorities in the UK. This prevented such articles from reaching the market by way of seizure and forfeiture proceedings (under section 3 of the 1959 Act), forfeiture stopped any of the titles deemed to deprave and corrupt from being prosecuted.

There is no full official record of either of the section 2 or 3 video nasty list in existence today as they were destroyed and not kept on file by the courts themselves after the implementation of the Video Recordings Act of 1984.

Abducted

(DPP Section 3) Banned in the UK
Also known as "Schoolgirls in Chains", "Girls in Chains" "Let's Play Dead".
Year of release: 1973
Writer: Don Jones
Director: Don Jones
R-rated USA
Tagline: "See it at your own risk!"
Main cast: Gary Kent (Frank Barrows), John parker (John Barrows), Stafford Morgan (Robert Matthews), Suzanne Lund (Ginger), Cheryl Waters (Bonnie), Merrie Lynn Ross (Sue).
Distributed by: Astra Video

Plot:
Brothers Frank and John Barrows are controlled by their overbearing, mentally unstable mother. These deranged brothers have a twisted sexual appetite and in order to satisfy those desires they abduct women and keep them locked in the cellar for their own amusement inflicting grotesque torture and brutal murder. This 1970's flick gives hitchhikers a reason not chance it!

Appraisal:
The film is basically a warning to hitchhikers across the globe in the 1960's/70's, hitchhiking was popular back in the 1970's and I assume that the number of people willing to accept a stranger into their car declined after this film. The two psycho brothers featured in this film are both twisted and just as bad as each other in their own way, they are believable as the twisted psycho pair in this exploitation flick which was deemed too bad for the British viewing public.

This film contains disturbing scenes of rape and abuse on women and you can see why it made the section 3 hit list. The film is shot really well and has a darkly disturbing feel to it. The actors (including the hillbilly brothers) are all on fine form here. Overall: good, but not a great horror film.

Abducted was seized under section 3 of the 1959 Obscene Publications Act on VHS in the early 1980's before the implementation of the Video Recordings Act of 1984 in the UK.

Abducted was only released on pre-cert VHS by Astra Video in 1982, there is no other official VHS release in existence; the only way you can get hold of a copy of the film is buying a US copy of the film, which is unrated.

-Tony Newton

The Aftermath

(DPP Section 3) Banned in the UK
Also known as "Zombie Aftermath".
Year of release: 1980
Writers: Steve Barkett and Stanley Livingston
Director: Steve Barkett
Unrated USA
Tagline: "Mutants – A savage encounter."
Main cast: Steve Barkett (Newman), Lynne Marguiles (Sarah), Sid Haig (Cutter), Christopher Barkett (Christopher), Alfie Martin (Getman), Forrest J Ackerman (The Curator).
Distributed by: World of Video 2000

Plot:
Steve Barkett's offering of The Aftermath sees astronauts Newman, Williams and Matthews return to Earth after they struggle to make contact with the planet. When the astronauts land they discover that a nuclear war has caused the end of civilization. Only mutants and a biker gang led by Cutter (Sid Haig) have survived this nuclear war.

Appraisal:
This film does have a really great sci-fi/horror feel to it and in my opinion is an extremely underrated movie. It's full of cheese, but the right kind of cheese like a strong cheddar melted on toast fresh out the from the grill. The Aftermath is a classic film but it does feel slightly dated in parts. For me the star of the film is Sid Haig who is better known for his role as Captain Spaulding in Rob Zombies "House of 1000 Corpses" and "Devils Rejects". Sid Haig is on fine form as an evil rogue in this horror classic.

The Aftermath has some gore and plenty of violence, in truth this film is a little known gem of a movie, the only thing that makes me chuckle is how much the male actor looks like Bennet from Arnold Schwarzenegger's 80's smash hit "Commando", Worth a watch just for that alone!

The Aftermath was seized under section 3 of the 1959 Obscene Publications Act on VHS in the early 1980's before the implementation of the Video Recordings Act of 1984 in the UK.

The Aftermath was only released on pre-cert VHS by World of Video 2000 in 1982, there is no other official VHS release or DVD in existence in the UK, it is worth tracking down an unrated US version of the film to add to your collection.

-Tony Newton

The Black Room

(DPP Section 3) Banned in the UK
Year of release: 1981
Writer: Norman Thaddeus Vane
Directors: Elly Kenner and Norman Thaddeus Vane
R rated USA
Tagline: "There is a room for rent in the Hollywood Hills......and the tenants are paying in blood"
Main cast: Stephen Knight (Jason), Cassandra Gava (Bridget), Jimmy Stathis (Larry), Clara Perryman (Robin), Charlie Young (Lisa), Geanne Frank (Sandy).
Distributed by: Alpha Video

Plot:
A room comes up for rent in the Hollywood hills but little do the tenants know that sibling landlords Jason and Bridget have provided this erotic setting in order for men to lure their mistresses back. Their dark secret is revealed as they drain the blood of their victims to satisfy their hunger for blood until the tenants begin to fight back!

Appraisal:
I can see The Black Room being remade especially with the current vampire craze or ironically the dying vampire craze of late. This film is different; It's a clever tale of love, family, strained relationships and sex all at the same time. "The Black Room" is shot well and does hold up today mainly for its original storyline. The film is not very gory or exceptionally violent but is a classic original horror film that raises the bar for the vampire genre we see today.

A lost gem here that is well worth re-visiting!

The Black Room was seized under section 3 of the 1959 Obscene Publications Act on VHS in the early 1980's before the implementation of the Video Recordings Act of 1984 in the UK.

The Black Room was only released on pre-cert VHS by Alpha Video in 1983, there is no other official VHS, DVD or Blu-Ray release in existence, this film is one of the hardest to track down - it was back in the day, and still is now.

-Tony Newton

An evocative and beguiling chiller, The Black Room is a kinky, consummate reinterpretation of the vampire myth. Just as George Romero used vampirism as a metaphor for teenage despondence in his 1976 gem Martin, here co-director's Elly Kenner and Norman Thaddeus Vane - the latter whom also scripted - use it to explore matrimonial problems and pre-AIDS attitudes to decadent sexuality. A somewhat legendary swordsman, Vane (whose other main genre credit is the endearingly naff, Theatre of Blood-aping slasher, Frightmare, starring a pre-Re-Animator Jeffrey Combs) was a regular on the party scene throughout swinging sixties and 70s London, New York, and Los Angeles. His playboy lifestyle as, at various times, a nightclub owner and editor of Penthouse Magazine served as his inspiration when piecing The Black Room together; as noted by author Stephen Thrower in is mighty Nightmare USA tome, and by blogger Sam Weisberg of hidden-films.com, it was during Vane's stint at Bob Gucione's notorious men's rag that he repeatedly cheated on his then-wife, sixteen year old model Sarah Caldwell, with numerous centrefolds at a similarly voyeuristic venue to the eponymous room of the title.

Upping the already sizzling sexual undercurrent inherent in the blood-sucker sub genre and making it far more explicit - yet never exploitatively so - The Black Room also switches fangs for a blood transfusion machine, and swaps the usual Transylvanian castle for a swanky Hollywood Hills mansion; a locale used to similar eerie effect in David Lynch's later Hollywood horror story Mulholland Drive. Our Dracula is Jason (Stephen Knight), a handsome and charismatic photographer - think Lugosi, Lee, and Langella all rolled into one - stricken with a rare blood disease, manageable only through fatally draining others of their plasma. "Jason's been sick his whole life, ever since he was a child... He had to constantly replenish his blood; every sixty days. Then once a month. Now, it's twice weekly," explains his sister Bridget, the film's singular answer to the old Count's buxom brides. Played by the stunning Cassandra Gava (best remembered as the sexy witch in Conan the Barbarian, and credited here under her real name Cassandra Gaviola), Bridget is Jason's carer, muse and, it is hinted at, his incestuous lover. She's also his accomplice, helping Jason lure in, kill and dispose of his potential blood donors.

Like Paul and Mary Bland, who murdered and robbed an assortment of "perverts" to bankroll their dream of owning a restaurant in Paul Bartel's released-the-same-year black comedy Eating Raoul, Jason and Bridget too have found the sexually promiscuous to be ideal victims. Renting out the titular space in their home, they've been taking their pick from the randy denizens who come, quite literally, to occupy it: "Restrictions? None. This isn't the YMCA," says Jason. "What the former tenants usually did was phone first; I'm always working in my studio. If you like, I can just pop in, light the candles, pour the wine; the rest is up to you."

Thrust into this scenario is Larry (Jimmy Stathis) and Robin (Clara Perryman); a couple whose marriage is growing a little stale. Though emotionally still in love with each other, their physical relationship has taken something of a beating, thanks to a mixture of boredom and the frequent interruptions of their attempted bedroom gymnastics by their two hyperactive children. Sexually frustrated, Larry soon finds himself Jason and Bridget's latest tenant, using the room as his basecamp for a bit of afternoon slap and tickle.

Whilst it would be easy to condemn Larry as simply a sleazeball letch, Vane instead throws in a curveball: suddenly Larry's illicit dalliances are being used to stoke the fires of wedded passion once more. Relaying his black room visits back to Robin, she - at Larry's insistence - treats them as nothing but fantasy; they're dirty talk, they're foreplay.

Seemingly as unsatisfied with Larry as he is with her, Robin's inner fox is repeatedly quelled by her husband's strange sense of coital morals: it's OK for him to indulge his appetite for exotic sex with strangers in the confines of his baroque hired hump den, but anything other than missionary on the marital mattress is strictly off limits with the Mrs. "Why aren't you ever [kinky] with me?" she asks. "Because," Larry replies, "I love you".

Though the probing of Larry's attitudes to sex and fidelity is the meat of the narrative, it's his handling (or not) of his marital repressions that results in Robin having the most interesting arc of the film. "Why don't you do to me what you said you did to that girl that you took to that black room?" she questions, upon her quiet discovery that her man's frisky fairy-tale shag pad is actually quite real. "I couldn't do that to you, it wouldn't be right. You're my wife," an oblivious Larry responds, dragging on a cigarette in bed. Barely masking her hurt and - more importantly - her disappointment, she pushes further, "I don't want to be your wife when we make love. I want to be your whore." Larry, of course, makes his excuses once again, "I don't see you in that room. You don't belong there, Robin." However, before long she's checking the place out for herself, with both her vulnerability and her own desires brought into question by a calculating Jason; one vampire who seems to *really* enjoy playing with his food...

In a contemporary context, The Black Room is akin to the offbeat oeuvre of House of the Devil director Ti West. The movie is character-focused and slow-burn, reliant more on sustained mood and powerful suggestion than graphic splatter; more Arthouse than grindhouse. Of course, when the blood does flow - in an early sangre-squirting gig for 80s gloop and latex specialist Mark Shostrom (From Beyond, Evil Dead II) - it's thrilling stuff. The Black Room certainly doesn't skimp on its horror, with the five-minute blood draining sequence being the undoubted, palm sweat-inducing highlight.

The first and only time we actually see Jason's full ritualistic process, it's a perfect and grotesquely poetic terror moment. It's a heavily eroticised set piece, fizzing with sexual energy and every bit as perversely titillating and as sensual as the entwined naked bodies on display throughout the rest of The Black Room. Constructed along the same edgy lines as the pre-sex shivers present during Larry's earlier initial encounter in his then newly acquired room - that simmer of nervous excitement, that feeling you get just before you rip someone's clothes off, is palpable in both instances - a heartbeat starts to pulse on the soundtrack, accompanied by composers James Ackley and Art Podell's throbbing, low synth score. Bridget and Jason smile at one another, their eyes meeting as his and drugged prostitute Sandy's (Geanne Frank) flesh is penetrated with prongs and syringes, hooking them up to the transfusion machine. Editor David Kern's cutting is rhythmic. Fetishistic glides over the machine and Sandy's surprising moans of ecstasy as her life-juice is sucked from her are the emphasised; the lines between pleasure and pain, and sex and death are blurred. Jason, meanwhile, is also in the throes of orgasmic posturing; sweat cascading over his brow, him squeezing Bridget's hand as, for all intents and purposes, he climaxes as Sandy's claret fills him. It's up there with Nekromantik as the most beautifully deranged ménage-a-trois ever committed to celluloid.

Introduced in a striking double murder sequence during the film's opening credits, the actual black room itself is also impressively realised, with cinematographer Robert Harmon's simple but effective use of a strange glowing coffee table, candlelight and inky black shadow conjuring up a rich air of genuine eroticism and danger. It's an intoxicating experience each time we're inside it; seductive and scary, flesh and fear dripping from its walls. A former on-set stills photographer, Harmon would later put his keen eye and unique sense of alluring unease to good use in his subsequent career as a director, with the gorgeously shot pair of brooding road-horror movies The Hitcher and Highwaymen but two of his credits.

Adding further ethereal elegance is the superb Steadicam work of the late Andrew "Jeff" Mart; as immersive and hypnotic here as Larry McConkey's use of it is in Donald Cammell's mystical desert slasher White of the Eye. Mart was the first person in the world to own such a rig privately and famously had a one handle barred bicycle that he would use for daredevil Steadicam shots. Throughout his career he'd work on several other great genre projects, like the fright fan favourite Pumpkinhead, Wes Craven's The People Under the Stairs and the cops-and-werewolves TV movie Full Eclipse, before his death at the age of sixty-six in 2009.

For connoisseurs of the more trashier end of the 80s horror spectrum, The Black Room is notable as one of the early features of delectable Scream Queen Linnea Quigley, popping up in a thankless and very minor role as somewhat doomed babysitter Milly. Though still a while off hitting schlock pay dirt thanks to her iconic turns in The Return of the Living Dead and Night of the Demons, it's an interesting echo of her earlier-still gig as Bondi's Mother in another sideways vampire flick, Don't Go Near the Park. A woeful dud, Don't Go Near the Park is nowhere near the thoughtful, charismatic excellence of The Black Room but nonetheless would make for a solid companion in a thematically similar double feature. The fact Don't Go Near the Park was actually one of the DPP's 'proper' Nasties too just sweetens the deal.

Passed uncut for theatrical release with an X rating by the BBFC in November 1982, The Black Room found itself on the Intervision roster. The videotape subsidiary of distributor Alpha Films, the Intervision label also included in its line up such seminal shock as Tourist Trap, Carrie and the early David Cronenberg trio of Shivers, Rabid and The Brood. Whilst they have all found their audience over the years thanks to multiple disc reissues and positive, sustained critical recognition, The Black Room has had neither; something that looks unlikely to change any time soon. Supposedly available in one of those Stateside bargain-bin multipack DVD bundles (though actually finding one with the film in it on the import market seems to be rarer than rocking horse poop), its fifth generation public domain transfer aside there'll be no Arrow Blu-ray special edition or even a no-frills disc: The Black Room's original negative is long rumoured to be lost, and the rights to it anyway allegedly tangled up in a mother load of unspecified legal hell. It's a damn shame and - if true - the most depressing end for a remarkable little picture that should get a hell of a lot more love.

Find the long out of print tape or pirate the thing; just make sure you see it before it's gone for good.

-Matty Budrewicz Writer/Author.

Blood Lust

(DPP Section 3) Banned in the UK
Also known as "Mosquito the Rapist", "Mosquito", "BloodLust", "The Vampire".
Year of release: 1976
Writers: N. Supasi and Mario D'Alcala
Director: Marijan David Vajda
Tagline: "….Will haunt the darkest corners of your mind!"
Main cast: Werner Pochath (The Man), Ellen Umlauf (The Mother), Birgit Zamulo (Young girl), Gerhard Ruhnke, Peter Hamm, Charly Hilti.
Distributed by: Derann

Plot:
Left deaf and dumb following a beating by his father as a child, Mosquito keeps himself to himself in his apartment decorated with his collection of dolls. In order to satisfy his inner demons Mosquito begins to break into mortuaries and mutilate women but when his secret love interest is killed in an accident this is no longer enough to suppress his appetite and that's when he takes to murder!

Appraisal:
This film seems similar to an Andy Warhol experimental film more than Andy Warhol's movies themselves, if anything the film seems at least ten years older than it actually is, it's dated but that being said does not detract too much from the film it's an underrated gem of a movie. "Blood Lust" has a very bizarre feel to it, quite surreal along with the main character's glass fangs, which he uses to suck blood. This film does have a Nekromantik feel to it, which is not a bad thing at all. I watched this film after I saw Nekromantik 1 and 2, which was on a bootleg tape; I do have a soft spot for this film, which dishes out in fair portions, sleaze, blood, and gore. It's something different, which shouldn't but does give the viewer something albeit in a bizarre way, a clever little film that you could easily see being remade in the next few years. Blood Lust was seized under section 3 of the 1959 Obscene Publications Act on VHS in the early 1980's before the implementation of the Video Recordings Act of 1984 in the UK.

Blood Lust was only released on pre-cert VHS by Derann in 1981, there is no other official VHS release in existence, the only way you can get hold of a copy of the film is buying a US copy of the film which is unrated from the USA.

The version that was released by Derann in 1981 was the cut cinematic version of the film so it's worth trying to find a uncut version of the film.

-Tony Newton

Blood Song

(DPP Section 3) Banned in the UK
Also known as "The Hunters" and "Dream Slayer"
Year of release: 1974
Writers: James Fargo and Frank Avianca
Director: Alan J. Levi
Rated 18, 89 mins. USA
Tagline: "….the last song you will hear."
Main cast: Donna Wilkes (Marion), Richard Jaeckel (Frank Hauser), Antionette Bower (Bea), Dane Clark (Sheriff Gibbons), Lenny Montana (Skipper), Frankie Avalon (Paul Foley).
Distributed by: Iver Film Services

Plot:
Blood Song is a 1980's slasher starring singer-turned-actor Frankie Avalon, who, after escaping from a mental institution, develops an obsession with Marion (a student who was handicapped in a car accident and received a blood transfusion from him). The crazed killer plays a blood song on his flute as he continues on this killing spree.

Appraisal:
Frankie Avalon plays a flute-playing killer – yes, a flute-playing psycho killer! Jethro Tull would be proud! This killer certainly doesn't tip toe around the daises! It's hard to take Avalon serious as the menacing character he attempts to portray on screen. I can't help but think of him in the film "Grease." He looks as menacing on screen as Frankie Howard would be in the same role.

This film is just one of a number of films which you could easily miss out from your video nasty collection, but if you let the bad acting and full on cheese of the early 80's hit you full on in the face then will find a fun little slasher here; we're not talking a groundbreaking cult movie but fun for fun's sake here!

Blood Song is very dated but a cool flick to watch with friends.

Blood Song was seized under section 3 of the 1959 Obscene Publications Act on VHS in the early 1980's before the implementation of the Video Recordings Act of 1984 in the UK.

Blood Song was only released on pre-cert VHS by Iver Film Services in 1982, the film is available 18 uncut in the UK and R-rated in the US.

-Tony Newton

The Blue Eyes of the Broken Doll

(DPP Section 3) Banned in the UK
Also known as "House of Psychotic Women" and "los Ojos Azules de la Muneca Rota".
Year of release: 1973
Writers: Carlos Aured and Paul Naschy
Director: Carlos Aured
R rated 89 mins. Spain
Main cast: Paul Naschy (Gilles), Diana Lorys (Claude), Eduardo Clavo (Doctor Pillipe), Eva Leon (Nicole), Ines Morales (Michelle), Antonio Pica (Inspector Pierre).
Distributed by: Canon

Plot:
The Blue House of the Broken Doll finds Paul Naschy (better known for his role in the film "The Werewolf and the Yeti") as an ex-convict plagued by disturbing nightmares. This murderous handy man has an MO, the victims of his murder spree all have blonde hair and blue eyes, which the killer collects as trophies!

Appraisal:
This bizarre euro trash offering that found its way onto the section 3 banned film list has a certain charm to it, a charm that as a youngster seeking out banned films I just didn't get or at least appreciate when I had a second generation copy and sandwiched the film between watching Faces of Death and The Texas Chainsaw Massacre. Now being a lover of foreign cinema, I adore this masterpiece! This is one of Paul Naschy's finest performances, once again Paul Naschy teams up with director Carlos Aured and both of them co wrote the films screenplay, I always had a soft spot for Paul Naschy, the Spanish actor who always seemed to give his all no matter how low the films budget was! This Giallo-esque offering does have some great shots and visuals which at times are lost due to the low budget, This sleazy Spanish horror flick does hit all the right notes and does deliver, the film is very underrated and only now I notice more and more people talking with a fondness for this little gem. This is a low budget horror but you can tell everyone involved making the film gave a 100% and the film was made with passion and a love of the craft!

The films effects are rather dated but this doesn't take anything away from the film, but all in all this is a cracking horror movie. The Blue Eyes of the Broken Doll features a disturbing pig slaughter, which is very prominent in the film - and disturbing - but doesn't stop this from being an enjoyable horror gem.

The Blue Eyes of the Broken Doll was seized under section 3 of the 1959 Obscene Publications Act on VHS in the early 1980's before the implementation of the Video Recordings Act of 1984 in the UK.

The Blue Eyes of the Broken Doll was only released on pre-cert VHS by Canon in 1982, the film is has not had a UK release on any other format since but is available in its unrated form in the US.

-Tony Newton

Brutes and Savages

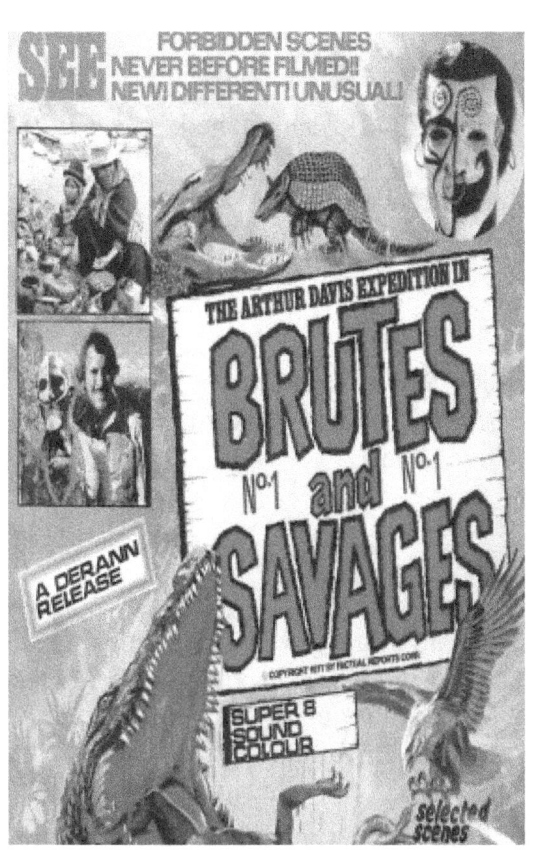

(DPP Section 3) Banned in the UK
Year of release: 1977
Writer: jenny Craven
Director: Arthur Davis
Unrated 92 mins. USA
Tagline: "See 1001 forbidden scenes never before filmed!! New! Different! Unusual!"
Distributed by: Derann

Plot:
Brutes and Savages is basically a social experiment, not dissimilar to the movie "Faces of Death". "Brutes and Savages" sees world explorer Arthur David explore deep in the jungles of Africa and South America with his crew. With the use of hidden camera footage this film documents the horrors they witnessed, with a mixture of both true footage and gruesome re-enactments.

Appraisal:
This is not a great Mondo film; it's filled with animal torture mixed with very bad effects looking at tribal rituals. "Brutes and Savages" is dire the only one good thing about it is the musical score. Mondo style full on pumping horror, well that's what I was told to expect, when I first saw this film I was shocked not at the amount of gore or how horrific the film was but how this bad knock off of Mondo Cane received any kind of status and attention and was anticipated and talked about even in school yards back in the day.

Brutes and Savages makes you wish that Arthur David hadn't taken a crew with hidden cameras to secretly film, you wish that he would have filmed the process of paint drying as it would have been a lot more entertaining!

In its defense, you do get that on the edge of your seat feeling, and anticipation although that's mainly waiting for the film to end. This is hands down the worst Mondo style film I have ever seen, lacking budget, talent and originality. The infamous crocodile attack in the film is laughable; there are some scenes of animal cruelty or killing, which just adds to make this one of the worst films on the list. Brutes and Savages was seized under section 3 of the 1959 Obscene Publications Act on VHS in the early 1980's before the implementation of the Video Recordings Act of 1984 in the UK. Brutes and Savages was only released on pre-cert VHS by Derann in 1980, the film is has not had a UK release on any other format since but is available in its unrated form in the US from Synapse films 2003 release.

The cut version of the film was released on VHS by Derann in 1980, so it's worth trying to track down a copy on the uncut film.

-Tony Newton

Cannibal

(DPP Section 3) Banned in the UK
Also known as "Last Cannibal World" and "The Last Survivor"
Year of release 1976
Writers: Tito Carpi and Gianfranco Clerici
Director: Ruggero Deodato
Unrated 82 mins. Italy
Tagline: "A stone-age world of horrors....ONLY ONE SURVIVED!"
Main cast: Massimo Foschi (Robert Harper), Me Me Lai (Pulan), Ivan Rassimov (Rolf), Sheik Razak Shikur (Charlie), Judy Rosly (Swan), Suleman (Native Chief).
Distributed by: Derann

Plot:
Cannibal is directed by Ruggero Deodato, who later directed "Cannibal Holocaust." In Deodato's first stab at the cannibal genre "Cannibal" a plane crash-lands in the jungle leaving the passengers stranded. When they stumble upon a group of cannibals devouring the remains of the bodies of their former associates they try desperately to repair the plane and leave the jungle before they suffer the same fate.

Appraisal:
As soon as I hear the word cannibal I think of Ruggero Deodato's classic Cannibal Holocaust, a film that will stay with me forever! Or at least memories of viewing the film for the first time at a young age. This film was made before Cannibal Holocaust and the film is laying the foundations to make his classic, but in truth that's all this film is!

This offering doesn't have the impact, the inventiveness, the shock horror factor and the love that came with the making of Cannibal Holocaust, which is a piece of modern art disguised as a film.

Cannibal is a great film; it's an adventure film that is very entertaining. The film is very similar to The Man From Deep River, which is not a bad thing. Overall the film is very good and does deliver; the animal cruelty is more toned down than Cannibal Holocaust. There are some great scenes in the film, which are thought provoking, it's well worth checking out!

This film contains lots of animal cruelty, which the primates would actually consume. This film sees these primates acting out the horrific and ritualistic life study. It's a good cannibal film but contains some very disturbing scenes one of which is the woman who bites on the umbilical cord of her newborn child and continues to toss it to an alligator. This is as disturbing as most cannibal films, the effects aren't too bad nor is the splicing of video.

Cannibal was seized under section 3 of the 1959 Obscene Publications Act on VHS in the early 1980's before the implementation of the Video Recordings Act of 1984 in the UK.

Cannibal was only released on pre-cert VHS by Canon in 1981, although this was the cut version of the film that was seized, the film is available in the UK with an 18 rating with cuts made by the BBFC.

-Tony Newton

Cannibals

(DPP Section 3) Banned in the UK
Also known as "Mondo Cannibale" and "White Cannibal Queen".
Year of release: 1980
Writer: Jesús Franco
Director: Jesús Franco and Franco Prosperi
Unrated 90 mins. Spain, Italy, France
Tagline: "Where the natives are pleased to meat you!"
Main cast: Al Cliver (Jeremy Taylor), Sabrina Siani (Lana), Jerome Foulon (Safari member), Lina Romay (Ana), Shirley Knight (Barbara Shelton), Anouchka (Lana as a child).
Distributed by: Cinehollywood

Plot:
Cannibals sees Dr. Jeremy Taylor travel to the Amazon with his wife and daughter, when his wife is captured and devoured by a cannibal tribe and his daughter is taken Dr. Taylor barely makes it out alive. Some years later Dr. Taylor returns to the Amazon only to discover that his long lost daughter is now Queen to the cannibal tribe!

Appraisal:
A father missing a limb returns to the jungle with help in tow to rescue his daughter the white queen from a cannibal tribe. This film has bad dubbing, even the good old countryside in Spain, as mentioned some of the same sets and even footage is from "Cannibal Terror" which was made alongside this film. This film has an all out funky soundtrack and for some strange reason even with bad editing, dubbing and effects (the pale cannibals) this is an enjoyable watch and a big plus to this film is the welcome lack of animal cruelty.

"Cannibals" gets a bad rap for its poor acting and bad effects but the idea at least seems okay. "Cannibals" isn't anywhere near the best cannibal film featured!, but for me it's not the worst either, though a lot of people would disagree with me there but, in my defense, I do have a soft spot for Jess Franco movies!

Franco's Eurocine effort is an okay film!, I like the idea here of a family being attacked, the wife murdered and during their escape the daughter gets captured by the cannibals, that in itself is a very suspenseful horror movie.

The whole film could have been executed better, but not as bad as everyone makes out at all!

Cannibals was seized under section 3 of the 1959 Obscene Publications Act on VHS in the early 1980's before the implementation of the Video Recordings Act of 1984 in the UK.

Cannibals was released on pre-cert VHS by Cinehollywood and EVC in 1981, although this was the cut version of the film that was seized, the film is available in the UK with an 18 rating uncut.

-Tony Newton

The Chant of Jimmie Blacksmith

(DPP Section 3) Banned in the UK
Year of release: 1978
Writer: Fred Schepisi and Thomas Keneally
Director: Fred Schepisi
X rated 120 mins. Australia
Tagline: "The chant of Jimmie Blacksmith is the chant of the underdog."
Main cast: "Tommy Lewis (Jimmie Blacksmith), Freddy Reynolds (Mort Blacksmith), Ray Barrett (Farrell), Jack Thompson (Rev. Neville), Angela Punch McGregor (Gilda Marshall), Steve Dodds (Tabidgi).
Distributed by: Walton Video

Plot:
The Chant of Jimmy Blacksmith is set in the 1900's and follows the plight of a mixed race Aboriginal heritage man (Jimmie) who decides to take revenge into his own hands after suffering years of injustices at the hands of white farmers after attempting to integrate into their community. "The Chant of Jimmie Blacksmith" is based on the serial killer "Jimmy Governor."

Appraisal:
The chant of Jimmie Blacksmith is a snap shot into Australia and the problems encountered by Aboriginal heritage people in society. This film covers racism but it has a twist that is rather disturbing. This film is a race drama with strong violence, it's a classic film that doesn't get enough exposure. The Chant of Jimmy Blacksmith is not a horror film it's more of a political race drama.

This film is shot well and the actors - especially Tommy Lewis - are all trying their best. This film is more for fans of "10 Years a Slave" than horror!

The Chant Of Jimmie Blacksmith was seized under section 3 of the 1959 Obscene Publications Act on VHS in the early 1980's before the implementation of the Video Recordings Act of 1984 in the UK.

The Chant Of Jimmie Blacksmith was released on pre-cert VHS by Walton in 1982 and Odyssey in 1984, although this was the cut version of the film that was seized, the film is available in the UK with an 18 rating uncut.

-Tony Newton

Have you ever wanted to know what it would look like if Merchant/Ivory made a revenge film? Then this is the movie for you. It's probably the most beautifully shot of the Video Nasties, but that doesn't make it any less hard to watch.

-Mark Miller   Seraphim Films

The Chant of Jimmy Blacksmith is another one of those films that quite frankly shows exactly how ridiculous the video nasties scare was. Not because the film is tame, because it's not... Not because the film is a genre film that may offend, because it's not and where it is offensive it's because it shows a world that should offend anyone too the core, particularly because it's a world that has its feet firmly planted in reality. The Chant of Jimmy Blacksmith follows the titular character, Jimmy Blacksmith, a half-caste Aboriginal brought up by a deeply religious white family in the late 1800's and his existence is not made easy by his being neither one race nor the other. On the one hand he identifies with his Aboriginal roots, he hangs out with them and spends time learning the old ways of hunting and tradition. But the community is soon seen to be a deeply scarred one. Blighted by poverty, sickness of sexual and other diseases brought to the country and stricken with chronic alcohol abuse amongst its people, the community is barely functional being subjugated not only by the white landowners but also by their inability to cope with the vices that have been introduced to them.

Then there are the colonists - aka the white folks. The casual racism on display is so matter of fact, done without thought, so instinctive to the white community that looking at from with today's point of view is deeply uncomfortable. The black community is literally regarded as sub human, no more than animals that can talk and do things that they are told to. Jimmy straddles the two communities, never belonging entirely to either and he struggles to find his feet wherever he is. As Jimmy grows up the schism of what's expected of him as a half white and how he's perceived and received because of his black blood widens.

He joins the police but faced with the injustices he sees and indeed commits against his fellow Aboriginals he ends up taking on manual work. He teaches himself fence laying, reading up on the materials and techniques, and he becomes remarkably good at the job but even after doing an impressive job for several clients he's on each occasion short changed by the landowners who make up any excuse not to fully pay him. His work also brings him into conflict with his tribe who take all his hard earned money for the community and the resentment on Jimmy's face is palpable.

Understandably he feels trapped, he can't save his money for making a better life and when he is earning he's being screwed over by the men he works for. When Jimmy ends up with a white girl, a local floosy who seems nice enough but not exactly picky, he finds himself a father to be. Building a house for them both and desperately trying to keep his pregnant wife fed he has a devastating blow when the baby turns out not to be his. Despite the ridicule from the white community he steps up and looks after his wife and the child until the local white families begin to humiliate him in front of his wife. This final straw makes Jimmy snap and with his friend he visits them to demand an apology. But things turn bad when the lady of the house is unrepentantly rude to him and Jimmy buries an axe in her shoulder. In a fit of insanity he goes on to kill all the women and children in the house with one exception.

Now beyond the point of no return Jimmy goes on the run but decides to revisits those who messed with him to settle some old debts and the rampage of murder that follows is as tragic as it is abhorrent.

Based on the true story of Jimmy Governor, an outlaw, or rather bushranger, of the Australian outback in the opening years of the 1900's Jimmy Blacksmith does take some liberties with the story. The basis of Governor's history, his struggles with the normalised racism and a rough outline of his life are what are taken forward into the story of Jimmy Blacksmith. It's not really historically accurate in short but seems intended to carry the social baggage of the real story and present that plight of the native Australians in shocking but familiar terms. Governor has some status as legend in Aboriginal culture. I'm only partially familiar with it so I can't state how much but the general consensus seems to be that although his deeds were not so much condoned, they were understood, even sympathised with. An existing member of the family he killed has even gone so far as to publicly forgive him even blaming her relatives poor behaviour towards Jimmy for being integral to the events.

The chant of Jimmy Blacksmith is commendable to a high degree in that it does have the decency to change the name of the lead character, it's not trying to deceive as so many films have done by using a 'true story' it's trying to focus on aspects of that story and covey a specific message, a message of the roots of Governors evil deeds.

Jimmy is a tricky character to pin down. In some ways he represents the native community of Australia but he's also part of the new community to some extent. It's probably more accurate to say Jimmy Blacksmith is representative of the collision of these communities; he's the tectonic fault line at which these two worlds strain against each other. He's a character that is lovingly built up in the first part of this movie as being a hard working, smart and conscientious young man who is then torn down by circumstances that spiral out of control.

It's this second, the moment when things turn tragic for all involved that Jimmy is transformed from being a decent man into reflecting the hatred and abuse of his black family back at the white community. But true to life he's not so simple a creature as to be able to describe him as blowback. His behaviour towards the black community is often as bad as the white community that he strives to be a part of. As a police officer he assaults several people with little apparent guilt, he even treats his family and friends abruptly when they offer up a protective totem because of his marriage to a white woman. Jimmy, like his real life counterpart Governor doesn't identify either way racially. He's never been integrated fully either way so like Governor he regards himself as neither, or both as historian Henry Reynolds points out...

"He did not like to be called a black fellow. He declared himself a mestizo, as much white as black."

Jimmy as a child is part of those ways, at least as much as he can be with his adoptive white father not approving, as a man he's more aligned with the ways of the white community. It's not when they reject *him*, it's when they reject his wife that he breaks, it's the insult to the only family he is truly, completely part of that tips his hand.

His personal struggle with his duality shows most prominently during his time on the run where he continues to struggle with the two worlds he straddles. He seems bothered by his brother's behaviour when leaving his colleagues behind, he protests loudly at the sacred site but he shows a high degree of competence in the old bush crafts and is able to survive quite comfortably where most white folk, including his hostage, struggle.

The last scene has a very chilling line, a line that says a lot about 'justice' back in those days and is delivered as Jimmy sits in a cell awaiting his fate. Before I tell you it though it's worth a brief discussion of the character of the butcher/executioner.... the guy does both for a living. He's very staid, very clinical about his discussion of his trade. The are several scenes in the film where he's being harassed by a journalist for information and a story on what will happen with Blacksmith when he gets to the gallows. The butcher is very calm and detached about the questions and the process though betrays a certain underlying emotion when forced to think about it. He's very much a professional about his grim task and has probably seen, or rather participated in the deaths of more men than we'll know. But it's when we hear his assessment of Jimmy Blacksmith, that line of dialogue 'His neck muscles appear to be more developed than the average black', I start to wander how many he strung up, and how many truly deserved it.

But it's surprisingly not all doom and gloom in this film. The Chant of Jimmy Blacksmith is set at a time when Australia was about to go through federation. It was a massive time of change and despite the hideous racism towards the native populace by many of the characters there are sparks of not only the various states and territories uniting, becoming one, but that maybe the races were starting to move closer together.

They're small things but they're there. As Australia becomes one and the generation of white settlers begin to identify as Australians there seems to be some connection and one less difference between the races. It's a little ray of hope in an often-bleak world.

The Chant of Jimmy Blacksmith is a beautiful film in all regards. The cinematography is gorgeous, the soundtrack with its use of Aboriginal instruments weaves together western and native Australian sounds. It's a beautiful musical parallel of Jimmy himself with a foot in both worlds. The story is well adapted from the original true story to have purpose and to extract the still relevant lessons of the time. Speaking of which this is one of the most remarkable things about this film. As Roger Ebert points out about this film it is a film that presents the world it portrays pretty much as it was. It doesn't try to shift the characters into a modern moral framework, the events speak for themselves. It's really us the audience that put these things into a modern context. Jimmy himself is an ambiguous character, a good man turned very bad and one who barely redeems his hideous action...but he's a sympathetic character, we can't hate him because we've taken the journey with him, seen the struggle he's gone through and seen what it took to turn him. This thing, this insight is what is most important about the film. Not its historical accuracy or otherwise, not whether Jimmy is a hero or a murderer, it's the realisation that a good person can be turned very bad by injustice in society, by being regarded as lesser for such trivial reasons as their heritage or sexuality/sex. Jimmy Blacksmith is the consequence of injustice and prejudice; the Chant of Jimmy Blacksmith shows us the origins of those consequences.

To know where we are, we must begin by knowing where we came from. (Roger Ebert on Jimmy Blacksmith) http://www.rogerebert.com/reviews/the-chant-of-jimmie-blacksmith-1981

-Glenn Criddle   Writer/Critic.

The Child

(DPP Section 3) Banned in the UK
Year of release: 1977
Writer: Ralph Lucas
Director: Robert Voskanian
R rated 82 mins. USA
Tagline: "Let's play hide and go kill…!"
Main cast: Laurel Barnett (Alicanne Del Mar), Rosalie Cole (Rosalie Nordon), Frank Janson (Nordon), Richard Hanners (Len Nordon), Ruth Ballan (Mrs. Whitfield), Slosson Bing Jong (Gardener).
Distributed by: VRO Video Network

Plot:
The Child is set in rural California and follows Rosalie, a young who possess telekinetic abilities and is hell bent on revenge for the death of her mother. New nanny Alicianne intends to create some stability for the young and tortured soul but she gets more than she bargained for when she attempts to help Rosalie!

Appraisal:
The Child is a mash-up of the zombie genre; it's atmospheric with plenty of horror and gore.

The Child is a great little known horror film made on a very low budget. The idea alone is fascinating, the effects and budget are cheap but the films actors are all on fine form if not a little annoying at times, I can't tell if they are good actors hamming it up in which it comes across on screen, or actually bad. The director does a great job in creating great atmospheric effects; all this saves the film, making it a decent horror/thriller.

The Child is a very low budget horror film that is all over the place editing and continuity wise, the low budget effects can be annoying at times. It's another bizarre horror, this 1977 horror film is a strange one, the idea sounds better than the actual film we see here, having said that if you can deal with the annoying girl, and the low budget there is some entertainment to be had here.

The scene with the scarecrow and carved pumpkin are very entertaining. The girl has strange psychic powers, promising to avenge her mother's death at her graveside and the ability to control objects including corpses, I love the ideas here and would not be surprised if we get a remake a full on zombie horror style film.

The Child was seized under section 3 of the 1959 Obscene Publications Act on VHS in the early 1980's before the implementation of the Video Recordings Act of 1984 in the UK.

The Child was released on pre-cert VHS by VRO Video Network in 1981. This was the uncut version of the film that was seized. The film is available in the UK with an 18 rating uncut.

-Tony Newton

Christmas Evil

(DPP Section 3) Banned in the UK
Year of release: 1980
Writer: Lewis Jackson
Director: Lewis Jackson
R rated 100 mins. USA
Tagline: "He'll sleigh you."
Main cast: Brandon Maggart (Harry Stadling), Jeffrey DeMunn (Philip Stadling), Dianne Hull (Jackie Stadling), Andy Fenwick (Dennis Stadling), Brain Neville (Marc Stadling), Joe Jamrog (Frank Stoller).
Distributed by: Iver Film Services

Plot:
When Harry discovers that Santa isn't real (Sorry folks!) and is traumatized by something he witnesses as a child he begins his obsession with Christmas, so much so that he makes his own rules for his very own naughty or nice list. This psycho dresses as Santa Claus himself and slashes his way through the naughty list! You'd better watch out!

Appraisal:
Christmas Evil will alter your perception of Santa Claus forever!
Christmas Evil is definitely one of the better Christmas slasher films out there. This film has a tongue in cheek comedy-esque feel to it but all this said the film is a watchable and enjoyable experience, one to watch this holiday season! Anyone working at a toy company probably would go mad, this man did! I love the fact that the killer wears a Santa Claus outfit, I think that is brilliant, taking an iconic trustworthy and much loved figure and outing an axe straight through it, literally.

Brandon Maggart does an outstanding job as Harry the psycho who has had enough, he has elements of the killer from "Don't go in the House" mixed with Norman Bates in his character. Welcome to the darker side of Christmas! This is a holiday you won't forget! This is one of the films you have to watch every Holiday season! This wasn't the first horror to cash in on the Christmas season "Black Christmas" and "Silent Night, Deadly Night" did quite a good job. I love the fact that the killer isn't completely evil and works well with the naughty or nice message throughout the film. Please be good for goodness sake! Although the film has a black comedy feel, it does seem to still work and does offer entertainment, well worth a watch this holiday season.

Christmas Evil was seized under section 3 of the 1959 Obscene Publications Act on VHS in the early 1980's before the implementation of the Video Recordings Act of 1984 in the UK.

Christmas Evil was released on pre-cert VHS by Iver Film Services in 1982. This was the uncut version of the film that was seized - the film is available in the UK with an 18 rating uncut.

-Tony Newton

A Clockwork Orange

(Withdrawn by Stanley Kubrick in 1973)
Year of release: 1971
Writers: Stanley Kubrick and Anthony Burgess
Director: Stanley Kubrick
Rated: X rated
Tagline: "Being the adventures of a young man…who couldn't resist pretty girls…or a bit of the old ultra-violence…went to jail, was re-conditioned…and came out a different young man…or was he?"
Main Cast: Malcolm McDowell (Alex), Patrick Magee (Mr. Alexander), Michael Bates (Chief Guard), Warren Clarke (Dim), John Clive (Stage actor), Adrienne Corri (Mrs. Alexander).
Distributed by: Warner Brothers

Plot:
A Clockwork Orange is an adaption from Anthony Burgess's novel about a totalitarian future in which Alex a classical music obsessed thug and gang leader is subjected to behaviour modification therapy after performing ultra violent and sexual attacks with his gang of droogs.

Appraisal:
Stanley Kubrick's A Clockwork Orange see's Malcolm McDowell play a bully and a rapist who the authorities try to get to see the error of his ways with the clockwork orange treatment. Apart from the disturbing rape scene and beating a tramp up this film isn't that shocking.. It's an amazing film but not as shocking as it was deemed to be at the time, for me the worse bit is when Malcolm McDowell's eyes are fixed open with metal rods, that really is disturbing. The unusual use of dialogue does work within the film and to be honest this is an all round great piece of celluloid history that you can easily watch over again and again. It doesn't feel dated in anyway and does hold up to the test of time, there are many stories why this film wasn't available for home viewing in the UK for so long, Was the film banned? Was it on the nasty list? As well of many stories centering around Kubrick himself, ironically it was Stanley Kubrick himself who actually banned this film here in the UK.

A Clockwork Orange was given an X certificate for the film to be viewed at cinemas in the UK but this was short lived when Stanley Kubrick received a threatening note, threatening his own family saying that violence was going to happen to his family, after this Stanley Kubrick withdrew this film. Everyone at the time assumed the British Board of Censors withdrew the film, but this was Kubrick's doing, which was very strange that he only withdrew the film from the UK itself. The films infamous tramp scene where they literally beat a tramp to death kicks this poor defenseless man is a very shocking scene, but for me does not even match the shocking rape scene where they are singing aloud to Gene Kelly's singing in the rain, Gene Kelly is reported to be appalled at this song being used in the way it was!

A Clockwork Orange was not allowed to be shown in the UK until after Stanley Kubrick's death in 1999. The film was re-submitted to the BBFC in 1999 and received an 18 rating without any cuts made to the film.

A Pure cult classic; now got make some eggy-weggies, crank up some Beethoven, while hunting for an old VHS copy of the film!

-Tony Newton

"Disturbed though we were by the first half of the film, which is basically a statement of some of the problems of violence, we were, nonetheless, satisfied by the end of the film that it could not be accused of exploitation: quite the contrary, it is a valuable contribution to the whole debate about violence".

- Stephen Murphy, BBFC's Secretary in 1971,

This wasn't so much a favourite of mine, but a lot of naked female flesh is plentiful enough for someone about to enter their teenage years and to stay in ones memory.

Watching the movie again you can see why it was banned when it was, but by today's standards, it's obviously very dated. But the blended mix of Kubrick's stylistic shots/cinematography, joyous classical music, and, crazy characters do make this movie unique in many ways.

Eagle-eyed viewers should also spot the vinyl soundtrack for Kubrick's sci-fi movie '2001' when the lead character is at the record store before his threesome with 2 female customers.

-Shaun Troke   Filmmaker.

I first saw *A Clockwork Orange* my sophomore year in college. Of course, I had known about the film for years, but was too terrified to watch it. I'd heard it was an incredible, groundbreaking film, daring and innovative. I'd also heard it was filled with some of the most disturbing scenes of violence ever filmed.

I could remember the first time I encountered *A Clockwork Orange*. When I was a little girl, I saw the poster on the wall in a video store. Back before Netflix, the only way to watch movies at home when we wanted to was to take a trip to the store and rent VHS cassettes. It was a much simpler time. I hid behind my mother and pretended not to be afraid of the horror movie posters that covered the walls. *Happy Birthday To Me, My Bloody Valentine, April Fools Day*--most of which I later realized were not nearly as scary as they look when you're a child. But there was one that stayed with me. The poster was terrifying and beautiful. A young man with a prominent eyelash under one eye and a thin, shiny blade.

A Clock Orange tells the story of Alex, who was according to the tagline, "a young man whose principal interests are rape, ultra violence and Beethoven." When I was old enough to read, the poster scared me even more.

"What's that movie about?" I asked my dad.

"It's about a guy who's really bad. And when they catch him, they try to program him to be good. Only it doesn't go so well. It's a scary movie, not for kids. But it's a really good movie."

My whole life, I was afraid to watch *A Clockwork Orange*, and as I sat in my dorm room while my roommate put in into the VHS player, I was still afraid to watch it.

Malcolm McDowell was handsome and charismatic, disturbingly so for a character who does nothing but physically and sexually assault people. Oh, and listen to Beethoven.

Alex was the narrator. Everything was coming from his perspective, including the violence. And he thought the violence was fun. As I watched, I realized that the violence was disturbing, not because it was so graphic, but because of the way it was presented. Alex thinks violence is funny, and when he shows it to the audience, they want to laugh.

So I watched it. I watched it again and again. During the day, between classes, and before I went to bed. It was funny and disturbing and brilliant, and every time I watched it, I saw something new.

A Clockwork Orange was not banned in the UK in the traditional sense. Stanley Kubrick, the director had it pulled in the UK and did not allow it to be shown. I was living in London in 1999 when Stanley Kubrick passed away. I got to see it when it was shown in the theater in the UK for the very first time.

-Rachel Grubb   Actress.

Communion

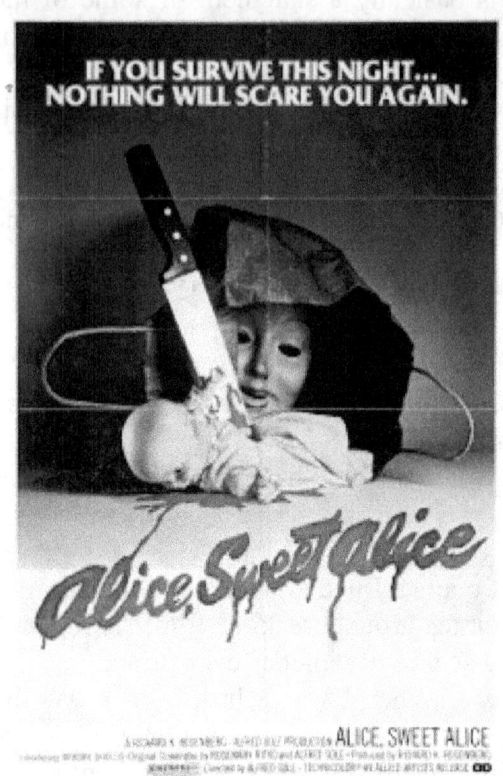

(DPP Section 3) Banned in the UK
Also known as "Alice Sweet Alice", "Holy Terror".
Year of release: 1976
Writers: Rosemary Rivto and Alfred Sole
Director: Alfred Sole
R rated 108 mins. USA
Tagline: "If you survive the night….nothing will scare you again."
Main cast: Linda Miller (Catherine Spages), Mildred Clinton (Mrs. Tredoni), Paul E. Sheppard (Alice Spages), Niles McMaster (Dom Spages), Jane Lowry (Aunt Annie DeLorenze), Rudolph Willrich (Father Tom).
Distributed by: VCL

Plot:
Communion is set in a church in 1961, Alice lives in the shadow of her younger sister Karen, so when Karen is found murdered before her first communion fingers being pointing at Alice. As the death toll rises, a thirst for blood and inventive methods of brutal murder continue but is sweet Alice really the culprit?

Appraisal:
The killer is strangely dressed in a yellow rain Mac complete with mask, which is not dissimilar to the ones used in the film "The Purge". The mask alone brings a certain eeriness to film. Communion is an unsettling horror film featuring a young Brooke Shields. The film features a church communion and a very young girl as the killer, which is obviously the reason it was banned. This film gets away with feeling dated as it is set in the early 1960's, and stands out as a great piece of horror cinema.

This is an all-round gem of a movie, this film scared the shit out of me as a kid, I had nightmares about the freaky masked killer in a yellow raincoat, this is a very disturbing film, which pays homage to Italian giallo films. The film is shot very well; the whole production oozes an eerie atmosphere and is a suspenseful slasher/horror thriller offering. In my eyes a very underrated film which delivers the goods and contains everything that a true horror film should have.

This film doesn't seem dated and does a great job holding its own against today's slasher horror offerings. The musical score works very well and only enhances your enjoyment of the film, any film for me that has an element of religion in this case Catholicism adds that extra creepiness to it. One of my favorite scenes from the film has to be the scene with the very creepy landlord who gets his comeuppance! For anyone who hasn't seen Communion it is a must watch for fans of the slasher genre, giallo and horror films in general.

Communion was seized under section 3 of the 1959 Obscene Publications Act on VHS in the early 1980's before the implementation of the Video Recordings Act of 1984 in the UK.

Communion was released on pre-cert VHS by VCL in 1982, this was the uncut version of the film that was seized, the film is available in the UK with an 18 rating uncut as of 2014.

-Tony Newton

Alice, Sweet Alice is an immortal feature that transcends time. It is just as meaningful today as it was upon its initial theatrical exhibition in 1976. But when making the film, director Alfred Sole had no expectation that Alice would exhibit the staying power it has demonstrated in the years since its release. "I had no idea that it would become a cult classic, I am actually quite surprised by it," remarked Sole when we reached out to him regarding the picture's longevity and status as a cult classic.

In addition to its staying power and status as a timeless cult classic, the film is noteworthy for being very much like an American-made giallo. All the key components of a giallo are there: At its core, Alice, Sweet Alice is a murder mystery that features an unseen killer who is ultimately revealed to be the last person the audience would suspect.

In discussing the film with Sole in the past, he has revealed to me that he didn't set out to make a giallo but in spite of that, the finished product is highly reminiscent of the gialli of the late '60s and early '70s. Sole attributes some of that resemblance to his fondness for the 1973 giallo-esque thriller Don't Look Now.

Though Alice, Sweet Alice was once categorized as a Video Nasty; it was not Sole's first battle over censorship. He was previously charged in the United States for transporting pornographic material over state lines due to his involvement with the X-rated title, Deep Sleep. Beyond the legal woes Deep Sleep caused, Sole was also excommunicated from the Catholic Church for being at the helm of that film.

It is somewhat curious that Alice, Sweet Alice made the Video Nasty list because it is far from graphic when compared to many of its counterparts and the body count of the film is substantially lower than what one might expect from a horror picture. Sole's reputation as a director of X-rated cinema may very well have played a role in Alice Sweet Alice being classified as a Video Nasty.

Aside from everything else, the film also raised eyebrows over the antics that took place during its production. In fact, actress Linda Miller—who plays Catherine Spages—slit her wrists on set. In the years since the film's release, Sole has been particularly outspoken about what a nightmare Miller was to work with.

When all is said and done, Alice Sweet Alice is a classic horror picture that has had a lasting impact on several generations of filmmakers and fans of genre film, alike. It stands as one of my personal favorites and is a title that I enjoy more every time I watch it. I discover something new to love about Alice, Sweet Alice every time I revisit it.

-Tyler Doupe´ Managing Editor at wickedhorror.com

Dawn of the Mummy

(DPP Section 3) Banned in the UK
Year of release: 1981
Writer: Daria Price and Ronald Dobrin
Director: Frank Agrama
Unrated 93 mins. USA, Egypt, Italy
Tagline: "They came from the dead…to feast on the living."
Main cast: Brenda Siemer Scheider (Lisa), Barry Sattels (Bill), George Peck (Rick), John Salvo (Gary), Ibrahim Khan (Hamid), Joan Levy (Jenny).
Distributed by: VideoSpace

Plot:
This is a classic Mummy horror film offering from the early 80s. In "Dawn of the Mummy" a group of fashion models and their photographic crew search the desert for the perfect setting for a photo shoot. When they happen upon an ancient tomb and hold the photo shoot a curse is aroused. The Mummy of the tomb is brought back to life along with its slaves who have a craving for human flesh!

Appraisal:
Director Frank Agrama's Dawn of the Mummy was made for around $500.000 you have to wonder what the money was spent on as the production is pretty poor and with funds equivalent to that today you would expect a Blumhouse production horror film, I can only assume the money is hidden in a sarcophagus somewhere! This feels like a complete rip off from Dawn of the Dead mixed with the cult classic The Mummy but without good actors or a killer plot, this is a campy horror film, I love Zombie films and anything to do with Mummies as much as the production is bad I kind of like this film, the sheer craziness of it the b-style horror is funny as hell you literally laugh out loud at some of the scenes, this film really introduced me to the kind of B-style schlocky style of films and that realization that you could get enjoyment from a film that wasn't technically perfect!

Dawn of the Mummy was shot in Egypt and features elements of gore and horror throughout. Models are hunted down by mummies, though there is surely not enough flesh to feast on, the film is very likable as daft as it may seem. The effects aren't great but the gore is the main saving grace of this film.

I do remember being scared watching this flick as a kid, my parents had this on VHS and I caught this when I was very really young, it's crazy the impact even the worst horror films can have on you at a young age, and when you are that young replaying the images on screen again and again every time you close your eyes in the dark. As crazy and as bad as this film is I have a secret soft spot for it, just for those early memories alone and the introduction to B-style cinema! Dawn of the Mummy was seized under section 3 of the 1959 Obscene Publications Act on VHS in the early 1980's before the implementation of the Video Recordings Act of 1984 in the UK. Dawn of the Mummy was released on pre-cert VHS by VideoSpace in 1983, this was the uncut version of the film that was seized, the film was re-submitted the BBFC in 1987 and was passed 18 with cuts, the film is now available in the UK with an 18 rating fully uncut.

-Tony Newton

Dead Kids

(DPP Section 3) Banned in the UK
Also known as "Strange Behavior", "Human Experiments", "Small Town Massacre".
Year of release: 1981
Writers: Bill Condon and Michael Laughlin
Director: Michael Laughlin
R rated 99 mins. (DVD) Australia, USA, New Zealand
Tagline: "Cuts up parts other movies just dislocate."
Main cast: Michael Murphy (John Brady), Louise Fletcher (Barbara Moorehead), Dan Shor (Pete Brady), Fiona Lewis (Gwen Parkinson), Arthur Dignam (Dr. Le Sange), Dey Young (Caroline).
Distributed by: Iver Film Services

Plot:
John Brady is struggling to come to terms with the suspicious death of his wife some years earlier. John works as the Chief of Police and when teenagers are found murdered his investigations find that the towns teenagers are the subjects of strange experiments, which have resulted in their transformation into psycho killers!

Appraisal:
Dead Kids directed by Michael Laughlin who later went on to direct 1983 film "Strange Invaders" is, in my eyes a very underrated director. After Strange Invaders he only directed one other feature in 1985 "Mesmerized" which starred Jodie Foster and John Lithgow. I love Dead Kids this film was always in my VCR player, it was one of those early 1980's stalk and slash films that I used to re-watch and re-watch as a teenager. The soundtrack by Tangerine Dreams is awesome, who doesn't like Tangerine Dream? Dead Kids is pure 1980's nostalgia, only a fucked up slice of 80's America. This clever little slasher does the job perfectly, I love its cheesiness, its tacky charm, I love the feel it has, its Halloween-esque vibe mixed with Scooby Doo feel to it. Dead Kids is a rare treat, something a bit different from the usual 80's slashers doing the rounds which is refreshing, not all 80's stalk and slash films feature dancing and bizarre fancy dress scenes.

Long live the slashers!

The soundtrack by "Tangerine Dream" enhances the film and it suits the picture well. It's is a classic, original horror and this film is a unique take on the slasher genre. This is an underrated film, it has a comedic element to it which works well and, in my opinion, "Dead Kids" should be up there amongst other 80's horror classics.

Dead Kids was seized under section 3 of the 1959 Obscene Publications Act on VHS in the early 1980's before the implementation of the Video Recordings Act of 1984 in the UK.

Dead Kids was initially released on pre-cert VHS by Iver Film Services in 1981, this was the uncut version of the film that was seized, the film was re-submitted the BBFC in 1986 and was passed 18 uncut, the film is now available in the UK with an 18 rating with cuts.

-Tony Newton

Death Weekend

(DPP Section 3) Banned in the UK
Also known as "The House by the Lake" and "Weekend Savage".
Year of release: 1976
Writer: William Fruet
Director: William Fruet
R rated 87 mins. Canada
Tagline: "They were going to rape her one by one. She was going to kill them…one by one."
Main cast: Brenda Vaccaro (Diane), Don Stroud (Lep), Chuck Shamata (Harry), Richard Ayres (Runt), Kyle Edwards (Frankie), Don Granberry (Stanley).
Distributed by: Vampix (Video Media)

Plot:
From the director of "Spasms" comes Death Weekend, which is a Canadian rape-revenge movie. Rich playboy Harry arranges a date with model Diane, they're almost run off the road by a gang of psycho biker yobs and when the yobs follow them back to Harry's home they terrorize the couple until the gang begin to realize that they have messed with wrong girl!

Appraisal:
This 1970's film is a rape revenge horror/thriller obviously inspired by the success of Straw Dogs, the film is very similar but does not live up to expectations after watching Straw Dogs, it just lacks a little something. This sleazy offering is a cult flick and a all-round good film, it is a bit slow to begin with but does pick up pace, The film's main star Don Stroud is on great form here. Death Weekend does stand out as a great Canadian movie and definitely the best film of director William Fruet's career. The atmosphere is created well here and the film is based on true events, which actually occurred in Canada.

Director William Fruet's Canadian offering is a classic home invasion thriller, which features a very cool car chase among some brutal visuals with local douchebags - just as a young couple are about to go on to an idyllic retreat. The local townsfolk seek revenge and begin to torture the couple both mentally and physically. This is a very good thriller along the lines of Straw Dogs, and touches on similar themes as rape revenge though is more of a home invasion flick, which features abuse. The film obviously tried to capitalize on Wes Craven's The Last House on the Left as well, but is something very different. A suspenseful little drama flick well worth a watch, it does come over a little dated though but is still a great little film.

Death Weekend was seized under section 3 of the 1959 Obscene Publications Act on VHS in the early 1980's before the implementation of the Video Recordings Act of 1984 in the UK.

Death Weekend was initially released on pre-cert VHS by Vampix in 1982, this was the uncut version of the film that was seized, prior to this the film was cut by the BBFC for its 1976 theatrical release, the film has not had a UK release on any other format since but is available in its unrated form in the US.

-Tony Newton

Death Wish

(Withdrawn)1987-2000
Also known as: "The Sidewalk Vigilante"
Year of release: 1974
Writer: Brian Garfield and Wendell Mayes
Director: Michael Winner
Rated: R rated
Tagline: "Vigilante, city style – judge, jury and executioner
Main Cast: Charles Bronson (Paul Kersey), Hope Lange (Joanna Kersey), Vincent Gardenia (Frank Ochoa), Steven Keats (Jack Toby), William Redfield (Sam Kreutzer), Stuart Margolin (Aimes Jainchill).
Distributed by: CIC

Plot:
The story of a young man seeking revenge after his family are brutally raped and attacked.
Appraisal:

Easily Michael Winner's best film! Death Wish is a vigilante cult classic. Charles Bronson as Paul Kersey is on fire; no one else could have played the role as well as Bronson – the one-man vigilante killing machine who outwits with both brains and brawn!

You feel for Paul Kersey and route for him all the way throughout the film. I find myself cheering at the screen as he gets revenge on these evil thugs. "Death Wish" is one of the most amazing vigilante films ever made, if not *the* best. This film sparked controversy over the rape scene and use of language throughout the film, Bronson's screen presence is outstanding, he simply owns every frame, even though Bronson has very little lines of dialogue within the film.

The theatrical release of the 1974 film was passed uncut with an X rating. The VHS was released in 1981 due to the fact that there were no rating systems in place at the time of release, the 1981 version was the exact same version as the cinema release in 1987 when "Death Wish" was submitted to the BBFC for certification the BBFC would not allow the uncut version to pass at a standard 18 certificate and thus being withdrawn from distribution. The only way you could get hold of "Death Wish" for 13 years was to get hold of an early pre-cert copy of the film. In 2000 a version was released with the rape scene cut. In 2006 the film was finally released uncut.

Death Wish was a representation of what was actually happening in the US at the time, crime levels were very high, Just a shame Charles Bronson wasn't actually there kicking some ass!

Death Wish was finally given an 18 rating and released fully uncut for its DVD release in 2006 by the BBFC.

-Tony Newton

Death Wish is probably my favorite movie. It has it all – Bronson out for vengeance! It doesn't get any better. I love the entire series. I don't care what would people say, but part 3 is a masterpiece! Even Death Wish V has its values – I can bet that Jack Nicholson stole Michael Parks' performance from this movie for his character in The Departed. Serbian title of the movie is "Paul Kersey doesn't forgive". Just love it. But this is not about Death Wish…

I was making a movie and had an honor of having a living legend as a star of my little film. Franco Nero! I was so excited to have him play badass character that fights evil mermaid. One night we were shooting a part of finale where Franco is on a boat and mermaid is attacking him. It was a stormy night, big waves, it was very difficult. So I was standing on the pier, giving directions, and Franco was on the boat, five meters away, on a restless sea, and he yelled something like "We did it first!" I was like "What is he talking about?" He pointed finger to my chest and said "Our movie was before Bronson's". I realized I have "Death Wish 3" t-shirt and that he is referring to that. He said "Check it out, it is called IL CITTADINO SI RIBELLA!" As soon as we wrapped the film, I looked for that film, and when I found out it was one of Nero Castellari's movies, I immediately ordered the DVD.

STREET LAW (which is the US title) is indeed the Italian version of Death Wish that was made before Death Wish. Although it was released on the same year, Street Law was first out. It is a story about an ordinary citizen that goes against criminals after he realizes that police cannot protect him, nor society. In the middle of crime wave, with some scenes based on the actual events from that period, here comes angry Franco Nero who goes after mafia. He is just a regular guy, he don't have a real chance. He's not American hero Bronson, so his attempts are filled with failure. He gets beaten up, dragged through mud, but eventually he explodes and kills them all. Amazing cinematography, with some of the best visual solutions by Enzo G. Castellari. Castellari always had fantastic camera work in his movies, especially when you watch those movies now – it looks so modern – but Street Law has probably the best shots he ever made. Franco is absolutely fantastic, and does a lot of physical action and also some real drama. There is a mandatory slow motion shot of Franco running toward camera. Also, there is a long fall down some sand hill in a mine or something. Franco told me he did it himself, without using a double. Amazing! The song "Goodbye my friend" is totally mesmerizing, and I still have it in my head. Italo-crime at its best! The narrative is not as strong as all the other aspects of the movie, but still very enjoyable and good movie in general. It's a crowd-pleasing vigilante action flick. A strong part of Franco's iconic filmography.

The tagline is: "Robbery. Assault. Murder. One man has had enough!" Hell yeah!!

-Milan Todorovic   Director.

Deep Red

(DPP Section 3) Banned in the UK

Also known as: "Profondo Rosso", "Susperia 2" and "The Hatchet Murders".

Year of release: 1975
Writer: Dario Argento and Bernardino Zapponi.
Director: Dario Argento
X rated 126 mins. Italy
Tagline: "When was the last time you were really scared? Psycho?, The Exorcist?, Jaws?... Now there's Deep Red."
Main cast: David Hemmings (Marcus Daly), Daria Nicolodi (Gianna Brezzi), Gabriele Lavia (Carlo), Macha Meril (Helga Ulmann), Eros Pagni (Supt. Calcabrini), Giuliana Calandra (Amanda Righetti).
Distributed by: Techno films

Plot:

When pianist Marcus witnesses the horrific murder of a famous psychic he decides to team up with reporter Gianna in an attempt to uncover the killers identity. Their lives hang in the balance as the murderer attacks. This killer is desperate to keep a secret buried, but what is the secret and who is the murderer?

Appraisal:

David Hemmings stars in Dario Argento's classic better known as "Profondo Rosso" around the globe. David Hemmings is on top form in this cult giallo horror classic. The music score is supplied by the fantastic "Goblin" which helps give the film its eerie and brutally creepy atmosphere. This film features some unique and chilling murders and has a great horror ambience, which is generally present in all Dario Argento's films, all in all a great horror classic from the master of horror!

In this, another classic giallo offering from the master himself Dario Argento we see the talented actor David Hemmings trying to solve a case of a medium being brutally murdered, This film was released in 1975 and still looks as fresh today, this film is nothing short of a psychic masterpiece, this is a full out claustrophobic, visceral thriller which does hit all the right spots. Goblin provides the heart-racing soundtrack, which fits perfectly to the film. Argento seems to work his magic here. The killer complete with black gloves is as mysterious as a killer could be. This film does have very strange things going on and I don't mean David Hemmings getting beaten by a woman at arm wrestling! The dolls and the children in this film are equally as scary! It's crazy to me how something as simple as a doll hanging us very effective onscreen (my Action Men never looked that good when they never quite made it to the end of the zip-wire). There are some very clever kills, which are both gory and not just gore for gore's sake. This is an all-round classy horror offering from the mind of Dario Argento, Stunning just stunning!

Deep Red was seized under section 3 of the 1959 Obscene Publications Act on VHS in the early 1980's before the implementation of the Video Recordings Act of 1984 in the UK.

Deep Red was initially released on pre-cert VHS by Techno Film (Fletcher) in 1982. This was the uncut version of the film that was seized. The film is available in the UK fully uncut with an 18 rating.

-Tony Newton

Demented

(DPP Section 3) Banned in the UK
Year of release: 1980
Writer: Alex Rebar
Director: Arthur Jeffreys
R rated 87 mins. USA
Tagline: "Revenge is sweet…and deadly."
Main cast: Sallee Young (Linda Rogers), Harry Reems (Matt Rogers), Deborah Alter (Annie), Katheryn Clayton (Carol), Bryan Charles (Dr. Dillman), Edward Tabolt Matthews (Mark).
Distributed by: Media

Plot:
In this rape-revenge flick, a young woman Linda endures a horrific gang rape. The rapists are caught but Linda becomes paranoid and begins to be plagued by visions of her tormentors. When Linda is attacked again something snaps inside of her and she transforms from an innocent victim to a crazed woman exacting revenge on her attackers.

Appraisal:
Demented never really knows what kind of movie it truly wants to be, at times it tries to be a standard horror flick but most of the time it's just outright bonkers. The director Arthur Jeffrey's didn't really do anything after this film, which is a shame as I did like this movie and would have loved to have seen more from the director. It's so truly bizarre. As a kid those masks freaked me out, big time! It's so bad it's good. Demented is a rather dated horror film, but does still grab your attention due to the sick and twisted theme of the film, nothing we haven't seen before though, the film features lots of blood and features overacting aplenty. This low budget horror is an okay film, it really gave me chills as kid watching this title as it has a really Eire feel to it, as we see the victim take revenge on her tormentors. Demented was seized under section 3 of the 1959 Obscene Publications Act on VHS in the early 1980's before the implementation of the Video Recordings Act of 1984 in the UK. Demented was released on pre-cert VHS by Media in 1982, this was the uncut version of the film that was seized, the film was again submitted to the BBFC in 1987 and is now available in the UK 18 with cuts made by the BBFC.

-Tony Newton

Demented is a film, which certainly grabs your attention from the start. Within the opening few minutes, pretty Linda (Young) is gang raped by four thugs (all of whom wear stockings over their heads, bank robber-style). No preamble establishing the characters. No threatening build-up of tension. No idyllic home life about to be shattered. Just brutal fucking in a stable. And bare tits. Linda is raped into a catatonic state and, after some time in a sanatorium, returns home to her bell bottom-wearing, Jaguar-driving surgeon husband Matt (Reems). Linda is still suffering mentally, as expertly shown by director Jeffreys in a series of brilliantly unconvincing hallucinations and some spectacularly rotten acting from Young. Worse still, her husband is secretly having an affair with Linda's sluttish sister Annie (Alter). *Even* worse still, a bunch of teen bastards menace poor Linda by threatening her with rape!

Anyone who's seen I Spit On Your Grave can guess what'll happen next. Will the cops reckon Linda is still nuts? Will mousy Linda turn into a stockings-clad killing machine? Will dirty bastard Matt get his comeuppance? Will your teeth be set on edge by Young's fucking annoying, screechy voice? The answer to most of these is pretty obvious, but the connoisseur will still find plenty to enjoy in this sleazy piece of magic.

True, this has none of the sheer savagery of, say, Last House on the Left or the slightly camp entertainment value of Thriller: A Cruel Picture but the script (by the Incredible Melting Man himself, Alex Rebar) throws in enough clangers to see you through the rather dull middle third. In a scene which had me scratching my head, Linda and Matt's touching post-meal chat soon descends into a bizarre discourse in rape/menstruation/sex. I had to rewind it twice to fully comprehend the lyrical majesty of lines like: "Matt, I was raped. I didn't get a frontal lobotomy...I'm a little edgy today – I started my period. I wonder, why on earth do they call it a period? Why not a comma?"

If you manage to sit through all this (and there are *just* enough skimpy nighties on display to hold the interest), your patience is rewarded by a superbly duff climax, where an obviously, err, demented Linda bloodily dispatches the teen idiots who have the misfortune to break into her house. Normally, in a rape/revenge film, the rapists themselves are messily killed by their victim. Rebar's masterstroke is that Linda's victims are innocent (the rapists, we are told, are in prison). Well, perhaps they're guilty of breaking and entering and, maybe, assault, but whereas we cheer as Camille Keaton cuts off that guy's cock and balls in the bath, here we're slightly nonplussed as Linda seduces one of the poor bastards before making him bark like a dog and castrating him. I've been a little unkind about Young's acting, but in the climactic scenes she is actually very good, moving from coquettish to unhinged pretty convincingly.

Rape/revenge films usually have a slight excuse in the violence shown because the rotten fuckers deserved being chopped up with a propeller or similar. It's never a particularly convincing argument, but at least they try. Demented, however, can make no such claim at all. Linda is patently suffering from the cinematic version of Post Traumatic Stress Disorder, and crazy killers always give the best value for money.

-Rich Flannagan   Writer.

The Demons

(DPP Section 3) Banned in the UK
Also known as "les Demons".
Year of release: 1973
Writer: Jesús Franco
Director: Jesús Franco
R rated 103 mins. France, Portugal
Tagline: "Erotic horror… torture…witchcraft."
Main cast: Anne Libert (Kathleen), Britt Nichols (Margaret), Doris Thomas (Mother Rosalinda), Karin Field (Lady De Winter), Cihangir Gaffari (Lord Justice Jeffries), Luis Barboo (Truro).
Distributed by: Go Video

Plot:
When a witch is convicted by the Inquisition she puts a curse on those responsible before being burnt at the stake "The Demons" follows a pair of orphaned sisters who have been raised as nuns following the burning of their witch mother. Will these nuns take revenge for the murder of their mother?

Appraisal:
Jess Franco's The Demons is so similar to Ken Russell's The Devil's in so many ways although it's not a patch on The Devil's which is one of my favorite films of all time. This film is a great, underrated horror, it's an unrelenting force of a non-stop sleaze horror romp. If you are a fan of Franco's you will love this film. The Demons was so hard to get hold of on VHS in the 1980's that it's great the film is out now on Blu-ray, it's a rare treat!.

The Demons has elements of torture, nudity and Nunsploitation what's not to like! The film has copious amounts of nudity and sexual that are within the context of the film these don't seemed forced just for the sake of it and flow well within the films structure.

Apart from the obvious comparisons to The Devils, if you look through that you will find a very entertaining film, Franco had a way to create an aesthetic all of his own a certain feel that just resonates throughout his productions, this film does contain a lot of torture scenes and nudity throughout the mix of this with witchcraft and the paranormal style really works here.

The Demons was seized under section 3 of the 1959 Obscene Publications Act on VHS in the early 1980's before the implementation of the Video Recordings Act of 1984 in the UK.

The Demons was initially released on pre-cert VHS by Go Video in 1981, this was the uncut version of the film that was seized, The film is now available in its full, uncut form rated 18.

-Tony Newton

The Devils

(Banned by Councils in the UK, Still not available in its full, uncut form to this day.)
Year of release: 1971
Writer: Ken Russell
Director: Ken Russell
Main cast: Vanessa Redgrave (Sister Jeanne), Oliver Reed (Urbain Grandier), Dudley Sutton (Baron De Laubardemont), Max Adrian (Ibert), Gemma Jones (Madeleine).
Distributed by: Warner Brothers

Plot:
Set in the 17th-Century The Devils sees Father Urbain Grandier played by Oliver Reed seeking to protect the city of Loudun from its corrupt establishment. All hell breaks loose when he is accused of witchcraft by a sexually repressed nun.

Appraisal:
As Ken Russell said himself "I am the savior of the British film industry", and I think he was!. I adore Ken Russell, I love all his work and re-visit his films all the time. Ken Russell's "The Devils" is a classic film, which pushes boundaries. "Women in Love" seems a far cry from this very controversial offering. The Devils is based on the non-fiction novel by Aldous Huxley "The Devils of Loudun" which focuses on demonic possession, unbridled sex, sexual repression, centered around Catholicism in the 17th century Loudum, France. Playwright John Whitling had previously adapted Huxley's novel into a play in 1960. Ken Russell had the ability to transport the viewer into another world, as he does with all his work. Ken Russell's films are like no other, there is always an air of unease and after viewing you feel like you have just recovered from a hit to the head and jolted back into this so-called reality, or the an LSD comedown. Ken Russell in my eyes was a genius and watching "The Devil's" reinforces this. When I first watched this film as a youngster and coming from quite a religious family it had a big impact and was a film that stayed with me and a film, which I regard as one of my all-time favourite films. The film stars Oliver Reed as (Urbain Grandier) and Vanessa Redgrave as (Sister Jeanne), they both give equally intense performances on screen and for both they give the best performances of their careers. Reed's character (Grandier) who shows his true love for God, (or is it sodomy?), just dominates the screen at all times. The films religious tone, which there's no getting away hits you and you can't escape the creepy feel which it brings. The film is deemed blasphemous most notably the scene which is more commonly known as the raping of Christ, does stand out in the film. This film is a visual rollercoaster ride and in my eyes doesn't lack substance as many critics have said in the past, but Ken Russell's unique style of filmmaking is shown here and Derek Jarman's sets are nothing short of stunning.

On its initial UK release and after a treacherous back and forth between director Ken Russell and the BBFC came what is now to be known as the X rated cut of "The Devils" which saw its theatrical release in 1971.

Upon the film's release came with it controversy not only in the UK, but also globally. The film was banned outright in many countries and even in America the film was heavily cut to then receive an R rating, notoriously cutting the X rated print and for years and years people who believed they were watching the original X rated version were in fact watching the R rated US version of the film. Only the UK VHS release by Warner Bros in 1997 was not only a stunning print of the film with crisp clear picture and good audio but the original print standard copy of the 1971 x rated version shown in cinemas.

The version containing the rape of Christ is still unavailable for home viewing. Although the full, uncut version has been shown in special cinema showings.

I am lucky enough to have seen the film in its full uncut glory and this is the way Ken Russell intended the film to be viewed, which is the director's cut including the infamous rape of Christ and charred tibia masturbation scene, as of now (late 2019) Warner Bros still refuse to release the full directors cut of the film. This is a true example of morally wrong and big brother in 2016.

Free "The Devils"!

#FreeTheDevils

-Tony Newton

#FREETHEDEVILS

Over the last 40 years, there have been shredded versions, mercilessly cut American bootlegs, scan-and-pans from internet glimpses, copies made from ancient VHS's, rip-offs that frustrated the people who owned the film (Warner Brothers, originally) and the generations who want to be allowed to see it intact.

Because of *The Devils* in 1971, I have been accused of Devil-promotion, nun-lust, torture-porn, church-desecration and bad taste. I plead guilty only to the last, which is proportionate to my good taste, in my humble opinion. I'm a good Catholic boy who finds it my duty to the Faith to question hypocrisy, chicanery, hysteria and mob decisions. Frankly, I don't know what the fuss is over *The Devils.* Shocking? Passionate? Brave? Noble? Isn't that a good thing?

I know in 1971 the censors weren't prepared for naked nuns and pubic hair. The Americans wanted every hair on the cutting room floor. Oh dear. I'd already given the actress-nuns £150 to shave their heads; it was too late to put them in underwear; the film was done. These were nun characters going from one extreme of shame-based behavior to the other, to exhibitionism. How could I write fig leaves into a script on truth? So I didn't, and the Americans cut out so much footage as to make the film disturbingly fragmented.

John Trevelyan, the official BBFC chief censor, old colleague, was more reasonable and circumspect. He asked only that a 12-minute segment in the middle be cut as well as a few masturbatory bits. Fair enough.

But I'd rather have the film seen, even censored.

-Ken Russell

12 March 2012 The full article was written by Ken Russell for The Times in 2012 copyright The Times / News Syndication, thanks to Lisi Russell.

Ken Russell's *The Devils* is a film whose reputation precedes it. Banned when it came out, and savagely cut by 14 minutes for the US version and 12 for the UK version, a complete version has been permitted a screening in the UK only 3 times for fear it would send people stark staring mad and create riots.

Why? Why is it so threatening, still, 40 years after its release? In 1971 it was given an X-rating and denounced as pornographic and anti-religion. That was not Ken's intention—he would assure you. "It's not a film against religion but against the abuses of organized religion. It's about the unpleasant tendency of mobs to relish sadistic displays of public torture and humiliation," he said. Ken Russell, an otherwise agreeable man, was accused of Devil-promotion, nun-lust, torture-porn, church-desecration and bad taste when it came out in 1971. Incredibly, as ahead of its time as it was, the film has become even more relevant today.

The film is so disturbing because in spite of taking place in 1634, the look of it and the behavior of the main protagonists are incredibly modern – from Derek Jarman's sculpturally futuristic, massive sets to the so-called "cures for the plague" – one of which (cupping) is Demi Moore's and Gwyneth Paltrow's current beauty fad – to Georgina Hale's gothic green lipstick – which Ken verified was actually a fashion statement in the 1630's – to the party-going sophistication of King Louis and his drag queens – to the exorcist wearing John Lennon glasses – to Oliver Reed's muscular and confident self in the main role – to Sister Jeanne's destructive cynicism.

There is no disguising that Ken meant the medieval action to feel current – to feel as though it were being lived now, without the comfortable distance he could have created by using moss-covered stonework or quaint customs. The film touches a nerve – it sits on the nerve and drills it. *The Devils* is about now – it's about 1634, and it's about 1971 when it was made – when student protests against war were raging, Charles Manson was sentenced and Jim Morrison overdosed – and it's also about 2013. It puts in the spotlight humanity's more lurid extremisms – its lusts, its lies, its power drives; its greed, vanity and arrogance; its torture, fetishes, superstitions, fake cures; its attention-seeking and specifically, its use of religion to make the world safer for hypocrisy.

Much of the film is ugly. Also, much of the film is excessively beautiful. See that last scene with the heroine, Madeleine, and compare it visually to Polanski's *The Pianist*, where the hero steps out of the Warsaw ghetto into a direct homage to Ken Russell. Impressions are laid on with a trowel in *The Devils,* vivid, fantastic, propelled by Maxwell Davies's avant-garde and discomforting score. The characters, played by actors with whom Ken developed lifelong relationships, are deep, complex, witty, venal, sharp and vulnerable.

The Devils is a story written and directed by Ken Russell, inspired by Jonathan Whiting's 1960 play, which Ken saw and which starred Dorothy Tutin – who had starred in Ken's film *Savage Messiah.* Ken primarily based the script – which was written without changes in 3 weeks, and refined in a day – mostly on the original book *The Devils of Loudon* by Aldous Huxley, author of *Brave New World.* Ken never met Aldous, who had died eight years before the film came out, but Ken is mentioned indirectly by Huxley in his letters, when he said: "I pity the poor fellow who is going to try and make a film out of *The Devils*."

The Devils is a true story, set in 1634 in 17th century France in the medieval town of Loudon, when an actual closed order, a convent of Ursuline nuns, claimed to be possessed by the Devil and his minions, and staged daily possession scenes to emphasize their plight. The circus atmosphere attracted the attention of the Catholic Church's inquisition in an effort to purge the devils. The possession began, coincidentally, when Sister Jeanne of the Angels, played magnificently by the brilliant Vanessa Redgrave, fell in love with the sexy priest of the sponsoring Church, played flawlessly by Oliver Reed, and asked him to be her order's confessor, a request he thoughtlessly took no notice of.

Sister Jeanne had revenge by claiming the Devil used Grandier's body to perform nefarious sexual acts at the convent – easy enough for some to believe, in that Grandier was known to be a sexually overactive priest who had seduced the daughter of a leading citizen, Trincant. This film is love in the time of the plague, where the tension caused by constant anxiety over the death count and the lack of hygiene, the sores and the incurability of it all, the pitiful attempts to use fires to fumigate the land, the abundance of corpses and the emergence under Louis XIII of the first absolute monarchy create a surreal atmosphere suited for panic, chaos and mass hysteria.

Above all the film is very angry. Ken called it his most and in fact his only political movie.

Ken's genius led him to hire extremely creative people, who were previously unknown, to fill key positions: he instructed his set designer Derek Jarman to make the walls look imposingly new; and to resemble the impact of the sets in *Metropolis,* his favourite film. Ken felt it was a cliché to present a medieval city as moss and stones, when to the inhabitants of Loudon in the 1600's, a new-built town would have been just that, brand-new and something to be proud of. Pinewood Studios still calls the set of *The Devils* on their back lot "the most impressive set design of the century" in their history. Ken read in Huxley's book that "the exorcism of Sister Jeanne was the equivalent of a rape in a public lavatory" – and you can see that source in Jarman's tile designs for the convent.

Ken hired the relatively unknown Peter Maxwell Davies to do the score – his first film score, as the sets were Jarman's first film sets – and the music is frightening, out of control, outrageous, piercing. He used David Watkin's stunning cinematography, the man who photographed Richard Lester's, Zeffirelli's, and Sidney Lumet's films as well as Ken's *The Boy Friend.* The whole is a feast for the senses and an affront to everything that would keep us safe and in denial. In this movie there is no place for denial. The whole is on display, the petty vanities, the adaptations made with governments gone drunk with power, the serious passions and quiet devotions which make life meaningful but which disturb the jealous and the greedy, the way in which sex repressed results in outrage and delirium…I don't think there's been a film with such a scope in telling the story of the sacred and profane, the personal and the public, love, sex, disease and crucifixes, with the unconditional union between a man and woman – between Grandier and Madeline – providing a counterpoint of sanity and consideration in the midst of the madness.

Louis XIII here is played by Graham Armitage as a self-indulgent, crafty homosexual, as he was said to be - a man fond of putting on musical pageants, and who popularised wigs for men. He was the son of a Medici, and he coldly exiled his Mother and executed her courtiers to come to absolute power. He taxed the people and stole their lands and to implement his quest for power used his Cardinal, Cardinal Richelieu – a man with his own private ambitions. King Louis XIII using Protestants for target practice may have been Ken's symbolic interpretation, but the image once seen is never to be forgotten, as are so many images in the film: Sister Jeanne's visions of Grandier as a voluptuous Christ, her exorcism by the spurious medical men – a barber, rather than a surgeon; the opening with King Louis performing the classical myth of the Birth of Venus; precious art being smashed for no purpose by the King's henchmen while Grandier is tested for witchcraft; Sister Jeanne spying on Grandier through the ground floor bars of the convent; unforgettable Murray Melvin as Father Mignon giving a conflicted kiss of absolution to Grandier; King Louis bringing the blood of Christ in a golden box.

Ken's favourite subjects were people who became great not because of their talents but in spite of their faults. Oliver Reed's Father Grandier is no exception. Reed suspected Ken of having a bit of a messiah complex himself, and called him Jesus throughout their long association. (Ken did, it must be said, wear sandals.) *The Devils* is an historical account of a charismatic and sexy Catholic priest called Father Urban Grandier, played by a magnificent Oliver Reed, who becomes a martyred hero in spite of his vanity, pride and compulsion to break his vows of celibacy with his attractive parishioners. He unwittingly comes up against the cloistered and claustrophobic order of Ursuline nuns headed by Sister Jeanne of the Angels, whose classic beauty is marred by a hump.

Father Grandier and Sister Jeanne, though they never meet except in Sister Jeanne's visions and only once very late in the film, precipitate and enflame a brewing political crisis between Church and State. The Catholic Cardinal Richelieu is pressuring King Louis XIII to give him the property rights to the fortified city of Loudon. Richelieu is furthering the King's agenda, to demolish the city in order to consolidate Catholic wealth and power; but King Louis wants to preserve the city as a promise to an old friend, who was once the Governor, and because he hates being told what to do by the slimy Cardinal. Only Father Grandier and a self-indulgent King Louis XIII stand between the city and the Cardinal's plan to capture it.

Power struggles propel the plot, both private and public – that between Louis and Richelieu, that between Grandier and Sister Jeanne, that between Grandier and Richelieu, that between Grandier and Philippe, the woman he has seduced, played by the lovely Georgina Hale. The sexual frustration and plague-provoked anxiety at the core of the story creates a surreal vortex of intensity. *The Devils* is about desire for property and control, unrequited love and the conclusion that hell hath no fury like a rejected nun.

What happens is the final word on mob hysteria and what people are capable of doing to get their own way, especially with the power of a corrupt institution to assist them – an institution which can just as readily turn against them.

When Sister Jeanne accuses Grandier, whom she has never actually met, of consorting with devils and of having his way with her in the form of a demon, her nuns fall in and proclaim the same, throwing off their habits and their inhibitions. The wicked head of the King's soldiers, Laubardemont, played with menace by Dudley Sutton, who incidentally lied to Ken that he knew how to ride a horse but still managed it expertly – cynically uses the possessed nuns to further the Cardinal's cause to strip Grandier of the influence he has over the city. Ken paid the actress-nuns £150 extra to shave their heads and he played them Stravinsky's "Rite of Spring" and Penderecki's "Die Teufel von Loudon" to get them in the mood for the orgy scenes. (He ensured Oliver Reed's shaved eyebrows for half a million.)

Forty years ago, in 1971, when *The Devils* was released, the censors weren't prepared for naked nuns and pubic hair. The Americans wanted every single hair on the cutting room floor. It was too late to put the nuns in underwear; the film was done. The nuns were characters going from one extreme of shame-based behavior to the other, from celibacy to exhibitionism. How could Ken write fig leaves into a script on truth? So he didn't, and the Americans insisted the film be cut and fragmented.

There remains a missing 12-minute sequence in the middle that has come to be known as "The Rape of Christ" sequence, when the nuns defile a statue of Christ on the altar. Top British film critic Mark Kermode instigated an Indiana-Jones type search for the missing footage deep into the vaults of Warner Brothers' archives, where he found a film canister with a note inside: "This shall never see the light of day," signed by a prominent executive. And so it hasn't, except four times – notably once in Asheville, NC, thanks to brilliant film writer Ken Hanke – when it was painstakingly restored by the original editor, Mike Bradsell, who worked with Ken closely for 50 years and whom Ken called his "psychic twin." The film is still being held in abeyance for public viewing by the powers-that-be.

Luckily, after a mere 40 years of petitions and storming the Warner Brothers archives, *The Devils* was released on DVD last year by the BFI in a UK Directors' Cut, without the "Rape of Christ" sequence, but otherwise intact. Ken felt it was more important to see the film as whole, in any state, to get the emotional impact of how intently Ken wedded images to music.

Ken pre-deceased the release of *The Devils'* DVD with extras by 3 months, but he knew it was coming.

"It's my masterpiece," he said. "Frankly, I don't see what the fuss is about. It's strong, yes. Shocking, passionate, brave, noble. Isn't that a good thing? It's not a blasphemous film; it's a film about blasphemy. "

He was very proud that the Jesuit priest Father Gene Philips taught classes on *The Devils* at Loyola University as "the best Catholic film." Ken was very angry that Alexander Walker, the film critic, savaged the film in print when he obviously hadn't watched it, describing Grandier as having had his testicles crushed. "That is not true; it's not in the film. The critics were out to get me," he said. On TV where Ken and Alexander Walker appeared together, Ken impulsively took Walker's review, rolled it up and hit Walker over the head with it, surely the most satisfying display of a director's response to his critics ever.

It was a blow to Ken that what he considered his masterpiece and what may be the greatest British film of all time was censored, hidden and reviled, its parts butchered in America, its motives misunderstood, much like what happened to Grandier in the film. Ken was not trying to shock. He found the events shocking. A Catholic himself, he wanted to make the distinction between the passionate and simple heart of faith that had led him to convert in his 20's and the political chicanery that he found permeating Church policies.

The Directors Cut itself has been too little seen. Five years ago it was shown at the BFI in London to a standing ovation with Ken in attendance, and last year it received a showing after his death. There have only been a few authorized screenings of the film. It is still considered scandalous, even after 40 years. There is something so powerful, so full-on, in his dissection of the hypocrisy of the Church, a film devised by a unique and visionary director at the height of his powers, working with his favourite actor, Oliver Reed, also at the height of his talents and doing the greatest acting of his career.

Oliver Reed did keep trying to sneak copies of the Latin text into the Communion bread or into slips of paper floating in the Holy Font, and Ken kept catching him and making him learn his lines. They had a good relationship and understood each other. In spite of the stress of the content, Ken and Mike both remember it as the most blissful film experience out of all of Ken's films, because it was so expertly conceived.

It is an important film. It is shocking, disturbing, hysterical, grotesque at times. It shows plague-ridden medieval France in a brilliantly imagined way. Georgina Hale, who plays Father Grandier's mistress Philippe, said only last month, "I don't think I can see it yet again – it upsets me so." The ideas are violent, vivid, forthright. Ken directs such enormous and overpowering anger at lies, corruption, torture and foolishness that you can feel the heat of his concerns, his identification as a humanist, his recognition of both the petty and profound at war in each person's chest. Ken celebrated truth and the simplicity of trust, and had righteous indignation for the power imbalances we support by telling lies and jockeying for position.

"Satan's boy I could never be," he'd sing out in a cinema, with the dialogue he wrote for the film.

Ken said: "Not one word of criticism written has ever altered in any way my scripts or my next project. I believe in what I'm doing wholeheartedly, passionately and what's more, I simply go about my business. I suppose such a thing can be annoying to some people."

Because Ken, of course, is Father Grandier. He was a Picasso, he was Gaudier-Brzeska, he was the British Fellini. If any man took on the whole of British film culture, it was Ken Russell, and he did it without flinching and in fact, without being thanked for it. To live with such a man was inspiring and delightful and infinitely sweet. I'm afraid I'm rather spoiled for good company now.

-Lisi Russell   Gorsewood Films & Ken Russell Productions.

Don't Answer the Phone!

(DPP Section 3) Banned in the UK
Year of release: 1980
Writers: Robert Hammer and Michael D. Castle
Director: Robert Hammer
R rated 94 mins. USA
Tagline: "Run – if you must. Hide- if you can. SCREAM but… he'll know you're alone!"
Main cast: James Westmoreland (Lt. Chris McCabe), Ben Frank (Sgt. Hatcher), Flo Lawrence (Dr. Lindsay Gale), Nicholas Worth (Kirk Smith), Denise Galik (Lisa), Stan Haze (Adkins).
Distributed by: Jaguar (World of Video 2000)

Plot:
Don't Answer the Phone sees an overweight Vietnam veteran, who has an interest in photography, stalking and killing women in Hollywood CA. It's a race against time for Lt. Chris McCabe to try and catch the killer.
Can anyone stop this psychotic strangler?

Appraisal:
In Don't Answer the Phone, the villain here is an overweight Vietnam veteran who doubles up as a photographer and serial killer. The film is as sleazy as it gets. Following an ex-Vietnam veteran into the realms of insanity. This film feels quite dated and could have been so much better which is disappointing. The main actor in this film is on top form and very believable in the role.

Yes we have another "Don't" flick here! I think my favorite has to be "Don't go in the House" but if you are a collector of the "Don't" movies like me this is one you must have in your collection.

I loved the trailer of the film; I think it was much better than the film itself. This film wasn't high art, but I'm a lover of early 80's stalk and slash flicks so I did get some enjoyment from it. What this film doesn't deliver on is good acting all round and suspense, although it does deliver on sleaze and all out craziness. If you love 1980's slashers you will enjoy this for its sheer bizarreness if nothing else.

Don't Answer The Phone was seized under section 3 of the 1959 Obscene Publications Act on VHS in the early 1980's before the implementation of the Video Recordings Act of 1984 in the UK.

Don't Answer The Phone was initially released on pre-cert VHS by Jaguar (World of Video 2000) in 1981, this version was the cut theatrical version of the film, the film is available with an 18 rating from the BBFC which is the US cut version of the film it is well worth trying to track down a unrated version.

-Tony Newton

Enter the Devil

(DPP Section 3) Banned in the UK
Also known as "Disciples of Death".
Year of release: 1972
Writer: Frank Q. Dobbs and David S. Cass
Director: Frank Q. Dobbs
PG 86 mins. USA
Tagline: "Then it's too late for exorcism!"
Main cast: Joshua Bryant (Glenn), Irene Kelly (Leslie), David S. Cass Sr. (Jase), John Martin (Sheriff), Carle Bensen (Doc), Norris Domingue (Chuy).
Distributed by: Inter-Ocean

Plot:
Enter the Devil sees Sheriff's Deputy Jason Brooks discover the existence of a robe wearing, Devil worshipping cult clan who operate under the name the "Disciples of Death". The Deputy teams up with an occult researcher and the two put themselves in grave danger to investigate the cult "Disciples of Death" who are making human sacrifices in the desert wastelands. Who will be their next sacrifice?

Appraisal:
Enter the Devil is an occult horror film from the early 70s. It's one of those films that would have probably drifted quietly into room 101 unnoticed if it wasn't for prominently being featured on the section 3 video nasty list.

This film does have a certain charm to it and certainly delivers with the visuals and gritty atmosphere which it tries its best to create throughout, all this is helped by the locations used within the film including the stunning California's Mojave Desert.

Enter the Devil in parts feels dated but that doesn't detract from the movie itself, it can feel like a slow burn at times but there are certain scenes which are brilliant and worth it just for the ending alone.

This is no "Race with the Devil" by any means, it just okay, which is a shame as occult horror movies are spread very thin and I have a huge soft spot for them.

If you are expecting "Devils Rain" you will be disappointed as this film may have some of the cheesiness but none of the killer effects and atmosphere which that film brings!

All that said I did get some enjoyment from this b-style horror offering, it's not the best occult film by any means, but this film does deliver some great cinematic shots and all the actors are on fine form.

Enter the Devil was seized under section 3 of the 1959 Obscene Publications Act on VHS in the early 1980's before the implementation of the Video Recordings Act of 1984 in the UK.

Enter the Devil was initially released uncut on pre-cert VHS by Inter-Ocean in 1983. There was no other version of this film ever released on any format in the UK.

-Tony Newton

The Erotic Rites of Frankenstein

(DPP Section 3) Banned in the UK
Also known as "La Maldicon de Frankenstein" and "The Curse of Frankenstein".
Year of release: 1972
Writer: Jesús Franco
Director: Jesús Franco
Uncertified 94 mins. Spain, France
Main cast: Alberto Dalbes (Doctor Seward), Dennis Price (Doctor Frankenstein), Howard Vernon (Cagliostro), Beatriz Savon (Vera Frankenstein), Anne Libert (Melisa), Fernando Bilbao (Monstruto).
Distributed by: Go Video

Plot:
The Erotic Rites of Frankenstein is another take on Mary Shelley's "Frankenstein". In this Jesús Franco giallo Dr. Frankenstein and his assistant Morpho are murdered soon after the re-animation of Frankenstein's monster. Cagliostro steals Frankenstein's monster; he plans to use the monster to create a master race!

Appraisal:
Dennis Price a familiar face of the 1970's plays Dr. Frankenstein very well alongside Howard Vernon who plays Evil like no other with his mad staring eyes. This is a very different take on a Frankenstein adaption. Don't expect classic Hollywood Frankenstein, The Erotic Rites of Frankenstein has an almost Hammer Horror-esque feel to it, which is a plus for this movie. Hammer regular Dennis Price makes it feel more Hammer although we didn't get this much blood or nudity in a Hammer offering at the time! This is a cheesy fun horror movie complete with the monster covered in silver paint, but it just works. is The Erotic Rites of Frankenstein is well worth a watch if you are a fan of 70's horror cult style horror and a fan of the legend that is Jesús Franco.

The Erotic Rites of Frankenstein was seized under section 3 of the 1959 Obscene Publications Act on VHS in the early 1980's before the implementation of the Video Recordings Act of 1984 in the UK.

The Erotic Rites of Frankenstein was initially released uncut on pre-cert VHS by Go Video in 1983, There was a cut version showing less nudity released in 2006 which was passed 15 cert by the BBFC. The version has the actors clothed for all the major scenes so it's worth tracking down the uncut version of the film.

-Tony Newton

The Evil

(DPP Section 3) Banned in the UK
Also known as "House of Evil".
Year of release: 1978
Writer: Gus Trikonis
Director: Galen Thompson and Gus Trikonis
R rated 89 mins. English, French
Tagline: "Witness it's awakening."
Main cast: Richard Crenna (C.J Arnold), Joanna Pettet (Dr. Caroline Arnold), Andrew Prine (Prof. Raymond Guy), Cassie Yates (Mary Harper), George O'Hanlon Jr. (Pete Brooks), Lynne Moody (Felicia Allen).
Distributed by: VRO-Video Network

Plot:
The Evil follows a psychologist and his wife, who buy an eerie mansion that is in desperate need of repair. When the restoration begins a demonic force is unleashed from the lower depths of the house and when the group become trapped in the chilling old mansion the murders begin and battle between good and evil ensues.

Appraisal:
This film could have been so much better than it was!, it's eerie in parts and paced quite well but some parts are just laugh out loud stupid, fun with a few mates and a few beers, it's an okay watch! "The Evil" stands out to me for the scene of the man who is on fire being buried alive. This film is a rather strange watch but for some reason I'm rather keen on it. The film does seem to get a bad rap but it is so bizarre it does keep you watching with its varying elements including supernatural, thriller. This B-movie- esque horror film is a fun film and feels like a cross between a grown up version of The Monster Squad and The Beyond meets 80's kids TV show "Rentaghost"!

This film is worth a watch just for the sheer bizarreness of the whole film. Director Gus Trikonis went on to direct episodes of "The Twilight Zone" 80's TV series "Beauty and the beast" and even 22 episodes of "Baywatch". Gus Trikonis' previous works include the 1970's crazy cult film "The Student Body" starring "Naked Fist" star Jillian Kesner, after directing that you can see why he later directed episodes of "Baywatch".

The Evil was seized under section 3 of the 1959 Obscene Publications Act on VHS in the early 1980's before the implementation of the Video Recordings Act of 1984 in the UK.

The Evil was initially released uncut on pre-cert VHS by VRO-Video Network in 1982. The film is now available in its full, uncut state with a BBFC 18 certificate rating.

-Tony Newton

The Executioner

(DPP Section 3) Banned in the UK
Also known as "Massacre Mafia Style" and "Like Father Like Son".
Year of release: 1978
Director: Duke Mitchell
Rated 18 79 mins. USA
Tagline: "Fingered by the Godfather, Nailed by… The Executioner."
Main cast: Duke Mitchell (Mimi Miceli), Vic Caesar (Jolly Rizzo), Lorenzo Dodo (Don Mimi), Louis Zito (Chucky Tripoli), Cara Salerno (Liz), Fred Otash (Bones).
Distributed by: Hello Video

Plot:
Directed by Duke Mitchell this Grindhouse classic "The Executioner" features a man hell bent on revenge on the mafia for exiling his father. When Mimi returns to L.A to take over its underworld activities he reconnects with childhood friend Jolly Rizzo, when the two kidnap the current L.A crime kingpin Chucky Tripoli for ransom a bloody war is waged as they attempt to gain control of the West coast underworld.

Appraisal:
The Executioner is rumored to be a collaboration of true stories! This film is rather unknown, although the film has elements without any meaning and strangely a big "Pulp Fiction" feel to it.

The Executioner is a very low budget offering, full on mafia madness, crazy exploitation film. This film gets a bad rap and is not that well known (to be honest I expected far worse but this is a fun and enjoyable watch.)

Imagine "Goodfellas" or "The Godfather" made on a very small budget, grindhouse style, that's what you get here. This film just works, don't ask me why, but it does! There are some great scenes in the film, some of my favorites are the disabled man being electrocuted in the urinal, in fact there is more than one, all the original kill scenes are great. This film is pure over the top exploitation mafia style, anyone is fair game in this film even Security guards and Lift Attendants all end up meat sacks. This films portrayal of a cold-blooded killer is on the money, when they kill people they don't even flinch or express any kind of remorse. There is an almost "Vincent Vega" quality to the killer though obviously "Pulp Fiction" was a lot later but Vincent Vega would not be out of place in this movie.

Duke Mitchell wrote and directed this film and was obviously inspired by "The Godfather" and classic gangster mafia films. If you haven't seen it already get out and grab a copy, if you have already seen it spin that disc again you know you want to!

The Executioner was seized under section 3 of the 1959 Obscene Publications Act on VHS in the early 1980's before the implementation of the Video Recordings Act of 1984 in the UK.

The Executioner was initially released uncut on pre-cert VHS by Hello Video in 1982, The film is now available in its full uncut state with a BBFC 18 rating.

-Tony Newton

Mimi Micheli, the deported son of a Mafia don decides to return to America to get back into the old game to take his slice of the American dream Teaming up with an old partner and friend Mimi begins to make his mark on the LA underground, muscling his way through the established families.

Success come quickly and initially Mimi is accepted back into the organised crime scene but when Mimi becomes obsessed with power and money he starts to overstep the bounds even for the families who hold back out of respect for his father. The guns are out and Mimi is about to put the old families back on the old path, if one thing is sure it's that things are about to get very bloody....

The Executioner, also known by the infinitely more entertaining title, Massacre Mafia Style is an interesting artefact in the world of independent films. Duke Mitchel wrote, directed and stars in this small but spirited tale of a gangster going back for his slice of the American dream. Opening to an energetic scene of Mimi and his partner rampaging through an office we have part of his character set up from the off. Mimi is ruthless in his work up until a point. Quite happy to execute bystanders at the drop of a hat he shows his limits when a young boy walks into the scene, Mimi has rules but they don't seem to be much of an impediment for sure. Women, cripples, janitors and other innocents are fair game but children, well that would be barbaric.

There is a perverse sense of honor amongst the characters here, Mimi abducts the number one man in the area, cuts off his finger and sends it to his relatives, extorts the local dons companions and then casually turns up at now digitally deficient sons wedding to nonchalantly discuss business... and it's all rather friendly. It paints a picture that is somewhat outrageous and alien and it's interesting to note that we have a rather ambiguous relationship with this brutal character, he's not exactly unlikeable, he certainly has charm but he's also vicious and rather gregariously arrogant. The world that is presented certainly has a high degree of romanticism about it and fittingly it's presented from Mimi's point of view which is why his actions are not exactly condemned and so we find the morality of the film is squarely from the heart of a somewhat psychotic character. He justifies some pretty despicable and selfish actions but then at the drop of a hat we find ourselves faced with a heartfelt though rather self-conscious exploration of what it means to be Italian.

It does feel a bit schizophrenic sometimes like this but because of how the film is presented it does make some sense.

Inspired by The Godfather and apparently informed by Mitchel's discussions with people from the real Mafia The Executioner has a rather perversely sentimental attitude towards the violence. In this world the crime families have been moving away from the mob game and Mimi's return brings with it a spiral back towards the bad old ways that he seems to crave and the story presents it with both gusto and a tone of regret. The screenplay is peppered with monologues that lament the image of the American Italian community which seems distinctly at odds with the joyous outbursts of serious violence that come only moments after several of them.

In this respect it does all feel like I say somewhat romantic and not a little naive. Talking about naïve there is a somewhat problematic element to this film, the dialogue sometimes slips into a rather racist tone. Now this isn't the first or the last time this has happened, Fight for your life for instance had far worse and to be honest although the language is rather casually deployed it sort of fits. On one particular instance Mimi's confrontation with a pimp seems oddly close in intent to a piece of stand up comedy by Chris Rock. Of course there is a racial licence with Chris Rock that arguably Duke Mitchel doesn't have but it does feel to me that his intent wasn't so much racist as it was misjudged. This would be more certainly true if it is in fact the case that Mimi's partner Jolly was as is claimed originally supposed to have been cast as a black man. But it has to be said it's all a little close to the knuckle by today's standards and the conflict of old and new which is coincidentally a minor theme of the movie, plays out in the form of what the movie meant in it's release date context compared to how it reads now. The film also seems to someone like me to so heavily rooted in a strange sense of sentimentality for respect on pain of violence that it feels rather uncomfortable and probably rightly so.

While it does have that uncomfortable allegiance going on it should be noted that this doesn't make it a bad film. In fact The Executioner is well paced, no longer than it needs to be and often quite exciting and fun. The opening, which is curiously placed as it's an event that doesn't happen until much later in the films timeline, is a brilliant piece of filmmaking. The rampage goes from room to room with some wonderful pacing and features some very enjoyable camera work as we follow Mimi at work. All of this is set to a jolly Italian folk song that counterpoints the brutality and reflects Mimi's devil-may-care attitude to the darker side of his work. This guy for all his lamenting on the consequences of what he does rather seems to enjoy the killing and is pretty bloody inventive when doing it, after all how many films can boast a scene containing a urinal electrocution. The rampage scene in particular is rather well edited being as it is accompanied by what feels like a rather gregarious folksy take on the 1812 overture. The gunshots punctuate the score like a enthusiastically inappropriate and kinda perverse drummer but damn it if it isn't a lot of fun. This is probably the most overtly celebratory moment of violence as it really gets into the character of Mimi and it'd be easy to see why the police may have taken some exception to it given that not only did they only have to watch the first couple of minutes of the film to get a handle on what the content was going to be like (in their superficial opinion) but because it really does celebrate the violence. As it stands I find it quite an alluring piece of film in it's own right and it's not surprising that the sequence was used almost verbatim as the trailer to the film.

Though the story, like I say, is a bit dubious in some respects, it does have some rather spectacular moments of violence the most remarkable of which include the pimp being crucified on a cross in the Hollywood hills to the strains of the Hallelujah Chorus, make of that what you will particularly given that the murder is done on Easter day, and there is the alternative poster moment where one of the mob guys is hung from a meat hook through the back of his head and protruding out of his eye socket which is gloriously grim.

The Executioner is a rather fun film and despite it's slightly dubious morality base it is a rather fun time sitting through it. Duke Mitchell makes up for the shortfalls in the films production values with a seemingly unrelenting enthusiasm for the story and the film does balance the action and story rather well elevating it above being a simple gangster film to being a film with a rudimentary but heartfelt commentary. Despite being a character that it's not entirely desirable to get behind Mimi is a charismatic guy and at the very least you can understand his motivations and reasoning. In many respects I like this portrayal because it's nice to have a character that you don't have to agree with but who's not entirely out of the realms of plausibility and understanding.

If there is one thing that characterises this film it's that it has a genuine sense of sincerity and enthusiasm. It's not entirely successful on all fronts, the story for instance is a bit overly dewy about the lifestyle that Mimi follows particularly considering how much he clearly enjoys it one minute and laments it the next but it's not all that common for a film of this nature to project the off screen excitement and commitment from the creative team. It looks pretty good, it has some enjoyable music and over all it's a well-made film given the budget and resources they were probably working with. The acting is generally fairly decent, especially from Mitchell even though a few times the turns do seem to stray into cliché, but the short comings just don't matter that much. Yeah it's a bit of a vanity project, Mitchell does come over as being the kind of guy with enough of an ego to fill the role and there are fairly strong traces of self-indulgence when it comes to the heartfelt monologues but I can't find it annoying or offensive. I genuinely think Mitchell wanted to make the best movie he could. That sincerity comes through strongly and makes the film feel less laden with ego than it could have. All in all The Executioner is very much worth a watch if you can find it. It seems to be rather rare at this point because of some apparent copyright wrangle that's going on and hopefully it will get it's day on DVD again soon because it does deserve having a fresh audience. If you like gangster movies then you should check it out. If you don't I'd have to say that it's still worth giving a visit to for the sheer joy of watching a film that's made by someone who really wanted the make a film for its own sake. In this regard it reminded me of the section 3 title GBH which I reviewed some time ago and that's in my opinion good company for this and about as high a compliment as I can give.

-Glenn Criddle Writer/Critic.

The Exorcist

(Withdrawn from Home Video for 11 years by the BBFC.)
Year of release: 1973
Writer: William Peter Blatty
Director: William Friedkin
Rated: R rated
Tagline: "Something beyond comprehension is happening to a little girl on this street, in this house. A man has been called for as a last resort to try and save her. That man is the exorcist."
Main Cast: Ellen Burstyn (Chris MacNeil), Linda Blair (Regan MacNeil), Max Von Sydow (Father Merrin), Lee J. Cobb (Lt. William Kinderman), Kitty Winn (Sharon), Jack MacGowran (Burke Dennings), Jason Miller (Father Karras).
Distributed by: Warner Home Video

Plot:
This is the story of Regan played by Linda Blair who becomes possessed by a demonic force. Regan's mother played by Ellen Burstyn enlists the help of two priests to try to rid her daughter of a demonic force from hell.

Appraisal:
William Friedkin's Exorcist see's a young girl being possessed by a demonic entity in this classic horror with a amazing unforgettable performances by all of the main lead cast. The film builds up nicely to a great ending which has its place in cult horror film history, most people can quote at least one line from the movie.

Director William Friedkin does an unmatchable job directing this cult horror masterpiece. The Exorcist is as fresh today as it was in the early 70's not only does it have a stellar cast performing great but the music score is amazing, the filming and lighting works perfectly to create a masterpiece. This film to me is like "Night of the Living Dead", no it's not a zombie film but should be the staple of films shown in film school, and it's crazy to think that this film was banned in the UK for so long. I remember seeing this for the first time at the cinema in London when half way through the film there was a technical fault the screen was a blur and there was a high pitched noise, every member of the audience thought it was part of the film, I even witnessed some people leave after that as if it was a sign or bad omen.

Linda Blair gives an amazing performance as the young girl who has the devil inside her literally! If you haven't seen the Exorcist then where have you been living? Get out there now and get a copy, and if you have already seen it watch it again, just because you can! Although the theatrical version of The Exorcist was passed fully uncut and given an x rating in the UK by the BBFC, the film was outed by local councils and catholic groups across Britain upon its early 1970's release, The BBFC's very own secretary at the time Stephen Murphy said the following, regarding the decision on receiving the X rating "It is a powerful horror movie. Some people may dislike it, but that is not a sufficient reason for refusing certification."

The film was release by Warner Home Video in 1981 and strangely enough never ended up on the video nasty wanted list or get caught up in the scandal any degree.

Although with the implementation of the new Video Recording Act and after waiting over four years for a decision to be reached by the BBFC, finally a decision was made, it was deemed unsuitable for home viewing because The Exorcist featured a young girl and these demonic acts actually happening to the girl character they thought younger viewers would be drawn more attention to the film, where the film was played at cinemas the rating could be easily reinforced making sure a younger audience didn't watch it, but at home this wouldn't be the case in 1988 the remaining videos were removed from the shelves of video stores and The Exorcist on home video was banned for 11 years until it received a rating from the BBFC.

-Tony Newton

THE EXORCIST

When my wife Wiescka and I saw The Exorcist in Stockholm we were both unnerved by it. We were renting a flat that, strangely, had rows of dining-room chairs all around the living-room. I happened to say to Wiescka before we went to bed "Wouldn't it be frightening if you got up in the middle of the night and there were people sitting in every one of those chairs, in the dark, perfectly still, and saying nothing?" I don't know why I said it. Horror writer's imagination, I suppose. But that night we were still creeped out by The Exorcist and neither of us got up until it was light, and in Stockholm in late September that doesn't happen until quite late!

We saw The Exorcist again a few years later and neither of us found it scary at all. Time had not been kind to it, and it seemed almost ludicrous. The one film that we did find disturbing, though, was The Ring — both the English-language remake and the original Japanese Ringu. There is something infinitely unsettling about children, especially children with long wet hair covering their faces crawling crablike out of your telly. I have often used children myself to create unsettling characters because they have not yet learned about morality and they cannot yet distinguish between reality and fantasy.

Of course I have to mention my own nasty, The Manitou, still available on DVD. First released in 1978, it has dated just as much as The Exorcist but I still have a fondness for the evil Native American shaman Misquamacus being reborn in the neck of a modern-day white woman to take his revenge on the palefaces. What I liked was that, in spite of an insane plot, every actor in the movie played it dead straight, which did make for one or two startling moments. But regrettably we could never put a remake together - Tony Curtis, Susan Strasberg, Burgess Meredith and Michael Ansara, who played the main characters, are all brown bread.

Never fear, my friend Fred Caruso, who was one of the producers of The Godfather, is developing my novel Demon's Door for me, about a very nasty Korean demon who threatens some unfortunate LA college students, so you have a chilling treat in store!

-Graham Masterton   Author.

Special Makeup Effects, The Exorcist, and Its Impact On My Life, and My Career

I got into makeup effects late in the game, at least by many industry standards. Many of the titans of the industry, as well as my peers, were plaster casting and smearing latex on their faces before they hit their teens. I, on the other hand, thought I was going to be an animator. Then when college rolled around, I decided on a career in industrial design (designing consumer products and such), given that animation was segueing quite rapidly to computers, and my passion had always been hand drawn cell animation. But my second term in college, specifically, is when fate intervened. One of my required courses that term was in special makeup effects. Throughout college there were 3 additional classes in effects, taught by the same teacher (a Mr. John Stuart). But it was that first effects class that cemented it in my mind. I decided then, that I would become a makeup artist, or more specifically a special makeup effects artist. Amazingly, until that class I never even thought that makeup effects could be a career. Not sure why, but I never did. College was a good starting point, and after that I went to makeup school, and then I started working.

I think a lot of people in the makeup effects industry were inspired by the classic Universal monsters and their films, and by assorted gore films from the 1970's and by work done on Planet of the Apes (work done by

John Chambers), as well as shows like The Twilight Zone. For me, as a makeup effects artist, the one singular film (at least as far as horror goes) that really impacted me, was The Exorcist. There were, of course, some gore effects, but for the most part the effects were of a more character, creature, or supernatural nature. There were other films that inspired me as a makeup effects artist, like Legend (work done by Rob Bottin), American Werewolf in London (work done by Rick Baker), Thinner (work done my Greg Cannom), and several others, as well as films in more recent years that were released after I entered the field. But, as far as horror goes, it was definitely The Exorcist. The work done by Dick Smith in that film was spectacular, and quite innovative for the time, if not even for the present day.

A fair few "professional" special makeup effects artists view Halloween as the pinnacle of their year. They worship zombies, and revel in blood and gore work. I am not that guy. Don't get me wrong, I do my share of horror films. Lord knows they pay the bills, and I love my work. However, the work that inspires me most are character makeup's, the art of transforming an actor into an interesting character, or aging them, or making a unique and interesting creature. I also love subtlety. Sometimes a little wrinkling or a prosthetic nose and a chin, or other small touches can completely change the way someone looks. I love innovating, whether it's making my own materials or figuring out a transformative effect. So The Exorcist really struck a chord. The possessed makeup was not over the top, but it was transformative. Nobody had ever seen anything, to date, as a spinning head, or words materializing on the skin, or projectile vomiting. More than anything, the aging makeup on Max von Sydow is spectacular, and held by many in the industry to be one of the best old age makeups of all time. Most people watching the film did not even realize he was in age makeup. He looks easily to be in his late 70's, but at the time of the film was only in his early 40's. Dick had to figure all of these things out. There were no manuals, nobody to go to for suggestions. It was just him. This was actually true of a great deal of Dick's work over the years. He pioneered so many techniques, many of which are now standard methods in the makeup effects industry. Not only that, but he built everything for the film with minimal assistants (primarily a young Rick Baker) in the basement of his home in Larchmont, New York. Absolutely incredible.

I think that today, we take for granted that, if push comes to shove, for almost, and I do say almost, anything, as an effects artist, there is someone you can call or email for advice on how to best achieve an effect. In addition, to some degree or another, almost any effect you can think of has probably already been done. Now, granted, there are always going to be new cool creatures and aliens to come along. One of my more recent favorites is the Pale Man from Pan's Labyrinth. Also, today, even with practical effects, we have the benefit of using CG enhancements where a 100% practical method just cannot achieve what is in the script. When The Exorcist came out, things were different, and I think that is one of the things that makes it so impressive. Today, we have 10 times the number of materials to choose from, and back then it was an epic adventure just trying to find a material that would work the way you needed. Sure, there are blood effects from the 80's that had never been seen before, and that era was when zombie culture really took root in our society and in the effects community. I still admire a well-executed blood effect and a well-crafted zombie, though I do think that cheap blood effects, and poorly executed or less interesting zombie makeups are now the bulk of low budget horror in our modern age. I also think, somewhat sadly, that for the average consumer, blood, gore, and zombies are what most think of when they think of "special effects." I probably have 20 slasher film scripts and 30 zombie film scripts come across my desk in any given year. So for me, these elements hold only limited appeal. And it's also hard when you read one that is actually kind of cool and then find out the production company cannot afford what it will cost to actually build the effects in the script so they look great, the way I envisioned when reading the script. Films like The Exorcist are few and far between. Other exorcism films have come along, though none have been nearly as captivating. The found footage method of making horror films has also taken some of the magic out of it. But all the way back in 1973, Dick Smith, William Peter Blatty, and William Friedkin achieved something truly amazing. Their work will live on in my memory for as long as I live. That spirit of creativity and innovation drives the approach I take with my work.

So, in conclusion, I would say, that had The Exorcist never been made, and had William Friedkin not pushed Dick Smith to never settle for less than perfection on his film, the special makeup effects industry and craft would not be where it is today, and the artists in it might not be who they are. In some ways, I liken films like this, at least for my craft, to the invention of the wheel or the harnessing of fire and electricity. They are a pivotal moment in time that sparked new innovations and progression of this craft that I love so much.

-Michael Dinetz   Haunted Dreams Effects Studio.

It seems somewhat mad that a film of such class, integrity, intelligence and artistic sensibility was ever persecuted as severely and for as long by the British censors, but thanks to the almighty for the films re-release in the UK in 1998, that audience could once again engage with this masterwork.

Directed by veteran filmmaker William Friedkin, this film is quite simply both genre defining and genre changing. Until this movie was made horror, with a few exceptions such as Rosemary's Baby (1968) and The Devil Rides Out (1968) had become a form of filmmaking that had slipped largely into parody. Fredkin's smooth, deft, atmospheric, and profoundly clever direction gave the genre the shot in the arm that it needed and even generated a whole new genre of its own, the "demonic child" genre.

Whole chapters in books on filmmaking have been produced about the movie's cinematography, especially its use of subliminal imagery, despite the decades on controversy that the movies cinematography has created. Every choice in tone and setting is so carefully made to create an imprint of fear on the viewer. Techniques such as the notorious subliminal imagery (which isn't actually subliminal at all) enhance the storytelling in a way that has never really been replicated.

The script written by William Peter Blatty from his 1971 novel of the same name and the book inspired by the 1949 "real" exorcism of Roland Doe is literary and profound, an intelligent and engaging commentary on the nature of evil. An authentic Post Morden theodicy expressed though the media of cinema.

The editing of the film is once again a real master class in filmmaking, it is paced wonderfully, and the use of special effects are even now still highly effective, although this is mostly down to the groundbreaking work of makeup artist Dick Smith. One of the greatest achievements of the special effects are the subtle ones…such as the ageing of Max Von Sydow.

The costume design does seem a little dated now, but this is easily glazed over by the location filming, which again is testament to the film's brilliance. From the opening shots in the Middle East with that iconic standoff between good and evil, to the grey autumnal filming in the U.S.A right through to the famous "Exorcist stairs" in many ways define the film for the audience.

The soundtrack, or famously lack of one has a fascinating history all of its own concerning its development, and again much has been written on the subject in other publications but once again the score and the use of sound effects and the hints of score in the film is almost unrivalled in movie making in regards to leaving a memorable impact on the viewer.

-Ian Young   Writer.

Final Exam

(DPP Section 3) Banned in the UK
Year of release: 1981
Writer: Jimmy Huston
Director: Jimmy Huston
R rated 89 mins. USA
Tagline: "Some pass the test…God help the rest!!!"
Main cast: Cecile Bagdadi (Courtney), Joel S. Rice (Radish), Ralph Brown (Wildman), DeAnna Robbins (Lisa), Sherry Willis-Burch (Janet), John Fallon (Mark).
Distributed by: Embassy

Plot:
Final Exam is a 1980's slasher film fresh off the back of "Friday the 13th" and "Halloween". It follows a similar plot to "Friday the 13th" with a psycho killer dressed in a green overcoat who wreaks havoc at a college campus when he begins to stalk the corridors to prey on a group of young students.

Appraisal:
Final Exam is one of a number of unoriginal slasher movies, although the video release is a very well known slasher piece. I am a big fan of stalk-and-slash films; this is not one of the better ones, though the acting isn't great and the plot needs more. Unfortunately it doesn't take much to see that this film was made to cash in on the "Friday the 13th" and "Halloween" films.

This early slasher offering which is set during, yes you guessed it when students are due to sit their exam finals, yet another slasher film from the 1980's this is a low budget offering and it shows here. This film is not one of the best slasher films from the 80's , this is a by the numbers stalk and slash offering, not much in the way of originality here. It's not a film I would regularly re-visit, it seemed a lot better the first time I viewed it as a youngster. I am a huge fan of the very over saturated slasher genre, this is the usual campus slasher it's kind of tongue in cheek and it's enjoyable for what it is, it's no high art but more of a fun camp 1980's slasher offering.

Final Exam was seized under section 3 of the 1959 Obscene Publications Act on VHS in the early 1980's before the implementation of the Video Recordings Act of 1984 in the UK.

Final Exam was initially released uncut on pre-cert VHS by Embassy in 1983, The film was submitted to the BBFC in 1986 and was certified 18 uncut. The film is now available in its full, uncut state with a BBFC 18 rating.

-Tony Newton

Foxy Brown

(DPP Section 3) Banned in the UK
Year of release: 1974
Writer: Jack Hill
Director: Jack Hill
R rated 94 mins. USA

Tagline: "Don't mess aroun' with Foxy Brown, Don't mess aroun' with Foxy Brown – She's the meanest chick in town!"

Main cast: Pam Grier (Foxy Brown), Antonio Fargas (Link Brown), Peter Brown (Steve Elias), Terry Carter (Michael Anderson), Katheryn Loder (Katherine Wall), Harry Holcombe (Judge Fenton).

Distributed by: Guild Home Video

Plot:

Foxy Brown is the classic and well-known cult Blaxploitation film featuring the famous Pam Grier as "Foxy Brown" getting justice the only way she knows how! Following the murder of her boyfriend Michael, Foxy Brown (the meanest chick in town) seeks revenge on his killers.

Appraisal:

Pam Grier is fantastic as the femme fatale vigilante Foxy brown. This film is packed with action and is actually one of the best Blaxploitation pictures ever made. If you're a fan of 1970's exploitation films you will love Foxy Brown. (Quentin Tarantino is obviously a fan). Foxy Brown is a classic which stole the hearts of exploitation cinema fans across the globe, "Foxy Brown" has to the be the Queen of the so-called Blaxploitation era, no other film can come close to this classic. Pam Grier is on fire in this film her on screen presence is amazing you just can't take your eyes off of her throughout the movie! Foxy Brown is a kick ass force not to be messed with. This film cuts away from the sleaze element and is a nonstop action packed cult movie. Although the film was made in 1974 it still holds up well even today, this is a slice of the 70s you want to consume again and again! Director Jack Hill also directed Pam Grier in the film "Coffee" in 1973, he does a great job here as he provides us with a true cult Blaxploitation classic. Antonio Fargas also does a great job

here providing one of his best speeches in his film career as Link Brown. Sid Haig also features in this movie, he was a regular in quite a few of Jack Hill's pictures. Sid Haig is famous for playing Captain Spalding in Rob Zombies "House of 1000 Corpses". This is a very violent film, you can see why this film caused controversy at the time, for me "Coffee" is equally as good as "Foxy Brown" and I would find it hard to choose my favorite between the two films. Both are timeless pieces of cult exploitation goodness! I cannot praise this film enough and just how important it really is as part of cinematic history, and how important Jack Hill was to the film industry and the progression of black cinema, bringing it into the mainstream and helping to change opinions and racism along the way, ironically Blaxploitation pictures made black actors like Pam Grier household names across the globe, and we saw more and more leading black actors in mainstream films roles, I still have my Foxy Brown Poster on the wall in my office today. Foxy Brown was seized under section 3 of the 1959 Obscene Publications Act on VHS in the early 1980's before the implementation of the Video Recordings Act of 1984 in the UK. Foxy Brown was initially released uncut on pre-cert VHS by Guild Home Video in 1982, The film is now available in its full uncut state with a 18 BBFC rating.

-Tony Newton

Foxy Brown banned in the UK? I never knew that before. Well, so now, Free at last! — as they say.

I knew that my first big hit film, "*The Big Doll House*", had been banned in London, despite it being rather tame - even by the standards of the time. The censors didn't really give any specific reasons, but just indicated that the picture was simply too outrageous for public viewing in some way. It seemed clear to me that the issue was that the movie featured *women* talking tough and being mistreated. I mean, well, you could lash the likes of Errol Flynn and Burt Lancaster on screen, but women — even with a wet towel — no, no, no way, not for delicate British sensitivities. That was blatant *sexism*, in my opinion (should I be saying that?), even back before the term was in vogue.

Foxy Brown was originally conceived as a sequel to *Coffee*, which had been a huge hit in the US, and was originally entitled "*Burn, Coffee, Burn*". But just before principal photography began, the AIP sales department declared that sequels were not doing well and proclaimed a change of title, and name of the central character, to *Foxy Brown*. I was appalled at first, as I felt that *Coffee* could have been a franchise, and I also objected to the new name for my Pam Grier character: I felt it was demeaning. (How wrong I was!)

I've also been astonished that *Foxy Brown* has become such a popular cult favorite, as I guess you'd call it (the concept of cult films didn't exist in those days), especially because at the time, I felt rushed into whipping out a script at the last moment, with insufficient time to work out a really good dramatic scenario — which I felt I had accomplished with *Coffee* — and was reduced to just trying to make the picture as entertaining as I could— let's say *really* outrageous -- and into the bargain cocking a snook at the studio, which was treating me with the same kind of disrespect that they held for the intended audience for their pictures (but that's another subject).

In the end, though, I was pleased that I could sneak at least some measure of social comment into *Foxy Brown*, as well as having fun with ideas like, for example, staging a typical Hollywood Western bar room brawl, but in a Lesbian bar — weaving in the kind of comedy which my growing up with Warner Bros films of the 40's has inspired most of my, um, *oeuvre (*dare I use the term?).

After the success I had with the black pictures, as they were called back then, I went for an interview with a producer who was interested in making one. He said to me, and this is an exact quote, "What do they like?" — "they" meaning the black audience — "I know they like to laugh. And I know the picture shouldn't be too good." Needles to say, I didn't pursue the matter any further with this guy.

At AIP, most of the mid-level executives, and even some crewmembers, as well as some of the white actors -- sad to say -- that I worked with seemed to have little but contempt for the "black pictures" that we were making, and for their target audience. I could see it in their faces and hear it in their voices — even when they first heard the music track — just hoping to get through it until they could move up to better jobs on higher-budget projects with more mainstream companies. This in contrast to the black actors, who were so happy just to be working, giving it their best every moment, although I could sometimes feel a sense that they were aware of the undercurrent of racism that surrounded them. It was always a struggle, both for them and for me as writer-director, to try to eke out some real quality and humanity in the pictures in an atmosphere of constant demands for "more action, more sex" — and oddly no mention of humour, probably because the studio people didn't understand what "they" would laugh at. I would like to think that both "they" and I shared a secret kind of bonding in the knowledge of what we were all working against — and for.

-Jack Hill   Director of "Foxy Brown".

Friday the 13th

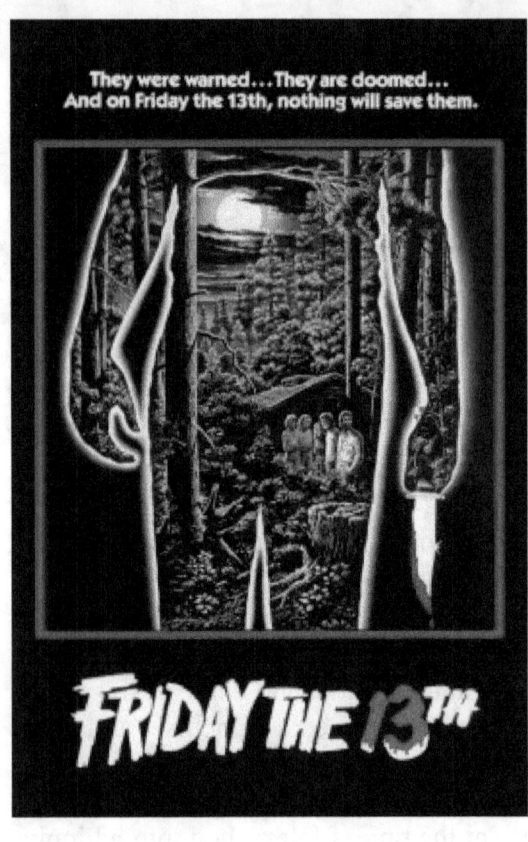

(DPP Section 3) Banned in the UK
Also known as "Long Night of Camp Blood".
Year of release: 1980
Writer: Victor Miller
Director: Sean S. Cunningham
X rated 95 mins. USA
Tagline: "You'll wish it were only a nightmare…"
Main cast: Betsy Palmer (Mrs. Pamela Voorhees), Adrienne King (Alice Hardy), Jeannine Taylor (Marcie Cunningham), Robbi Morgan (Annie), Kevin Bacon (Jack Burrel), Harry Crosby (Bill).
Distributed by: Warner Home Video

Plot:
Friday the 13th is the story of Jason Voorhees the pillowcase-wearing (later hockey mask) king of the stalk and slash movies. This movie started the franchise, which is cherished by horror fans across the globe. Pamela Voorhees takes revenge on summer camp leaders for the death of her son Jason Voorhees, Jason drowned at the Camp Crystal Lake whilst camp leaders were busy trying to fulfil their sexual urges. "Friday the 13th" sees the debut of Hollywood star Kevin Bacon.

Appraisal:
1980, the year we were first introduced to Jason Voorhees, the legacy was born and what a legacy it was! This film is unique as Jason Voorhees mum "Betsy Palmer" is the "spoiler alert" killer. This film is a classic in every way, unlike most stalk and slash films it takes itself seriously, ok! It still has some annoying teens but as with most films it's great seeing them picked off one by one, that was always my favorite part of the 80's slashers wishing the most annoying ones would get killed first. "Friday the 13th" global phenomenon and it's easy to see why, the film features enough suspense, shocks and sexual scenes to keep the viewer entertained. Although most affiliated with the psycho killer Jason Voorhees is his hockey mask we had to wait until "Friday the 13th part 3" until Jason actually wore the mask. Most of the sequels are interesting enough slasher films featuring the iconic killer, in 2001 we say "Jason X" a strange sci-fi offering of the series in which we see Jason cryogenically frozen.

This is hands down one of the best slasher films of all time. There are two benchmarks for the slasher genre, Friday the 13th and "Halloween". Writer Victor Miller had originally called Jason Josh but this was later changed to Jason as the name was deemed too friendly (I don't think Josh would have had the fear inducing quality that Jason has to it), "Freddy Vs. Josh" just wouldn't have worked, Josh sounds like a teen high school jock. This movie has continued to influence filmmakers today and will continue for future generations, this film doesn't date it's a timeless classic. This haunting horror film has everything you want from a good horror, shock, scares, heart racing scenes, and a amazing horror atmosphere which is created by the director, this is a masterpiece! The films franchise is one of the longest running in film history, director and co-writer Sean S. Cunningham is a true master of the craft, every scene is well shot and executed. Sean S. Cunningham previously produced the 1972 film "The Last House on the Left" and the remake in 2009. Sean S. Cunningham also produced "Freddy Vs. Jason" in 2003 and was an executive producer on "Jason X" in 2001 and "Jason goes to Hell: The Final Friday" in 1993.

Betsy Palmer who played the role of Pamela Voorhees was nothing short of amazing, she looks and acts like a psycho bitch-just perfectly! Actress Adrienne King as Alice Hardy is up there as one of the greatest scream queens of all time, she's feisty and a true force to be reckoned with. The film also stars a very young

Kevin Bacon when he wasn't annoying us with bad TV ads. This films does get a lot of stick the new Jason Voorhees fans expecting the hockey-masked killer wielding his machete. This film sets everything up perfectly and has an underlying creepiness which the other films don't have, my love of this film comes from my childhood watching this at a young age freaked me out and that horror has stayed with me, this is a great slasher film! Friday the 13th is one of the best horror films of all time and was withdrawn in 1984 leaving Warner Bros to wait a long time before the BBFC made a final decision on the films fate. When the film was submitted for classification it was stated as the full, uncut version but it actually had 11 seconds of cuts, these 11 seconds were deemed to gory and were missing from the original VHS and cinematic release in the UK.

Friday the 13th was seized under section 3 of the 1959 Obscene Publications Act on VHS in the early 1980's before the implementation of the Video Recordings Act of 1984 in the UK.

Friday the 13th was initially released uncut on pre-cert VHS by Warner Home Video in 1982, prior to this the UK theatrical version of the film was passed in 1980 with cuts made. The film is now available in its full, uncut glory with a 18 BBFC rating.

-Tony Newton

When Sean S. Cunningham, the director and producer of *Friday the 13th*, edited the film for television, he was surprised to discover that he only had to trim twenty seconds, and anyone familiar with the film knows where those twenty seconds came from. Annie's throat-slashing. The Kevin Bacon arrow-through the-throat sequence. Bill hanging from the generator cabin door, full of arrows. The decapitation of Mrs. Voorhees. Those were the good old days.

Instead of lingering over these sequences, the TV version presented them in sharp, short jolts. This was precisely the effect that Cunningham was striving for when he initially conceptualized *Friday the 13th*, and while I have the greatest admiration for effects legend Tom Savini and his groundbreaking work in the film, it was this version of *Friday the 13th* I saw first and which has retained its poignancy in my memory, more than thirty years later.

I was nine years old when I saw *Friday the 13th* for the first time, on a Friday night in 1982, in my living-room, and that viewing endures as the most visceral experience I've ever had watching a film, in any genre.

What happened to me on that Friday night? Oblivious, at my age, to the newly-minted slasher film genre that *Friday the 13th* popularized, I was excited and startled as the would-be camp counsellors at Camp Crystal Lake were whittled down, one by one, in the most bizarrely-inventive and shocking ways I'd ever seen, even minus the twenty seconds, even with commercial breaks, all of which were punctuated by the *Friday the 13th* block logo exploding through glass.

When Alice, *Friday the 13th*'s heroine and lone survivor, barricades herself inside the main cabin towards the end of the film, I was paralyzed with fear alongside her, wondering where the invisible killer was, and how they were going to attack next. When the killer was revealed to be Pamela Voorhees, a middle-aged woman, it blew my mind. As played by Betsy Palmer, Mrs. Voorhees was the scariest villain I'd ever seen, and I still get scared just thinking about her.

When I went to bed that night, I hid under the covers, the first and last time I'd ever been so scared of a film. When I went to school on Monday, I discovered that the other kids had also seen the film and this begun a phase when *Friday the 13th* took on a mythic status for me and my friends at school. In the abstract, I can see now that *Friday the 13th* isn't a very good film at all, but in the way it affected me and my friends back then, and defined that era, it was, and remains, a touching experience.

Banned by my mother from watching horror films in 1984, for an indefinite term, watching *Friday the 13th* required a measure of dexterity and stealth on my part through the mid 80s. On another Friday night, in 1985, while my parents were upstairs in bed, I was downstairs in the living-room again, pretending to watch wrestling, but although I was a big WWF fan, I was really waiting for *Friday the 13th*, keeping the volume low, flipping back and forth between the channels, the Record lever on the Beta machine pressed down, listening for sounds of my mother, too scared to watch the film alone in the basement.

Beta remained in our house until the late 80s, which was about the same time I started renting *Friday the 13th* at my local video store. Watching the theatrical version on tape, it was a revelation to see the effects as they appeared in theaters, but the element of surprise was lost, and this marked the beginning of an era when I started looking at *Friday the 13th* through a nostalgic lens, even though I was only a teenager.

I also started reading the magazine *Fangoria* around this time, and it was within *Fangoria*'s pages that the curtain of horror movie magic was lifted and I started reading interviews with all of the actors and filmmakers responsible for the horror films that had affected me so greatly growing up, including *Friday the 13th*.

Ironically enough, in 2002, I was the first journalist to do a retrospective on the 1980 film, which was published in *Fangoria*. 2004 saw the publication of my first book, *Making Friday the 13th*: *The Legend of Camp Blood*, a book that covered the entire *Friday the 13th* film series, and 2013 saw the publication of *On Location in Blairstown*: *The Making of Friday the 13th*, a book devoted to the filming and planning of *Friday the 13th*, the first film, the only one I love.

So I have quite a long history with *Friday the 13th*, personally and professionally, and I can no more believe that the film is approaching its 35th anniversary than I can believe that I'm now 41 years old. As a journalist, I can look at the film objectively and see that it has a lot to answer for, in terms of its effect on the genre. It brought the slasher genre into the mainstream and changed the way Hollywood did business, at least for a brief period in the early 80s. It inspired a legion of copycats, and was ultimately most responsible for the backlash against horror and violence in cinema that took flight in the 80s.

In terms of content, it's amazing what Cunningham and Savini were able to get away with, within the confines of the R rating, particularly with the decapitation scene and the Kevin Bacon effect. For his part, Cunningham is shockingly complimentary towards the MPAA ratings board and the way it treated him and *Friday the 13th*. "We have in the MPAA," said Cunningham, "one of the greatest political gifts to artists in the world. Because of the MPAA, any person can make a movie about anything he wants. He can make it any way he wants. The MPAA stays sensitive to the mood swings of the country so they can adjust their ratings. I think it's wonderful we live in a culture where you can do anything in a movie, whatever it is. Nobody tells you that you can't do something, except the marketplace."

I agree with Cunningham, and believe the ratings system, however arbitrary and flawed, serves a necessary function, and one of *Friday the 13th*'s most impressive achievements is how the film skated by the certification process virtually unscathed, an oversight for which 1981's severely compromised *Friday the 13th Part 2* and many other post-*Friday the 13th* slasher films were made to suffer.

The violence in *Friday the 13th* is graphic and shocking, but it falls squarely within the prism of fantasy and horror and serves the purpose of taking the audience on a roller coaster ride rather than wallowing in sadism and torture, as Cunningham's previous horror effort, *Last House on the Left,* was accused of doing, and was the case with post-*Friday the 13th* filth like *I Spit on Your Grave* and *Mother's Day*. As gory as it was *Friday the 13th* played by the rules of the horror genre by redrawing the rules.

On a personal level, *Friday the 13th* has taken on the same persona as one of those half-forgotten, long-lost kids I grew up with during our elementary school years, so many years ago now. Like those kids, I've lost touch with the film over the years, watching it only sporadically, once every few years, but it will always be a part of me, just like the nine-year-old boy I was.

-David Grove, author of *Jamie Lee Curtis*: *Scream Queen* and *On Location in Blairstown*: *The Making of Friday the 13th.*

Why this film is banned will always make me shake my head and laugh. Out of the four film essays I have written, this one perhaps reflects my daily life in horror journalism, broadcasting and culture. Created as a money making effort post John Carpenter's classic slasher tale "Halloween", director/writer Sean Cunningham, writer Ron Kurz, writer Victor Miller, EFX artist Tom Savini, composer Harry Manfredini and an incredible cast and crew constructed a story that amped up what "Halloween" had been missing… some gore, guts and balls. Not to say that Carpenter's creation isn't amazing, tense and a landmark, it is! To be honest, I enjoy "Halloween" much more than "Friday the 13th" on many levels including the man/monster, pacing, performances, score, influence on genre and impact on my life.

One of the underlining truths to the horror culture and genre is that a lot of the time, these films happen by happenstance. Things falling into place, the right audience, staying power, review, memorable scenes or lines, hell just horror happening! It's the only genre where you can show reality, truth and emotion to the different crowds and get different and unique reactions. "Friday the 13th" did that for me and it would be the location also where I broadcast in Blairstown, New Jersey. Just like the film and the location, this quiet throwback town has never really changed in personality or style. Walking down the streets as much as I can, the town holds a legend and distinction given to it after many different audiences have watched this film over generations.

Is "Friday the 13th" the best horror slasher film of all-time? My answer is no. Does this film deserve to be banned? Again, I would say no. Is it a film that affected many people's growth and development? Oh hell ya! For that, it deserves the recognition it gets with each viewing whether on DVD, Blu-Ray or my original VHS tape I bought years ago. Just like "Night of the Living Dead", it's film that had its bump and bruises along the way, when it was released it was shocking, unsuspected and influenced so many filmmakers and fans for decades. It has done the same for me not only over my five years on Home Grown Radio NJ (which use to broadcast from Blairstown and I still do) but it is one of those films that takes a simple formula that I appreciate and creates a nightmare of tension, blood, cult status score, cinematography and shocks that is so much fun to experience!

Again, the truth is that this film does not deserve to be on the banned list by any stretch of the imagination but I understand why people would have it on there. My life was influenced by this film, and it sits like a dark seed in my soul knowing that on dark nights with friends or alone I would watch the scares, laugh and enjoy true horror filmmaking. I thank those involved with the film for that and how "Friday the 13th" has been another film that has taken me down that dark path to the lifestyle I love of horror!

-Jay K (The Horror Happens Radio Show on HGRNJ).

Friday the 13th Part 2

(DPP Section 3) Banned in the UK
Year of release: 1981
Writers: Ron Kurz and Victor Miller
Director: Steve Miner
R rated 87 mins. USA
Tagline: "Just when you thought it was safe to go back to camp….."
Main cast: Amy Steel (Ginny), John Furey (Paul), Adrienne King (Alice), Kirsten Baker (Terry), Stuart Charno (Ted), Warrington Gillette (Jason).
Distributed by: CIC Video

Plot:
Friday the 13th Part 2 is the second installment in the long running Jason Voorhees's saga. This movie takes place back at Camp Crystal Lake where we discover that Jason Voorhees isn't dead and has been living in nearby woods. With a new group of students at Camp Crystal Lake and Jason hell bent on revenge for the murder of his mother will anyone get out alive?

Appraisal:
In "Friday the 13th Part 2" Jason Voorhees is in full swing as the pillow case wearing psycho killer. In my opinion this film is equally as good as the first and brings us back at the start of the film reliving what happened last year and to the victims. This film is a classic 1980s slasher, full of scares, and jumps in all the right places, which are just brilliant in an all round classic 1980's stalk and slash movie.

Steve Miner directed this offering; Miner delivered his best directional piece of his career in my eyes. Miner also went on to direct part 3 of this franchise and "Halloween H Twenty" in 1998, Miner also directed the 2008 remake of George A Romero's "Day of the Dead". Friday the 13th Part 2 is an amazing slasher film which holds its own against the original film. We get to see actress Adrienne King's fate as (Alice) as she is attacked in her own city apartment far away from camp, then 5 years on Jason unleashes hell on the teens and countless others at Camp Crystal Lake. This film has one of my favorite jump scares from any horror film. You once again get all that you could want from a good horror film here. Amy Steel as Ginny is fantastic and she went on to star in the horror classic "April Fool's Day". Kirsten Baker as Terry is also great but didn't have much of an acting career after this film. This film has nudity, sex, blood, gore and shocks everything you expect and love from a 80's stalk and slash epic. Easily one of my favorite sequels from the franchise, to me this film is on a par with the original, although the hockey mask is still a twinkle in Jason's rather crazy eyes, the cloth sack really does work and gives a rather disturbing quality to the killer. A great horror film, grab the popcorn but don't drop any, with the jump scares!

Friday the 13th part 2 was seized under section 3 of the 1959 Obscene Publications Act on VHS in the early 1980's before the implementation of the Video Recordings Act of 1984 in the UK.

Friday the 13th Part 2 was initially released on pre-cert VHS by CIC Video in 1982. The film is only available in the MPAA R Rated version in both the US and UK.

-Tony Newton

Beginning the Jason era of F13 films, FRIDAY THE 13TH PART TWO might have made a couple of missteps regarding the introduction to the character (he took a trip into the city to kill Alice?!), but it's a much better and more terrifying film than the first film. It also introduced viewers to one of the best "final girls" of all time: Amy Steel's Ginny Field character. One of the smartest and most memorable characters to have faced Jason Voorhees (this time wearing a sack on his head, a la: THE TOWN THAT DREADED SUNDOWN), Ginny goes through hell, has all of her friends brutally murdered by Jason, and is still quick witted enough to not only stand up to Jason, but to play mind games with him.

Showcasing some of the best kills in slasher history (the wheelchair bound mark getting a machete to the face and falling down the long stairway is brutal and worthy in itself to be included in the video nasties list), FRIDAY THE 13th PART TWO is one of the most entertaining and easily one of the best film in the entire franchise. It's a bloody and terrifying film, one that never loses its horror charm.

-Jerry Smith   Editor in Chief/Writer Icons of Fright.

G.B.H (Grievous Bodily Harm)

(DPP Section 3) Banned in the UK
Year of release: 1983
Writer: Cliff Twemlow
Director: David Kent-Watson
Unrated 73 mins. UK
Tagline: "Not for the squeamish."
Main cast: Cliff Twemlow (Steve Donovan), Jane Cunliffe (Tracy), Anthony Schaeffer (Murray Parks), Brett Sinclair (Chris), Jerry Harris (Keller), Lenny Howarth (Connor).
Distributed by: World of Video 2000

Plot:
The 1983 film G.B.H is a cult home video which follows the exploits of Manchurian nutcase Steve Donovan (Salford's finest ex-bouncer) who is called in to resolve conflicts with a vicious gang led by Jewish crime boss Keller who is extorting the clubs of Manchester. The body count rises as the two settle the score once and for all.

Appraisal:
Although the acting is not that great and the film is made on a seriously low budget you can tell actor Cliff Twemlow put his all into the movie. G.B.H is deemed as Manchester's answer to "The Long Good Friday". I do have a soft spot for this film it's not dissimilar to an excessively bloody episode of "Sweeney" or "Minder", there's lots of fighting and British charm displayed on-screen.

Well worth a watch and always interesting reading up on Cliff Twemlow who was a character himself.

G.B.H (Grievous Bodily Harm) was seized under section 3 of the 1959 Obscene Publications Act on VHS in the early 1980's before the implementation of the Video Recordings Act of 1984 in the UK.

G.B.H (Grievous Bodily Harm)was initially released uncut on pre-cert VHS by World of Video 2000 in 1983, There has been no releases of the film in the UK since its initial release on VHS.

-Tony Newton

Graduation Day

(DPP Section 3) Banned in the UK
Year of release: 1981
Writer: Anne Marisse and Herb Feed
Director: Herb Freed
R rated 96 mins. USA
Tagline: "Graduating from high school has never been so deadly….."
Main cast: Christopher George (Coach George Michaels), Patch Mackenzie (Anne Ramstead), E. Danny Murphy (Kevin Badger), E. J Peaker (Blondie), Michael Pataki (Principle Guglione), Richard Balin (Mr. Roberts).
Distributed by: Iver Film Services

Plot:
Graduation Day is an early 1980's slasher movie. There is a black-gloved serial killer on the loose, killing high school teen track stars. After a teen student dies from a heart attack after running a 30 second 200-meter race.

Appraisal:
Graduation Day, yes another campus slasher movie! The film centers around graduation day but who will graduate? as there's a killer on the loose!

Graduation Day is your run of the mill campus slasher but it has received a lot of bad press however which makes me slightly dubious about admitting to actually quite liking this film, it's humorous in parts and does use some inventive murdering techniques. I find this a very fun stalk and slash movie! That does deliver even through the campiness on Campus!

Overall this film is nowhere near as bad as a lot of the 80's slasher offerings.

Grab out the old VHS, dig out the Wham bars, and hunt for Tab Clear!

It's 1981 goddammit!

Graduation Day was seized under section 3 of the 1959 Obscene Publications Act on VHS in the early 1980's before the implementation of the Video Recordings Act of 1984 in the UK.

Graduation Day was initially released on pre-cert VHS by Iver Film Services in 1982, The director's cut which was re-edited which was passed 15; this is the cut version of film.

-Tony Newton

Happy Birthday to Me

(DPP Section 3) Banned in the UK
Year of release: 1981
Writer: John C.W. Saxton
Director: J. Lee Thompson
R rated Canada
Tagline: "Because of the bizarre nature of this birthday party, pray you're not invited."
Main cast: Melissa Sue Anderson (Virginia Wainwright), Glenn Ford (Dr. David Faraday), Lawrence Dane (Hal Wainwright), Sharon Acker (Estelle Wainwright), Frances Hyland (Mrs. Patterson), Tracey E. Bregman (Ann Thomerson).
Distributed by: RCA/Columbia Pictures.

Plot:
Virginia Wainwright has recently returned to the Crawford Academy after being involved in a major car accident in which she was seriously brain damaged, after undergoing a radical new procedure she re-joins her friends at the academy, it's then that Virginia's clique of friends (the "Top Ten") are murdered one by one but just who is responsible for slaughtering them?

Appraisal:
Happy Birthday to Me is the much-loved 1980's cult horror film. It follows the stalk and slash adventures of a psycho. The video cover features a man with a kebab skewer being violently shoved down his throat, this cover was always going to grab the attention of the censors.

Happy Birthday to Me is a big budget slasher film with twists and some great gory moments and features some inventive methods of murder.

Happy Birthday to Me directed by J. Lee Thompson is another early 80's slasher flick, which I adore!

I love the films tagline, "six of the most bizarre murders you will ever see." This film is fantastic and it's a great fast paced slash fest of a film with a great body count and some of the most original kills you will see in an 80's slasher movie, including death by shish kebab!

This is such a fun little horror movie, which I always revisit time after time.

Pure 1980's stalk and slash heaven!

This is a true classic for all fans of 80's slasher films, well worth a watch!

Happy Birthday to Me was seized under section 3 of the 1959 Obscene Publications Act on VHS in the early 1980's before the implementation of the Video Recordings Act of 1984 in the UK.

Happy Birthday to Me was initially released uncut on pre-cert VHS by RCA/Columbia Pictures in 1982, The cut US R rated version which was passed 15 without extra cuts, this is the cut version of film.

-Tony Newton

I was hired by J Lee Thompson in his house in Malibu. I didn't even have to read. He talked to me for a bit and said, OK. I said, "What's OK?" He said, you are hired! He used to call me CRAZY, that was my name on set. I earned it because we were doing a scene that had a big wide shot of hundreds of kids running to go see a skeleton head that had just been found. I was supposed to run through the extras, hit my mark at the edge of everyone, stop and look very concerned. Well, they set the shot, everyone ran and just as I was to hit my mark, an extra pointed with her arm and I ran directly into it, it hit me directly in the throat and I started to laugh but continued the scene. Oh Lee was furious with me! I had ruined the shot!! Well, the moment that I RUINED ended up being the reason they changed the entire ending of the movie to make me the murderer. My character was originally killed half way thru the movie. Interesting how life works. I really loved making the movie and everyone associated with it. I have kept in touch with someone of the actors through the years. I will never forget Lee Thompson or the experience of making my first movie.

-Tracey E. Bregman   Actress in "Happy Birthday to Me".

As a Canadian, I think of *Happy Birthday to Me* as being a time capsule of both the short-lived post-*Friday the 13th* and *Halloween* slasher boom in the early 80s and the slash-for-cash tax shelter era that defined Canadian cinema during that same period. As a viewer, it was a film whose reputation preceded it, and it was that reputation that filled me with an obsession to see it.

Happy Birthday to Me had been on television several times throughout the 80s, but I was never able to watch it, and I couldn't find a video store that carried the film on Beta, up until 1988, when I found a store that carried it in Beta and asked my mother to rent it for me. Much to my surprise, she agreed, but before she could get it for me, I arrived home after school one day and found the film listed in *TV Guide*.

It was shown late on a Saturday night, and I slept through the first act, my mother eventually slapping me awake, not wanting to have to rent it for me. Watching the rest of the film, I wasn't impressed. It was derivative, grimy and featured the silliest plot and denouement I'd ever seen in a slasher film up to that point, with the possible exception of *Killer Party*.

And yet there was something bizarrely compelling about the experience of watching it that made me want to watch the entire film again, which I was able to do when the film was shown on television again, in 1990, when I was in senior high. This time, I watched the film from the beginning, and I also recorded it on VHS, *Happy Birthday to Me* joining my fledgling library of Beta and VHS taped horror films that I watched over and over again. You never forget those films, including the commercial cuts, especially the commercial cuts.

I found *Happy Birthday to Me* morbidly fascinating in the way the film approaches badness from so many ingenious directions. The ad's promised "Six of the most bizarre murders you will ever see" and the film certainly delivers, in a scene where a character has a barbell dropped on his throat and in a scene involving a death by shish-kabob rammed down his throat. It's silly but effective.

Happy Birthday to Me was directed by J. Lee Thompson, of *The Guns of Navarone* fame, and the cast featured Melissa Sue Anderson, then starring in the television series *Little House on the Prairie*. Anderson was joined in the film by Hollywood legend Glenn Ford, but if the makers of *Happy Birthday to Me* thought they could legitimize the project by enlisting someone as distinguished as Ford, it didn't work, although the film's elevated pedigree is one of its most disarming elements.

Happy Birthday to Me was responsible for one of the most genuine moments I've ever had as a moviegoer. After buying a VHS copy off EBay in 2004, I skimmed the film once and then put it on the basement wall, where it gathered dust until one pitch black Saturday night in 2008 when I decided to revisit the film out of the blue. With the VHS image blown-up on my plasma screen, I laughed all the way through the film, talking back to the actors, repeating the dialogue, celebrating the film, its badness and the era it now symbolizes. It was one of the best times I've ever had watching the film, and it wouldn't have been possible on DVD or Blu-Ray.

-David Grove   Author of *Jamie Lee Curtis: Scream Queen* and *On Location in Blairstown: The Making of Friday the 13th.*

The Headless Eyes

(DPP Section 3) Banned in the UK
Also known as "Bloodthirsty Butchers".
Year of release: 1971
Writer: Kent Bateman
Director: Kent Bateman
X rated 78 mins. USA
Tagline: "See the terrifying spectacle of the eye-gouger…"
Main cast: Bo Brundin (Arthur Malcolm), Ramon Gordon (Gordon Ramon), Kelley Swartz, Mary Jane Early, Larry Hunter (Harry Silver).
Distributed by: Sapphire Video

Plot:
The Headless Eyes is an early 1970's gritty New York horror film, which follows an artist who turns to murder after losing his eye, which was gouged out by his victim whilst he attempted to rob her. This killer has a taste for blood and a fascination for human eyeballs.

Appraisal:
The Headless Eyes follows a serial killer who loses his eye whilst breaking into a New York apartment, this premise alone is crazy as hell and what follows is even crazier!

The Headless Eyes was filmed on a very low budget, it's a shame that what started out as a great idea falls flat in many parts, although the film is seedy and gritty. This is a very early example of seedy and gory serial killer film. The Headless Eyes has a unique idea focusing on an eyeball collector but that alone is not enough to make it a success, it falls flat toward the end but for some strange reason you are left wanting more!

This is well worth a watch if you're a fan of psycho slasher films but it just doesn't hold up and feels very dated.

On the plus side the VHS sleeve is really cool, but that's the best thing about the movie!

Headless Eyes was seized under section 3 of the 1959 Obscene Publications Act on VHS in the early 1980's before the implementation of the Video Recordings Act of 1984 in the UK.

Headless Eyes was initially released uncut on pre-cert VHS by Sapphire Video in 1983, There has been no re-release in the UK since its initial VHS release but you can get hold of an unrated US version of the film.

-Tony Newton

Hell Prison

(DPP Section 3) Banned in the UK
Also known as "Escape from Hell"
Year of release: 1980
Writer: Sergio Chiusi
Director: Eduardo Mulargia
Rated 18 93 mins. Spain, Italy
Tagline: "The warden's just handed down a stiff sentence."
Main cast: Anthony Steffen (Doctor Farrell), Ajita Wilson (Zaira), Cristina Lay (Vivienne), Cinita Lodetti (Katie), Luciano Pigozzi (The Warden), Serafino Profumo (Martinez).
Distributed by: KM Video

Plot:
Hell Prison sees the prisoners of a women's prison camp located deep in the tropical rain forest endure torture at the hands of the prison guards. The inmates are raped and beaten on a daily basis. The prisoners, determined to breakout enlist the help of the camp Doctor to plan their escape.

Appraisal:
Hell Prison see's women being brutally tortured and abused and features more naked flesh than a soft-core porn film. You get the feeling that this film is just there for its flesh and women being abused for the sake of it, all in all this is not a great film or even one of the better women's prison offerings.

This film is full on exploitation for exploitation sake, although I am huge fan of Italian cinema, this one doesn't deliver the goods!

Hell Prison was seized under section 3 of the 1959 Obscene Publications Act on VHS in the early 1980's before the implementation of the Video Recordings Act of 1984 in the UK.

Hell Prison was initially released uncut on pre-cert VHS by KM in 1982, prior to this the film was banned had its theatrical release banned by the BBFC, the film was released on VHS again in 1987 with cuts made by the BBFC rated 18.

-Tony Newton

The Hills Have Eyes

(DPP Section 3) Banned in the UK
Also known as "Blood Relations".
Year of release: 1977
Writer: Wes Craven
Director: Wes Craven
X rated 89 mins. USA
Tagline: "They burned the father, killed the mother, and raped the sister!"
Main cast: John Steadman (Fred), Janus Blythe (Ruby), Peter Locke (Mercury), Russ Grieve (Big Bob Carter), Virginia Vincent (Ethel carter), Suze Lanier-Bramlett (Brenda Carter).
Distributed by: Thorn EMI

Plot:
The Hills Have Eyes is a 1970's Wes Craven classic horror masterpiece. This a disturbing tale of a family who are driving across country on vacation. When they take a shortcut through New Mexico they break down and are consequently left stranded in the middle of nowhere. The hills are occupied by inbred cannibal rednecks, and the family find themselves fighting for survival.

Appraisal:
This film is a total classic from start to finish; everything about this film is great. The Hills Have Eyes never feels dated, it delivers everything needed for a clever and thrilling horror film, which is atmospheric to boot! The film is shot well and captures the feeling of being deserted and falling prey to the psycho's very well. The Hills Have Eyes is now a cult classic, It was much talked about in the 1980's and was on every horror fans wish list. I remember before watching the film feeling apprehensive to watch it, only to find that it wasn't covered in gore or the usual take on cannibalism but a really good horror/thriller where you were rooting for the family to survive and exact revenge on the sick and twisted mutant freaks! The Hills Have Eyes is easily one of Wes Cravens best films, a true horror film in every sense of the word, it's a masterpiece that shocks, scares and brutally attacks all of your senses, pure class! Just how horror should be!

This unrelenting horror flick is the staple of horror films; everything about this film is perfect! The film shows every element of how a horror movie should be from start to finish!

I watched this film when I was really young and it freaked me out. Since then I added the film to my yearly Halloween movie-athon, and re-visit this horror classic every year!

The Hills Have Eyes was seized under section 3 of the 1959 Obscene Publications Act on VHS in the early 1980's before the implementation of the Video Recordings Act of 1984 in the UK.

The Hills Have Eyes was initially released on pre-cert VHS by Thorn EMI in 1977 and also released by Jaguar Video in the UK in 1981, prior to this the film was cut by the BBFC for its theatrical release, it was the theatrical version that was featured on the VHS releases, The film is available rated 18 from the BBFC but this version is the US R Rated print of the film which still contains some cuts.

-Tony Newton

August 30th, 2015 was a sombre day for horror aficionados the world over. *Wesley Earl Craven* died, leaving a massive void behind him, and the world mourned one of the boldest visionary filmmakers of our times. While he reached a fairly ripe old age of 76, it still didn't feel like his time. I grew up with Craven, films such as A Nightmare on Elm Street and The Serpent & The Rainbow providing the backdrop for my own adolescence and, while none of his features would make my all-time top twenty, a fair number of them populate my top one hundred. As well as being astute in his craft, former humanities professor Craven was also a kind, gentle man and well considered by his peers. The horror industry may currently mourn him but I prefer to celebrate his numerous achievements. Thus, I have decided to appraise one of his finest and most controversial films.

The Hills Have Eyes arrived at a time when 70s exploitation provided the midnight screenings at countless drive-ins all over the United States. Craven made no secret of his adoration of *Tobe Hooper's* 1974 exploitation classic The Texas Chain Saw Massacre and intended to pay affectionate homage to it. This also meant reusing many of the props as art director *Robert A. Burns* cut his teeth working on Hooper's debauched classic. Craven's film was placed under similar scrutiny by the censors, with the MPAA demanding several cuts in order to award it the R-rating required to reach a wider audience. Frustratingly, like so many other movies of its era, the absent footage has long since been misplaced, meaning that the true director's cut will never be seen.

Under the working title Blood Relations, the film was originally intended to be set in woodlands, with most of the cannibals being juveniles and the purpose of their skulduggery being ritualistic, as opposed to survivalist. Eventually, Craven opted for a desert location in Nevada, much to the crew's displeasure, as the temperature was prone to reach up to 120 degrees in the searing mid-afternoon heat. While they struggled with the conditions, it was *Michael Berryman* who drew the shortest straw. Suffering from Hypohidrotic Ectodermal Dysplasia means that, aside from a lack of body hair, he also doesn't possess a solitary sweat gland. After five months of shooting in unbearable conditions, I would imagine that unhinged glare of the promo art to be entirely authentic.

The feral family depicted are based loosely on a fifteenth-century clan led by *Sawney Beane* who roamed the Scottish highlands, cannibalising passing transients, before being captured and executed without trial. While they populate the red corner, the Carters prove a surprisingly formidable opponent in the blue. These comprise former lawman Bob *(Russ Grieve),* his homemaker spouse Ethel *(Virginia Vincent),* minors Bobby *(Robert Houston),* and Brenda *(Susan Lanier),* eldest daughter Lynne *(Dee Wallace),* her husband Doug *(Martin Speer)* and their newborn infant Katy *(Brenda Marinoff).* On the surface they appear to be just your average bickering nuclear family but there's nothing like watching on as half of your loved ones are harshly decimated to stoke the fires for some good old all-American retribution.

Having received directions from gas station attendant Fred *(John Steadman),* and finding themselves marooned in an abandoned airfield, the brood has become sitting ducks for any resident Neanderthals and it just so happens that Fred's nearest and dearest fit that particular bill rather inconveniently. Patriarch Papa Jupiter *(James Whitworth),* rules a roost which comprises three spiteful sons, Mars *(Lance Gordon),* Pluto (Berryman), and Mercury *(Pete Locke),* and want-away daughter Ruby *(Janus Blythe).* The clan make up with survival instinct what they lack in airs and graces and it isn't long before they sniff out the Carters and infiltrate their happy motor home.

From the offset, Craven imbues his film with a sense of isolation, using shots of the vast, desolate wasteland to set the tone before reigning it back in and focusing on the penned-in Carter livestock. Once their homely Winnebago becomes compromised, it's game on, and the family feud commences. This is where The Hills Have Eyes finds a rattlesnake pace which it relentlessly maintains for the remainder of the feature. It's like playing draughts with the Mansons, and playing fair isn't in Papa Jupiter's game plan. However, he does have smarts, thus the primary port of call is to flambé his opposite number Bob before the very eyes of his mortified loved ones and wrestle that home advantage. There's nothing like a flame-grilled head honcho to disassemble your family unit.

While pops is still smoking in the clearing, Jupiter's boys are wrecking merry havoc in the trailer, unbeknownst to those attempting to douse the flames outside. This scene is particularly torrid when you consider that the numbers are whittled down so swiftly and unceremoniously. Round one definitely goes to the hills and the Carter's are left to count any cost to their obliterated collective. By forcing them to confront the aftermath, Craven's film hits on a far more personal level, as we put ourselves in their sorry shoes and ask ourselves whatever next? How does one ever bounce back from such a visceral exhibition of malicious intent? The Hills Have Eyes poses these discomforting questions and then reminds us of snatched bairn Katy and our maternal instincts kick in full throttle.

We only need cast our minds back to 1971 and *Dennis Weaver's* backbitten commuter David Mann from *Steven Spielberg's* restive rod movie Duel to be granted with the necessary perspective. Mann's resolute rearguard was one thing, but ultimately he was the only one threatened with missing his p.m. appointments. Speer even looks a little like Weaver if you squint your eyes but his exasperation is far more intense and, once cause graduates to effect, he becomes the true hero we hang our hats upon. Lanier and Houston both contribute also, but theirs is more of the Kevin McAllister mild mischief variety, where Doug is prepared to really get his nails grimy. It's a fascinating showdown and the second half of The Hills Have Eyes is unapologetically unflinching.

This is all well and good but what of the unruly opposition? What do our resident heathens bring to the game? Berryman must never have dreamed that one day he would become one of the most deliberated poster boys of the decade. While not destined to be seen squeezing his rump into a pair of pre-shrunk 501 denims at the local Laundromat any time soon, his boggling eyes were ideal to stare at us from within such gritty hills and that image still haunts my soul to this very day. As for his brothers in arms, what they lack in charm they more than make up for with smarm, while their dental plan is questionable at best and table manners leave something to be desired. I've always found budgerigars to be rather purposeless as domestic pets but they do evidently make for delightful finger foods.

After his debut feature The Last House on The Left had detractors spitting feathers, his second foray into horror is even more mean-spirited in many respects. Its perpetrators lack any kind of reason and their crimes can be considered even more heinous, should you play the numbers game. However, The Hills Have Eyes didn't leave the same obnoxious tang on my palate. There is simply no time to mourn our fallen comrades and it rewards at a far brisker pace than its forebear. Also notable is that five years had passed by the time this hit the marketplace and audiences were becoming a little more battle-hardened. Craven used the interim learning to grasp his directorial reigns with a little more conviction and it is visible in an end product which positively oozes rough justice.

If you look back on the plethora of appraisals I have constructed for Craven's other works, you will be aware that I never considered him to be in the leagues of the Romeros, Carpenters, or Argentos. This may well be so, but I revere him to the moon and back for supplying me with so many reasons not to slumber in tranquillity come nightfall. The Hills Have Eyes may not be the kind of movie to encourage repeat views but it is a significant gear in the 70s exploitation mechanism and reason not to take that cross-country jaunt across Nevada. In acknowledgement of the great man himself, Pluto joins Krueger, Krug, and their entourage in my subconscious each time I nestle my weary head into the pillowcase and, for that, I will always be indebted. Rest well my friend and I'll be seeing you soon in my nightmares.

Dedicated to Wes Craven (1939-2015)

-Keeper of the Crimson Quill   (Rivers of Grue)

You may not recognise the name of actor Michael Berryman but when you see his face you will know exactly who he is. He is B-movie royalty & starred in the 1977 video nasty supreme The Hills Have Eyes.

On a budget of less than $250,000, Wes Craven created a violent slice of cinema history which has been followed & remade ever since, with the latest movie, a re-make of the original being released in 2006.

The plot is simple. Break down in the desert. Family cut off. Strange cannibal creatures in the hills. Mayhem, murder, a major body count & a substantial volume of acting blood. B-movies don't come much better than this.

Michael Berryman gives the performance of his life as the mutant human-muncher Pluto & the scenes as our stranded family try to escape the hungry 'pack' are unforgettable.

I must have been pretty young when I first watched it as I remember his face more than anything else. But you know what, it's was not in scary, Freddy Kruger kind of way – I always quite liked him & his crazed character. That's probably why I ended up writing horror.

So, find this movie. If you have to dig out a VHS tape, insert that cassette & enjoy a trip back to the 70s when horror was gruesome, budgets were tight but the hills most certainly had eyes. If you can't take the time trip, try the 2006 version – it's reasonable if slightly more lame.

-Sean T. Page,
Author of The Zombie Survival Manual & The Alien Invasion Manual, both from Haynes Publications.

The legend of 15th-century Scottish cannibal Sawney Bean and his inbred clan may not have been entirely true — and that I find this disappointing may mean there's something quite wrong with me — but that hasn't stopped it from inspiring gobs of retellings. For my tastes, none are more harrowing than 1977's *The Hills Have Eyes*, director Wes Craven's follow-up to his debut, *The Last House on the Left*.

The set-up is bare-bones simple: en route to California, the thoroughly middle-American Carter family takes an ill-advised route through the southwestern desert and snaps an axle, becoming sitting ducks for the predatory attentions of a murderous tribe led by Papa Jupiter, a sun-baked patriarch of Old Testament dimensions. The movie is an obvious low budget effort, and we wouldn't have it any other way. As with the original *The Texas Chain Saw Massacre*, its simmering desolation feels so authentically hostile that the film stock itself seems to have been seared in the process.

Even by the standards of its era, *The Hills Have Eyes* isn't that overtly violent or bloody. Despite a few shocking scenes, any number of contemporary films from Sam Peckinpah and Clint Eastwood topped it on those terms. Instead, it seems plausible that *Hills* may have earned its "video nasty" status for reasons similar to the odd rationale Hollywood's MPAA gave for refusing to grant an R-rating to the low-key *Henry: Portrait of a Serial Killer*: an intangible transgression they called "disturbing moral tone."

Underlying it all is the creepy, mythic backstory of how Papa Jupe came to be, filled in by his father, a grizzled old man eking out his days in a decrepit gas station past the edge of nowhere. Jupiter emerged into the world as a 20-pound baby, "hairy as a monkey," who nearly tore his mother apart. After enduring a decade of increasingly barbaric conduct, his father bashed his face open with a tire iron and left him out for the elements to finish off. Puny elements! Jupiter is a force of nature with a grudge, who likely stole a wife to sire his own family out in the desert wastes and name his dimwit sons after planets. There's a primal mojo to this, which exploits our modern fear of anyone who not only thrives where the rest of us would perish, but scorns us for the civilizing influence that keeps us from guzzling a canary like a juice box.

Then again, the proficiency of the surviving Carters in fighting back recalls the thoughts of Henry David Thoreau: "The savage in man is never quite eradicated."

The Hills Have Eyes' greatest strengths are never more apparent than in comparison to the 2006 remake. On its own, the later version isn't a bad movie by any means. It's a good, solid, gritty horror film, which benefits from fine casting, including the ever-dependable Ted Levine as the ill-fated Big Bob Carter. Still, in seeking to push the extremes, the remakers appear to have lost sight of the fact that it's often subtleties and small things that resonate the most. They were content to merely stretch out the surface, instead of trying to go deep, as well.

They devised a bigger, more topical backstory to explain the existence of their desert clan, but it still can't match the archetypal power of the original's tale of Jupiter as a "devil kid."

The makeup effects are more grotesque, but there's still nothing as weird as actor Michael Berryman for real.

Its mutants ratchet up the ultraviolence, but nothing they do is as disturbing as the original's first look at Mars' shambling, subhuman behavior during the trailer attack.

There's a supermarket fridge full of human remains, but this is nowhere as appalling as the original Mama's joyous reception when her dutiful sons bring home the "tenderloin baby."

In fact, there's no matriarchal presence in the remake at all, beyond a glimpse of a bald, television-dazed woman combing a wig. Which gets to the heart of where it falls short where the original works best. Although the remake hurls more cannibals at the Carters, it's essentially devoid of any sense of them interacting as a tight-knit family. They're mostly each off by themselves, doing … ehh, mutant things. It's as if being a mutant is just a really crappy job. Sadly, the whole fertile family-versus-family dynamic (or, if you prefer, family-versus-the-most-ungodly-fucked-up-frat-house-ever) falls by the dusty wayside.

In contrast, the original's late-night dinner scene — with the clan presumably snacking on the roasted body of Big Bob, while Papa Jupiter rants at his charred head and everyone cheers him on — has to be one of the greatest perversions of everyday family custom ever committed to film. Jupiter's triumphant snarl of "I'm gonna watch yer goddamn car rust out!" is so totally from his frame of reference it seems alien. Who *thinks* like that? *These* people. *These* weirdoes do.

The remake does introduce one change that works at least as well, with the character of clan-daughter Ruby. In the original, she's a sorta hot young woman who, feral wardrobe aside, comes off as normal and conscientious enough that there's a theory she wasn't the clan's daughter by birth, but rather a victim they spared as a little girl and raised as their own. The 2006 Ruby is still a child and, without any doubt, one of *them*, but wordlessly longs for the normality she sees in the Carters. It's a poignant portrayal that tugs at the heart.

Otherwise, the remake keeps its hill clan at a comfortable remove from audience sensibilities. They're such gnarled, misshapen loners, they're as impossible to identify with as reptilians stepping off a starship.

The original provides no such escape hatch. *This is us*, it seems to be saying. Stripped of niceties, of opportunity, of education, of electricity, bereft of civilizing influence and the need to conform enough to get along with the neighbors, this could be any of us.

Now dinner is served.

-Brian Hodge   Author

Home Sweet Home

(DPP Section 3) Banned in the UK
Also known as "Slasher in the House".
Year of release: 1981
Writer: Thomas Bush
Director: Nettie Peña
Rated 18, 85 mins. USA
Tagline: "Be it ever so humble, there's no place to HIDE."
Main cast: Jake Steinfeld (Killer), Vinessa Shaw (Angel), Peter De Paula (Mistake), Don Edmonds (Bradley), Charles Hoyes (Wayne), David Mielke (Scott).
Distributed by: MEDIA

Plot:
In this retro slasher Home Sweet Home a psychopathic murderer escapes an insane asylum on thanksgiving weekend. When a family gather to celebrate thanksgiving at a secluded ranch they get more than they bargained for when this psychopathic killer goes on a bloody rampage! Who will be left standing?

Appraisal:
This is a crazy little early 1980's slash n' kill film! Home Sweet Home is very by the numbers, killing for kills sake and the characters are quite annoying. The killer isn't convincing enough and just plays it for laughs literally!. Home Sweet Home is one of the worst slasher flicks out there, complete with an annoying teen who is as annoying as is his clown/ KISS-esque make-up, crazy to think the one thing that stood out for me in this film was the annoying guy in the makeup. It has its moments a cheese ball comedy style 80's horror flick why this was banned is beyond me!

Some scenes are so funny that if you want a laugh give this film a spin, instead of a comedy VHS!

Home Sweet Home was seized under section 3 of the 1959 Obscene Publications Act on VHS in the early 1980's before the implementation of the Video Recordings Act of 1984 in the UK.

Home Sweet Home was initially released uncut on pre-cert VHS by Media in 1982. The film is available fully uncut and with an 18 rating from the BBFC in the UK.

-Tony Newton

Honeymoon Horror

(DPP Section 3) Banned in the UK
Year of release: 1982
Writer: L.L. Carney and Harry Preston
Director: Harry Preston
R rated UK
Tagline: "'Til death do us part".
Main cast: Paul Iwanski(Jeff), Bob Wagner (VIC), Cheryl Black (Elaine), Philip Thompson (Dwayne), James Caskey (Gary), Bill Pecchi (Sheriff), Gerry Meagher(Deputy), William Clarke(Tourist), Margi Curry(Kay).
Distributed by: AVI

Plot:
Three young newlywed couples on an idyllic island honeymoon retreat are in for the fright of their lives when a crazed killer starts picking of the women one by one, this is one Honeymoon they will never forget.

Appraisal:
Honeymoon Horror is an early 80's horror slasher flick obviously made to capitalise on both the trend in slasher horror features and the rise in home video sales across the globe, as bad as this film is Sony made a few quid on the home video rental market with this feature which is very surprising.

This Scooby Doo style slasher lacks heart, well quite a lot really, this low budget offering is full of bad acting annoying characters that you are only too happy to see get killed on screen and an shower killing scene with an axe that is a knock off from psycho that has to be the worst shower kill in the history of horror films.

I love slasher films but this film was disappointing normally even if the film is bad you can get some enjoyment on other levels but this film lacked comedy and campness that normally can save a low budget slasher.

Do yourself a favor and re-spin The Burning instead!

Honeymoon Horror was seized under section 3 of the 1959 Obscene Publications Act on VHS in the early 1980's before the implementation of the Video Recordings Act of 1984 in the UK.

Honeymoon Horror was initially released uncut on pre-cert VHS by AVI in 1982, The film has not since it's successful Sony VHS release in the states had a reissue on any format!

-Tony Newton

Inseminoid

(DPP Section 3) Banned in the UK
Also known as "Horror Planet", "Planet Terror".
Year of release: 1981
Writer: Nick Maley
Director: Norman J. Warren
R rated UK
Tagline: "The Horror-birth spawned in space!"
Main cast: Robin Clarke (Mark), Jennifer Ashley (Holly), Stephanie Beacham (Kate), Steven Grives (Gary), Barrie Houghton (Karl), Rosalind Lloyd (Gail).
Distributed by: Brent Walker Video

Plot:
Inseminoid is a sci-fi, horror set in space where scientists begin an archaeological excavation. This 1980's gore-filled shocker follows an unfortunate group of scientists who encounter alien beings. When one of the scientists is impregnated by the alien life form she begins to murder them all one by one.

Appraisal:
Inseminoid is another "Alien" style knock-off, complete with a woman who plays host to an alien being. The film itself is very watchable and very entertaining, if you are a fan of sci-fi/ horror you should definitely give this a watch. The film contains just enough gore to quench your daily horror needs and a stellar cast.

Inseminoid has a very dark feel to it throughout but it's easy to see that it was filmed on a low budget, that said for some reason this film just works, It's nice to see more sci-fi based horror films making an appearance on the video nasty lists.

Norman J Warren is definitely an underrated UK film director, his films have a feel all of their own; he has his own unique stamp that he puts into each production.

Inseminoid was seized under section 3 of the 1959 Obscene Publications Act on VHS in the early 1980's before the implementation of the Video Recordings Act of 1984 in the UK.

Inseminoid was initially released uncut on pre-cert VHS by Brent Walker Video in 1981, Prior to that a shortened version of the film was released for its theatrical version. The film is available fully uncut and with a 15 rating from the BBFC in the UK.

-Tony Newton

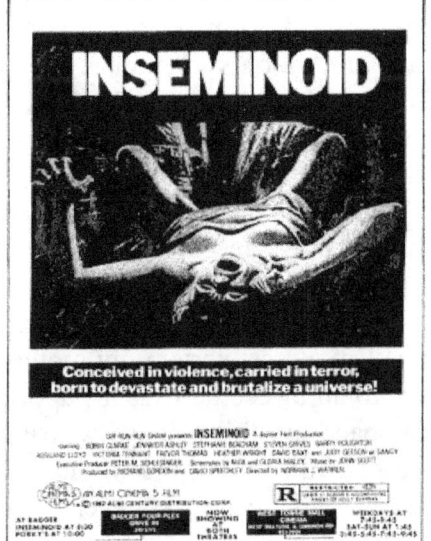

Inseminoid (renamed Horror Planet in the United States) opens with a kaleidoscopic mix of starfields and space imagery and dated synthesiser music as the voice of Stephanie Beacham's character records a log about the discovery of alien tombs on a frozen planet.

The parallels between 'Inseminoid' and Ridley Scott's 'Alien' are extremely recognisable, even if they have been officially denied. The opening excavation scene in 'Inseminoid' is reminiscent of the scene where the crew of the Nostromo are exploring the crashed Space Jockey's ship (or Engineer's ship, if you recognise the 'Prometheus' retconning as part of the canon), and the film even has an alien cocoon exploding in the face of a crewmember in a scene that is set out almost identically to Jon

Hurt's impregnation scene. What's interesting in 'Inseminoid' is that the Earth scientists seem to know the ancient history of the dead alien race, from their early religious beliefs to archaeological points of interest. This plot element, although interesting, is bizarre and rather difficult to swallow. Stephanie Beacham is playing some sort of journalist who is documenting the crew's expedition, every so often interviewing them and recording their (very flat) responses into her rather un-futuristic tape recorder. Beacham is no stranger to British horror and some of my favourite films of hers include 'And Now The Screaming Starts' and 'Dracula A.D 1972', however she will always be known to me as the holographic love interest of the malevolent Moriarty in 'Star Trek: The Next Generation'. Speaking of which, another Trek hologram stars in 'Inseminoid', Judy Geeson, who appeared in some episodes of 'Star Trek: Voyager' as the owner of a holographic French bar.

The guy who had the alien pod blow up in his face wakes up and runs out of the ship in a mad frenzy, the crew try to track him on their black-and-white view screens but lose him once he re-enters the ancient alien tomb. A little bit of drama ensues with another character being clumsy and getting her foot stuck under a rock as the air lock is being shut, confusingly another crew member gives her some odd instructions to free herself by connecting the blue and yellow leads on her wrist watch. All through the panic, Beacham's character continues to dictate to her little tape recorder what is happening. It's revealed, in voiceover, that the wires were to supposedly bypass her thermostat, but she ignores that direction and cuts her leg off with an electric knife! Confusing? Stephanie Beacham also seemed confused, having darted from the spaceship to try to rescue this crewmember only to find her dead, deep-throating a whopper of a pipe. Why was this girl sucking on a pipe? Then it goes back to the 'Alien' parallels, with Beacham taking on the emotional guilt of being the one responsible for shutting the airlock to keep the infected man outside when she was only following regulations, just as Ellen Ripley did. The archaeological mission continues after they hold a funeral service for the deep throating leg-cutter. Two of the crew are attacked by an unseen monster, and as one guy is ripped to shreds by it, the camera jumps to Judy Geeson laying naked in a laboratory with a syringe looming over her. All the plot elements are there in 'Inseminoid', but I think they were just thrown together in the edit because there is no flow from scene to scene; it just jumps from one scene to the next with no explanation and I often wonder if a lot was cut from the final edit and some scripted scenes were perhaps dropped from the shooting schedule. Why was Geeson suddenly naked on a table with the ship's doctor sticking a giant drinking-straw up her butternut-squash and filling her with what looks like, mushy peas? What does it have to do with the pod-explosion and the weird monster that attacked them? None of it continues directly from the previous scenes. After Judy's unusual insemination scenes, things go back to normal for the crew with no mention of the dead crew members, people are back to work and cataloguing artefacts they have uncovered when Geeson starts showing the early signs of pregnancy. After having morning sickness, she goes to the ship's doctor who confirms she is indeed carrying a child, during this examination she clarifies with the doctor that it was he who injected her but strangely it's never explained. Later on in the ladies toilet, Judy Geeson smashes a mirror with the power of her mind and attacks a female crewmember with an item from her makeup bag, she instantly regrets it and breaks down in tears. Another crewmember sees the aftermath of Geeson's attempt at being Carrie White and reports it to her superior, what a snitch. Meanwhile, Geeson knocks out all the CCTV cameras so nobody can watch the bitch fight she has planned with Stephanie Beacham, Geeson continues to bash poor Stephanie's head against the dirt until two guys come in and break the fight up. What is strange is what happens next, all the remaining crew have a staff meeting about how to discipline Geeson's character and Stephanie Beacham blarts out "We have to kill her!" and a colleague adds that they can't kill her as she is pregnant and that wouldn't look good on their report. What ever happened to a verbal warning? The main bulk of the movie is a mixture of scenes showing various crewmembers finding the pregnant Geeson, feeling sorry for her and trying to help her only to get brutally tortured or murdered by her. I'm almost certain my mother didn't act this way when she was carrying me. Geeson eventually gives birth, to an awesome rubber puppet, and her offspring attacks what's left of the characters. The film ends with a spaceship full of guys wearing cowboy hats (well, it was the 80's) landing at the dig site and venturing into their doom. On the whole, the film is good and I'll always enjoy watching it because of the gratuitous gory death scenes, it never quite knows where it sits on the grand scale of British horror as it's not quite mainstream and it's not quite indie, but 'Inseminoid' will always have a space in my list of personal favourites.

My favourite moments:
1) Watching Carry On England star Judy Geeson attack a crewmember with a welding iron.
2) Hearing Stephanie Beacham talk about using chainsaws to stop a murderous pregnant woman.

-Nathan Head   Actor

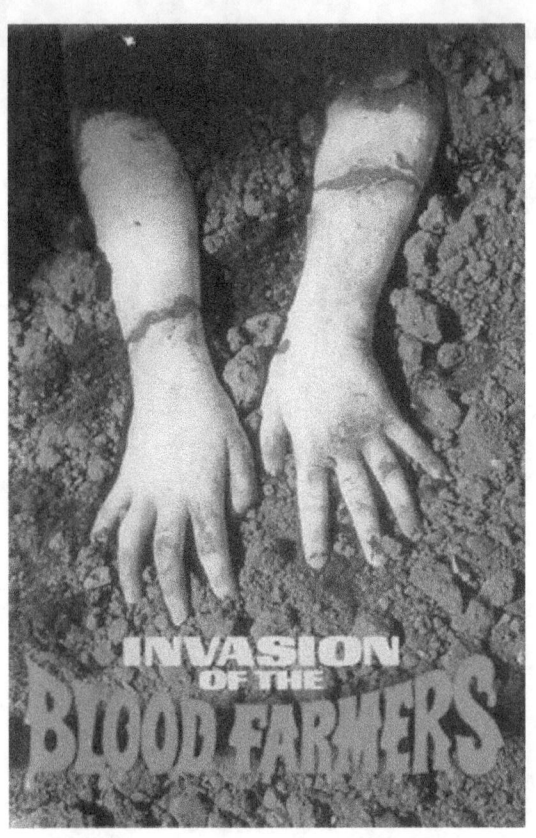

Invasion of the Blood Farmers

(DPP Section 3) Banned in the UK
Year of release: 1972
Writer: Ed Adlum and Ed Kelleher
Director: Ed Adlum
15 rated 84 mins. USA
Tagline: "They planted the LIVING and harvested the DEAD!"
Main cast: Norman Kelley (Dr. Roy Anderson), Tanna Hunter (Jenny Anderson), Bruce Detrick (Don Tucker), Paul Craig Jennings (Creton), Jack Neubeck (Egon), Richard Erickson (Sontag).
Distributed by: Rainbow(Mountain)Video

Plot:
Invasion of the Blood Farmers is a 1970's cult movie! This difficult to track down movie follows a group of druids living in a sleepy American town who terrorize and murder their innocent victims in ritualistic killings in order to drain their blood and keep their Queen alive!

Appraisal:
This film was full of hype and in the 1970's it was a rare find. This is one of those films that you wish you didn't waste your time watching or hunting for but!, it looks cheap which is unfortunate as it's a unique idea but poorly executed throughout.

These modern day druids see a cult who are searching the state of New York for a certain blood type with which to bring back their dead druid cult leader of their bizarre cult.

Invasion of the Blood Farmers is a cult little horror flick, it's great for all the wrong reasons! It's fucked up fun all the way through! Shocking horror heaven!

If you are a fan of films like "Color Me Blood Red" and Schlock you will love this movie!

It's dated, the overall production and acting is dire but the film is such a bizarre flick that you can't help but love it!

Invasion of the Blood Farmers was seized under section 3 of the 1959 Obscene Publications Act on VHS in the early 1980's before the implementation of the Video Recordings Act of 1984 in the UK.

Invasion of the Blood Farmers was initially released uncut on pre-cert VHS by Rainbow(Mountain)Video in 1981, There has not been a further release in the UK since its initial VHS release in 1981.

-Tony Newton

The Killing Hour

(DPP Section 3) Banned in the UK
Also known as "The Clairvoyant".
Year of release: 1982
Writer: Armand Mastroianni and B. Jonathan Ringkamp
Director: Armand Mastroianni
R rated 97 mins. USA
Tagline: "Beyond the five senses lies a sixth. To possess it is to see the unseen. If she see's you…..you're dead."
Main cast: Perry King (Paul McCormack), Norman Parker (Det. Larry Weeks), Elizabeth Kemp (Virna Nightbourne), Kenneth McMillan (Detective Cullum), Jon Polito (Detective Sporaco), Joe Morton (Detective Rich).
Distributed by: LU Productions (World of Video 2000)

Plot:
When a mysterious "Handcuff killer" strikes in New York a talk show host and police detective team up to investigate, with the help of clairvoyant art student Virna (who foresees the murders before they occur).Can they all work together to track down the serial killer and discover his identity?

Appraisal:
The Killing Hour was directed by "He Knows You're Alone" director Armand Mastroianni. This gialloesque horror slasher style piece is a great little film, if anything underrated.

The Killing Hour doesn't seem dated at all and is a very original film. The actress playing the clairvoyant is very believable in the role and also very likable which helps you to have compassion with her character. The film is well worth checking out and has a great feel to it and stunning scenery as it is filmed in Italy.

The Killing Hour is a hard-hitting crime drama with violence and nudity rather than a brutal slasher, the film is rather bloodless but that doesn't take away from it as in The Texas Chainsaw Massacre we thought we saw a blood soaked piece of celluloid but most of the film is played in the mind. The Killing hour does feature nudity, amazing cinematography and twists and turns what's not to like here! a great little unique film.

This stalk and slash crime drama does give a very unique take on both slasher films and the gialli. I love Armand's work, this film does not disappoint, I love the sleaze and atmosphere that is created in this film showing New York at its sleazy best!

I think I remember seeing two different cuts of this film, one with the implementation of a forced sex act which was obviously the reason the film got banned in the UK, which is crazy even the premise for such acts was deemed too much for UK viewers and we're not talking full on porn here, I suppose what you imagine in your head is far worse! Which Armand used to his advantage for both that scene and the kills themselves! If you haven't seen The Killing Hour get out there and see it!

The Killing Hour was seized under section 3 of the 1959 Obscene Publications Act on VHS in the early 1980's before the implementation of the Video Recordings Act of 1984 in the UK. The Killing Hour was initially released uncut on pre-cert VHS by (World of Video 2000)in 1983, The film is now rated 18 in the UK by the BBFC but this is with cuts of 1 minute 19 seconds to the film.

-Tony Newton

Immediately after I made He knows You're Alone, I was approached by several producers, including MGM, about doing another film. William Friedkin director of The Exorcist also approached me asking me to do a movie for his company and I told him about an idea I had for killer loose in New York City, he liked it, and we made The Killing Hour. Later on, the producers of He knows you're alone, Lansberry and Beruh came on board and produced the film. I knew from the beginning that I wanted to make a suspense thriller dealing with a dark secret. The Killing Hour has been likened to the Giallo films from Italy but it was never my intention to make one at the time...I'm flattered by the comparison. The films plot revolved around the "seemingly" accidental murder of a prostitute and the four men involved with her that night. The entire scene is depicted through the eyes of an art student who is clairvoyant and begins to see pieces of the murder as she draws images from that night. In order to expose the dark side of these four men I chose to make the scene graphic and violent. Tame by today standards, at the time the scene did raise objection from the ratings board when I showed it to them. After deleting several shots of the sex act that leads to the death of the young woman they gave me an R rating allowing the film went on to open in the theaters.

I was unaware of the fact that the film was featured on the section 3 obscene publications act in the UK. I had no idea of this and I'm kind of surprised because I don't think the film really crossed the line that much. The scene wasn't an arbitrary sex scene but a pivotal point in the plot to depict the depravity of the individuals involved. I tried to make it as realistic as possible and have the audience feel the suffocation of the victim. Rather than salacious, I thought it was horrific. I'd be interested to know if it was the sex or the violence or the combination of both that they objected to. Times and attitudes have changed and certainly there have been many films that have gone way further than The Killing Hour. I only hope that filmmakers continue making the films they want to make, how they want to make them and have individuals, instead of the censorship board, decide for themselves how they feel about them.

-Armand Mastroianni   Writer/Director of The Killing Hour.

The Last Horror Film

(DPP Section 3) Banned in the UK
Also known as "Fanatical Extreme" and "The Fanatic".
Year of release: 1982
Writer: Judd Hamilton and David Winters
Director: David Winters
R rated 87 mins. USA
Tagline: "Inescapable fear descends upon the French Riviera."
Main cast: Caroline Munro (Jana Bates), Joe Spinell (Vinny), J'Len Winters (Girl in jacuzzi), John Kelly (Man in theatre), Simone Overman (Woman #1 in theatre), Malgosia Casey (Woman #2 in theatre), Patty Salier (Woman #3 in theatre).
Distributed by: Alpha Video

Plot:
The Last Horror Film features aspiring filmmaker Vinnie "Maniac" star (Joe Spinell) as a New York City cab driver who becomes obsessed with a horror movie actress Jana Bates (Caroline Munro). When Vinnie slowly begins to lose his grip on reality, Jane receives death threats and is stalked by the wannabe filmmaker, then people close to her begin start to disappear one by one.

Appraisal:
The Last Horror Film features "Maniac" star Joe Spinell teamed with his co-star Caroline Monroe. The film follows Caroline Monroe as an actress who receives death threats and then stalked by a crazed fan played by Joe Spinell. The film (as cheesy as it is) is quite a good send up to the movie industry itself.

This Last Horror Film isn't high art by any stretch of the imagination but for me Joe Spinell can do no wrong; he's a sensational actor.

All in all "The Last Horror Film" is well worth a watch if you are a fan of scream Queen Caroline Monroe and cheesy horror flicks.

The Last Horror Film was seized under section 3 of the 1959 Obscene Publications Act on VHS in the early 1980's before the implementation of the Video Recordings Act of 1984 in the UK.

The Last Horror Film was initially released uncut on pre-cert VHS by Intermission in 1983, The film is available fully uncut and with an 18 rating from the BBFC in the UK.

-Tony Newton

The Last Hunter

(DPP Section 3) Banned in the UK
Also known as "the Hunter of the Apocalypse" and "Ultimo Cacciatone".
Year of release: 1980
Writer: Gianfranco Couyoumdjian
Director: Antonio Margheriti
X rated 96 mins. Italy
Tagline: "The most horrific war movie ever made!"
Main cast: David Warbeck (Capt. Henry Morris), Tisa Farrow (Jane Foster), Tony King (Sgt. George Washington), Bobby Rhodes (Carlos), Margit Evelyn Newton (Carol), John Steiner (Maj. Cash).
Distributed by: Inter-Light Video

Plot:
The Last Hunter was originally intended to be the sequel to the 1978 war drama movie "The Deer Hunter". When Captain Henry Morris ventures deep into the jungles of Vietnam in order to prevent a radio tower from broadcasting anti-war propaganda he gets more than he bargained for when he discovers a cannibal tribe, they're hunting down intruders and sacrificing them to their cannibal god!

Appraisal:
The Last Hunter is a classic war film, which is rumored to be an unofficial sequel to "The Deer Hunter", with obvious connections running through the film. "The Last Hunter" gives a perspective on the Vietnam War, however this film is rarely mentioned it is always overlooked. It's filled with action, violence and explosions(pretty much everything expected of a war film).

This all-out action 80's war frolic is a great watch for fans of "Rambo" and "The Deer Hunter" with a drink, popcorn and a movie-athon you'll love it.

The Last Hunter was seized under section 3 of the 1959 Obscene Publications Act on VHS in the early 1980's before the implementation of the Video Recordings Act of 1984 in the UK.

The Last Hunter was initially released uncut on pre-cert VHS by Intervision in 1980. The film is available fully uncut and with an 18 rating from the BBFC in the UK.

-Tony Newton

The Love Butcher

(DPP Section 3) Banned in the UK
Also known as "O Jardineiro Assassino"
Year of release: 1975
Writers: Mikel Angel and James M. Tanenbaum
Directors: Don Jones and Mikel Angel
R rated 85 mins. USA
Tagline: "He wants more than your love…"
Main cast: Erik Stern (Caleb), Kay Neer (Flo), Jeremiah Beecher (Russell), Richard Kennedy (Don), Robin Sherwood (Sheila), Eve Mac (Pat).
Distributor: Intervision

Plot:
The Love Butcher is a 1970's slasher film which tells the story of an elderly gardener named Caleb. Caleb hides a dark secret as his alter ego (a handsome brother named Lester) seduces and murders young women. The Police desperately attempt to uncover the killer's identity but can anyone stop Caleb and his split persona Lester before more innocent women fall victim to the Love Butcher?

Appraisal:
This is a strange 1970's horror piece and actually stands out because it features a mentally retarded man who has an alter ego exacting revenge on those that have wronged him (something a bit different for a video nasty!). This film is worth a watch but once is enough; this is not a film to regularly re-visit. The Love Butcher gives an uneasy element of comedy and horror that is very different to any horror film out there; the retarded character looks like "Ernest" in those fucked up 80s films! Let's just thankful he didn't look like Pee Wee Herman!

The Love Butcher was seized under section 3 of the 1959 Obscene Publications Act on VHS in the early 1980's before the implementation of the Video Recordings Act of 1984 in the UK.

The Love Butcher was initially released uncut on pre-cert VHS by Intervision in 1979. There has not been a further release in the UK since its initial VHS release in 1981.

-Tony Newton

The Mad Foxes

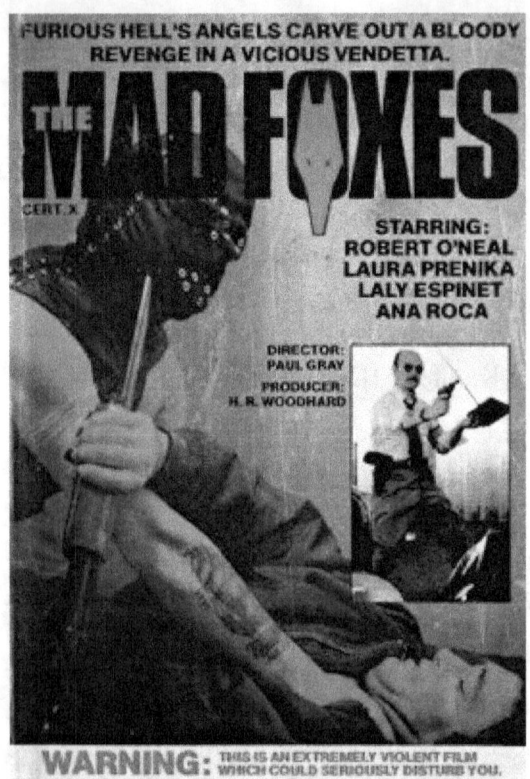

(DPP Section 3) Banned in the UK
Also known as "Stingray 2" and "Los Violadores"
Year of release: 1981
Writer: Hans R. Walthard and Paul Grau
Director: Paul Grau
Uncertified 77 mins. Spain, Switzerland
Main cast: Jose Gras (Hal Walters), Laura Premica (Silvia Godo), Andrea Albani (Babsy), Peter John Saunders, Brian Billings, Hank Sutter.
Distributed by: Merlin/(VCL)

Plot:
This 1981 Spanish revenge exploitation offering sees just what gruesome lengths lead character Hal will go to in order to exact revenge for the attack on himself and his girlfriend at the hands of a local biker gang. When this gang of bikers savagely beat Hal and brutally rape his girlfriend Silvia Hal enlists the help of his martial arts expert friends in order to take vengeance.

Appraisal:
This film is a crazy non-stop action exploitation piece of grindhouse gold. The Mad Foxes is out there and very entertaining although it's dated and yes cheesy, it's literally a hoot with nonstop entertainment all the way through to the very end. This unclassified film is a much better watch in its truly uncut form.

This is full on exploitation here with this film you get comedy, and tones of it, add the violence and over the top murders with Kung Fu and Nazi bikers, who couldn't love this low budget offering? The film has an overall camp feel to it which makes it even more enjoyable, if you're going balls out to make an exploitation film this is how you do it! This little known gem is begging to gain a cult status, which it deserves. The Mad Foxes was seized under section 3 of the 1959 Obscene Publications Act on VHS in the early 1980's before the implementation of the Video Recordings Act of 1984 in the UK. The Mad Foxes was initially released on pre-cert VHS by Merlin (VCL) in 1982, The film was also heavily cut for its theatrical release in the UK, it was the cut version that featured on the UK VHS releases. There has not been a further release in the UK since its initial VHS release in 1982.

-Tony Newton

Maniac

(Banned for cinema in 1981 and for video in 1998)
Year of release: 1980
Writers: C.A Rosenberg, Joe Spinell
Director: William Lustig
Rated: R rated
Tagline: "You can lock your windows and doors…But you can't lock the madman out of your mind."
Main Cast: Joe Spinell (Frank Zito), Caroline Munro (Anna D'Antoni), Abigail Clayton (Rita), Kelly Piper (Nurse), Rita Montone (Hooker), Tom Savini (Disco boy).
Distributed by: Intervision

Plot:
When a man who suffered child abuse starts killing women in New York City, he begins to collect their scalps as trophies.

Appraisal:
Maniac is one of my all time favorite horror films the dirty sleazy dark feel of this film is just beautiful in its own dark sadistic way.

Joe Spinell plays psychopath Frank Zito in this classic early 1980's slasher film, Joe Spinell is amazing on screen as the child like figure who struggles to find a place in the world following the death of his mother, Joe Spinell (who also appeared in the gritty film "Taxi Driver) is very underrated as an actor and it's refreshing to see him in the lead role here. Once again New York looks a dirty and unwelcoming place here providing the perfect backdrop for this slice of cult horror. This classic horror film is an original film and there are some great scenes throughout, the stand out seen for me is when Frank puts the scalps of his victims on mannequins and tales them to bed with him.

This down beat horror is a refreshing change to the other early 1980's slasher offerings, which at times could be a little samey.

The 2012 remake starring Elijah Wood playing Frank Zito's role was also very well done and a homage to this classic cult horror film.

Director William Lustig went on to direct the very underrated film "Vigilante" and the "Maniac Cop" series. This is a must own for fans of slasher films and an inspiration for filmmakers across the globe.

In 1981 the BBFC totally banned the theatrical release of this film, there were even cases of imports of the uncut VHS being confiscated in customs from as early as 1983 and as late as 1999.

This film was released with 58 seconds of cuts in 2002 in the UK and was passed uncut in 2004 by Umbrella Entertainment in the US.

-Tony Newton

Mark of the Devil

(DPP Section 3) Banned in the UK
Also known as "Hexen Bis Aufs Blut Gequalt"
Year of release:1970
Writers: Michael Armstrong and Adrian Hoven
Directors: Michael Armstrong and Adrian Hoven
R rated 96 mins. West Germany
Tagline: "Rated 'V' for Violence"
Main cast: Herbert Lom (Lord Cumberland), Udo Kier (Count Christian Von Meruh), Olivera Katarina (Vanessa Benedikt), Reggie Nalder (Albino), Herbert Fux (Jeff Wilkens), Johannes Buzalski (Advocato).
Distributed by: Intervision

Plot:
Mark of the Devil is a 1970's controversial graphic exploitation movie which is professed to be based upon three real-life accounts of witch burnings, from the director of "The Haunted House of Horror".

Christian, is an apprentice witch finder to Count Cumberland but when they are called to an Austrian town to rid it of its suspected witches Christian falls in love, but when the young lady he's in love with is accused of being a witch by the towns sadistic resident witch finder Albino, Christian attempts to aid her in her escape but will they make it out of the town alive?

Appraisal:
Mark of the Devil is a cult horror film from the director of "The Haunted House of Horror". This film has elements of the film "The Witchfinder General" and a feel of Ken Russell's "The Devils"-esque theme. This film does have some strange elements of torture, this hammer esque film is a very good horror film for 1969 some of the torture scenes are even uncomfortable to watch, because the film is set in a time period of yesterday the film does not seem dated, look out for a young Udo Kier. This film even had its very own vomit bag that was given out because of the gut wrenching gore scenes.

Mark of the Devil is a must watch on this list! Michael Armstrong does a great job directing this classic piece of horror, the cinematography is excellent you are drawn into the grim settings and lurid horror world that is "Mark of the Devil". A true classic that continues to inspire the horror genre. Another plea of classic horror cinema that they deprived us of in the full uncut glory for far too long! A great addition to any horror film collection!

Michael Armstrong's "Mark of the Devil" is a cult classic hard hitting piece if cinema that still packs a punch today, it is an all round solid film that provides shocks and moments that make you squirm. The film was released in 1970 and seems way ahead of its time.

Mark of the Devil is set in 18th century Austria and centers around Herbert Lom playing a witchfinder along with his apprentice the young Udo Kier. Herbert Lom and Udo Kier will hunt down anyone suspected of devil worshiping. This film is somewhat of a nod to the slightly earlier "Witchfinder General" starring Vincent

Price but the "Witchfinder General" seems like a happy family film compared to this offering. There are scenes of torture and rape including a woman's tongue being pulled out, people being tortured with bizarre instruments. Director Michael Armstrong worked as Michael reeves assistant on the "Witchfinder General" and it is rumored that Michael Reeves was set to direct this film but died before filming began. I couldn't imagine Michael Armstrong not directing this classic; only he could have brought his own script to life like this. Having Herbert Lom in the film gives an almost hammer quality to the film, imagine watching a 1970's hammer film but adding your deepest darkest fears and this is what you get. The film even came with its own sick bag (now that is a good piece of marketing).

Udo Kier is fantastic in this film but it's strange seeing him have an almost naive quality about his person, something we don't usually see from him. Overall this is a fantastic horror film that does not date due to the fact it is set in a much earlier time than it was made, a must see for all horror fans. Mark of the Devil was seized under section 3 of the 1959 Obscene Publications Act on VHS in the early 1980's before the implementation of the Video Recordings Act of 1984 in the UK. Mark of the Devil was initially released uncut on pre-cert VHS by Intervision in 1981, Prior to this the film was given an x rating by the BBFC for its theatrical release but the film suffered heavy cuts and a much shortened running time, the film is available uncut with an 18 rating from the BFFC in Britain.

-Tony Newton

CENSORING *MARK OF THE DEVIL*

Whither went the true meaning of Free speech?

Censorship is as much one of Man's fashionable follies as is his taste in clothes, beliefs, opinion's and just about anything else he can his destructive little hands can get their self-righteous moralising fingers on.

Each new generation is laughed at by the next for those things it considered so morally shocking they needed to be censored or banned outright.

Below is a piece I wrote in the late autumn of 1983 attacking the *Daily Mail* for one of its moral campaigns against the burgeoning video market years before DVD and Blu-rays appeared on the scene. It was published in the magazine *Film on Screen and Video*. This occurred thirteen years after I had made *Mark of the Devil* which had been banned outright in the UK. I feel it may be of interest as a historical document of the period.

-Michael Armstrong   Director of "Mark of the Devil"

HYSTERIA AND THE NASTIES
(First published in *Films on Screen and Video* in October 1983)

The recent hysteria campaign conducted by the *Daily Mail* over video 'nasties' has been as irresponsible as it has been ridiculous. Of course one is concerned about the protection of children from exploitation and exposure to potentially corruptive material but the *Mail*'s approach to this problem has deliberately merged fact with supposition and sweeping generalisations in such an emotive manner of reportage that it has totally blurred the numerous factors involved into such a serious distortion of the Truth as to deserve the label of bigotry. Were such prejudiced attitudes applied in a political or racial context, there would be far more serious labels one could attach to the paper's methods of presenting information before the public. A personal point of view stated is one thing: emotive colouring and prejudiced selectivity of news items is another. Hitler, Stalin and the Inquisition employed similar approaches to problems that concerned them. That is not what one expects from one of Britain's leading newspapers.

In the August 12th issue, the *Mail* reported on the collapse of Astra Video Ltd with the headline: 'The £100,000 fall of video nasties 'king'.' For a start, Astra Video Ltd distributed titles other than *Snuff* and *I Spit On Your Grave* including children's product. The *Mail*'s accusation that this was purely to clean up Astra's image may or may not have justification. However, it should be remembered that there is no trading company, which does not, at some point, try to improve its image in one form or another in order to move up-market. Motives for this are usually for the improvement of business dealings rather than creating a respectable front in order to camouflage dubious activities. Criminal organisations often operate behind respectable fronts but surely the *Mail* is not accusing Astra Video of that? The fact that the company was distributing amongst its other titles, one or two exploitation films of appalling bad taste is not in question. Nor are the Mail's attempts to have them withdrawn from public circulation. What is questionable, however, is the *Mail*'s attempts to escalate the news into something of a national scandal by making suppositions over Behr's motives for distributing children's product by their label 'King of the Video Nasties' and by phrases selected for their emotive content: "Magistrates were told that the film … was a violent, shocking story of bloody revenge". A by-line that could equally be used to promote *Hamlet* commercially. Likewise, "Public outrage forced Mr Behr to withdraw *Snuff*". What public outrage? The principal outrage seemed only to come from the *Mail*'s own editorial policy.

Similar biased selectivity of information has continued throughout. The case of Miss Pam Jeff's screening of *The Texas Chainsaw Massacre* at a children's home may have a ludicrous sense of irresponsibility about it, particularly when she is quoted as saying she did not know what the film was about. With a title like that? But the *Mail*'s delight in quoting the poor girl's mother as saying: "When she saw it was evil she stopped it" and phrases designed to associate the film with a larger and more terrifying bogey-man: "She allowed video nasties to be shown" and "to see part of the horrific *Texas Chainsaw Massacre* video" all contribute to a biased piece of reporting when certain information regarding the film is not released. To lump the movie in the public's mind along with snuff movies and the like is grossly unfair and misrepresentative. The film is not a recent sexual sadism piece. It was made in 1974 and has been screened throughout the country in cinemas since that time and with a censor's certificate. It was directed by Tobe Hooper, received many excellent reviews around the world and has now achieved a cult status in many film circles. Whether or not it is a particularly good film within the genre of exploitation horror is purely a matter of personal opinion but it is certainly not 'evil' nor has it any right to be called a 'video nasty'.

Continued reportage in the *Mail* on just about any case it could dig up where some potential psychotic, usually with a long case-history of sexual violence, had been known to have seen a horror film on video has been blown up out of all proportion to imply that watching screen violence crates violence. Whilst this has as yet to be proven, the *Mail* seems to have taken it for granted and set about its crusade accordingly. By creating this 'nasties' monster that is threatening our very lives, the *Mail* is merely putting words and ideas into our minds of the very people most likely tube affected by such things.

A typical example is that of rapist Christopher Meah, whose wife is reported in the *Mail I as saying:* "He was always watching video films but two in particular, *The Thing* and *The Last House On The Left* really twisted his mind. One was about multiple sex attacks, and not long after watching it he was raping and stabbing an unfortunate woman. It's sickening what these things can do to a person." The fact that prior to the attack he had been taking drugs and drinking and had, in 1978, suffered brain damage in a road accident probably had far more to do with his resultant actions than watching *The Thing* which, incidentally, features an entirely male cast beset by a special effects alien – hardly an inducement to sexual arousal and rape fantasies. Yet it is tossed indiscriminately amongst the 'video nasties' as another highly corruptive and dangerous incitement to rape and murder. Again, the film has respectably played in the cinemas throughout the country with a censor's certificate. Maybe *The Last House On The Left* was catalyst for that one particular attack but judging from his past history and the drunken drug-ridden state that he was in, his excitement could just as well have been aroused by a phrase in a book, a painting or photograph, reportage in a newspaper … To imply that it was solely the responsibility of the video film is far too over-simplistic and certainly no argument for indiscriminate banning and panic mongering.

If Christopher Meah had been "inspired" by a video film, how does that apply to a Peter Sutcliffe who claimed to have been "inspired" by God? Indeed, inspiration by God or the Bible has served for many psychotics. What is the answer to that one? – ban God? –label the Bible as a 'literary nasty'? Sex, violence and horror have existed in drama since the beginning. To start claiming that this is in any way responsible for violence and horror in real life is as naïve as it is ridiculous. The vast catalogue throughout history of Man's atrocities have been motivated by greed, jealousy, power-lust, ambition, bigotry, ignorance; not by going to the theatre and witnessing cannibalism (*The Bacchae*), eye-gouging (*King Lear*), the rape and mutilation of women (*Titus Andronicus*), beating and crucifixion (*The Mystery Plays*) – the list is endless. Whatever one would like to think, the Arts and entertainment as a whole have done little else but to amuse, sometimes inform or reflect upon Man's lighter or darker sides to his nature and the Society in which he functions and that is all: unlike philosophers, religious or moral leaders, politicians, revolutionaries, tyrants or scientists. You do not change a man's appearance by altering his reflection in a mirror. All you do is disguise the Truth. Violence in life can be horrific and it should be portrayed accordingly not doctored to appear palatable. That can have far more dangerous consequences.

On August 4th the *Mail* published a particularly emotive piece of biased journalism by Vivien Harding opening with: "While evidence is slowly building on how video horror films encourage violence in real life …" First, it is interesting to note how the 'nasties' tag is now compatible with horror films. What was once used to describe pornographic sexual sadism has now encompassed the whole catalogue of films designed to frighten people. Suddenly the words 'nasty' and 'horror' are made to mean the same thing with all the accompanying emotive associations built up over weeks by the *Mail*'s campaign. The article goes on to quote a doctor who has come to the rather obvious conclusion that horror films can frighten people including children. He refers to the case of a psychologically disturbed child he had been treating and appears surprised that the child should have been upset by watching a horror film at a family wedding. The incident led the doctor to speculate upon the possible long-term effects exposure to disturbing images can have on a child. His feelings that children under the age of ten would be better served by not being exposed to adult horror films are entirely commendable. Which is more than can be said to the *Mail*'s approach to the story.

Plastering the whole centre-spread with headlines: 'The men who grow rich on blood-lust', 'How the films are made and the damage they did to the mind of one little boy', 'Taken over by something evil from the TV set', the *Mail* places the doctor's musings beside a lurid account of a video 'nasty' being made in America with caption headings: 'The Godfathers of Gore: Bill Lustig 'For five bucks people get somebody to act out their fantasies … Everybody wants to kill someone@ and a poster for *Vigilante* behind him. *Vigilante* being a straightforward thriller with a censor's certificate. Other captions read: Simon Nuchterne: 'In America, success is the thing … no matter how you arrive at it'. Mort Zarchi: 'I don't have any moral responsibility for the effect of films on the audience'. Charles Kaufman: 'cashing in with a decapitated head and butcher's knife'. Filmmakers Tom Duran (left) and Brendan Faulkner 'call for more blood for victim Joan-Ellen Delany. Make-up man Arnold Garguilo obliges'.

These captions of carefully selected quotes in some cases totally out of context with what the various named people were actually saying are designed entirely towards one aim – to present an image of men who are unleashing dangerous goods onto a public and whose only motives are the amount of money they can make. \it is the kind of heartless, evil image normally reserved for drugs dealers and purveyors of arms to terrorist organisations. The often realistic and sensible statements of Lustig, Zarchi and the others are surrounded by emotive descriptive passages: 'Inside a secluded woodland cabin a young woman lies sprawled on a couch. Her throat has been ripped out and blood soaks her yellow blouse', 'Children will be able to watch the same sickening scenes', 'stomach-turning', 'hacks, bludgeons and castrates her assailants in a welter of blood'.

None of this kind of biased reporting is helping anyone or, indeed, the situation the *Mail* is seeking to see brought within some kind of control. By lashing out in all directions, hysterically latching onto the slightest excuse for furthering its cause, creating confusion in the public's mind between respectable films bearing censor's certificates and banned, uncertified violent pornography, the *Mail*, having adopted scare-mongering tactics have only aggravated the problem and turned serious journalism into a three-ring circus. When Manchester police can feel justified in raiding a video shop and seizing copies of the 15 certified Zeffirelli film, *Endless Love* because the cassette cover bore the catch-line 'She is 15. He is 17' then it is time to stop encouraging such irresponsibility and turn one's rancour upon more deserving causes. Perhaps the Manchester police should go back to the shop and seize the other Zeffirelli film about teenage lovers, *Romeo and Juliet*. In that the kids are even younger.

New legislation regarding obscene tapes is already being prepared by the Government after which the industry will be answerable to a code of censorship as operates quite successfully in the cinema. Journalistic hysteria is not required to control the issue. The sooner the *Mail* realises the vast difference between the perfectly legitimate horror film and a tape produced solely to promote sadistic pornography then it may cease to inflict its naïve, half-baked theories and patronising concept of morality upon a public and an industry which is predominantly run in a highly responsible manner and is as concerned as the *Mail* about the abolition of corrupting and obscene material.

-Michael Armstrong   Director of "Mark of the Devil".

Martin

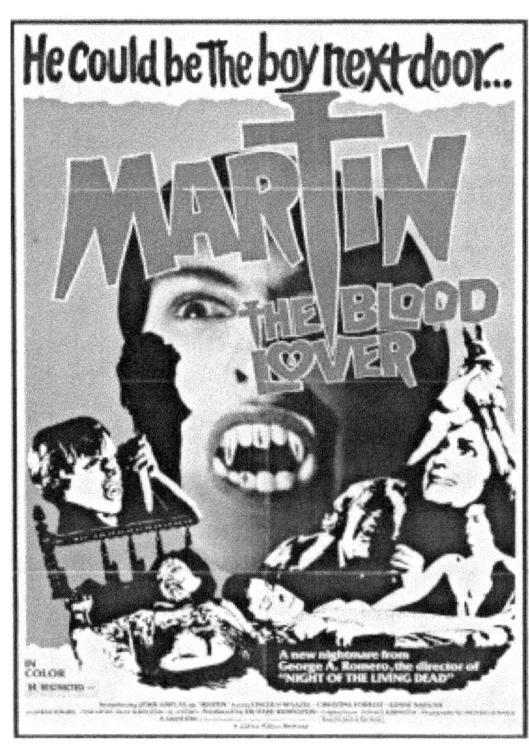

(DPP Section 3) Banned in the UK
Year of release: 1976
Writer: George A. Romero
Director: George A. Romero
R rated 95 mins. USA
Tagline: "Heir to the blood lust."
Main cast: John Amplas (Martin), Lincoln Maazel (Cuda), Christine Forrest (Christina), Elyane Nadeau (Mrs. Santini), Tom Savini (Arthur), Sara Venable (Housewife victim).
Distributed by: Hello Video

Plot:
Martin is a 1976 movie, which is directed by the godfather of zombie movies George A. Romero. "Martin" provides an alternative take on the vampire genre. "Martin "tells the story of a socially awkward young man who possesses vampire characteristics, as he attempts to control his condition by using syringes to knock out his victims before draining their blood and feasting on them.

Appraisal:
Martin is a different take on the vampire genre. Martin is a vampire who is trying to control his condition using syringes to sedate his victims instead of brutally killing them alive.

Martin still holds up, mainly because of the uniqueness of this film, it was fresh, it was new, it has a feel and atmosphere all of it very own, mix this with the fantastic job done by actor John Amplas who portrays Martin and you have a stunning very underrated horror movie. The film features a young Tom Savini, always great when Savini pops up in a movie, though nothing beats him in "From Dusk Till Dawn" That death scene is killer!. Tom Savini not only appears in the film itself as Arthur but also provides the special effects for the film. "Martin" is a cult film, which deserves everything that it gets in the way of recognition. This is nothing short of a masterpiece. John Amplas gives a captivating performance throughout and portrays a 84-year-old vampire this film.. or is he? The film tackles human relationships which as we all know can be much darker than any monster, Martin is as vulnerable as he is a psycho vampire killer with a razor blade smile! This is a must watch for horror fans of all genres, even if you're not a huge fan of Romero's zombie features you will still love this film!

George A. Romero as we know is an amazing filmmaker who likes to think outside the box, the subject here Vampirism is tackled very different to the films we were used to at the time, Romero one to make his own rules up where filmmaking is concerned and creates a new era of vampires, this film is a far cry from the Hammer Horror-esque Christopher Lee or even the classic Bela Lugosi before. Martin is one of the best vampire films of all time and a timeless horror classic. Martin is essentially a new breed of vampire who uses needles instead of the classic hypnotism and where normal vampires use their fangs Martin uses razor blades, of the latest fest of vampire films that are just the same more love than lust and more talk than blood and definitely no soul. Please take a look at this classic refreshing look at the genre. I love the use of Martin as The Count on the radio talk show as we get closer to finding more about Martin himself, but not just not enough.

Martin was seized under section 3 of the 1959 Obscene Publications Act on VHS in the early 1980's before the implementation of the Video Recordings Act of 1984 in the UK. Martin was initially released uncut on pre-cert VHS by Hello Video in 1982, The film is passed 18 uncut in the UK by the BBFC.

There are two versions of Martin in existence the Italian version and the original cut, both of these versions are passed uncut in the UK.

-Tony Newton

In 1976 I starred in what became, in my estimation the most important film of its kind. George Romero's Martin. A psychological and sociological character study of a young man plagued by old world myth and superstition played out during a period of time in a place that was suffering from an inability to stave off the change it was forced to face. Martin was made into who he became, by the fears of the society he was born into. Martin is a film that appropriately ends with a question. That's the job of art isn't it, not to answer but question. 38 years later this film keeps finding new audiences. I keep thinking about its meaning. It will be a part of me and ultimately be part of my humble legacy in the world of film. I am proud of it".

-John Amplas   Martin in the 1976 film "Martin"

George A Romero is undoubtedly one of the very best horror filmmakers of our time. The term zombie, whilst not exclusive to or even inspired by him, has become largely his intellectual property and, decades after he made them relevant, it is Romero whose blessing is called for when making a zombie movie. His long-running dead saga is still considered the template to be measured against and the first three entries into his series have stood the test of time largely because of their rich social commentary. Night, Dawn and Day are the epitome of perfection and it would be easy to assume that they are his most significant works. However, just before gifting us Dawn of The Dead and with bankruptcy looming large, he gave us his own personal darling Martin. I'm thankful that he did.

Martin is essentially a vampire movie although unlike any other you may have previously seen. It single-handedly augmented a trend, later elaborated on through The Hunger and The Addiction, for films whereby vampirism is more metaphorical than historically accurate. Instead of portraying its count as a sexually overpowering force against nature, his film focuses on a protagonist bearing none of his Nosferatic forefathers' dominance. Garlic and crucifixes are ineffectual in his tale; Romero scoffs at tradition and stumps on ambiguity by allowing his addressee to come to their own conclusion as to whether or not Martin is actually a vampire at all. His character debunks folklore openly despite claiming that he is 84 years old and possessing some worrying characteristics such as a penchant for blood.

His gentle demeanor belies that of a bloodsucker and, as one character informs him when referring to him as an alley cat of sorts, there is something almost feline about him. Cautious, concentrated, and always committed to his immediate surroundings; he can be initially standoffish but warms to a little harmless petting over time. However, rub his fur the wrong way, and he will likely flee with a bushy tail. As a hunter he is by no means decisive and this is demonstrated via a mesmerizing opening scene aboard a train bound for

Pittsburgh where he struggles to overcome his cornered prey. There is an innocence about him but, at the same time, an arrogance that suggests a lifetime of experience in his chosen field. It's a delicate balancing act but one which a twenty-eight year-old *John Amplas* manages quite remarkably and utterly conclusively.

I first watched Martin at ten years old and his performance resonated with me even then. In my opinion, there have been few turns in cinematic history so exquisitely understated and fewer still as pitch perfect as his. With searching eyes, rosebud lips and floppy locks which hang like dainty drapes about his baby face; he has all the tools to convince us as to his authenticity. What is more compelling is the way in which he utilizes said tools. Being a man of few words, it's his face, which chronicles for the most part. The part was originally intended to include such narration but Romero declined to implement this approach upon realization that the actor was already so expressive without the need for verbal signposting. For any director this would be a wet dream and the fact that Amplas returned for parts in Knightriders, Creepshow, Dawn, and, in a larger capacity, Day of The Dead, suggests just how moved his director was by his portrayal. He's not alone.

"There is no magic – it's a disease."

The whole film and its success rests squarely on his young shoulders and he accepts this burden in much the same way as Martin welcomes his own perpetual anguish. Outside of the tormented young man, Romero provides us his gatekeeper, the seemingly deluded Cuda *(Lincoln Maazel)*, who is convinced that his bloodline is cursed and prepared to snuff Martin out at any given moment the very second he falls out of formation. Female characters, in particular Christina (Romero's spouse *Christine Forrest*) and bored housewife Mrs Santini *(Elyane Nadeau)*, are critical to proceedings and Martin's relationship with the latter is potent as it shows his reluctance to capitulate to his primal urges. There is a repression to his actions, which suggests impotence, while latent necrophilia informs that he prefers to traverse the sexual mine field without the distraction of pulse.

As he toys with the idea of uncorking his pent-up frustration we are transported to another time via black and white flashbacks to a lifetime ago when he embraced his birth right. As these play out in his own mind, we are still not entirely convinced as to whether or not he is, in fact, a vampire at all. This is always intentional on Romero's part as his film embraces the romanticism of vampiric folklore without purely bowing to convention. He intended the entire film to be shot in black and white but was urged against it; a decision which is entirely justified in my mind as the washed-out palette of inner city fabric is deliciously offset by the rare emergence of deep 1970's red. Blood tantalizes him and, considering we are his passengers throughout, it does so to us also. There is only ever under ninety seconds of bloodletting to be gleaned from Martin, even in that misplaced 165 minute cut, but it punctuates the silence all the more effectively as a result.

The suburban playground is representative of the death of youth. It's a bleak and morose wasteland for neutered teenagers not afforded with an identity, hopes or dreams; and feels constrictive at all times. Being the proverbial alley cat affords him the ambiguity required to explore his nocturnal lusting without society blinking an eye even when folk start showing up on the sides of milk cartons with alarming regularity. One such ensnared soul is Christina, whose dysfunctional relationship with Arthur *(Tom Savini)* is one merely of convenience and remains trapped by the traditional values of older townsfolk like Cuda. She becomes intrigued by Martin's single-minded independence and increasingly embittered against her grandfather for the ignorant views, which restrain her. It's another affiliation played beautifully and validates his decision to be a little different.

Martin is a tale most tragic and, in this respect, is faithful to its own heritage. We are hypnotized by Amplas and afforded the chance to quench with him each time he nourishes but then a stake is rammed through our rib cages just as we grow accustomed to his idiosyncrasies and the candelabra ultimately dims in the most heart-aching of fashions. At nearing four decades matured, it won't appeal to many and will likely be considered too long in the tooth to all but the most refined tastes. I would debate that, despite evidently aging, it is the timeless performance of Amplas, which holds us captive. How a young man cutting his teeth for the first time achieved such a feat is still beyond me almost forty years down the tracks. The knowledge that he now teaches as Associate Professor of performing arts at Point Park University, ironically in downtown

Pittsburgh, enables Keeper to sleep at night although, due to his commanding turn as Martin, I still do so with one eye open.

-Keeper of the Crimson Quill   (Rivers of Grue)

Sure, I love Romero's zombie films as much as anyone else, with special appreciation for *Day of the Dead*, but his non-zombie work has always been his strongest in my estimation. *Creepshow* (1982) is easily one of the best horror anthology films, and one of the best horror films of its decade. *Monkey Shines* (1988) is another underrated, and nasty piece of work that has a lot more going on than it appears at first glance: a crippled man and a killer monkey. *Season of the Witch* a.k.a. *Hungry Wives* is an interesting look at the domestic life of women in the suburbs of America when women's liberation was more than a derogatory phrase flung from the political right wing in the United States. There was real momentum to challenge the very idea of being female in American society. Perhaps that film is more prescient today in light of the political climate with the treatment of women in the United States, specifically in terms of reproductive health; an issue it seemed was settled the year after *Hungry Wives'* release?

That now brings us to *Martin*, my favorite film from Romero, a quiet study of the titular teenager, beautifully portrayed by soon to be Romero regular John Amplas. The film is a portrait of the economically depressed modern America, specifically, Braddock, Pennsylvania and old world superstition and religion, and whether the two can ever exist harmoniously. Young Martin has come to the steel town to live with his elder cousin, Cuda (Lincoln Maazel, father of the famed conductor, Lorin Maazel) after some trouble at home. It seems Martin is "cursed", and is believed to be a vampire. Yet it's never made clear if Martin believes this because of the old stories, mental illness, or is he truly a murderous monster? Cuda does nothing to dissuade Martin of this thinking, whatever the cause, and we do witness Martin attacking a woman on the train over. But what are we to make of this attack? It doesn't seem traditionally vampiric, as Martin stabs his victim with a syringe of tranquilizer so he can engage in the "sexy stuff" and slit her wrist with a razor blade. It's more akin to a sex crime than anything in Stoker.

With the key phrase, "There is no magic." Amplas' tortured teen reminds us of the power of the mind, and what humans are able to talk themselves into, regardless of evidence and the potential outcomes of the belief systems they choose to cling to. Perhaps it is this troubling concept that religion can be the cause of a problem instead of the solution that has caused the film to float in such troubled waters over the years. Yet without these battling ideals, the film would not hold so much to treasure.

Apart from the religious aspects, sex is another hot button the film touches upon in interesting ways. On the surface, Martin is everything a woman would want. He is young and handsome, a bit shy, with an unfettered sensitivity about him. Most teenagers are sexually and socially awkward, yet things are taken to an extreme in Martin's case. It's the thrill of the hunt, literally, which is just as exciting as the satiation of desire it seems. On the other side of the animal, Martin is deeply caring and does what he can to minimize his victims' suffering, hence the injections. As soon as the rush of pleasure is had, he seems depressed again, knowing he has caused the death of an innocent person, his innocence forever lost, perhaps never experienced as he has struggled with this for too long already.

However one approaches *Martin*, there will surely be questions not answered, and left floating in the mind as the movie ends. That is one of the greatest gifts art can give, the chance to think about the unknown, and untouched in all of us. Martin is more than a teenage vampire, a victim of a family story, a product of a violent America, a loving America. Martin is the mystery of humanity…

-Derek Botelho   Author

George A. Romero is famous for his zombie films, but one of my personal favorites is Martin.

Released in 1978, Martin tells the story of a young man who also happens to be a vampire. In the opening scene, Martin accosts a woman on a train, shoots her full of drugs, and proceeds to drink her blood.

Many critics see Martin as a "deconstruction" of the vampire myth, as Martin displays absolutely no outward signs of his affliction: He doesn't have fangs, he walks in the sunlight, and holy objects have no effect on him. To me, however, Martin is portrait of mental illness, religious hysteria, and stubborn tradition. I don't want to ruin the end, but let's just say, it caught me off guard. And, to be honest, it left me shaken.

-Joseph Rubas   Author

Martin is gloomy at its most superb, a reminder that low budget can often work in the favour of the horror moviemaker. So few Romero actors are ever found anywhere else, they exist as actors only for Romero, yet John Amplas is so brooding, or maybe sulky and affecting, in this. I could also have seen John Lydon taking the role, in the way he played the manipulative psychopath in another forgotten, but intriguing, film Order of Death. the end is horrific because it seems so real. Before horror movies started pretending to be documentaries, Romero was creating a very similar effect.

-Robin Ince   Writer/Comedian

Massacre Mansion

(DPP Section 3) Banned in the UK
Also known as "Mansion of the Doomed", "The Terror of Dr.Chaney".
Year of release: 1976
Writer: Frank Ray Perilli
Director: Michael Patak
R rated 89 mins. USA
Tagline: "What happens is so horrifying we can't even hint at it in this poster."
Main cast: Richard Basehart (Dr. Leonard Chaney), Gloria Grahame (Katherine), Trish Stewart (Nancy Chaney), Lance Henriksen (Dr. Dan Bryan), Al Ferrara (Al), JoJo D'Amore (Georgio).
Distributed by: Vipco

Plot:
Massacre Mansion tells the story of an eye surgeon whose daughter loses her sight in an horrific car accident, her father proceeds to remove eyes from unwilling victims for his daughter, the only trouble is that the eyes don't work for long which leaves the surgeon on a continuous hunt for fresh eyes.

Appraisal:
Yes, this film is as bad as it sounds; its daft plot and full on cheesy horror all the way through and through. You do get to see a young Lance Henriksen, which is a plus; if you are a lover of cheesy horror films you will love this, it's so daft, it's good! This film has a dark feel to it throughout, it does look cheap and the actors are not on top form; but, all that said, this film is really good! For some reason, it just works.

This film was banned in the 1980's, Anyone who collected VHS tapes and banned films in the 80's and 90's would know the cover with the clenched fist and two eyeballs sticking out the top, I remember buying a copy of this film through a magazine, well in the back of the magazine wanted ads then again purchasing a real copy complete with the cover through an ad in Dark side magazine I think the later was in the 1990's!

A cult little VHS hit with a fantastic memorable cover!

Massacre Mansion was seized under section 3 of the 1959 Obscene Publications Act on VHS in the early 1980's before the implementation of the Video Recordings Act of 1984 in the UK.

Massacre Mansion was initially released uncut on pre-cert VHS by Vipco in 1983. The film is passed 18 uncut in the UK buy the BBFC.

-Tony Newton

Mausoleum

(DPP Section 3) Banned in the UK
Also known as "The Terror of Dr. Chaney" and "Mausoleu".
Year of release: 1983
Writers: Robert Barich and Robert Madero
Director: Michael Dugan
R rated 96 mins. USA
Tagline: "What evil lives in the…mausoleum."
Main cast: Marjoe Gortner (Oliver Farrell), Bobbie Bresee (Susan Walker Farrell), Norman Burton (Dr. Simon Andrews), Maurice Sherbanee (Ben the Gardener), LaWanda Page (Elsie), Laura Hippe (Aunt Cora Nomed).
Distributed by: Filmtown, Videospace

Plot:
Are you brave enough to enter the Mausoleum? Following the death of her mother Susan gave her soul to the Mausoleum and it turned her into a demon! Susan is unable to prevent the evil forces that have taken her body as the host. Can anyone stop this demonic force before it consumes her?

Appraisal:
This film has a B-movie quality about it, the acting isn't great but there are enough bizarre scenes in the film to grab the attention of horror film fans out there, it's not a top ten but what a bizarre watch!

This 1983 movie is quite enjoyable on the first watch but doesn't lend itself to repeat viewing. It's a fun camp horror movie which cannot be taken seriously, this film is a tale of demons, possession and is a total clusterfuck of a movie, the effects range from fantastic to strange amateur throughout the film, no Oscars where going to be given out for the performance in this film either. The main star is Bobbie Bresee who had a very short career as a lesser-known scream queen. Bobbie Bresee also appeared in "Ghoulies" and later "Surf Nazis" must die and also appeared in the cult classic "Evil Spawn". "Mausoleum" is a strange low budget film that could have been so much better than it was. The execution of the beast was to be the films downfall. On paper this sounds like a great film when I first watched this film many years ago I expected to be scared but instead I entered into yet again strange B movie underworld of the bizarre.

Masoleum was seized under section 3 of the 1959 Obscene Publications Act on VHS in the early 1980's before the implementation of the Video Recordings Act of 1984 in the UK.

Masoleum was initially released uncut on pre-cert VHS by Videospace in 1982, Since then the film was passed by the BBFC uncut rated 18.

-Tony Newton

Midnight

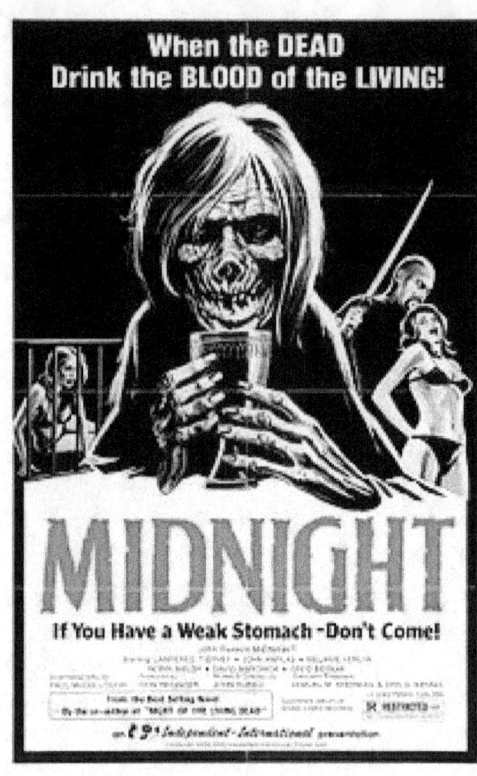

(DPP Section 3) Banned in the UK
Year of release: 1982
Writer: John A. Russo
Director: John A. Russo
R rated 91 mins. USA
Tagline: "When the dead drink the blood of the living."
Main cast: Melanie Verlin (Nancy Johnson), Lawrence Tierney (Bert Johnson), John Hall (Tom), Charles Jackson (Hank), Doris Hackney (Harriet Johnson), Bob Johnson (Reverend Carrington).
Distributed by: Alpha Video

Plot:
Midnight features a backwards serial killer, satanic rituals, resurrection, all over seen by equally crazy law enforcement and young fun loving teens warned to stay away but didn't listen. Hitchhiking leads Nancy to being captured in a cage as part of a sadistic satanic ritual. The sadistic family keep the corpse of their deceased mother in a rocking chair in the attic!

Appraisal:
Midnight is a watchable and enjoyable horror film, but not director John A. Russo's finest hour, the film has an almost cult following and is loved by horror fans across the globe, Tom Savini make up FX effects are great.

Midnight was filmed on a low budget but manages to give a certain creepiness but once again it's a good idea poorly executed due to the fact of the low budget. Some of the ideas from this film are great at any time you cannot trust any of the characters which is a great touch, though the music score is more comical overall not what I expected. The first time I watched this movie because of John A Russo's "Night of the Living Dead" I just expected more, as "Night of the Living Dead" is one of the best horror films of all time!.

Too many ideas and things that happen off screen, okay that worked for The Texas Chainsaw Massacre with the kills but just not for this film as you can obviously see that scenes and things deemed to be happening off screen are because of the low budget. It sounds like I hate this film but actually it's not bad by any means nor is it the worst film on the list and is well worth tracking down.

Any film focusing on the occult or religion I'm a big fan of, there's a shortage of these elements in horror films. This film shows the real dangers associated with religion and occults.

John A Russo's Midnight: A Novel of Terror book is a fantastic read, I much prefer the book and really like the pacing of John A Russo's writing and the way he delivers the macabre on the page. Definitely give it a watch if you haven't already! Midnight was seized under section 3 of the 1959 Obscene Publications Act on VHS in the early 1980's before the implementation of the Video Recordings Act of 1984 in the UK.

Midnight was initially released uncut on pre-cert VHS by Alpha (Intervision) in 1983, Midnight is currently available fully uncut from Arrow Video, and was given an 18 rating by the BBFC.

-Tony Newton

Connected with one of the most famous walking dead/zombie films of all time "Night of the Living", John A. Russo is a man who has done and created so much for horror fans between writing, film, culture and more. Russo, who has stayed in the Pittsburgh, Pennsylvania area for decades, has developed and been a part of many of the famous projects in the nearly 50 years of horror. Accepting the invitation to come on as a live guest to my horror radio show (The Horror Happens Radio Show), I delved deep into the works of Russo in prep and study. For the most part, "Night of the Living Dead" has been one of my all-time favorite films and I had only connected to more of his Russo's written work after listening to Russo, Russ Streiner & Judith O'Dea do a live panel at a convention called Infect Scranton in Pennsylvania. In retrospect, not only am I glad I had the chance to have him on live but actually listen to him speak and get to know him some at different convention appearances. Those chances and meetings brought me to a film called "Midnight" released in 1982. While many fans and horror journalists will discuss "Night of the Living Dead", I mind "Midnight" a much more interesting film but found it to be his best work.

Written and directed by Russo, this cult, grindhouse thriller is staple of what is right with bare bones indie horror filmmaking. Upon viewing this film, I was impressed with Russo's fearless writing, blend of humor and tension, featuring of taboo subject matter (race, sexuality, freedom, choices, rednecks, abuse, etc.) and defining performances especially by genre actor John Amples and legend Lawrence Tierney. The story of "Midnight" revolves around an abusive relationship within a family home between stepdaughter Mel Verlin (Nancy) and her stepfather Tierney (Bert). Upon escaping the house after Bert's heavy drinking binge, Nancy hitches a ride with two guys (white and African American) on spring break. She ventures in a van (nothing to racial, sexual or creepy about it) across country with all those crazy and zany adventures both legal and not. Upon some criminal acts, confessions and secrets, the trio stops to camp in the back woods area near a group of Satanists! From there, a family including Amples as Abraham and his brother (posing as police) abducts, tortures and murders the trio in the backwoods with Bert chasing them down to a tense, tragic and disturbing end!

The performance of Tierney, who is despicable as a drunken sleazy cop at first only to end up the vigilante hero in the end is one of the best in the film. Also Amples, who I believe was the prototype for the back woods satanic psycho in films to come, shows diversity in character from the famed scientist in George A. Romero's "Day of the Dead" or the vampire type in "Martin". Talking with Russo and Amples over the last couple of years, you find that "Midnight" is a remarkable genre film for all that went wrong and the lack of resources they didn't have. Even with these factors that affect many indie projects over the different decades, the film has also survived decades and was released during a time when the slasher genre of horror was very successful. Surviving over the years, "Midnight" grew in cult status and again for me it connects to the 1980's horror films I love and pushed the boundaries being a staple of grindhouse cinema. It continues to be one of Russo's best efforts and according to Russo is looking to be remade with the same intensity and grit.

-Jay K   (The Horror Happens Radio Show on HGRNJ).

Naked Fist

(DPP Section 3) Banned in the UK
Also known as "Firecracker".
Year of release: 1981
Writers: Ken Metcalfe and Cirio H. Santiago
Director: Cirio H. Santiago
R rated 77 mins. USA, Philippines
Tagline: "She'll blow you away."
Main cast: Jillian Kesner (Susanne Carter), Darby Hinton (Chuck Donner), Rey Malonzo (Rey), Ken Metcalfe (Erik), Peter Cooper (Pete), Don Gordon Bell (Japanese Karate fighter).
Distributed by: VRO Video Network

Plot:
In this low budget exploitation movie we see actress Jillian Kesner as Susanne Carter a martial arts teacher who travels to the Philippines to investigate the suspicious disappearance of her sister Bonnie, once there she's pointed in the direction of drug kingpin Erik, she discovers the arena of death and teaches the mafia a lesson they will never forget!

Appraisal:
With a tagline like "She'll blow you away." this films sounds like a 1970's porn film that Linda Lovelace would star in but the film is anything but that!

Jillian Kesner the lead lady is very likeable and does a great job keeping your eye fixed on her, she owns the screen and makes the film watchable. At times the film is badly edited and even the sound is awful in parts. You don't see a woman in her underwear normally kicking a bad guys ass but you do in this flick, well worth a watch!

Naked Fist also known as "Firecracker" Jillian Kesner is on fire well is a Firecracker in this cult classic martial arts epic, that is somewhat understated and seems to go under the radar.

The film is knocked for its choreography but to be honest this goes unnoticed as Jillian Kesner's on screen presence takes over and you go on a journey with her as she fights the Mafia and teaches them a lesson they will never forget. Jillian Kesner(Susanne Carter) goes to the Philippines in search of her sister who is missing and was last seen doing an interview relating to the drug cartel. This film does have a lot of over the top fight scenes, which are very entertaining. This is full on exploitation fun all the way through. "Naked Fist" is a must see, I may be biased as I am a fan of martial arts movies and exploitation flicks so this to me is just fantastic all round hard hitting entertainment 80's exploitation on high kicks! This film seems to be a remake somewhat of the directors earlier film "T.N.T Jackson" who female lead goes in search of her brother killer-you guessed it drug dealers. Then in 1993 director Cirio H. Santiago released "Angelfish" which is basically a remake of "Naked Fist" but lacks it's exploitation charm and just feels like a low budget flick, then later in 2005 the director released "Blood Fist 2050" which sees a role revived as this time a male lead is in search of his brothers killer. If you are not a Naked Fist fan after your first watch I'd be surprised. It's a classic exploitation, high-kicking action flick - a great all round fun and thrilling movie! Naked Fist was seized under section 3 of the 1959 Obscene Publications Act on VHS in the early 1980's before the implementation of the Video Recordings Act of 1984 in the UK. Naked Fist was initially released uncut on pre-cert VHS by VRO Video Network in 1982, No UK re-release though you can get the uncut version from the US and appears in the Roger Corman's Cult Classics DVD box set.

-Tony Newton

Released as FIRECRACKER here in the United States, NAKED FIST had a very strange history. The first actress shipped to the Philippines refused to perform her nude scenes as contracted and was quickly flown back to the US, where she promptly filed a lawsuit against Roger Corman for sexual harassment (which she lost). Roger grabbed onto my friend, Jillian Kesner, and asked her if she would hop on a plane straight away. Jillian was game, but confessed to Roger that she had no martial arts training whatsoever. Roger arranged for her to take a short Karate lesson and then booked her on the twenty-plus hour flight to Manila. He told Jillian to practice whatever she had learned (in her single lesson) in the aisles of the plane… it'll help pass the time.

Jillian made it through the movie, but when she returned Roger discovered that the Filipino filmmakers had failed to shoot any nude scenes with Jillian… the very reason she was sent there in the first place!

Corman quickly set up a small shoot at the New World lumber yard where Jillian, with a fledgling director and crew, would kung-fu a handful of stunt men and, piece by piece, lose all of her clothes until she was fighting in nothing but her panties. It was quite a sequence.

She must have impressed Roger, because the girl who flew off to the Philippines with but a single Karate lesson to her credit, suddenly became the "Winner of the Black Belt Olympics", an impressive sounding competition that didn't even exist. Still, it made for great hype on the poster. In a freaky twist of fate, Jillian immediately became known as a "martial arts actress" and picked up work in RAW FORCE, OPERATION COBRA and a stint on TV as John Ritter's judo obsessed girlfriend on THREE'S COMPANY.

-Fred Olen Ray   Director of Hollywood Chainsaw Hookers. Director producer, screenwriter, actor, and cinematographer.

The Nesting

(DPP Section 3) Banned in the UK
Year of release: 1981
Writers: Daria Price and Armand Weston
Director: Armand Weston
R rated 104 mins. USA
Tagline: "What's outside brings terror. What's inside means death."

Main cast: Robin Groves (Lauren Cochran), Christopher Loomis (Mark Felton), Michael David Lally (Daniel Griffith), John Carradine (Colonel LeBrun), Bill Rowley (Frank Beasley) David Tabor (Abner Welles).

Distributed by: Vipco

Plot:
The Nesting tells the story of agoraphobic novelist Lauren. In order to overcome writers block Lauren decides to rent an old Victorian mansion in the countryside but when eerie and unexplained things start to occur in the mansion and the people around her meet horrific ends the sordid history of her new home is uncovered.

Appraisal:
The Nesting is a different take on the slasher genre; this film sees a mystery writer who is suffering from agoraphobia finding a new house to work on a novel with disastrous results. This is a cult slice of horror that does taste good. The gore effects are well done and story is very entertaining and intriguing throughout. John Carradine plays the owner of the house who is very creepy and captivating on screen. This mystery horror offering does feel a bit dated in parts but is quite different to any film on the list, it's not one of the best on here but a good enough watch to be enjoyed. This film seemed to fly under the radar for many years, but seems to have had a resurgence of late with the film being released on Blu-ray and viewed by a new audience of horror fans. The film has a great atmosphere throughout.

This film is often forgotten and always gets a bad rap, I think because I first saw this film at an impressionable age that it had quite an effect. The film has elements of supernatural and brutal horror, Kind of so bad that it's good! Well worth checking out and not half as bad as people make out, it has a great 80's vibe.

The Nesting was seized under section 3 of the 1959 Obscene Publications Act on VHS in the early 1980's before the implementation of the Video Recordings Act of 1984 in the UK.

The Nesting was initially released uncut on pre-cert VHS by Vipco in 1982, In 1986 the film was re-submitted to the BBFC and all versions since 1986 have been passed uncut and with an 18 rating.

-Tony Newton

The Nesting was the only non-adult film ever directed by Armand Weston and a good alternate title might have been Hell Hath No Fury...

When a bunch of whores are gunned down by some hooligans, what's the only logical solution? Communicate from beyond the grave to the only living offspring of the head madame via dreams, so the offspring becomes agoraphobic and has to find the house she's been dreaming about, be mercilessly tormented by spirits, only try to leave once all the men in her life are dead, and then find out it was all an elaborate setup by the ghosts because the men in the offspring's life were the same men who killed the whores in the first place. Tale as old as time.

I don't know what it is about this movie, but it had a profound effect on me as a child. At 7 years old, I was definitely far too young to watch it, but that's proven true of many of the films I've seen. Eraserhead at age 12? Too soon!

As a result, I feel like this film has informed a lot of my peculiar fascinations. I love old architecture. I love urban exploring. I love haunted house films. The Nesting has all of that and more.

The house in which this film takes place might win for best haunted house location of all time. Sure, the Amityville house is iconic, but it's got nothing on the chill factor of the grand maison in this film. With its domed top and bulbous wrought-iron fixtures, it's almost Russian in its design and yet it doesn't particularly seem as though it belongs to any specific era or geographical location.

It's because of this house that, to this day, I cannot pass a ramshackle 2-story home without stopping to stare.

Well, that, and the fact that there's a scene that's forever burned into my brain. A scene which haunted me since childhood and carried through to my adolescence. I first saw the film on a Sunday matinee on television. Midway through the film, our lead actress (the offspring in question) becomes trapped outside the top floor of this distressing old house. A friend pulls up (one of the aforementioned men in need of dispatching) sees her in peril, and tries to save her. But when the specter one of the dead whores appears from inside the house laughing maliciously at him, the man falls to his death impaling himself on a weathervane.

For years I sought the film out unable to remember the name or anything else about it save for this one haunting scene. I searched high and lot, to no avail, watching everything I could get my hands on to try and find it. I even took to posting to "Name that movie" Internet forums. Finally, at a video store closeout I came across a Warner Bros. Clamshell edition of something called "THE NESTING". It looked like fun. And it was only $1. How could I resist?

That was the best $1 I ever spent. The second I saw the house, I knew it was the movie I'd been searching for.

And unlike so many films that you watch as a child which can lose their magic or power over the years, this one grew more powerful as I watched it.

The acting is hammy as hell. The logic is barely there. And the story is loopy enough to make you dizzy at times. But the scares are effective. The ghosts in this movie are mad as hell and it comes off on screen. They're not done up in any kind of makeup. They're not spectral. They appear, for the most part, as corporeal beings, and they take no small joy in tormenting the men that are stupid enough to come back to this place. As a result, the sheer glee with which they enact their revenge is actually quite startling.

While the film isn't gratuitously violent or sexual, it does earn its R rating. Though I'm not quite sure it deserved the attention it received from the DPP, it certainly boasts the requisite violence against women that seemed to be the prominent focus of the prosecutors of the day. Regardless, I'm happy I finally have a chance to speak about the film. It's far from perfect, but it doesn't pull any punches and if you're in the mood for a great bad movie night, I recommend giving The Nesting a try.

-Mark Miller   Seraphim Films.

The New Adventures of Snow White

(DPP Section 3) Banned in the UK
Also known as "Grimm's Fairy Tales for Adults" and "Grimm's Marchen Von Lusternen Parchen"
Year of release: 1969
Writer: Jacob Grimm and Wilhelm Grimm
Director: Rolf Thiele
Uncertified 78 mins. West Germany
Tagline: "The naked truth at last!"
Main cast: Marie Liljedahl (Snow White), Eva Reuber – Staier (Cinderella), Ingrid Van Bergen (Queen), Gaby Fuchs (Sleeping Beauty), Kitty Kino (Cinderella's 1st step sister), Evelyn Dutree (Cinderella's 2nd step sister).
Distributed by: Mountain Video

Plot:
This 1969 offering "The New Adventures of Snow White" is pretty much a gruesome and erotic German twist on the classic well-known fairy tales of "Cinderella", "Snow White" and "Sleeping Beauty". This movie is truly grim!

Appraisal:
This film is very enjoyable fun romp! fairy tales are and always will be very dark. This film is not as dark as it could be; it's more a tongue-in-cheek sex romp. The film plays more like a Russ Meyer offering than anything else. It's neither here nor there, a good idea poorly executed, a fun daft watch but nothing else. You wouldn't watch this film more than once unless you were on a bad trip or smoking pot.

There were a lot of these style films popping up in the late 70's, I never really got much enjoyment out of them instead of being erotically charged for some reason they creeped the hell out me, with the surrealistic undertones.

The New Adventures of Snow White was seized under section 3 of the 1959 Obscene Publications Act on VHS in the early 1980's before the implementation of the Video Recordings Act of 1984 in the UK.

The New Adventures of Snow White was initially released uncut on pre-cert VHS by Mountain Video in 1980, No UK re-release, though you can get the uncut version from the US.

-Tony Newton

The Brothers Grim are making their way across the land, minding their own business and just trying to get where they're going. Along the way they meet a strange selection of people who get them involved in all sorts of wacky situations. Snow White tends the needs of the seven dwarfs, Sleeping beauty requires something a bit more involved than a kiss to break her spell, Cinderella's sisters are hacking off bits of their bodies to trick the prince and the creatures of the woods are all a bit too frisky.

Well.....it had to happen at some point or another...I'm reviewing porn... Don't worry though I shall guard your delicate sensibilities in accordance with good taste, not that that will be hard to do as The New Adventures of Snow White is about as tame as it could be, well the version I have is and as far as I can tell it is the pre-cert version as it's under the same title and in English language, I'm definite that there is a hard core version out there but this ain't it, not by a long shot.

The film seems to open with the trailer. I wish I joking, but the beginning of the film could be taken verbatim and put up as a self-contained trailer.

Coming from the golden age of porn, the late 60's and into the 1970's, The new adventures of snow white at the very least is a good example of the imagination that went into porn back in those days, the most contemporary example of the kind of film we have here is really to be found in the spoof remakes that popped up so frequently in the 90's. Nowadays the internet has rather rained on the parade of porn film making as the majority is delivered free with no cumbersome plots to hinder the spectacle of fucking, ironically the films that make a decent attempt at a story to contextualise the sex can now make it into the 18 category with on screen penetration and all sorts of other formally forbidden acts.

At the time of the Video Recordings Act being mid way through the process of being read in the commons a great deal of attention was suddenly being focused on titles such as this. If Mary Whitehouse, Sir Bernard Braine and Prime Minister Margaret Thatcher had their way then this would not even have been possible in the R18 category. Putting this into context, this is less explicit than Basic Instinct, hell this is less explicit than some 15-certificate stuff I've seen. For all this and the MP's lack of thought on the subject they did at least make sure that there was to be an R18 certificate available under the terms of the VRA. Graham Bright himself publicly opposed the push to a prohibition on sexual material on video cassette and duly Maggie Thatcher and her puritan posse of Bernard Braine, Leon Brittan and Mary Whitehouse were told in no uncertain terms that that was a step too far... 'By all means ban the bloody stuff we don't like but leave us our right to porn' was the slightly amusing response coming from Westminster. Just for amusement I'm going to treat you to the comment on porn by Graham Bright and let you ponder on the maturity of the kinds of responsible men and women who were and are in charge of the country...

The sort of film which hon. Members witnessed in the House last week would be banned totally. R(18) material applies to the blue movie. Whether we like it or not, many people enjoy watching such films. I had never watched a blue movie, but I must admit that when I was in Sweden I was led astray by some Swedish politicians and I did not enjoy the experience at all. I have no wish to see blue movies. I acknowledge that some of my hon. Friends may wish to do so.

Graham Bright HC debate 11, November 1983

These days, The New Adventures of Snow White would probably, well almost definitely, make a certificate in the cut that I witnessed at least, as even the more troublesome content is so mild as to be harmless. But enough discussion of the merits and political battles of the golden age of porn, lets look at the film itself.

The New Adventures of Snow White carries a rather strong Benny Hill overtone to it, and it barely goes much further than the classic comedian other than it either other than actually having nudity and the more plainly portrayed sexually explicit implications, and boy do we get some implied stuff that is rather...fringe on occasions. We're first introduced to the Brothers who act as out link between the various stories in this fantasyland. They are rather buffoonish but likeable enough to want to follow. They bumble their way through the countryside making dubious trades and interacting with characters that could almost be better described as tertiary rather than secondary.

But when they finally get to interact with the main names in the film it gets rather fun. They really do little more than bump into Snow White, and a rather suggestive cow milking scene ensues, but they do get to wake the homely and erroneously named Sleeping Beauty and they also get to blow the uglies' deception amongst other things.

The first main character we're introduced to is Snow White herself. On the run from the evil queen who wants her sex appeal she's pursued by a hunter until she eventually escape into the woods, where all the animals appear to be transformed princes that need to get laid in order to transform back. Snow White is of course the target of their urgent need to engage in sexual relations, and that's more than a little weird to sit through. A wolf, a frog, a snake and a bear all try to get with Snow White who by this point is barely covered by her less than substantial arrangement that passes for clothing. She is quickly united with the seven dwarfs and in the meantime the Queen gets a meal of what the hunter says lying is Snow Whites ...ahem... lady bits. It's implied stuff like this that really makes up the majority of the more adult content of the film rather than explicit stuff even the nudity in the film is largely limited to breasts and the film is more on the erotic side rather than pornographic.

The queen duly tucks in and only finds out about Snow White still being alive when she consults the magic mirror then has to go off on a couple of occasions to do the job her self. This is one of those places where the film shows its humour.

The Dwarves, after the queens first assassination attempt on Snow White, revive her with what looks like a sensual mud massage...fair enough, though the second time it doesn't work and it takes the handsome prince to come and save her this time and the pair ride off semi clothed of course.

The thing with this film is as odd as it may sound, sexing up a fairy tale, this movie is actually much closer to the original tales than Disney have ever been. The original fairy tales were seriously bloody things and when we get to the Cinderella tale here, well it goes old school.

When the prince comes to find the girl who fits the slipper the uglies hack off parts of their feet in order to try and fit into them, it's pretty grim, no pun intended, as is the barrel full of body bits that the brothers discover. Of course there would have been a bit more mileage in this aspect of the film had they gone with older, more traditional tales which believe me are bloodier and more repulsive than the majority of the films I've reviewed, or am likely to review. Sleeping Beauty in this is unbelievably tamer than the original folk tales had her story, and this is 70's porn.

The overwhelming aspect of the film as a whole is not really the gore anyway, as surprisingly good as it seems to be through the grainy picture quality. No, what comes over as the most outstanding element here is the humour. This film really treats everything as a bit of fun, though there are a couple of darker moments, but for the most part it just revels in the frivolity of some simply bizarre situations. For instance during Snow Whites escape she meets a host of cursed princes in the forms of the woodland creatures. They all try to get with the girl to lift their curse but Snow White is less than understanding about this situation and refuses then because as she says "All you want from me is sex!"

It will never cease to amaze me quite how anything like this could be considered offensive. It's only problem is that of course it's not suitable for kids and because the likes of Disney have claimed all these tales in the name of children, effectively denying the origins of such material in the process, and the powers that be seemed to have a problem with an adult take on the tales. The cover does make it pretty clear what the nature of the film is though and when it comes to be misleading it can safely be said that this film doesn't try to deceive.

Whilst almost all the films of this kind were never likely to be classics, a couple of exceptions being the notable titles of Deep Throat or Behind the green door for instance, it is interesting to note that there are some lost and obscure films out there that are worthy of some attention. The New Adventures of Snow White is more than a little shaky in several places but it remains an entertaining piece of filmmaking. While I've been calling this porn throughout the review it's fairer to call it erotica as it's got much more going on than the single-minded goal of titillation. Where porn provokes a narrow range of response, The new adventures of Snow White is a story that has sexual content, tacked on in many cases of course, but it's almost peripheral to the main thrust of the film. This is to the extent that as these things go it feels rather innocent, it certainly is playful and there isn't a bad bone in the body of it at all.

Of course the chances of it getting a release are slim to none due to its obscurity and some kind of legal action that was taken against it, which is a shame. As obscure cult films go this is probably one of the more entertaining for many reasons and certainly stands out as one of the more unusual takes on the classic fairy tales. If you can find it, I recommend giving it a watch.

-Glenn Criddle   Writer/Critic.

The New York Ripper

(Outright Banned for its cinema release in 1982)and the film famously had a police escort out of the country, so no copies of the film could be made and distributed in the UK).

Year of release: 1982
Writers: Lucio Fulci, Gianfranco Clerici, Dardano Sacchetti
Director: Lucio Fulci
Rated: R rated
Tagline: "New York City: It's a nice place to visit, but you wouldn't want to die there!"
Main Cast: Jack Hedley (Fred Williams, Almanta Suska (Fay Majors), Howard Ross (Mickey0, Andrea Occhipinti (Peter Bunch).
Distributed by: No original VHS release

Plot:
There's a killer on the loose in the streets of Manhattan, this killer is targeting women who, in his opinion, deserve to be killed; the killer decides this in his own bizarre way.

Appraisal:
The New York ripper see's a deranged killer terrorizing the mean streets on Manhattan, Who is safe? (No One) definitely not those with a penchant for perversions!

Some of the victims are involved in bizarre sex acts, small crimes and even a woman who performs live sex shows. No one is truly safe from the New York ripper's clutches.

Lucio Fulci's "The New York Ripper" is a true classic horror from the 1980's, although this title never officially made the video nasty list, this film is a true video nasty. When the film was submitted to the BBFC the film was initially rejected and the film was even given a police escort out the country and completely removed from the country to ensure that it didn't fall into the wrong hands and be distributed in any form or be seen by anyone thus not being able to corrupt anyone on British soil, so this film is definitely nasty! Trying to get your hands on a copy of "The New York Ripper" in the early to late 1980's was near impossible. The film was passed with cuts made to the film due to strong sexualized violence in 2002 and even today there is not a full, uncut version available in the UK though foreign uncut versions of the film are available.

The New York Ripper is directed by the late, great director Lucio Fulci who is a true master of the horror genre, and this film is no exception. The violence toward women is very strong and the BBFC were known to be against this kind of violence in films so the fate of the film in the early 1980's was no surprise. The film's most controversial scene features a woman restrained as the killer tortures her with a razorblade, this doesn't fail to shock even by today's standards. The strangest part of this film has to be the killer talking like a duck or rather like Donald Duck; I suppose the quacking adds to the complete package of the deranged psycho killer who has completely lost the plot. Seeing New York as a sleazy, gritty, mean streets city like this does add to the film, especially when contrasted with the glamorous women.

The New York Ripper is a giallo style gore slasher flick that just works, it's not Fulci's best work but it's definitely a contender. This is a must see horror classic which certainly doesn't hold anything back as far as gore, nudity and shocks go. Banned for its cinema release in 1982. Most famously escorted out of the country once it got rejected for its cinema exhibition in the UK.

The film was later released with 22 seconds of cuts in 2002 with a runtime of 86 min 36secs, the best release is the latter Argent/Shameless release of 2011 with a runtime of 90min 25secs and with only 29 seconds of cuts, the above version had new footage added and is the best version available in the UK.

-Tony Newton

This is Lucio Fulci at his best. I couldn't get enough of this outrageous film, there is so much gore and sleaze thrown in this it should keep any genre fan happy! This is a must watch! If you've not seen this just go and watch immediately.

-Jason Impey   Filmmaker.

Nightbeast

(DPP Section 3) Banned in the UK
Year of release: 1982
Writer: Don Dohler
Director: Don Dohler
R rated 80 mins. USA
Tagline: "His hands tear through flesh and bone!"
Main cast: Tom Griffith (Sheriff Jack Cinder), Jamie Zemarel (Jamie Lambert), Karin Kardian (Lisa Kent), George Stover (Steven Price), Don leifert (Drago), Anne Frith (Ruth Sherman).
Distributed by: VIPCO

Plot:
This movie is a throwback to classic B- monster movies from the 50's. When an alien spaceship passing through our solar system crash lands its occupant wreaks havoc on the residents of a small town in America. Sheriff Jack Cinder is called in to investigate but no one is safe as this alien continues to obliterate the town's residents.

Appraisal:
You can tell Don Dohler was obsessed with 1950's sci-fi and monster movies. This is a great all out monster flick! The monster complete with its ray gun causes havoc ripping off body parts. To me this film is how a monster movies should be, when I watched this film as a kid I always thought how cool it would be if some of the 1950's monster flicks had more gore in them just like this film. Don Dohler ran a magazine called Cinemagic for movie making wanabees. JJ Abrahams of "Lost and "Super 8" and now "Star Wars" fame corresponded with Don Dohler and asked the young JJ Abrahams to supply music for the film "Night Beast", this is JJ. Abrahams first film credit.

This film is a sequel to Don Dohles "The Alien Factor", "Night Beast" is a far better offering complete with a sheriff whose job is to stop the residents from being killed by the evil alien being. This film is a fun watch and a must see if you are a B style monster movie fan!

Nightbeast doesn't feature much gore but there are some scenes that are quite gruesome.

Nightbeast was seized under section 3 of the 1959 Obscene Publications Act on VHS in the early 1980's before the implementation of the Video Recordings Act of 1984 in the UK.

Nightbeast was initially released uncut on pre-cert VHS by Vipco in 1983, and all known versions of Nightbeast have been passed fully uncut, 18 cert in the UK.

-Tony Newton

The notion that Nightbeast, a schlocky rubber creature oriented Don Dohler movie could feature on Fascist documentation (the Video Records Act) alleging potential moral corruption of the population defies belief, especially considering Dohler had the demeanour of a tired bureaucrat and a reluctant acceptance of his cult status – hardly a character to invoke mass amorality. His career could best be summed up as a handful of low budget films, all made with a great amount of heart and a whole lot of passion. Born in Baltimore in 1946, Don was a fan of the genre from an early age being an avid reader of Famous Monsters of Filmland. By 1972 he had launched his own magazine called Cinemagic which featured illustrated step-by-step guides to create your own amateur special effects. The magazine ran for 11 issues before being purchased by Starlog in 1979, but its legacy was lasting with many contemporary Hollywood filmmakers such as J.J Abrams citing it as an influence.

His first foray into making his own films came with The Alien Factor in 1978. It was a fairly simple idea with a crashed alien spaceship leading to a horde of extra-terrestrials invading small town USA and mutilating the townsfolk. Despite its meagre budget it was surprisingly a notable success due to the popularity of Star Wars. With George Lucas' film raking in big bucks in the cinemas, the American public found themselves with an insatiable desire for anything sci-fi orientated and Dohler's film quenched that thirst just fine. The Alien Factor went on to appear at selected cinemas, not to mention a stint on that famed Grindhouse strip of 42nd Street, while a healthy TV syndication ensured that Don received some much needed coin in his direction.

With the general consensus that there was always a core audience for horror, Dohler then went into production on Fiend (1980). Little was changed by way of production, he still used friends, family and familiar locations and with the finished product and he decided it might be worth his time seeking out Lloyd Kaufman to seal a nationwide video distribution deal with Troma. Kaufman, despite being impressed with what Dohler brought to him opted to pass on Fiend saying that his audience demanded more nudity and explicit content – something Dohler himself wasn't too keen on integrating into his films. However, having decided that if that's what it'll take he set about creating his next project – Nightbeast.

Nightbeast actually turned out to be pretty much a more polished and professional looking version of The Alien Factor. With many of the original cast of that movie reprising their roles there are a lot of similarities, especially in the narrative, which takes many of the plot points from the original, not least the alien spacecraft crash landing in a small town. From here we meet the heroic Sheriff Jack Cinder (Tom Griffith) who arrives on scene with the local militia to investigate the disturbance only to be attacked by the alien. Cinder decides to make a stand, and along with the lovely Deputy Lisa (Karin Kardian) and a handful of townsfolk the battle is on to defeat this extra-terrestrial invader.

While the plot doesn't exactly feature much in the way of originality, the charm of Nightbeast lies firmly in its homemade nature. We have a spaceship crafted from polystyrene and paper, while much of the film is shot in a patch of woodland adjacent to Dohler's back garden so they could run the power lines for the lights into his house! The supporting cast are largely made up of neighbours, friends, his aunt's hairdresser and let's not forget his children as well. The film is bursting with Ed Wood style moments such as the scenes he had to extend to pad the film out that show his kids with a six month age difference looking notably physically different in terms of height and weight.

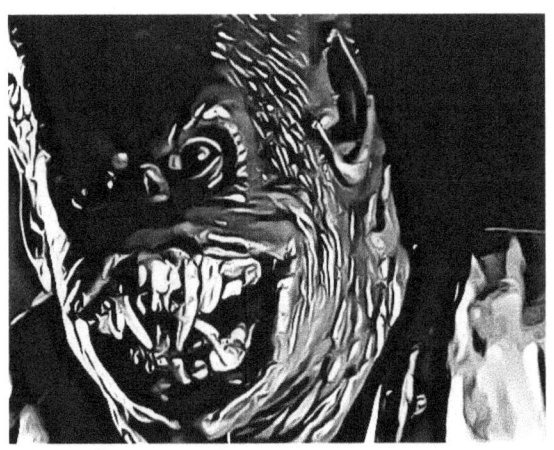

One of the most talked about scenes in the film though is undoubtedly the sex scene Lloyd Kaufman suggested Dohler put into his film as "that's what people want". I implore you to watch this moment of insatiable erotica and tell me that it's quite possibly the most anti-erotic sex scene ever filmed. Sheriff Jack, whilst running for cover from the marauding alien happens to sustain a mild injury to his leg. It needs attention though, and Deputy Lisa suggests they stop off at a nearby cabin to get it cleaned up and bandaged. For whatever reason, Tom Griffith dispatched with the dated but functional long hair he sported in The Alien Factor for the most ridiculous prematurely greying perm you are ever likely to see. We're talking aged Napoleon Dynamite here. During this first aid session, Deputy Lisa gets ravenously horny and reveals her tan lines whilst off comes the Sheriff's ill-fitting y-fronts. With his beer gut and handlebar moustache, this steamy lovemaking session is about as erotic as watching your Mum and Dad having sex; but oddly, all it does is solidify your appreciation of what Don Dohler pulled together.

Nightbeast was released in the UK by Vipco having been passed with no cuts made in 1983. Why would they make cuts though? It really is virtually a blood free zone apart from a few incidents of very tame low budget gore. I can only think that its remarkably iconic sleeve featuring the John Dods (Ghostbusters II, Alien Resurrection) - designed creature conjured up the idea that the film might contain something more 'corrupting' than it actually does. It was reclassified (again without cuts) in 1996 for a release on retail VHS in

Troma's brief sojourn into the UK home entertainment industry. Troma's US release of it is well worth picking up as you can get it on a cool double feature alongside John Paul Kinhart's excellent Blood, Boobs, and Beast documentary which examines Dohler's career.

Despite its low budget nature, Nightbeast is looked back on as the pinnacle in of Don Dohler's career. Granted, that may be akin to saying that Glen or Glenda is the pinnacle of Ed Wood's career but nevertheless - for a guy that made movies in his own town, with his friends and family and handmade special effects, Nightbeast represents quite an achievement. Don Dohler only made seven films in his career, and after having production problems on Blood Massacre (1991), which found the film land in other people's hands for completion he decided to back out of the industry with only the occasional return. Harvesters (2001), which he co-wrote is certainly worth a look for those low budget aficionados amongst you.

Don died of cancer aged 60 in late 2006, and it's only since his death that I became aware of the legacy he left. The fact that legacy includes a position on a Section 3 DPP list is a genuinely surprising one. It's such an inoffensive little film that the average viewer would more likely mock and disparage as opposed to question its morality. However, if the recognition it gets from this infamy creates a few more Don Dohler fans then it might just be worth the attention.

-Dave Wain   Writer.

Night of the Living Dead

(DPP Section 3) Banned in the UK
Year of release: 1968
Writers: George A. Romero and John A. Russo
Director: George A. Romero
Unrated 96 mins. USA
Tagline: "Pits the dead against the living in a struggle for survival!"
Main cast: Duane Jones (Ben), Judith O'Dea (Barbara), Karl Hardman (Harry), Marilyn Eastman (Helen), Keith Wayne (Tom), Judith Ridley (Judy).
Distributed by: Alpha (Intervision)

Plot:
Night of the Living Dead sees radiation from a satellite cause the dead to reanimate. On a trip to visit their father's grave siblings Barbara and Tommy encounter the reanimated corpses of the dead and they're hungry for flesh! Barbara joins a group of mismatched survivors as they attempt to stay alive in this zombie flick by the master George A. Romero.

Appraisal:
This film is amazing full stop. The film itself being black and white makes the special effects look so much more believable than they actually are. As a young lad I was more used to watching the Marx Brothers or Norman Wisdom films in black and white. The Night of the Living Dead was a new experience and opened up a portal for me into classic early black and white horror films. The films script and direction is flawless! The whole film comes over so well especially when you consider the budget they had to work with. Every actor takes the whole thing seriously and gives outstanding performances. The ending of the film is as classic as the start and even to this day I think that it's one of the best shock endings ever! George Romero paved the way for the whole zombie genre making the rules that would stick, only Romero has the talent to make slow moving zombies a real threat by building great characters intertwined with a great story, effects and suspense. George A. Romero's decision to cast Duane Jones as the lead protagonist leading crazy white people amidst a zombie pandemic in the movie works so well. clearly there are underlying messages of racism in the film. The 1960's saw civil rights protests that were going in the country, the ill fated end to Ben surely was a depiction of the assassination of Malcolm X and Martin Luther King Jr. Although in interviews Romero says he was just the best actor for the job, which he was for sure! That ending will always haunt me!

This film should be a staple of filmmaking and shown in schools (maybe not to pre-teens) but those student filmmakers of any kind. This just goes to show what you can do with passion and talent and even a small budget, what you have the potential to come up with. This is easily hands\-down the best low budget horror film of all time! Night of the Living Dead was seized under section 3 of the 1959 Obscene Publications Act on VHS in the early 1980's before the implementation of the Video Recordings Act of 1984 in the UK. Night of the Living Dead was initially released uncut on pre-cert VHS by Alpha (Intervision) in 1979 and 1981, As it stands the film is now rated a 15 cert by the BBFC in the UK fully uncut.

-Tony Newton

As the sound recordist and one of the first ten investors in the original 1968 version of Night of the Living Dead I had the opportunity to observe most every component of the films creation, At the ripe old age of

Twenty or twenty one, I got to be there ever day of the pre-shoot and post production. I got to watch the big guys, the twenty eight year olds as they crafted the story of one of the greatest films ever made.

Night of the Living Dead came before the rating system and who knows what part it actually played in getting a rating system implemented. There was the Roger Ebert review that asked the question "Should we be letting our children watch these movies"? but as I remember it when the story was being created and then it went into production, I can't remember much attention being paid to censorship.

Not because we were rebel filmmakers but because we were naïve filmmakers. We were accustomed to working with advertising agencies that took care of that kind of stuff, so off we went with no real adult supervision!

I have never been much of a fan of the studio system, but they are one of the early forms of censorship in the film business and being that we were the epitome of independent filmmakers we never had that input either. So off we went on our blissful merry way.

Decisions were not made for reasons of political correctness, but more on did it make the film scarier?

Flash forward a year and the film is made and ready to be screened for potential distributors, with tons of things these people had never seen before. As luck would have it they were hung up on the fact that the film was black and white, more than an African/American man was slapping a white woman or that there was a nude shot or two or even there was actual simulated flesh eating going on.

When Walter Reid decided they wanted to put Night of the Living Dead on the silver screen and they choose Continental as the distribution force behind the film, there were other distractions that must have a played a part in them over looking all it's censorable issues.

I am of the opinion that Night of the Living Dead, got to be a cult classic because of the fact it was a very good script to start with but then those powerful moments got to stay in the film and that gave the viewer something that they weren't able to see in other films.

Lot's of things go into the success of anything, I'm just thankful Night of the Living Dead got the breaks it needed to be a crucial influence on the horror world.

-Gary Streiner   Sound engineer on "Night of the Living Dead" 1968.

It shouldn't still scare me, but it does. The opening minutes, with the brother and sister squabbling in the graveyard; the immortal line: "They're coming to get you, Barbra," the thrilling orchestral score and the tall guy walking slowly in the background—who could be just another visitor. My heart beats faster as the tension builds, until Barbra (Judith O'Dea') reaches the house.

Inside the house my fear becomes dread; as the alpha male, Ben (Duane Jones), and the scared weasel guy, Mr Cooper (Karl Howdman), argue over who will rule the kingdoms of the house and the cellar. In some shots Barbra looks more zombie than human. The occupants' reason, kindness and common sense are consumed by their fear of the relentless 'ghouls' and I remember: none in the house will survive.

-Nicholas Vince   The Chatterer in Hellraiser -Actor and author.

Night of the Living Dead is the movie that started it all. The first film to depict a true flesh eating undead "zombie", *Night* was released in 1968 and singlehandedly created the zombie genre.

Filmed on a budget of only 114,000, *Night of the Living Dead* reaped over 42 million at the box office.

Written and directed by George A. Romero and John A. Russo, two amateur filmmakers from Pittsburgh, Pennsylvania. A commercial smash, *Night* nevertheless generated controversy for a number of reasons. Violence was depicted in graphic detail, cannibalism was freely shown, and the leading man, Duane Jones, was black, something that was virtually unheard of at the time. *Variety* magazine called it an "...orgy of sadism" while a prominent *New York Times* reviewer labeled it "junk."

Despite initial misgivings, critics eventually accepted *Night* as a groundbreaking horror film with wide reaching influence; not only did it launch the career of the zombie, it also revolutionized horror filmmaking as a whole, paving the way for such films as *The Texas Chainsaw Massacre* (1974), *Halloween* (1978), and *Friday the 13th* (1980).

In 1999, *Night of the Living Dead* was inducted into the Library of Congress's National Film Registry, an honor reserved for "culturally, historically, or aesthetically" important films.

What makes this film so memorable isn't its violence; it's its lack of it. *Night* is built on dread and suspense. What little gore there is might have been shocking to more conservative viewers, but it made up a very small percentage of the film. *Night* was about terror, not gore, and it delivered on the terror.

And, to this day, still does.

-Joseph Rubas   Author.

The Night of the Living Dead: I first saw this early feature from George Romero when I was about 10 years old. Since then I have been scarred and hooked by the horror genre. The original black & white manages to capture a sort of reality that it loses in color. This is one I should go back and watch again but probably will not. Okay, I admit that it still scares the crap out of me.

-Jeffrey Littorno   Author.

No one film has been so connected to so many lives as George A. Romero's 1968 independent living dead spectacular "Night of the Living Dead". Featuring a narrative based around an outbreak of reanimated corpses near Pittsburgh, Pennsylvania. The story follows a group of individuals fight trapped in a farmhouse who must fight through the night for survival. Featuring realistic gore, the fear of what our bodies can do to us and performances that have stayed with us through generations, the film stands as a bench mark for what a filmmaker can do on so many levels and the ability to dare to make a statement. That statement came from different angles including the casting of African American actor Duane Jones as the leading man in arguably one of the most powerful and shocking performances in horror film history. The mindset of revolution and overthrowing the traditional ways and means was at the heart of this film. Also, the understanding that no one was safe whether dead or alive!

Romero, Russ Streiner, John Russo, cast and crew created a world that had never been seen by film and horror audiences before. In retrospect, as a horror film fan, writer and radio show host (The Horror Happens Radio Show), this film has stuck with me through most of my adult life going back as early as ten years of age. "Night of the Living Dead" was part of my growth and even influenced my early decision making as a horror film fan that has stuck with me over the years. How, you ask? When I was ten years old, I was taken out for school clothes shopping at the local mall; it was one of my favorite times of the year! My knowledge of horror was so limited as a youngster but "Night of the Living Dead" which I had seen on some cable television station stuck in my mind and heart.

With that influence, I made the choice of picking up a copy of the film on VHS tape asking my aunt to buy this for me instead of school clothes. Upon getting the okay (and a look), I went home to watch it and still to this day still have the tape watching it for decades now. It's funny to look back and see how so much in my life has changed with time but certain things continue to stay with me like love I have for horror films, the New York Yankees, pro wrestling, my family and this film.

Even more evidence to the impact of this film on me and no doubt generations of families who fall anywhere in the dark sea of horror fans, this film has been one of the many stops along the way to establish me as a professional in all the dark corners of horror impacting my mindset and taste in the genre and lifestyle. Even meeting such legends as John Russo, Russ Streiner and Judith O' Dea, I marvel at their tales, memories and paths created from this film. Why not all of Romero's work is to the quality of his earlier work, I still have a place in my heart for the tension, storytelling, emotion, love, gore and fear that I view every time I watch this film. Impact is not strong enough of word to state the way "Night of the Living Dead" has moved my life and goals ahead as part of the dysfunctional family of horror.

-Jay K   (The Horror Happens Radio Show on HGRNJ)

Nightmare City

(DPP Section 3) Banned in the UK
Also known as "Incubo Sulla Citta Contaminata."
Year of release: 1980
Writers: Antonio Cesare Corti and Luis Maria Delgado
Director: Umberto Lenzi
Unrated 92 mins. Italy, Mexico, Spain
Tagline: "Now they are everywhere! There is no escape!"
Main cast: Hugo Stiglitz (Dean Miller), Laura Trotter (Dr. Anna Miller), Maria Rosaria Omaggio (Sheila Holmes), Francisco Rabal (Maj. Warren Holmes), Sonia Viviani (Cindy).
Distributed by: VTC

Plot:
Nightmare City is another entry in the zombie movie craze of the early 1980's. A radiation spillage causes mayhem when a swarm of flesh hungry zombies emerge from a plane which has been exposed to nuclear radiation. TV news reporter Dean Miller attempts to reveal the truth about the zombie outbreak to the public but General Murchison has other ideas. There's no escape and the only thing that can stop them is a bullet to the brain!

Appraisal:
This classic film with zombie like beings sucking blood and killing victims in every way imaginable, The infected here can run fast, they can attack people with weapons as well. These beings are a major threat, which gives the movie a great realistic feel throughout! You can feel what it would be like, having to face this evil threat, these monster like zombies mean business. you can tell that Quentin Tarantino's Planet Terror was certainly inspired by this great film.

Umberto Lenzi has put his hand to many styles of film, for me this is my favorite piece of work by him. How anyone can dislike this film is beyond me, everything about this movie is awesome!

Dean Miller the television reporter is played excellently by the fantastic Hugo Stiglitz, who survives when a plane carrying a cargo of radioactive zombies go on the rampage immediately after landing. If you haven't already seen "Nightmare City" go and do so! This is a great addition to anyone's horror collection, a must own!

Let the Nightmare begin!

Nightmare City was seized under section 3 of the 1959 Obscene Publications Act on VHS in the early 1980's before the implementation of the Video Recordings Act of 1984 in the UK.

Nightmare City was initially released uncut on pre-cert VHS by VTC 1982. The film was re-submitted to the BBFC in 1986 was released by Stablecane LTD with a running time of 83 mins. 5s with approx. 3min 5s of cuts, In 2003 Anchor Bay released the uncut version rated 18 by the BBFC with no cuts made with a running time of 88mins. 5secs.

-Tony Newton

In 2003, British director Danny Boyle shocked the world with 28 Days Later - perhaps the most terrifying (and utterly plausible) "zombie" film ever made. In it, a government-engineered virus sweeps the British Isles, turning ordinary people into mad, mindless killing machines.

28 Days Later was hailed for its originality. Apparently, depicting zombies are infected humans was a really innovative concept (although George A. Romero's The Crazies, 1973, did just that, and thirty years earlier).

Only it wasn't.

There was The Crazies, of course, but there was also another film.

In the wake of Dawn of the Dead, another Romero film that was hugely popular in Europe, a thousand European filmmakers set out to produce their own zombie films, most notably Lucio Fulci.

In 1980, Umberto Lenzi's Nightmare City (also known as City of the Walking Dead) appeared in Italy. The plot is simple. A reporter and his wife are caught up in an epidemic of violence as radioactive zombies overwhelm the city and the outlying countryside. What sets these zombies apart is this: They aren't dead, and they aren't dumb. In fact, Nightmare City contains countless scenes of zombies wielding axes, clubs, and, yes, even firearms. How many movies show zombies shooting victims with assault rifles?

Nightmare City, like so many other Italian zombie film of the era, was filmed on next-to-nothing and features...well, bad acting. Might as well be honest. It doesn't skimp on gore, and as such was banned in many countries. In the UK, it was certified as a "Video Nasty," though a UK Stablecane release was passed on home video in 1986 with just over three minutes cut.

It's readily available today, especially on the Internet, where it can be viewed in its entirety. I believe I watched it on YouTube. Back then, I was under the impression that it was the first film to feature "running" zombies. It's not. Like I said, the "zombies" are really just people. And, yes, the acting is stiff, the dubbing is out-of-synch, and there really isn't much of a plot, but it's still an interesting film from a historical perspective.

And, everything else aside, it's fun.

-Joseph Rubas   Author

Oasis of the Zombies

(DPP Section 3) Banned in the UK
Also known as "The Treasure of the Living Dead".
Year of release: 1982
Writers: Jesús Franco and Ramon Llido
Director: Jesús Franco
Unrated, France, Spain
Main cast: Manuel Gelin (Robert Blabert), Eduardo Fajardo (Colonel Kurt Meitzell), France Lomay (Erikia), Jeff Montgomery (Ben), Lina Romay (Kurt's wife), Myriam Landson (Kurt's wife).
Distributed by: Filmland

Plot:
When a group of treasure hunters led by Herr Kurt search the African desert for a lost fortune of Nazi gold buried by the German Army during WW II they get more than they bargained for when they encounter an army of zombie Nazi's guarding the treasure.

Appraisal:
A Jesús Franco zombie film! This is nothing you would expect. This film gets a bad rap, but I think this is a different take on the zombie film genre. The idea is great although poorly executed due to the low budget, the film seems rushed but is not the abomination it's made out to be. This film has some great cinematography like the iconic zombies in the desert with a backdrop of sun and sand. Jesús Franco directed the film for the producer Marius Lesoeur. Jess Franco also made extra scenes including new actors and a different soundtrack for the Spanish market. I saw the original first so this is my favorite of the two cuts.

Jess Franco's has a varied body of work, okay most of it is exploitation, but I just adore his filmmaking he had a certain quality that only he can deliver in film, a true stamp of his own.

Oasis of the Zombies was seized under section 3 of the 1959 Obscene Publications Act on VHS in the early 1980's before the implementation of the Video Recordings Act of 1984 in the UK.

Oasis of the Zombies was initially released uncut on pre-cert VHS by Filmland 1983. No re-release so far in the UK though you can get the US unrated version.

-Tony Newton

Parasite

(DPP Section 3) Banned in the UK
Year of release: 1982
Writers: Alan J. Adler and Michael Shoob
Director: Charles Band
R rated 85 mins. USA
Tagline: "Once it gets inside you, it will do anything to get out!"
Main cast: Robert Glaudini (Dr. Paul Dean), Demi Moore (Patricia Welles), Luca Bercovici (Ricus), James Davidson (Wolf the Merchant), Al Fann (Collins), Tom Villard (Zeke).
Distributed by: Entertainment in Video

Plot:
Unfortunately scientist Paul Dean has a lethal parasite, which has attached itself to his stomach. The race is on to destroy the Evil but the parasite is not the only problem as government agents and rednecks are in hot pursuit.

Appraisal:
Parasite is set in the 1990's and sees a parasitic monster unleashes its wrath! Demi Moore stars in this crazy post alien offering, featuring blood, guts and gore!

This is not the abomination that some people make it out to be. Stan Winston provides some great looking effects, which are visually stunning.

This film was originally released in 3D though the version released on VHS doesn't provide that extra 3D kick which it needed, to stand out! This B Movie send-up to Masters of Yesteryear is a fun offering that doesn't scare.

All this said it's a good film and well worth hunting down.

Parasite was seized under section 3 of the 1959 Obscene Publications Act on VHS in the early 1980's before the implementation of the Video Recordings Act of 1984 in the UK.

Parasite was initially released uncut on pre-cert VHS by Entertainment in Video 1983, since then all known versions of the film have been passed uncut by the BBFC.

-Tony Newton

Phantasm

(DPP Section 3) Banned in the UK
Also known as: "The Never Dead".
Year of release: 1979
Writer: Don Coscarelli
Director: Don Coscarelli
R rated 88 mins. USA
Tagline: "This ball wants to play with you… for keeps!"
Main cast: A. Michael Baldwin (Mike), Bill Thornbury (Jody), Reggie Bannister (Reggie), Kathy Lester (Lady in Lavender), Terrie Kalbus (Fortune teller's Granddaughter), Kenneth V. Jones (Caretaker).
Distributed by: VCL

Plot:
In this epic horror film children encounter a mortician who has more than one dark side, this man has created a gateway between Earth and the afterworld and is harvesting souls to become slaves in this other dimension! The children and Ice Cream man are soon on a quest to stop the evil that is The Tall Man and his minions from hell.

Appraisal:
Phantasm introduces the tall man (menacingly played by Angus Scrimm) who is up there with the likes of legendary horror characters such as Freddy Krueger, Pinhead, and Leatherface!

This film is awesome, you feel for the young lad who has just lost his parents, Reggie Bannister (the ice cream man) is awesome in this film as he joins with the youngster to fight the tall man. The music is creepy and haunting and the film has an eerie feel, as the tall man is so scary, for me, the tall man and the old man from Poltergeist 2 were the stuff of nightmares. The spheres that kill are amazing; they really make this film very unique indeed! Killing with a sphere has never looked so good! This film spawned many a sequel but the first film is the better offering and a classic horror film all round, not the kind of film you would expect to be withdrawn, or banned but the sphere killing scenes are enough to see why. For me "Phantasm" has its charm and then some, it's low budget feel gave the film a very gritty feel to it, "Phantasm" hands down is one of the best horror films, I love this movie so much, There is more than just charm but a certain magic to this film much like shoving E.T in the VCR player, I can flip the old VHS cassette in and be transported to the 80's evoking the scares and same feelings once felt watching this classic! The Tall man creeped me out so much, and he is just as nasty as Mr. Krueger himself - if not creepier. When the sequel was put together 11 years later, the film obviously had a much bigger budget and outstanding special effects but a lot of the original charm and heart was lost in the process of making the film which money just couldn't buy.

Phantasm was seized under section 3 of the 1959 Obscene Publications Act on VHS in the early 1980's before the implementation of the Video Recordings Act of 1984 in the UK.

Phantasm was initially released uncut on pre-cert VHS by VCL 1981, prior to that rated x for its theatrical release in the UK and then given an 18 rating for its VHS release in 1989, distributed by VCL and passed uncut by the BBFC, since then all known versions of the film have been passed uncut by the BBFC and the film is now rated 15 in the UK.

-Tony Newton

The first time I saw and experienced Phantasm I was 12 years old. It was the mid 1980's. I was living in Long Island, New York. Around this time in the states a TV movie called ADAM exploded on the airways. It was a true story about a kidnapping and murder of a 7 year old boy. After the film aired it was immediately followed by numerous photos of missing children. That TV movie freaked out. Strangely enough a few months later on my block, three kids were chased by a van that failed to abduct them. Because of this event and Adam, I would isolate my self in my house watching movies, strangely enough mostly horror. I was terrified that I was going to be kidnapped by that van.

I'll never forget the first time I rented Phantasm in the middle of this scare. The hike to the video store wasn't too far, so I rode my ass off on my bike there a few times a week to get my horror fix. The Phantasm VHS tape I rented was missing the first 40 minutes of the film. It started right after Jodie cuts the Tall Mans fingers off. I didn't realize at the time that I was missing most of the plot, but it didn't matter. I was immediately transfixed into this film. Phantasm blew my mind.

It felt like this film was made for me. It was an R-rated children's horror film. This movie also reeked of cool. It was like Halloween or Friday the 13th with guns and a badass car. For once the kid character was cool and doing things that you'd never usually see. He was driving and repairing cars, making weapons and firing off guns. This kid was kicking ass.

I never had that type of visceral feel from a horror film before. Mostly because I could relate so much with the younger brother character Jodie. He was around my age and was being stalked by this menacing Tall Man. The fact he wasn't wearing a mask made it even more eerie. This is a scary man that wants to take you away. Like in my head, with that van, I always looking over my shoulders thinking I was being stalked.

This movie fell in my lap at a strange time in my young life. It added extra terror to my early teen years and it also comforted me. In the climax of the film, Jodie would tell himself "don't fear." Some days riding to the video store, that would be the mantra in my head. Thanks to Phantasm.

-Stephen Scarlata   Film producer.

Phantasm does what a lot of horror movies at the time failed to do, which is build a compelling mythology around its villain. The wacky pseudo-Lovecraftian logic that encapsulates the Phantasm universe is why it is still watchable to this day, partially because the world is never fully explained. This element of the unknown is a hard thing to pull off, but in the case of Phantasm, it helps to elevate the atmosphere considerably and gives The Tall Man a genuine air of dread. Like *The Evil Dead*, it has a low-budget grit that adds to the charm, but it's the thought that went into the universe that makes it a classic.

-Steven Kostanski   Astron-6.

Angus Scrimm is a scary looking man. A scary looking Tall Man. Even today, one look at a still from Phantasm sends creeping finger nails down my twitching spine. I think when Death finally comes calling for me, this is what he is going to look like. Phantasm is a proper cult film. Not a huge box office success but enough fan fervour to generate a series of sequels. And why not? It has iconic horror images. The Tall Man himself, a ghoul of an undertaker bringing back the dead as poison dwarfs. The dwarfs, looking like a clan of

Hell-spawned Jawas. And of course that deadly silver ball with the lethal spikes. I always wondered if James Caan would have survived the Rollerball arena if that's what he'd had to play with.

But is it a good movie? I think it was. It dealt with the issue of death in an up front and open way. The lead bad guy was a true dealer of death, being a mortician. By having the protagonist as a young teenage boy it taps into that deep-rooted fear of the day we die. Yes, it is weird. And yes, the special effects in retrospect were done on the comparative cheap. More importantly, it was influential. It resonated with the audience and the characteristics of it can be seen in such films as the Freddie Kruger series. Is it a true Video Nasty? Compared to some, it is not as nasty as maybe it could have been but it certainly has its moments. And if the whole film wasn't absolutely nasty, then that Tall Man certainly was. And in the dark of night when I cannot sleep, he still is.

-Craig Jones   Author.

My Video Nasty adulation started in the early 1980s. I remember with fondness trips to my Grandmas where we were free of parental regulations and as my Aunty lived at home with her Mum and Dad and had a friend of a friend of a friend who could get their hands on "pirate" VHS videos, our Saturday afternoons were the highlight of the week. How many laws could be broken of an afternoon, underage viewing (I was 11), pirate VHS videos and often it would be a banned "nasty" – ah, them were the days.

The film that sticks in my mind from those pre-teenage Saturdays is Phantasm for many reasons, its opposing contrasting features, a tall man, a very tall man turning the dead into dwarf zombies – if the tall man, the very tall man had a modicum of sense he'd have created a new race of tall, very tall people or was he saving money on wood for coffins? And then the heroes, the young protagonists being a young boy, his older brother and his mate "Reggie", everyone knew a "Reggie" and to top it all off he was an ice cream man, completely transforming my perception of the profession which had been tarnished by the child catcher in Chitty Chitty Bang Bang.

Phantasm is my guilty pleasure in horror, for me, no matter what horror films I see, there's nothing like it in terms of storyline, plot, humour and even though true to horror form each sequel gets progressively worse I'll never forget a quote from Angus Scrimm, the guy who played the tall man, the very tall man, he said that the film "gives expression to all the insecurities and fears of all 10-13 year old boys" – he hits the nail on the head and hammers it into one of his dwarf coffins!!

-Paul Stevenson   Editor, Haunted: After Dark Magazine.

When I think back to all the horror films I devoured starting in the late 70's and culminating throughout the 80's, Phantasm was high on my list. Firstly, the originality of the concept kept me spellbound, proving repeat viewings were warranted – but the Tall Man was the real reason behind my infatuation.

Deftly played by actor Angus Scrimm, the Tall Man as he was dubbed in the film becomes the pariah to young Mike (A. Michael Baldwin). His relentless pursuit of the young boy takes up the bulk of the film, and it's hard to argue over how engrossing this chase becomes when you factor in all the creepy settings. Worse yet, Mike must come to terms with this nightmarish bogeyman while clinging on to his older brother Jody (Bill Thornbury). I think the bigger dilemma is the fact that Jody wants to split, leaving Mike all alone to face the growing onslaught of the Tall Man.

Phantasm was a film that built a surrealistic story structure into a paradigm of recurring nightmares – evidently since the same story gets played out in three further sequels. Don Coscareli directed all these films, and I must hand it to him for staying on point with the series. The original is arguably the best of the lot, especially since it cultivates those youthful fears of abandonment and more specifically introduces us to the Tall Man and his flying spheres. In my mind this is probably one of the most original horror films ever made.

-Kenneth Gallant   Editor-In-Chief Horror Metal Sounds.

Phantasm was, and still is, absolutely bonkers. It plays out like a fever dream and I absolutely adore it to this day. I think the first time I saw Phantasm was on a cable channel in the US called USA. I roped my little brother into watching with me when it came on a second time, and therefore deranged another mind. He also has found memories of the shotgun, which morphed into a quadruple barrel. We also both thought that the Hemicuda was the most badass car we'd ever seen in a film—or anywhere! And of course, the compressed alien corpses, who are "short, brown, and low to the ground!" Some entries in the series are better than others, and it seems like we are going to get a fifth film—hopefully it will premiere while Angus Scrimm (The Tall Man) is still with us. If you're looking for something extremely weird and original, Phantasm is your bag!

-Izzy Lee   Filmmaker.

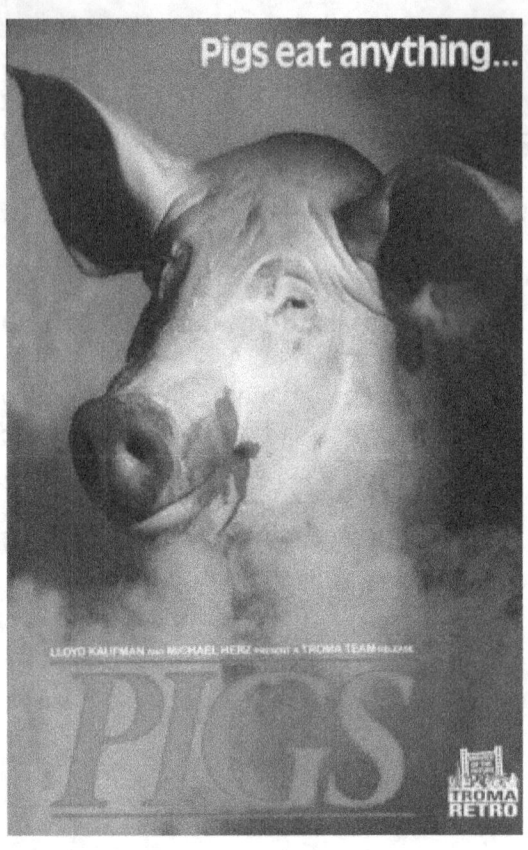

Pigs

(DPP Section 3) Banned in the UK
Also known as "Daddy's Deadly Darling".
Year of release: 1972
Writer: Marc Lawrence
Director: Marc Lawrence
Tagline: "If you go down to the woods today… you're in for a PIG surprise."
Main cast: Toni Lawrence (Lynn Hart), Jesse Vint (Sheriff Dan Cole), Catherine Ross (Miss Macy), Paul Hickey (Johnny), Iris Korn (Annette), Walter Barnes (Doctor), Erik Holland (Hogay).
Distributed by: Iver Film Services

Plot:
In this early 1970's horror we meet Lynn Hart (played by Toni Lawrence). Lynn was institutionalized after murdering her abusive father, she manages to escape the insane asylum and begin a new life for herself, but Lynn has been scarred by her father's actions and consequently begins to take revenge on those who remind her of him. With the help of her new friend Zambrini, they destroy the evidence by feeding the victims' bodies to the pigs!

Appraisal:
Pigs centers around Lynn seducing vulnerable men and enjoying killing them. Pigs isn't all that bad; when I first watched it I expected something completely different, pig masked killers maybe or even animal cruelty which is not uncommon in video nasties but instead we get a just an okay psycho killer film with a twist, that it's a woman doing the killing instead of men who normally dominate this type of role. Don't expect high art or groundbreaking cinema but considering the low budget this film it's actually watchable.

Pigs was seized under section 3 of the 1959 Obscene Publications Act on VHS in the early 1980's before the implementation of the Video Recordings Act of 1984 in the UK.

Pigs was initially released uncut on pre-cert VHS by Iver Film Services 1982, No re-release in the UK though Troma released the film uncut and unrated in the US.

-Tony Newton

PIGS aka DADDY'S DEADLY DARLING mixes incest, murder, cannibalism, bad music, bad acting, and of course, pigs all into one insane hodgepodge of bad tasting madness. And I loved every second of it.

The film stars and was also written and directed by Marc Lawrence, whose film credits are FROM DUSK TIL DAWN, MARATHON MAN, THE MAN WITH THE GOLDEN GUN, and THE ASPHALT JUNGLE. Here he plays Zambrini, the owner of a diner/pig farm which catches the eye of some snooping neighbors who question what Zambrini feeds his pigs to make them so bulky and aggressive. When a woman on the run arrives at the diner out of the blue, it's revealed that the suspicions of Zambrini's neighbors were pretty spot on.

But this film takes the unconventional route narratively, which is part of its charm. Before Zambrini is introduced, we are told the backstory of the woman, Lynn Hart (played by Lawrence's real life daughter, Toni Lawrence). After killing her rapist father, Lynn is committed to the most poorly guarded insane asylum I've ever seen. Lynn escapes and makes her way to the Zambrini farm where she is hired on as a waitress. So on top of the murderous butcher owning the diner, now an escaped man-killer is hired there as well. When customers and the local sheriff start asking questions about missing people, the threat increases two-fold as both Zambrini and Lynn begin offing folks in their own different ways.

I don't know if director Lawrence is able to keep things straight with the plot as it does get a bit convoluted towards the end, but at its core, PIGS turns out to be a pretty straightforward tale of revenge, madness, and dark, dark secrets. Zambrini and Lynn are seemingly drawn to one another's murderous nature, respecting each other's secrets and trying to cover for one another when outsiders pry too much. The tone of this film is dour to say the least, and like many grindhouses, there is an air of sleaze especially that this is a story about a father raping his daughter being played out by a real life actual father and daughter. It's even creepier that Lynn is in ill fitting and scantily clad clothing for most of the film. The scene where Lynn dreams that Zambrini is attacking her with a straight razor is given another level of ookiness given the relationship between these two actors.

Though the production value and acting in this film leaves a lot to be desired, I have to give Lawrence credit for making PIGS wallow in the creep like a…well like a pig in slop from start to finish. Later brought back en vogue in rap videos, Lawrence uses fish eye lenses and bizarre camera angles to cause a palpable sense of unease, claustrophobia, and paranoia here to great effect. Pigs is less about swine and more about fucked up people, I'd recommend this freaky little number to any fan of twisted grindhouse theater. Though the gore is low in PIGS, the shear perversity at play makes up for it in spades. And the title song, "Somebody's Waiting for You" sampled in the trailer, may be scarier than the film itself. I found myself humming the horribly catchy jingle days after watching the film.

-Mark L. Miller

Pink Flamingos

(Pink Flamingos was convicted under the Section 3 of the Obscene Publications Act in the mid 1980's.)
Year of release: 1981
Writers: John Waters
Director: John Waters
18 UK with cuts
Tagline: "An exercise in poor taste. The filthiest people alive! Their loves, their hates and their unquenchable thirst for notoriety!"
Main cast: Divine (Divine/Babs Johnson), David Lochary (Raymond Marble), Mary Vivien Pearce (Cotton), Mink Stole (Connie Marble), Danny Mills (Crackers), Edith Massey (Edie), Channing Wilroy (Channing).
Distributed by: Palace/Castle VHS

Plot:
John Waters' cult smash hit featuring the notorious criminal Divine as she struggles to keep her title as the filthiest person alive, when she faces (or is that *faeces*) a sleazy married couple who do their best to humiliate her, as Divine faces losing her crown, will Divine be the queen of filth?

Appraisal:
Where do you start with this cult classic? John Waters' Pink Flamingos is a work of genius, John Waters was not afraid to try something different and made a film that he wanted to make without limits and that would shock the audience from the off.

The premise alone caught my attention when I was really young, two families competing for a title that surely no one in their right mind would want "The filthiest people alive".

Living in the UK trying to get a copy of Pink Flamingos uncut on VHS was harder than buying crack from the pope, The film had a life of its own even before it was properly released in the UK the myth and legend that was Pink Flamingos was talked about in school yards across the country and what was supposed to happen in this film from Divine eating Dog Shit to a man doing tricks with his singing anus! Well I just had to try and get a copy of this film this was the kind of filth every teenager wanted to see! It sounded like the grossest film of all time and it did not disappoint! John Waters is a cult film icon who went on to inspire filmmakers across the globe. John Waters single-handedly invented filth films to the mass market; these schlocky, bad taste, filth movies, which are, trash heaven! I'm a huge fan of John Waters and although he has a vast body of work Pink Flamingos is my favorite mainly because it was the first of his movies I ever watched! John Waters and Divine go together like peanut butter and jelly - or is it a dog shit sandwich?!

Pink Flamingos was released in 1981 as part of The John Waters collection and distributed by Palace Video, but the film was not submitted for classification after the British rating system was introduced, no distributor in their right mind would have submitted the film as the film would have been cut to shreds and with the filth taken out what would be the point and instead Pink Flamingos was convicted under the Section 3 of the Obscene Publications Act in the mid 1980's.

Pink Flamingos was distributed in a rather bizarre way in the mid 80s, you couldn't get hold of a copy in any video rental store but the distributor set up a rather nifty way of getting customers to view the film and make cash at the same time you had to send a blank tape on which the film would be recorded on, they in turn sent back to the customer minus any packaging at all just the film on the tape. I remember the copy I was lucky enough to watch must have been a 5th generation one, it was almost black and white but it still had the ability to shock me and make me feel sick to my stomach, but still wanting more and more John Waters movies!

Then, in 1989, the film was submitted for classification by the BBFC, and in 1990 they approved it; after much debating, a cut version, which was cut by over 3 mins surfaced. The film was submitted again 1997, and a cut was approved that lost only two minutes and forty-two seconds of footage. It was was then again submitted in 1999 with cuts to a edited print with two minutes and eight seconds taken out. That is crazy, as I can remember watching a full, uncut cinema release in 1997 - complete with the singing anus! I thought the singing nun was bad enough but John Waters might have topped it! The force that is divine mixed with John Waters' vision makes for the trash epic, which is amazing! Camp filth at its finest! This movie really is *Divine*!!

-Tony Newton

Prey

(DPP Section 3) Banned in the UK
Also known as "Alien Prey".
Year of release: 1981
Writers: Max Cuff and Quinn Donoghue
Director: Norman J. Warren
Unrated 78 mins. UK
Tagline: "His savage hunger makes us all… Alien Prey."
Main cast: Barry Stokes (Anders), Sally Faulkner (Josephine), Glory Annen (Jessica), Sandy Chinney (Sandy), Eddie Stacey (1st Policeman), Jerry Crampton (2nd Policeman).
Distributed by: Vampix

Plot:
Norman J Warren of "Inseminoid" fame directs this sci-fi horror. A young couple are attacked by an extra-terrestrial being whilst on a date in the woods. The young man (Anders) is killed and his body used as a host for the alien. With the alien now assuming Anders identity it inadvertently stumbles upon the pad of lesbian lovers Jessica and Josephine.

Appraisal:
The alien's methods of surveillance are very strange; yes he spies on the women having sex and tries to track down a fox!

But surely this is what every alien would do on their arrival on earth in rural England in the early 80s, I wonder if the director previously watched a video nasty and it was that in which corrupted his mind.

Prey is set in Britain and I wouldn't assume that the first thing an alien would do is spy on lesbians and kill a fox, dress up in drag (well they might if it's the weekend). If you are expecting an alien all out kill fest with blood, Gore or even horror you won't get it here.

There was an influx of this kind of film in the 70's and 80's, my favorite being "The Man Who Fell to Earth" starring David Bowie which was made long before this film.

I can only assume that this film featured on the list because of the sex scene featuring two women and some strange violence and sex at the end of the film. If you are not expecting extreme scenes of gore but you are a fan of 1970's TV plays like "Play for Today" you will enjoy this film, it's well acted and has a great twist at the end, overall a bizarre little film that even though it has many flaws is highly enjoyable on a lot of levels!

I think just because this film was banned and is featured on a video nasty section 3 banned list you just expect so much more blood and gore, it got to the point that the censors were just banning horror films for the sake of it in the early 1980's. No this film should not have been banned, and if I were to come across this movie late on TV and watch as a standalone horror sci-fi movie it's amazing, but as a video nasty it's well not nasty at all, I suppose the bar is set high with video nasties with films like Faces of Death, I spit on Your Grave, Cannibal Ferox and Cannibal Holocaust. So as a teen every time I tracked down a banned nasty I thought they were going to be as sick and shocking as the above titles!

I actually love this film, for all its quirky charm. I'm obsessed with 1970's and 80's British horror movies like this; I think it spawned from watching Psychomania on TV late one night. I own three different versions of Prey on VHS video, DVD and now Blu-ray. Prey was seized under section 3 of the 1959 Obscene Publications Act on VHS in the early 1980's before the implementation of the Video Recordings Act of 1984 in the UK.

Prey was initially released uncut on pre-cert VHS by Vampix 1981, prior to this the film was given an x rating for its theatrical release in 1977, The film was then released by Stablecane LTD in 1986 with the BBFC giving the film an 18 rating with 10s cuts, the films latest UK release was in 2004 by Anchor Bay which was the extended version uncut and rated 18 by the BBFC.

-Tony Newton

Prom Night

(DPP Section 3) Banned in the UK
Year of release: 1980
Writers: William Gray and Robert Guza Jr.
Director: Paul Lynch
R rated 92 mins. Canada
Tagline: "There's a special night in the lives of all of us. A night to be beautiful. To be desirable. A night we can break all the rules and make our own. Prom night."

Main cast: Leslie Nielsen (Mr. Hammond), Jamie Lee Curtis (Kim), Casey Stevens (Nick), Anne-Marie Martin (Wendy), Antionette Bower (Mrs. Hammond), Michael Tough (Alex).

Distributed by: Embassy

Plot:
Leslie Nielsen and Jamie Lee Curtis star in this 1980 classic stalk and slash offering from director Paul Lynch.

A strange game leads to the murder of a young girl; 4 years later someone is seeking revenge on prom night of a group of young students. It's not just the prom that the killer is intent on ruining, in this classic 80's slasher. Will anyone discover the killer's identity and stop them before it's too late?

Appraisal:
Jamie Lee Curtis is great as usual as the teen scream queen put through her paces in this run of the mill slasher horror offering. This is not a top ten slasher and the music and feel of the film are very dated and stands out like a saw thumb, however this film is quite good and provides enough scares and suspense, although some are very predictable. It's not that gory or gruesome and you do wonder why this film featured on the section 3 nasty list as it's one of the tamer films on the list. The cover had some great artwork that probably prompted the films removal from the shelves all across the UK. A masked killer holding a knife up to his face with only his eyes showing, worth a watch for classic horror fans!

If you are expecting extreme horror this is not for you!

Prom Night was seized under section 3 of the 1959 Obscene Publications Act on VHS in the early 1980's before the implementation of the Video Recordings Act of 1984 in the UK.

Prom Night was initially released uncut on pre-cert VHS by Embassy 1982, Prior to this the film was given an x rating for its theatrical release in the UK.

Embassy re-submitted the film to the BBFC in 1987 and the film was passed 18 uncut since then all known versions of the film have been passed without cuts in the UK.

-Tony Newton

Prom Night means everything is all right…right? Well no, not if you find yourself in the middle of an '80s high school slasher flick. Following in the footsteps of some pretty influential high school horror movies (Carrie, Halloween etc.) *Prom Night* came along with horror's hottest scream queen (Jamie Lee Curtis) at the forefront and promised teen carnage galore. It came out at a time when the standard for slasher was high and an appetite for more was well and truly whetted.

Prom Night was a little different to its predecessors, the story took its time (some might say it took its *damn* time), there aren't many on-screen deaths and there are some very questionable dance moves. For these reasons it may not be at the forefront of people's minds when thinking of the video nasty era, but when you look at the time scale, *Prom Night* played an intricate part of that really exciting time.

This first time I saw this film was not long after my first viewing of *Friday the 13th* so expectations were high. I had "borrowed" a VHS copy from my brother and watched it alone. I remember the grainy look of the opening scenes in the old high school as the children played their nasty game, and for me, as much as the story progressed and the deaths got grizzlier, nothing compares to the opening scene. The chants of "Kill! Kill!" ringing through the halls were terrifying; this was a perfect beginning to a slasher! The movie has a slow build up of suspense with the caller ringing his victims, reminiscent of *Black Christmas*, but it seemed like a whole lot of nothing until there was murder on the dance floor. The surprise beheading before the announcement of the prom king and queen came out of nowhere and most likely jolted you out of a slump while watching the film considering how middle of the road the previous hour had been. All the action happening in the last ten minutes, although rushed, at least gives Jamie Lee Curtis the platform to kick some ass…even if it was to *that* song.

This film may not be the best there is of the genre, but it had the cheesy campiness that would be taken further in the likes of *Sleep away Camp* and *My Bloody Valentine*. It has the scream queen of the era in a setting that perfectly fits the format of a slasher movie and for that, it is worthy of its place here.

-Charlotte Stear   Writer.

Rabid

(DPP Section 3) Banned in the UK
Year of release: 1977
Writer: David Cronenberg
Director: David Cronenberg
R rated 91 mins. Canada
Tagline: "Pray it doesn't happen to you."
Main cast: Marilyn Chambers (Rose), Frank Moore (Hart Read), Joe Silver (Murray Cypher), Howard Ryshpan (Dr. Dan Keloid), Susan Roman (Mindy Kent), Roger Periard (Lloyd Walsh).
Distributed by: Alpha Intervision

Plot:
In David Cronenberg's classic horror "Rabid" a beautiful young woman Rose is injured in a motorcycle accident. Rose undergoes plastic surgery at the hands of Dr Dan Keloid but following the experimental operation develops a rather scary taste for blood, whoever she bites turns into a rabid corpse infecting others and further spreading the infection.

Appraisal:
If anyone had to be featured on the DPP list for me it had to be David Cronenberg, which I think is a badge of honor, his films are shocking and gory but always stand out from the crowd. David Cronenberg is a fantastic director and this film is no exception with this feature from 1977 shows just how good he really is. Rabid feels very familiar and feels like "Shiver" which was completed just before this film and has the same themes throughout. The film is somewhat overlooked as not being one of Cronenberg's best works but personally I think it is a great horror film with the right amounts of gore and shocks. The films theme of infection spreading fast throughout Montreal works perfectly, well worth a watch and yet another great addition to your horror film collection. This film has obviously inspired many filmmakers across the globe with its theme.

Rabid was seized under section 3 of the 1959 Obscene Publications Act on VHS in the early 1980's before the implementation of the Video Recordings Act of 1984 in the UK.

Rabid was initially released uncut on pre-cert VHS by Alpha Intervision 1981, Prior to this the film was given an x rating for its theatrical release in the UK in 1977.

The film was re-submitted to the BBFC in 1986 and the film was passed 18 uncut since then all known versions of the film have been passed without cuts in the UK.

-Tony Newton

David Cronenberg's Rabid is a beautiful film. Cronenberg's movies seem to all co-exist in an alternate reality which is similar to our world, but heavily skewed. From the incredible names he gives his characters (for example, Stathis Borans, Allegra Geller, Darryl Revok and, in this movie, Dr and Mrs Keloid) to the almost too-clinical buildings and landscapes, from the moment you start watching, you know you're watching a Cronenberg film. You also know it's likely to be damned uncomfortable – but usually incredibly rewarding – viewing.

Rabid tells the story of a young woman who, as a result of undergoing experimental plastic surgery, develops a strange new vagina-like organ in her armpit and goes on to infect people, turning them into rabid zombie-like creatures. Sounds ridiculous, doesn't it? In the hands of any other director, it'd probably *be* ridiculous. But Rabid isn't. Rabid is a damn scary and unsettling movie.

There are similarities here with Shivers (aka They Came From Within), Cronenberg's previous film, but for me, Rabid is a far more satisfying watch. Marilyn Chambers (a former adult movie star) gives a great performance here as Rose: perfectly balancing her vulnerable and predatory sides. On the face of it, the plot of the movie is deceptively simple, but as with a lot of Cronenberg's work, it's the complex themes below the surface, which really have an impact here. To my mind, Rabid is one of the first films, which considered the other side of the zombie/vampire equation: What do *they* think? What do *they* feel? All too often the undead or bloodsucking monsters are just that – monsters – and we feel little for them and care about them even less. Rabid presents us with a very different scenario, because we're behind Rose all the way, and we know she's as big a victim as the people she goes on to infect.

You might look at the film's blurb and think you're getting a run-of-the-mill infection/pandemic movie with Rabid, but believe me, you're most definitely not!

-David Moody   Author of Autumn.

Rosemary's Killer

(DPP Section 3) Banned in the UK
Also known as "The Prowler" and "Pitchfork Massacre".
Year of release: 1981
Writers: Glenn Leopold and Neal Barbera
Director: Joseph Zito
Unrated 89 mins. USA
Tagline: If you think you're safe… you're DEAD wrong!"
Main cast: Vicky Dawson (Pam MacDonald), Christopher Goutman (Mark London), Lawrence Tierney (Maj. Chatham), Farley Granger (Sheriff George Fraser), Cindy Weintraub (Lisa), Lisa Dunsheath (Sherry).
Distributed by: Entertainment in Video.

Plot:
When a soldier returns from World War II he receives a Dear John letter informing him that his wife Rosemary has grown tired of waiting for him and found herself a new man. Hell-bent on revenge he murders both Rosemary and her new lover at the graduation dance. Some years later the graduation dance is to be held for the first time since the horrific murders but someone is stalking college students and the masked prowler begins murdering the students one by one.

Appraisal:
Rosemary's Killer sees a psycho killer with a unique mask for a horror film (a world war II United States issue helmet). This stalk and slash offering is a cult classic hit, the killer returns 35 years later to the college dance, which he previously sabotaged. Joseph Zito who made "Friday the 13th the Final Chapter" brings us this stalk and slash offering that was very popular in the early 1980's. Rosemary's Killer stood out for me mainly because of the killer's outfit it was an original take on the genre at the time. Tom Savini provides the effects for this film and they are gory FX and original killings.

This film is a sleazy slasher, easily one of the best of the best, a truly great film with a brilliant twist at the end and one of the greatest head exploding scenes in a 1980's which is easily up there with Scanners!

Overall this is definitely worth watching if only for Tom Savini's amazing FX work and some gruesome original kills! Grab yourself a slice of 80's nostalgia with this classic slasher offering. But be sure to get hold of a copy that is fully uncut!

Rosemary's Killer was seized under section 3 of the 1959 Obscene Publications Act on VHS in the early 1980's before the implementation of the Video Recordings Act of 1984 in the UK.

Rosemary's Killer was initially released on pre-cert VHS by Entertainment in Video in 1983, with a runtime of 87 mins, this version was heavily cut and it was almost impossible to find a version fully uncut in the UK, I remember buying a Australian DVD which seems to be the closest to the full uncut version of the film.

-Tony Newton

Savage Terror

(DPP Section 3) Banned in the UK
Also known as "Primitif", "Primitives".
Year of release: 1980
Writer: Imam Tantowi
Director: Sisworo Gautama Putra
Unrated 90 mins. Indonesia
Tagline: "Captured by flesh-eating savages!"
Main cast: Enny Haryono (Rika), Barry Prima (Amri), Johann Mardjono (Tommy), Rukman Herman (Bisma), Jafarpree York (Lahang), Novita Rully.
Distributed by: Go Video.

Plot:
When a group of students go on an expedition to study the primitive tribes inhabiting the jungle their worst nightmares are realized when they head off to find the mysterious cannibal tribe rumored to live there. Following a rafting accident the group is split; will they escape the clutches of the terrifying cannibal tribe, which is hunting them down?

Appraisal:
Savage Terror is another cannibal offering known more widely as Primitives.

If you're looking for a cult horror like Cannibal Holocaust or Cannibal Ferox you won't find it here. Savage Terror tries so hard to be a film like Cannibal Holocaust but it couldn't be further away. Savage Terror is a by the numbers cannibal film, yes you get the stock footage that was doing the rounds at the time and yes we get the animal cruelty, one scene that stands out is the alligator scene which is brutal but some of the laugh out loud scenes soon make you forget what you have just witnessed.

This is a jungle adventure and as that it's an entertaining film, just don't approach Savage Terror as if it were Cannibal Holocaust! The violence and terror is toned down and it's a bizarre film.

Savage Terror was seized under section 3 of the 1959 Obscene Publications Act on VHS in the early 1980's before the implementation of the Video Recordings Act of 1984 in the UK.

Savage Terror was initially released on pre-cert VHS by Go Video in 1982.

-Tony Newton

Scanners

(DPP Section 3) Banned in the UK
Year of release: 1981
Writer: David Cronenberg
Director: David Cronenberg
R rated 103 mins. Canada
Tagline: "There are 4 billion people on Earth. 237 are Scanners. They have the most terrifying powers ever created… and they are winning."
Main cast: Jennifer O'Neill (Kim Obrist), Stephen Lack (Cameron Vale), Patrick McGoohan (Dr. Paul Ruth), Lawrence Dane (Braedon Keller), Michael Ironside (Darryl Revok), Robert A. Silverman (Benjamin Pierce).
Distributed by: Guild

Plot:
This Canadian science fiction horror piece was written and directed by David Cronenberg and stars Patrick McGoohan from the cult TV series "The Prisoner". "Scanners" see's a man with incredible psychic powers on the hunt for others like himself with disastrous results.

Appraisal:
The film see's Michael Ironside's character with super telepathy powers amongst normal civilians and shows his lack of control of his abilities, with the constant ability to hear others thoughts it's enough to drive anyone crazy!

Scanners is a fantastic film, which often receives bad press because the acting is not up to scratch. This aside, Michael Ironside and Patrick McGoohan are on top form as ever! These two characters carry the whole film. Scanners contains enough gore for the gore hounds and fans of David Cronenberg especially the amazing, groundbreaking exploding head scenes!

This film is a cult classic which still stands up today, it's a must watch on the video nasties list. I always re-visit this film and I just seem to get more and more enjoyment from it each and every time!

One of my favorite early 1980's horror films. Crank out that old VHS copy and give it a spin!

Scanners was seized under section 3 of the 1959 Obscene Publications Act on VHS in the early 1980's before the implementation of the Video Recordings Act of 1984 in the UK.

Scanners was initially released on pre-cert VHS by Guild home video in 1981, Prior to this the film was given an x rating for its theatrical release in the UK in 1981 by the BBFC.

The film was re-submitted to the BBFC in 1987 and the film was passed 18 uncut since then all known versions of the film have been passed without cuts in the UK.

-Tony Newton

I love Michael Ironside. There, I've said it. In public. In print. But why shouldn't I love him?

Top Gun, V, Starship Troopers, The Machinist, Total Recall (the good one), I can even forgive him for doing Free Willy, that strong is his movie CV. The guy personifies the word villain. He makes Walken look like your nice uncle. This guy is a powerhouse. And before he starred in any of those blockbusters he was making people's heads explode in Scanners.

Scanners are basically the next step in human evolution. Telepaths who can read or 'scan' others' thoughts and even take control of their bodily functions (why blow up someone's head when you can make them crap themselves? Is there a Family Guy cut away in waiting?) The film tried to be many things. Sci-fi, Horror, Thriller, Spy flicks. What it kind of ends up being is one massive special effect after another. But man, oh man, are they memorable. My brothers had seen the film before me and had to wait until our parents went out to show ne the infamous head/ watermelon explosion. We watched, rewound and paused it so many times that the videotape actually snapped. It got fixed with a tiny screwdriver and some sticky back plastic like a banned episode of Blue Peter and the video hire shop never knew any difference but of course I never got to see the rest of the film. But for my kudos, I didn't need to. I'd seen the iconic moment, the one to talk about in school the next day, because that was the part everyone wanted to see. And that was unfair. No, it wasn't Cronenberg's best (for me that was The Dead Zone) but when I finally watched it in full some years later I understood more of the depth, more of the social commentary and saw it for the fast paced action horror that it was. A Video Nasty? Yes. You see a head explode and the final telepath duel is brutal so of course it is. It was more the timing of the release than the overall content that earned it that moniker. The censor's attention had been piqued and banning an exploding skull was always likely to be a no brainer!

-Craig Jones   Author.

Scanners was the second grown-up horror I saw. At the time, like most of us, I was excited by the blowing up head. I loved reading about how the effect was made. False head fill, it with offal, someone shoots a shotgun at it. So much better than CGI. Since then, Cronenberg has become one of my favourite directors, I can think of no other horror director, indeed few directors of any genre, who have been so intellectually adventurous. His ability to take the money for exploitation and make something enigmatic and dramatic is remarkable. His worlds are fully formed. He is one of the great artists of imaginative cinema.

-Robin Ince   Writer/Comedian.

What makes David Cronenberg's Scanners so immediately compelling is that it's lead character Cameron Vale is sequentially personality blank. A telekinetic so inundated with other people's thoughts and feelings, that he has no room for an identity of his own. This simultaneously makes us wonder if he could learn to be as dangerous as the films other psychic villains, while it also frees audience members, from all walks of life, to be able to almost instantaneously graft themselves into the roll, that is ingeniously left blank for them to inhabit. This adds to the almost interactive nature of the story, because this is the same way that "scanners" can themselves inhabit other people's minds and nervous systems. However, once in, you are open to an unnerving world, where the next enemy you encounter, may read your thoughts or even control your body to the extent that they can light you on fire, explode your blood vessels, eyeballs, and in one early yet terrifyingly shocking scene, your head. There is no protection from these threats, and you can feel it in every scene of the movie. Later we find that these freaks of nature are the result of doctors and their experimental pregnancy drugs that were tested on human subjects too soon. This makes the film both a tale in the tradition of Frankenstein, and a commentary on society's fear of modern pharmaceuticals, impacting humanities future in ways we may not be able to stop.

-Christopher Moonlight   Moonlight Art Magazine.

Scream for Vengeance

(DPP Section 3) Banned in the UK
Also known as "Vengeance".
Year of release: 1980
Writer: Bob Bliss
Director: Bob Bliss
Unrated USA
Tagline: "Everyone has a boiling point… then comes the…."
Main cast: Walter Addison (Mason), Leonard Belove (Tony Lomas), Bob Elliot (Luke), Susie Gardner (Shari Lomas), Nicholas Jacquez (Mark), Sally Lockett (Jenny).
Distributed by: Intervision

Plot:
When four thieves break into the home of an exceedingly wealthy jeweller, things go from bad to worse as they turn to murder, rape, and even taking hostages in this tale of greed.

Appraisal:
Scream For Vengeance is a little lost gem, which never rightly gets that much press but is often overlooked. Scream, for Vengeance is directed by Bob Bliss, who I don't think actually ever directed anything else. This is a brutal tale of the length's people will go to, to get money. This film has many different acts to it, at first we get the family held hostage then we cut to the robbers fleeing the scene and as luck would have it one of the thieves hostages is related to a senator, this then turns to the criminals seeking a large ransom for the release of the hostages. This film is made on a very low budget and this shows but the story and acting just seem to work, this is a well-paced slick revenge style thriller that is well worth checking out!

Scream for Vengeance was seized under section 3 of the 1959 Obscene Publications Act on VHS in the early 1980's before the implementation of the Video Recordings Act of 1984 in the UK.

Scream for Vengeance was initially released uncut on pre-cert VHS by Intervision in 1982, The film was also banned for its theatrical release in Australia and the Australian VHS distributed by Video Classics was cut by around 2 mins. The UK release by Intervision is the full, uncut version. There has been no UK re-release.

-Tony Newton

Shogun Assassin

(DPP Section 3) Banned in the UK
Year of release: 1980
Writer: Robert Houston and Kazuo Koike
Director: Robert Houston
R rated 85 mins. Japan USA

Tagline: "Lone wolf and son. The greatest team in the history of mass slaughter."

Main cast: Tomisaburo Wakayama (Lone Wolf), Kayo Matsuo (Supreme Ninja), Minoru Oki (Master of Death), Shogen Nitta (Master of Death), Shin Kishida (Master of Death), Akihiro Tomikawa (Daigoro).

Distributed by: Vipco

Plot:
Shogun Assassin see's an aging samurai warrior who goes by the name of Lone Wolf pursue revenge for the murder of his wife. Lone Wolf takes work as an assassin whilst travelling with his 5-year-old son trying to evade the ninjas, who have been sent to take the lives of himself and his young son.

Appraisal:
Ninja's I can't get enough of them, the 80s brought an influx of ninja movies in the 1980s one being this shogun assassin. This is a true classic ninja action film that is very entertaining. The 1980's brought with an influx of ninja VHS rental shelves were full of them but for a lot of the time there was one film missing "Shogun Assassin" the daddy of all the ninja films and the film every martial arts fan was always talking about. This film was a long way away from your usual martial arts mayhem blockbuster that Hollywood was cashing in on. I was much late to join the "Shogun Assassin" party than most. I thought Bruce Lee's "Enter the Dragon" or Michael Dudikoff in "American Ninja" or "Revenge of the Ninja" were the only martial arts and Ninja films out there! It was my love of "Shogun Assassin" that made me spend a lot of my youth tracking down older ninja films, martial arts and other lost samurai films, many of these being black and white films. Long before Quentin Tarantino's "Kill Bill" this was the film you associated with samurai swords. The shogun along with his son Daigoro and his cart full of Booby traps is fantastic. The shogun himself who goes on the run after his wife is brutally murdered with his young son he encounters Shogun assassins. This gore filled cult classic is enjoyable today as the first time I viewed it on an old VHS. This film is just a thrill ride that you never want to end, a cult smash hit, a slice of Ninjasploitation cut with he sharpest samurai sword. Shogun Assassin was seized under section 3 of the 1959 Obscene Publications Act on VHS in the early 1980's before the implementation of the Video Recordings Act of 1984 in the UK.

Shogun Assassin was initially released uncut on pre-cert VHS by Vipco in 1981, Prior to this the film was cut by around 2 seconds by the BBFC for its theatrical version. Since then the film has been given an 18 rating by the BBFC, which was basically along the lines of the cinematic release.

-Tony Newton

Shogun Assassin - A great synth score is just icing on the cake in this lightning-paced rollercoaster of samurai hack-n-slash. Watching a Mortal Kombat style line-up of villains get cut down by what is essentially the Japanese Punisher (with the fun addition of having an adorable toddler in tow) is about as awesome as it gets. Having the kid narrate is a genius move, providing a weird juxtaposition against the onscreen violence. The moment where the final Master of Death gets slashed, and then has an inner monologue about how ridiculous it is that he just got his throat slit, is one of my all-time favorite movie moments.

-Steven Kostanski   Astron–6.

There's chambara films (samurai sword play films), and then there's Shogun Assassin. Where to begin with this amazing bit of Asian cinema? Based on the manga Lone Wolf and Cub it tells the story of a betrayed Ronin (a samurai with no master) and his son in a baby cart you won't find at kids R us traveling japan on the run from an insane emperor who made the reeeeeeally bad choice of mistaking our samurais wife for him and killing her. I say on the run.... But it's the emperor who should be running.

Sure... It's a chambara film... But it's also one of the wettest films of all time, it's inspired EVERY movie with a katana sword in it since (ask Quentin T, cough Kill Bill, cough) and with great reason It takes everything you'd love from a kuresawa film and then piles on the exploitation of a Shaw Bros film or a later Tsui Hark film.

It's got heart galore, the scene with young Daguro forced to choose between the sword and a ball.... To choose the ball is death.

To choose the sword is to join his father on a long road to vengeance (this scene as well as countless others are sampled on GZA, the genius's, first solo album liquid swords).

Now I could go on and on about the film but I was asked to talk about it's meaning to me (and I imagine if you're reading this... You've seen the damn thing a few times!)

I saw this movie on VHS when I was 12 from the mom and pop video store that was my church down the road from my moms, while I was already a blue belt in kenpo karate it inspired me to pick up a katana sword and learn all I could.

I mean I'd seen samurai movies but NOTHING like this!

It had more gore then ANY Friday the 13th film or nightmare or Halloween film combined! But it wasn't till I was about 19 or so at a horror convention in New Jersey at a table full of bootleg DVDs I saw them ...

My interest piqued, I asked the sweat pants-wearing guy in a Basket Case t-shirt (you know this guy horror fans... he's at EVERY convention the world over.

"So is this like a sequel to shogun assassin?"

And in true comic book guy from the Simpsons fashion he looked at me like I had ten heads and dropped a bombshell on me

"No... Shogun Assassin is these 14 movies cut into one."

WHAAAAAAAT? WTF? How did I not know this?

Well safe to say I bought them all, and watched them straight for two days. And man how us yanks got fucked!!! Each one of these is gold... And for who knows why they picked and chose key scenes to make ONE film out of fourteen!!!

I guess that's why Shogun Assassin has that shoddy ending? Gone is Daguros' narration... Well technically gone is ANY English voice as it was never dubbed (the way it should be) and the subtitles could be better but regardless ...EVERY ONE of them is gold, and I cherish them all to this day. Now.... (Ha! Ten paragraphs later, I get to the point of this piece) the "video nasty" ... again... being a yank, we never had a banned list of films. In fact, the only reason I ever even knew about it to begin with is a few articles back in the day in Fangoria about a lot of movies being cut to hell or just not even released at all in the UK and Australia, which is just utter insanity!! No grown ass man or woman should EVER be denied the right to see something because some stuck up fuck has deemed it "inappropriate " Who is one person.... Or even a group of people to decide what a nation can watch in the privacy of their own home? It's just wrong. And some of the titles on that list are just flat out silly to "ban" They're not even THAT violent! They're cheesy as hell at best!! And... all you're doing is making people want to see it EVEN MORE! It's like the parental advisory explicit lyrics sticker on CDs Yup... You just helped that artist sell twice or even triple the amount of CDs !!! But, in Shogun Assassin's case? Ok... I guess if you're gonna go out of your way to ban violent movies... You'd probably start with this one I mean... The "Asian artery spray" was invented here where all of the body's blood is evacuated out of the neck in one blast!!! I can't think of one exploitation style director who isn't inspired by this film... Whether they know it or not.

The thing that makes a true classic is if it can hold up over time And there's no doubt that this film is JUST as kickass now in 2014 as it was in the 70s when it was released I mean now you see it and it's like "oh, cool, every 5 mins, someone's neck is opened up" You've seen it a MILLION times, no biggie right? But imagine seeing it BACK THEN??? Audiences must've been bugging out!!!!! I know when I was a kid I was!

And that's the biggest thing I look for in a film now... Make me feel like a kid again when I'm watching your film ... Give me that sense of wonderment ... Make me forget I work in this industry and I know just slightly out of frame there's a microphone recording sound and a entire crew of people... Make me get lost in a great story and EVERYTIME I watch the Babycart films or just Shogun Assassin ... I do just that.

-Nick Principe   Actor/Filmmaker.

"Shogun Assassin" (1980) was one of those films that showed up on VHS in video stores in the mid-80s. Most people in the US had never heard of the Lone Wolf and Cub series and probably picked it up out of curiosity more than anything else. Some filmgoers may have been familiar with the Kurosawa samurai flicks by then, but nothing prepared them for the bloodletting in Shogun Assassin. It outdid anything seen in this country before, including Sam Peckinpah's films. What made it even more shocking is that the violence all happens while the lone wolf samurai (Tomisaburo Wakayama) pushes a baby cart around the countryside, containing his little son Daigoro (Akihira Tomikawa). The film developed a cult following and even appears on a TV screen being watched by Bill (David Carradine) in Tarantino's Kill Bill II. But it's really a schlocky cut-and-paste job, made up of scenes from two films from the Lone Wolf and Cub series, namely "Sword of Vengeance" (1972), and "Baby Cart at the River Styx (1972)." You're better off tracking down these, along with the other four of the six film series. There's nothing quite like them.

-John M. Whalen   Author of Vampire Siege at Rio Muerto.

Street Killers

(DPP Section 3) Banned in the UK
Also known as "The Mad Dog Killer", "Beast with a Gun", "Ultime Violence", and "La Belva Col Mitra".
Year of release: 1977
Writer: Sergio Grieco
Director: Sergio Grieco
Unrated 91 mins. Italy
Tagline: "Out of prison…Out of control…and totally out of his mind!"
Main cast: Helmut Berger (Vitali), Marisa Mell (Giuliana), Richard Harrison (Santini), Marina Giordana (Carla), Luigi Bonos (Pappalardo), Vittorio Duse (Caroli).
Distributed by: Astra

Plot:
When brutal murderer Nanni Vitali and three of his sadistic henchmen escape prison the group begin a rampage of robbery, rape and murder. Nanni Vitali is desperate to exact vengeance on the man whose testimony lead to his incarceration but police officer Giulio Satini has other ideas as he is intent on putting a stop to the gangs trail of destruction.

Appraisal:
This crazy Italian horror film is quite entertaining and follows escaped convicts as they go on a killing spree, causing mayhem including rape, abduction and burglary. This sleazy horror film has a good pace and the acting is on fine form, Helmet Berger is fantastic on screen as Vitali in this exploitation cult classic. This film has a great heist scene, which is a bit farfetched but none the less entertaining. All in all this film is well worth a watch.

Street killers was seized under section 3 of the 1959 Obscene Publications Act on VHS in the early 1980's before the implementation of the Video Recordings Act of 1984 in the UK.

Street killers was initially released uncut on pre-cert VHS by Astra in 1982, not currently available in the UK as it was never re-released.

-Tony Newton

Suicide Cult

(DPP Section 3) Banned in the UK
Also known as "The Astrologer".
Year of release: 1975
Writer: John Cameron (based on the novel)
Director: James Glickenhaus
R rated USA
Tagline: "He's the gypsy king of the carnival men! To be famous he lies, cheats, steals, even sometimes kills!"
Main cast: Bob Byrd (Alexei), Mark Buntzman (Kajerste), James Glickenhaus (Spy), Alison McCarthy, Al Narcisse, Monica Tidwell (Kate Abarnel).
Distributed by: Mega Films

Plot:

Schizophrenic cult leader Kajerste is a wanted man in several countries for the ritualistic and sacrificial mutilations he has inflicted. Scientist Interzod member Alexei Abernal discovers that Kajerste's was destined for evil and that his wife Kate has the same rare zodiacal configuration as the Virgin Mary. Will anyone stop the sadistic cult leader before it's too late?

Appraisal:

In Director James Glickenhaus entry we see a scientist fighting against an evil suicide cult of devil worshipers, mix this with scientist Alexei who is having breakthroughs in scientific history merging astrology with the advancements of computer and technology. This film although sometimes slow in parts is very entertaining and keeps the viewer in their seat, this is one of the lesser-known films on this lest. Director James Glickenhaus went on to direct the cult smash "The Exterminator", this film although it has a low budget is put together well and does have a good mix of scares and features the occult which is always a good thing.

Suicide Cult was seized under section 3 of the 1959 Obscene Publications Act on VHS in the early 1980's before the implementation of the Video Recordings Act of 1984 in the UK.

Suicide Cult was initially released uncut on pre-cert VHS by Mega Films in 1977, not currently available in the UK, this film was never re-released in Britain.

-Tony Newton

Superstition

(DPP Section 3) Banned in the UK
Also known as "The Witch"
Year of release: 1982
Writers: Galen Thompson and Michael O. Sajbel.
Director: James W. Roberson
Unrated 85 mins. Canada
Tagline: "The victims who died were the lucky ones."
Main cast: James Houghton (Rev. David Thompson), Albert Salmi (Inspector Sturgess), Lynn Carlin (Melinda Leahy), Larry Pennell (George Leahy), Jacquelyn Hyde (Elvira Sharack), Robert Symonds (Pike).
Distributed by: VTC

Plot:
Superstition sees a family relocate to a new home, but it's not long before they discover that their home was the site of a witch execution. A witch who was sentenced to death in 1962 and executed at that very site returns to exact revenge!

Appraisal:
Director James W Roberson's classic horror film, released on the famous VTC video label as a pre-cert, was one of the most anticipated films and is still an iconic, cult hit today. The film had a very short-lived theatrical release going by the name of "The Witch". This film delivers in all the right places the terror and atmosphere is spot on and the actors do a great job too. Overall this is a very good horror film. Rev David Thompson didn't expect such horror when he moves into this new home on finding out that a witch haunts the nearby pond. The witch was killed in 1962; she takes revenge on anyone she can!

This low budget film is a gem of a movie and still looks great today. The journey the viewer goes on will keep you on the edge of your seat and teamed with a fantastic musical score it sets the film up perfectly, a little underrated gem here!

Superstition was seized under section 3 of the 1959 Obscene Publications Act on VHS in the early 1980's before the implementation of the Video Recordings Act of 1984 in the UK. Superstition was initially released uncut on pre-cert VHS by VTC in 1982, then later submitted to the BBFC in 1984 and given an 18 rating with a title change entitled The Witch, the latest release saw the film return to its original title of Superstition, the partially re-edited version was released by Momentum pictures in 2005, the film is available in the UK rated 18 uncut.

-Tony Newton

I was introduced to Superstition by way of Anchor Bay's DVD release in 2006, when they were the go-to distribution company when it came to pumping of vintage horror films to *connoisseurs who were looking to build a library of the best of esoteric genre titles. Being that I was older the first time viewing it, the movie had a lot going against it since I was looking at it through adult eyes and not the raw innocence of a child. I was not familiar with the director, nor the actors involved, which was nice for a change, so I could concentrate on the story at hand.*

I've always loved the more visceral side of horror; the one that goes for the throat, sometimes literally, that fully embraces the power of the grand guignol theatre of spectacle. But I also have a soft spot for the cerebral too. Thanks to flicks like The Omen and Friday the 13th, the creative kill was at the forefront of the pictures being released at that period, and Superstition has a few humdingers: my favorites being the exploding decapitated head in the microwave, bisection by a shard of glass and a buzz saw through a chest!

Superstition is more than just another splatter flick from the early '80s, because when there is not a lot of the red stuff spraying about, there is a tremendous amount of restraint from director James W. Roberson; and that is admirable for a film that is heavily influenced by the product of its time. The mise-en-scèneon *display is a thing of beauty and something that was sorely missing from almost every hack 'n slash thriller being made in the United States. The thick atmosphere laid down is like a breath of fresh air, making it more like a Hammer title, and not the gore romp that most fans think it is. Perhaps because Superstition is produced by Mario Kassar and Andrew G. Vajna, there is a European flavor that elevates it and puts it on the same table with the likes of Lucio Fulci's The Gates of Hell (City of the Living Dead). The wicked witch seeking vengeance from beyond the grave is smartly nestled in the shadows and is kept hidden behind a cloak; the most you see of her is her monstrous arms and razor-sharp claws.*

Priests die. A kid bites the big one. Two teens spend most the running time in scantily clad outfits. There's a hangin' in an elevator shaft. A drowned sorceress with bladders pulsating from her forehead wreaks havoc upon mankind as nihilism reigns supreme as evil dominates good in this classic from the 'golden age of gore' that plays well as a double bill with Ulli Lommel's The Devonsville Terror. The hand reaching out of the lake in the epilogue harkens back to Carrie, and it is truly a chair-jumping scene!

-Jason Bene   Writer.

Suspiria

(DPP Section 3) Banned in the UK
Year of release: 1977
Writers: Dario Argento and Daria Nicolodi
Director: Dario Argento
X rated 98 mins. Italy
Tagline: "The only thing more terrifying than the last five minutes of this film are the first 90!"
Main cast: Jessica Harper (Suzy Bannion), Stefania Casini (Sara), Flavio Bucci (Daniel), Miguel Bose (Mark), Barbara Magnolfi (Olga), Susanna Javicoli (Sonia).
Distributed by: Thorn EMI

Plot:
Suspiria tells the story of an innocent young ballerina named Suzy who travels to Germany to join a prestigious school of ballet, but as the students are picked off one by one, Suzy begins to investigate, unveiling the schools deep, dark secret. The ballet school is a cover for a savage coven of witches!

Appraisal:
When Suzy (Jessica Harper) arrives in Germany to join a strict ballet school, things go from bad to worse as her fears unfold in front of her eyes.

Suzy becomes obsessed that there is more than meets the eye and a terrible secret that's hiding behind the ballet schools past, as people begin to die around her Suzy gets closer and closer to the dark secret that the ballet schools teachers are hiding.

It's hard to define such a film as Suspiria as it hits the spot on so many levels, not only is this movie visually striking, as the main thing that stands out in this movie is Dario Argento's use of colour within the film itself that in a way creates it's very own universe that you are not only a visitor in but you feel trapped from the very start.

Suspiria has a certain feel of claustrophobia, the viewer experiences many situations just as the lead character does, you feel like you are on a journey with her from the very start of the film. Goblin's soundtrack literally makes the movie into a living nightmare; this film has every element strategically laid bare to put the viewer into pure terror. I'm a huge fan of the band Goblin but I can't think of a time Goblin's music has ever suited a movie than in this film masterpiece. It's just sheer perfection. Dario Argento's 1977 cult horror classic is loved by most horror fans and with good reason, this film is very well paced and visually stunning, a truly haunting piece of cinema. Suspiria is up there as one of Argento's best pieces of work! Thinking of taking up ballet, you may want to have a re-think. Suzy Bannian, a new student at a posh ballet school encounters murder's and a secret coven of witches behind the scenes, the soundtrack makes this film a roller coaster ride you just don't want to end. The soundtrack provided by Goblin is stunning they are at their finest here.

I don't think there is a Dario Argento film that I haven't got some kind of enjoyment from but Suspiria has to be his true masterpiece. Suspiria made Dario Argento a master of horror.

The unique ways in which we see people get killed in this film is nothing short of shocking, there are shocks ahoy, scares and jumps throughout, this is one of the best horror films of all time undoubtedly Suspiria is a true example of how to make a horror film, pure class and so damn stylish no VHS collection would ever be complete with the masterpiece which is Suspiria.

I love and adore Giallo films, Suspiria is one of those films which strikes a big debate, yes Suspiria is made by a true master of the Giallo film, but strictly speaking Suspiria isn't a giallo film it has giallo elements throughout and giallo influences in both cinematography and the use of colours from the crime genre but Suspiria isn't a Giallo film it's a suspense horror film dealing with the paranormal.

That's my two penneth'. I've seen Suspiria on countless lists of films cited as the best Giallo film of all time, I think somewhere along the way modern giallo films have used Suspiria as a staple for the giallo and the modern giallo film owes its roots to Suspiria. Whatever this beast is it's a thing of beauty throughout. I'm taken back every time I watch Suspiria, shocked at just how great this film really is and I always find something I missed on a previous watch!

The gore in this film is just spot on, in all the right places there's no gore for gores sake and the effects are great. This film stands out today and does not feel dated in anyway, of course the film is of its time but one of the best from the 1970's, there are some great scares and scenes that make you jump and many stand out visuals. My all time favorite scene is the hand coming through the window and the girls head being pushed through the glass window then repeatedly stabbed and hung, it's very clever and well executed, cut to the other unlucky victim who has a steel girder through her throat and glass through her eye, this is why Dario Argento is one of the best out there, this provides clever and original ideas to the horror genre giving the viewer suspense, stunning atmospheric visuals, shocks, jumps and gore all within a few minutes. A true classic horror, which is a timeless classic.

Suspiria was seized under section 3 of the 1959 Obscene Publications Act on VHS in the early 1980's before the implementation of the Video Recordings Act of 1984 in the UK.

Suspiria was initially released on pre-cert VHS by Thorn EMI in 1982, Cut by the BBFC for its theatrical and video release in 1977, and given an X-rating since 1990. The film has been given an 18 rating by the BBFC.

A true thing of beauty, a masterpiece of horror!

-Tony Newton

Oh my god! Little did I know what to expect when myself and a group of friends rented this to watch over at one of our parent's houses when we were all about 17/18. It was a period where we regularly rented whatever looked gory/horrific/dangerous from our local video rental shop on a Saturday afternoon. Looking back at what is now one of my favourite horror movies, all I can really remember is staring in awe at the TV screen at the amazing visuals and having to drive back home in the dark, down fairly remote country roads, in utter and total fear. That was probably the only movie that got under my skin in that period - as opposed to just a fun, gory video session, which would be instantly forgotten even before I took the VHS back to the shop.

-Charlie Adlard   The Walking Dead Artist.

If you are looking for a visual masterpiece then look no further than Suspiria. Dario Argento has created a work of art that people will either love or hate. From the colour to the music, everyone has an opinion about the film, so now its time for me to chip in mine.

Originally Dario Argento wanted to cast younger girls, but the studio didn't feel this would be right or work, Argento didn't change the dialogue so if you feel some of the things the women say are childish - you're right! Also look out for the door handles, they are hirer up than normal so they give the effect of a child reaching up to open the doors.

Personally I love the look of the film, each scene has a range of different colours and they heighten the tension and mood, then this adds to giving you an off balanced feel. Mix that with the music and you have a whole whirlwind of crazy tension. Goblins soundtrack is there to keep you on the edge of your seat and as you watch the actresses in the scene its like they are also reacting to the music (Maybe this is because Goblin were on set and playing some of the music live). This makes you almost go through the feelings of fear and the stress the girls go through, the colour and music draw you in to the film and you soon feel a part of the film, joining the girls on their journey.

I understand why people don't enjoy the film but you have to appreciate what the film did for cinema, Dario Argento has such a creative eye and his shots are often imitated but never matched.

-Sian Richter   Writer.

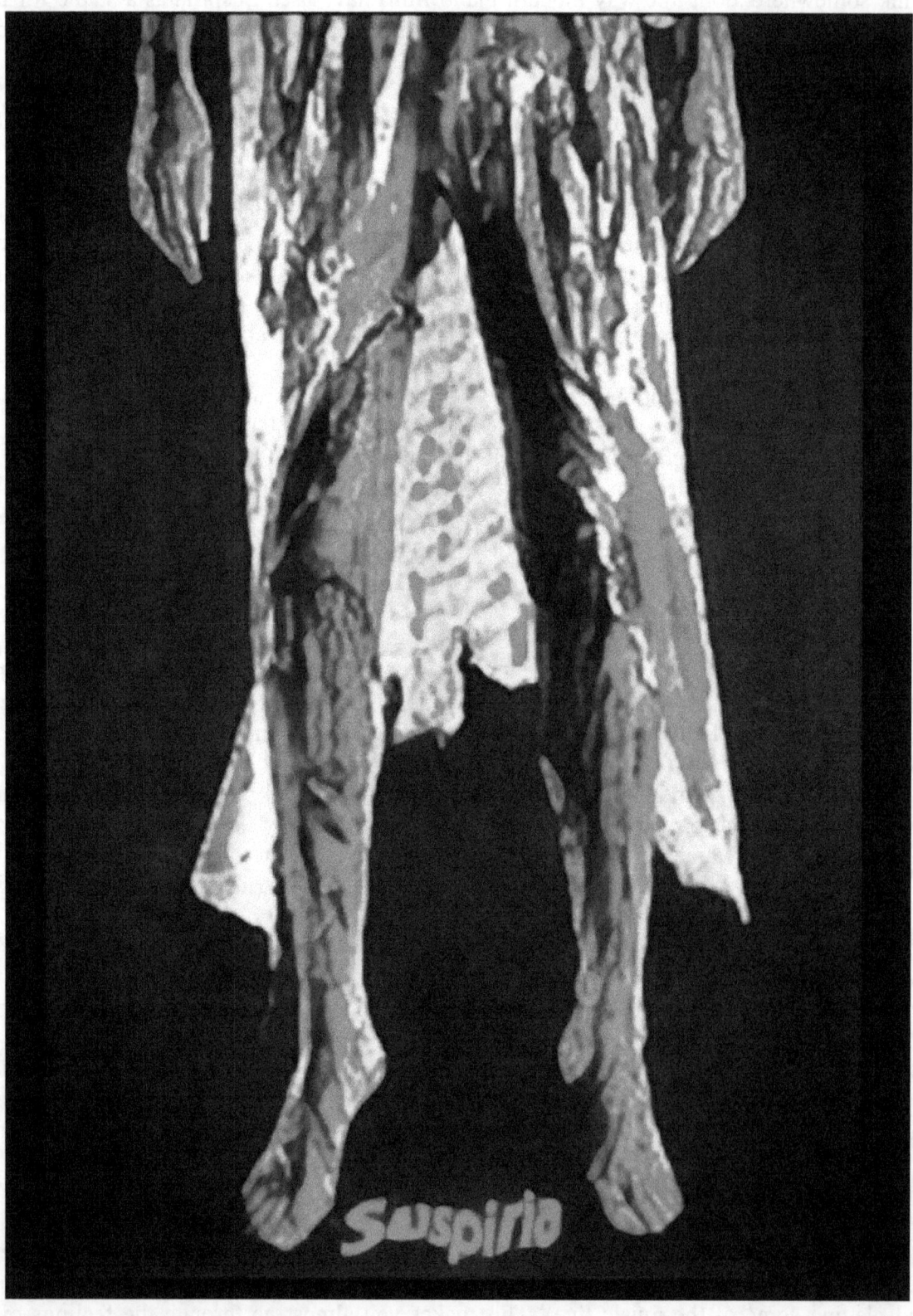

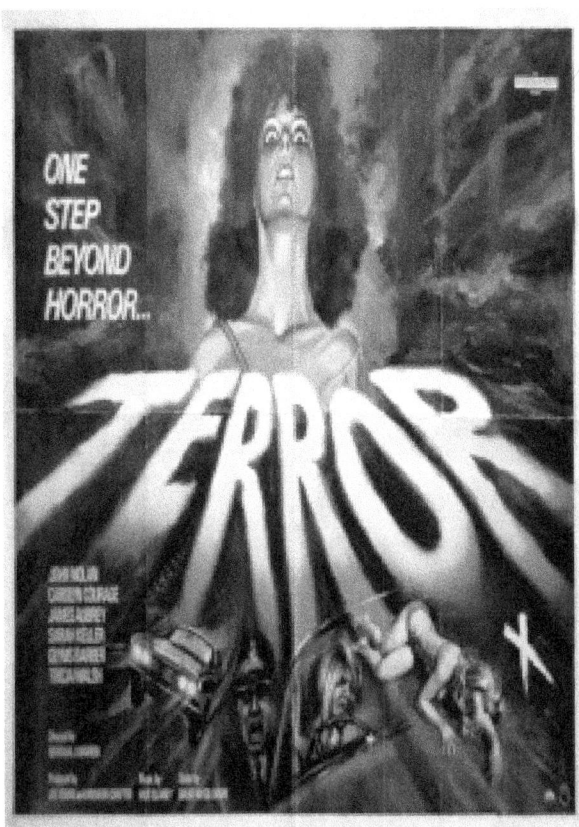

Terror

(DPP Section 3) Banned in the UK
Year of release: 1978
Writer: David McGillvray
Director: Norman J. Warren
R rated 84 mins. UK
Tagline: "Have you ever felt an evil presence all around you...?"

Main cast: John Nolan (James Garrick), Carolyn Courage (Ann Garrick), James Aubrey (Philip), Sarah Keller (Suzy), Tricia Walsh (Viv), Glynis Barber (Carol Tucker).

Distributed by: Hokushin

Plot:
A filmmakers new project is a bit too close to home as he tells the story of a witch burned at the stake many years ago and the curse she placed upon a family which resulted in their strange and gruesome deaths. Cousins James and Ann are plagued by the curse placed on their family by the witch dubbed Mad Molly; those closet to Ann and James begin dying in mysterious and gruesome ways!

Appraisal:
Norman Warren's Terror is classic horror, which has giallo-esque qualities mixed with supernatural. This is a very underrated film that in full of suspense and atmosphere throughout, this film often gets overlooked but is actually one of director Norman J Warren's best pieces of work. This is non-stop hell ride of a movie that will have your heart pumping. The giallo elements make it very enjoyable. This slice of 1970's horror is best served with more Norman J Warren films directly after (optional). This was my first taste of a Norman J Warren film. I love all his work; he is a true master of horror, so underrated, and one of the best living British

film directors of our time. My favourite has always has been "Inseminoid" but it has long since changed to "Terror" as this and the 1976 film "Satan's Slave" are easily his best pieces of work, but then again who doesn't love occult/witches and slowly losing your sanity?

The very underrated Norman J Warren does shine here in this rather unsettling original offering.

Norman J Warren is one of the best horror filmmakers alive today, I adore his work and I would put him up there alongside the very best filmmakers on the video nasty list!

If you are also a lover of Norman J warren's work there has just been a box set released of his horror films entitled Bloody Terror: The Shocking

Cinema of Norman J Warren (1976-1987), well worth checking out! The set definitely gets a thumbs-up from me!

Terror was seized under section 3 of the 1959 Obscene Publications Act on VHS in the early 1980's before the implementation of the Video Recordings Act of 1984 in the UK.

Terror was initially released uncut on pre-cert VHS by Hokushin in 1981, Available uncut 18 rated in the UK since 1997.

-Tony Newton

The Texas Chain Saw Massacre

(DPP Section 3) Banned in the UK
Year of release: 1974
Writers: Kim Henkel and Tobe Hooper
Director: Tobe Hooper
R rated 83 mins. USA
Tagline: "For five young friends, a typical summer afternoon drive becomes a terrifying nightmare."
Main cast: Marilyn Burns (Sally Hardesty), Allen Danziger (Jerry), Paul A. Partain (Franklin Hardesty), William Vail (Kirk), Teri McMinn (Pam), Edwin Neal (Hitchhiker).
Distributed by: Iver Film Services.

Plot:
Concerned that her Grandfather's grave is amongst those that have been vandalized Sally, her brother Franklin, her boyfriend Jerry and friend Pam set off to investigate, they pick up an psychotic hitchhiker along the way, but there's worse to come as the group come face to face with a monstrous chainsaw wielding man wearing the face of another human being as a mask. Will anyone survive Leatherface and his family of cannibals, or will they all succumb to his mighty chainsaw?

Appraisal:
The Texas Chain Saw Massacre is a fantastic horror film, easily hands down one of the best horror films of all time! This film will never date and every time I see Leatherface wielding that chainsaw it sends chills down my spine.

Leatherface was the original scary face of horror, the first big horror icon. The large figure stumbling along wielding a chainsaw combined with the most terrifying face of all. Before this franchises like Dracula played by Bela Lugosi and Christopher Lee, and universal monsters were the faces of horror and the stuff of nightmares, Leatherface was that bit different he was truly horrifying and would be the first of the modern horror icons such as Jason Voorhees and Michael Myers, soon he had many of horror's iconic figures to join him and compete for the role including, Freddy Krueger and Hellraiser to name but a few.

Leatherface still holds his own to this day, and in my eyes is the worst person I would want running into me in a dark alley!

The Texas Chain Saw Massacre is so well made/shot you end up thinking you have seen far more blood and gore than you actually have in the film, most of this actually happens off screen, leaving your imagination to run wild! I don't think there is a horror film out there that can fully capture the atmosphere Tobe Hooper manages to create on screen. This film is a terrifying piece of cinema that is so well executed.

Leatherface is obviously based on real serial killer Ed Gein as Ed Gein would wear a similar mask made of real human skin, although Ed Gein didn't use a chainsaw to kill his victims he used a pistol.

Ed Gein wore the face and scalp of his victims he would also wear a vest made of the human skin with the victims breasts attached and had the female genitalia placed directly over his own.

There is no doubt that Tobe Hooper's Texas Chainsaw Massacre from 1974 had such an important role in the video nasty period. The Texas Chain Saw Massacre was a groundbreaking film that inspired horror filmmakers and revived interest at the time in horror films. There is no doubt that The Texas Chain Saw

Massacre we entered a darker, seedier, grittier side of horror filmmaking that was born when this film was made.

There is something uneasy about The Texas Chain Saw Massacre, I think the film has a feel of its own, everything from the sound production to aesthetic of the whole production is unique in building suspense and managing to send chills down your spine, I watched The Texas Chainsaw Massacre when I was around 10 years old and every time I re-watch the movie I'm transported to watching it through those same eyes! It's crazy how even a certain sound of a chainsaw starting up can install pure terror into the viewer.

Unlike most serial killer flicks before Leatherface wasn't like the slick calm killer you would see in films like Brighton Rock, Peeping Tom or even Psycho, he was a fucking nutcase 24/7, I think the use of the mask covering his face the whole time added to the suspense and in so many horror films when they have a reveal like Scooby doo what's behind the mask is never as terrifying as what we imagined. Kudos to the actors in the film as they filmed in the summer in Texas and the heat was kicking up a 100 degrees if you look close enough you can see the sweat pouring of the actors in the film. It's reported the film cost around $300,000 to make, and would go on to gross over $30 million in the America alone. The Texas Chain Saw Massacre was seized under section 3 of the 1959 Obscene Publications Act on VHS in the early 1980's before the implementation of the Video Recordings Act of 1984 in the UK. The Texas Chain Saw Massacre was initially released uncut on pre-cert VHS by Iver Film Services in 1981, Available uncut 18 rated in the UK. The film was banned by the BBFC for its theatrical release and famously local councils across the UK passed it certificate x with a local cert, many attempts were made by distributors to try to gain a certificate but the BBFC refused, the film was banned in the UK until 1999.

Famously the film was initially given an x rating in the US before the film was cut and given a R-Rating, The Texas Chain Saw Massacre was the last film in the US to receive an X rating certificate before the implementation of the NC-17 rating system by the MPAA.

Horror cinema at its finest!

-Tony Newton

The Texas Chainsaw Massacre, directed by Tobe Hooper is an unrelenting, unflinching assault on the viewer. It is also one of the most streamlined and sadistic horror films ever made. At the time of its release, there was nothing like it, with its semi-documentary style and some of the most prolonged scenes of sustained horror ever captured on camera. Upon first viewing it in 1974 I found it inexplicably terrifying and still do today. The psychological torture during the dinner scene is absolutely gut-wrenching. What separates this from other slasher films is that it relies on suspense to create the on-screen terror. It's not what we see, but what we think we see that engulfs us in a nightmare from which we cannot escape. It's a milestone in exploitation horror cinema with barely any blood on screen. Leatherface, the film's lead villain, would become one of the most iconic horror villains in history and the film would go on to influence many filmmakers including myself.

-Armand Mastroianni   Director "The Killing Hour".

We had no idea the little indie film we were doing would do anything. At that time there were no instant playbacks because everything was on film, pre-digital era. We never saw anything until after it was released. They ran out of money twice and had to shut down filming. An initial two week shoot went to five weeks. There were no storyboards. It was a miracle it came out of the can. No one knew it would do anything, however we all poured our hearts into our work. We took what we were doing very seriously and worked very hard to get things right. They gathered a talent cast and crew of serious artists who cared.

The UK BBFC banned TCSM as well as many other films from '71-'99, 25 years under Ferman's directorship. TCSM wasn't alone by any means. Clockwork Orange, The Last House On The Left, Straw Dogs and many more were also banned. I imagine many producer/directors stopped resubmitting their films over the years, as did Kubrick, frustrated first by the BBFC's Stephen Murphy and then by James Ferman's refusals and strict denials to lift the bans, but I don't know that as a fact except with Kubrick. (During James Ferman's time, the title of the chief executive officer at the BBFC changed from "Secretary of the Board" to the current "Director") All these films broke ground. 1974 was a completely different day and age. Although the violence in TCSM is mainly inferred, not shown, but left to the viewer, it was quite controversial to show terrorizing people and violence in such a blatant manner. Chainsaws, meat hooks, that's pretty disturbing even now.

-Teri McMinn   (Pam) in the original "Texas Chainsaw Massacre" 1974, The Orginal Chainsaw Gal.

I am part of this franchise, THE TEXAS CHAINSAW MASSACRE, THE BEGINNING, and without this trend-setting style of shock horror/suspense the genre would not have given us the continued thrills we experience with these films. I feel that without the stalking effect of, Leatherface, our horror genre would be less than. I can't imagine this original film, not being presented to the public, and scaring them to question reality or fiction.

-Lew Temple   Actor.

Summary: Five Scooby-Doo wannabes in a piece of crap Volkswagen van fall victim to chainsaw-wielding Leatherface and his inbred family of backwoods cannibals.

This is *the* quintessential low-budget indie horror flick. Filmed on location in the boondocks of central Texas during the sweltering summer of 1973 by a group of scruffy hippies, *The Texas Chainsaw Massacre* has proven to be one of the most enduring horror films ever made. Gritty, brutal (for 1973), and unsettlingly realistic, *Chainsaw* has spawned three sequels (with another in the works), a remake and *its* sequel, comic books, Halloween costumes, and spoofs on everything from *The Simpsons* to *Robot Chicken*. Its director, Tobe Hooper, has gone on to do great things himself, including directing Stephen King's *Salem's Lot* in 1979 and *The Poltergeist* in 1982.

Not bad at all.

Now, *Chainsaw* is a great movie, but it owes at least some of its astronomical success to a lie. That's right, once and for all: the events depicted in this movie *did not happen*. There was no Leatherface, no Pam, no Kirk, Jerry, Sally, or Franklin. Hell, that black trucker in the end wasn't even real. It was a movie. It was as based on true events as *The Blair Witch Project*. Even today, people are still wondering whatever happened to ol' Leather and his brood. It was all a gimmick, guys - just a way to draw more people into movie houses. It was *not* based on a true story.

It was *inspired* by one. Big difference.

Back in 1957, a Wisconsin farmer was arrested on suspicion of murdering a local hardware store owner, Bernice Warden: her son, who just happened to be sheriff, dropped by, and found his mummy gone, a pool of blood on the floor and the cash register MIA. Checking the receipts, he discovered that her last costumer was Ed Gein, the local weirdo. Ed was arrested at a friend's dinner table, and the lawmen that went out to his house were scarred for life. They found Worden hanging from a meat hook in the shed, decapitated and disemboweled. Inside the house itself, they found a cache of horrors that would shock a nation: lampshades made of human flesh; skull-tops converted into bowls; dried faces adorning the walls like fine art; and much, much, much more. Oh, it got worse, trust me. They even found a suit made out of a woman (featuring breasts and a vagina) that Eddie would don, probably so he could pretend to be his dead mother. And then there was the shoebox moldering in the corner…what was in there? Female parts - a half dozen or so.

A local writer turned Gein's story into the beloved suspense classic *Psycho* (or, rather, Alfred Hitchcock turned the book into a beloved suspense classic), and then, drawling on the case, Tobe Hooper created one of the greatest low budget films ever made. (The chainsaw part came from Hooper's own depraved urges: one Christmas, trapped in a mall by a hoard of shoppers, he saw a chainsaw, and imagined himself snatching it up and running through the crowd).

What I loved most about *Chainsaw* (and, indeed, most indie films) is the realism. This movie wasn't made by some fat cat with deep pockets. They couldn't afford luxuries like props. That chainsaw Leatherface is running around with? That's real, my friend. That broom handle the old man beat Sally up with? Real too. And he really hit her with it. And it *really* hurt. He also really hit the hitchhiker with it. And poor old Sally…when she was running through the woods from Leatherface, most of the blood she was coated in was real; there were briers out there and they ripped her flesh.

This is why indie films are superior to their Hollywood counterparts. Fake guts *look* fake. Pig guts, however, look real. Plus, fake guts cost money. Why put out dough when you could find a butcher or slaughterhouse that would happily give you the same thing for free?

The Texas Chainsaw Massacre is the perfect film. The story is shocking and tragic, the actors lived and breathed their roles, and the atmosphere is the very definition of macabre. The effects are…well, very effective, and you know what? There aren't that many, because this movie doesn't rely on blood and guts. *Chainsaw* isn't meant to gross you out; it's supposed to leave you shaken.

And it does that *very* nicely.

-Joseph Rubas   Author.

The Power of The Texas Chainsaw Massacre

Of all the video nasties, the one that holds the most power while being actually extremely implicit in its delivery is The Texas Chainsaw Massacre (Tobe Hooper, 1974).

Filmed in an almost documentary style of intimacy, a car full of teenagers encounters a family of crazy, redneck cannibals on the back roads of Texas. Cast offs from a closed slaughterhouse, the family consists of the cook (Jim Siedow), the hitcher (Ed Neal), a nearly comatose Grandpa (John Dugan) and the chainsaw-wielding, face-wearing Leatherface (Gunnar Hanson).

Despite its disturbing premise, the gore content of this horror masterpiece is practically zero. As a teenager, I swore to see the most extreme and gruesome scenes that are just not *there*, and never were.

This film gets inside your mind and it is exaggerated by your imagination. It is a testament to director Tobe Hooper that he is able to play sleight of hand with your brain. I have seen nearly every horror film on the Video Nasty list, and none scared me more than this film. The performances, the gritty realism and the prospect of no escape on an obscure acre of Texas backwoods makes this required viewing for anyone who considers themselves a true horror film fan.

Based heavily in the true crime case of Ed Gein.

-Terry M. West   Author.

Not only one of the best horror films ever made, but straight up one of the best films ever made PERIOD, Tobe Hooper's THE TEXAS CHAINSAW MASSACRE was actually a film that I stayed clear of growing up, having been terrified of it as a kid. Picked up from elementary school, I sat in the backseat of our family vehicle, as my father and uncle discussed the "TRUE STORY" horror film they had just watched prior to picking me up, the film being TCM. Obviously my father didn't do his homework regarding how much of a "true" story the film was, because he swore up and down that the exploits of Leatherface and his family were exactly as they played out onscreen.

By the time I finally had the nerve to watch it, I had actually already seen TCM 2 and LEATHERFACE: THE TEXAS CHAINSAW MASSACRE III, but had not even attempted to sit through the original film, as that scary car ride as a child really spooked me away from it. I was 27 when I finally DID see it, and was recently divorced and was trying to impress a girl who was a big fan of the film, so I said "of course I've seen it", pretty much lying to her face. We sat down, and watched it, and it was by far one of the most profound experiences of my life, right up there with the birth of my children. It's an excellent example of what can be done with little money but with a clear and ambitious vision. THE TEXAS CHAINSAW MASSACRE is one of the very few PERFECT films in my opinion, one that is still as terrifying today as it ever was. I didn't get lucky that night, because Leatherface and his crazy family left me creeped out. Enthralled, but heavily creeped out. I absolutely adore the film and it's one that I watch quite regularly. Thanks to Tobe Hooper, I walked home frustrated by the lack of scoring, but happily gaining an addition to my favorite films of all time.

-Jerry Smith   Editor in Chief/Writer Icons of Fright.

The Texas Chainsaw Massacre is the most deeply affecting and utterly mean-spirited rotting hunk of celluloid that I have ever had the good fortune of being subjected to. Period! Forget about **The Last House On The Left** and **I Spit on Your Grave.** They may both be accomplished movies in their own right but both were culpable of displaying more than enough ineptitude to cancel out a lion's share of the good work done. Not the case here, not in the case of **The Texas Chainsaw Massacre…**

Tobe Hooper has had a chequered career in filmmaking to say the least. For every other **Poltergeist** there's been a **Crocodile** for Hooper, and not all his works have been held in the same lofty regard at this. Take **Lifeforce** for example…a cataclysmic mess, as many critics would wrongly have you believe, it is actually a truly masterful B-Movie, which deserved so much more than the indifference it received. One thing that nobody can take away from him is that he has supplied Horror buffs with the most taut and nerve-jangling movie experience in many of their existences. Put simply, this film was more menacing and brutal than anything else I have ever watched. Perhaps most remarkably, it did so without the need for bloodshed or visual imagery.

Its brutality lied solely in what you knew was happening behind that rickety sliding door. It came from the brief glimpse of the meat hook behind said door and from the 'twitch of the death nerve' in one of Leatherface's hapless victims. It also came courtesy of the seemingly endless chase scene (in which *Marilyn Burns* gave such a tangible performance because… she was truly fucking horrified). But then it had the audacity to force you into chortling from the pit of your abdomen just minutes later (courtesy of *Jim Siedow's* demented turn). All of the brutality you were exposed to lied in the Director's cut, which your mind's eye conjured. No two versions of this will ever be the same as they depend eventually on everyone's interpretation of the events. Me? I dropped acid for the first time at sixteen and since then my mind goes wherever it damned well pleases whether I like it or not so, needless to say, I'm sitting at the table, banging my condiments down as I scream *"Where's my cake, Bedelia?"*

Now there have been sequels, prequels, and reboots with different Directors each in turn attempting to expand on what we know already about the real life family who are depicted loosely here. Some have been good (Superior prequel **The Beginning**) and others shambolic (laughably bungling **Next Generation**) but one thing is true of all of them. They can never hold a candle up to the original and I state that, not to be pompous and arrogant. I simply speak the truth.

The less we know the more realistic and distressing the concept becomes of being in such an ungodly place, discovering the room of bones (complete with hanging teeth mobiles), being in audible range of that sliding door opening behind you or waiting for Gramps to get a better grip on that hammer and give your crown a well-placed dig. It is the material from which sleepless nights derive and anyone familiar with my Appraisal method by now should be aware that I'm actually relatively easily scared if the correct approach is taken.

Texas took the correct approach. Tobe used a lot of improvisation during his shoot and he would never be able to coax the performance he did out of his leading lady if she wasn't actually beside herself with panic and anguish. I'm sure she has forgiven him since as his decision made the experience all the more unsettling, but I'm also convinced that the whole traumatic episode must've haunted her for a considerable period of time after shooting had wrapped up. *Teri McMinn* also endured a considerable amount of pain for her art as she dangled excruciatingly on the meat hook with nylon cord between her legs throughout her character's downfall).

For anybody waiting feverishly for a plot synopsis, I regret to inform you that you won't find one here. There are plentiful sources for those who wish to know the plot (the title really does sum it up to perfection). All you Texas newbies really should watch this with an unsullied perspective and remember kids – the less you know the more you stand to gain.

One closing point I wish to make is that Texas is presented now on Blu-Ray with a superior transfer and looking extremely crisp. That's great but I would be just as happy watching it on its grainy VHS print. That says a lot for its raw depiction of unbridled human terror. It is grimy, filthy even and deserves to be seen both ways to truly appreciate the different experiences. If you haven't had either, then I urge you robustly to dust off your old VHS player one last time and share an evening with the true 'Video Nasty'.

Without a shadow of a doubt this is right up there with the very meanest-spirited of the nasties. However, there's hardly a drop of **Grue** in the entire duration. This attests that the most imperative factor of *Tobe Hooper's* raw masterwork is the feeling you get deep in your abdomen whilst watching. All the decapitations and disembowelments in the world can't compare with that feeling.

-Keeper of the Crimson Quill (Rivers of Grue).

The Thing

(DPP Section 3) Banned in the UK
Year of release: 1982
Writers: Bill Lancaster and John W. Campbell Jr.
Director: John Carpenter
R rated 109 mins. USA
Tagline: "What you fear most... is among you."
Main cast: Kurt Russell (R.J MacReady), Wilford Brimley (Dr. Blair), T.K Carter (Nauls), David Clennon (Palmer), Keith David (Childs), Richard Hallahan (Vance Norris).
Distributed by: CIC

Plot:
When a group of scientists are confronted by a shape-shifting alien, a race for survival on the desolate Antarctic base ensues. Paranoia runs rife throughout the group no one is safe from the thing.

Appraisal:
John Carpenter directs this classic sci-fi horror and is undoubtedly his finest hour; this film is also John Carpenters personal favorite of his own work. A group of scientists are confronted by an alien, which can shape shift into the unlucky host. A race for survival on the desolate Antarctic base entails, complete with paranoia throughout the group - no one is safe from the thing - it's a recipe for a sci-fi horror epic!

The Thing originated from John W Campbell Jr.'s novella "Who Goes There" which in turn was adapted for the 1951 film "The Thing From Another World". This is a long way from a B-movie anything but! The effects in this film are second to none and, hands down, it has the best effects than any other video nasty out there. The effects make this film what it is, the acting is first class complete with Kurt Russell as Macready. The music score works perfectly throughout. For me this film is one of the best if not the best 1980's film, the pacing, scenery and filming are second to none. The film has an almost alien like quality to it "In space no one can you scream" or can they in the Antarctic?

The desolate setting makes the film, you find yourself as the viewer being put in the same situation they are by the clever use of great cinematography and sound, a huge cluster fuck of claustrophobic delight! You have to watch the film with the lights out!

Tobe Hooper and Kim Henkel are rumored to have written a draft of the film set underwater before director John Carpenter worked his magic on it, it's hard to imagine that we would not have had "The Thing" as we know it, we would have probably got a film like The Abyss" with more monsters and gore though I would have liked seeing "The Thing" merge with a shark, octopus or a whale (Ok, maybe that's just me), those beards would never have looked so good under water!

The Thing is pure class from start to finish. It was seized under section 3 of the 1959 Obscene Publications Act on VHS in the early 1980's before the implementation of the Video Recordings Act of 1984 in the UK.

The Thing was initially released uncut on pre-cert VHS by CIC in 1983. Prior to that, the film was given an X rating for its theatrical release by the BBFC in the UK in 1982. CIC submitted the film to the BBFC in 1987 and it was given an 18 rating and was released uncut. Currently available uncut 18 rated in the UK.

-Tony Newton

For many different reasons, this may be my favorite horror film. I think it was one of the first real, over the top type horror films I had ever been allowed to see. Not only is it a favorite for specific elements within the film, but also for everything I associate with the movie when I first watched it. It's simply a great film. The cast, the score, the effects, everything comes together. I have a soft spot for creature features, and while this may not be the typical definition of one, it hits all the right marks for me. Kurt Russell is great. He had already busted out of his Disney persona with Escape From New York and was well on his way to his badass action hero phase, but MacReady was much more of a reluctant hero making him all the more relatable to the viewer.

The real star of the film though is the effects. It seemed light years ahead of anything else I had seen in a horror film. I remember watching it for the first time with my father. I had been bugging him to let me watch more horror films, so the next trip he made to the video store resulted in him bringing home The Thing. I remember all of the gags. The dog in the kennel, the spider head, everything, but most of all, my father laughing. Not because he was not impressed, but because he was so blown away at the time by the effects and the levels they went to, it was his honest reaction. He may also have been overcompensating for me, to try to lessen the impact. Either way it's one of my favorite memories. I had been nervous about watching it and I remember when the film was over, he said to me "If you can watch that, then you will be able to watch any horror movie you ever want to" It kind of became an event as opposed to just a film, which is probably why it stands out to me as my favorite. At the time it was like a badge of honor.

I've already watched again with my son. The effects are still great, but just not the same as what is remembered. He loved the film though, and randomly "Window's, blast them!" can be heard from the basement.

-James Fler   Raven Banner Entertainment.

John Carpenter's The Thing is in many ways the perfect storm: a tight focus on the essential elements of a horror movie. The polar station makes for a quintessentially isolated environment to trap the characters – and the viewer – in. The creature has an infinite repertoire of nightmarish shapes – all monsters in one. At the same time, it could be anyone, the monster hiding amongst us. Taut and suspense-filled direction and special effects that still hold up make this an enduring classic."

-Adrian Tchaikovsky Author.

John Carpenter's The Thing is one of my top five favorite films. The terror comes from the realization that the creature can be anyone. The direction of the suspense and pacing are exceptional and the music by Ennio Morricone is top-,notch.

-John Borowski   Filmmaker.

I can hardly believe this film is on the list. This is not only my favourite horror movie of all time but easily in my top 5 all-time favourite films. Admittedly, this was a film I saw at the cinema first, and after seeing it with a friend, we went out and made our own horror move on a super8 camera I owned. I think that attests to the influence the film had on me straight away, and it continues to do so. The Thing is certainly the pinnacle of Carpenter's career. He never made anything since bordering on the genius of this film. And, as great and eye-poppingly gory Rob Botin's effects are, I think we forget just how brilliantly intense the film is.

And that ending...

It's amazing to think that in 1982, two of the most seminal movies of all time - The Thing and Blade Runner - were box office flops. Everything fell before the feel good onslaught of ET. Thankfully history has proved its initial "failure" to be wrong, and The Thing [and Blade Runner] is now hailed as a classic.

-Charlie Adlard   The Walking Dead Artist.

Born from the short story Who Goes There and following the 1950's B movie "Thing From Another World", this tail of paranoia and self preservation is masterfully crafted, and driven home by the gore and ingenious practical effects work of Rob Bottin. While video nasties were being attacked as nothing more than cheap exploitation, corrupting the morals of societies youth, I believe that it was features like The Thing, with it's dog faces blooming into flowers of blood and severed heads walking around like spiders, placed into a compelling story with first rate acting, that really disturbed and threatened the fragile minds of those who would see them band. What would it mean for the NVALA if an "obscenity" could validate itself in the manner that John Carpenter's now classic, had.

-Christopher Moonlight   Moonlight Art Magazine.

Oh, what a beautiful slice of cinematic gore!

The makeup effects in *The Thing* are fantastic! Rob Bottin's prosthetics are slimy, gooey, and sticky in equal measure. Enough to make me gag on the pepperoni-and-cheese pizza I was consuming during my first viewing!

This movie is not content with the usual head-exploding, limb-hacking, eye-gouging monotony of so many other movies of the period. *The Thing* takes the word "splatter" and gives it all new meaning!

Dogs explode into swarms of snake-like veins, scrabbling for their next victim. A dying man's chest cracks open like a huge, hungry mouth and bites off the arms of the doctor applying shock-paddles to it. The same man's head detaches from his body and crawls out of the room on spider-legs, screaming as though offended by its own profane existence.

Every gory tableau is a work of art. The scene where Dr. Cooper cuts open the dead dog, only to find a mangled grotesquery of fused flesh and bone, never fails to make me go all Indiana Jones and growl; "That belongs in a museum!"

The movie isn't all gore, though. There's a nape-prickling sense of paranoia the whole way through, as the characters question whether or not they can trust one another, and Kurt Russell puts in a brilliantly bearded performance as one of the classic '80s leading men, RJ MacReady.

But, at the end of the day, it's all about the juicy stuff, and *The Thing* delivers it in sloppy bucket-loads!

-Joe Ramshaw   Writer.

Tomb of the Living Dead

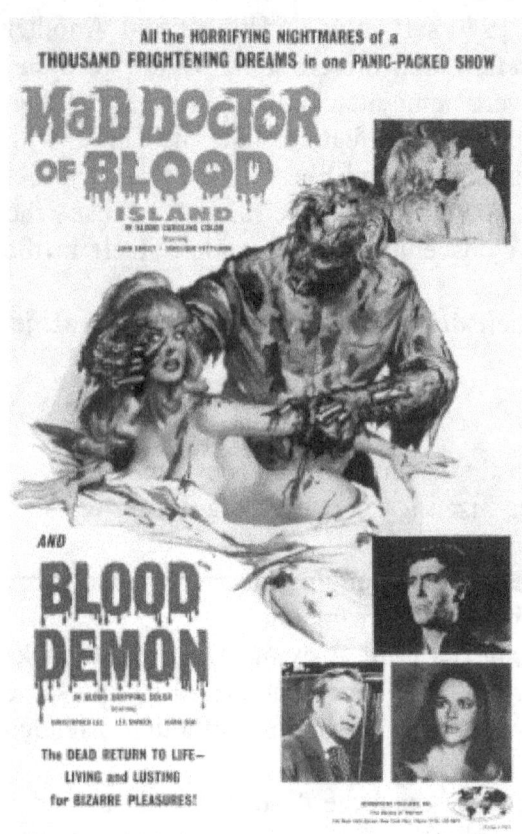

(DPP Section 3) Banned in the UK
Also known as "Mad Doctor of Blood Island".
Year of release: 1968
Writer: Reuben Canoy
Directors: Gerardo de Leon and Eddie Romero
M rated 85 mins. USA, Philippines
Tagline: "No waiting. No appointment. No escape!"
Main cast: John Ashley (Dr. Bill Foster), Angelique Pettyjohn (Sheila Willard), Ronald Remy (Dr. Lorca), Alicia Alonzo (Marla), Ronaldo Valdez (Carlos Lopez), Tita Munoz (Mrs. Lopez).
Distributed by: Horror Time

Plot:
When Bill Foster and his girlfriend Sheila head to Blood Island they discover that Sheila's father has been living as a drunk in the camp of scientist Dr. Lorca. Dr Lorca is using his expertise to experiment on the islands inhabitants in search of the key to eternal life, but what he creates is something far more sinister than he could ever have imagined!

Appraisal:
Tomb of the Living Dead is more commonly known as Mad Doctor of Blood Island in the UK.

This 1960's horror is a fun romp that from the off takes homage of early 1950's sci-fi films, which is not a bad thing! This does feel dated and feels very alien being on the section 3 banned video nasty list. Lovers of classic horrors like The Texas Chain Saw Massacre and 80's slashers may not welcome its charm but if you're a fan of B movies and have a penchant for cheeky horror you will love this!

For me, it felt like I was watching an afternoon TV old horror sci-fi flick that you would see as a kid, but this film features boobs! I think that sums the film up!

It's entertaining enough. The change of the title from Mad Doctor of Blood Island to The Tomb of the Living Dead was genius, you end up with Romero and living dead on the cover sleeve and I'm sure a lot of people bought the flick because of that, thinking they were getting something like Night of the Living Dead by George Romero!

Director Eddie Romero was a great director; I'm a huge fan of his work. My favorite being Black Mamma, White Mamma starring Pam Grier and 1974's Sausage Sisters! Eddie Romero was an exploitation king and, if anything underrated! This campy offering does get a lot of shit, but it's a fun romp of a film!

Long live the exploitation genre!

Tomb of the Living Dead was seized under section 3 of the 1959 Obscene Publications Act on VHS in the early 1980's before the implementation of the Video Recordings Act of 1984 in the UK.

Tomb of the Living Dead was initially released uncut on pre-cert VHS by Horror Time in 1983, The film is available rated 18 with cuts by the BBFC re-titled as The Mad Doctor of Blood Island.

-Tony Newton

The Toy Box

(DPP Section 3) Banned in the UK
Year of release: 1971
Writer: Ronald Victor Garcia
Director: Ronald Victor Garcia
18 rated 89 mins. USA
Tagline: "He twisted women in his hands as though they were toys!"
Main cast: Sean Kenney (Ralph), Ann Perry (Donna), Neal Bishop, Debbie Osborne (Sally Howard), T.E Brown, Lisa Goodman.
Distributed by: TCX

Plot:
The Toy Box is a bizarre offering, when a young woman attends a party she gets more than she bargained for. We enter a strange swinging party.

Appraisal:
"The Toy Box isn't your average keys in the bowl affair!". I think that should have been the perfect tagline! The film features some bizarre scenes including someone performing weird sex acts in front of the party's host, and yes the host is a corpse! A true mindfuck of a movie!

"If you perform well enough you receive a gift from the toy box"

I think I'll pass! Although I'm still bitter that I didn't receive my invite to the party!

This bizarre slice of sexploitation is actually a fun little film. Unlike any sexploitation film out there, with various elements of this bizarre film making it grab your full attention, it's strange, it's weird, it's strange it's low budget fodder, but worth watching for its bizarreness alone.

The Toy Box was seized under section 3 of the 1959 Obscene Publications Act on VHS in the early 1980's before the implementation of the Video Recordings Act of 1984 in the UK.

The Toy Box was initially released uncut on pre-cert VHS by TCX in 1981, The film is not available in the UK as it never got re-released but you can get a German 18 rated version or the unrated and uncut US version.

-Tony Newton

Werewolf Woman

(DPP Section 3) Banned in the UK
Also known as "Naked Werewolf Woman".
Year of release: 1976
Writers: Rino Di Silvestro and Anthony La Penna
Director: Rino Di Silvestro
R rated 79 mins. Italy
Tagline: "A true story so brutal and horrifying it was kept from the public for over a century!"
Main cast: Annik Borel (Daniela Neseri), Howard Ross (Luca Mondini), Dagmar Lassander (Elena Neseri), Tino Carraro (Count Neseri), Elio Zamuto (Psychiatrist), Osvaldo Ruggieri.
Distributed by: Cinehollywood

Plot:
Daniela is a victim of abuse; she is mentally unstable and believes herself to be the descendant of a werewolf. Her dreams become a reality when she lures men into her bed only to rip out their throats with her teeth. After being institutionalized for some time things begin to look up for Daniela and she's ready to put the past behind her, but when things go horribly wrong Daniela reverts to her old ways once again.

Appraisal:
Werewolf Woman does seems to get a lot of hate, people kind of brush this film of as pure Italian sleaze and not much else. Of course the film is going to garnish that kind of taint because the director famously made "Deported Women of the SS" in the same year as "Werewolf Woman". The same director made "Love in a Woman's Prison" in 1973, so people would just assume the film was going to be sordid. The film is more sexually charged and steamy than full on sleaze, which we get from the majority of the directors other work. It's a good mix of horror and exploitation in all the right places - a nice slice of Italian cinema from a somewhat underrated director.

Werewolf Woman was seized under section 3 of the 1959 Obscene Publications Act on VHS in the early 1980's before the implementation of the Video Recordings Act of 1984 in the UK. This film was cut in the UK for both the cinematic release and the VHS release.

Werewolf Woman was initially released on pre-cert VHS by Cinehollywood in 1981, prior to its VHS release the film was given an X rating by the BBFC for its theatrical release in the UK after cuts made by the BBFC.

The version that featured on the VHS releases in the early 1980's in the UK wasn't uncut and had around 5 minutes of footage missing from the film. Werewolf Woman was later given an 18 rating with further cuts made by the BBFC for its 1986 VHS release under the title of "Naked Werewolf Woman". At present you can only get the cut version in the UK, but you can get hold of the US print which is uncut and unrated.

-Tony Newton

Wrong Way

(DPP Section 3) Banned in the UK
Year of release: 1972
Director: Ray Williams
X rated 78 mins. USA
Tagline: "Lured...! Abused!...Abandoned!"
Main cast: Laurel Canyon, Candy Sweet, Forrest Lorne, Ray Wray, Ron Namkram, Kurt Ames.
Distributed by: Inter-Ocean

Plot:
When their car breaks down two young women find themselves lost in the middle of nowhere. The girls are kidnapped by a couple of drug-fuelled hippies and taken back to their gang where its members rape them. Just when the horrific ordeal comes to an end and they attempt to make their way back to civilisation the girls quickly realise that their nightmare is far from over, when they happen upon a deranged cult leader!

Appraisal:
Wrong way is a rather forgotten exploitation piece! It's very similar to The Last House on the Left and early 70's exploitation pieces, but not very well produced or acted and the whole feel of the production is very low, this film is an okay exploitation offering but at times it leaves the viewer thinking what the fuck! not explaining a lot of things, which you could assume this is due to running out of money on the set and their plans had to try and include a very long script and little money to produce it and rushing different scenes then just editing it together. The film is cut at strange times and you go from one scene to another, the next scene has nothing to do with the last. The film starts of really well and is a hippie-fueled exploitation mind fuck, complete with annoying folk style music and inbred nutters with half a brain cell between them. The music is a big part of this film and is used to set up each scene but the crazy music score really does make you feel like you are on a bad acid trip, there is a very bizarre rape scene featuring two women who must have the worst luck in the world, this scene does drag on far too long and is very disturbing to watch. The whole film is basically two girls going out of the frying pan and into the fire, things just get worse and worse for them, this is a very different film to any other video nasty.

When I originally watched it I was expecting a rape revenge style horror film, the film is basically missing the revenge part, which makes the viewer feel uncomfortable throughout, the rape scenes are brutal to say the least. Those the girls encounter are the most evil, sick, depraved people in existence; by chance, the girls happen to run into every one of them. After my first watch of the movie, I thought that was just a full on exploitation film trying to cash in on Drugsploitation, sexploitation and basically trying to hit on any 'sploitation they could. After I watched the film the second time I wondered how much of the film was serendipitous, or was this film made this way on purpose? The bad cuts, the bad production, the really awful choreographed rape scenes, bad acting, the almost documentary feel to it, the whole aesthetic of the movie! Is this film so ahead of its time that what we are actually watching is pure grindhouse exploitation gold? The jury is still out! If Troma and Rob Zombie had a love child in the 1970's this film would be the product!

I'm torn with this film; is this an exploitation masterpiece way ahead of its time, or is it just bad!?

Wrong Way was seized under section 3 of the 1959 Obscene Publications Act on VHS in the early 1980's before the implementation of the Video Recordings Act of 1984 in the UK.

The BBFC cut the film for a theatrical release in 1980, cutting well over 15 minutes of footage and giving it an X-rating.

Wrong Way was initially released on pre-cert VHS by Inter-Ocean in 1981, It's one of the hardest VHS titles to get hold of, the film never got a re-release in Britain, but you can get this on a US unrated DVD release but well worth checking out!

-Tony Newton

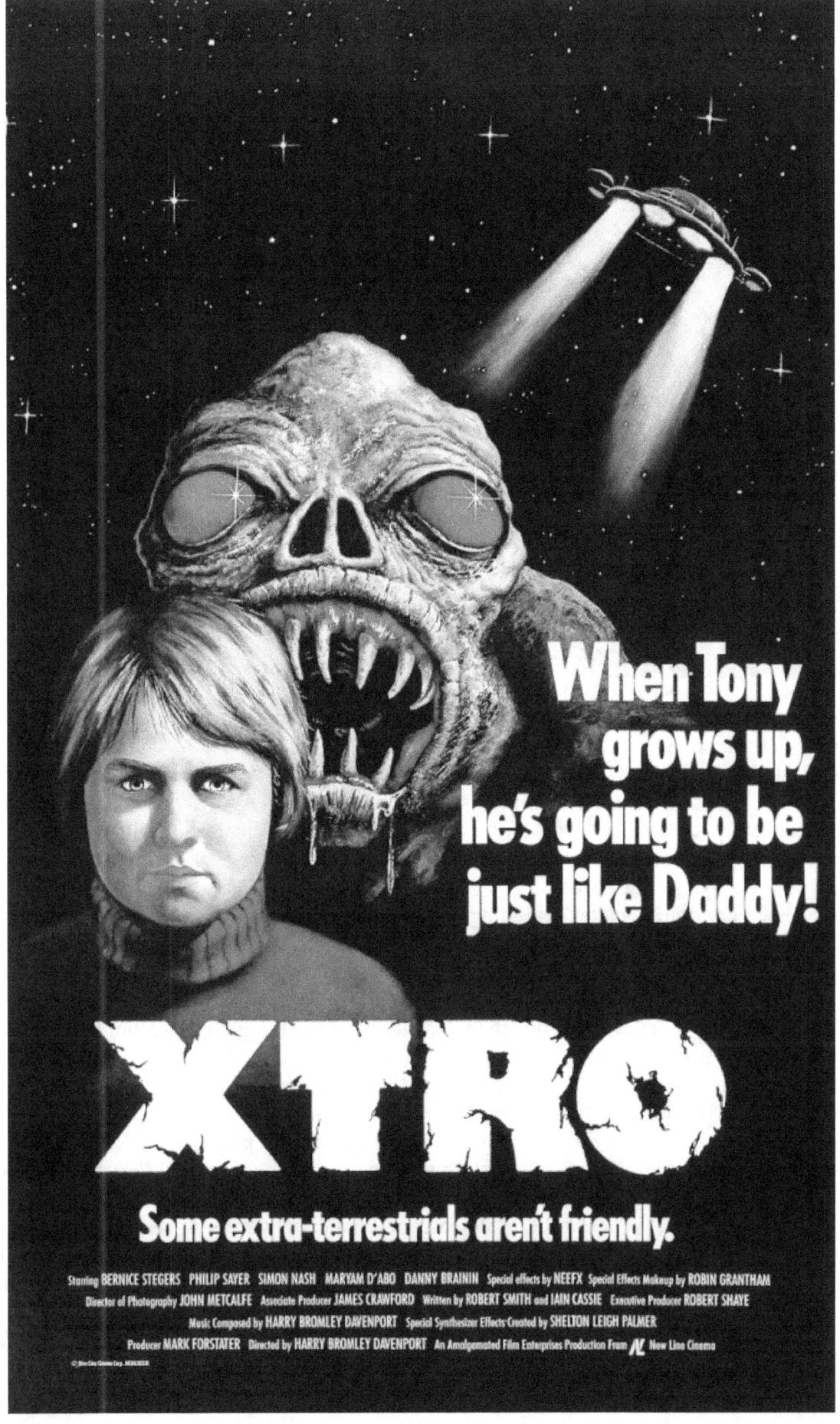

Xtro

(DPP Section 3) Banned in the UK
Year of release: 1983
Writers: Harry Bromley Davenport and Iain Cassie
Director: Harry Bromley Davenport
R rated 84 mins. UK
Tagline: "A brutal excursion in terror."
Main cast: Philip Sayer (Sam Phillips), Bernice Stegers (Rachel Phillips), Danny Brainin (Joe Daniels), Maryam D'abo (Analise Mercier), Simon Nash (Tony Phillips), Peter Mandell (Clown).
Distributed by: Spectrum (Polygram)

Plot:
In this British sci-fi horror classic, a man returns to Earth following his mysterious abduction 3 years earlier. Sam is keen to reunite with his son Tony and wife Rachel but finds that Rachel has long since moved on. The bond between Tony and his father grows as a Doctor struggles to explain Sam's disturbing behaviour, will Tony convert his son into an alien being and continue with his plans to return to the alien world with his son?

Appraisal:
Xtro pays homage to many films; it's even compared to E.T, but anyone expecting a film like E.T will be in for a shock as I was when I watched this film as a youngster.

Xtro is a lost classic and I personally think it never really got the attention it deserved; "Xtro" doesn't have too much gore and contains the usual amount of sex you would expect from a video nasty. This film has a very dark feel throughout and dare I say one of the most out there films here on the list! The film is very dark, powerful and an experience to watch. you can't look away from the screen, there are bizarre moments, creepy, horrifying ones and shocks throughout!

Xtro has some very quirky and surreal things going on all the way through the movie, all of which make me love this movie all the more. You can't turn away from the screen for a minute. The scene when the action man/G.I Joe style figure is attacking a woman is one of the most surreal scenes in a horror film ever, the ending is sheer brilliance and the effects are solid throughout, every cast member is on top form and Harry Bromley Davenport does a fantastic job directing this cult hit! That is a long way from E.T the cute alien!

For me the woman giving birth to the full grown man has to be one of the highlights of the film, as well as the life size action man going on his killing rampage, the acting in this film is great, everyone takes the film serious and this shows and gives it more of an Eire feel throughout.

Xtro is a very underrated film, this film broke the mould and went places others films never dared too, for some reason it just works, this is a cult film that I always watch again and again! Pure Sci-Fi and Horror VHS Heaven!

Xtro was seized under section 3 of the 1959 Obscene Publications Act on VHS in the early 1980's before the implementation of the Video Recordings Act of 1984 in the UK. Xtro was initially released uncut on pre-cert VHS by Spectrum in 1983. The original UK theatrical release was passed 18 and uncut by the BBFC. The film was submitted to the BBFC in 1987, gained an 18 rating, and was distributed uncut.

-Tony Newton

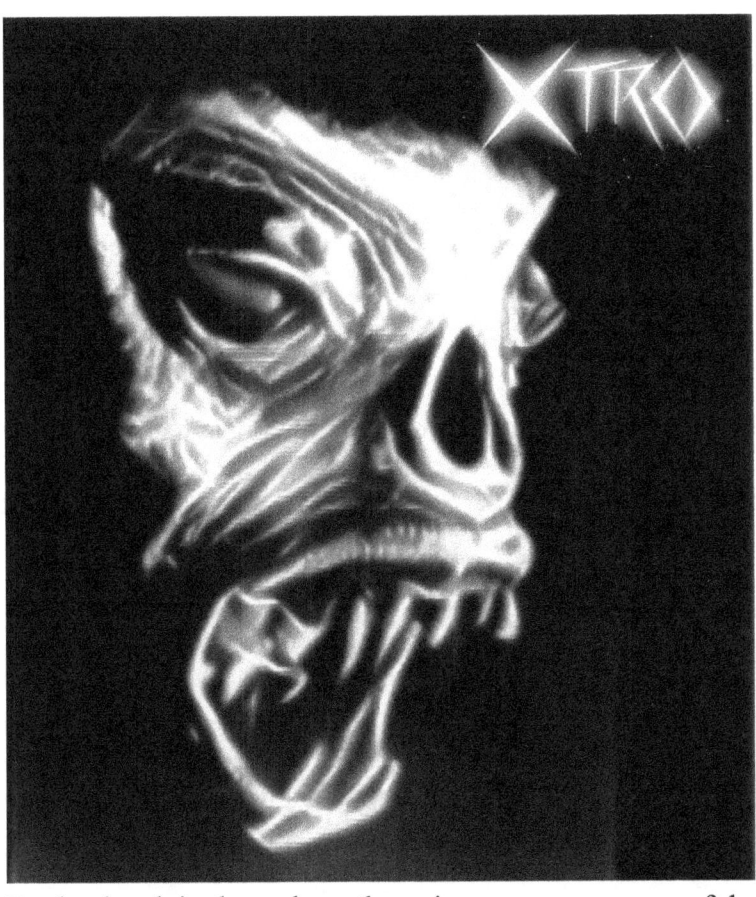

Xtro was my second feature film. My first was called "Whispers of Fear" and some smart critic said it should have been called "Screams of Boredom," which is a very funny remark - but it crushed me at the age of twenty-three.

So I determined that Xtro would not be boring. In fact, I made a chart on graph paper to be sure that we achieved what the Hollywood movie business endearingly refers to as "Whammies" every 5 minutes.

Action director Rennie Harlin once said to me at a party that his formula is as follows: "First act - small Whammies. Second act - Whammies mount. Third act - all Whammies." That's surprisingly astute advice.

The guiding force behind the first Xtro was to be as outlandish as we possibly could. In my hubris, I took it as read that I would make a "good film", but I reckon that all we achieved was to shock a few people. I was disappointed with the end result … and the shortcomings were all my fault. I was inexperienced. It was a union film and we could only work for 8 hours per day, so it took 36 days to shoot. That was in England and, in those days, the unions were very powerful.

Now I live in Los Angeles and there is an entire parallel industry populated by non-union technicians. It's a different world. In the US, I've been able to make a film every two years or so. In England, I couldn't get a job. After the success of Xtro, no respectable agent wanted to meet me. Thank goodness for Mark Forstater, an American ex-pat living in London who produced Xtro. He was in possession of an imagination and, dare I say, intellect, who financed multiple scripts and lunatic ideas that I brought to him. I owe a lot to Mark who is one of the good guys.

We were all greatly surprised that, when the film was released in theaters, it did well. I was excited to see the title in the Variety top 50 films of the week. I am still astonished that the film has lasted so long and that people still remember it. I am told that it has a strange atmosphere. Well, I think that's the atmosphere of chaos, which you get when you don't know what you are doing.

I wish it were a better film.

Only recently, 30 years after the shoot, have I come around to appreciating the kind people who ask me if I'm the guy who directed Xtro. I used to shrink into a corner. But I now realize that this film was seen by many people when they were young, and it was probably the most shocking film they had ever seen. Of course, now it looks very tame. But I have learned that, perhaps, the film has an undercurrent of lunacy where you never know what the insane filmmaker is going to do next.

In any event, I'm going to be making another Xtro in the near future - yes, really - and hope that we will manage to squirt enough imagination into it for it to be as insane as the first one. But you can't plan "atmosphere", or whatever it is, so I'm going to do something, which, like the original, jumps like a demon from the awful depths of my subconscious.

Damn the torpedoes … full speed ahead.

Wish me luck. Please.

-Harry

Acknowledgements: Bob Shaye, Michel Parry, Iain Cassie, Robert Smith, Andrew Mollo, Christopher Hobbs, Nicolas Gaster, Vivien Pottersman, John Midgley, Tom Harris, Phil Sayer, Bernice Stegers, Maryam D'Abo, Tik & Tok, John Metcalfe, James Crawford and others who are blessed with far greater creative talent than me.

We all suffered together because, although it was only a little monster movie, it was OUR MOVIE and, despite its shortcomings, these were top-notch people who worked on the film. I can't imagine why but, in case any of them read this, I send them all my best affection.

-Harry Bromley-Davenport. Hollywood, USA. October 2014

I'm not even really sure what a 'Video Nasty' actually is in terms of 1980s movies, because looking at what was deemed offensive and possibly reprehensible back then now more often than not seems no worse than what can be seen on TV or YouTube today. To be honest, I was never really interested in that kind of gross-out, torture porn genre of horror movies like *Cannibal Holocaust, SS Experiment* at all. My enjoyment came from Hammer and Amicus movies from the '60s and '70s and a liberal sprinkling of Sci-Fi from those decades and the 1980s too.

So it was an interesting twist of fate that led me to playing a very bad alien in a movie that ended up on the DPP Section 3 list! Back in the early 1980s I was half of a successful mime and music duo called Tik and Tok. We were known for our 'Robotic' style of movement that we had pioneered and perfected and as a result we'd appeared on a lot of TV shows as well as many live performances. The big gig of early 1982 was the two of us (because of our mime training) playing featured creatures in *Star Wars - Return Of The Jedi*. A massive experience on every level, believe me! We would also, when available, do a 30 minute appearance on a Friday and a Saturday night at a fairly posh cocktail bar and restaurant named Coconut Grove behind Oxford Street for £30 each and a couple of free exotic drinks, following us terrifying innocent diners with our machine-like movements and extravagant make up and clothing.

One night, after completing our act, we were approached by a couple of dudes who told us over a drinkie or two that they were putting together a low budget British Sci-Fi/Horror movie and they wanted us to be in it. Wow, that doesn't happen every day! Naturally we said yes after they told us that I would play an Action Man who comes to murderous life and Sean (Tok) would be a ghastly and hungry alien. The money was crap and the script changed every day virtually due to the somewhat 'Altered' state of those in the script and directorial departments. Originally the film was called *The Reaper* and then inexplicably overnight it became *Xtro*. I suggested that visually it might look more weird and frightening if the alien, instead of being a mime artist creeping about upright in a monster suit, was actually on all fours in a backwards crab position. Oh, they loved the idea! Then, to my horror it was decreed that I would play the alien and Sean would be the bayonet wielding life-size plastic soldier! Damn!

I went to the workshops of a company in South London called NEFX (I think) to have my whole body cast in plaster in a backwards crab position on a plastic sheet on the floor. I was allowed to keep my underwear on but despite copious amounts of Vaseline being applied there were many stray pubes and body hairs imbedded in the rock hard plaster. Ladies, I KNOW what it feels like to have a Brazilian! My head was also cast in two halves so that the crew could mould the alien skull to fit my own. It was a ghastly, claustrophobic event that even now I shudder to recall.

My scenes were filmed outside in a wood in Buckinghamshire, England in March late at night. I tell you, if you're encased in a tight rubber suit you get cold, very cold. I did. No real provision was made for me in terms of comfort or safety and I became increasingly angry at the indifference of the director and his cronies. Because the head had to go on backwards I could only see where I'd been not where I was going, which was a challenge believe me when you're crawling on all fours along the mucky and leafy floor of a damp wood!

The director comes out with a bright idea a few days later. This involves me as the alien emerging headfirst in slo-mo from a pool of brackish water. They've created said puddle somewhere in a clearing deep in the heartless and chilly forest, lit it and now the crew stamp their cold feet, exhale the breath of the privileged and warm and await my shivering arrival. I ease my body into the tepid water and have my *Xtro* head applied. I then, against every instinct of my goose-pimpled body, submerge myself under the scummy surface and allow the contents of the pool to flood in through the eye and mouth sockets in the mask. I can just about make out the Director's distant and muffled shout of "ACTION!" and I slowly; slowly raise my head up from the swampy water. It's a revoltingly claustrophobic and genuinely frightening experience, as I could actually very easily drown doing this, and I realize that no one has had the foresight to prepare for this possibility. I do the action once again for luck and that's it. There will be no more! Even if the world's largest hair is jammed in 'The Gate'. You are not paying me enough to undergo this. Fuck you very much and goodnight. I'm home by 6 A.M. and I vow never, ever to do that kind of dangerous, underpaid wank ever again.

The scene that primarily caused this now somewhat charmingly oddball Brit movie to be considered a possible contender for 'Video Nastiness' was the moment that the girl that I'd orally impregnated with my extra terrestrial jizz in her country cottage (but because of the backwards head thing I couldn't savour the moment) begins to give birth. But what emerges from between her now motionless thighs is the naked torso of a fully-grown man! Yep, complete with masses of lumpy blood, afterbirth and a gristly umbilical cord that he chews through when he's Homo erectus.

Back then this moment alone caused people to run from theatres aghast with their hands over their mouths. If you couple that with a naked Maryam D'Abo hung up in a bathroom like a birthing cocoon plopping out alien eggs into the tub, an unstoppable Action Man come to life who bayonets an old lady to death, a ghastly midget clown, a blood-drenched young boy with newly developed psycho-kinetic powers, a corridor-strolling, completely superfluous black panther and much more other weirdness you've then got a movie that was so out there then but today it just fits right in there. These days I really enjoy it on the rare occasions that I watch it but back in 1983? Different story altogether!

-Tim Dry   Writer, Actor

Tim Dry is a writer, mime, musician and photographic artist, best known for appearing in *Star Wars Episode VI: Return of the Jedi*, the cult Sci-Fi/horror movie *Xtro* and for being half of a duo, Tic and Took, that popularized robotic mime in the UK in the 1980s.

Tim is the author of two published books of memoirs and his first novella *Ricochet* is due for release in 2015 by Theatrum Mundi. He also has short stories in three Horror anthologies. Namely: *The Bestiarum Vocabulum* (Western Legends Press), *Demonology* (Static Movement) and *Phobophobias* (Dark Continents Publishing). Tim has also contributed articles for Forbes magazine.

Many, many years ago, when my only source of horror news was Starburst magazine, I read about a film called XTRO. Though I knew I had little chance of seeing it, I was so intrigued by the bizarre images (a woman trapped in a cocoon giving birth to eggs over a bath, an alien with inverted knee and elbow joints, and a full-size Action Man on the rampage to name but three) that I made a promise to myself to see the film. It took me around thirty years, but I finally managed it. And it really is an oddity.

Here's the story in a nutshell: after throwing a stick for his dog to chase (seriously – it's that kind of movie) a chap called Sam is abducted by aliens. He unexpectedly returns three years later and is reunited with his wife (now living with another man) and son. Things are understandably awkward between the main characters, and then the situation deteriorates as Sam begins to have an increasingly bizarre effect on his young son. Throw in a few sex scenes, a supporting cast of nosy neighbours and the like, a midget clown (like I said, it's that kind of movie), and a woman giving birth to a fully-grown man, and you're just about there.

And I loved it. Unlike the majority of horror movies, which see the light of day today (I'm looking at you endless remakes, sequels, reboots and re-imaginings), XTRO is jam-packed with originality. Though it takes its inspiration from some familiar sources (there's more than a hint of Invasion of the Body Snatchers and it was marketed as the anti-ET at the time), it's refreshingly different. It moves along at a decent pace and frequently doesn't make a huge amount of sense, but it's never boring. The effects are remarkably good, particularly for the early 1980s, the score (by director Harry Bromley Davenport) is effective in a John Carpenter-esque way, and there are a few scenes that'll make you question what you've just watched and have you skipping back a couple of minutes to check you weren't imagining things and having particularly hallucinogenic dreams.

Like I said, with XTRO you're not going to get the most coherent movie experience, but you will get a film chock-full of ambition and originality, and to my mind that's hugely important. And if one XTRO movie's not enough for you, XTRO 2 and 3 were also made (though apparently there's no connection other than the name and the reviews are less than glowing...). And be warned, as recently as 2010, Harry Bromley Davenport was promising XTRO 4. I wait with bated breath!

-David Moody   Author of Autumn.

Zombie Holocaust

(DPP Section 3) Banned in the UK
Also known as "Doctor Butcher M.D.".
Year of release: 1980
Writers: Fabrizio De Angelis and Romano Scandariato
Director: Marino Girolami
R rated 84 mins. Italy
Tagline: "Not for the faint hearted…."
Main cast: Ian McCulloch (Dr. Peter Chandler), Alexandra Delli Colli (Lori Ridgeway), Sherry Buchanan (Susan Kelly), Peter O'Neal (George Happer), Donald O'Brien (Dr. Obrero), Dakar (Molotto).
Distributed by: VTC

Plot:
When Lori Ridgeway and Dr. Peter Chandler venture to the Moloto islands to investigate the mysterious transformation of one of the hospitals male nurses what they discover is far worse than they could ever have imagined. They discover a mad scientist (Dr. Obrero) who is creating zombies in a quest for immortality but with cannibals inhabiting the island who will win in the battle of cannibals Vs. zombies?

Appraisal:
The idea here sounds totally amazing! A film capitalizing on not only zombie but also cannibal films too! And that's exactly what this film is, okay it's executed rather strangely but you can't help but adore this crazy zombie feature film.

This film could have literally been so much more! Zombie Holocaust is rumored to be shot on the same set as Lucio Fulci's "Zombie Flesh Eaters", which, in itself, is very interesting!

Though this film could not be compared to "Zombie Flesh Eaters"! As Lucio's masterpiece is far superior in so many ways!

This Italian offering is full of blood and gore and that's really the only thing going for it! Strangely enough I love this film, although you have to except it for what the film is, a cheesy run of the mill zombie flick made to cash in on the popular genre! The film delivers on an entertaining level for the gore alone, and does seem to attract a good following of fans, which is surprising!

The music featured in the film is the same music that appeared in Emmanuelle and the Last of the Cannibals by Nico Fidenco, I love the music, 70/80's cheese at its finest! The zombies in the film are crazy as hell!

Goofy zombies, good effects in parts, mainly the saw taking the women's scalp off! the zombies look like they have shit on their faces most of the time, but this film is a fun watch for pure exploitation pleasure and comedic qualities alone!

An enjoyable watch, through and through!

Zombie Holocaust was seized under section 3 of the 1959 Obscene Publications Act on VHS in the early 1980's before the implementation of the Video Recordings Act of 1984 in the UK.

Zombie Holocaust was initially released on pre-cert VHS by VTC in 1983. The version released in the UK by VTC in 1983 was cut by 3 mins. 24 secs, the film was released uncut on VHS in 2000 in the UK and every version since has been rated 18 uncut in the UK.

-Tony Newton

In a rain-sodden (and badly lit) teaching hospital deep in the heart of New York City (the home from home for 80's lo-fi Italian movie makers) someone has been helping themselves to various body parts belonging to the cadavers marked for use in the daily anatomy class, much to the chagrin of the grumpy surgeon who uses the incidents as an excuse to shout "You've all failed!" at his students and fuck off down the pub (possibly).

The gorgeously glamorous (in a Kay's catalogue way) Lori Ridgway (the frighteningly fish lipped Delli Colli) and her colleagues are baffled by this spate of icky thefts and reckon that the answer must be prank-playing students. But lo, the truth is far more sinister (and oh so slightly racist) when they discover the token, bowl haired Asian doctor (who looks disturbingly like a porn movie version of Erik Estrada) is caught sitting in the dark eating a corpses heart. Spooky. Erik decides the best course of action is to evade capture by throwing himself out of a window then cunningly turning into a shop window mannequin before he hits the ground (with a satisfying plastic echo it must be said).

After a leisurely trip to street level in the lift Ridgway bags the body and returns to work to start her examination.

Of the corpse that is, she's not taking her driving test or anything.

It's whilst examining the aforementioned corpse, that Ridgway — who also happens to be a student of anthropology, lucky that — recognizes a strange (for strange re: shite) tattoo on the dead man's chest—a tattoo that just happens to be (are you paying attention?) exactly the same as a symbol found on a ceremonial dagger given to Ridgway for her sixth birthday by the housemaid that looked after her when she lived on the tropical island of Kitkatoo.

Which by a strange coincidence is where the heart-eating doc was from too. Phew!

And if that wasn't plot contrivance enough it turns out that the dagger has recently been stolen! I mean what are the chances of that?

Feeling there's more to this than just an isolated incident, Lori decides to ask famous scientific 'investigator' and generally suave stud muffin Dr. Peter Chandler (genre god and owner of the world's best ginger comb-over McCulloch) for help in solving the macabre mystery. After much ooing and aahing, Chandler reckons the best way to get to the bottom of things is to organize an all-expenses paid holiday, sorry expedition to the island alongside a crack team of experts (well alongside Lori, her assistant George (the credits say Peter O'Neal but I swear it's a pre Dead Ringers Jon Culshaw) and tough tomboy reporter Susan (the lank-haired, boy-trousered, but infinitely bonk-able Buchanan).

Non-entities one and all but infinitely more charismatic than anyone featured on I'm A Celebrity.

Deciding to visit the big island next to Kitkatoo (Dogpoochone?) first our fantastic foursome spend a few days staying with the trampish Dr. Jeff Obrero (screen legend O'Brian, looking like Wilfrid Brambell's buffer brother), a piss stained and pooh breathed gone to seed medical researcher with a great line in open neck shirts who's been living among the natives for years.

Well in their bins by the look of him.

Although stinky as hell he still has some manners and, after tea, cakes and a severed head (though' it may have been a mouldy potato) in Laura's bed he offers not only the use of his boat but a trio of Beatle haired native bearers and his big-created 'man friend' Moloto (Barrera, essaying his role in Zombie Flesh Eaters but in a cheaper outfit), as their guide. As is the way in such movies, nothing goes according to plan. The boats engine overheats stranding the group not on the isle of Kitkatoo but on the smaller (and slightly less dangerous) Kitkatoow...or so Moloto claims.

Chandler however is beginning to suspect that Moloto isn't being entirely honest about the situation but as he goes to confront the guide a loin-clothed band of scary cannibals jump out of the bushes and attack our heroes. The native bearers are the first to fall (but isn't that always the way?) giving Chandler and co. time to leg it into the trees. Contacting Dr. Obrero, the survivors are told to make their way to a handy abandoned church further inland and to lock themselves in whilst awaiting rescue.

As Chandler and his merry (if slightly smaller than earlier) band make their way through the jungle (well, producers garden) they seem surprised to find that the cannibals have been following them and stand around screaming when they attack again and after a particularly threadbare struggle George ends up eyeless whilst slinky Susan (being the most attractive woman in the movie) is carried away by the arse bearing natives. Suddenly (almost as if the director has remembered the film's title) a gaggle of shuffling zombies turn up and scare the natives to buggery (not literally), and the survivors make it to the church on time to find Obrero waiting for them.

Convincing them that Susan is probably enjoying the attentions of the sausage fingered cannibals, he hands Lori and Chandler a map showing the quickest way to New York and points them in the direction of a handy rubber dingy left on the beach. Even though Chandler's suspicions of foul play are getting stronger by the second he decides that it probably would be safer to just head home and forget about everything.

Plus he realizes that it'll just be him and Lori in the dingy for weeks...the dirty wee dog.

His sinful thoughts of hot sea-based sex are interrupted though when a zombies attacks them on the beach, leaving an angry (and no doubt sexually frustrated) Chandler to dispatch it with a handy outboard motor. With a look of grim determination usually only seen in Sheepdogs our hero slowly realises that the only way he's ever gonna pull Lori is to solve the island mystery so with a heavy heart – and a raging horn - Chandler heads back to the church to confront the mad doctor...

With more cuts available than Richie Manic, Marino Girolami's cult classic is probably the only Italian gore-a-rama to feature not only cannibals but also zombies and a mad as a lorry doctor too, so you effectively get three movies for the price of one. It's just a pity that none of them are any good. On the plus side, Ian McCulloch is in it and as we all know he would never appear in anything too shady, standing around in a selection of Primark suits looking worriedly ginger (or is that gingerly worried) and let's be honest, he could stand around in his undies painting a wall and he'd still be infinitely watchable.

Donald O'Brian on the other hand is the complete antitheses of McCulloch's subtle acting style, a perfect example of an eye rolling, scenery chewing and wee stained madman. His fantastically realized Dr. Obrero is an utter joy, so convincing is his performance that you can almost taste his fishy breath. Of the other cast members, the plump mouthed star of Fulci's New York Ripper, Alexandra Delli Colli, is only there to look good in her cream suspenders whilst pouting, her most difficult acting scene is where she's required to look vaguely scared whilst a group of Filipino tramps smear her naked body in face paint and strap her to a big paper Mache wheel.

This she manages with great aplomb I'm glad to say, whilst Sherry Buchanan comes across as a dirtier (but less mental and with more teeth) Margot Kidder.

Wearing her dads clothes and with hair that hasn't seen shampoo for about six months she still manages to exude an air of clumsy back alley sexual hijinks (even when strapped to a table after being scalped which would be a tall order for most actresses).

The rest of the cast are kinda just there really, which is enough, I guess.

As for the cannibal tribe, well it's the first time I've ever seen scary natives dressed only in thongs fashioned from rashers of bacon and mop top wigs but who's to say this isn't a realistic depiction of an ancient civilization? Not me that's for sure. Now to the zombies hordes (well I say hordes but there are only five of them, one of which is the directors mum) who, with make-up that is a triumph for the seven year old hired to produce it using only the contents of the class arts and craft cupboard and accompanied at all times by a synth score that consists mainly of samples of a small boy farting whilst a dog with throat cancer barks backwards these undead terrors are guaranteed to strike mild apathy into the hearts of even the most hardened viewers. Essential viewing.

-Ash Loydon   Illustrator, writer.

Zombies: Dawn of the Dead

(DPP Section 3) Banned in the UK

Also known as "Dawn of the Dead" "Zombie". "Zombies" "Zombie: Dawn of the Dead", "Zombi" "Dawn of the Living Dead"..

Year of release: 1978
Writer: George A. Romero
Director: George A. Romero
Unrated 127 mins. Italy, USA
Tagline: *"When there's no more room in hell,* the dead will walk the earth."

Main cast: David Emge (Stephen), Ken Foree (Peter), Scott H. Reiniger (Roger), Gaylen Ross (Francine), David Crawford (Dr. Foster), David Early (Mr. Berman).

Distributed by: Alpha Intervision

Plot:
During the zombie apocalypse a mismatched group of survivors seek refuge in an abandoned shopping mall with dire consequences.

Appraisal:
George A. Romero's Dawn of the Dead is hands down the best zombie film ever made, no film even comes close to this gem of a movie. This film never seems to age and is a slice of the 70's that we all want to consume. George A. Romero always has an underlined message in his films, the nod to consumerism in this film works very well, the hidden message I took from the film was this is how you make a zombie! A lot of zombie films can be a clusterfuck of everything going on for no reason, this includes blood and gore in all the wrong places the pointless decisions the survivors make, with Dawn everything is spot on just sheer perfection here!. This film uses gore when it's needed and not just gore for gore's sake. For me the craziest part of Romero's film is that humans who are not infected or have been bitten trying to kill each other, in reality this is what it would be like, humans and there greed, lust and hunger are far more dangerous than any zombie virus. This film is not only one of the best films here on this list but one of the best horror films ever made. It's crazy to think this amazing slice of cult horror cinema was banned in the UK for so long , the myth surrounding the film growing up and in school yards could not prepare you for the first time you see it through your own eyes. I literally can't pick fault with this movie, this is pure gruesome fun on every level with a big hint of genius thrown in, the mysteriousness about this plague makes the film work, it's the not knowing what spreads this pandemic which makes the film work . The soulless beings that walk the Earth seem a lot less frightening than Tom Savini and the gang of crazy biker psychos. This film will get under your skin and have you question your own values. All the actors are fantastic and mostly likable, you seem to be drawn to actor Ken Foree whose presence on screen is fantastic, he has a cool, calm air about him and is how everyone wishes they could handle the zombie apocalypse life if they were faced with the same ill fate.

This film is an example of how to make a horror film the right way. Even if you are dealing with a subject matter that may not appeal to all horror fans. I've met a lot of horror film fans who say they hate zombie films but adore "Dawn of the Dead". If you haven't seen "Dawn of the Dead" yet! you are in for a real treat, if you are already familiar with this film visit it again and again.

It is crazy to think that a film of this standard was banned in the UK. The first time I saw "Dawn of the Dead" was a third generation copy from a video that some lucky owner had kept, this seedy transaction of me purchasing the VHS added to the whole viewing experience, even watching a bad copy, I enjoyed every minute of the film and was left wanting more. One thing I hate the censors for is that I actually watched

George A. Romero's "Day of the Dead" before watching "Dawn of the Dead" ruining the order of things for me. I was blown away by "Day of the Dead" but even more so by the slick "Dawn of the Dead", you find yourself wondering what you would do if you were held prisoner by the undead in a shopping mall! This film is rumored to have cost $650,000 to make and grossed $55 million worldwide. Tom Savini's visual make up effects in the film are fantastic none greater than a hatchet to the head and the head being blown off in the beginning of the film and helicopter zombie guy, I could go on forever damn this film is just so good! This film will always be director George A. Romero's masterpiece!

George A. Romero's Dawn of the Dead is my favorite movie of all time.

Dawn of the Dead, the video nasty was previously banned and only surfaced many years later. It has to be the scariest, most shocking and possibly the greatest film of all time. Without George A. Romero we would not have zombies as we know them, although Night of the Living Dead was an amazing film and up there as my second favorite zombie movie of all time. Dawn of The Dead had it all: bright colors, amazingly shocking effects, blood, gore and enough tension to give you a heart attack; you were with the survivors in the mall from looting and defending themselves to the loneliness and terror which the survivors endured.

Dawn of the Dead is like a comfort blanket you can play the film and instantly you feel good!

Do yourself a favor and give it another watch - you know you want to!

Zombies Dawn of the dead was seized under section 3 of the 1959 Obscene Publications Act on VHS in the early 1980's before the implementation of the Video Recordings Act of 1984 in the UK.

Zombies: Dawn of the dead was initially released on pre-cert VHS by Alpha Intervision in 1981, under the title of Zombies: Dawn of the Dead, The film was cut and given an X rating by the BBFC in 1979 for its UK theatrical release and VHS release both versions of the film had 3mins. 46secs of cuts these included the famous scene of the lady having her shoulder bitten and the exploding head during the SWAT raid and the famous Tom Savini hatchet scene.

The film was submitted to the BBFC by distributor Entertainment in Video in 1989 and gained an 18 rating with 12 seconds of cuts these were in addition to the already cut film, BMG submitted a longer cut to the BBFC and the film gained an 18 rating with 6 seconds of cuts made in 1997, BMG re-submitted the film to the BBFC in 2003 and the film was passed fully uncut rated 18.

-Tony Newton

When we worked on "Dawn of the Dead", none of us had any idea that it would go down in cinema history as the iconic zombie film that it became. As a struggling actor working in Pittsburgh theatre in the 1970s, I had been doing all manner of odd jobs just to keep my career going.

That's why it was like a ray of sunshine when Tom Savini, who also lived in Pittsburgh, asked me about doing a role in the new George Romero film, Dawn of the Dead. It was a job with pay and a role in the field where I wanted to work.

Tom and I had gone to college together in Pittsburgh and also worked in the same theatrical productions in the 1960s. Now Tom is world-famous. He has acted, directed and even developed his own school of makeup and special effects. His students regularly appear on the Face Off television series, competing for big bucks as they demonstrate their effects skills.

In the 1970s, however, Tom was still a school chum and George Romero was still best known for his groundbreaking "Night of the Living Dead," released in 1968. While today it is recognized as the horror classic, at the time many considered Night of the Living Dead a gruesome cult film. With acting work sometimes scarce, and reputations always fragile, you could not be sure that working on a similar film might brand you as undesirable for other types of films. It might negatively affect your future employment options.

That was not a problem for me. As someone who grew up on all the Universal horror films and Japanese monster movies, I idolized iconic actors like Boris Karloff and Bella Lugosi. Just having the chance to be part of a horror film was a huge thrill, although I had no idea how extensive the makeup preparation would be.

I had been used to facial makeup, but not to having my entire head cast in plaster while I was breathing through a straw for half an hour as the plaster hardened. Tom did the casting in his workshop, in the basement of his parents' home in Pittsburgh. He called a couple of days later to say that the plaster had cracked. We had to repeat the process. Photos and illustrations of the process, as well as many of his other creations, are in Tom's book "Bizarro" or "Grand Illusions."

Within two weeks I was on set for Dawn at the small Monroeville airport about 10 miles from the mall where the majority of the shooting was being done. I had had no exposure to the other actors or how the zombies moved. My first day on the set was mostly sitting around watching scenes being shot. As I recall it was a bit overcast and drizzly outside, so a lot of shooting was done in the wooden hangar and in the small block office building near the unpaved, grassy runway. Makeup was being done inside the block building, so we stayed out of sight in the back room there.

On the second day, I was getting a bit nervous. If it rained, they might have to cancel my scene. On a film with a tight budget and tight deadlines, there were not a lot of second chances, so I was prepped. It took about an hour to get into the prosthetics and garb. A second set of clothes was handy in case we needed a second take.

George Romero and Tom Savini worked together very well at the Monroeville Airport, the only location where I was present. There was a relaxed flow to the work, which probably belied the pressure they were both under at the time. Since Tom had devised the scenario for my decapitation, George gave him the lead on making the effect happen. I believe George had me come out from under the airplane wing on the far side of the field, then, once I arrived at the crates near the helicopter, Tom took over direction. Timing was important, because the piece of the apparatus on top of my head, which had been cut into chunks and threaded together with monofilament line, needed to be pulled away off-camera at the same time the blood started to pump. That's what would create the illusion of the helicopter blade slicing off the top of my head as I stepped onto the crates.

The two streams of blood came from two hand-held pump-type fire extinguishers held by Tom and one other person behind the crates. Tom called out the directions and I climbed the crates. I stumbled a bit on the climb, because the crates were loosely stacked. Quick recovery, stand up tall, cue the off-camera line-tugger, and start pumping the blood.

The two lines of blood streamed down my face as I collapsed on the boxes. It was a gusher.

It was all done in one take. There was applause afterward from the crew and others on set, because it looked good immediately. We were all pleased and relieved, and all I could think was, "It's over? Now I go home? After all that? I only hope the scene makes it into the final cut."

Getting into character as a zombie was easy enough for me. There wasn't the modern plethora of zombie character types to choose from, however. It was all new. My memory went to folklore and maybe a few older films for some ideas, to the concept of actually being a flesh-eating ghoul. And, George didn't call them zombies, anyway. They were the undead.

But, in my heart, in my struggling actor's ambition and hope and dreams, I was going to be the best possible zombie I could be. Whatever I had internally to prepare was called upon for those all-too-brief moments. This was to be my moment. I was lucky, very lucky. The moment became an iconic part of the film and has been listed as one of the top five zombie death scenes. Bravo Network listed it as one of the top 100 moments in horror movie history.

Pretty cool.

I remain good friends with Tom Savini and hope to work with him again. I see George Romero at a few conventions and we always have a warm chat. At a panel we once shared, he said wanted to include more humor in Dawn than in Night, and my scene was part of that levity. The other actors who worked on Dawn have remained good friends, even though I knew many of them before Dawn from working in theatre in Pittsburgh. When we get together on the convention circuit, we tend to celebrate the fact that together we were part of something groundbreaking and special to each of us in a unique way.

The appreciation of fans across the world is amazing to me. When people tell many how many times they've watched Dawn, how it influenced, amazed or frightened them, I just feel a deep thrill for having been a small part of something that is now part of cinematic history. But, more than that, it was an experience that has continued to touch the psyche of film buffs for many decades. I am honored and humbled to be part of it. It has been a blessing to be enveloped in the fold of this wonderful film. I still watch it. I still enjoy it. I am glad so many others continue to watch, too.

-Jim Krut   Helicopter Zombie in George A. Romero's 1978 "Dawn of the Dead".

From the first time I read the script, I was impressed by George's brilliant handling of exposition. Exposition is the information a viewer, or reader, needs to understand a story. Writers are constantly challenged by the need to impart that information without putting off the story too long, or bogging it down too much.

George's solution was to break it up among several characters and embed it within a frantic situation. The various people at the television station have strong objectives, which are essential to strong performances, and are dealing with strong obstacles, including fear and chaos. These are the ingredients of compelling drama.

In the case of Dr. James Foster, my own character, the objective was to persuade the world, as encapsulated by the TV station personnel and even further by the interviewer played by David Early, that the zombie crisis is real and that they must take specific action. His obstacles are their need to deny the facts and their outright hostility toward hearing them.

So Dr. Foster is blessed with a strong objective and equally strong obstacles, again the ingredients of compelling drama. The actor's job is to play that objective for all it's worth—to do everything he can to persuade the people in that studio, and by extension the public at large, that zombies must be acknowledged and dealt with.

The trap in a scene like this is to play an emotion, which in this case would be anger. All actors know to focus on objectives rather than emotions, because objectives are richer and more varied and more interesting than emotions. They move the story along. Emotion brings it to a screeching (or roaring or weeping or agonizing) halt. Emotions happen, sure, but they're always a reaction to events, not the prime mover.

I'm proud to this day that I focused on Dr. Foster's objectives and not his emotions. And David Early, playing Mr. Berman, focused on his. And so our encounter seemed real and interesting. It's an ordinary thing—a couple of actors doing their job—but I'm delighted that it made a bit of a contribution to a great movie.

-David Crawford   Dr. Foster in "Dawn of the Dead" 1978.

You survived the Night of the Living Dead. Now what? What do you have to do; to survive the day, next week or the months of a pregnancy?

For me, the most moving moment is early on, when a S.W.A.T. team member Peter (Ken Foree) must execute a dozen or so zombies. He becomes sick with himself. This self-questioning is the spur for him to join teammate Roger (Scott H. Reiniger) – who simply wants to escape the insanity around him – and a couple from a TV station.

In the shopping mall, these survivors work hard to create a haven from the zombies, the government, and raiders. But the question festering under all their efforts is, "What are we doing here?"

As the audience we must ask, "What would I do?"

-Nicholas Vince   The Chatterer in Hellraiser, Actor, and author.

Zombie Lake

(DPP Section 3) Banned in the UK
Also known as "Zombie Lake".
Year of release: 1981
Writers: Julian Esteban and Jesús Franco
Director: Jean Rollin
Unrated 83 mins. France, Spain
Tagline: "God help us if they rise again!"
Main cast: Howard Vernon (The Mayor), Pierre-Marie Escourrou (German Soldier), Anouchka (Helena), Anthony Mayans (Morane), Nadine Pascal (Helena's mother), Youri Radionow (Chanac).
Distributed by: Modern Films (Mountain).

Plot:

Young women are disappearing without a trace in a lakeside town and due to its haunting past the locals begin to blame "The lake of ghosts". But the lake holds a dark secret; German soldiers were thrown into the lake by the resistance and are coming back to life as flesh eating zombies.

Appraisal:

The makeup used in this film is terrible, it features some of the worst zombies made up on screen. The plot isn't great either!

This film features many scantily clad women mainly being ravaged by zombies. The mayor of this unnamed French village is played by Howard Vernon, a regular horror exploitation actor, who is at least entertaining in the role. As bad as this film sounds on paper it's not, I actually enjoyed this movie (no I'm not crazy) a great movie to watch with a few beers and some friends, it's not scary but very fun indeed and not the abomination most people say it is but not a serious horror or zombie film, so if you're looking for laugh out loud schlocky fun you've found it here!

Zombies Lake was seized under section 3 of the 1959 Obscene Publications Act on VHS in the early 1980's before the implementation of the Video Recordings Act of 1984 in the UK.

Zombies Lake was initially released uncut on pre-cert VHS by Modern Films (Mountain) in 1981, under the title of Zombies Lake, releases as Zombie lake in 2004 from Arrow Films uncut and with an 18 rating by the BBFC.

My favourite release is the big cardboard Wizard Video US release, it's so damn cool one, one my favorite VHS cover art sleeves of all time!

-Tony Newton

Welcome to 1970's exploitation Europe and an oh-so-slightly scummy lake somewhere in France, the sun is glistening over the discarded condoms, fag boxes and pop cans as an incredibly buxom beauty is frolicking through the trees and gaily throwing her clothes behind her. Stripped naked and enjoying the sun (unless you're watching the 80's UK 'Modern Films' Betamax edition where she's sporting big grey granny pants) she suddenly notices a 'danger' sign near the water's edge. Tossing it aside she dives into the welcoming waters of the lake. Little does she realise that it is, in fact, a lake of death. Or, more correctly, a lake of zombies. A 'zombie lake' if you will.

Sexily splashing away to a frankly fantastic Euro-porn organ soundtrack and making sure to keep her ample breasts in shot at all times, our wet 'n' wild wench doesn't notice the shadowy figures lurking just below the surface. Well she wouldn't, would she, seeing as all those shadowy figure bits have been filmed miles away and weeks later at a disused public swimming baths. Anyway, back to the action where without warning - unless you count the sudden burst of 'spooky' organ music that is - a green hand grabs for the girl's leg and pulls her below the surface to her doom. Which is quite scary, if I'm honest, though not as scary as the loud pops and scratches that constitute a smooth transition to the next scene, which appears to be made up of someone's holiday super8's of a quaint (if not a little seedy) public house somewhere in Normandy. Most probably the town of Domfront* if I'm not mistaken.

Inside this marvellous example of early 19th century Orne architecture another, totally different buxom lady (she's blonde for one thing) is serving huge jugs (snigger) of beer to the locals who are busy eating snails and gossiping about the sheer amount of young girls who go missing near the local lake. "She probably met some young stud eh?" remarks Claude, the big burly Brian Blessed alike as his drips piss weak French lager down his plaid shirt. His rat-like companions twirl their moustaches in agreement before deciding to go see the Mayor if she hasn't shown up by closing time. I mean come on; those tables aren't going to clean themselves.

Morning dawns and the Mayor (who it appears is played by Ren Hoek from The Ren and Stimpy Show) is rudely awakened from his garlic-fuelled fantasies by Claude and his chums loudly banging on his door. It seems that after much frantic searching there's been no sign of the girl except her discarded clothes, so Mayor Ren decides to call in the police from the next village - his town being so small that they don't have any of their own. Meanwhile, out near the (zombie) lake another busty young woman is busily spending her day pushing a milk churn in a wheelbarrow across a bridge whilst wearing orthopaedic shoes. Which if I'm honest is reason enough to stay in the EU alone. Unfortunately she is so deeply involved in her obviously important job that she totally fails to notice the fact that a shadowy green figure is watching her from the lakeside. A shadowy figure, which is revealed to be a one-eyed zombie in a Nazi uniform. Well I say Nazi uniform but it's really a pair of mouldy Quick-Fit overalls with Swastikas painted on them topped off with a pair of Wellington boots but at least the thought was there.

If not the budget. The hideous Hun quickly grabs the woman and grapples her to the ground before clumsily exposing her hideous brown bra to the world and finally messily nuzzling her neck. She screams, kicking off her horrendous clogs in the struggle as the zombie dribbles poster paint over her throat in a cacophony of hisses, scratches and pops that suddenly cut to her prone body being laid (but not in that way, though I wouldn't put it past the French) on the Mayor's patio by an ever sweatier than earlier Claude.

"I know how you feel about your daughter," Mayor Ren tells her distraught dad as he shuffles about his daughter's corpse desperately trying to cover her big white pants. Which is nice.

As the fumbling father heads off into the bushes for a tearful wank and a garlic frogs' leg flavoured Pot Noodle the gathered crowd (all six of them) stand motionless gazing longingly at the Mayor for what seems like an eternity. Before it gets too uncomfortable, there's another cack-handed cut and we're suddenly watching Ren sitting on a bridge, his sinewy wrinkled arms wrapped around two obviously terrified young boys as he slowly drags them ever closer to his quivering, sweat covered lips.

It turns out that the boys have witnessed something strange near the lake and the Mayor wants all to know all the facts straight from their pretty mouths. And probably a 'special ' cuddle too.

Meanwhile back at the pub, ace reporter, Janet Ellis (Annouchka) has arrived in town determined to uncover the mystery of the 'ghostly lake' and heads over to Claude's table to pump him for information. "You call it the Lake of Ghosts." Announces Janet. Claude grunts, strokes his droopy moustache and lets loose a very eggy fart before realising that this would probably make a better title for the film. So impressed by Janet's use of words—and her hairy back and arse—he quickly offers to take her up the Mayors house. Which is sadly not a euphemism for field-based barebacking, although it really should be. Once there, Janet wastes no time (OK maybe a minute or so) introducing herself before explaining that she's working on a story regarding the legends of the lake and surrounding area for a local TV show called Zombing About. Probably. Ren tells her she's talking bollocks, which she counters by whipping out a huge book detailing the legends of the lake (and other stuff) from her tiny handbag. "Now I'm intrigued!" a visibly aroused Ren exclaims, rubbing his bony hands together with glee. His pleasure is soon curtailed when he begins reading through the tome before deciding it's too vague to be of any use. "The book is too out of date to be useful" he cries. You heard it here first kids; any books not written within the last forty minutes must be obsolete and should therefore be burned. Janet, not being an inbred hick, argues that legends and folktales like these are usually based on fact. "But they are the very stuff of books." Ren cryptically (and nonsensically) replies, before launching into a tale from the heady days of the Second World War...

Through the magic of the 'wobbly dissolve' (that's the actual technical term for it, go on check) we're quickly transported back to the 1940's where a crack squad of German soldiers are battling an (unseen) airplane with pellet guns whilst yet another busty blonde stands screaming at the chaos and bloodshed going on just out of shot.

Noticing how the sunlight glistens on her ample breasts, the sexy blond Nazi-boy (is there any other kind?) in charge runs through the ensuing explosions to save her, grappling her to the ground as a 'huge' (ahem) bomb goes off. Later that evening she shows her gratitude by having sex with him in a barn to the strains of romantic choral music. As morning breaks the lovers prepare to go their separate ways - her to explain to her dad why she's having sex with a Nazi, him to slaughter some more Jews, the disabled etc. - she gives him a huge pendant to remember her by. Which begs the question who knew they had pound shops in 1940's France? Anyway, after what seems about 3 days' worth of footage of the Nazi's fighting in the snow against (invisible) Russians and driving around aimlessly in a badly painted milk float, Aryan boy returns to the village to find that his 'lady friend' is heavily pregnant. On discovering this fact—and being a black clad bad boy—he kisses her goodbye and leaves almost immediately to re-join his jackbooted buddies for a bit more killing. Cue even more shooting at imaginary foes and driving down deserted country lanes to a slightly sinister soundtrack. Fear not though, because before too long - probably due to the rocking motion in the back of the van - the crack troops are all desperate for a toilet break and a quick ciggie. Just like the audience. But, unlike the said viewer the soldiers joy is cut short by Claude and his buddies who leap out of the trees and shoot them all dead before dumping their bodies in the local lake. See? it's all coming together now.

In a case of spooky coincidence - or plot contrivance take your pick - blond boy's squeeze dies at exactly the same moment. Though this may have more to do with the fact that she's giving birth to a ball headed baby than some supernatural quirk of fate. Janet, unable to hide her disappointment at such a shite story makes her farewells and heads back to the pub with only an evening of cheap drink and the chance of Claude pawing at her underwear with his sweaty sausage fingers for comfort. Which, if I'm honest sounds a pretty good night. Meanwhile back at the lake a local all-girl volleyball team have decided to stop for a picnic followed by some nude cavorting to a jaunty Hammond organ score. As groups of women together are known to do. Giggling, combing each other's hair and throwing a ball around (in glorious boob bouncing close-up) they're all blissfully unaware of the evil lurking nearby. And I'm not talking about Claude.

As is always the way in these situations there's usually one person for whom jiggling about in the nude is never enough, so a cry of "Let's all go for a swim in this inviting and zombie-free lake!" is soon heard and the ladies cheerfully dive in for more ball based, giggly fun. But down below the zombies are on the move. Not too quickly though as they appear to be enjoying the underwater shots of the girls swimming, doing star jumps and kicking their legs wide open as much as we are.

The zombies soon remember that this is meant to be a horror film though and soon enough decide to attack, fondling the ladies' soft thighs as they drag them to their doom at the bottom of the lake. Luckily one of the team has been sitting on the banks painting her nails so manages to run screaming and wobbling towards the village clad only in a big (and I mean BIG) pair of blue pants.

Claude and his posse are enjoying a quiet beer or three (now there's a surprise) when she bursts into the pub screaming before promptly collapses on their table. Obviously impressed by the service and totally enamoured by her choice of underwear Claude orders his pals to take her 'up the stairs' (I don't know if this is a particularly French sexual activity but we never see her again) whilst at the same time top 'tecs, Spitz and Moran, arrive on the scene, stopping by the pub to ask directions to Mayor Ren's residence. It's all go in this town isn't it?

Mayor Ren cracks under the good hair/bad hair double act and reveals the full sordid history of the 'Lake of the Damned' and how it's evil has stretched back as far as the middle ages and maybe even earlier. Though probably not as far back as lunchtime though because that would be silly. Spitz and Moran unfortunately think he's talking complete shite and decides to go back to the pub to, um, 'interview' people. As all this is going down (as the yoof say) our favourite Aryan zombie has taken a break from all the killing and decided to go and visit his now-grown-up (well 12 year old) daughter. Surprisingly, she takes his re-appearance quite well, seeing as he's now a green skinned, undead beast in a (possibly very damp smelling) German uniform. The lack of surprise is only equalled by the films lack of logic, I mean it's now the 'modern' (well the 1980's) day, so how come she's not in her early 40's? Ignoring this vexing plot point they exchange knowing glances and he heads back to the lake. But what of Europe's greatest detective duo? Well Spitz and Moran, now bored with getting pissed and annoying the locals elect to go and investigate the disappearance of the basketball team everyone's talking about, especially upon hearing that they were nude. Heading out to the lake, the dynamic duo soon come across an abandoned camper van and piles of ladies' clothes. "Do you think it's foul play?" asks Moran as he wipes his now flaccid member on a discarded t-shirt. "It beats me," Spitz replies, "There's no clue to what happened." Save the bloodstained shoes and claw marks on the benches obviously. Shrugging at each other in a manner usually reserved for impatient waiters the pair proceed to rifle through the team's discarded handbags no doubt in order to pocket lipsticks, blusher etc. to give to their wives. But as this blatant abuse of police power continues the zombies are slowly rising from their watery graves and preparing to attack killing the detectives. But this is only the beginning of their lust for vengeance (and lust for blood and possibly big pants too) as the unstoppable zombie horde starts to shuffle towards the village...

You can't imagine the sheer ecstatic pleasure I feel every time a young film fan inadvertently discovers the joy of Jean Rollin's infamous no-budget zombie 'epic', directed under the frankly fantastic pseudonym 'J.A. Lazer' and starring Rollin regular, the frighteningly ferret like Howard Vernon, what Zombie Lake lacks in budget, plot, effects, editing, coherent storytelling etc. it more than makes up for with lots of long, lingering nude scenes (not found in the original, bulky-boxed Betamax UK Modern Films release) alongside scenes of such mind numbing bizarreness that you'll be flicking back to make sure you really did see them. And then just flicking away in general. Seriously it's that good.

Experience the crew forgetting to turn the lights on till halfway through a scene! Recoil in horror as Nazi zombies in green emulsion stomp about in a swimming pool! Swoon as grannie-haired Annouchka sits in the pub with a sweating moustached man! Go open another bag of crisps as the unnecessary love story subplot (complete with soft focus 'lurve' scenes) unfolds in bum numbing detail! Strain your ears trying to decipher the almost Lynchian dialogue and get a headache attempting to figure out how it relates to the action on screen! Get slightly uncomfortable as you watch the antics of the nude female basketball team unfold to a cheesy 'Europorn' score and much more besides!

You know you're onto a winner when you realize that Rollin was in fact using a completed different script to the one his actors had (he admitted as much in a 1981 interview in Starburst Magazine number 48...go find it out, it's the special Zombie issue fact fans) meaning that for the majority of the films shoot people were just looking at him blankly as he barked out directions at them. If only Jennifer Kent had had the same problem during The Babadook we might have had a halfway decent movie.

Usually at this point I spend ages ripping a film apart and making puerile jokes at the crew's expense but in all honesty, I can't do it with Zombie(s) Lake because it's so damn wonderful. No, really. Essential Friday night viewing for fans of Eurotrash horror, anyone who thinks they've already seen the worst movie ever or those who really enjoyed 'Bloody Moon'. Sheer genius.

* Domfront is a very pretty hill town in the south of Normandy full of ancient ramparts and a quaint old town centre with half-timbered houses, an historic church and a breath-taking castle. There is also a popular - and cheap - market on Friday mornings. More importantly I once kissed a girl from there named Cécile in the Zigzag toilets in Birmingham back in 1986. She then asked me to move to France with her but being really young and nervous I declined, though I've no idea if that's a reason to love Zombie(s) Lake or not.

-Ash Loydon   Illustrator, writer.

Chapter 13: VHS Lives

My Favourite VHS titles that weren't banned but had such a huge impact on me and lived in my VCR player. I would not have the love I have for VHS now if it wasn't for the video nasties and these accompanying titles!

Due to so many horror films being banned in the UK, and those titles actually being available in the UK, they were huge over here, and the staple of every teenager's video collection, be it original copies, bootlegs, or weekly rentals from the video store!

-Tony Newton

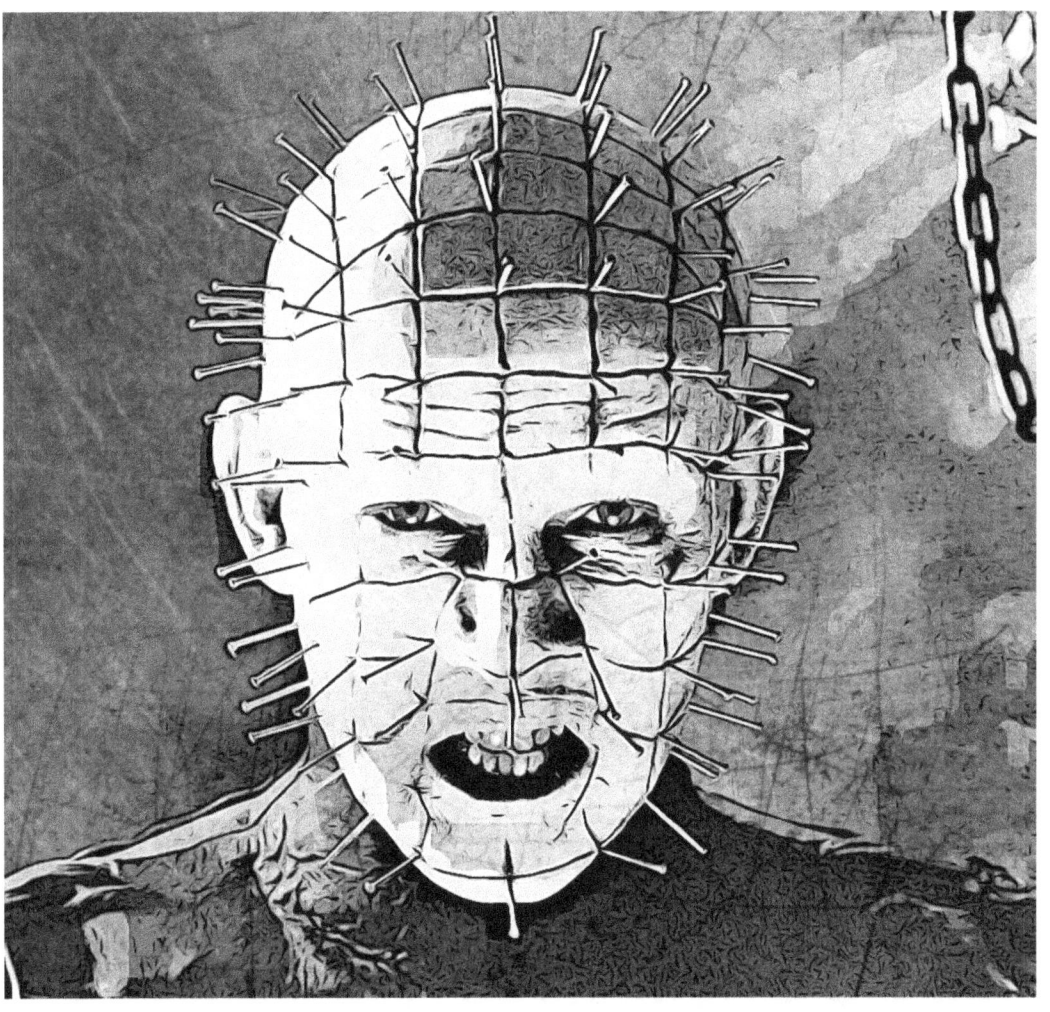

Hellraiser

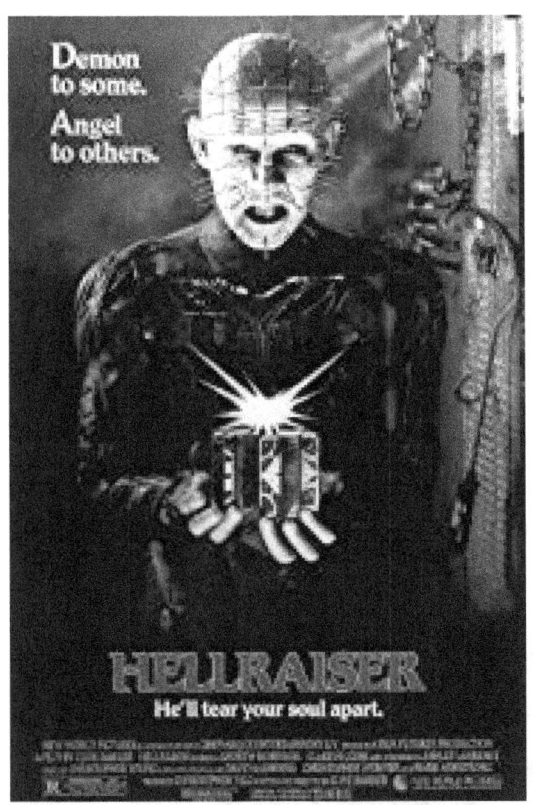

Year of release: 1987
Writer: Clive Barker
Director: Clive Barker
Rated: R rated
Tagline: "He'll tear your soul apart."
Main Cast: Doug Bradley(Pinhead), Andrew Robinson (Larry), Clare Higgins (Julia), Ashley Laurence (Kirsty Cotton), Sean Chapman (Frank), Oliver Smith (Frank the monster), Robert Hines (Steve).
Distributed by: New World Video

Plot:
A man seeking the ultimate experience in pleasure, unleashes hell on earth!

Appraisal:
Clive Barker's classic 1980's cult horror Hellraiser is a groundbreaking slice of gore and sadomasochism hell. Hellraiser is up there alongside Leatherface, Freddy Krueger and Jason Voorhees and he could definitely hold his own against the lot of them. The start of this film is very memorable: Traveler Frank seeks sexual depravity in any and all forms and hunts for the ultimate in pleasure. When Frank gets his hand on the mysterious puzzle box and solves the ultimate puzzle, he unleashes much more than he bargained for, unleashing pure hell in the form of an alternative universe. Frank is soon ripped apart by hooks and chains by the evil cenobites. This is only the beginning as Frank's brother and family get caught up with the zombie-like Frank.

Frank's brother Larry has an accident when he decides to return to his family home dripping blood into the attic floor, which the blood resurrects Frank. Larry's wife Julia who previously had an affair with Frank falls under his spell once again bringing back men to drain their blood so that he can be fully restored.

Doug Bradley is instantly recognizable as Pinhead; his look is amazing - the full leather clad Hellraiser and Cenobites are as terrifying as you can imagine and bring a hell-like quality with them with almost all the seven deadly sins molded into them.

Ashley Laurence as Kirsty the daughter steals the show and is always captivating on screen. This film spawned a number of sequels the first three are undoubtedly the best, later on in the franchise when Hellraiser was replaced and not played by Doug Bradley it was just a joke. Bradley is the one and only Pinhead. This film never dates and feels as fresh now as it was on the first watch. I have a soft spot for all of the first three Hellraiser films, they were fresh something new, to be honest I can't pick a favorite of the three, each are a thing of dark beauty, yet different in every way, The first film we lack Hellraiser and his cenobites and keep yearning for more screen time, but still the film is a masterpiece, which sets up the franchise perfectly! Growing up for me most kids loved Freddy Kruger as did I, but Hellraiser was darker less comical and was less popular than the Nightmare on Elm Street series for your casual horror fan child, you knew your friends were real horror fans if they could conjure up a Hellraiser quote in the playground!

The Hellraiser films were dark, twisted and that bit different to everything on offer, Clive Barker will literally tear your soul apart with this masterpiece.

I love all of the Hellraiser films (with Doug Bradley); they are so dark, they literally do tear your soul apart!

Although I watch 1, 2 and 3 more than any of the other films in the series!

All on good old-fashioned VHS!

-Tony Newton

Hellraiser Film Series

"He'll tear your soul apart" reads the almost iconic tag line for the poster for this British horror film written and directed by Horror maestro Clive Barker… The Poster almost gives you the impression that the now iconic Pinhead is some kind of slasher, akin to the Friday the 13th or, Halloween franchises, but despite this the audience receives something much more complex, a box of gothic and sadomasochistic delights await!

This perfectly paced movie based on Barkers novella, The Hellbound Heart, is imbued so strongly with his own style, never has an author from the horror genre adapted his own material so successfully. From the very outset the movie is full of horrific atmosphere.

This atmosphere is reinforced by the cinematography, which is just sublime. The camera focuses on such incredible detail, which is artistic, nuanced and full of esoteric meaning. Another striking element of the cinematography which works superbly has to be the setting, and the sensible choice of shooting the movie in real suburban locations, which helps the movie, send the viewer the message… "don't be fooled by the utopia of suburbia, it's really hell on earth!" these elements help create a truly memorable slice of horror.

The script is impeccable; every element of its essentially perfect plotting is tight and means that every scene moves the story forward. The characterisation is naturalistic and creates an air of plausibility to the overall effect of the film helping even the crazier plot points more credible for the viewer. The script also contains strong thematic elements… a black sense of humour and wit along with some interesting commentary on the concepts of sexual awakening go on to overall make the script is highly quotable.

The editing of the film is again almost as flawless as is possible to be and the plot flows extremely well. Although today some elements of the special effects appear dated…for the most part they are still of a very high standard.

One of the great visual strengths of the film is the costume. The Coenobites are still both as enticing and repellent as they have ever been, and the costume/special effects of arch villain Frank Cotton are amazing, and just by this characters evolving look the audience gets a very three dimensional view of him, in fact this is true of the whole cast from Julia's 1980s power dressing to protagonist Kirsty Cotton almost virginal costume.

The score is another element that helps to cement this movie into its classic horror status, although not the initial choice for the score (the original commission was given to the industrial band Coil) Christopher

Young's score is amazing…it adds suspense…enhances the thematic and atmospheric elements of the movie and rounds off a perfect horror movie of the era.

-Ian Young   writer.

It's amazing to me the effect Chatterer has had on people. I look at the mask and see a piece of rubber foam with plastic teeth and remember the claustrophobia when wearing it.

The audience sees a man who's had his face ripped, perhaps with his eyes gouged and only able to chatter his teeth in frustration or delighted anticipation of Frank and Kirsty's suffering. I know he's caused people nightmares, as they tell me when I meet them at conventions. Some even tremble as they talk to me. A friend's girlfriend, when introduced to me a year after the film's release; ran from the pub and didn't return for 20 minutes.

To promote Hellraiser, the crew from Image Animation did a make-up demonstration in London. It was hosted by a comics shop: Forbidden Planet, and they placed one of the manikins – the desiccated victim from whose mouth maggots tumble onto Kirsty – in their shop window. They had to remove it as the police had received a complaint. At the event, I was dressed as Chatterer, complete with mask and teeth, and sat behind a twelve-year-old girl who was watching the demonstration. I tapped her on her shoulder. She turned and screamed. But as my Mum, who was there, said - she loved it! Perhaps because she was there with her Dad and ultimately felt safe.

Marketing horror films must be tricky. The designers must find images, which convey the chills on offer, without offending too many people and so reducing the size of the potential audience. Because these images are disturbing.

On Hellbound: Hellraiser II, we did a photo shoot with all four Cenobites for the film's marketing. When the film came out, they produced a wonderful standee featuring Butterball, Pinhead, and the Female cenobite. None of the lobby cards showed Chatterer either, and I was told he was simply 'too disturbing' to be used.

Chatterer really is only meant for darkened cinemas and living rooms. And for your dreams.

-Nicholas Vince   The Chatterer in Hellraiser -Actor and author.

Memories of Hellbound: Hellraiser II

I remember going to see the first *Hellraiser* movie back in 1987. It was considered a major part of a regeneration of the British horror film industry. Clive Barker was also the new sensation in British horror literature. As an actress and an aspiring writer, I wanted to see what Mr Barker could throw at me.

To be honest, I was never a visceral horror fan. My favorite genre was Sci-fi, although Sci-fi horror was coming back with a vengeance at the time — *Alien* being the prime example in 1979. My interest in conventional horror extended to classic black and white films, such as *The Innocents* (1961) and *The Haunting* (1963) — still two of my favorites.

So, what did I think of *Hellraiser*? I was astounded, taken aback, deeply disturbed… The Cenobites were a new breed of monster that I'd never seen before, never imagined before, never dreamt of in my worst nightmares. Yet, although they were horrific, there was something so reserved about them, so dedicated to "sweet suffering" that I could understand how they could worm their way into our hearts and become enduring horror icons, especially Pinhead (played with diabolical relish by Doug Bradley). One always longs for a bad guy who knows how to throw out a good quip at a trembling heroine. And frankly, he was pretty sexy in that scarred, pinned and leather-suited way.

But weren't the humans the true monsters of the piece? Uncle Frank (Sean Chapman) with his dubious and murderous sexuality, and Julia (Clare Higgins) metamorphosing from mousy housewife to lust-obsessed diva, eagerly whacking innocent men -- with a hammer to the back of the head, no less — so her dead lover could get his skin back. Gosh, you have to admire that kind of dedication!

The other thing that struck me about *Hellraiser* was that there were three powerful female roles in the movie: Kirsty (Ashley Laurence) the heroine and the two baddies: Julia and the Female cenobite (Grace Kirby). This was another unusual aspect of the film that I thought was really effective.

However, when I got the call from my agent to audition for the part of a cenobite in *Hellbound: Hellraiser II* in 1988, I almost didn't go. My memory of the Cenobites in the film was dominated by the image of the Chatterer (played by Nicholas Vince in *Hellraiser I & II*): those horribly exposed clattering teeth, blood-soaked, leather jumpsuit and sewn-shut eyes. Yuk! At the time, I was helming *The Small Screen*, my own video review program on late night UK TV and I didn't want to play a monster, for goodness' sake. But a friend of mine urged me to go and in the end, I met with director Tony Randel and got the part of the Female cenobite.

The following weeks were filled with makeup tests and costume fittings. When my first day on set finally rolled around, it was one of the worst ones I'd ever experienced, simply because my plane was delayed coming into Heathrow for 24 hours (I'd been visiting my folks back in the States for Christmas) and I ended up coming straight from the airport to Pinewood in a taxi, arriving around 8 AM, where an exasperated makeup crew was waiting for me. Not the best way to start a job, but in the end, it worked out fine. After four hours in the makeup chair and a half an hour being laced into my cenobite costume (smeared with Kensington Gore and KY Jelly for that lovely slimy shiny monster-look), I was ready to go on set. But instead, I waited for hours, as is normal in the filming process.

The cameras finally rolled on my first scene six hours later, at 6 PM, which meant that I'd been up for around 34 hours. I was feeling pretty lifeless, which was perfect, because when I asked Tony Randel for my "motivation" (I still can't believe I asked him that! Cheesy or what?), he just said: "you're dead." Fabulous!

My initial scene was when Pinhead & Co. first appear in *Hellraiser II*. Tiffany (Imogen Boorman) is playing with the puzzle box, and Dr Channard (Ken Cranham) and Julia are hiding in a secret alcove. The lights flicker, the walls part and the Cenobites enter, to the accompaniment of Christopher Young's extraordinary score and a ton of fake fog. I'm sharpening my knives in preparation for skewering Tiffany's lovely young flesh and then Pinhead, spoilsport that he was, stops the proceedings. "No!" he thunders. "No?" I whinge. And then comes one of the best lines of the film: "It is not hands that summon us. It is… DESIRE."

That moment still chills me and I was there, filming, with a crew, a director, the stink of the smoke machine in my nostrils and everything else that should make an actress know that this is all make-believe, but it was still a definitive moment.

Looking into the mirror every morning after my transformation from big-haired, 1980s TV presenter-actress to a High Priestess of Hell was a peculiar experience for me. Sometimes I felt like crying because… well, where was *me*? Bald, blue-fleshed, pierced with pins and wires, and with that rather dubious bloody wound in my throat. Hell, let's call a spade a spade: that "vagina" wound in my throat. (By the way, my makeup crew nickname on set was "Deep Throat", which was deemed too rude by the American producers to be my character name on the cast list. Pinhead, Chatterer and Butterball (Simon Bamford) were all makeup crew nicknames that did appear on the cast list of *Hellraiser II*.)

On other days though, I'd look into the mirror and feel very powerful. After all, I was a monster. I was a demon from hell. I ripped peoples' skin off for my pleasure and then took their souls. What's not to love about that job description?

Of course, at the end of the film, when Channard cenobite's "penis" tentacle pierces that "vagina" throat, resulting in my gruesome death, I'm sure that Freudians around the world rejoiced at that lovely conundrum. (And how could I die? I was already dead. I always wondered about that one.)

Years later, in the wake of the horrific murder of James Bulger, a TV show would use a clip from *Hellraiser II* to illustrate the effect of scary movies on children. I felt very uncomfortable watching this program. The kids interviewed seem to yearn for their parents to exert some control, to intervene and say "hey, you're too young for this movie" and turn the channel over to *The Sooty Show*, or something similar. (A show that I also appeared in, by the way. Yes, that's my "Kids' TV Claim to Fame": I taught Sooty how to do robotic mime.)

Even now, at horror conventions, fans come up to me and say: "You scared the hell out of me when I was eight years old." And I always reply (with a smile, of course): "What were your parents thinking of?!" But the fans seemed to have survived intact and the extraordinary *Hellraiser* mythology lives on in late night screenings on the Horror Channel, amazing artwork on the Internet, the Boom! Comics, the *Hellbound Hearts* Anthology (in which "Sister Cilice", a story of mine about a female cenobite, is featured) and the sequels. And of course, that mythology lives on in people's minds and nightmares as well.

Hellraiser and *Hellbound* both received an "18" rating from the censors in the UK and they were rated "R" in the USA when they were released back in the 1980s. I somehow think that it wasn't the violence that would have traumatized the censors (even though it's pretty graphic), but the obsessive and explicit sexual desire expressed in the film. There's also a fair amount of S&M subtly — and not so subtly — implied in the movie. Censors always seem to be more worried about sex than violence, a dichotomy that never fails to puzzle (and amuse) me.

I think that the difference between *Hellraiser* and many of the more extreme examples of horror movies is this: the genius of Clive Barker. However you might view the Cenobites and those humans that foolishly wanted to explore the ultimate in sensual suffering, it was done in a very intelligent and artful way — and also with great humour. If you read Clive's original novella on which the film is based, *The Hellbound Heart*, you'll find a beautifully written story about love and obsession and death that is truly a classic of its genre. And you'll have to agree with Stephen King, when he wrote: "I have seen the future of horror, his name is Clive Barker".

-Barbie Wilde   Author and actress (The Female Cenobite).

Demons

Year of release: 1985
Writer: Dardano Sacchetti and Dario Argento
Director: Lamberto Bava
Rated: Unrated
Tagline: "They will make cemeteries their cathedrals and the cities will be your tombs."
Main Cast: Urbano Barberini (George), Natasha Hovey (Cheryl), Karl Zinny (Ken), Fiore Argento (Hannah), Paola Cozzo (Kathy), Fabiola Toledo (Carmen).
Distributed by: Avatar

Plot:
A large group of unexpecting theatregoers are trapped inside a theatre in Berlin during a screening of a horror film. But, real horror awaits when demons begin to possess the humans one by one and multiplying at an uncontrollable rate.

Appraisal:
The premise alone is amazing. A large group of strangers trapped in a movie theatre and one by one they are hunted by demonic beings, once possessed by the demons, the victim turns into one of them. Demons are very similar to zombies and this film does get compared to other famous zombie films. The demons grow in numbers just as zombies do when the host is taken over by the demonic force of the demons.

This film is produced by the legendary Dario Argento and directed by Lamberto Bava, the soundtrack is great although the film is not strictly a zombie film it does come across as one, you get the same feeling as if you were watching one, think "Night of the Living Dead" but being trapped inside a huge Berlin theatre.

The whole feel of this film is on the money the effects are superb and the pacing is perfect, it's fun throughout, it's not shit your pants scary but it's one hell of a ride. The contrast from what is going on onscreen in the theatre itself works so well against the audience in this film and sets up the film well. Bobby Rhodes stands out and steals the show throughout the whole movie, the demons stand out with the teeth and nails and eyes, the gore is great and just enough in all the right places. A VHS everyone should own.

-Tony Newton

Demons is a 1985 blockbuster movie directed by Lamberto Bava, whose father was one of the greatest Italian directors, Mario Bava. Production was signed by Dario Argento, Italian maestro of *giallo* horror and one of the greatest horror movie directors alive. At the time, movie was screened in Belgrade cinema "20th October", that, unfortunately is no more active. It used to be only cinema where you could watch horror movies and where I used to spend a lot of time as a boy, basically, since I was four years old. Although there used to be parental advisory warnings, with the help of my father's friend who worked there, I could watch every movie I desired. They also used to screen whole "Friday the 13th" series, which I was terrified by, but I somehow enjoyed during whole movie, must admit it, sometimes peeking through my fingers. Mostly I was terrified by special effects, such as decapitations or body parts amputations and mutilations.

Since my childhood, "Demons", besides "The Thing" is the movie that influenced me the most. Especially the work of special effects genius, Sergio Stivaletti. It was maybe the first impression I've got about horror genre. By time, after I have seen certain amount of horror movies, I can say that Savini and Stivaletti became my idols, when it comes to special effect, especially bloody and gore effects.. Stivaletti's work with transforming people into demons was incredibly terrifying for me, all together with animatronic puppets, teeth fallouts, nails breaking, eyes digging out, etc. For the complete effect, I have to mention the unforgettable music of a composer Claudio Simonetti, who usually composed music for Argento movies. When I saw it for the first time, I thought it was American movie, it wasn't like other Italian movies I have seen before. Otherwise, it was censored version, later you could find uncensored on VHS tape, which was revealed to me by Dejan Ognjanović, Serbian best horror genre expert.

Shortly before the projection of "Demons", the cinema was half full and we all were excited for the famous movie we heard so much about, that only the bravest kids have seen.

With the beginning of the famous Rosemary transformation scene, in which actress Geretta Geretta was brilliant, (she really won the fans all over the world) nothing was the same as before. Beside her, actor Bobby Rhodes was also phenomenal, appearance of those two at the very moment left all cinema audience in fear. Upheaval scene in the cinema is unforgettable. In that scene, Rosemary takes demonic mask from the cinema lobby, cuts down on it while she was taking it off; she can't stop the bleeding, and soon afterwards she transforms into demon. It all began with the snapping of her face ulcers (which caused indescribable fear in the audience faces), with *a la Exorcist* scene and vomiting green fluids, scratching present people with her claws and infecting them, like zombies do. By that time, we got used to watch zombies infecting all around, but it seems to me that "Demons" were the first time that I have seen infection spreading and activating so fast.

Watching movies such as "World War Z" or scene with the fast zombies in the "Dawn of the Dead" remake, I realized that "Demons" introduced us with the running zombies revolution.

And when the bloody feast of infection spreading began, audience started to leave the cinema. All friends of mine left, but I craved to stay until the end. I couldn't remember that so many people left cinema so quickly ever! Watching that cinema screen, I wished to close my eyes, but I couldn't do it. I had the strong feeling that only by just watching the movie I will get infected. And I have. The infection spread through all my being. After that projection, I just knew that movie mask and the horror genre would become - and remain - important parts of my life. Forever.

Years after, I had the honor of meeting Sergio Stivaletti, as a special guest at the Serbian Fantasy Film Festival 2011. Mister Stivaletti, while he was visiting my work studio, joked that we could work together on a future project, movie named "Demons vs. Zombies".

That's how dreams become reality.

-Miroslav Lakobrija   Effects Artist.

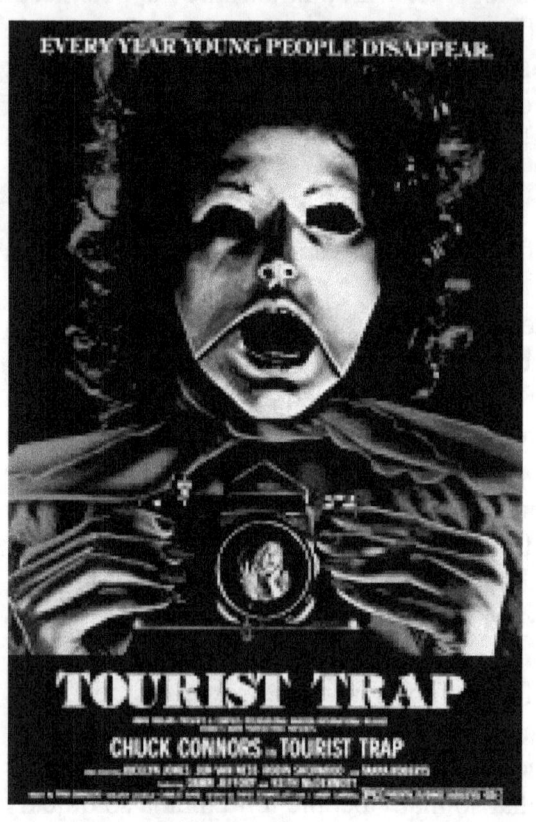

Tourist Trap

Also known as: "A Ratoeira", "Horror Puppet".
Year of release: 1979
Writers: David Schmoeller and J. Larry Carroll
Director: David Schmoeller
Rated: PG rated
Main cast: Chuck Connors (Mr. Slausen), Jocelyn Jones (Molly), Jon Van Ness (Jerry), Robin Sherwood (Eileen), Tanya Roberts (Becky), Dawn Jeffory (Tina).
Distributed by: Media/ Intervision/ Full Moon Features

Plot:
When a group of young friends get lost and stranded, they take refuge in a roadside museum, the owner is not quite as nice as he appears to be, as they soon find out he is a psychopathic killer who has the ability to control his mannequins for murder!

Appraisal:
Damn, I love this movie, I still watch this on VHS to this very day and collect different VHS versions of the film for my collection. No, this isn't a video nasty in the truest sense, but hell, this is a *nasty* video!

Chuck Connors stars as the psycho killer Mr. Slausen and does the most wonderful job of putting fear into the audience; this is as odd as it is unsettling.

I did read that John Carpenter was initially up for directing the movie, whether this is true or not is neither here nor there, but at least very interesting, I love hearing stories like this and it does make you wonder what different beast the film would have been had Carpenter to the helm.

This often underrated and forgotten horror gem to me is up there alongside the greatest horror movies. This is an original take on the stalk and kill genre, this film has elements which are similar to "Texas Chainsaw Massacre", "Halloween" and "The House of Wax" and is very similar to Rob Zombie's "House of a 1000 Corpses", I wonder if this lost horror cult classic, inspired Mr Zombie in anyway?. The film seems to be getting the attention it deserves now due to Shudder playing it and you can watch it on there with or without Joe Bob Briggs commentary...I would opt for the Mr J.B.B. commentary every day of the week!

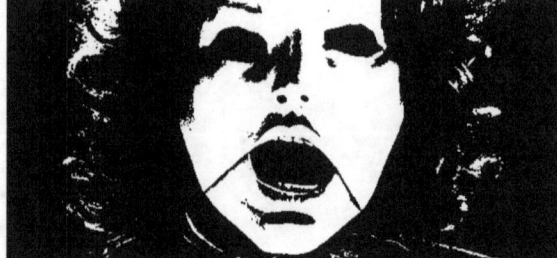

The film provides a great atmosphere that is enhanced by the creepiness of the musical and visual effects and of course the creepy mannequins.

The scary mask the killer wears is fantastically creepy, the mask is instantly recognizable by horror fans, the mask and mannequins are nightmare fuel for any age group. When I first watched this film at a young age, I needed more than warm milk to get to sleep. The effects are great throughout the film and do stand out even today, yes there is some hammy acting by the unlucky victims but no more than in any other horror flick of today. Charles Band of later "Puppet Master" fame produced this classic film and you can even see some of the puppets and dolls have the Charles Band's Puppet Master look about them. This film is a fantastic addition to your horror collection and a film that has influenced many stalk and slash modern horror movies today.

-Tony Newton

YOUR VIDEO NASTY CHECKLIST

Below is the complete list of the Section 2 Video Nasties, This is a list that would be part of my life for a long time, in the 1980's there were different variations as films were dropped or prosecuted it was sometimes hard to keep track of the video nasties, but this is the definitive video nasty list of the DPP section 2 banned Videos.

The list was like Holy Grail for fans and VHS collectors and became a checklist for VHS collectors and horror fans.

1. Absurd
2. Anthropophagous
3. Axe
4. The Beast In Heat
5. The Beyond
6. Blood Feast
7. Blood Rites AKA "The Ghastly Ones"
8. Bloody Moon
9. The Bogey Man AKA "The Boogeyman"
10. The Burning
11. Cannibal Apocalypse
12. Cannibal Ferox
13. Cannibal Holocaust
14. The Cannibal Man
15. Cannibal Terror
16. Contamination
17. Dead & Buried
18. Death Trap
19. Deep River Savages
20. Delirium
21. The Devil Hunter
22. Don't Go In The House
23. Don't Go In The Woods
24. Don't Go Near The Park
25. Don't Look In The Basement
26. The Dorm That Dripped Blood AKA "Pranks"
27. The Driller Killer
28. The Evil Dead
29. Evilspeak
30. Exposé
31. Faces Of Death
32. Fight For Your Life
33. Flesh For Frankenstein
34. Forest Of Fear
35. Frozen Scream
36. The Funhouse
37. Gestapo's Last Orgy
38. The House By The Cemetery

39. The House On The Edge Of The Park
40. Human Experiments
41. I Miss You, Hugs And Kisses
42. I Spit On Your Grave
43. Inferno
44. Island of Death
45. Killer Nun
46. The Last House On The Left
47. Late Night Trains
48. The Living Dead At Manchester Morgue
49. Love Camp 7
50. Madhouse
51. Mardi Gras Massacre
52. Night of the Bloody Apes
53. Night of the Demon
54. Nightmare Maker
55. Nightmare in a Damaged Brain
56. Possession
57. Prisoner of the Cannibal God
58. Revenge of the Bogey Man
59. The Slayer
60. Snuff
61. SS Experiment Camp
62. Tenebrae
63. Terror Eyes
64. The Toolbox Murders
65. Twitch Of The Death Nerve AKA "Bay of Blood"
66. Unhinged
67. Visiting Hours
68. The Werewolf and the Yeti
69. The Witch Who Came From The Sea
70. Women Behind Bars
71. Zombie Creeping Flesh
72. Zombie Flesh Eaters

Top Ten Video Nasties:

As soon I was asked to list my top ten video nasties I knew I would I struggle, what with there being so many of my favourite movies on the list of fiendish and forbidden flicks that caused outcry amidst the uptight right wing government during my formative years...

So, I've kinda cheated a little: sometimes listing multiple, slightly related titles as one choice. Also, I've included titles that were on the dropped list.

I'm unable to list in any particular order as I hold all these movies in high regard, for various reasons...

1) Axe

I'm a huge fan of this grubby little gem from Frederick R. Friedel, the scenes of Lisa's blood soaked hallucinations and chicken slaughter highlight her psychosis well and the Tarantino style hoods are a lot of fun in their attempts at recreating William Tell.... Anyone for soup?

2) Bay Of Blood / Tenebrae

Double dose of Giallo at its finest here from master Mario Bava and protégé (and one of my personal favourites) Dario Argento.

Great style on show from Bava, as to be expected, with this gem that was to set the blue print for the slasher genre lurking in the shadows of the home video boom...

One of Argento's finer efforts, I originally saw this in it's cut form under the title Unsane. In any form this is a fine movie with some great Dario murder set pieces, genius camera work and one of Goblin's best scores.

3) Cannibal Apocalypse / Cannibal Ferox / Cannibal Holocaust / Prisoner Of The Cannibal God

The good old cannibal flick - great exploitation fodder from those fellas in pasta land. I've had to go multiple choice with this, as they are all so good!

Vietnam vets spread cannibalistic virus? Sweet!

Giovanni Lombardo Radice as the bad guy drug dealer in Ferox? Awesome!

Deodato's unflinching found footage epic? Amazing!

Ursulla Andress covered in honey? Need I say more?

4) The Beyond / The House By The Cemetary / Zombie Flesh Eaters

Fulci, zombies, little boys with bad hair and girls voices, death by tarantula, swarms of maggots, a shark, more zombies, really, really gross, rotten looking zombies and zombies... Bobby! Bobby? Bobby???

5) House By The Edge Of The Park / I Spit On Your Grave / The Last House On The Left / Late Night Trains

The home invasion / rape revenge movies and their Italian knock offs proved hugely popular while providing politicians and busy bodies with all the fuel they needed for a full scale war against the corrupting nature of the video nasty.

Whenever I'm asked what is the scariest kind of horror I always think of these, no monsters, just real people shaped by the society they've grown up in and the lengths their victims will go to for revenge...

6) The Living Dead At The Manchester Morgue / Zombie Creeping Flesh

Here we have both one of the best and one of the worst examples that European undead cinema had to offer.

One is high in style and atmosphere, well cast and brilliantly acted, and the other is directed by Bruno Mattei.

Zombie Creeping Flesh is a guilty pleasure of mine, with it's attempts to rip off Dawn Of The Dead and hilarious scenes of gung-ho zombie slaying, crazy dialogue and one of the best death by hand in mouth and out through eyes scenes ever!

7) Nightmares In A Damaged Brain / Island Of Death

The list is a funny thing, some of the films banned are quite laughable, with their shoddy effects, dreadful dialogue and wonky camera work, it's hard to see how they were banned in the first place.

On the other hand, some films were worthy of the nasty label and these two serve as perfect examples.

Nightmare is one of those films that makes you want to take a shower after watching. I was quite young when I first saw this and it stayed with me for a long time after. Quite grim and frowned upon enough to see a man put behind bars for it's distribution in the UK.

Island Of Death, incest, murder, goat rape, torture, golden showers and more compete for your disgust in this Greece set shocker.

8) Contamination

Yet another Italian movie - and yet another rip off. This time Luigi Cozzi takes on Alien with Zombie Flesh Eaters and Zombie Holocaust star Ian McCulloch trying to survive while people explode all around him. Lots of laughs to be had with this one!

9) The Evil Dead

One of my top films of all time and one I would watch again and again as a teenager. Also, one of the few on the list to have gained such a huge legacy, which even includes a stage musical! Groovy!

10) Inferno

The second in Argento's Three Mothers trilogy, which unfortunately lost it's way by the third outing, is as enchanting as it is frightening.

As in Suspiria, we are sucked in, despite the unease and confusion, to a world of witchcraft where there is no such thing as a linear landscape and terror lurks at every turn. Instead of Argento's usual musical collaborators Goblin the score here is provided by Brit keyboard wiz Keith Emerson, perfectly befitting the sense of fear portrayed by Irene Miracle, also seen jumping out of a moving train in Night Train Murders.

-Gary Baxter   Actor/Filmmaker.

1. Cannibal Holocaust
2. Night of the Living Dead
3. Andy Warhol's Frankenstein
4. The Texas Chain Saw Massacre
5. The Evil Dead
6. The Thing
7. Phantasm
8. Prom Night
9. Suspiria
10. I Spit on Your Grave

-John Penney   Screenwriter

1. The Thing
2. Dawn of The Dead
3. Phantasm
4. Suspiria
5. Deep Red
6. Shogun Assassin
7. Zombie Flesh Eaters
8. Zombie Holocaust
9. The House By the
10. Dead and Buried

-Charles Colyott   Author

1. Cannibal Holocaust (Ruggero Deodato)
2. The Texas Chainsaw Massacre (Tobe Hooper)

3. Evil Dead (Sam Raimi)
4. The Beyond (Lucio Fulci)
5. Tenebrae (Dario Argento)
6. Possession (Andrzej Zulawski)
7. Zombie Flesh Eaters (Lucio Fulci)
8. Bay of Blood (Mario Bava)
9. The Burning (Tony Maylam)
10. Cannibal Ferox (Umberto Lenzi)

-Matt Wavish   Writer

Top 10 Classic Film Nasties List (Pre-1999)

1. Maniac – 1980 (Directed by William Lustig)
2. Henry: A Portrait of a Serial Killer – 1986 (Directed by John McNaughton)
3. The Fly – 1986 (Directed by David Cronenberg)
4. Faces of Death – 1978 (Directed by John Alan Schwartz)
5. The Last House on the Left – 1972 (Directed by Wes Craven)
6. Bloodsucking Freaks – 1976 (Directed by Joel Reed)
7. The Brood – 1979 (Directed by David Cronenberg)
8. Cannibal Holocaust – 1980 (Directed by Ruggero Deodato)
9. A Clockwork Orange – 1971 (Directed by Stanley Kubrick)
10. Frenzy – 1972 (Directed by Alfred Hitchcock)

-Jay K   (The Horror Happens Radio Show on HGRNJ)

1. I Spit on Your Grave
2. Last House on the Left
3. Clockwork Orange
4. The Driller Killer
5. Delirium
6. Inferno
7. The Beyond
8. Don't Go in the House
9. The Toolbox Murders
10. Don't Go in the Basement

-Lilith Stabs   Actress

1. Dawn of the Dead
2. The Evil Dead
3. Cannibal Holocaust
4. Zombie Flesh Eaters
5. The Texas Chain Saw Massacre
6. Night of the Living Dead
7. The Last House on the Left
8. The Beyond
9. I Spit on Your Grave
10. The Burning

-Tony Newton

About the Authors

Facebook: Tony-Newton-275305769170265/
Instagram: @TonyNewton1
Twitter: @TonyNewton1

Tony Newton is a UK-based writer, filmmaker, film producer, and an avid VHS collector.
Owner of Vestra Pictures, Schlock Films and Body Bag Films.
Author of Horror Movie Poetry, Terror Rhymes, Splatter Video, The Zombie Rule book: A Zombie Apocalypse Survival Guide, #I'm Zombie: A Zombie Mosaic Novel and Producer of the films VHS Lives: A Schlockumentary, VHS Lives 2:Undead Format, VHS Lives 3: VHS NASTY, Virus of the Dead, 60 Seconds to Die trilogy and Troma's Grindsploitation films.

With VHS Nasty touching on his beloved subject of not only VHS but also video nasties themselves.

Tony has a collection of over 2,000 VHS Tapes—mostly horror, exploitation, monster movies, and science fiction.

David Bond –
An award-winning scriptwriter, author, essayist, film producer and festival curator, David Bond recently produced the feature EXTREMITY for Dark Elegy Films, co-writing the screenplay with Rebecca Swan (MASTERS OF HORROR) for acclaimed director Anthony DiBlasi (DREAD, LAST SHIFT).
Bond also co-produced the legendary extreme-cinema anthology THE PROFANE EXHIBIT, and oversaw the reboot of Ulli Lommel's 1980 cult horror hit THE BOOGEYMAN. He currently has multiple film and television projects in development through his own production company.

A very special thanks to the contributors to this book, all of whom have made this book a reality:

David Del Valle, Lloyd Kaufman, Colin McCracken, Ash Loydon, Paul Draper, Shane Ryan, Taylor Sprow, Joseph Rubas, Mark Campbell, Glenn Criddle, Joe Ramshaw, Craig Jones, Alyse Wax, Graham Fletcher-Cook, Courtney Button, Charles Colyott, Kenneth J. Hall, Jon Ford, David Magowan, Robin Ince, David Moody, Keeper of the Crimson Quill (Rivers of Grue), Leigh Dovey, Shawn Conn, Christopher Moonlight, Peter Goddard, Troy Howarth, John Thomson, Frederick R. Friedel, Nigel Maskell, Marc Wright, Dante Tomaselli, David Grove, Shaun Troke, David Brown, Dave Wain, Brian Steward, Ruggero Deodato, Richard Stanley, James Cullen Bressack, Matt Wavish, Mark Miller, Eric Weston, Ramsey Campbell, John Penney, Edoardo Margheriti, Max Weinstein, Bracken MacLeod, Lilith Stabs, Donald Farmer, Jerry Smith, Dale white, Jason Meredith, Chris Yardley, Charlie Adlard, Courtney Button, Izzy Lee, Ulli Lommel, Rich Flannagan, Gary Sherman, Joey Keogh, Tony Timpone, Steven Kostanski, Aaron Moorhead, Lew Temple, Kenneth Gallant, Andy Soar, Pete Von Sholly, Mark Pidgeon, Joe Yanick, Sergio Martino, Aaron Eischeid, Margit Newton, Brian Bankston, Dustin Austen, Amy Lynn Best, Martin Grund, Maria Olsen, Merlyn Roberts, Jim Towns, Tedi Sarafian, Dan Brownlie, Ted Newsom, John Borowski, Steve Wright, Glenn Criddle, Aaron Sterns, Buddy Giovinazzo, Tristan Risk, Mitchell Altieri, Zack Parker, Matty Budrewicz, Mark Miller, Shaun Troke, Rachel Grubb, Tyler Doupe', Milan Todorovic, Rich Flannagan, Lisi Russell, Michael Dinetz, David Grove, Jay K, Tracey E. Bregman, Sean T. Page, Brian Hodge, Nathan Head, Armand Mastroianni, Michael Armstrong, John Amplas, Derek Botelho, Joseph Rubas, Robin Ince, Fred Olen Ray, Gary Streiner, Nicholas Vince, Jeffrey Littorno, Craig Jones, Stephen Scarlata, Steven Kostanski, Paul Stevenson, Kenneth Gallant, Mark L. Miller, Charlotte Stear, Nick Principe, John M. Whalen, Jason Bene, Terry M. West, Teri McMinn, Adrian Tchaikovsky, Harry Bromley-Davanport, Tim Dry, Jim Krut, David Crawford, Ian Young, Graham Masterton, Dustin Ferguson, James Fler, Shane Ryan, Jason Impey, Sian Richter, Gary Baxter, Barbie Wilde, Milan Todorovic, Miroslav Lakobrija.

Kerry Newton

Writer and researcher for the book: Shane Ryan

Black and white Video Nasty art by Shane Ryan, Shane Ryan has been a horror artist since he was old enough to grasp a pencil in his creepy little claws. He has been developing and honing his dark craft for over three decades, with the last eight years in the killing fields as a free-lance artist working on various horror genre projects. Shane's disturbingly macabre creations have haunted the walls of several exhibitions, both at home in Australia and internationally and have gouged an intensely sinister presence onto the pages of many genre publications and websites.

Ash Loydon

Ash Loydon is a UK based Artist and blogger his cult iconic artwork has been used for film festivals, book covers DVD and Blu-Ray cover art and storyboards.

Colin McCracken

Writer and screenwriter.

Glenn Criddle for his extensive research into video nasties.

Artist Paul Draper

Paul Draper is a UK based artist and has had work featured in horror film books and magazines across the globe.

Thanks to (Full Moon Features) Wizard Video for sending over the old sell sheets and VHS advertisements for use in the publication.

Special thanks to Lloyd Kaufman and David Del Valle for the forewords.

Copyright © 2020 Tony Newton

All rights reserved.

HORROR MOVIE POETRY
TONY NEWTON
OUT NOW!
Via Amazon.

US: https://www.amazon.com/dp/1081899816

UK https://www.amazon.co.uk/Horror-Movie-Poetry-Tony-Newton-ebook/dp/B07VM4759V

A HellBound Books LLC
Publication

www.hellboundbookspublishing.com

Printed in the United States of America

www.ingramcontent.com/pod-product-compliance
Lightning Source LLC
Chambersburg PA
CBHW081342070526
44578CB00005B/691